**RAMSEY ZARIFEH** (right, beside the line testing and diagnostic shinkansen known as Dr Yellow) was born in the UK but has spent most of his working life abroad. Graduating from Magdalene College, Cambridge, he worked in Japan on the Japan Exchange and Teaching (JET) scheme, before writing the first edition of this book. He currently works for Al Jazeera English and often returns to Japan. In 2015 he presented *Off the Rails*, a documentary for Al Jazeera on Japan's love affair with its train network.

**ANNA UDAGAWA** (left, at Kawaguchi-ko below Mt Fuji) was born in Sussex. After graduating she worked at the BBC in London before heading off to explore the world, gradually travelling further east. She went to Japan initially to visit a friend but was soon inspired to prolong her stay, working in Tokyo and also Yokohama as an English-language teacher. She met her future husband in Japan but after getting married they came back to Britain. However, Anna returns whenever she can.

**ANDREW PICKNELL** (right, at the top of Mt Fuji) first visited Japan as an English teacher after working at the National Maritime Museum and the BBC. He taught and has travelled in places as varied as Hokkaido, Kyushu and Shikoku. Now teaching history in Leicester, he goes back regularly to explore more of Japan's past and continue to indulge his passion for its language, art and landscape.

**JAMES HODGSON** (right, in the tea-producing region of Uji) read geography at Cambridge and studied Japanese for a year in Kyoto where he rapidly fell in love with the diversity of Kansai culture, food and trains. He now works in the UK writing business plans for railway companies.

uthors

W9-AAC-629

**Japan by Rail**
First edition: 2002; this fourth edition July 2016

**Publisher**
Trailblazer Publications   🖳 www.trailblazer-guides.com
The Old Manse, Tower Rd, Hindhead, Surrey, GU26 6SU, UK

**British Library Cataloguing in Publication Data**
A catalogue record for this book is available from the British Library

**ISBN 978-1-905864-75-1**

© Ramsey Zarifeh 2002, 2007, 2012, 2016
Text and photographs unless otherwise stated

The right of Ramsey Zarifeh to be identified as the author of this work has been
asserted by him in accordance with the Copyright, Designs and Patents Act 1988

**Maps** © Trailblazer 2002, 2007, 2012, 2016
**Colour photographs** © as indicated: AU = © Anna Udagawa, KU = © Kazuo Udagawa,
RU = Rikki Udagawa, TK = Toshiaki Kasai, JH = James Hodgson,
J&RL = © Jill & Roderick Leslie, LR = Lucy Ridout, RZ = Ramsey Zarifeh
**B&W photographs**: p73 © Andrew Picknell; p320, p400 & p522 © Anna Udagawa;
all other B&W photographs © Kazuo Udagawa

The haiku at the start of each chapter in this book is reproduced with the permission of:
Tohta Kaneko: p29; Minako Kaneko: p463; Kazuko Konagai: p88; Professor Makoto Ueda
and University of Toronto Press (*Modern Japanese Haiku – An Anthology*): p53 & p412.

**Editing and proofreading**: Nicky Slade and Anna Jacomb-Hood
**Cartography**: Nick Hill
**Layout**: Anna Jacomb-Hood
**Japanese proofreading**: Kenichi and Kazuo Udagawa
**Index**: Anna Jacomb-Hood and Jane Thomas

All rights reserved. Other than brief extracts for the purposes of review no part of
this publication may be reproduced in any form without the written consent of the
publisher and copyright owner.

Every effort has been made by the author and publisher to ensure that the information
contained herein is as accurate and up to date as possible. However, they are unable
to accept responsibility for any inconvenience, loss or injury sustained by anyone
as a result of the advice and information given in this guide.

**Updated information** will be available on: 🖳 www.japanbyrail.com

**Photos – Front cover and this page**: Mt Fuji from Fujinomiya,
Fuji-Hakone-Izu National Park; photo © Akira Tagami/Aflo/Corbis
**Overleaf**: Raked gravel, Takayama Jinya; photo © Anna Udagawa
**Back cover**: Komachi (series E6) shinkansen at Tazawa-ko station (© AU)

Printed in China; print production by D'Print (☎ +65-6581 3832), Singapore

# Japan
## BY RAIL

RAMSEY ZARIFEH & ANNA UDAGAWA

**FOURTH EDITION RESEARCHED & UPDATED BY**
**ANNA UDAGAWA, RAMSEY ZARIFEH**
**JAMES HODGSON, ANDREW PICKNELL**
**ANTHONY ROBINS, KENICHI UDAGAWA,**
**KAZUO UDAGAWA & YUKI AKITA**

TRAILBLAZER PUBLICATIONS

## Dedication

Anna Udagawa dedicates this edition to the memory of her mother, Honor, and sister-in-law, Elizabeth.

## Acknowledgements

**From Ramsey**: Thanks are due to the Central Japan Railway Company (JR Central/JR Tokai), without whose generous support the first edition of this book would never have been written, and to the Japan National Tourist Organization (JNTO).

Special thanks to Anna Udagawa for masterminding this edition and for her hard work on the road and back home updating much of the book, to Anthony Robins, Andrew Picknell, James Hodgson and Kenichi Udagawa for their invaluable contributions, and to Kazuo Udagawa for his assistance.

For the haiku (poems) at the start of each chapter I should like to thank: the President of the Modern Haiku Association (Japan), Tohta Kaneko; the President of the British Haiku Society, David Cobb, whose introductions, haiku suggestions and general advice were invaluable; Kazuko Konagai for supplying and translating a wide range of appropriate haiku; and the late Patricia Major for liaising with everyone above and for making the final selection. I am also very grateful to Ichie Uchiyama for providing the calligraphy for the book title. Thanks also to my parents and to my brothers, Alex and Andrew.

**From Anna**: Particular thanks to Kylie Clark and everyone at JNTO; Kohei Ohno and Tadayuki Shibuya at Tokyo Convention and Visitors Bureau; Keith Kelly and everyone at Japan Local Government Centre; also to everyone at JR East, to Yoshitaka Ito at JR Hokkaido, and to Simon Metcalfe at JR Kyushu.

Special thanks to James Hodgson, Andrew Picknell, Anthony Robins, Yuki Akita, Kazuo Udagawa and Kenichi Udagawa for their help updating this edition – and to Ramsey for giving me the opportunity to spend more time in this amazing country.

I am very grateful to Louise Archer, Helen Atkin, Mary-Ann Bartlett, Malcolm Fairman, Hitomi Goto, Stephen E Little, Sarah & David Nave, Lucy Ridout, Ben Storey & Alex Chambers, Angelina Oguma, Georgie Tongue, Rikki Udagawa, Kristina Watanabe and Steven Wedema for their contributions.

**From Andrew**: Thanks to all of the people associated with Trailblazer, especially Anna and Ramsey, for their advice and insights as well as the kindness of the station café lady in eastern Hokkaido who unexpectedly offered me a bag of cherries and iced water as I waited for the train in the hot sun.

For help with producing this edition the authors would jointly like to thank: Nicky Slade for her thorough editing and proofreading; Nick Hill for doing a wonderful job with the many map changes; Kenichi and Kazuo Udagawa for the Japanese proofreading; Lucy Ridout, Toshiaki Kasai, Rikki Udagawa, Jill & Roderick Leslie for the photos, and also the publisher, Bryn Thomas, for his invaluable input.

## A request

The author and publisher have tried to ensure that this guide is as accurate and up to date as possible. Nevertheless things change. If you notice any changes or omissions that should be included in the next edition of this book, please write to Ramsey Zarifeh at Trailblazer (address on p2) or email him at ramsey.zarifeh@trailblazer-guides.com. A free copy of the next edition will be sent to those making a significant contribution.

# INTRODUCTION

## Why take the train?

Think of Japan and one of the first images you're likely to conjure up is that of a bullet train speeding past snow-capped Mt Fuji. For many, what lies beyond this image is a mystery. But hop on board that train and you'll quickly discover what the country has to offer.

The fascination of Japan lies in its diversity: remote mountain villages contrast with huge neon-lit cities that never sleep; the vast natural landscape of unspoilt forests, volcanoes and hot springs more than compensates for the occasional man-made eyesore; the silent oasis of a Shinto shrine or a Buddhist temple is not far from the deafening noise of a virtual-reality games arcade. Nowhere else in the world do past and present co-exist in such close proximity as in this relatively small country.

The ideal way of seeing it all is by rail, whether on one of the famous bullet trains (*shinkansen*), on the wide network of local trains, or even on one of the many steam trains. An early 20th-century guidebook advised visitors to 'make travel plans as simple as possible. The conditions of travel in this country do not lend themselves to intricate arrangements'. Today, however, nothing could be further from the truth. Trains run not just to the minute but to the second, so itineraries can be as complicated or precisely timetabled as you wish. Or you can simply turn up at the station and plan your journey as you go.

**The real secret to touring the country is the Japan Rail Pass, deservedly recognised as the 'bargain of the century'.**

The real secret to touring the country is the Japan Rail Pass, deservedly recognised as the 'bargain of the century'. Rail-pass holders can travel easily almost anywhere on the four main islands.

Japan need not be too expensive as, apart from your rail pass, you can cut costs by staying in hostels, *minshuku* (Japanese-style B&Bs), or business hotels (mostly Western style). For those with a

**Above**: Futons laid out for the night in Hoshi Ryokan in Tsuwano. (© AU)

larger budget, staying in *ryokan* (upmarket minshuku) can be an amazing experience, but if you prefer there are world-class five-star hotels throughout the country.

Unexpected pleasures also await the traveller: where else do railway staff bow to you as they enter the carriage and also look as smart as they do in Japan? And where else can you buy cans of hot coffee from a vending machine at the top of a mountain, or sip sake whilst sitting in an open-air hot spring bath? It's said that no *gaijin* (outsider) can ever fully know Japan but only by visiting and seeing for yourself can you discover what the country is really like: somewhere between the images of traditional past and hi-tech future which flicker worldwide on the small screen.

# Routes and costs

## ROUTE OPTIONS

So you know you're going to Japan: the next step is to work out what you want to see and how much ground you want to cover once you've arrived. This guide shows you how travelling around Japan by rail is the best way of seeing the country close up and in full colour.

And there are few places in the world where it really can be as much fun to travel as it is to arrive. Welcome to Japan by rail.

*... there are few places in the world where it really can be as much fun to travel as it is to arrive.*

INTRODUCTION

**Below**: The red-lacquered Shinkyo Bridge, across the Daiya River; the bridge originally provided the main gateway to the shrines and temples in Nikko. (© AU)

# Japan by Rail
## Selected highlights

—— Shinkansen line
···· Other rail line

**Takayama**
Streets with Edo-period buildings; wonderful festivals; access to picturesque Shirakawa-go, known for its houses with steep thatched roofs

**Kanazawa**
Kenrokuen, one of Japan's great gardens; temple, samurai and former geisha districts

**Tottori**
Japan's 'desert' – almost 16km of beautiful sand dunes; optional camel ride

**Osaka**
The antidote to Tokyo: easy-going; 1960s kitsch; 'eat-till-you-drop' food culture

**Miyajima**
Scenic island known for the 'floating' torii gate

**Hiroshima**
A-bomb dome and Peace Memorial Park

**Kyoto**
Kinkaku-ji (Golden Temple); Nijo-jo; scenic Arashiyama

**Nagasaki**
Beautiful port city with reminders of its international links; Peace Statue

**Takamatsu**
Ritsurin garden; access to art island, Naoshima

**Koya-san**
Mountain-top temple town; overnight in a temple

**Kagoshima**
Access to Sakurajima (volcanic island) and Ibusuki (natural hot-sand bath)

**Himeji**
The picture-postcard-perfect Himeji Castle

**Nara**
Todai-ji housing Japan's largest Buddha statue; deer park

*WESTERN HONSHU*

Tottori ○

Kanazawa ○

● Hiroshima

Takayama ▲

Miyajima ●

Himeji ●

● Kyoto

Takamatsu ●

**OSAKA** ○ Nara

*SHIKOKU*

*KANSAI*

○ Koya-san

Nagasaki ○

*KYUSHU*

Kagoshima ○

**Noboribetsu-onsen**
Hot spring resort town; Jigokudani (Hell Valley)

*HOKKAIDO*

**Kakunodate**
Former samurai town

○ Noboribetsu-
onsen

○ Hakodate

**Dewa Sanzan**
The 'three mountains of Dewa'; pilgrimage route for spiritual cleansing

**Hakodate**
Attractive port city with historic buildings

*TOHOKU*

**Hiraizumi**
Historic temple town; 'Pure Land Garden' at Motsu-ji

**Nagano**
Zenko-ji temple; access to the snow monkeys

**Kakunodate**

○ Dewa   ○ Hiraizumi
Sanzan

**Nikko**
Opulent Toshogu shrine complex; former Imperial villa

○ Nagano

**Nikko** ○

*CENTRAL HONSHU*

**Kawaguchi-ko**
Multiple ways to see Mt Fuji including its reflection in this lake

awaguchi-
ko
akone ○ **TOKYO**
○ **Kamakura**

**TOKYO**
Asakusa's Senso-ji temple;
Tsukiji fish market;
Tokyo Skytree tower; Meji Shrine;
Akihabara for technology & anime;
Shibuya/Harajuku for shopping;
Shinjuku for neon lights and nightlife

**Kamakura**
Largest open-air statue of a Buddha; lovely seaside town

**Hakone**
Scenic beauty and Mt Fuji; myriad of transport options

0      100      200km

## Using this guide

Japan Rail (JR) boasts that its network covers every corner of Japan's four main islands. If you look at the maps in JR's timetable you'll see what appears

**Japan Rail (JR) boasts that its network covers every corner of Japan's four main islands.**

to be something like a bowl of spaghetti. The choice of routes is, if not infinite, at the very least overwhelming. And that is only the JR lines – there are also lines operated by private railway companies. In some places the private railways provide the only service available and in others their stations are in more convenient places for sightseeing; for this edition there's additional information about these lines.

To simplify travel planning and to reassure the first-time visitor that a qualification in orienteering is not needed, this guide splits the largest island, Honshu, into regions – Central Honshu, Kansai, Western Honshu and Tohoku (North-eastern Honshu) – and suggests (connecting) routes for each of these as well as for the other three main islands: Hokkaido, Kyushu and Shikoku. For example, if you are following the route round Western Honshu you will pass through Okayama, the starting point for the route guide around Shikoku.

Each section begins with an introduction to the area, with information on regional highlights and suggested stopping-off points. Routes can be followed

Mt Fuji; this photo was taken from a shinkansen as it was speeding past this iconic mountain. (© RU)

in reverse but in this case all points of interest from the train will be on the opposite side.

Though it's possible to travel every route by local train, it's assumed that most travellers will have a rail pass so will use the shinkansen and/or limited express (LEX) services. It is not possible to mention every station so, as a rule of thumb, only stops served by limited expresses (or by shinkansen if the route follows a shinkansen line) are included. Stations served solely by local trains are listed only if they, or the

area around them, are of particular interest. The fastest point-to-point journey times are provided for each section of the route.

Even though each route has been divided into different sections it may not be necessary to change train as you go from one section to the next. Occasionally, however, it is essential to change train in order to complete the route described. Such instances are denoted by the following symbol ▲. Places which are served by local trains only are marked ♦.

Sample itineraries are provided on pp41-7.

For the main shinkansen, limited express and local JR services see the summaries on pp504-13.

## COSTS

Contrary to popular belief, a visit to Japan doesn't have to be expensive but it is important to plan your budget as it is an easy country to spend money in.

Package tours which include travel by rail (see pp37-9) rarely offer better value than organising an independent trip. From the UK you're probably looking at a mini-

**Contrary to popular belief, a visit to Japan doesn't have to be expensive but it is important to plan your budget**

mum of £3000 for a 14-day tour including return flights, rail travel, accommodation in basic Japanese inns, some meals and the services of a tour guide. Given the price of a 14-day rail pass (¥46,390: £290/US$408), it would certainly be more cost effective (and more fun) to organise your own trip.

Though the cost of a Japan Rail Pass (see box p30) may seem high, a pass can almost pay for itself in just two journeys on a shinkansen. For example, a 7-day rail pass costs ¥29,100 (£182/US$256; free seat reservations) but the

---

❏ **Sample daily budgets**

**Note**: The budgets below do not include general travel costs because they assume you have a Japan Rail Pass. The exchange rates are rounded up/down for convenience.

**Low**

| | |
|---|---|
| Accommodation | ¥3000+ (£19/US$26+): dorm bed in a hostel, no meals |
| Breakfast | ¥600 (£4/US$5): coffee and toast |
| Lunch | ¥600 (£4/US$5): sandwich or snack and drink |
| Dinner | ¥1200 (£7/US$11): noodles/pasta, or a hostel meal |
| Sightseeing# | ¥1700 (£11/US$15): less if you mainly visit free attractions |
| **Total** | **¥7100+ (£44/US$63+)** |

**Mid-range**

| | |
|---|---|
| Accommodation | ¥6000 (£37/US$53)+ for a single room, ¥9000 (£56/US$79)+ for two sharing in a business hotel (breakfast is usually included); ¥8000pp (£50/US$70)+ in a minshuku (half board) |
| Breakfast* | ¥800 (£5/US$7): egg, ham, toast and coffee |
| Lunch | ¥1200 (£7/US$11): lunch deal in a café/restaurant |
| Dinner | ¥1700 (£11/US$15): set evening meal at a restaurant |
| Sightseeing# | ¥1700 (£11/US$15): more if you visit lots of galleries/museums |
| **Total** | **¥11,400+ (£71/US$100+)** |

**High**

| | |
|---|---|
| Accommodation | ¥12,000+ (£75/US$106+) for a single room, ¥20,000+ (£125/US$176) for two sharing in an upmarket hotel; ¥16,000+ (£100/US$141) per person half board in a ryokan |
| Breakfast* | ¥2200 (£14/US$19): buffet breakfast |
| Lunch | ¥4000 (£25/US$35): a three-course meal |
| Dinner | ¥6300+ (£39+/US$55+): à la carte meal |
| Sightseeing# | ¥9000+ (£56+/US$79+): guided city tours and entry fees |
| **Total** | **¥33,500+ (£209/US$295+)** |

* If not included in room rate    # including a one-day tram/bus/subway pass

return fare including reserved seat on a shinkansen between Tokyo and Hiroshima costs ¥37,120 (£232/US$327); even just going to and from Kyoto costs ¥27,200 (£170/US$239). A return journey to Kagoshima-chuo by shinkansen from Tokyo works out at ¥59,720 (£373/US$526), more than the cost of a 14-day pass (see p13). For additional sample fares, see box p99.

# When to go

In general, Japan has a mild climate, though it's difficult to talk at all generally about a country which stretches for some 3000km north to south. It can be below freezing and snowing in Hokkaido while southern Kyushu is enjoying sunshine and mild temperatures.

**April and May are often considered the best time to visit ...**

April and May are often considered the best months to visit, when the worst of the Hokkaido winter is over and the rest of Japan is not yet sweltering in humidity. The **cherry blossom season** is eagerly anticipated and the Japan Meteorological Agency (JMA; 🖳 www.jma.go.jp) has an internet page dedicated to reporting when the blossoms are forecast to flower. Although each year is different, the season starts in Kyushu, generally mid to late March, and progresses northwards climaxing in Hokkaido in May.

Families, friends and colleagues gather to celebrate the fleeting appearance of the cherry blossom with *hanami* (blossom-viewing) parties, picnicking under the trees. (© LR)

However, try to avoid the school/university holidays from late March to early April and the so-called **Golden Week** (29th April to 5th May), which includes four national holidays and can feel as if the entire country is on the move; hotels and trains are booked out and prices rise to meet demand. The latter part of May is a lovely time to be in Japan as the weather is often good but it isn't too hot.

The **rainy season** in June/ July (with occasional typhoons) marks the change from spring to summer but the showers are soon replaced by heat and humidity. Humidity is high throughout the summer months so carry bottled water if you are planning long days of sightseeing at this, the hottest, time of the year. Hokkaido is by far the coolest and least humid place in summer, which also makes it one of the busiest. The school holiday season in August is another busy time, particularly around mid August during the Obon festival when people head back to their home towns.

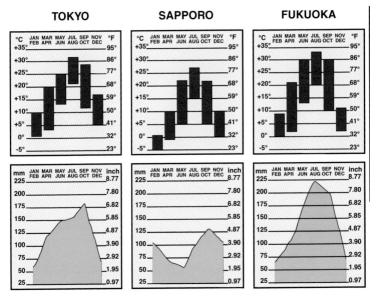

**TOKYO**  **SAPPORO**  **FUKUOKA**

**MAX/MIN TEMPERATURE CHARTS (°F/°C) AND AVERAGE RAINFALL (MM/INCH)**

The high temperatures and – particularly in the south – blistering heat can last well into September and often there is a lot of rain then. **Typhoons** strike coastal regions, particularly in Kyushu, Shikoku and Kansai in late summer. Fortunately these are usually predicted a day or two before they hit so it's unlikely you will be taken unawares.

By the beginning of October things usually cool down and dry up. Late October and November are the months for viewing the **autumn leaves** (*koyo*); this can be a spectacular time to visit. The sky is often clear so views are better and you also have more chance of seeing Mt Fuji. The autumn colours begin their magnificent display in Hokkaido and gradually move south through the islands, in the opposite direction to the cherry-blossom wave.

If you don't mind the cold, December and January are also good times, especially for skiing.

Skiing at Gala Yuzawa (see p352) in Honshu. This is the only ski resort directly connected to a shinkansen station. The main ski areas are in north-eastern Honshu and Hokkaido; the season usually lasts from November/December to April/May. (© AU)

INTRODUCTION

A rice planting festival takes place in May at Shirakawa-go village (see pp224-5), famous for its steep-roofed thatched houses. (© AU)

**New Year** is another major holiday period and even though the weather may be fine many places get crowded.

## NATIONAL HOLIDAYS

Japan observes 16 national holidays when all banks, offices and post offices, and most shops are closed. Museums and tourist attractions are usually open but will close the next day. If a holiday falls on a Sunday, the following day is a holiday. Nearly everything, apart from public transport and larger shops, closes from 31st December to 3rd January for the **New Year** holiday. The period from 29th April to 5th May is called **Golden Week** and is a prime holiday time, as is **Obon** (around 11th-16th August though the dates vary depending on the region).

● **1st January**  Shogatsu (New Year's Day) – traditionally people visit a shrine; many women dress up in a kimono
● **Second Monday in January** Seijin no hi (Coming of Age Day) – girls who have reached the age of majority (20) don gorgeous kimonos and visit the local shrine
● **11th February**  Kenkoku Kinenbi (National Foundation Day) – commemoration of the legendary enthronement of Japan's first emperor, Jimmu
● **20th March**  Shunbun no hi (Vernal Equinox Day) – graves are visited in the week around this day

Koinobori (carp streamers) and kites are flown on Children's Day, 5th May. (© KU)

● **29th April**  Showa no hi (the late Emperor Hirohito's birthday)
● **3rd May**  Kenpo kinenbi (Constitution Day)
● **4th May**  Midori no hi (Greenery Day) – to celebrate the former Emperor's (Emperor Hirohito) love of nature
● **5th May**  Kodomo no hi (Children's Day) – kite-flying events are held all over the country; also expect to see koinobori streamers flying near rivers
● **Third Monday of July** Umi no hi (Ocean Day)

● **11th August**  Yama no Hi (Mountain Day) – celebrating the country's many mountains; this is a new holiday from 2016
● **Third Monday of September**  Keiro no hi (Respect for the Aged Day)

- **Around September 23rd**  Shubun no hi (Autumnal Equinox Day)
- **Second Monday in October**  Taiiku no hi (Health and Sports Day) – this commemorates the opening day of the 1964 Tokyo Olympics
- **3rd November**  Bunka no hi (Culture Day)
- **23rd November**  Kinro kansha no hi (Labour Thanksgiving Day)
- **23rd December**  Tenno no tanjobi (The Emperor's Birthday)

## FESTIVALS AND EVENTS

Japan is truly a land of festivals (*matsuri*); hardly a day goes by when there is not a celebration taking place somewhere. These can be huge, lively, atmospheric events attracting thousands of visitors – such as Sapporo's Snow Festival, Aomori's Nebuta, Tokushima's Awa Odori Festival, or Kyoto's Gion Festival – or local festivals in towns and villages which are little known outside the area.

Yabusame Festival (horseback archery) takes place in April in Tsuwano (see p285). (© KU)

Parades of large floats, street processions to the tune of taiko drummers, firework displays, and colourful costumes are all part of the festival experience. Eating and drinking while walking around in public is generally frowned upon but this rule is broken at festival time; street stalls serve foods such as yakisoba, takoyaki, okonomiyaki.

Listed below is a selection of the many festivals and events that are worth including in your itinerary if you are in Japan at the correct time of year. For more details see the relevant city guides. JNTO also publishes a comprehensive list (⌨ www.jnto.go.jp/eng/location/festivals).

The dates for religious festivals, which are based on the lunar calendar, vary every year but other festivals are held on fixed dates.

- **February**  Yuki Matsuri (Snow Festival), **Sapporo**, Hokkaido; Fuyu Matsuri (Winter Festival), **Asahikawa**, Hokkaido.

**Setsubun** (3rd Feb) is held in temples and shrines everywhere; people throw soy beans around to celebrate the end of winter (by banishing the evil spirits) and welcome the start of spring.

- **March-May**  The **cherry-blossom season** is a highlight of the year. Popular spots for *hanami* (blossom-viewing) parties (see p14), include: Ueno Park and Shinjuku-gyoen, **Tokyo**; **Kamakura**; Tetsugaka-no-michi (Philosopher's Way), Heian Jingu and Maruyama-koen in **Kyoto**; **Yoshino-yama**; **Nagoya Castle area**, Nagoya; **Kakunodate**; and **Hirosaki**.

- **April**  **Takayama** Spring Festival; Yayoi Festival, **Nikko**; **Kamakura** Matsuri; Yabusame Festival, Washibari-Hachimangu Shrine, **Tsuwano**; Hi-watarishiki

Sanja Matsuri takes place over the third weekend of May at Asakusa, Tokyo. This important Shinto festival is one of the biggest in Japan. Central to the event is the parade in which participants carry the three portable shrines which give the festival its name. (© TK)

(fire-walking ceremony), Daishoin Temple, **Miyajima**.

● **May**  Hakata Dontaku Festival, **Fukuoka**, Kyushu; Sanja Matsuri, **Asakusa**, **Tokyo**; Aoi Matsuri, **Kyoto**.

● **June**  Hyakumangoku Festival, **Kanazawa**; Yosakoi Soran Festival, **Sapporo**.

● **July**  Hakata Gion Yamakasa Festival, **Fukuoka**; Gion Matsuri, Yasaka Shrine, **Kyoto**; Tenjin Matsuri, **Osaka**.

● **Late July and August Fireworks (hanabi) festivals** Spectacular firework displays are a feature of most summer festivals. The largest in **Tokyo** is the Sumida River Fireworks Display. The National Japan Fireworks Competition is held in **Omagari**, Akita, at the end of August.

Taiko drummers at Aomori's Nebuta Matsuri (festival) which takes place in August. (© KU)

● **August**  Nebuta Matsuri, **Aomori**; Neputa Matsuri, **Hirosaki**; Kanto Matsuri, **Akita**; Tanabata Matsuri, **Sendai**; Yosakoi Festival, **Kochi**; Awa Odori Festival, **Tokushima**; Asakusa Samba Carnival, **Tokyo**.

● **September**  Yabusame at Tsurugaoka Hachimangu Shrine, **Kamakura**.

● **October**  **Takayama** Autumn Festival; Toshogu Shrine Autumn Festival, **Nikko**; Jidai Matsuri, Heian Jingu, **Kyoto**.

● **October to December**  Well-known places for **viewing autumn leaves** (see p15) include: **Daisetsuzan**, Hokkaido; **Nikko**; **Hakone**; **Miyajima**; Arashiyama and Philosopher's Way, **Kyoto**.

● **November**  Hi-watarishiki (fire-walking ceremony), Daishoin Temple, **Miyajima**; International Balloon Festival, **Saga**, Kyushu.

● **December**  Kasuga Wakamiya's On-matsuri, **Nara**.

**Opposite**: A *maiko* (apprentice *geisha*) in Gion, Kyoto. This photograph was taken during the cherry blossom season which is perhaps why this maiko has chosen pink flowers for her hair ornament (*kanzashi*). (© LR)

Japan by rail – the best

**Best gardens**

- **Kenrokuen, Kanazawa** (see p226)  Rated one of the top three landscape gardens in Japan, the others being Korakuen and Kairakuen (both below)
- **Korakuen, Okayama** (p297)  Okayama Castle forms the perfect backdrop
- **Kairakuen, Mito** (p143)  Best known for its many plum trees and particularly popular in Feb-Mar when they are in blossom
- **Adachi Museum of Art, Yasugi, near Matsue** (**pictured here**, © AU, see also p316)  Unusual because it is also an art gallery; should be on everyone's itinerary
- **Ritsurin-koen, Takamatsu** (p480) Landscape garden set below wooded Mt Shiun

## Best of Tokyo

- **Asakusa's Senso-ji temple** (p118)
- **Niju-bashi entrance to Imperial Palace** (**top**, © AU, p105)
- **Akihabara** (p114) District known for technology, anime and manga
- **Tokyo from a water-bus** (p120) A great way to see the city (**top right**, © LR); some routes pass Tokyo Skytree (p121, **middle right** © AU)
- **Odaiba** (p106) Artificial island with Miraikan (museum for the latest in robot technology), shopping, and modern architecture such as Fuji TV's observatory (**middle** © RU)
- **Markets** Tokyo's famous fish market (Tsukiji p116) may soon close to the public, but there are other general markets such as Ameyoko, p114 (**middle left**, © RU)
- **Museums** Tokyo National Museum (p114) and Edo-Tokyo (p120)
- **Nightlife** Head to Shinjuku (p110), or Shibuya (p109, **bottom** © KU)

21

**Best castles**

- **Hikone** (**pictured here** © AU, and see p236) Located by Lake Biwa, this is one of the few original castles in Japan.
- **Himeji** (p272) Also known as Hakuro-jo (White Heron Castle) as it resembles a heron with wings outstretched.
- **Matsumoto** (p213) Considered one of the finest castles in Japan and unusual because it is built on a plain.
- **Matsue** (p313) Surrounded by a moat, Matsue Castle was designated a National Treasure in 2015.
- **Inuyama** (p204) Set on a hilltop, this is the oldest standing castle in Japan though not fully original.
- **Matsuyama** (p490) Another of the few remaining original castles in Japan and you can reach it on a chair-lift.

## Best shrines

● **Itsuku-shima, Miyajima** (**top left**, © RU, p309) Its torii gate stands in the sea

● **Kumano Nachi Taisha, Nachi** (p242) One of Japan's most important shrines, **Top right**: pilgrimage path through the cedar forest; incense burner (© AU)

● **Toshogu Shrine, Nikko** (p324) An opulent shrine and mausoleum for Ieyasu Tokugawa, founder of the Tokugawa shogunate

● **Fushimi Inari, Kyoto** (**bottom**, © RU, p256) Notable for its long series of tunnels with thousands of torii gates, made famous in the film *Memoirs of a Geisha*

**Best temples**

- **Kinkaku-ji, Kyoto** (top, © KU, p251) Also known as the Golden Temple
- **Ryoan-ji, Kyoto** Famous for its 16th-century rock garden (p252)
- **Daibutsu, Kotoku-in, Kamakura** (bottom, © RU, see p136) Kotoku-in has the largest outdoor Buddha in Japan
- **Senso-ji, Asakusa** (p118) Tokyo's most popular temple
- **Naritasan Shinsho-ji** (p141) Notable for its daily fire ceremony
- **Byodo-in, Uji** (p265) A temple since the 11th century; like many it was originally built as a villa

### Best experiences

- **Seeing the 'snow' monkeys, Nagano (right**, © AU, p212) The wild monkeys that bathe in the hot springs at Jigokudani-kaen koen are particularly photogenic in winter but are here year-round.
- **Staying in a temple, Koya-san** (p158) The journey to Koya-san is an experience in itself, but the highlight is staying overnight at a temple here.
- **Bathing at an onsen or rotemburo** No visitor should miss the experience of bathing at an onsen or, even better, a rotemburo (open-air bath). Among the best onsen are Hakone (p165), Gero (p192), Noboribetsu-onsen (375), Beppu (p426), Yufuin (p428) and Dogo-onsen (p494). The best for a rotemburo with a view are Takaragawa (**pictured below** © JRL, p178), Saki-no-yu (p245) and Kawaguchi-ko (p140). Urban onsen experiences include Tokyo (p107) and Osaka (p146).
- **Hot sand-bath, Ibusuki (right**, p461) Get below the surface of Japan with a naturally hot sand-bath. A great place for this is Sunamushi Kaikan 'Saraku'.
- **Tottori sand dunes (top**, © AU, p317) Japan has a couple of areas of extensive sand dunes but the 'desert' at Tottori is the most impressive; you can even have a camel ride here.
- **Visiting Hiroshima** (p302) and **Nagasaki** (p442) Both have moving peace museums displaying tragic reminders of the horrors of the atomic bomb. **Far right**: Nagasaki's Peace Statue (© RU).
- **Naoshima, scenic 'art island' (bottom right**, © AU, p485), also home to a James Bond museum and an eccentric bath-house.

**Some typical Japanese dishes** (*clockwise from top left*)

● **Okonomiyaki** お好み焼き (© AU) Savoury pancake (see p498); oysters are a common topping in Hiroshima (see p308)

● **Sashimi** 刺身 (© KU) Sushi is now common worldwide but sashimi (raw fish) served with a shiso leaf, shredded *daikon* (radish) and wasabi is often part of a ryokan meal (see p498)

● **Soba** そば (© KU) Noodles, here served cold with a separate sauce but can be hot (see p498)

● **Ekiben** 駅弁当 (© JH) Lunch box for a train journey (see box p102)

● **Matsusaka beef** 松阪牛 (© AU) Several areas of Japan are known for their wagyu beef; the large amount of fat makes it a melt in the mouth experience

● **Tonkatsu** トンカツ (© KU) Deep-fried breaded pork cutlet with shredded cabbage (p498); plastic models like this are often displayed in a restaurant's window to show what is available

● **Katsu kare** カツカレー (© JH) Tonkatsu with *kare* (curry sauce); see curry rice (p497)

● **Tempura** 天ぷら (© KU) Prawns and vegetables deep fried in a batter (see p498)

● **Ramen** ラーメン (© KU) Noodles in a shoyu (soy) or miso broth (see p498)

● **Kuro tamago** 黒卵 (© AU) Eggs boiled at Hakone's Owakudani (see p167)

● **Yakitori** 焼き鳥 (© KU) Food on a bamboo stick barbecued over a charcoal fire (see p499)

## Rail passes

The original and still the best-value pass available to visitors is the Japan Rail Pass; this covers all four main islands and permits travel on most shinkansen services; for further details see below. See box p31 for details of the only other JR pass valid for the whole country.

Apart from JR Central (JR Tokai; see box p32) all companies in the Japan Rail (JR) Group offer their own range of passes. These are available for a range of periods, generally not more than a week, and are useful if you're intending to focus on a specific area; for details of these regional passes see pp31-6.

Several of the private rail companies also have passes but these are all for regional areas; details are given where relevant in the text.

### THE JAPAN RAIL PASS

The Japan Rail Pass is truly the bargain of the century, assuming you plan to use several shinkansen (bullet train) services. It entitles the pass-holder to travel freely on: almost all JR services including shinkansen, other than the Nozomi (Tokyo to Hakata) and Mizuho (Hakata to Kagoshima-chuo); the ferry service to Miyajima (see p309) operated by JR; and some of JR's bus services, though not their highway bus services. JR has a dedicated website (💻 www .japanrailpass.net) which provides up-to-date information about the Japan Rail Pass and all regional passes.

### Who can use the pass?

The pass can be used by any non-Japanese tourist visiting Japan under 'temporary visitor' status and by some Japanese nationals not residing in Japan. It cannot be used by anybody arriving in Japan for employment.

### Buying the pass

At the time of writing the most important rule concerning use of the pass is that it **cannot be purchased in Japan**. It is sold, in the form of an Exchange Order, through autho-rised agents (see pp36-9) outside Japan. However, for a trial period sometime in 2016 it will be available in Japan. For further information visit the Japan Rail Pass website (see above).

*Kyoh! screaming aloud*
*this train runs into*
*the fresh green midnight*
(TOHTA KANEKO)

きよお！と喚いてこの汽車はゆく新緑の夜中

## JR RAIL PASS PRICES

### Japan Rail Pass

| | GREEN CLASS | ORDINARY CLASS |
|---|---|---|
| 7-day | ¥38,800 (£243/$342) | ¥29,110 (£182/US$256) |
| 14-day | ¥62,950 (£393/$554) | ¥46,390 (£290/US$408) |
| 21-day | ¥81,870 (£511/$721) | ¥59,350 (£371/US$523) |

### JR East

| 5 days (in 14) | Tohoku Area Pass | ¥19,000* (£119/$167) |
|---|---|---|
| 5 days (in 14) | Niigata, Nagano Pass | ¥18,000* (£112/$158) |
| 3-day | Tokyo Wide Pass | ¥10,000 (£62/$88) |

### JR East & JR West

| 7-day | Hokuriku Arch Pass | ¥24,000* (£150/$211) |
|---|---|---|

### JR East & JR Hokkaido

| 6 days (in 14) | JR East-South Hokkaido Pass | ¥26,000* (£162/$229) |
|---|---|---|

### JR West

| 7-day | Sanyo San'in Area Pass | ¥19,000* (£119/$167) |
|---|---|---|
| 7-day | Kansai-Hokuriku Area Pass | ¥15,000* (£94/$132) |
| 5-day | Kansai Wide Area Pass | ¥8500* (£53/$75) |
| 5-day | Kansai-Hiroshima Area Pass | ¥13,000* (£81/$114) |
| 5-day | Hiroshima-Yamaguchi Area Pass | ¥11,000* (£69/$97) |
| 4-day | Sanin-Okayama Area Pass | ¥4500# (£28/$40) |
| 4-day | Hokuriku Area Pass | ¥5000# (£31/$44) |
| 1-day/2-day | Kansai Area Pass | ¥2200§ (£14/$19) / ¥4300§ (£27/$38) |
| 3-day/4-day | Kansai Area Pass | ¥5300§ (£33/$47) / ¥6300§ (£39/$55) |

### JR West & JR Central (Tokai)

| 5-day | Takayama Hokuriku Area Pass | ¥13,500 (£81/$119) |
|---|---|---|
| 5-day | Ise Kumano Area Pass | ¥10,500 (£66/$92) |

### JR Hokkaido

**Hokkaido Rail Pass**

| 3-day | ¥16,500 (£103/$145) | 5-day | ¥22,000 (£137/$194) |
|---|---|---|---|
| 4-day (flexible) | ¥22,000 (£137/$194) | 7-day | ¥24,000 (£150/$211) |

### JR Kyushu

| 3-day/5-day | Northern Kyushu Pass | ¥8500 (£53/$75) / ¥10,000 (£62/$88) |
|---|---|---|
| 3-day/5-day | All Kyushu Area Pass | ¥15,000 (£94/$132) / ¥18,000 (£112/$158) |

### JR Shikoku

**All Shikoku Rail Pass**

| 2-day | ¥6300 (£39/$55) | 4-day | ¥7900 (£49/$70) |
|---|---|---|---|
| 3-day | ¥7200 (£45/$63) | 5-day | ¥9700 (£61/$85) |

NOTES

* The pass costs an additional ¥1000 if bought in Japan;
# additional ¥500 if bought in Japan; § additional ¥100-200 if bought in Japan.
● Apart from the Japan Rail Pass all passes are available for Ordinary Class only
● Children aged 5 and under travel free providing they do not occupy a seat; those aged 6-11 pay half the adult rate.
● Prices are fixed in yen, but the charge is payable in local currency. The prices in brackets are for guidance only. The dollar ($) rates are US dollars.

First you need to decide whether you would like a **7-day**, **14-day** or **21-day** pass (see box opposite). The pass runs on consecutive days from the date you start to use it but there is no limit to the number of passes you can buy.

The next step is to choose which class you'd like to travel in. There are two types of rail pass: the **Ordinary Pass** is valid for standard-class rail travel, which is likely to be more than adequate for most people. Seats in Ordinary Class are very comfortable and have ample legroom; on some trains they are as good as first-class rail travel elsewhere in the world. The **Green Pass** is for those wishing to travel in more style. Green-class carriages (known as 'Green Cars') offer wider seats and even more legroom; they also often include extras such as slippers, personal TVs and laptop power points as well as free tea/coffee. However, there are no Green Cars on most services on the Sanyo shinkansen line (Shin-Osaka to Hakata), or on Tsubame shinkansen (Hakata to Kagoshima-chuo) in Kyushu. Most limited express services have Green Cars but local/rapid trains generally only have Ordinary Class.

## REGIONAL JR RAIL PASSES

The main features of the many regional JR passes are outlined on pp32-6. These can either be purchased before arrival through agents (see pp36-9), or in some cases online through the company's website, or for a slightly higher cost in Japan at the main airports and some stations in the relevant region and occasionally in other regions. As for the Japan Rail Pass you need to have 'temporary visitor' status, though Japanese who live abroad are eligible for the JR Kyushu passes.

**PLANNING YOUR TRIP**

### ❏ JR Seishun Juhachi Kippu

Apart from the Japan Rail Pass, the only other pass (ticket) that is valid for travel on all four main islands is the near-legendary JR Seishun Juhachi Kippu ('Youth 18 ticket'). This is a seasonal ticket, permitting travel on local and rapid trains only. It is aimed at young people travelling around in holiday time, but there is no upper age limit. The ticket (¥11,850) is a card which can be used by one person travelling on any five days within the period of validity, or five people on one day, or any combination of two/three in between; it is stamped per day of use or per person. Two disadvantages, unlike for other passes, are that there is no discount for children and the tickets are valid only during three designated periods of the year: for travel between 1st March and 10th April (on sale 20th Feb to 31st Mar); for travel between 20th July and 10th September (on sale 1st July to 31st Aug); and for travel between 10th December and 20th January (on sale 1st Dec to 10th Jan). The opening of the Hokkaido shinkansen meant that the ticket could not be used for travel to Hokkaido so JR Hokkaido has introduced an option ticket, called **Seishun 18 Kippu Hokkaido shinkansen ticket**, for ¥2300. This permits travel in an unreserved seat between Okutsugaru-Imabetsu, the last stop on Honshu, and Kikonai, the first stop on Hokkaido. It also covers the private South Hokkaido Railway line between Kikonai and Goryokaku, from where you can connect with the JR network in Hokkaido.

Effectively a day's travel with a normal 'kippu' is equivalent to ¥2370; if you are happy to spend about 8½ hours on local/rapid services going from Tokyo to Kyoto you would save ¥5840 on the normal fare and much more compared to a shinkansen.

If you know you want to travel in a limited area only the regional passes can be better value than a Japan Rail Pass; one or more can also be combined quite easily which would widen the area you can discover. However, the huge range of passes makes it much harder to work out what will be best value for your itinerary. If in Japan for 14 days the difference between a 7-day and a 14-day Ordinary Class Japan Rail Pass is ¥17,280 so it wouldn't make sense to spend more than that on a regional pass for up to 7 days. Also many of the regional passes don't include free seat reservations, though if not travelling in peak periods that may not be a concern. Every now and then the companies introduce special promotional passes/tickets so it is always worth checking their websites.

## JR East rail passes

The JR East network covers the Tokyo metropolitan area and extends north and east of Tokyo including the route around Tohoku (see pp318-53) as far as the northern tip of Honshu; it does not include Hokkaido. The main passes include travel on the Narita Express (N'EX) from Narita airport and the Tokyo Monorail from Haneda airport. They are also valid on Tobu Railway's Limited Express services to Nikko. Some of JR East's passes are also valid to places covered in the Central Honshu section such as Matsumoto, Atami and Odawara (though for the latter not using the Tokaido shinkansen), and on some private lines such as the Izu-kyuko line to Izukyu-Shimoda (for Shimoda).

A seasonal option (Apr-Nov) available with any JR East pass is the Tateyama Kurobe Option Ticket (see p184).

For full details of all the passes ☐ see www.jreast.co.jp. JR East also offers passes in conjunction with other JR companies; see opposite.

● **JR East Pass (Tohoku area)** (See box p30)  In addition to the network area outlined above the two main other lines this pass is valid on are the Iwate Galaxy Railway and Aoimori Railway. It is also valid for reserved seats in the Hayabusa and Komachi shinkansen – and of course all the other shinkansen in the region. Note that this pass is not valid on the Hokuriku/Nagano shinkansen

---

**❏ JR Central**

JR Central (JR Tokai), which operates the Tokaido shinkansen line between Tokyo and Shin-Osaka, and other mainline services, is the only JR company not to offer its own rail pass valid year-round, but it does offer a pass in conjunction with JR West (see p35) and the following:

● A **Central Japan FLEX-Rail ticket** valid for round-trip travel (day trip or up to seven days) on any shinkansen service between Tokyo and Kyoto/Shin-Osaka; the ticket gives approximately a 20% discount on the normal fare.

● A variety of **shinkansen tour packages** (from ¥21,000), some of which include accommodation (3-5 nights).

E-vouchers for these must be bought before arriving in Japan. For further details see ☐ english.jr-central.co.jp/shinkansen.

● **Alpine-Takayama-Matsumoto Area pass**  A seasonal pass (Apr-Nov; 5 days ¥17,500) introduced in 2016 for travel between Nagoya, Toyama, the Tateyama Alpine route, Shinano-Omachi and Matsumoto; see ☐ touristpass.jp for more details.

beyond Sakudaira, nor is it valid on any JR buses. For an itinerary suggestion see pp44-5.

● **JR East Pass (Nagano, Niigata area)** (See box p30) This pass is valid on the routes outlined opposite but for the Tohoku shinkansen only to Utsunomiya, the Hokuriku/Nagano shinkansen only to Joetsu-Myoko and the Niigata shinkansen to Niigata. In the ski season months it is also valid between Echigo-Yuzawa and Gala Yuzawa (see box p352).

For an itinerary suggestion see p45.

● **Tokyo Wide Pass** (See box p30) This permits unlimited travel in the Tokyo metropolitan area as well as Ordinary Class travel on JR East's shinkansen (except the Hayabusa and Komachi services) from Tokyo to: Sakudaira (Nagano shinkansen), Echigo-Yuzawa (Niigata); and to Nasu-Shiobara (Tohoku). It is also valid on some private lines. In effect this pass covers everywhere shown on the Around Tokyo map, other than the Hakone region. The designated area includes: Nikko (JR or Tobu services); the Kawaguchi-ko area; Kawagoe; to Odawara (for Hakone) but not on the Tokaido shinkansen; to Izukyu-Shimoda (for Shimoda); Kamakura; Yokohama; Narita and Haneda airports; the New Shuttle line (to the Railway Museum). In the ski season it is also valid between Echigo-Yuzawa and Gala Yuzawa (see box p352); pass-holders are entitled to some discounts at the resort.

If this pass is used on shinkansen services on one day at least and you don't mind doing day trips rather than staying over this pass provides excellent value, It means you can be based in Tokyo for several days but do a lot of sightseeing and then possibly only need a 7-day Japan Rail Pass for a 14-day holiday.

### JR East & JR West rail pass

● **Hokuriku Arch Pass** (See box p30) This pass is valid for travel between Tokyo (inc Narita and Haneda airports) and Osaka (inc Kansai Airport) using the Hokuriku shinkansen (Tokyo to Kanazawa) and the Thunderbird Limited Express (from Kanazawa to Osaka). The pass is also valid on JR lines in the Tokyo Metropolitan District; in the metropolitan areas of Osaka, Kyoto, and Kobe (Keihanshin area), but also including Nara and for some side trips from the Hokuriku shinkansen. The seasonal Tateyama Kurobe Option Ticket (see p184) is also available with this pass.

If travelling for a week and only really wanting to visit Tokyo, Kanazawa and Kyoto/Osaka this provides better value than a 7-day Japan Rail Pass.

For further details see 🖳 hokuriku-arch-pass.com.

### JR East & JR Hokkaido rail pass

● **JR East-South Hokkaido Rail Pass** (See box p30) This is basically valid for the same area as the Tohoku pass but also includes the shinkansen to Shin-Hakodate-Hokuto as well as JR Hokkaido services to Sapporo and also on the Otaru route. It is not valid for JR buses, or on the private South Hokkaido Railway (Kikonai to Goryokaku). This pass is good value if you have a 14-day holiday and want to focus only on these areas. For further details see 🖳 www.jreasthokkaido.com; for an itinerary suggestion see p45. See also pp35-6.

### JR West rail passes

● **Sanyo Sanin Area Pass** (See box p30)  This pass includes travel on the shinkansen between Shin-Osaka and Hakata (with reserved seats) as well as on limited express services in the designated area, which is most of Western Honshu and some of Kansai.

For a 14-day holiday in Japan this pass combined with the Hokuriku Arch Pass (see p33) would cost about ¥3000 less than a 14-day Japan Rail Pass. However, the downside would be that you can't see Kyushu beyond Hakata, nor can you spontaneously head off to Shikoku, both of which you could with a Japan Rail Pass. For itinerary suggestions see pp45-6.

● **Kansai Hokuriku Area Pass** (See box p30)  Valid on Sanyo shinkansen from Shin-Osaka to Okayama, services to Shingu (inc Kansai Airport) from Osaka, Kyoto or Nara as well as services on the Thunderbird LEX up to Kanazawa and from there on the Hokuriku shinkansen (excluding Kagayaki services) east to Joetsu-Myoko. The pass is also valid on some non JR lines as long as the pass-holder only stops at the stations that link with the JR lines.

It is important to note that services to Takayama are not included; nor is the reserved seat fee for any shinkansen service; nor is the pass valid for the Tokaido shinkansen between Kyoto/Maibara and Shin-Osaka. For itinerary suggestions see p46.

● **Kansai Wide Area Pass** (See box p30)  This pass is valid for unreserved seats on the Sanyo shinkansen (Shin-Osaka to Okayama) and also on several limited express trains in the Kansai region including south to Shingu, east to Tsuruga/Nagahama, west to Kurashiki and to Takamatsu on Shikoku.

---

### ❑ Kansai Thru Pass

Around Kansai, JR stations are often peripheral and onward transport is usually required at additional expense. The Kansai Thru Pass (🖥 www.surutto.com; ¥4000/5200 2-/3-day) offers unlimited travel on most private railway lines and bus services in the region, but its true value comes from the inclusion of all subway and bus lines at your origin and destination which collectively are often more expensive than the inter-urban element.

The pass is valid as far west as Himeji and also includes Kobe, Osaka, Kyoto, Nara and Koya-san. In addition it can be used to and from Kansai International Airport on the private Nankai railway (but you have to pay a supplement to ride Nankai's 'rapi:t' express service). Foreign tourists or Japanese nationals who live abroad, as well as anyone accompanying them, can buy this pass. The pass also comes with a coupon book with small discounts (around ¥100) off many Kansai attractions. The 3-day ticket can also be used on non-consecutive calendar days (not 24-hr periods), which is a huge advantage. Also note that, as for most passes, if you lose your ticket it will not be reissued.

An excellent way to maximize the value of a Japan Rail Pass, with which short-distance travel around Kansai is poor value, is to fly into Kansai and use a Kansai Thru Pass before or after the Japan Rail Pass validity period. The pass can be bought at Kansai Airport, Kyoto Station Bus Ticket Center and visitor information centres in Osaka; check the website for other possibilities. All attractions in the Kansai city guides can be reached with a Kansai Thru Pass; the nearest private line station is specified.

● **Kansai-Hiroshima Area Pass** (See box p30) This has the same validity as the Kansai Wide Area Pass, but includes travel west to Hiroshima on the shinkansen and to Iwakuni on ordinary services. It also includes the ferry to Miyajima.

● **Hiroshima-Yamaguchi Area Pass** (See box p30) Includes travel in unreserved seats from Mihara shinkansen station to Hakata and mainline services from Onomichi station but also up to Masuda and Tsuwano. It also includes the ferry to Miyajima.

● **Hokuriku Area Pass** (See box p30) Valid on Hokuriku shinkansen between Kurobe-Unazukionsen and Kanazawa, in non-reserved seats; also on conventional lines down to Johana, up to Himi/Wakura-onsen and west to Tsuruga.

● **Sanin-Okayama Area Pass** (See box p30) Valid only for stops on conventional lines between Okayama/Kurashiki and on the Sanin coast between Tottori and Masuda. One advantage is that this pass includes travel on the Chizu Express Line which means it is possible to go from Okayama to Tottori without paying an additional fare.

● **Kansai Area Pass** (See box p30) Useful if you're spending only a few days in and around Kyoto or Osaka and plan to make a couple of short excursions. It covers travel on local trains only between Kyoto, Osaka, Kobe, Nara, Himeji and Kansai Airport. It is also valid for non-reserved seats on the Haruka LEX to Kansai Airport. However, the Kansai Thru Pass (see box opposite) is fractionally cheaper and can also be used by Japanese resident abroad.

For more details on all these passes, see 🖥 www.westjr.co.jp

### JR West & JR Central (Tokai) rail passes

● **Takayama Hokuriku Area pass** (See box p30) Includes unlimited travel from Kansai Airport to Kyoto/Osaka and on to Kanazawa; also on Nohi and Kaetsuno buses to the Shirakawa-go area from either Kanazawa or Takayama; non-reserved seats on the Hokuriku shinkansen between Kanazawa and Toyama and also on conventional line services between Nagoya and Toyama.

● **Ise Kumano Area Pass** (See box p30) Valid for unlimited journeys on JR train services from Nagoya down to Kii-Katsuura and also to Ise-shi and Toba; this also includes the non-JR section between Kawarada and Tsu. Also can be used on bus services in the valid area operated by Mie Kotsu (including the CAN bus), and Kumano Kotsu. The pass also includes free seat reservations for up to four journeys.

**Notes**: Both these passes must be bought before coming to Japan. If flying to/from Kansai or Nagoya airports and only planning to see places in the central part of Honshu these would provide a good base for a 10- to 14-day holiday. For more details see 🖥 touristpass.jp/en.

### JR Hokkaido rail passes

(See box p30) The passes are valid on all JR Hokkaido trains (inc with reserved seats) but not on the Hokkaido shinkansen and therefore not for the journey from Honshu to Shin-Hakodate-Hokuto (for Hokkaido). The Hokkaido Rail Pass is available as a **3-, 5- and 7-day pass**, or a **flexible 4-day pass** that can be used on any 4 days in a 10-day period from the date of issue. All can be bought in Hokkaido or at JR East Travel Service Centers.

JR Hokkaido also sells a **7-day Hokkaido Round Tour Pass** (Hokkaido Furii Passu), which costs ¥26,230 (£164/US$231). The ticket – which, unlike the other rail passes, can be purchased by anyone – offers 7-day unlimited rides in the Ordinary Car unreserved carriages of express/limited express services as well as on some JR Hokkaido buses. You can make up to six seat reservations for free during the validity of the pass. However, the pass cannot be used during peak holiday seasons: Golden Week (29th April-5th May), Obon (mid August), and New Year.

See also 🖳 www.jrhokkaido.co.jp and for itinerary suggestions see p46.

### JR Kyushu rail passes

(See also box p30)  JR Kyushu has two main pass options: one is valid for the **northern part of the island only** (including Nagasaki and Kumamoto on the west side and to Oita on the east coast); the other covers the **whole island**. Both can be used for travel on Mizuho services, which the Japan Rail Pass does not permit. However, neither can be used on shinkansen services north from Hakata (Fukuoka) as they are operated by JR West. Up to 10/16 free seat reservations can be made for the 3-day/5-day passes.

Non-Japanese tourists as well as Japanese who have permanent residency in another country can use these passes and they can be bought in Japan.

For more details see 🖳 www.jrkyushu.co.jp; for itinerary suggestions see p46.

### JR Shikoku rail pass

(See also box p30) The **All Shikoku Rail Pass** permits unlimited travel (2-5 consecutive days) on all JR Shikoku services (up to Kojima station on Honshu) as well as those provided by private rail companies (Kotoden, Iyotetsu, Tosaden, Tosa Kuroshio and Asato). The pass can be bought in Japan.

See also 🖳 shikoku-railwaytrip.com and for itinerary suggestions see p47.

### GETTING A RAIL PASS

The Japan Rail Pass has to be bought outside Japan (but see p29) Most regional passes can now be bought in Japan, though generally for an additional charge (up to ¥1000). Note that for all passes the price is fixed in yen; what you pay will depend on the exchange rate used by the authorised agent – it is worth contacting a few to check their prices and also their postage charges, if any.

The travel agencies listed are some of the many worldwide **authorised to sell the Japan Rail Pass** (some also sell the regional passes); most also book flights and accommodation, operate tours to Japan and can organise tailor-made holidays as well as special experiences such as the tea ceremony or dressing in a kimono. If flying with either ANA or JAL it is possible to get a rail pass through the airline.

The full list of authorised agents is available at 🖳 www.japanrailpass.net. Some online agencies, such as JR Pass (see opposite) can send passes worldwide.

### In the UK and Republic of Ireland

● **AWL Travel** (🖳 www.awlt.com)  Have a range of tours from half a day to six days and can also book flights.

● **Discover Japan** (🖳 www.discover-japan.co.uk)  Focuses on the luxury end of the market.

● **Ffestiniog Travel** (🖳 www.myrailtrip.co.uk)  Also sell the JR East and JR Kyushu passes. Occasionally operate escorted tours (including a 21-day Japan Rail Pass).

● **H.I.S. Europe** (🖳 www.his-euro.co.uk)  Is part of the H.I.S. Group, a travel agency with branches all over Japan. H.I.S. also sells the regional JR rail passes. A variety of package tours is available through **ViaJapan Holidays** (🖳 www.viajapan.co.uk).

● **Inside Japan Tours** (🖳 www.insidejapantours.com)  Their website has a blog page with interesting articles about travel in Japan. The company offers a wide range of tours and can arrange a number of cultural experiences.

● **International Rail** (🖳 www.internationalrail.com)  An online agency.

● **Into Japan Specialist Tours** (🖳 www.intojapan.co.uk)  Enquiries about the Japan Rail Pass must be by phone (☎ 01865-841443). Have an office in Tokyo.

● **Jaltour** (operated by Euro Creative Tours; 🖳 www.jaltour.co.uk)  Also sells most of the regional JR passes.

● **Japan Experience** (🖳 www.japan-rail-pass.com)  Also agent for the regional JR passes. Japan Experience (🖳 www.japan-experience.com) also offers a house rental service (see p73) and can provide Suica/Pasmo cards, pocket wi-fi and pre-paid data SIM cards in advance of travel.

● **Japan Journeys** (🖳 www.japanjourneys.co.uk)  Arranges independent, special interest and tailor-made tours.

● **Japan Travel Centre** (🖳 www.japantravel.co.uk)  Can book flights and accommodation; offers tours and can arrange a pre-paid data SIM card.

● **JRPass** (🖳 www.jrpass.com)  An online agency with a very useful travel tips section, an interactive map and videos. Also offers pocket wi-fi rental.

● **JTB** (Japan Travel Bureau; 🖳 www.japanspecialist.co.uk)  JTB is a travel agency with branches all over Japan. It also sells the regional JR passes and is one of a few agencies authorised to sell tickets for Ghibli Museum.

● **My Bus** (🖳 www.mybus-europe.jp/myBusUK)  Part of the JTB group and provides the same services.

● **Rail Tour Guide** (🖳 www.railtourguide.com)  Also offers the JR East and JR West passes.

● **STA Travel** (🖳 rail.statravel.co.uk)  Also sells several of the regional JR passes and can book flights and accommodation.

● **Unique Japan Tours** (🖳 www.uniquejapantours.com)  Offers a range of tours including self guided. Has offices in Dublin and London.

### In continental Europe

● **Belgium** **Fuji Travel** (🖳 www.fujitravel.be); **Japan P.I. Travel** (🖳 www.japanpitravel.be).

● **Denmark** **JTB** (🖳 www.japanspecialisten.dk).

PLANNING YOUR TRIP

● **France**  Destination Japon (🖳 www.destinationjapon.fr); **H.I.S.** (🖳 www
.his-tours.fr); **JRPass** (see p37); **JTB** (🖳 www.specialistejapon.fr); **Vivre le
Japon** (🖳 www.vivrelejapon.com) also provides house rental and many other
services (see Japan Experience, p37).

● **Germany**  Fuji Tours (🖳 www.fujitours.de); **H.I.S.** (🖳 www.his-germany
.de); **Japan Experience** (🖳 www.der-japan-rail-pass.de, 🖳 www.japan-experi
ence.de), see also p37; **JRPass** (see p37); **JTB** (🖳 www.japanspecialist.de);
**STA Travel** (🖳 www.statravel.de/bahntickets-bahnpass.htm#japan).

● **Italy**  H.I.S. (🖳 giappone.hisitaly.com); **Japan Experience** (see p37);
**JRPass** (see p37); **JTB** (🖳 www.jtbitaly.eu); **Miki Travel** (🖳 www.giap
poneviaggi- miki.it).

● **The Netherlands**  H.I.S. (🖳 www.hisgo.nl); **Japan Experience** (see p37);
**JRPass** (see p37); **JTB** (🖳 jtbjapanspecialist.nl); **Tozai Travel** (🖳 www
.tozai.nl).

● **Spain**  H.I.S. Viajes (🖳 www.his-spain.com); **Japan Experience** (see p37);
**JRPass** (see p37); **JTB Viajes** (🖳 www.viajesajapon.net).

● **Sweden**  JTB (🖳 www.japanspecialisten.nu).

● **Switzerland**  Harry Kolb Travel (🖳 www.harrykolb.ch/3513/japan);
**H.I.S.** (🖳 www.his-swiss.ch); **Japan Ferien** (online agent; 🖳 japan-ferien.ch).

## In the USA

Some of the agencies listed have branches nationwide; check the website for
details of your nearest office.

● **H.I.S.** (🖳 www.hisgo.com/us)  Also offers the regional passes. Part of the
H.I.S. Group (see p37) and has several branches in the USA.

● **IACE Travel** (🖳 www.iace-usa.com)  Operates escorted and unescorted
tours and can arrange flights, hotels and accommodation including in a temple.

● **Inside Japan Tours** (🖳 www.japanrailpass.us)  See p37.

● **Japan Rail Travel Network** (🖳 www.japanrailtravel.com).

● **JRPass** (🖳 www.jrpass.com)  See JRPass, p37.

● **JTB USA** (🖳 www.jtbusa.com)  Part of the JTB group and provides a wide
range of tours; authorised to sell tickets for Ghibli Museum (see box p115).

● **Kintetsu International Express** (🖳 www.kintetsu.com).

● **Nippon Travel Agency** (🖳 www.ntainbound.com)  Also offers most of the
regional passes as well as a range of tours; can book accommodation.

● **Sankei Travel** (🖳 www.sankeitravel.com)  Offers several 1-/2-day tours.

● **Society of International Railway Travelers** (🖳 www.irtsociety.com)  Doesn't
sell rail passes but is the first American company to charter the Seven Stars train
(see box p97). They also offer a de luxe tour without the Seven Stars extension.

● **STA Travel** (🖳 rail.statravel.com)  Also offers several of the regional passes
and can book flights and accommodation.

● **TTA** (🖳 www.ttasfo.com)  Can tailor-make holidays as well as booking
flights and accommodation.

### In Canada

● **Elite Orient Tours** (💻 www.elitetours.com) Arranges several tours.

● **H.I.S.** (💻 www.his-canada.com) Part of the H.I.S. group; see p37.

● **IACE Travel** (💻 www.iace-canada.com) See opposite.

● **Jade Tours** (💻 www2.jadetours.com) Can also provide pocket wi-fi rental.

● **JTB International** (💻 www.jtb.ca) Part of the JTB group and authorised to sell Ghibli Museum tickets (see box p115).

● **Kintetsu International Express** (💻 canada.kiecan.com/en).

● **Nippon Travel** (💻 www.nippontravel.ab.ca) Also provides tours.

### ● In Singapore

**H.I.S.** (💻 his.com.sg); **JTB** (💻 www.jtb.com.sg); **Sankei Travel Singapore** (💻 www.sankeitourist.com.sg); **STA Travel** (💻 www.statravel.com.sg).

### ● In South Africa

**Planet Africa Tours** (💻 www.visitjapan.co.za).

### In Australasia (Oceania)

● **H.I.S.** Australia (💻 www.traveljapan.com.au); New Zealand (💻 www.traveljapan.co.nz) Also sells the regional rail passes.

● **International Rail** (💻 www.internationalrail.com.au) An online agency.

● **Japan Package** (💻 www.japanpackage.com.au) Offers packages for every interest and budget.

● **Japan Rail Pass Now** (💻 www.japanrailpass.com.au) An online agency.

● **JTB Australia** (💻 www.japantravel.com.au) and **JTB New Zealand** (💻 www.jtboi.co.nz) Also sell the regional rail passes, can book flights and accommodation and run some rail-based escorted tours.

● **Kintetsu International Express** (💻 www.kintetsu.com.au).

● **Rail Plus** (💻 www.railplus.com.au) Also sells the regional rail passes.

● **Sachi Tours** (💻 www.sachitours.com.au) Also offers most regional passes.

● **STA Travel** Australia (💻 www.statravel.com.au); New Zealand (💻 www.statravel.co.nz).

## EXCHANGE ORDERS

When you buy the Japan Rail Pass (and any regional pass bought outside Japan), what you actually receive is an exchange order, which you turn in for the actual pass once in Japan.

Exchange orders are valid for three months from the date of issue, so only purchase one less than three months before you plan to start travelling by rail. When purchasing the exchange order you will receive a guide to using the pass.

### How and where to turn in the exchange order

Once in Japan, take your exchange order to any **JR Travel Service Center** authorised to handle the Japan Rail Pass. The most obvious ones are at the JR stations in airports such as Narita/Haneda (Tokyo) and Kansai (Osaka).

Major JR stations such as Tokyo, Nagoya, Kyoto, Osaka, Shin-Osaka, Sapporo and Hakata have travel service centers, but, except at peak holiday periods, it's often easiest to sort your pass out at the airports even if you're not going to start travelling immediately. Staff there are used to handling rail-pass requests and are extremely efficient. However, be prepared for long queues at busy periods (March/April and November).

At the time of exchange you will need to provide the date you want to start the pass (this can be any day within one month of the day you turn in the exchange order). Once the rail pass is issued the date cannot be changed so the staff will carefully check you understand the dates it will be valid. They will also ask to see your passport to check that you have been admitted on 'temporary visitor' status; Japanese passport-holders resident abroad should bring proof of their address.

Assuming you are going to start using your pass immediately staff at the office will be happy to make seat reservations for journeys for that day. If they

PLANNING YOUR TRIP

### ❏ Overcoming the language barrier

One of the biggest worries for first-time visitors to Japan is the language barrier. How difficult is it to make yourself understood and navigate your way around the country? The answer is that it's surprisingly easy; most Japanese can understand some English, even if not everybody speaks it.

You don't need to be able to read Japanese characters (*kanji*) to find your way around: **station names** are written in English on every platform and on-board announcements are made in English on all shinkansen and many limited express trains and even on local trains in tourist areas; the vast majority of hotels and ryokan have their names written in English outside; in most towns and cities, road signs and street names are in both Japanese and English. The kanji for most places of interest is included in this guide, but if going off-the-beaten track ask hotel reception or tourist information staff to write down the name of the place you're heading for, so you can show it to taxi drivers or passers-by when asking for directions.

If you're travelling with a smartphone or tablet you can make use of some very useful **Japanese-language apps**. Touchscreens allow you to draw kanji to find out their meaning as well as look for definitions in the normal way. *Imiwa* (🖳 www.imiwaapp.com; free on iTunes) has a comprehensive dictionary of words and kanji. It is very easy to use and can be used offline; it can be fascinating simply to run in random English words and see what kanji are used to make up the Japanese word. A similar app called *JED* (🖳 www.umibouzu.com/jed) is available for Android smartphones. Google Translate has free apps for both Android and iPhone and Japanese is one of the 90 languages you can download in advance so not having wi-fi won't be an issue. A useful **online dictionary** is 🖳 jisho.org though some prefer the original version 🖳 classic.jisho.org. There are also various phrasebook apps with useful recorded **sound files**: try *Japanese Phrases & Lessons* (free on iTunes, or £6.99 with a much-expanded set of phrases).

For a list of railway-related words and phrases see p502.

are not busy they may also be happy to make seat reservations for travel on other days.

**Important**: JR will not replace lost passes so treasure your pass. If you do lose it on a train or at a station, the advantage of being in Japan is that there is a good chance someone will hand it in to a Lost and Found office (see p101).

## HOW TO USE THE RAIL PASS

Once you've received the pass, all you do is show it whenever you pass a ticket barrier and JR staff will wave you through. Since the pass is not computerised it cannot be fed through automatic wickets, but there is always a manned gate on one side of the entrances/exits to the platforms.

Unless you are boarding a train which contains reserved carriages only (see p101), seat reservations are not necessary as you can just turn up for any train and sit in the unreserved carriages. However, on some trains, and at certain times of the day/year (see pp14-16), it's a good idea to make a reservation in order to guarantee a seat and avoid the hassle of having to find one, especially if you are not getting on at the first station. Since holders of a Japan Rail Pass can make any number of seat reservations for free (see pp100-1 for details) it's worth doing so in any case.

A few JR trains run on sections of track owned by private companies and rail-pass holders are supposed to pay a supplement to travel on these sections. In practice you will only have to pay if a conductor is checking tickets at the time the train is running along the non-JR track. Where relevant, this is highlighted in the route description.

# Suggested itineraries

With such a vast network of rail services, one of the hardest tasks in planning a trip to Japan is working out how much you can fit in. **One week** is really too short to attempt anything more than a quick shuttle between Kyoto and Tokyo, with perhaps a day trip to Nara, Hakone or Hiroshima. To get anything like a sense of what the country is really about, and to give yourself time to get over jet lag and/or culture shock, plan for at least **two** but preferably **three** weeks.

The following itineraries are neither prescriptive nor are they intended to be the last word on rail travel in Japan. Their purpose is to give a flavour of what can be accomplished. Several of the itineraries listed include a lot of moving around; the aim being to give an idea of what is possible. However, when planning an itinerary it is likely to be more relaxing to choose certain cities as a base (such as Tokyo, Nagoya, Kyoto, Sendai, Okayama and Kumamoto) and do day trips from there rather than moving on every night.

When planning an itinerary it is worth knowing what festivals and events will be on when you are in Japan; for details see pp17-18.

## GENERAL ITINERARIES

The following general itineraries are for holders of **7-, 14- and 21-day Japan Rail Passes** and do not include days before/after the rail pass is used. The itineraries are arranged to start from and end in Tokyo, but most include Kyoto so could be adapted if you are arriving at Kansai Airport.

### Seven-day itinerary: the classic route
● **Day 1**  Spend the day and night in **Tokyo**, Japan's dynamic capital.
● **Day 2**  Take a shinkansen west to Mishima to see some of the **Hakone region** (Mt Fuji and Lake Ashi) then continue on to Kyoto, Japan's ancient capital, for the night. If the weather is bad go straight to **Kyoto**, best known for its temples.
● **Day 3**  Spend the day and another night in Kyoto.
● **Day 4**  Spend the day and another night in Kyoto, or have a day trip to scenic **Arashiyama**, or to **Nara** to see Japan's largest statue of the Buddha at Todai-ji temple.
● **Day 5**  Take a shinkansen to **Himeji** and visit the stunning and recently restored castle; continue to **Hiroshima** and visit the Peace Memorial Park. Overnight in Hiroshima.
● **Day 6**  Visit **Miyajima**, an island famed for its scenic beauty, Itsukushima shrine and for the torii gate that rises out of the sea. Then take the shinkansen back to Tokyo, perhaps stopping at Okayama to visit **Korakuen**, one of Japan's 'three great gardens'.
● **Day 7**  Spend the day in Tokyo, or go to **Kamakura** to see the second largest statue of a Buddha in Japan.

### Seven-day itinerary: off-the-beaten track
● **Day 1**  Take a shinkansen from **Tokyo** to Nasu-Shiobara and then transfer to a JR bus to visit **Shiobara-onsen**, an onsen town popular in the past with the Imperial family because of its fresh air.
● **Day 2**  Hop on a bus back to Nasu-Shiobara and then take a shinkansen to Ichinoseki and go to **Hiraizumi**, a compact town with some historic temples in scenic surroundings, for the night.
● **Day 3**  Take a shinkansen back to Tokyo and then transfer to the Nagano (Hokuriku) shinkansen and go to Nagano for the night.
● **Day 4**  Pick up the Wide View Shinano LEX to Nagoya and stop off at **Narai**, one of the traditional post towns in the Kiso Valley. Continue on to Nagiso and then take a bus to **Tsumago**, another post town where a number of traditional inns cater for the weary (rail) traveller.
● **Day 5**  Walk to **Magome** (2-3hrs) along the path used in the past to go between Kyoto and Edo (now Tokyo), and then pick up a bus to Nakatsugawa, or return to Nagiso and take the train to Nagoya from there. Spend the night in Nagoya.
● **Day 6**  Pick up a Kodama shinkansen as far as Kakegawa. Transfer to the conventional JR Tokaido line to Kanaya for a side trip on the **Oigawa steam railway**. Return to **Tokyo**.
● **Day 7**  Have a day trip to **Narita Town** to experience the Goma (Sacred Fire), ceremony at Naritasan Shinsho-ji.

## Fourteen-day itinerary: into the mountains and along the coast

● **Day 1** Spend the day and night in **Tokyo**, Japan's dynamic capital.

● **Day 2** Have a day trip north to **Nikko**, home to the opulent Toshogu Shrine, or south to **Kamakura**, home to the largest open-air Buddha.

● **Day 3** Take a shinkansen to Nagano and then transfer to a Shinano LEX and go to **Matsumoto**, site of one of Japan's best-preserved castles.

● **Day 4** On the Shinano again, continue south to Shiojiri and change to a local train to reach the old post town of **Narai**. By late afternoon, carry on to **Nagiso**, from where it's a short bus ride to **Tsumago**.

● **Day 5** After an early morning wander around Tsumago, return to Nagiso and continue south to Nagoya. Then take a shinkansen to **Kyoto** for the night.

● **Day 6** Spend the day and night in Kyoto, Japan's ancient capital.

● **Day 7** Spend a second day in Kyoto or have a day trip to **Arashiyama**, or **Nara**.

● **Day 8** Make the brief hop by shinkansen to Shin-Osaka (for **Osaka**). Though a city of commerce rather than tourism, Osaka is worth a visit; theme-park enthusiasts will enjoy **Universal Studios Japan**.

● **Day 9** Hop back on the shinkansen and spend some time in **Himeji**, fêted for its picture-postcard castle. Continue by shinkansen to **Okayama** for the night.

● **Day 10** Early morning is the best time to visit Okayama Castle and **Korakuen** the city's famous garden. In the afternoon pick up a westbound shinkansen and alight in **Hiroshima**.

● **Day 11** Have a day trip to **Miyajima**.

● **Day 12** Spend the morning in Hiroshima at the Peace Memorial Park. Pick up a westbound shinkansen to **Hakata** (Fukuoka) in Kyushu and then transfer to a Kamome LEX train to Nagasaki.

● **Day 13** Spend the day in **Nagasaki**, a beautiful port city but probably better known as the location for the dropping of the second atomic bomb in 1945.

● **Day 14** Finally retrace your steps back to **Tokyo** (you'll have to change at Okayama or Shin-Osaka), covering a distance of 1175km in just over six hours.

Other than buses to/from Tsumago/Magome, this itinerary only includes rail travel on JR services; if you are prepared to spend a bit more for travel on private lines with/without a pass, consider going to Hakone (see pp165-8), Kawaguchi-ko (pp138-41), and/or Koya-san (pp156-8).

## Itinerary for a 21-day pass

Make the most of a 21-day rail pass by combining the 14-day itinerary outlined above with a week focusing on one of the regions described below.

The 14-day itinerary gets you to Nagasaki on Day 13 so you're perfectly placed to continue with a third week of travel around **Kyushu** (see p46). If you prefer to spend the extra week exploring the island of **Shikoku** (see p47), the starting point is Okayama (reached on Day 9 of the 14-day itinerary). Another option would be to return to Tokyo (as on Day 14) and then continue north and explore the **Tohoku** region (see pp44-5), or go to **Hokkaido** (p45).

Alternatively, consider the 21-day itinerary (see box p44) followed by a couple of readers.

❏ **A 21-day itinerary including hot springs, Kyoto and a mountain temple**
Using a 21-day Japan Rail Pass and the Hakone Freepass we started our holiday in **Tokyo** and visited Shinjuku, the Meiji Shrine and Ueno, **Yokohama** and **Kamakura**. We then had two nights at a ryokan in **Takaragawa-onsen** (wonderful hot springs and forest/river walks) and one night in **Okayama** before continuing to **Nagasaki** for two nights. Back east to **Kyoto** for five nights (we would have been happy to stay even longer) and then on to **Koya-san**, a mountain retreat, for two nights in Jofukuin Temple. This enabled us to experience *shojin ryori*, the delicious vegetarian food associated with Buddhist temples. From Koya-san we went to Odawara and then used the Hakone Freepass to explore the **Hakone/Mt Fuji region** and had a night in Moto-Hakone, on the shores of Lake Ashi. We then moved on to **Nikko** for two nights before returning to Tokyo from where we had a fantastic day trip to **Narita**. A great way to end the trip.                              **Jill Rowe and Roderick Leslie**

## REGIONAL RAIL PASS ITINERARIES

The following are suggested itineraries for the main regional rail passes (see pp32-6), but can also be followed with the Japan Rail Pass. Since several of the passes permit a fixed number of days' travel within a certain time period it is best to plan to use shinkansen services on those days and local trains or buses – or your feet – on the other days. If you have just arrived in Japan and are feeling jetlagged you might prefer to spend two or three days in Tokyo at the beginning of your holiday, rather than at the end.

### JR East Pass (Tohoku): 5 days' travel in a 14-day period
● **Day 1**  Spend day in **Tokyo**.
● **Day 2 (Travel day 1)**  Take a shinkansen to Utsunomiya and change to the JR Nikko Line for **Nikko**, home to the opulent Toshogu Shrine.
● **Day 3**  Spend day in Nikko.
● **Day 4 (Travel day 2)**  Return to Utsunomiya and pick up the shinkansen to **Ichinoseki**.
● **Day 5**  Have a day trip to the temple town of **Hiraizumi**, a compact town with some historic temples in scenic surroundings; return to Ichinoseki for the night.
● **Day 6  (Travel day 3)**  Take a shinkansen to Akita (you may need to change train at Morioka) and consider stopping en route at **Tazawa-ko**, to see Japan's deepest lake, or at **Kakunodate**, a former samurai town.
● **Day 7**  Have a day trip to **Senjojiki** (or beyond) on the Ou Line (Hirosaki to Kawabe) and then on the Gono Line (between Kawabe and Senjojiki). The Resort Shirakami train operates on these lines at weekends/in holiday periods.
● **Day 8**  Akita to **Aomori**, Honshu's northernmost city, best known for the Nebuta Matsuri (Nebuta Festival) in August.
● **Day 9**  Spend day and another night in Aomori.
● **Day 10 (Travel Day 4)**  Take a shinkansen from Shin-Aomori to **Sendai**.
● **Day 11**  Day trip either to **Matsushima**, one of the top three scenic spots in Japan, or **Yamadera**, a hillside temple.

- **Day 12 (Travel Day 5)** Sendai to **Tokyo** by shinkansen.
- **Days 13 & 14** Spend remaining time in and around Tokyo.

## JR East Pass (Nagano, Niigata): 5 days' travel in a 14-day period

- **Days 1-3 (inc Travel day 1)** Same as for Tohoku Pass (see opposite).
- **Day 4 (Travel day 2)** Return to Utsunomiya, take shinkansen to Tokyo and then to Nagano.
- **Days 5 & 6** Visit Zenko-ji temple in **Nagano** and the **snow monkeys** in Jigokudani Monkey Park.
- **Day 7 (Travel day 3)** Travel from Nagano to Takasaki and then to Niigata by shinkansen; stay in **Niigata**.
- **Day 8** Have a day trip to Dewa Sanzan; three sacred mountains, a popular pilgrimage place.
- **Day 9 (Travel day 4)** Return to Tokyo.
- **Days 10-12** Tokyo and around including Narita, Kawagoe and/or Kamakura.
- **Day 13 (Travel day 5)** Day trip to Matsumoto or Izukyu-Shimoda (for Shimoda).
- **Day 14** Tokyo

## JR East-South Hokkaido Pass: 6 days' travel in a 14-day period

- **Days 1-3** Tokyo and around.
- **Day 4 (Travel day 1)** Tokyo to **Nikko**, home to the opulent Toshogu Shrine.
- **Day 5** Spend day in Nikko visiting the shrines and the former Imperial villa.
- **Day 6 (Travel day 2)** Nikko to Sendai via Utsunomiya.
- **Day 7** Have a day trip either to **Matsushima**, one of the top three scenic spots in Japan or **Yamadera**, a hillside temple.
- **Day 8 (Travel day 3)** Sendai to Kakunodate via Morioka by shinkansen.
- **Day 9** Walk around **Kakunodate**, a former samurai town.
- **Day 10 (Travel day 4)** Kakunodate to Hakodate
- **Day 11** Spend day in Hakodate and visit its morning market and Motomachi, the city's old quarter with several Western-style buildings.
- **Day 12 (Travel day 5)** Hakodate to Sapporo
- **Day 13** Spend day in **Sapporo**, also consider a visit to **Otaru**.
- **Day 14 (Travel day 6)** Sapporo to Tokyo

## JR West Sanyo Sanin Area Pass: 7 consecutive days' travel

- **Day 1** Starting in **Osaka** (Shin-Osaka), take a westbound shinkansen to **Himeji** and visit the picture-postcard castle; continue on to **Hiroshima** for the night.
- **Day 2** Spend day (and night) in Hiroshima or go to **Miyajima**.
- **Day 3** Take the shinkansen west to **Shin-Yamaguchi** and then take the Super Oki LEX (at weekends and in summer a steam locomotive operates on this route) to the picturesque town of **Tsuwano**.
- **Day 4** Take the Super Oki to **Matsue**, known as the 'city of water'.
- **Day 5** Spend day exploring Matsue before taking a sunset cruise around **Lake Shinji**. Alternatively have a trip to Adachi Museum of Art and/or Tottori.

PLANNING YOUR TRIP

- **Day 6** From Matsue, pick up the Super Yakumo LEX which cuts across Honshu to **Okayama** and spend the night there.
- **Day 7** Spend last day in Osaka.

## JR West Kansai Hokuriku Area Pass: 7 consecutive days' travel
- **Day 1** From Kansai Airport to Shin-Osaka (Osaka)
- **Day 2** Spend day in **Osaka** discovering Dotombori, Osaka's eccentric entertainment district or visit Universal Studios, or Osaka's popular aquarium
- **Day 3** Take a limited express service to **Kanazawa**.
- **Day 4** Top priority in Kanazawa is the stroll garden, Kenrokuen, but also worth visiting are Myoryu-ji, better known as the Ninja Temple, the samurai district and Higashi-chaya, the former geisha district.
- **Day 5** Take a limited express service to **Kyoto**.
- **Day 6** Spend day in Kyoto visiting one of the main temples.
- **Day 7** Visit **Arashiyama**; return to Kyoto and then to Kansai Airport.

## JR Hokkaido Pass: Hokkaido highlights
- **Day 1** Explore **Hakodate**, a port town with a wonderful morning market.
- **Day 2** Take a train to Oshamambe and transfer there for the alternative route to Sapporo; stop off at **Otaru**, a beautiful seaside town; continue to Sapporo.
- **Day 3** Spend day in **Sapporo**, known for its snow festival and clock tower.
- **Day 4** Get an early train to **Asahikawa** and either visit the zoo or make an excursion to **Asahidake** in Daisetsuzan National Park.
- **Day 5** Head to **Furano**, known in summer for the fields of lavender and in winter for snow, and spend the night there.
- **Day 6** Go to **Noboribetsu-onsen** for the night.
- **Day 7** Return to Sapporo or Hakodate.

The itinerary above is for a 7-day pass (see pp35-6); recommended stops for a 5-day pass are Hakodate, Otaru, Sapporo, Asahikawa and Noboribetsu-onsen, for the flexible 4-day pass are Hakodate, Otaru, Sapporo and Noboribetsu-onsen, and for a 3-day pass are Sapporo, Hakodate and Otaru. See the Hokkaido route guides (pp367-93) for full details.

## JR Kyushu Pass: Kyushu highlights
- **Day 1** Starting from Kyushu's capital, **Fukuoka (Hakata)**, take the Kamome LEX west to **Nagasaki**.
- **Day 2** Spend the morning in Nagasaki and then travel to **Kumamoto**.
- **Day 3** Spend the morning in Kumamoto then travel to **Kagoshima**, access point for both the island of **Sakurajima**, with its active volcano, and **Ibusuki** for its naturally hot sand-bath.
- **Day 4** Take a train to Miyazaki and then continue to **Oita** for the night.
- **Day 5** Spend the morning in **Beppu** visiting the 'burning hells' then take a train back to Fukuoka (Hakata).

The itinerary above is for a 5-day All Kyushu pass (see p36); recommended stops for a 3-day pass are Nagasaki and Kumamoto or Kagoshima. See the Kyushu route guides (pp412-33) for full details.

PLANNING YOUR TRIP

## All Shikoku Pass: Shikoku highlights

● **Day 1** At **Takamatsu** visit the magnificent garden at Ritsurin-koen.
● **Day 2** Travel to **Tokushima**, known for its summer dance festival, and have a side trip to the whirlpools at **Naruto**.
● **Day 3** Visit **Oboke Gorge** en route to **Kochi**; in Kochi go to see the castle.
● **Day 4** Take the scenic Yodo line for the bull-fighting city of **Uwajima** or continue to **Uchiko**, for its well-preserved old quarter and Noh theatre.
● **Day 5** Travel to **Matsuyama**; be sure to go to **Dogo-onsen** to relax in the historic hot springs before completing the rail circuit back to Takamatsu.

The itinerary above is for a 5-day All Shikoku Rail Pass. Recommended stops with a 4-day pass are Takamatsu (two days), Tokushima & Matsuyama, with a 3-day pass visit Takamatsu, Tokushima & Matsuyama, and with a 2-day pass Takamatsu & Matsuyama. Details of all routes and sights are given in the Shikoku route guides (pp463-80).

# Before you go

## BOOKING A FLIGHT

Flights to Japan (see box below) can be booked direct through an airline, through a travel agency (see pp37-9), or online through discounted ticket outlets such as: Cheap Flights (🖳 www.cheapflights.com), Expedia (🖳 www.expedia.com), or Opodo (🖳 www.opodo.com). Discounted fares for students are also offered through STA Travel (🖳 www.statravel.com/worldwide.htm) and Travel CUTS (🖳 www.travelcuts.com). Some low-cost (budget) airlines operate international services to Japan but only from Asia.

---

❏ **Airports in Japan with international flights**
The three major airports in Japan are: Narita (Tokyo; NRT; see pp126-7), Haneda (Tokyo; HND; see p127), and Kansai (Osaka; KIX; see p151). All have flights from a large number of places worldwide.

Both Nagoya (Central Japan International Airport; 🖳 www.centrair.jp/en), and Fukuoka (🖳 www.fuk-ab.co.jp) have some flights from Europe but mainly from Asia.

Airports with flights from some destinations in Asia include: Hiroshima (🖳 www.hij.airport.jp); Sapporo (New Chitose Airport; 🖳 www.new-chitose-airport.jp); and Kagoshima (🖳 koj-ab.co.jp).

At the time of research there were no direct international flights to any city on the island of Shikoku.

The many code-sharing flights available now mean it is much easier to fly into one airport and leave Japan from another; the bonus is that this makes planning an itinerary without spending too much time backtracking much more straightforward. Also, once in Japan, there are domestic flights to virtually every city which can help if your time is limited.

---

PLANNING YOUR TRIP

## PASSPORTS AND VISAS

All visitors to Japan must have a passport that's valid for at least six months from the date of entry to Japan.

If visiting for the purposes of tourism, citizens of the following countries do not need to apply for a visa and can stay in Japan for up to 90 days under the 'reciprocal visa exemption' scheme: Australia, Austria, Belgium, Canada, France, Germany, Ireland, Italy, Netherlands, New Zealand, Singapore, Spain, Switzerland, UK, USA. Many other countries come under the same scheme. Exceptions include citizens of Hong Kong (though SAR and BNO passports are

### ❑ TOURIST INFORMATION

The best source of tourist information prior to arrival in Japan is the **Japan National Tourist Organization** (🖥 www.jnto.go.jp); it has a comprehensive website as well as a YouTube channel (🖥 www.youtube.com/visitjapan). JNTO's worldwide offices are information centres only; they do not sell any tickets or rail passes. Some are open for visitors to pick up brochures but all are happy to post maps and brochures, though a lot of information can be downloaded from their website. The main thing JNTO produces which isn't available online is a very useful map of Japan.

JNTO has offices in: **Australia** (🖥 www.jnto.org.au); **Canada** (🖥 www.ilove japan.ca); **China** (🖥 www.welcome2japan.cn; Hong Kong 🖥 www.welcome2 japan.hk); **France** (🖥 www.tourisme-japon.fr); **Germany** (🖥 www.jnto.de); **Indonesia** (🖥 www.jnto.or.id); **Korea** (🖥 www.welcometojapan.or.kr); **Singapore** (🖥 www.jnto.org.sg); **Thailand** (🖥 www.yokosojapan.org); the **UK** (🖥 www.see japan.co.uk); and the **USA** (🖥 us.jnto.go.jp).

### Other online sources of information

● 🖥 **www.japan-guide.com**  A truly wonderful resource as it provides comprehensive and up-to-date tourist information.

● 🖥 **www.japanvisitor.com**  Information about all aspects of travelling – as well as living and working – in Japan.

● 🖥 **www.att-japan.net**  Extensive information for visitors and residents; also produces a quarterly magazine distributed to tourist information offices in Japan.

● 🖥 **digjapan.travel**  A medley of pages about eating, shopping, sightseeing and more in Japan.

● 🖥 **taiken.co**  Blogs on a range of topics related to sightseeing.

● 🖥 **www.tsunagujapan.com**  A listings website with guides to all aspects of travel and sightseeing in Japan.

● 🖥 **japanican.com**  A JTB Group website which is primarily for booking accommodation and tours, but also has various travel guides.

● 🖥 **www.japantrends.com**  A fascinating website with links to articles about all the new trends and technological developments in Japan.

● 🖥 **www.japan-zone.com**  Features pages on popular and traditional culture as well as practical information.

● 🖥 **www.newsonjapan.com**  Compiles news stories on Japan from both the Japanese and international press and therefore is a great way of finding out what is happening.

● 🖥 **www.japannatureguides.com**  A useful website about flora and fauna in Japan.

OK), and Malaysian citizens who don't have a biometric passport; they need to apply for a tourist visa from the Japanese embassy in their home country.

Citizens of Austria, Germany, Ireland, Switzerland and the UK can apply for a further 90-day extension while in Japan.

Visa requirements change periodically, so before making travel arrangements check with the Japanese embassy in your home country.

Details about visa requirements as well as a complete list of Japanese embassies and consulates can be found at 🖥 www.mofa.go.jp. See pp64-5 for details of arrival procedures.

Note that in Japan you must carry your passport with you at all times.

## HEALTH AND INSURANCE

No vaccination or health certificate is required to enter the country (except for those arriving from a yellow fever zone) and there's no need to worry about diseases such as malaria, which are not endemic in Japan.

Unless specified (such as on trains), tap water is safe to drink everywhere in Japan. However, bottled water is readily available in convenience stores (sparkling/carbonated water is harder to find than still) and from vending machines.

Don't arrive in Japan without a comprehensive travel insurance policy. Japanese hospitals invariably offer high standards of care and most doctors speak English, but diagnosis, treatment and prescriptions can be prohibitively expensive.

If you're on medication, bring a copy of your prescription. This may be needed if Customs inspect your bags but will also be useful if you need a repeat prescription. Note that many international drugs are sold under different brand names in Japan. Also some medications are illegal in Japan so you need to prove whatever you have is legitimate.

## WHAT TO TAKE

The best advice is to **pack as little as possible**. Travelling light makes life much easier when you are getting on and off lots of trains; having a small suitcase should mean it is easy to fit your luggage into a locker (see p101) at the station. Also many accommodation options have laundry facilities.

It's really worth bringing **slip-on shoes** as you're expected to take your shoes off in the entrance hall at Japanese-style accommodation and also often when going around castles and temples. Guests walk around either in the slippers provided or, if these are too small, just in **socks** (pack a few pairs without holes!). Guests in most Japanese-style accommodation, as well as business hotels, are provided with a small towel which doubles as a flannel; if you prefer a large towel it might be better to bring one.

**Nightwear is not essential** as guests in most forms of accommodation, apart from hostels, are provided with a *yukata* (a cotton robe tied with a belt) that can be worn in bed and which is used as a dressing gown to go between

PLANNING YOUR TRIP

your room and the bathroom – in onsen towns/resorts it is also acceptable to walk around in the streets wearing a yukata. Yukata (and Japanese-style towels) can often be rented or purchased from the front desk if they are not provided.

**Pack according to the season** and the region in which you're likely to be travelling (see pp14-16). As a general rule, shorts and T-shirts are fine in the summer, though you'll probably need a sweater or two in the spring and autumn. Take warm clothes for the winter, especially if travelling in northern Japan.

At any time of the year, it's worth packing **a few smart clothes** – older Japanese people in particular are generally well dressed (even when on holiday themselves). If you forget anything, clothes and shoes are relatively cheap as long as you avoid the designer-label boutiques, but it's not always easy to find large sizes. **Don't bother packing an umbrella** as disposable ones are readily and cheaply available in convenience stores. Outdoor tourist attractions, as well as minshuku and ryokan, usually have a supply of umbrellas for visitors to borrow. If you want an unusual souvenir of your trip, take a **notebook** (see box below).

## MONEY

Japan is a **cash-based economy** so when travelling around it's best to ensure you always have a supply of cash. Easiest access to cash is via the thousands of post office **ATMs** around the country, all of which accept foreign-issued **debit cards** (including Maestro and Visa) and have instructions in English, as do branches of the 7-Eleven convenience store (see box p84).

Note that when you are being given change in a shop, hotel or restaurant, staff are likely to use a calculator to show what the bill came to and then what change is due; you will be given the relevant bank notes first and then coins, so don't panic if it seems you are just being given notes.

---

❏ **'Stamp' collecting around Japan**

'Stamp' collecting is a popular pastime in Japan, though the most popular stamps are not of the postage kind. Virtually every tourist attraction, and railway station, has its own stamp and ink pad at the entrance. Some towns organise seasonal 'stamp rallies', when tourists are invited to follow a trail from one attraction to another, collecting stamps as they go. Small souvenir prizes are sometimes doled out to those who completely fill their 'stamp cards' (a gesture of thanks for contributing to the local tourism industry). In Japan, it's almost as if you only know you've really been somewhere when you can bring back the stamp to prove it.

'Stamps' are particularly popular on the railway. JR East has created a 77-station stamp series for all the stations in the Tokyo metropolitan area. Even the tiniest rural station will more than likely have a stamp in the waiting room or by the ticket desk. Paper is not provided so pack a blank notebook in your luggage. Try to forget your image of the nerdy stamp collector; by collecting stamps as you go you'll have an instant souvenir of your rail trip around Japan as well as a useful record of your itinerary.

**Credit cards** are accepted in most major tourist places but don't rely on this. Upmarket hotels/ryokan generally accept (foreign-issued) credit/debit cards but cash is the preferred currency in hostels, minshuku, budget ryokan and business hotels. (See also pp78-9).

## SUGGESTED READING

A very useful reference list for books about Japan can be found at ⌨ www .japanvisitor.com/japan-books.

### History
● *Modern Japan, A Very Short Introduction* Christopher Goto-Jones (OUP, 2009) Covers the period from the early 1800s, when Japan started to open up, to the modern day – useful as a background read before you arrive.
● *A History of Japan: From Stone Age to Superpower* Kenneth Henshall (Macmillan, 2012) Scholarly but very readable.
● *A Traveller's History of Japan* Richard Tames (Interlink Publishing, 2008) A great, pocket-sized book that's ideal to dip into as you travel around.

### Travel narratives
● *The Roads to Sata* Alan Booth (Kodansha, 1997) The late Alan Booth walked the length of Japan, from Hokkaido to Kyushu, looking for beer. Equally absorbing is his *Looking for the Lost: Journeys Through a Vanishing Japan* (Kodansha, 1996), a series of travel narratives taking in parts of Japan that most foreigners never see.
● *The Japanese Chronicles* Nicholas Bouvier (Eland, 2009) The chronicles are based on three decades (1950s-70s) of living and travelling in Japan.
● *Rediscovering the Old Tokaido: In the footsteps of Hiroshige* Patrick Carey (Global Oriental, 2000) The story of a nostalgic journey on foot along what remains of the road that linked Edo and Kyoto in the days before the Tokaido railway line.
● *Hokkaido Highway Blues* Will Ferguson (Canongate, 2003) Ferguson travels from southern Kyushu north to Hokkaido following the path of the cherry blossom; an irreverent account of life on the open road.
● *Japan Through Writers' Eyes* Elizabeth Ingrams (Eland, 2009) Arranged according to place and includes extracts from travellers' experiences through a wide variety of historical periods.

### Life in Japan (non-fiction)
● *Geisha* Liza Dalby (Vintage, 2000) Based on Dalby's year as a geisha in the 1970s. She was subsequently a consultant on the film adaptation of *Memoirs of a Geisha* (see p52).
● *Geisha: The Secret History of a Vanishing World* Lesley Downer (Headline, 2001) This is a personal account of the months Downer spent in the Gion tea houses, befriending the *mama-san* who hold the purse strings and manage the careers of trainee geisha. She gets closer than any commentator to a revelation of life behind the enigmatic smiles and painted faces of geisha in Kyoto.

● *A Geek in Japan: Discovering the Land of Manga, Anime, Zen and the Tea Ceremony* Hector Garcia (Tuttle Shokai, 2011) An insight into life in contemporary Japan, with plenty of photos and illustrations.

● *Kokoro: Hints and Echoes of Japanese Inner Life* Lafcadio Hearn (Tuttle, 2009) The best introduction to Irish writer Lafcadio Hearn's experiences of life in Meiji-era Japan (see p56).

● *Xenophobe's Guide to the Japanese* S Kaji, N Hama and J Rice (Oval Books, 2010) A pocket-sized humorous guide to what makes the Japanese tick.

● *The Blue-Eyed Salaryman: From World Traveller to Lifer at Mitsubishi* Niall Murtagh (Profile Books, 2006) Amusing insight into what office life is like for a foreigner working in Japan.

● *Rice, Noodle, Fish: Deep Travels Through Japan's Food Culture* Matt Goulding, Nathan Thornburgh (HarperWave, 2015) An exploration of aspects of Japan's culinary history focusing on seven regions including Kyoto (kaiseki), Hiroshima (okonomiyaki) and Fukuoka (ramen). Also in effect a travel guide focusing on food; all accompanied by lots of colour photos.

## Life in Japan (fiction)

● *The Last Concubine* Lesley Downer (Corgi, 2009) A tale of Japan in the 1860s and the life of Sachi, a village girl, who becomes the last concubine of the reigning shogun.

● *Memoirs of a Geisha* Arthur Golden (Vintage, 1998) Golden's novel about a trainee geisha's life has become a modern classic and a Hollywood blockbuster. Sayuri is born in a fishing village but is sold to a Kyoto geisha house from where she rises to become one of the city's most famous and sought-after geisha.

● *Number 9 Dream* David Mitchell (Sceptre, 2002) The British novelist, who taught English in Hiroshima for eight years, presents an extraordinary post-*Blade Runner* Japanese world which has been variously described as terrifying and exhilarating.

● *In the Miso Soup* Ryu Murakami (Bloomsbury, 2005) A gritty, frightening story about life in the backstreets of Tokyo.

## The railway

● *Early Japanese Railways 1853-1914: Engineering Triumphs That Transformed Meiji Japan* Dan Free (Tuttle, 2014) A well-illustrated and detailed account of the railway's early days.

● *Shinkansen: From Bullet Train to Symbol of Modern Japan* Christopher Hood (Routledge, 2006) A comprehensive and readable account of the history of the bullet train. See also 💻 www.hood-online.co.uk/shinkansen.

## Fauna

● *Birds of East Asia* Mark Brazil (Helm/Princeton Field Guides, 2009) A comprehensive, well-illustrated guide; the author lives in Hokkaido.

● *A photographic guide to the birds of Japan and North-east Asia*, Tadao Shimba (Helm Photographic Guides, 2007) The first photographic field guide in English.

# JAPAN

# 2

## Facts about the country

### GEOGRAPHY

Japan is made up of over 3000 islands, a total land mass almost as large as the state of California. The four main islands are: **Honshu**, the largest; **Hokkaido**, the most northern and also the least populated; **Kyushu**, the southernmost; and **Shikoku**, the smallest. Stretching 3000km from north to south, the northernmost regions of Japan are subarctic, while the extreme south is subtropical.

Four-fifths of the land surface is mountainous and rural; most of the 127 million people who live on the four main islands are packed into the coastal plains. This has led to the development of so-called 'urban corridors', of which the longest, and perhaps the most densely inhabited in the world, is the Tokaido belt between Tokyo and Osaka.

Japan is a hotbed of **volcanic activity**. Even though world-famous Mt Fuji last erupted in 1707 and many don't think it will erupt again, it is actively monitored as if it did it could cause massive damage. Hokkaido, in particular, has several active volcanoes but there's no need to panic as the island's hiking routes and paths are always closed at the first sign of smoke. Both Sakurajima, off the coast of Kagoshima, and Mt Aso, in Kyushu are active.

### Earthquakes

Japan is located where the Eurasian and Pacific plates meet so is prone to earthquakes. The most powerful (8.9 on the Richter scale) since records began happened on 11th March 2011 off the north-east coast of Honshu and caused a devastating tsunami (see box p329). On April 16th 2016 a series of earthquakes caused considerable damage in Kumamoto (Kyushu), but fortunately not too many fatalities.

Earthquakes, of course, are not seasonal, nor can they be accurately predicted. They are, however, a fact of life in Japan and most cities have an earthquake centre equipped with a simulator room where Japanese can prepare for any eventuality by experiencing the full force of the Richter scale. There are monitors all along the shinkansen tracks, which means that trains can stop within 70 seconds if signs of an earthquake are detected. Minor quakes/tremors

*To the butterfly in the sky all buildings on the temple ground are upside down*
(BOSHA KAWABATA)

蝶の空七堂伽藍さかしまに

are very common in Japan but unless you're particularly sensitive you'll probably only hear about them the next day. In the very unlikely event you find yourself waking up to a sizeable quake, the best thing to do is to **get under something solid, such as a table**. Major quakes are extremely rare and not worth
becoming paranoid about – they occur roughly once a century.

## HISTORY

Space permits only a condensed 'bullet
points' history of Japan. For recommended books on the history of Japan,
see p51.

> ❏ **Japanese names**
> Japanese put the surname (family
> name) before the Christian (given)
> name, but for this guide the
> Western style is followed.

### Birth of a nation: myth and reality

Nobody knows exactly when Japan was first inhabited by humans but estimates
range from between 500,000 and 100,000 years ago. The **Jomon period**, named
after a rope pattern found on the oldest form of pottery in the world, began
around 10,000BC but the country was not unified until the 4th century AD, when
the **Yamato dynasty** was established and the title of emperor first used.

### A capital is established: 710-794

Up until the 7th century, tradition dictated that the capital was changed every
time a new emperor ascended the throne. But in 710, the Imperial Court decided to settle in Nara, a city still proud that it was the capital of Japan and the
home of seven emperors in just 77 years before the court was moved to
Nagaoka (in Niigata prefecture) in 784 and then to Kyoto in 794.

The **Nara period** was marked by influences from China and the growing
popularity of its imported religion, Buddhism. The main Chinese influence is
visible today in Todai-ji: this temple boasts the largest wooden building in the
world and contains Japan's biggest Buddha statue, a bronze image cast in 752.
Religious riches and treasure aside, hunger and poverty were commonplace outside the Imperial Court, though there was worse to come in later centuries.

### Flourishing of the arts but rivalry outside the court: 794-1185

Nara was soon overrun with temples and Shinto shrines, and Emperor Kammu
could no longer bear being closeted there. So a new capital was established, in
794, in Heian (present-day Kyoto), where it remained until 1868. A symbolic
fresh start was assured by a complete reconstruction of the city on a grid layout.

Japan's most famous literary work, *The Tale of Genji* by Murasaki Shikibu,
was written during the **Heian period**, as was *The Pillow Book*, a revealing
account of life at the Imperial Court by a woman very much on the inside, lady-
in-waiting Shonagon Sei. It was not just literature that flourished, but painting,
sculpture and poetry; the emperor hosted outdoor parties at which guests would
be invited to compose haiku over cups of sake.

Outside the walls of the Imperial Court, far from the parties and poetry
gatherings, a new warrior class was emerging: the **samurai**. The bloodiest military campaign of all for national supremacy raged between two rival clans the

JAPAN

Minamoto (also known as Genji) and the Taira (or Heike). The epic war, now steeped in as much legend as historical fact, finally climaxed in a decisive sea battle in 1185, and the Tairas were routed. But peace was short lived and the feudal era had begun.

## The first shogun: 1185-1333

The bloody corpses of the defeated Taira had hardly washed away before **Yoritomo Minamoto**, victorious leader of the Minamoto clan, moved the capital to Kamakura and was sworn in as the country's first shogun. The Imperial Court remained in Kyoto but real power had shifted geographically and politically to the samurai. Government of the country remained in the hands of successive shoguns for the next 700 years, until the Meiji Restoration of 1868.

The popularity of Buddhism grew during the **Kamakura period**. The Zen sect in particular, with its emphasis on a life of simplicity and austerity, appealed to the warrior class, which had always been ill at ease with the effete world of Heian culture. Instead of ushering in a new era, Yoritomo Minamoto's death in 1199 prompted his widow and her family to assume control. The political capital remained in Kamakura until 1333, when Emperor Go-Daigo succeeded in overthrowing the shogunate.

## Eruption of civil war, West and East meet: 1336-1575

The Emperor's moment of triumph turned out to be unexpectedly brief. He was soon booted out of Kyoto by **Takauji Ashikaga**, the military turncoat who had defected from the Kamakura court in time to become the Emperor's right-hand military man and assist in the rebellion against the Kamakura shogunate. Rightly or wrongly expecting credit for this assistance and anticipating the title of shogun as due reward, Ashikaga was aggrieved when Go-Daigo completely overlooked him. Seeking revenge, Ashikaga forced Go-Daigo into mountain exile and appointed a new emperor, who was gracious enough to name him shogun.

The Golden and Silver pavilions, two of Kyoto's major tourist draws, were constructed as villas for the shoguns during this period. As in the Heian period, culture and arts took centre stage, with Noh theatre, the tea ceremony and flower arranging all being established in the latter half of the **Muromachi period**. But war was also becoming commonplace as rival feudal lords clashed over territory and isolated skirmishes spiralled into full-scale civil war.

As the nation fought with itself, Christianity made its first appearance in Japan when the missionary **Francis Xavier** sailed into Kagoshima in 1549, carrying with him enormous ambition: to convert emperor and shogun alike. He failed, but relations with the West developed further in Nagasaki, where the port was opened to trade with the Portuguese.

## Reunification: 1575-1603

The long road to reunification began in 1568 when **Nobunaga Oda**, descended on Kyoto. He soon cemented his authority by building the first castle stronghold and setting a trend that was to be repeated by feudal lords all over Japan. Castles, each one grander and its defences safer than the last, became a must-have for every lord needing to prove his power over the people he ruled. Sadly, only a few original examples remain intact today, notably at Himeji and Matsumoto.

Nobunaga Oda hardly had time to settle into his own castle before he was assassinated in 1582. His successor, **Hideyoshi Toyotomi**, picked up where Oda had left off and continued with efforts to reunite the country, a task largely completed by 1590. Flushed with success at home, Toyotomi rebranded himself as an international warrior during two ill-fated attempts to capture Korea.

After his death, his son and heir, Hideyori, was swept aside by the warlord **Ieyasu Tokugawa**, who went on to establish his own government in Edo (present-day Tokyo).

## Closing down on the outside world: 1603-1853

The Kamakura shogunate had shown itself open to attack from rival clans but Ieyasu Tokugawa and his successors tolerated no intruders. Some 300 feudal clans across Japan were forced to travel to Edo for regular audiences with the shogun and to pay their taxes (see box p456). The expense and length of such journeys, nearly three centuries before the rail network would shuttle anyone to Tokyo within a day, ensured that feudal lords were never able to build up the power or finances to mount a challenge to the Tokugawa shogunate.

Strict laws of personal conduct were enforced and a social hierarchy developed with the shogun at the top and peasants and merchants at the bottom. Sandwiched in between were the samurai, though they too were restricted in movement and activity by their own strict code. In 1639, Japan suddenly closed all its ports to international trade, with the exception of a tiny Dutch enclave (Dejima) in Nagasaki. The policy of self-seclusion also prohibited all Japanese from leaving the country. Despite, or perhaps because of, the 'no vacancies' sign held up to the outside world, the **Edo period** was one of the most peaceful in Japanese history. Once again, the arts flourished, kabuki theatres opened and merchants traded in lacquerware and silk. But peace and prosperity at the price of national isolation could not last forever; by the middle of the 19th century, the feudal system was looking increasingly outdated. Not for much longer could the shogun keep the outside world at bay.

## The era of modernisation: 1853 to the present

**Commodore Perry's** arrival in 1853 accompanied by the 'Black Ships' of the US Navy was to alter the course of Japan's history for ever. The ships were laden with gifts but Perry's visit was anything but a social call. The Americans demanded that the ports be opened to trade and it became increasingly clear that the authorities would not be able to resist the influx of technology from the outside world. The Tokugawa shogunate clung desperately to power for another decade but was finally overthrown in 1867. In the following year, **Emperor Meiji** was restored to the throne, ushering in what was to become known as the **Meiji Restoration**. The Emperor himself remained politically powerless but he presided over a period of astonishing and fast-paced change. Edo, by now renamed **Tokyo**, became the official capital and Japan embarked on a long period of modernisation. One of the most notable achievements was the building of a national railway, an account of which begins on p88. But the education system was also completely overhauled, inspiration for which came from Western models. The period was also marked by the introduction of universal conscription, and there was wholesale overhaul of the army and navy.

As the country began to catch up with the rest of the world, the last remnants of the *ancien régime* were cast away. The land owned by feudal lords was carved up into the prefectures that still exist today. Swordless samurai were deprived of their status and forced to find work elsewhere – even their trademark top-knot hairstyle had to go. A new Western-style constitution was instituted in 1889 and compulsory education introduced. Wealthy Japanese parents sent their children to Oxford or Cambridge university, while engineers from the West were drafted in to provide the initial technology which would one day turn Japan into an economic superpower.

However, by the end of the first decade of the 20th century, British and other foreign engineers had all but disappeared (the Japanese learned the skills, then learned how to do better themselves). An increasingly confident Japan sought to gain a foothold in Asia; by the time of Emperor Meiji's death in 1912, the country had already engaged in wars with China and Russia. These wars were inspired, in part, by the fact that Japan saw how Britain – an even smaller island nation – had managed to acquire a huge empire and imagined it could do the same.

Elsewhere in the world, Japan was keen to promote its culture and traditions; for six months in 1910, the new international face of Japan was displayed to an intrigued British public at White City in west London. Over eight million visitors caught a glimpse of a country in transition. There were demonstrations of judo, kendo, karate and sumo. A tea house, replica Japanese gardens and Ainu village were constructed, along with a white-knuckle ride, called the Flip-Flap, which gave visitors a bird's eye view of London.

The end of the first half of the 20th century was dominated by Japan's involvement in **WWII**. When France fell to Nazi Germany in 1940, Japan moved to occupy French Indo-China. Japan's attack on the US Pacific fleet at Pearl Harbor in 1941 – which led the US and its allies to declare war on Japan – remains one of the most infamous chapters of the country's WWII history. In the following year Japan embarked on an expansionist campaign across Southeast Asia, occupying a succession of countries including The Philippines, Dutch East Indies, Burma and Malaya. The war culminated in the devastating atomic bomb attacks on the cities of Hiroshima (6th August) and Nagasaki (9th August) in 1945. It is estimated that over 140,000 people had died in Hiroshima by the end of that year, and more than 70,000 people in Nagasaki. **Emperor Hirohito**, who had ascended the throne in 1926, announced Japan's surrender.

Under American occupation after the war, the country embarked on another period of sweeping reform. By the time the **Tokyo Olympics** opened in 1964, and the bullet train was speeding between Tokyo and Osaka, Japan's rise to economic superpower was complete. Over the next two decades, the rest of the world could only watch in amazement as the country that had been closed to outsiders for more than two centuries became the fastest-growing economy in the world.

The economic downturn of the late 1990s worried the Japanese and put pressure on politicians to produce a magic formula and wipe away the lingering recession in an instant. By the early years of the 21st century it became clear that there would be no quick fix; the real challenge was to try and stem what appeared to be a long and painful process of economic decline. The other formidable challenge is the increasing economic and political might of China. The regional battle for global influence and economic supremacy has only just begun.

## POLITICS

For over 50 years Japanese politics was dominated by the ruling **Liberal Democratic Party (LDP)**, founded in 1955. Though the LDP has been widely credited for Japan's economic success, it has also been dogged by accusations of cronyism and corruption.

Kakuei Tanaka, prime minister in the 1970s, was dubbed the LDP 'kingmaker' and the country's political powerbroker. He was also seen as one of the most corrupt politicians of modern times; his greatest achievement – having a shinkansen line built from Tokyo to Niigata solely because Niigata was his constituency – bankrupted the entire national railway.

Throughout the 1990s, as the country was searching for a way out of the economic doldrums, the LDP showed no signs of reforming itself. Change finally arrived in 2001, in the figure of Junichiro Koizumi, Japan's 11th prime minister in just 13 years. Considered an outsider, Koizumi remained popular with voters for his maverick style and reformist agenda and lasted for nearly 5½ years (a remarkable achievement in modern Japanese history) before passing the baton to Shinzo Abe, in 2006. Abe – who became the country's youngest prime minister at the tender age of 52 – brought a return to a more familiar political era, one where grey-suited prime ministers came and went with relative speed and anonymity.

By 2009 the country seemed ready for a genuinely new direction. In the election that year, the opposition **Democratic Party of Japan** swept to power, with the bouffant-haired Yukio Hatoyama – nicknamed 'space alien' for his prominent eyes and at times otherworldly ideas – at the helm. But he was to last barely nine months before throwing in the towel. His successor, Naoto Kan, faced the biggest political challenge of a generation when he had to respond to the devastating 2011 earthquake and tsunami as well as the ensuing nuclear fallout (see box p329). Within months of the quake he too resigned, leaving his successor Yoshihiko Noda, to set the path to recovery. Noda lasted barely a year in office before handing power back to Abe, who – when he took charge of the country for a second time in 2012 – became the first former Prime Minister to return to office since 1948. Abe spent his second term in the top job implementing a raft of economic reforms – his policies were dubbed 'Abenomics' by the media – and, more controversially, strengthening the role of Japan's armed forces, whose mandate had been severely curtailed in the decades following

WWII. Abe's attempt to reinterpret the country's pacifist constitution was driven through parliament despite public protest, but the move won him plaudits in Washington, where in 2015 he was accorded the honour of becoming the first Japanese Prime Minister to address a joint session of the US Congress.

## ECONOMY

When Japan's bubble economy finally burst in the early 1990s, the nation and world reeled in shock. Throughout the previous decade the country's economy had seemed unstoppable. At 2.5%, interest rates were the lowest in the world, making money easy to borrow. Banks assisted in pumping up the bubble by offering loans to virtually anybody with little or no scrutiny of their personal finances. As a piece of real estate, Japan was worth the whole of the US seven times over. The value of land was pushed artificially high and companies staked their livelihood solely on the soaring price of the square feet they owned. This made them profitable on paper but bankrupt the moment the bottom fell out of the property market.

The gloomy economic outlook extended well into the 21st century, but by the middle of the first decade there were signs of cautious optimism and a renewed sense that Japan was finally back in business. This mood did not last long. Japan may have remained in self-imposed isolation from the outside world for hundreds of years, but it could not shield itself from the impact of the global recession at the end of the first decade of the new century. In 2010, the country suffered a huge psychological blow when the Chinese economy officially overtook the Japanese economy for the first time in history.

In the 1980s Japanese manufacturers were teaching the world to be competitive and the country's industries were global bywords for quality and efficiency. The years since then have been more challenging for Japanese companies as many have suffered from the twin effects of the global slowdown and increased, cheaper, competition. Despite all the odds – including the economic downturn in the Tohoku region following the 2011 tsunami and nuclear disaster – nobody is yet writing off Japan Inc.

## RELIGION

The two main religions in Japan are **Shinto** (literally, 'the way of the gods'), Japan's indigenous religion and **Buddhism**, imported from China.

Shinto's origins extend as far back as Japanese mythology, to the belief that all aspects of the natural world (water, rocks, trees and wind, for example) have their own spirit/deity (*kami*). Shinto was the official state religion until 1945, up to which time the emperor himself was considered to be a divine being. There is no founder nor are there any scriptures. Buddhist places of worship are temples, the names of which in Japanese mostly end with the suffix '-*ji*' but some end '-*in*' and '-*dera*'. In Shinto, places of worship are shrines and are much plainer in design than the often brightly coloured temples. Shrines are most obviously distinguished from temples by the *torii* (gate) which marks the entrance to the shrine precinct. The names of shinto shrines end with a variety of suffixes but the most common are *-jinja*, *-gu* and *-taisha*. The harmonious relationship between Shinto and Buddhism means it is not unusual to see a shrine and a temple on the same site.

Despite numerous attempts by foreign missionaries, **Christianity** has made few inroads into Japan, though the Western white wedding is popular. Some of the churches and chapels you might see in Japan have been built solely for white weddings and are not consecrated for religious services.

## THE PEOPLE

Of the over **127 million** people living in Japan, the vast majority are Japanese by birth. Commentators liken Japan to an exclusive club; only rarely is anyone from outside the circle given the much sought-after membership card – a Japanese passport. History disputes the much-touted fact that the Japanese are an entirely homogenous people since the country is said to have been first settled by migrants from various parts of mainland Asia. The Ainu, an ethnic minority who are culturally and physically distinct from the Japanese, are further proof that Japan is much more multicultural than it may at first seem. Believed to have inhabited northern Honshu and Hokkaido since the 7th century, the Ainu began to dwindle in number as the Japanese colonised the north of the country. For more on the Ainu, their cultural heritage and battle for survival, see box p408.

It would be wrong to assume that the 'closed shop' nature of Japanese nationality means the people are hostile. On the contrary, it would be hard to find a more friendly and welcoming country. The traditional image of the polite, but formal, hard-working Japanese is only partially accurate. Indeed, generalisations about the Japanese rarely hold water. Even the briefest (rail!) journey here proves that the people are as diverse as the landscape is varied.

JAPAN

❏ **Omotenashi**

The concept of *omotenashi* (at its simplest meaning hospitality) has been part of Japanese life for hundreds of years but came to the fore for foreigners when it was mentioned by Christel Takigawa (a Japanese/French television news journalist) as part of the presentation for Tokyo's bid to host the 2020 Olympics.

Hospitality is not unique to Japan but once you have been there you know there is something different about it. The word omotenashi stems from the verb *motenasu*; this means to welcome, to entertain and to offer hospitality. In general the host should look after their guest(s) selflessly, attentively and unobtrusively. Examples of omotenashi in Japan can be seen through many simple things: when you enter a restaurant, staff will call out *irrashaimase* (welcome); many hotels and tourist attractions provide umbrellas that can be borrowed; in shops even the simplest of things are wrapped up beautifully; retail and train staff bow to show respect; if you ask for directions whoever you ask is likely either to accompany you to where you want to go or at least go overboard to make sure you find what you want. Fortunately omotenashi is something all visitors experience, not just those who will be at the 2020 Olympics.

❏ **Longevity record**
Japanese women are the world's longest lived – and have been for over two decades. They enjoy an average life expectancy of 86.6 years, while Japanese men can expect to live about 80 years; Japan now has 60,000 centenarians. The health ministry puts this down to a healthy diet, rich in vegetables and fish products and relatively low in animal fats. But the figures may not remain so impressive, given the high number of smokers and the Westernisation of their eating habits. And the long-life expectancy is not all good news: combined with a falling birth rate, it is creating considerable problems for Japan's economy.

## SPORT

### Traditional sports

Perhaps the best-known traditional Japanese sport is **sumo**. Two wrestlers (who usually weigh between 90kg and 160kg each) attempt to push each other out of a 4.55m-diameter clay circle; the winner is decided when any part of a wrestler's body apart from the soles of his feet touches the ground, or if he steps or is pushed out of the ring. Sumo wrestlers are divided into six divisions, the highest rank being that of *yokozuna*. There are six sumo tournaments (known as *basho*) every year and each lasts for 15 days. Basho are held in Tokyo (January, May and September), Osaka (March), Nagoya (July) and Fukuoka (November). Tickets for ringside seats are expensive and usually sell out weeks in advance but the public broadcaster NHK provides live coverage of the tournaments. For more information visit 🖳 www.sumo.or.jp.

Of all the martial arts, **aikido** is perhaps the one most steeped in religion. Created in Japan by Morihei Ueshiba (see p246), aikido combines the disciplines of judo, karate and kendo. Practitioners of aikido attempt to harness an opponent's *ki* (spiritual power), which is said to enable them to throw their adversary to the ground with little effort. **Judo** follows a similar principle though the techniques are very different. Much of the basic judo training involves throwing your opponent to the floor and holding them down. Judo has been a regular Olympic event since the Tokyo Olympic Games in 1964 and is now practised worldwide. There are 10 ranks, called *dan*, which are internationally recognised.

**Karate** originated in China and only reached mainland Japan in the early 1920s; today it exists in many different styles. **Kendo** (literally, 'the way of the sword') is sometimes known as Japanese fencing. Opponents wear protective masks, chest gear and gloves while using a bamboo stick *(shinai)* or metal sword *(katana)* to strike each other. **Kyudo**, or Japanese archery, is one of the oldest martial arts and can be performed on the ground as well as on horseback, when it is known as **yabusame**.

### Modern sports

**Baseball** (yakyu) is taken as seriously as it is in the USA, with 12 professional teams divided into Central and Pacific leagues; six in each league. Each team plays at least 140 games a year. The regular championship season starts in late March and the championship team of each league is decided by about the beginning of October. Then the top three teams of each league play in a post-season championship; finally the top two of these postseason teams of each league play the Japan Series and the overall champion team of the year is then decided. The sport also attracts large numbers of amateur, school and university clubs. Traditionally baseball is associated with men but a professional women's league started in 2010. For details about going to a game in Hiroshima, see box p306.

**Rugby** has a smaller following, but is growing in popularity as the country makes its mark on the international stage. Japan's rugby team for the 2015 World Cup provided possibly the biggest surprise when it beat the South African team in its opening game. So, it seems very appropriate that it will host the 2019 World Cup. **Soccer (football)** has taken off in a big way since the launch of the J-League in 1993. A measure of the sport's success came when Japan successfully co-hosted the 2002 World Cup with South Korea. However, it is the women's national team that has had the most success.

## CULTURE

Japan is known as much for its ancient traditions as its futuristic technology. The following is a brief guide to the country's highly distinctive culture.

### Traditional culture

**Ikebana**  Perhaps the most celebrated of Japan's ancient cultural traditions is ikebana, or the art of flower arranging. Ikebana was once synonymous with the formality of the tea ceremony, when participants would contemplate the beauty and careful positioning of the flowers decorating the tea room. Just as there are different schools of judo and karate, so too there are some officially recognised schools of ikebana in Japan. Both men and women practise ikebana; indeed, it was even considered an appropriate pastime for the samurai. For more information visit the Ikebana International (💻 www.ikebanahq.org) website.

**Chanoyu**  Commonly known as the tea ceremony, chanoyu is one of the country's most highly regarded aesthetic pursuits. Considered to be a form of mental training as well as a means of learning elegant manners and etiquette, *sado* ('the way of the tea') is much more than just an elaborate way of pouring a cup of tea. While the powdered green tea is whipped up with boiling water using a special bamboo whisk and poured into the serving bowl, guests are offered a small cake or sweetmeat to prepare themselves for the bitter taste of the tea. The ceremony, which can last a couple of hours, is held in a simple tatami-mat room decorated with hanging scrolls and discreetly positioned flowers, all of which will have been chosen to reflect the season. Many travel agencies, such as JTB, and upmarket hotels now offer tea-ceremony demonstrations.

**Kabuki, Bunraku and Noh**  Probably the most accessible form of traditional theatre in Japan is **kabuki**, a kind of dance drama with music, which dates back to the 17th century. A knowledge of Japanese is not necessary to enjoy the

❏ **Geisha in the 21st century**

*Maiko*, apprentice geisha, train for up to six years for the right to be called a geisha (*geiko* in Kyoto). During this time the maiko-san will learn how to play traditional instruments, such as the shamisen and koto (see below), how to dance and how to dress in a kimono. Above all the trainee is required to become skilled in the manners and comportment associated with the geisha world, since every one of them will be judged by the customers whom they are sent to entertain in the evenings. Up until WW2 a maiko's virginity was auctioned and they had little control over their sexual relationships but nowadays any relationships they have are up to them.

In the 1920s there were about 80,000 geisha and a steady flow of new trainees. Today, fewer than 5000 brave the long hours and difficult working conditions. However, more and more young professional women, dressed in platform heels and forever chatting on their mobile phones by day, are now moonlighting as a new breed of geisha after only the briefest crash course in technique. Customers unwilling or unable to pay for an evening with a traditional geisha can opt instead for one of this new breed who charge a fraction of the price. They are different from hostesses in a bar in the sense that they dress in a kimono and go to their client's premises rather than the client going to a bar.

colourful performances, where men dress as women, the make-up is as bright as the costumes are lavish, and members of the audience frequently shout out their appreciation when actors take to the stage, strike a dramatic pose or deliver a famous line.

The kabuki theatre comes equipped with a *seridashi*, a trap door in the floor which allows actors to enter the stage from below, as well as a gangway through the audience which lets the actors make a dramatic, sweeping entrance, their silk costumes rustling behind them as they step gracefully towards the stage. It would be hard to find a more lively or entertaining theatrical experience in Japan. A useful website with more information and details of what performances are on, and where, is 🖳 www.kabuki-bito.jp.

Also originating in the 17th century and closely related to kabuki is **bun-raku** (puppet play). Puppets up to two-thirds the size of humans are dressed in costumes which are just as elaborate as those worn by actors on the kabuki stage. The puppets are operated by three stage hands while a fourth narrates the story to the tune of the traditional *shamisen* (see below).

Less immediately accessible than kabuki is **Noh**, a classical form of theatre which dates back more than 600 years. Performances combine music and dance: movements are highly stylised and the dancing is choreographed to represent actions such as crying and laughing and is accompanied by flutes and drums. Most of the actors wear masks depicting a range of expressions and emotions. Performances, on a special raised stage with a roof and a sparse set, often take place by firelight during the summer months in the precincts of Shinto shrines.

**Shamisen, koto and taiko** Proficiency on traditional Japanese instruments such as the **shamisen** (a wooden instrument covered in cat skin with three strings made of silk) and the **koto** (Japanese harp) was once as much a test of a geisha's talent as her ability to dance. Partly because of the cost of purchasing and maintaining such instruments, their popularity has faded. But one traditional instrument that remains popular for its infectious rhythm is the **taiko** drum. Bare-chested taiko drummers beating a furious rhythm while drenching themselves and their instruments in sweat are a staple sight and sound at most Japanese festivals, where the noise is the perfect accompaniment to a summer parade through the streets. Shaped like a cylinder, the body of the taiko drum is hollow and covered at both ends with leather. Smaller hand drums, known as *tsuzumi*, are often used in Noh and kabuki.

## Popular culture
**Manga and anime**  Manga (comic books) are big business in Japan, with an annual turnover of about ¥400 billion; they cover every theme and genre so appeal to all sections of the population. *Manga kissa* (manga cafés) are popular places for people to read manga but these days manga are also available online as webmanga.

One of the best-known manga is *Tetsuwan Atomu* (called Astro Boy outside Japan) by Osamu Tezuka; he is also credited as the father of anime as he adapted this manga for the television screen. *Doraemon*, a blue robot from the 21st century, is another manga character that was developed into anime. The genre was then expanded by Miyazaki Hayao; his company, Studio Ghibli (see box p115), has created some of the most successful anime movies.

**Pachinko parlours**  Another popular form of entertainment is a trip to the pachinko parlour. Players sit in front of upright pinball machines and feed them with tiny silver ball bearings. The machines then rattle a lot and, with luck (little skill seems to be involved), more silver balls pour out through the slot into a tray; these can be exchanged for prizes like washing powder and tins of ham. These unglamorous prizes are then traded in for cash at a semi-hidden booth outside. It's illegal to play for cash in the pachinko parlours so owners get around the law by allowing customers to exchange the prizes for money off the premises. The noise coming from the parlours mean they are not hard to find.

# Practical information for visitors

## ARRIVING IN JAPAN

Japan has three major international gateways: Narita Airport (see box pp126-7), east of Tokyo; Haneda Airport (see box p127), near central Tokyo; and Kansai Airport (see p151), near Osaka. Don't confuse Osaka (Itami) Airport with Kansai Airport; the latter is the one you are likely to arrive at even though the former has some international flights from destinations in Asia. Other airports with international flights include Fukuoka (see p438) and Nagoya (see p203).

Immigration and Customs are efficient at all the airports but don't expect to rush through the formalities. All foreigners entering Japan (apart from diplomats, children under 16 and US military personnel serving in Japan) are fingerprinted and photographed at immigration, whether or not they have a visa. Tourists will have a 'Landing Permission' stamp confirming their 'Temporary Visitor' status put in their passport.

All airports offer ample facilities for changing money and are connected to the Japan Rail network, so you can exchange your rail pass and begin your journey soon after touching down.

## TOURIST INFORMATION

The staff in the main **tourist information centres (TICs)** at the airports and in Tokyo, Osaka and Kyoto speak English and can provide information on onward travel throughout Japan. Most towns and cities have a tourist information office (look for the 'i' logo), though it may be called something else, such as 'Question and answer office'. Though the staff at offices in less touristy areas do not always speak English they can almost always provide maps and town guides in English.

A network of **'goodwill guides'** operates in a number of towns and cities. These are English-speaking volunteers who guide foreign tourists around local sights; the service is free but volunteers generally ask for their expenses to be covered. They can usually be contacted via the local tourist information office.

> ❏ **TIC information line**
> If you're stuck anywhere in Japan and need assistance in English, call the JNTO Tourist Information Center (TIC; ☎ 03-3201 3331; daily 9am-5pm, except 1st Jan). The staff are very knowledgeable and will help with any travel or tourism enquiry.

## GETTING AROUND

**By rail**  See pp93-102.

**By air**
If you're pushed for time and are planning to travel long distances it can make sense to combine use of the rail pass with a domestic flight. However, it may work out quicker to take a shinkansen once you factor in the time it takes to get to and from the airports.

Japan's two major airlines, All Nippon Airways (ANA; 🖳 www.ana.co.jp) and Japan Airlines (JAL; 🖳 www.jal.co.jp), operate a comprehensive network of domestic flights. Budget airlines include: Skymark (SKY; 🖳 www.skymark .jp); Peach (🖳 www.flypeach.com) and JetStar (🖳 www.jetstar.com/jp).

In recent years the price of domestic flights has fallen as a result of more competition, but it still pays to book ahead for the best deals. Both ANA and JAL offer discount 'air passes' for foreign visitors, which are worth considering if you are planning to take two or more flights. See also box p47.

JAPAN

## By bus or tram/streetcar

The **bus** service in Japan is almost as efficient as the rail service. In fact, some urban buses are operated by JR, so Japan Rail Pass holders travel free on those.

On most urban buses, you enter at the back and take a ticket from the machine by the door. In cities there is often a flat fare but in rural areas the fare depends on the length of your journey. To work out how much the fare is, just before your stop, match the number on the ticket with the fare underneath the corresponding number on the board at the front of the bus. Leave the bus at the front, throwing the exact fare and your ticket into the box by the driver; if you don't have the correct money and your fare is less than ¥1000 you must change a note (or ¥500 coin) to coins by using the change machine nearby.

Several cities and large towns still have a **tram/streetcar** service. On most trams fares are collected in the same way as on buses.

It is often possible to get a **one-day pass** (or longer) which makes life easier and is often good value. But you still may need to pick up a ticket as you enter the bus or tram and also put your pass through the ticket machine as you leave, or show it to the driver.

## By taxi

Taxis are usually available outside even the tiniest of stations but it's also fine to flag one down in the street if the red light in the lower right-hand corner of the windscreen is on. The starting fare is around ¥650 for the first 2km plus ¥100 for each additional 500m; a surcharge (up to 30%) is added between 11pm and 5am. Though taxis are not cheap if you are on your own, they can be very good value if there are three or four of you, especially in rural areas where bus

---

❏ **IC cards**

IC (smart) cards make travel a lot easier as they mean you don't need to worry about working out the fare for journeys on trains (see p99), buses, subways or trams/streetcars. Increasingly IC cards can be used in shops and convenience stores, and for vending machines and coin lockers which show the relevant logo. Even if you have a JR pass it can be useful to have an IC card to pay for any journeys on non-JR lines.

JR East's **Suica** (Super Urban Intelligent Card) was the first to be introduced and is perhaps the best known. A Suica can be bought at Narita and Haneda airports, or at any JR station in the Tokyo Metropolitan area. A basic Suica costs ¥2500 (pre-loaded with ¥2000 plus ¥500 refundable deposit). To use it place your card over the IC card sign and wait to hear the beep showing it has been recognised. You can top your card up to a maximum of ¥20,000 at machines with the Suica sign.

Other IC cards are: the **Pasmo**, issued by Tokyo's public transport operators other than JR; **Toica** (JR Central); **Icoca** JR West (see p151); **Kansai One Pass** for travel in Kansai on both JR and private lines; **Kitaca** JR Hokkaido; and **Sugoca** JR Kyushu. All operate in a similar way to the Suica and are compatible with each other so can be used in virtually any part of Japan. Whichever card you get, and whether you get it from a human or a machine, you can choose whether to register your details (name, date of birth, sex, telephone number) in the card. It's simple and easy to register and it means a replacement card can be issued if you have lost yours.

❏ **Cable cars and ropeways**
An important point to note is that in Japan a **cable car** is called a funicular/mountain railway and a **ropeway** is what many others consider a cable car (ie carriages suspended from a cable).

services are limited. Most drivers wear white gloves and peaked caps, and you don't even have to open the door yourself because the driver operates the rear passenger doors from the front. In fact they will be upset if you do try to open or close the door!

### By bicycle
It is possible to rent a bike at many stations; details are given where relevant. If you rent a bicycle in an urban area, note that there are strict rules about parking, so always check for signs saying parked bikes may be removed and impounded.

### Hitchhiking
*'There is no reason to hitchhike. That's why we built the bullet train.'*
**Will Ferguson** *Hokkaido Highway Blues* (abridged edition 2003)
The extensive rail network in Japan does mean it is easy to get around but railway lines do not go everywhere. So, if you want to head off-the-beaten-track hitchhiking is worth considering, especially as the chances are high that anyone who offers you a lift will do their best to get you as close as they can to where you want to go. As in most countries, you should be particularly careful if hitchhiking on your own.

## ACCOMMODATION

There is a wide range of possibilities and accommodation is almost always of a high standard.

**Rates** quoted throughout this guide are generally the lowest you should expect to pay. However, they can drop a lot if business is quiet so it is always worth checking, even if the rates quoted in this guide seem more than you'd like to pay. Not surprisingly, in holiday periods rates increase considerably.

It's wise, though not essential, to **book accommodation**, at least for the first few nights, before you arrive in Japan as it means when you are there you can focus on sightseeing. If planning to visit places such as Kyoto in March/April (cherry blossom time) or October/November (autumn leaves) it is worth booking well in advance. Whenever you book it's best to do so either through the relevant hotel/ryokan's website or by email, clearly stating dates and room requests. Telephoning may be complicated and anyhow hoteliers much prefer to have your requirements in writing; the few places now that don't have email may prefer to receive a fax. Another option is to use an online booking agency (see box p69). Always make sure you receive written confirmation and take that with you to show at check-in.

The city guides and, where relevant, route guides feature places to stay and contact details. Alternatively, see box p70 for details of the main hotel chains in

Japan. If you do turn up without a place to stay most tourist information centres have an accommodation list and some can make same-day reservations. Staff will also be able to tell you where the closest JTB (Japan Travel Bureau) office is as they can make reservations for the whole of Japan.

If you book online through an agency payment may be taken immediately through your credit card, but if you book direct you probably won't have to pay till you check-in – or leave. In general accommodation places in Japan still prefer payment in cash, though most upmarket places accept credit cards.

**Check-in** usually starts **from 4pm** and **check-out** is **by 11am** (10am in many business hotels); most places let you leave your luggage with them for free if you arrive or leave outside those times, so you don't always have to fork out for a locker. Most ryokan and minshuku prefer, or even insist, that you reserve ahead, especially if you want meals.

## Hostels and temple lodgings

The cheapest places, particularly if you are on your own, tend to be **hostels**. The majority of hostels belong to **Japan Youth Hostels** (JYH; 🖳 www.jyh.or.jp), which is part of Hostelling International/YHA (🖳 www.hihostels.com).

Expect to pay from ¥3000 per person (pp); non-members may have to pay about ¥600 extra per night so bring your card if you are a member. A few hostels accept members only but you should be able to join (¥1500) on the spot.

Hostels are great if you want to meet other travellers as many organise a programme of events, evening sing-songs and the like. However, JYH hostels in particular get booked up with young Japanese during Golden Week (see p14) and in the summer. Also, if there are two or more of you it may be as cheap to stay in a business hotel by the time you have factored in the almost inevitable cost of getting a bus to and from the hostel (most are not centrally located). Having said that, some of the hostels in rural areas are very atmospheric.

All hostels provide dormitory accommodation; some also offer private rooms (ideal for families travelling together). Most provide breakfast (from ¥600) and an evening meal (about ¥1200); many have communal kitchen facilities. It's wise to make a booking since managers may not appreciate it if you turn up unannounced.

There are now several **backpacker hostel chains** with branches in the main tourist cities – these are often more centrally located than JYH hostels. Expect to pay about ¥3500pp for a bed in a dorm, ¥5500-6500pp inc half board. Chains include: J-hoppers (🖳 j-hoppers.com) and K's House (🖳 www.kshouse.jp). In Hokkaido it is worth checking out the Toho Network (🖳 www.toho.net).

A few JYH hostels, such as those in Takayama and Nagano, are attached to, or in, **temples**. At these it may be possible (if you ask) to join early morning prayers or participate in a session of Zen meditation with resident monks. Certain temples which are not hostels also accept paying guests, offering an excellent insight into Japanese culture and a chance to eat *shojin ryori* (vegetarian cuisine that originated in Zen temples). Koya-san (see pp156-8) has many options, but also consider Yoshino-yama (see p156) and Dewa Sanzan (see pp350-1).

## Minshuku and pensions

**Minshuku** are small, family-run inns where the rate usually includes half board (an evening meal and breakfast); expect to pay ¥7000-9000pp, with a reduction for children. Rates are often available for room only, or for bed & breakfast.

Urban minshuku are usually fine but are often less personal and characterful than rural ones, which might be in old farmhouses so offer a great experience of being in a traditional Japanese home. Rooms are Japanese style (futons on tatami-mat flooring); see box p72. There are no en suite facilities and you may not be provided with a towel, or *yukata* (see p49), though you can probably rent one. Most have a TV in the room and many now offer internet access/wi-fi. Meals are eaten at set times (usually 6 or 6.30pm for supper and about 7.30am for breakfast), occasionally with the family. Invariably the food is Japanese, so be prepared for (raw) egg, fish and miso soup at breakfast! However, many minshuku in touristy areas also offer a Western breakfast.

**Pensions** are the Western-style equivalent of minshuku and are popular with Japanese. Like minshuku, they are usually small, family-run affairs but they offer beds rather than futons. Rates also start from around ¥7000pp including (a Western) breakfast, but not an evening meal.

## Hotels

Often conveniently located near railway stations (if a hotel's name includes 'ekimae' it may literally be opposite, or less than a 10-minute walk from, the station), **business hotels** have plenty of single rooms in addition to twins and doubles, and occasionally triples/quads. They should not be confused with Japan's infamous capsule hotels (see p73), since you get a proper room.

Most rooms are Western style, en suite, and are clean and tidy, but, as they cater for business travellers, they rarely have much space to move about in or hang your clothes. A yukata, TV, internet access/wi-fi and coffee-/tea-making

---

❏ **Online accommodation agencies**

● **Jalan** (🖳 www.jalan.net)  The listings on the English page are not as comprehensive as on the Japanese but it is still a useful resource.

● **Japan Hotel Association** (🖳 www.j-hotel.or.jp) A wide range of upmarket hotels offering Western-style accommodation.

● **Japan iCan** (🖳 www.japanican.com) Part of the JTB group and the site lists over 4000 hotels and ryokan.

● **Japan Ryokan and Hotel Association** (🖳 www.ryokan.or.jp) Lists independently owned places.

● **Japanese Guest Houses** (🖳 www.japaneseguesthouses.com)  Focuses on ryokan but also lists some of the temple lodgings on Koya-san.

● **Japanese Inn Group** (🖳 www.japaneseinngroup.com) A nationwide directory of ryokan & minshuku (not a chain of inns) that are used to dealing with foreign guests.

● **Rakuten** (🖳 travel.rakuten.com)  One of the biggest online accommodation reservation companies in Japan.

● **Selected Onsen Ryokan** (🖳 selected-ryokan.com) Over 200 ryokan and hotels that have hot-spring facilities. However, the website does not always say how to reach the onsen by train even though this is often possible; a bus journey may also be necessary.

facilities are almost always provided. The (compact) toilet/bath units generally include towels, toiletries and a hairdryer; shaver sockets are less common.

Facilities in the hotel usually include vending machines (soft drinks, beer, sake, and perhaps pot noodle and ice-cream), laundry facilities and a couple of computers with internet access. Guests may also be able to use a microwave oven and trouser press. Some of the newer ones offer a no-smoking floor and a

---

### ❏ HOTEL CHAINS

#### Business hotels

The majority of the hotel groups listed below have branches all over the country and offer online booking through an English website.

● **APA Hotels** (🖥 www.apahotel.com)  APA (Always Pleasant Amenity) provide a Japanese buffet-style breakfast and their hotels have a common bath.

● **Dormy Inn** (🖥 www.hotespa.net/dormyinn)  A highly recommended chain; a wonderful feature of these hotels is that they all have an *onsen*-quality bath, often also a *rotemburo*. They provide an excellent breakfast which may feature local specialities; the chain also offers free noodles (yonaki soba) in the evening.

● **Hotel My Stays** (🖥 www.mystays.com)  A feature of the Hotel My Stays chain is that the rooms have a kitchenette (though this can be quite basic). Breakfast may not be provided but a voucher can be bought for breakfast at a local café or restaurant.

● **Route Inn** (🖥 www.route-inn.co.jp)  Offers a buffet-style breakfast. All branches have a common bath, some of which are onsen.

● **Super Hotel** (🖥 www.superhotel.co.jp)  Rates include a bread-based breakfast. Worth looking out for are their hotels with onsen. Some branches close completely between 10am and 3pm.

● **Tokyu Hotels** (🖥 www.tokyuhotelsjapan.com)  The Tokyu group has hotels for all budget groups: Tokyu Bizfort, Tokyu Resort, Tokyu Inn, Excel Hotel Tokyu, Tokyu Hotel as well as The Capitol Hotel Tokyu. They also have a membership scheme (Comfort Members; ¥500 to join) offering discounts on rates and check-out up to noon.

● **Toyoko Inn** (🖥 www.toyoko-inn.com)  One of the best budget hotel chains in Japan, where most of the staff (including management) are women. The rate includes a simple buffet breakfast (based on *onigiri*). The furnishings are similar in every branch and rooms are always clean and well equipped. For ¥1500 you can become an 'International' Toyoko Inn Club member; this entitles you to discounted rates, one free night's stay for every ten, and early check-in.

#### Upmarket hotels

The majority of hotel chains listed below offer upmarket Western-style accommodation but some also have brands offering more reasonable options.

Japanese chains include: **Nikko/JAL Hotels** (🖥 www.nikko-jalcity.com/domestic) with the Okura brand; **Mielparque** (🖥 www.mielparque.jp); **Richmond Hotels** (🖥 www.richmondhotel.jp); **Solare Hotels** (🖥 www.solarehotels.com) includes the Chisun and Loisir brands; and **Washington Hotels** (🖥 www.wh-rsv.com).

Also at the top end of the market are Western hotel chains such as **Hyatt** (🖥 www.hyatt.com), **Hilton** (🖥 www3.hilton.com) and **Marriott** (🖥 www.marriott.com). Other Western hotel groups in Japan include **Best Western** (🖥 www.bestwestern.com), **Choice Hotels** (🖥 www.choicehotels.com), including the Comfort Inn brand, and **Intercontinental Hotels Group** (🖥 www.ihg.com) including the Holiday Inn and Crowne Plaza brands.

JAPAN

❏ **The JR Hotel group**

Anyone with a Japan Rail Pass will receive a list of JR-run hotels – the main brand names vary with each JR company, but the hotels are all Western style and range from standard business to top-class luxury. Rooms always have a good range of amenities and free wi-fi is generally available. JR-pass holders get a small discount (usually around 10% off the rack rate).

JR hotels are particularly convenient since they're nearly always right outside the station (or in some cases, above it). See the city guides for individual hotel details, or check the website 💻 www.jrhotelgroup.com.

few have a ladies-only floor or rooms specifically for women. The newest even boast automatic check-in where you feed your money into a slot and receive an electronic key card in return.

Rack rates vary from ¥5000 for the most basic singles up to ¥8000 for a room with slightly more breathing space. Expect to pay ¥8000-13,000 for a twin or double room. Online rates are often less than rack rates and since many business hotels accept online bookings and have websites in English it is worth booking in advance. Most also offer rates including breakfast; in general this is a buffet-style meal, though the quality and range of options varies. Many **business hotel chains** operate nationwide; for more details, see the box opposite.

Other **Japanese hotel chains** include the JR Hotel group (see box above) and those listed in the box opposite. In addition there are many **Western hotel chains** (see also box opposite) in Japan. The best way to find out about independently owned hotels is through an accommodation agency (see box p69).

**Accessible Japan** (💻 www.accessible-japan.com) has useful information on hotels which offer specially adapted rooms for the disabled and also on sightseeing with a disability.

### Ryokan

Ryokan offer the most traditional Japanese accommodation and you really should plan to stay at least one night in one. They are more upmarket and have better amenities than minshuku. Rooms are generally spacious and may include *shoji* (sliding paper-screen doors) and an alcove (*tokonoma*) or two containing a Japanese fan, vase or scroll. Often you will also have a lovely view over a garden, though admittedly that may be a very small one.

In luxury ryokan particularly, where per-person (pp) rates start from around ¥20,000, every guest is a VIP. From the moment you arrive you're waited on by your own kimono-clad maid, who will pour tea as you settle in, serve you meals (usually in your room) and lay out your futon. You may also have en suite facilities and your own Japanese-style bath. But you don't have to stay in a luxury property to enjoy first-class service. Standard ryokan charge around ¥9500-12,500pp including half board (breakfast and an evening meal). However, note that if you are travelling on your own it may be hard to book a room, especially for a Saturday night, without paying a higher per person rate, or even the rate for two people.

Many ryokan have their own *onsen* (hot spring), which may or may not include a *rotemburo* (open-air hot-spring bath), the perfect place to unwind after a hard day's sightseeing. Ryokan may not have wired internet access in the rooms as the idea is you are there to relax. However, increasingly wi-fi will be available though you may have to go to the reception area for this.

Evening meals are nearly always Japanese and the dishes are prepared so that they are as much a visual treat as a gastronomic one and often feature local produce/specialities. A typical meal might include some tempura, sashimi/sushi, grilled fish, a meat dish, vegetable dishes and pickles, and will always include miso soup and rice; dessert is likely to be slices of fresh fruit. All this can be

---

### ❏ Ryokan and minshuku etiquette

A stay in a Japanese inn is a wonderful experience and thoroughly recommended, but it's worth bearing the following in mind. You'll find a row of **slippers** waiting in the entrance hall; this is where you're expected to leave your outdoor shoes. The slippers can be worn anywhere except on the tatami-mat floor of your room and in the toilet/bathroom. If you're heading out for a stroll around the local area, *geta* (wooden clogs) may be provided as an alternative to putting on your outdoor shoes.

Before you enter the toilet or bathroom make sure you take off the house slippers because toilets in particular have their own slippers. These are hard to miss as they are usually plastic, have 'toilet' written on them, and come in bright blue or pink. Don't forget to switch back to your other slippers when you leave.

The **bedding** is stored in cupboards in the rooms. At most ryokan staff lay your futon out each night and put it away in the morning (usually while you are having supper/breakfast), while at minshuku you're expected to do it yourself. Don't be surprised to find that the pillow is very hard – traditionally pillows are filled with rice husks – and, in winter, that a blanket is put below the duvet part of the futon. If you find what has been put out is too hard on the floor you will often find extra futon in the cupboard.

Also in the room you'll find a hand towel and a *yukata* (a dressing gown/pyjama combo). Remember to cross the yukata left over right (the opposite way is for the deceased). In the winter months a *hanten* (a jacket) may also be provided.

Bathrooms are nearly always communal but this doesn't necessarily mean you have to share your bath time with complete strangers. In the majority of places used to foreign guests the bathroom can be locked from the inside. The bath is often large enough to accommodate two or three and made of stainless steel though in a ryokan it may be made of cedar-wood and the water scented with pine or mint. The golden rules for **having a bath** are: wash outside the tub, only climb in once you're clean (staff will already have filled the tub with piping hot water), and never let the bath water out! When you enter the bathroom you will find bowls, stools and taps/shower heads; pick up a bowl and a stool and sit in front of a tap. Soap and shampoo are usually provided; use your small towel as a flannel and scrub as hard as you can.

**Tipping** is not encouraged but if you've enjoyed exceptional service you might want to leave a small amount of money (notes only) in an envelope or wrapped in tissue paper in your room; it is considered rude to give something without wrapping it up.

If the **breakfast** is Japanese you are likely to have miso soup, grilled fish, pickles, some kind of egg, and rice. If you see a bowl with an egg in its shell it is almost definitely a raw egg. The Japanese break that into their rice bowl and mix it with soy sauce and then eat it.

washed down with beer or sake (for which there will be an additional charge) and/or Japanese tea. Some ryokan offer a choice of Japanese- or Western-style breakfast, the latter is now often a buffet meal.

## Other accommodation options

**Renting an apartment/house** is a brilliant way to get an idea what living in Japan would really be like. Japan Experience (🖳 www.japan-experience.com) has over 50 properties (in Tokyo, Kyoto, Kanazawa and Fukuoka); each sleeps up to four people (¥7500-44,300 per night). All have standard Japanese cooking facilities. A major benefit is their Travel Angel service; you will be met at the property by an 'angel' and they will help you settle in to your accommodation and will be happy to answer queries throughout your stay. If booked in advance many can also act as a tour guide.

**Airbnb** (🖳 www.airbnb.com/s/Japan) has become very popular in Japan but, as in many other parts of the world, the hotel industry is unhappy about the loss of custom; also here some residents have complained as they feel their local areas are becoming overwhelmed with foreigners. This means it is possible legislation will be introduced banning stays for less than a week. Tomareru (🖳 stay japan.com) is a Japanese equivalent to Airbnb.

If all else fails and you're stuck for accommodation in a city, find out the location of the nearest **capsule hotel** (¥3000-4000pp), good for a one-off novelty but not recommended for claustrophobics and the majority are for men only. However, in places such as Kyoto and Tokyo, capsule hotels for tourists have opened, but men and women may be in separate sections.

Alternatively, consider a **manga kissa** (manga café) – these are meant for people who want to play computer games so aren't necessarily the quietest place, and you will need to 'sleep' in a chair, but they are cheap (¥1000-2000pp) and often soft drinks and light snacks are provided for free.

Sleeping compartments in a capsule hotel

A final option might be a night in a Japanese **love hotel**. During the day, rooms are rented by the hour, but from around 10pm they can be booked for an overnight stay (¥6000-12,000). Like capsule hotels, you'll find love hotels in big cities and sometimes around mainline stations. They're easy to spot because the exteriors are usually bright and garish. The over-the-top design continues inside with a variety of themed rooms, which may contain bizarre extras such as rotating beds, tropical plants and waterfalls. The service in these places, by contrast, tends to be very discreet and you are unlikely ever to see a staff member. A display board at the entrance lights up to inform guests what rooms are available. You then go to pay at a counter, after which a mysterious hand passes you the key to your room. It is not nearly as seedy as it might sound; the arrival process is designed to protect the customers' anonymity and a night here is just as much an experience of Japan as is a stay in a traditional ryokan.

JAPAN

## WHERE TO EAT

Eating out in Japan can seem a daunting prospect but with so much on offer it's also a great opportunity to try a variety of cuisines.

Japanese restaurants tend to specialise in a particular kind of food, so it's more common to find a *sushi* restaurant or *soba* (noodle) shop than a generic 'Japanese restaurant'. The only places that have a mixture of kinds of food are *shokudo* and family restaurants; see below for details of both.

Note that many restaurants close early, often by 10pm; for late-night eating head to an *izakaya* (bar), or a fast-food place.

### Japanese food

For a guide to Japanese food and drink, see pp497-9.

A quick and cheap breakfast is served in **coffee shops** advertising 'morning service' or 'morning set' – usually coffee, toast and a boiled or fried egg. Chains to look out for include UCC, Tully's and Doutor; Starbucks continues to spread inexorably across Japan. There are also lots of independent coffee shops.

To save time and money for lunch, **convenience stores** (known as *konbini*) are a good bet; all stock sandwiches, *onigiri*, noodles and the like, and nearly all are open 24 hours and have microwaves. Major convenience-store chains include 7-Eleven, Lawsons/Natural Lawson, Heart-in, ampm and Family Mart; in Hokkaido, look out for Seicomart. (See also box p84).

Other good places for snack-style food are **bakeries** (every large station has at least one), **supermarkets** (Ito Yokado, Daiei, Jusco and Fresco; these also often have a microwave for customers so you can easily heat up anything you buy), and department store **food halls** *(depachika),* usually in the basement. Snacks nearly always come with the appropriate eating implement. In supermarkets, food halls, and stations, you'll find take-out **lunch boxes** *(bento)* which are cheaper than eating at a restaurant. For details on the *ekiben* (railway station lunch box), see box p102.

The cheapest sit-down meals are at counter-service noodle shops selling **ramen**, **soba** and/or **udon**; a bowl of either costs about ¥400. Alternatively, try a **shokudo**; these restaurants serve a variety of economical dishes (plastic models of which are displayed outside) and are often found in and around station areas. Other inexpensive places to eat include the nationwide chains of *gyudon* **restaurants** (bowls of rice with beef and onions cooked in a slightly sweet sauce) such as Yoshinoya and Sukiya, where dishes cost from ¥300.

❏ **Travelling in Japan as a vegetarian**

Vegetarians are rare in Japan so be sure to make any dietary requirements clear to restaurant staff. It may be assumed, for example, that as a vegetarian you eat fish or even chicken. It's advisable to explain exactly what you can eat rather than simply say you're a vegetarian (see Useful Phrases p503). The best place for a truly vegetarian meal is a Buddhist temple. The superbly crafted *shojin ryori* prepared by monks can be tried at the temple town of Koya-san (see pp156-7), for example.

## ❏ Eating out and how to order

Many Japanese restaurants hang a *noren* (split curtain) at the entrance whenever they are open. In the evenings, bars show they are open by hanging or illuminating a red lantern outside. Before entering the restaurant take a look at the window display showing plastic models of the dishes on offer. As you go in, don't be alarmed by the loud greeting that is often shouted not just by the waiters but by the entire kitchen staff. After the chorus of 'Irasshaimase' ('Welcome') dies down you'll be taken to a table and handed the menu along with hot towels and glasses of cold water or Japanese tea (all part of the service).

If you're lucky the menu will contain pictures of what's on offer (this is always the case at family restaurants). If not, staff are usually happy to go outside with you to see which of the plastic models has tickled your fancy. At some (noodle) places you choose what you want from a list on a machine at the entrance, buy a ticket, hand it to the person behind the counter and then take a seat.

If you see a bell on your table you should ring it when you are ready to order.

The city and route guides include restaurant recommendations but two useful websites for finding particular restaurants are 🖳 gurunavi.com and 🖳 tabelog.com. For help reading a menu in Japanese see the food glossary on pp497-9.

The **canteens** in city halls are subsidised and meant for the staff but are open to anyone. They're often on the top floor, which means you get a cheap meal and a decent view thrown in.

Look out for **stalls** in the evenings and at festivals which sell savoury snacks such as *yakitori*, *takoyaki*, *okonomiyaki* and *yakisoba* as well as sweet things such as candy floss (*wata-ame*) and *kakigori*. Fukuoka is known for its *yatai* (see p439), stalls selling ramen and gyoza.

Japan's best known culinary export is sushi; the cheapest **sushi restaurants** are *kaiten-sushiya*, where you sit around a revolving counter and help yourself to plates of sushi (different colour plates denote different price bands). At the end of the meal the restaurant staff count how many plates you've taken and tell you how much to pay. It's usually possible to eat your fill for less than ¥1500. In most you can also order anything you would like but can't see – either using an iPad or a special form.

Restaurants specialising in *tonkatsu* and *kare-raisu* (curry-rice; look out for the CoCoCurry chain) are also a culinary mainstay; there are usually one or two in large stations. *Tempura* restaurants tend to be a bit more expensive than these.

All **department stores** have at least one 'restaurant floor' where you'll find a variety of Western and Japanese eateries; most offer a daily set lunch which can be very good value. Restaurant floors tend to stay open until 10pm, though the department stores themselves close earlier. At main meal periods there is almost always a queue at the popular places.

### Other foods

In major cities you'll rarely be far from **restaurants** serving ethnic cuisine, the most popular being Chinese, Indian, Italian and French. Italian places tend to be cheap and in some cases offer fusion-style (Italian and Japanese) food; Indian

---

### ❏ Vending machines

Vending machines (*jidohan-baiki*) are on every street corner, as well as in unexpected places such as mountain tops, temple precincts and remote villages. The vast majority sell drinks, both hot and cold, with a bewildering range of options. However, you are unlikely to find white coffee without sugar; only the black coffee in cans has a sugar-free option. Check that fruit juices say '100% juice' or you might get a sweet syrupy concoction. Beer and sake vending machines generally close at 11pm. Some machines are now touch screen and many accept IC (smart) cards (see box p66) as well as cash.

Several vending machines sell ice-cream and snacks and a few have noodles/pasta dishes; less common but not unknown are ones with bananas and eggs.

You can even get prepaid SIM cards from vending machines but these are mostly at the international airports.

---

restaurants serve relatively authentic curries, though you may prefer to try kare-raisu, the Japanese version (see p75). French food is considered classy and therefore is expensive; luxury hotels invariably have at least one French restaurant. Malaysian and Thai restaurants are popular, though the spiciness you might expect is often toned down to suit the Japanese palate.

For **fast food**, McDonald's is everywhere, but look out too for the Japanese chain Mos Burger, and also Wendy's. In big cities you'll find branches of Lotteria and KFC.

Don't reject out of hand the large number of so-called '**family restaurants**' that seem to be everywhere. The menu at these places is a mix of Western and Japanese, such as spaghetti, steaks, pizza, noodles, tonkatsu and curry rice. Some places also offer a salad bar and all-you-can-drink soft drinks bar. Popular family restaurant chains include Royal Host, Jonathan's, Denny's, Gusto, Ringer Hut and others which are found only in specific regions.

## NIGHTLIFE AND ENTERTAINMENT

Japan has its fair share of clubs, discos and bars. Some are ultra-exclusive and expect you to part with a wad of cash in the form of a cover charge before you even see the drinks menu but many more offer good value for money. Every town and city has its own entertainment district, which often radiates out from the area around the main railway station. To find the nightlife look for the large numbers of businessmen staggering about at dusk in search of their favourite karaoke bar or izakaya.

For details of traditional Japanese entertainment see pp62-4.

**Karaoke** Some people have never forgiven Japan for inventing karaoke but its presence in every town and city is unavoidable. In the early days karaoke was available in bars where everyone could hear you sing. It is now much more common to rent a room in a place dedicated to karaoke. The main chains are Big Echo (🖥 big-echo.jp) and Karaoke-kan (🖥 karaokekan.jp), but there are karaoke places everywhere; look out for カラオケ. Note that even within a chain some branches are better than others.

Rates vary depending on a variety of factors such as: whether you go during the day or in the evening; the size of the room and what facilities there are; and whether you choose a package with just one drink, or unlimited (soft) drinks – some permit you to take your own food and drink. Many places also offer food. The main chains are likely to be better equipped and thus more expensive. During the day expect to pay from ¥300 an hour or in the evening ¥500-3000 per hour; some places charge per 30 minutes. You can usually extend your time if you are enjoying yourself.

Virtually all karaoke machines have instructions in English and also a mass of English songs programmed into them (usually a mixture of traditional pop, rock and contemporary music).

**Izakaya and robotayaki** Izakaya are small atmospheric Japanese-style pubs (bars). They are often filled with locals who go along after work for a few beers and an evening meal. Don't be surprised if you see rows of sake or whisky bottles stacked up behind the bar; most bars operate a 'bottle keep' system for regulars. A typical izakaya consists of seating along a counter, with tables squeezed into any other space available.

The menu changes according to what the owner (known as the 'master') has bought in from the market but there's nearly always a choice of fresh fish and meat, as well as salads, tofu dishes and *edamame* (soy beans). Everything is served in snack-size portions so it is a good chance to try a variety of things; dishes usually cost from ¥350 each. Keep track of what you are ordering if you are bothered about your budget as it is easy for the bill to mount up. If the menu is only in Japanese you will probably find the kanji in the food glossary (see pp497-9) useful; alternatively you can look at what others are eating and point at that. Izakaya are great places to meet people and it is unlikely anyone will mind you pointing at their food; in fact it may be a great way to start a conversation. These places don't tend to open much before 6pm and close around 1am or even later; to find them, look for the tell-tale red lanterns hanging outside.

**Robotayaki** offer similar food and drink; the main difference is that the food is displayed between the 'chef' and guests; you point to what you would like and it will then be cooked for you.

**Beer gardens** The name is a bit of a misnomer because beer gardens are almost always on the roofs of department stores and large hotels rather than on the ground. For a fixed price (around ¥3500) most places offer an all-you-can-eat-and-drink beer-and-buffet deal for a set time (90-120 minutes).

Beer gardens are open only from the end of May to early September and are highly recommended as places from which to escape the summer humidity.

## MEDIA

Four English-language daily **newspapers** are published in Japan, of which the best are the *Japan Times* (🖳 www.japantimes.co.jp) and the *Daily Yomiuri* (🖳 www.yomiuri.co.jp); you can find copies at kiosks in most large stations. Outside the Tokyo metropolitan and Kansai areas, they may be a day late.

The main national broadcaster of **television** programmes is NHK (Nippon Hoso Kyokai; 🖳 www3.nhk.or.jp/nhkworld), the Japanese equivalent of the BBC. NHK operates two digital channels, NHK-G (the main channel) and NHK-E with mainly educational programmes. Private broadcasters such as TBS, Fuji and TV Asahi fill the rest of the airwaves with game shows and soaps. Both the *Daily Yomiuri* and *Japan Times* carry TV listings in English.

**Radio** is not as popular as TV and most programmes are broadcast only in Japanese. A few cities produce selected pop music shows in English.

## ELECTRICITY

The electric current in Japan is 100 volts AC, but there are two different cycles: 50Mhz in eastern Japan (including Tokyo) and 60Mhz in western Japan. Plugs in Japan are of the flat two-pin variety (like American plugs).

## TIME

Japan is GMT + 9 so at 9pm in Tokyo it is noon in London, 7am in New York, 4am in California and 11pm in Sydney (all same-day times, not taking summer daylight-saving times into account).

## BANKS AND MONEY MATTERS

The unit of **currency** is the Japanese yen (¥). Bank notes are issued in denominations of ¥10,000, ¥5000, ¥2000 and ¥1000. Coins are ¥500, ¥100, ¥50, ¥10, ¥5 and ¥1; the ¥50 and ¥5 coins have a hole in the middle.

For such a sophisticated economy, banking practices remain somewhat archaic. Banks are open Monday to Friday from 9am to 3pm only.

---

### ❏ Hi-tech attention to the call of nature

There are free, clean toilets (restrooms), generally with toilet paper, virtually everywhere you go in Japan. Most are now Western style, though on some older trains, particularly local services, and occasionally in public toilets you'll still find Asian squat toilets. Most of the Western-style toilets have a control panel as there are usually several functions; many of these now have English translations but if they don't the following may be useful.

On even the most basic models the seats are heated and in addition to the lever for the flush 流す (on many toilets now there are two levels of flush, though if you turn the lever the wrong way nothing dramatic is likely to happen), there is likely to be a button that activates a warm-water spray おしり. There may also be a button so you can adjust the pressure of the spray 水勢調節つまみ and move its position/angle おしり洗浄用ムーブスイッチ. Other functions you may find are: power deodoriser パワー脱臭, nozzle-cleaning ノズルクリーン; a choice of background music 音姫 or a flushing sound 洗水音, to hide your own natural noises; and a built-in bidet ビデ. When you have had enough of any of these press the stop switch 止.

Big hotels try to outdo their rivals by fitting guest rooms with futuristic lavatories so expect to experience even more amazing functions.

Japan has always been a **cash-based society** and although things are changing credit cards are not as popular as in many other countries so check that any hotel, restaurant or shop accepts them before you go in. However, you can use foreign-issued credit cards to buy JR train tickets. If you are expecting to use lockers and buses and don't have an IC card (see box p66), it is worth keeping a supply of ¥100 coins, though buses do have change machines.

| ❏ Exchange rates | |
|---|---|
| £1 | ¥161 |
| €1 | ¥126 |
| US$1 | ¥111 |
| Can$1 | ¥86 |
| Aus$1 | ¥85 |
| Sng$1 | ¥82 |
| NZ$1 | ¥76 |
| Zar1 | ¥7.3 |
| To get the latest rates of exchange check: 🖳 www.xe.com/ucc | |

Many **ATMs** at banks do not accept foreign-issued cards and, with very few exceptions, are not open 24 hours. The good news is that all 26,000 post office ATMs across the country (including small branch offices) as well as branches of 7-Eleven convenience stores accept Visa, MasterCard, Diners Club, American Express, Cirrus, and Plus; Maestro cards with IC chips may not be accepted. On-screen instructions are available in English. The normal hours for post office ATMs in major cities are Monday to Friday 9am-7pm, Saturday 9am-5pm, Sunday 9am-noon. For more information see 🖳 www.jp-bank.japan post.jp and click on 'Service information'. ATMs at 7-Eleven convenience stores are open 24 hours a day.

## POST AND TELECOMMUNICATIONS

### Post

**Post offices** open Monday to Friday 9am-5pm; main branches also offer a limited service in the evening and at weekends. Post offices in Japan are identifiable by a red '〒' sign outside.

Japan's **postal service** is fast and very efficient but not all that cheap. Postcards cost ¥70 to send abroad and ¥60 within Japan.

Japanese write addresses with the country first, then the post code and the name of the recipient last; for any postcards you send make sure the destination

---

❏ **Taxes and tipping**
**Consumption tax** (called *shohizei*; 8%, but 10% from April 2017)) is levied on near-ly all goods and services in Japan, but you won't necessarily notice it in shops because the tax is already included on price tags. However, foreign tourists can buy many goods tax-free – look for the sign saying 'Japan Tax-free shop' in shop windows. You will need to show your passport but the advantage is that the tax will be deducted immediately.

Hotel rate-cards usually show room charges excluding and including tax; charges quoted throughout this guide refer to the room rate including tax; see also box p130. Additionally, upmarket hotels levy a **service tax** of between 10 and 20% on top of the consumption tax. Room rates quoted in this guide do not include these.

There is no culture of **tipping** in Japan, but see box p83.

country is clear and you add an airmail sticker. You may also be charged more if anything other than the address is written on the address side of the postcard.

## Wi-fi and internet access

**Wireless access (wi-fi)** has exploded in Japan in recent years. Free wi-fi is now available in most tourist/urban areas, though in some cases you will have to register (give your name and email address) before accessing it. When you connect to a hotspot, a splash page will usually appear asking you to input your name and email address. Sometimes these pages are shrouded in impenetrable kanji, but generally there's a little link showing the instructions to turn to English; finding this will make gaining wi-fi access much easier.

The **Japan Connected-free wi-fi app** (🖥 www.ntt-bp.net/jcfw; for both Android and iphones) will, once you are registered, guide you to free wi-fi in an area. As long as you provide the relevant personal details it will also save you inputting these each time you register. **Travel Japan wi-fi** (🖥 wi2.co.jp/tjw) is another app giving free access to thousands of wi-fi hotspots; the full list can be accessed if you get the premium code from a partner store or city in Japan – look for the Travel Japan sign in the shop window. For a full list of wi-fi hotspots visit 🖥 www.hotspot-locations.com.

Softbank (🖥 www.softbank.jp/en/mobile/special/freewifi) offers a **free wi-fi passport** to anyone with a mobile device that supports W-CDMA and whose mobile phone contract covers international service. Alternatively if you have an unlocked iPhone (3G and newer) you can rent a **SIM card** (🖥 www.softbank-rental.jp; rental fee ¥110/day, unlimited data from ¥970/day). Global Advanced Communications (🖥 www.globaladvancedcomm.com) also offer SIM rental for both iPhone and Android as well as **Pocket wi-fi rental**; see their website for more details. PuPuRu (🖥 www.pupuru.com/en/service/emobile), eConnect (🖥 www.econnectjapan.com) and Rental wifi (🖥 www.rentalwifi.com) also offer pocket wi-fi rental as do some rail pass agents (see pp37-9), so you can arrange wi-fi access in advance of travel to Japan.

**Wired (LAN) access** is available in most Western-style hotel rooms (you may need to borrow a LAN cable from the reception desk), but not always in Japanese-style places. Access is generally free for guests (except in some upmarket hotels). Most Western-style hotels also have a computer with internet access that guests can use, but in every city and town it won't take you long to find an **internet café** ネットカフェ. The rate (around ¥400 per hour) often includes free soft drinks and snacks. A few places require you to become a member by paying an additional charge (¥100-200) and by showing proof of identity such as a passport (a copy of the relevant pages is usually accepted). *Manga kissa* マンガ喫茶 (comic-book cafés) are good places to access the internet. They are often near railway stations and usually open 24 hours a day; they can also be a good place to crash for the night (see p73).

## Phone

**Mobile (cell) phones** 携帯電話 (*keitai denwa*) are the ultimate everyday accessory in Japan as around the world. Most phones with 3G or 4G (and assuming any contract you have includes roaming) are now compatible with the Japanese network, but you won't be able to use your own phone if it is GSM because there is no GSM network in Japan. If this is the case the best option if you have an unlocked phone is to **rent a SIM card** from a Japanese provider; these services are usually only available at airports: SoftBank (see opposite) has counters at the main airports. You can turn up and rent a SIM card for an iPhone (from ¥110/day, phone calls from ¥110/min, texts ¥15 in Japan, ¥150 if international). If your phone is locked you can also **rent a mobile phone** (from ¥260/day) immediately, but for both if you book at least three days before you arrive, you can be informed of the number for your rented SIM card/phone and you can then give that to family and friends before you leave for Japan.

You'll need to provide proof of identity (such as your passport) when you pick up any SIM card/phone you rent and you will need a credit/debit card.

Alternatively it is now possible to get a **pre-paid SIM card** (nano & micro ¥3000/4000 1.0G/2.0G 30/90 days) from a vending machine at the airport, or around the country in convenience stores, such as Newdays. Even if you do rent a SIM card it is likely to be cheaper to make calls from a public phone.

マナーモードに
設定の上、通話は
ご遠慮ください。

Please set your mobile phone to silent mode and refrain from talking on the phone.

NTT DoCoMo (🖳 www.nttdocomo.co.jp/en glish/service) has a roaming agreement with phone companies in most countries; see their website to check if it will work with your phone.

On almost every railway line in Japan mobile phones must be on **silent mode**; if you really need to talk to someone you need to go to the area between carriages.

The proliferation of mobile phones has not yet led to a decrease in the number of **public telephones**. These are installed on all shinkansen and some limited express services, though a surcharge is levied and you may get cut off in tunnels. National and international calls are possible from some green phones and the grey ones. Both these phones accept ¥10 and ¥100 coins and/or telephone cards. It's best to use only ¥10 coins for local calls since change is not given. Local calls cost ¥10 per minute. **Prepaid telephone cards** (¥1000) are sold at some shops, kiosks, and from vending machines inside some phone boxes. Many cities and individual tourist attractions sell their own souvenir phone cards, which make great collectibles.

**Making a call** When calling **city-to-city** in Japan dial the area code first (all phone numbers in this guide include the area code). The area code can be omitted if calling a local number (for example, if you call a Tokyo number from within Tokyo omit the 03). Numbers starting 0120 or 0088 are toll free.

To make an **international call**, dial 010 followed by the country code, area code (minus the initial '0') and telephone number. Making overseas calls is cheaper at night as well as at weekends and on public holidays.

> ❏ **The Japanese calendar**
> Traditionally the Japanese have named and counted their years by the length of an emperor's reign. The count starts with each new emperor. The year 2016, for example, is known as Heisei 28; Heisei being the name that refers to the current emperor's era, and 28 being the number of years that have elapsed since he ascended to the throne; the year 2017 will be Heisei 29. While the Western system of counting years is widely used, the Japanese system is often found on official documentation such as train tickets and seat reservations, as well as some hotel/restaurant receipts.

## LANGUAGE

Japanese is one of the most difficult languages to learn to read and write, mixing as it does Chinese characters, known as *kanji*, with two different syllabaries, *hiragana* and *katakana* (the latter is used exclusively for writing words which the Japanese have borrowed from other languages); see pp500-1 for a guide to these scripts. That said, basic greetings and phrases are not difficult to remember (see pp500-3) and any efforts to speak Japanese will be appreciated. The Japanese always seem amazed and impressed that foreigners can speak their language, especially given the various levels and subtle nuances that need to be used in certain situations.

A misunderstanding sometimes arises over the meaning of the Japanese word 'hai' which is translated into English as 'yes'. Anyone who has had contact with the Japanese business world knows that the Japanese do not like to commit immediately to a straightforward 'yes' or 'no' answer to a proposal, at least during a first meeting. Thus, 'hai' often means 'yes, I am listening' (this also applies when talking on the phone) rather than 'yes, I agree'.

Although nearly everyone in Japan learns English at school, this does not mean they can speak it. Despite efforts to bring more native English speakers into Japanese schools as 'assistant language teachers', the classroom emphasis continues to be on written English and grammar, rather than spoken skills.

If you need help, try talking to younger people rather than older. If you can't make yourself understood, try writing your question down; many Japanese find reading English much easier than listening to, or speaking, it. And consider downloading a dictionary app or two on to your smartphone or tablet (see box p40).

## ASSISTANCE

You'll almost certainly find that the Japanese are delighted to help you: all you need to do is ask; generally younger Japanese are more confident speaking English (see above). Another option is to call the TIC information line, see box p65. You can expect **police officers** to be polite and helpful. Even the smallest villages have a street-corner *koban* 交番 (police box), where

> ❏ **Emergency numbers**
> **Police** (emergencies) ☎ 110
> **Fire/Ambulance** ☎ 119

you can ask directions. **Pharmacies** (chemists) are everywhere and can be recognised by the green cross outside the store. Few pharmacists speak much English but sign-language will generally do the trick.

---

#### ❏ Cultural tips

Perhaps the most important piece of advice to remember when visiting Japan is that foreigners are not expected to know the conventions that dictate how the Japanese behave in public. Nobody's going to care, for example, if you haven't mastered the art of bowing. Indeed, people would probably be more concerned if you did know exactly how low to bow on every occasion since it might suggest you know more about the culture than the Japanese themselves (which is a far greater sin). The following tips may help, however.

● The Japanese prefer consensus over disagreement and rarely show strong emotions. Flaring into a temper if your hotel room is not ready, for example, would be considered inappropriate behaviour and people might not know how to react.

● Take your shoes off as you enter a minshuku, ryokan, temple, or someone's home; shoes and slippers are never worn on tatami mats.

● It's understood that foreigners are unable to sit on their knees for long periods of time so if you have to sit on the floor it's fine to sit cross-legged; just don't point your legs towards anyone.

● Chopstick etiquette is important to the Japanese. Pitfalls to avoid include 'spearing' food with chopsticks, allowing them to cross over each other or using them to rummage through dishes. Avoid passing food between pairs of chopsticks and never stick them upright in a bowl of rice as these actions are associated with ceremonies observed after a cremation.

● Slurping noodles is supposed to improve the flavour and is encouraged; it's also common to bring the bowl up to your mouth to ensure you don't spill the liquid.

● If drinking beer or sake with a group, it's polite to pour someone else's glass and wait for yours to be filled.

● Eating while walking along the street is becoming less taboo, but should be avoided if possible. However, eating at a festival is OK.

● Blowing one's nose used to be considered rude – sniffing was seen as a demonstration of your ability to resist temptation. However, it is much more common now.

● Business cards (known as *meishi*) are almost sacred. Though tourists are not expected to carry a supply, they're still worth bringing with you. If you are offered a business card, it's considered very bad form to put it straight in your pocket and even worse if you get out a pen and scrawl notes on it. It's best to look at it for a while before putting it away.

● If you're expecting to visit someone's home, a souvenir from your home country is appreciated: tea, chocolates, biscuits, and coasters or tea towels or other things with famous landmarks on, would be perfect.

● When visiting a shrine or temple the most important thing is to be quiet and respectful. At both you should purify yourself before praying. At a shrine this means cleaning your hands at the *temizuya*, a stone basin filled with clean water; ladles are always provided. At a temple purify yourself by waving your hands over the incense in the burner so that you fan the smoke towards yourself. If you want to pray throw a donation into the offering box. At a shrine ring the bell (to let the gods/spirits know you are there). To pray bow twice, clap twice, and bow again.

For details of etiquette in a ryokan/minshuku, see the box on p72.

See the box on p72.

JAPAN

> ❏ **Floor confusion**
> A point of confusion, particularly for the British, is the way floors in Japan are num-
> bered. '1F' means the ground floor, and is not the same as the '1st floor' (which is
> really the 2nd floor); the style used in this guide is 1st/ground floor. 'BF' indicates the
> basement and B1F the first floor of the basement (there are often two).

## SHOPPING

**Department stores** open daily from 10am to around 7 or 8pm, but are closed
one day a month (usually Wednesday or Thursday but rarely Sunday). If you
arrive as the store opens, dozens of eager staff will be standing in position to
greet and bow to you. If you can negotiate your way through their ranks (realis-
ing as you go that this is how Japan achieves its low unemployment figures),
you'll eventually find departments that sell everything from furniture to food,
from digital cameras to kimonos. The biggest stores often encompass several
buildings and the variety of goods can be overwhelming but they are great places
for discovering Japan's latest fashions and craziest inventions. Souvenir hunters
will certainly not be disappointed: watches, silks, bamboo and lacquerware, pottery, woodblock prints, Japanese fans, dolls, kimonos, and chopsticks can all be
found under one roof; any gift you buy will almost certainly be beautifully
wrapped. As if selling goods were not enough, department stores also stage exhibitions of art or ikebana and sometimes even fashion shows. Some have roof-top
playgrounds, amusement arcades and beer gardens (see p77) in the summer.

Every town or city has its own **shopping street/arcade** *(shotengai)*; these
are often near railway stations and many are pedestrianised. Traditionally they
are identified by the plastic flowers (the colour of which varies according to the
season) that are suspended from lamp posts. In major towns and cities many are
now covered, which makes them particularly appealing when it is cold, wet, or

> ❏ **Convenience stores – one stop for everything**
> Most associate convenience stores (*konbini* in Japan) as a place to get a snack, or a
> missing ingredient, instead of going to a supermarket. Convenience stores in Japan of
> course provide this but also much more including being open 24 hours a day. Some
> food is sold hot but if you want, staff will heat up a ready-made meal; whether heat-
> ed or not chopsticks or plastic cutlery will be provided. They also sell soft drinks (hot
> and cold) and alcohol, the latter though only to people aged over 20.
>
> Many have ATMs (particularly branches of 7-Eleven) so you can get cash.
> Virtually all have a multi-function copy machine so you can copy something, or print
> photos. These can also be used to get and print out tickets for concerts, films
> (movies), theme parks and sports games such as baseball. At branches of 7-Eleven
> use the Seven Ticket function on the multi-copy machine; at any Lawson use their
> dedicated ticket machine, Loppi; and at FamilyMart use their equivalent, Famiport.
> Instructions are in Japanese only but, if requested, staff are certain to help.
>
> Most also have a toilet which you can use for free and free wi-fi. Some are also
> a collection point for Black Cat delivery services (see box opposite).

JAPAN

---

❑ **Luggage delivery**
If you end up buying too many souvenirs you may like to use a luggage-delivery service to get your suitcase transferred to your next hotel, or to the airport. There are several such services in Japan, but the one you will see everywhere is Yamato's (🖥 www
.kuronekoyamato.co.jp) **Ta-Q-Bin**, commonly called Kuroneko (literally '**Black Cat**') as their logo shows a black cat. Luggage can be delivered door-to-door anywhere in Japan – and internationally. Depending on the distance, delivery can be the same day, but it may be the next day. For a standard-size suitcase expect to pay from ¥1500. Many hotels act as collection points, but also shops and convenience stores – just look for the Black Cat symbol! Alternatively look for the 'Hands-free travel' sign: 🖥 www.jnto.go.jp/hands-free-travel.

---

even too hot, outside. Shopping streets have a variety of shops as well as cafés, restaurants, pachinko parlours, and sometimes a post office.

Worth looking out for are the **hyaku-en** (¥100) shops. Strictly speaking this is a misnomer as consumption tax (see box p79) is added to the ¥100. There are thousands of these shops all over Japan and they offer some great bargains and are a useful place to pick up souvenirs and presents.

The many **open-air markets** provide another great shopping experience. As at most markets they sell locally made goods, traditional handicrafts and fresh produce. Tourist information offices can provide details of the market day(s) in a particular town or city.

## MUSEUMS AND TOURIST ATTRACTIONS

Most museums and tourist attractions are open on Sundays and national holidays but closed on Mondays. If a public holiday falls on a Monday, museums are closed on Tuesday instead. Typical opening hours are 9.30am-5pm with last admission 30 minutes/one hour before closing. The opening hours quoted in this guide are for the full day so bear this in mind when planning your day.

Admission prices quoted are for standard adult tickets. The child rate (up to age 12, or sometimes 16) is usually 50% of the adult rate. Seniors (over 65, or sometimes 60) are also often entitled to a reduction. University students sometimes qualify for small savings so it's worth showing an ISIC card at the entrance. Some regional rail passes, such as the Kansai Thru Pass (see box p34), as well as one-day bus, or tram/streetcar, cards entitle you to discounts, but even just being a foreigner may be enough in a few places.

---

❑ **Smoking**
Smoking is now banned in many places in Japan, including in the open air in some urban areas. Unless specified – look for a sign on the door – it is legal to smoke in bars/restaurants; many restaurants have designated non-smoking and smoking areas but bars (izakaya/robotayaki) generally don't. There are also designated areas for smoking in trains and on platforms. Always check before you light up.

---

JAPAN

## ❏ Japanese gardens: a potted history

Japanese gardens (*teien*) were first developed during the 8th century, in what is now Nara Prefecture. Inspired by Buddhists from China and Korea they were designed to imitate **natural scenes**, in particular the seashore, and often featured ponds large enough to go boating on, with rocks for islands and stones representing sand.

In the Heian era (794-1185), when the capital moved to Kyoto, gardens became simpler though the boating ponds remained and waterfalls were added; gardens in this period were not intended for walking around. Background, or **'borrowed' scenery** became an important design feature and one which pertains to this day; Korakuen (see pp297-8) is an example of this, making fine use of Okayama Castle for its backdrop.

The **dry garden** (*kare-sansui*) came to the fore in the Muromachi period (1333-1568). In these gardens sand and fine gravel were used to represent water, and rocks and stones symbolised islands. Dry gardens were common in Zen temples, the idea being that they should be viewed from a particular place and used for contemplation. Probably the best-known example is Ryoan-ji (see p252) in Kyoto.

The **tea-ceremony garden** developed in the Momoyama period (1568-1603). It was only then that gardens were designed to be walked through – on the way to a tea house. Konchi-in in Nanzen-ji (see p255), Kyoto, is a well-known example.

The concept of the **stroll garden** evolved further in the Edo period (1603-1868), this time incorporating a variety of areas, each with a different view, for *daimyo* (feudal lords) and their guests to wander around. Many gardens also had a tea house and ponds but the latter were by now too small for boating. These were 'secular' gardens in that they were not associated with temples. The main feature of the Meiji era (from 1868) was the spread of Western influences throughout every aspect of Japanese life. In gardens this was seen through the introduction of lawns and parks; a good example of a stroll garden is Fujita Memorial Japanese Garden (see p344) in Hirosaki.

In general in Japanese gardens, trees are trained and pruned to show their best qualities and natural landscapes are reproduced in miniature.

## ACTIVITIES

Japan's mountainous terrain provides opportunities for a wide range of adventure activities. The Japanese Alps (Honshu) and Hokkaido offer the most spectacular **hiking**; routes and paths are nearly always well signposted and almost always well trodden. See 🖳 japanhike.wordpress.com for more details.

It's worth trying **skiing** in Japan, if only for half a day – where else in the world can you get bowed off a chair-lift? The season lasts from November to May and there are ski resorts in Hokkaido and throughout the Japanese Alps (Honshu); the most convenient to reach on Honshu is Gala Yuzawa (see box p352) as it is attached to a shinkansen station. For everything you need to know check 🖳 www.snowjapan.com. Other possibilities include **white-water rafting** to **canyoning**, **mountain-biking** to **snowboarding**. For more information on the great outdoors, see 🖳 www.outdoorjapan.com.

### Relaxing in a hot spring or public bath

Hot springs, known as **onsen**, are hugely popular among Japanese, who consider the chance to relax in a hot tub the perfect escape from the stresses of life.

Natural hot springs, where the water is often pumped direct from a bubbling pool of volcanic rock, are found everywhere. Diehard onsen lovers travel the country in search of the perfect hot spring; open-air baths, **rotemburo**, are the ultimate. Some ryokan and minshuku in rural areas have rotemburo, and there are also some free, public ones, usually high in the mountains, without any facilities. In theory these are mixed but in general they are mostly used by men. At the other extreme are Japan's onsen resorts, such as Beppu (see pp426-7) in Kyushu, where luxury hotels operate themed bath-houses.

Onsen generally include several indoor baths of varying temperatures, a sauna, plunge pool, Jacuzzi, and, where possible, a rotemburo. If you're lucky with the location, this will afford sweeping views of the mountains and surrounding countryside.

At a public onsen you will need to pay to enter (at the counter or from a vending machine) and to rent a flannel-sized towel if you don't have one. Then head for the segregated changing rooms (for the Japanese characters for male and female see p501). As when taking a bath in a minshuku or ryokan, you're expected to wash before entering the water (see box on p72); soap is generally provided. Swimming costumes are not worn but you can use your towel to protect your modesty when walking around. The onsen experience does not end the moment you step out of the bath. Changing rooms are often equipped with massage chairs, weighing machines, combs, brushes, aftershaves, scents, industrial-sized fans to help you dry off, and vending machines.

With so many hot springs scattered around Japan, it's hard to know where to start; see p26 for some suggestions but in general wherever you go in Japan there are likely to be some good places.

Another option is to go to a **public bath-house** (*o-sento*). Here the water is not naturally hot but in other respects the experience is the same. Unlike onsen most people in a sento are likely to know each other and thus they can have a very communal feel. For further information visit ⌨ www.sentoguide.info.

---

### ❏ Women travellers

Japan is one of the safest countries in the world and it's unlikely women travelling alone will have any problems. However, in crowded commuter trains women might

find themselves being groped. The best thing to do is shout out – the offender will be embarrassed – or try to move away. As a result of this some trains (both overground and subway) have dedicated women-only carriages during peak periods.

The best advice for safe travel is the same as for anywhere else in the world: don't take unnecessary risks, know where you're going if someone invites you out, and always arrange to meet in a public place.

JAPAN

# 3

# THE RAIL NETWORK

## Railway history

When Commodore Perry appeared off the coast of Japan in 1853 with the US Navy's 'Black Ships' (see p56), the country, like many others, had no railway whatsoever. But in the years since Japan ended its policy of self-isolation, its rail network has become the envy of the world. This transformation, given the country's topography and history of devastating earthquakes, is nothing short of extraordinary.

### PIONEERING EARLY DAYS

One of Perry's gifts on his second trip to Japan in 1854 was a quarter-size steam locomotive and accompanying track. However astonishing the sight of this miniature railway set up on the beach must have been, it would be a mistake to believe that the Tokugawa shogunate was entirely ignorant of technological developments outside Japan.

From the tiny Dutch enclave in Nagasaki, the only point of contact with the outside world in 265 years of self-imposed isolation, the Shogun had received an annual report on developments in the rest of the world. In 1865 Thomas Glover (see box p441) brought the first steam railway locomotive to Nagasaki and tested it on a line he built there. But it was not until the Meiji Restoration of 1868 (see pp56-7) that the idea of constructing a proper railway in Japan began to take root.

The Japanese government employed a number of British engineers and pioneering railwaymen to assist in the development of the country's rail network, notably Edmund Morel (1841-71); Morel was appointed chief engineer but died a year before the opening of Japan's first railway line.

In October 1872, 92 years before the inauguration of the Tokaido shinkansen between Tokyo and Shin-Osaka, Emperor Meiji and his entourage set off on the country's first official train ride, a 30km journey from Shimbashi, in Tokyo, to Yokohama, though services from the then Shinagawa station had been operating for a month. The driver for this historic journey was British and the coach the Emperor rode in was made in Birmingham. Some Japanese

蒸気機関車マリゴールドの野を過ぎる

*The steaming locomotive passing across the field full of marigold at night*
(KAZUKO KONAGAI)

guests, it is reported, upheld tradition by taking off their shoes before boarding and so travelled to Yokohama in their socks.

The use of foreign engineers was not without its complications, not least of which was the language barrier. British railwaymen accustomed to grey skies and drizzle also found it hard to adapt to Japan's hot and humid climate. Edmund Holtham, writing about his time as a railway engineer, describes how the summer heat made work 'rather a burden … in spite of running down to Kobe for a game of cricket and a plunge in the sea, I fell out of condition' (*Eight Years in Japan*, 1883).

A significant turning point came in the spring of 1879, when Japanese drivers were allowed to operate the trains between Tokyo and Yokohama – though on about one-sixth of the salary. However, it wasn't long before the Japanese were taking over from the British and other Western engineers. By 1904, as the last British railwayman set off for home, the country had embarked on an unprecedented expansion of the railway network.

## NATIONALISATION AND EXPANSION

As the railway expanded, people began to move around at previously unimaginable speeds. The old Tokaido road, for centuries the only way of getting between Edo (Tokyo) and Kyoto, was quickly abandoned after the opening of the Tokaido line in July 1889. A journey which had taken 12 or 13 days could now be completed in just 20 hours. By 1906, when a 'super express' was introduced, the journey time was cut still further to 13 hours 40 minutes. The year 1906 was significant in another way; 8000km (5000 miles) of track had been laid in just 34 years, though the majority of this was in the hands of private rail companies.

Under pressure from the military, who were finding it increasingly difficult to move around the country at any speed when they had to wait for connections between the private railways, the government passed the 1906 Railway Nationalisation Act, giving itself the authority to purchase the 'trunk' lines, while allowing private railways to own local lines. The railway (Japan National Railway; JNR) was to remain a nationalised industry until 1987.

---

❏ **The Japanese Railway Society**

The Japanese Railway Society (💻 www.japaneserailwaysociety .com; 💻 www.facebook.com/japanrailsociety; 💻 twitter.com/ JapanRwySociety) was founded in 1992 and now has members all over the world. The society takes an interest not just in the old steam days, but in the state of Japan's railway today as well as how it might look in the future. Members receive a quarterly journal, *Bullet-In* and a variety of events are held throughout the year; if interested in joining visit the website for details.

The society organises occasional **rail trips** to Japan generally through either Ffestiniog (see p37), or Railway Touring Co (💻 www.railwaytouring.net).

## ARRIVAL OF THE BULLET TRAIN

### Electrification

A nationwide network of trunk lines was well on its way to completion by 1910 but major electrification of the railway had to wait until after WWII, during which many lines sustained severe damage from bombing raids. In the early 1950s the journey between Tokyo and Osaka took most of a day and there was an observation car at the back with armchairs for passengers to enjoy the view. The Tokaido line, running through what had become Japan's major industrial corridor, was electrified in 1956. It was also in the mid 1950s that the idea began to surface for a new, high-speed link between Tokyo and Osaka. The proposal was not just for an upgrade of the existing line but for a completely new railway that would allow a top speed of 250kph. Crucially, businessmen in Tokyo and Osaka would be able to commute between the cities and return home the same day.

### Picking up speed

There is no more instantly recognisable symbol of modern Japan than the *shinkansen* (literally 'new main line'), known throughout the world as the bullet train. A particular design feature of this new line is the gauge of 1.435m rather than the standard 1.067m; it was decided to have a wider gauge as it would mean greater stability for the trains.

When the government finally gave its approval for the project in 1958, Japan National Railways (JNR) had six years to prepare the line in time for the opening ceremony of the 1964 Tokyo Olympics. The deadline was made and the ribbon cut at precisely 6am on October 1st 1964, but the construction bill had spiralled from an original estimate of ¥200 billion to ¥380 billion. Initial design faults also meant passengers experienced ear pain whenever the train darted into a tunnel and, more alarmingly, gusts of wind blowing up through the toilets.

The foreign press corps was taken for a test run, however, and appeared suitably thrilled. A *Times* journalist gushed on cue to his readers, remarking that the shinkansen fully lived up to the boast of a 'new dimension in train travel': 'In the airliner-style seats one groped subconsciously, but in vain, for the safety belt as the train hummed out of Tokyo, rather like a jet taking off in a narrow street. Bridges, tunnels, even passing trains flash by, thanks to the air-tight doors, as in a silent film. It is uncannily smooth ... So much tends to the vulgar in modern Japan that it is pleasant to report the superb fittings and finishing in this train ... Ablution facilities dazzle, with winged mirrors, and three lavatories per car set, one of them Western-style' (*The Times*, 28th September 1964).

Two services began operation in 1964: the *Hikari* ('Light'), which initially took four hours and stopped only in Nagoya and Kyoto, and the stopping *Kodama* ('Echo'), which took five hours. The new line was an instant success and tickets sold out weeks in advance. The construction deficit was overturned and by 1972 the line had been extended west to Okayama.

## Out of control

As the shinkansen spread further and sped faster, JNR's debt grew larger. Though the Tokaido shinkansen was a financial success, the rest of the network was in meltdown. The railway's total deficit year on year throughout the 1970s and '80s spiralled into thousands of billions of yen. Fares became daylight robbery, particularly in comparison with those offered by private railways, the network was grossly over staffed, labour relations were poor and morale low. Some pointed the finger at greedy politicians. Such was the glamour of the shinkansen, reported *The Times* in January 1987 (23 years after it had enjoyed that free test ride), that 'every politician of note feels he needs a shinkansen station in his district ... Over the years, promises of shinkansen services have brought in innumerable votes for the ruling Liberal Democratic Party. And with every new shinkansen put on to a marginal or loss-making line, JNR's deficit has increased.'

At midnight on April 1st 1987, the whistle was finally and literally blown on all this by the president of JNR, who rode a steam locomotive back and forth near Shimbashi in Tokyo on a symbolic last journey for the nationalised industry. JNR, undeniably the ultimate political pork barrel in Japan, had not made money for 20 years. Its liabilities on that April Fool's Day stood at ¥37 trillion (£160 billion), more than the combined debts of Brazil and Mexico, and £12 billion more than the US budget deficit of the previous year.

**Privatisation** of the railway was achieved by carving up the network into six regional passenger railway companies and one nationwide freight company, to be known collectively as the JR Group. In a bid to reduce some of the debt, unprofitable lines were closed, railway land was sold and staffing levels reduced. No longer constricted by the rules governing a nationalised company, the JR companies have since diversified into everything from department stores to hotels, hospitals, helicopters and also a bakery chain and ski resort.

## Future expansion

In the 21st century, expansion of the shinkansen continues apace: the Seikan Tunnel linking Honshu and Hokkaido has been adapted to accept shinkansen and services from Shin-Aomori to Shin-Hakodate-Hokuto in Hokkaido started in March 2016. Approval has been granted to extend this line as far as Sapporo; work should be completed by 2035. The Hokuriku shinkansen extension from Nagano to Kanazawa opened in spring 2015; work started in 2012 on extending this line to Fukui and Tsuruga; services should start by March 2026 but the line may then be extended to link with the Tokaido shinkansen (Tokyo to Shin-Osaka). In Kyushu, work has started on a West Kyushu shinkansen line from Shin-Tosu to Nagasaki via Takeo-onsen, but this is unlikely to be operational before 2023.

But new technology is not the preserve of the shinkansen. Fuel-cell trains powered by hydrogen are being tested in the hope that they can one day replace diesel services on lines not yet electrified. And one JR company, JR Central (JR Tokai), is already looking beyond the shinkansen towards the next generation of high-speed travel. It's hoped that the driverless **Maglev**, or 'superconducting magnetically levitated linear motor car', will one day travel at over 500kph – in January 2016 on a test run it created a new record going at just over 600kph – along an as yet only partially constructed line, bringing Shinagawa (Tokyo) and Nagoya to within 40 minutes of each other. Arguments persist over funding for the project (the total construction cost is estimated at ¥5.5 trillion) but construction has already begun deep underground at Shinagawa station; in fact most of the line will be underground. The Chuo shinkansen, as it is called, is not expected to open fully until 2027 (with an extension from Nagoya to Osaka to

---

## ❏ STEAM LOCOMOTIVE (SL) OPERATIONS

The following is a list of major preserved steam operations in Japan. JR rail passes are valid for most of the services below but seats have to be reserved; book early as the services are very popular. For up-to-date information visit 🖥 steam.fan.coocan.jp.

### Hokkaido
● **SL Fuyu no Shitsugen (C11 171/C11 207)**  Kushiro to Shibecha or Kawayu-onsen (one round trip a day late Jan-Feb). A good chance for a ride through the snow!

### Honshu
● **Oigawa Railway (C12-164/C10-8/C11-190/C11-227/C56-44)**  Shin-Kanaya to Senzu. Operated by the private Oigawa Railway (see pp174-5), this is one of the busiest preserved steam operations in the country with year-round services.
● **SL Banetsu-Monogatari (C61-20/C57-180)**  Niigata to Aizu-Wakamatsu on the Banetsu-Sai line (approx 4hrs). See pp328-9.
● **SL Ginga (C58-239)**  Hanamaki to Kamaishi on the Kamaishi Line. Operates seasonally at weekends (4½hrs); the journey's length means the service operates to Kamaishi on Saturdays and returns on Sundays; see pp335-6).
● **Mooka Railway\* (C11-325/C12-66)**  Shimodate (JR Mito Line) to Motegi (weekends and hols year-round; 1½hrs). The chance to experience a nostalgic branch line journey and see the steam-engine-shaped building at Mooka.
● **Chichibu Railway Paleo Express\* (C58-363)**  Kumagaya to Mitsumine-guchi (weekends and hols May-Oct; 2½hrs).
● **SL Minakami (D51-498 or newly restored C61-20)**  Takasaki (see p177) to Minakami (p178; Joetsu Line; 2hrs; runs quite frequently at weekends and holidays Mar-June).
● **SL Usui (D51-498/C61-20)**  Takasaki (see p177) to Yokokawa (60 mins; runs quite frequently at weekends and holidays Mar-Apr). A good way to reach Yokokawa's railway museum (see p178).
● **SL Kita-Biwako (C56-160)**  Maibara to Kinomoto on the Hokuriku line (typically operates once a day on just a few days including 29th April to 5th May). See p234.
● **SL Yamaguchi (C57-1, nicknamed Lady of Rank)**  Shin-Yamaguchi to Tsuwano on the Yamaguchi line. See p281.

### Kyushu
● **SL Hitoyoshi (8620-58654)**  Kumamoto to Hitoyoshi (Mar-Nov weekends and some additional days). Originally called the SL Aso Boy; see p454.

**\* Note**: reservations for the Chichibu (¥710) and Mooka (¥510) railways can be made at JR East offices as well as at the companies themselves. Chichibu also has a ¥510 non-reserved supplement for the Paleo Express, but it **does not** guarantee you a seat!

be completed by 2045), but it's already predicted to become the most expensive transport project in the world.

As room to expand at home reaches saturation point, the JR companies are looking to sell their technology and expertise abroad. A consortium including JR East signed a contract with India in December 2015 to build a 520km shinkansen line between Mumbai and Ahmedabad. Both JR Central and JR East are bidding to build, and/or provide trains for, high-speed lines in the US and other countries.

## STEAM RAILWAYS

In 1936 around 8700 steam locomotives were in operation across Japan. Complaints about the emission of black smoke, along with technological advances, brought about the demise of the commercial steam railway, as more efficient diesel and electric trains were brought into service after WWII. By 1976 steam had all but disappeared.

For years, many steam locomotives (known in Japan as SLs) were left to rust away in museums, or were shunted into corners of public parks and quietly forgotten. Perhaps because the Japanese now have the psychological room to look back on the nation's history of modernisation, restored SLs have made a comeback. In the late 1980s and '90s, with the vocal and financial support of nostalgic rail fans and local authorities, steam trains began to reappear as tourist attractions on rural lines. No longer the exclusive preserve of *tetsudo mania/otaku* (rail enthusiasts), of which there are thousands in Japan, preserved steam operations now cater to the tourist trade.

# The railway

## JAPAN RAIL TODAY

The railway in Japan is one of the most efficient in the world and it reaches nearly all parts of the four main islands. The bulk of the railway network is operated by six regional companies known collectively as the JR Group (hereafter known

---

❏ **Rail museums**
Rail museums of varying size and interest are spread throughout Japan; space does not permit a nationwide listing but some worth visiting are:
● **Honshu**: Railway Museum, Omiya (see p231-2); Tobu Museum, Tokyo (see p124); Linear Tetsudo Kan (Linear Railway Hall; also known as SCMAGLEV and Railway Park), Nagoya (see p202); Kyoto Railway Museum, Kyoto (see p256); Usui Pass Railway Heritage Park, Yokokawa (see p178).
● **Hokkaido**: Otaru Transportation Museum, Otaru (see p374).
● **Kyushu**: Kyushu Railway History Museum, Moji (see p416).

as JR). For the holder of a Japan Rail Pass, the six companies can be considered one national company because the pass is valid on virtually all trains across the JR network. Additional lines are operated by private and third-sector railways; third-sector lines are generally owned by local or central government, they may also be former JR lines, but are operated by private companies.

Every day, about 26,000 JR trains travel on a network which covers about 20,000 kilometres. These range from some of the fastest trains in the world to one-carriage diesel trains on remote rural lines. JR well deserves its reputation for **punctuality**; it is extremely rare for any service to run late. In the UK a train is judged to be on time if it leaves or arrives within five or ten minutes of the scheduled time – and most passengers are just grateful it is leaving (and arriving) at all. In Japan trains are officially late if they are more than one minute off the published schedule. On some lines they are meant to stay within 15 seconds and drivers assiduously check the time and any deviation from the schedule as they pass each station. Most services have a window built in to their schedule so that any lost time can be made up along the way. If there is a delay, likely never to be more than a few minutes, staff will make frequent apologies. The only time when there is a risk of major disruption is after a serious earthquake or in the event of extreme weather conditions. Warm water is sprayed on to the tracks on the Tohoku shinkansen east of Tokyo to ensure that snow does not

❏ **Japan by rail on the web**
Useful websites include:
● **HyperDia:** 🖳 **www.hyperdia.com** An indispensable website. Input your origin and destination points for anywhere on Japan's rail network and this site will come up with possible itineraries, including transfers, journey time, fare, and seat reservation charge where relevant. You can also specify if you want to travel via a particular station. Unless deselected the search results will also show flights and private rail services, where they are a relevant option. In addition you can see the station timetable (ie all the services leaving from that station), the train timetable (ie all the stops on the journey) and the interval timetable (ie how often that service operates). There is also an app for both iTunes and Android.
● **Jorudan:** 🖳 **www.jorudan.co.jp** A similar but more limited service.
● **JP Rail:** 🖳 **jprail.com** An unofficial but extremely useful website about how to make the best use of the Japan Rail Pass, but also about rail travel in Japan in general including details of the seasonal services.
● **The man in Seat 61:** 🖳 **www.seat61.com/Japan** General information about all aspects of train travel in Japan, including the Japan Rail Pass (which can also be bought through the website).
● **JNTO:** 🖳 **www.jnto.go.jp/eng/arrange/transportation** JNTO's page devoted to transportation in Japan.

All the companies in the JR Group have websites in English: **JR Central** 🖳 jr-central.co.jp; **JR East** 🖳 www.jreast.co.jp; **JR West** 🖳 www.westjr.co.jp; **JR Hokkaido** 🖳 www.jrhokkaido.co.jp; **JR Kyushu** 🖳 www.jrkyushu.co.jp; **JR Shikoku** 🖳 www.jr-shikoku.co.jp. These have details of the rail passes, tickets and package tours available to foreign tourists for their area; some also have timetables and/or up-to-date service information.

affect service, but in north-eastern Honshu and Hokkaido severe snow in winter occasionally does cause problems to these and other services.

Rail companies around the world must envy JR's track record for **safety**: not a single fatality on the shinkansen due to derailment or an accident since services began in 1964. In all these years shinkansen have only ever derailed twice. Special shinkansen, nicknamed the 'Dr Yellow' for Tokaido/Sanyo shinkansen lines and the EASTi for JR East's shinkansen services, inspect the track and overhead wiring; if any problems are found a small army of engineers is sent out to do the necessary repairs. They have only six hours each night to carry out all essential track maintenance.

Not only is JR the most efficient rail network in the world, the trains are also some of the **best maintained**. It's worth turning up early for your shinkansen (at the beginning of a route) to see the swarm of uniformed **cleaning staff** who, within about seven minutes, ensure the carriages are swept, the toilets cleaned, and all the seats turned round to face the direction of travel. At stations, platforms are always spotless, floors are constantly swept, wiped and disinfected, dustbins emptied before they are ever full and escalator rails wiped (staff seem to be employed exclusively for this task).

## THE TRAINS

### Shinkansen

JR's flagship trains are, of course, the shinkansen, better known as the bullet train because the front of the very first shinkansen train looked like a bullet, but also of course because it travelled very fast – up to 210kph. The fastest now are the Hayabusa (E5), used between Tokyo and Shin-Aomori, as they are able to go up to 320kph (200mph). Nozomi (N700A), which run between Tokyo and Hakata, can go up to 300kph, though on the Tokaido part of the line the maximum is 270kph. The Hokuriku (Kagayaki E7/W7; Tokyo to Kanazawa) and Mizuho (800 series; Hakata to Kagoshima-chuo), can both go up to 260kph. The E6 series (Komachi) used on the Akita and Yamagata 'mini' shinkansen can go up to 130kph.

The first shinkansen may have resembled a bullet but since then they have become much more stylish, particularly the Hayabusa and Komachi with their approximately 15m-long nose. The Komachi was designed by Ken (Kiyoyuki) Okuyama, who designs Ferraris.

The shinkansen offers what is almost certainly the smoothest train ride in the world as the train appears to glide effortlessly along the line; this is largely because, apart from the Akita and Yamagata shinkansen, the trains run on special tracks and the lines were built with as few bends as possible.

The Ordinary Class **seating** configuration is 3 x 2 or 2 x 2 and, as with most trains in Japan, seats can be turned round so that a group travelling together can face each other. Green Class seating is either 2 x 2 or 2 x 1.

**Facilities** on board include: public telephones (though expect to pay a premium rate); Japanese- and Western-style toilets; and a nappy-changing room which can be used as a sick bay by anyone who is not feeling well – the key is

> ❑ **Luggage space**
> On all shinkansen and most limited expresses there is an area at the back of each car for luggage, as well as airline-style overhead storage bins or racks. Since the seat spacing is usually very good, if your luggage is not too large you can probably keep it with you. If it is too big for that, or too heavy to lift up, ask to have a seat at the back of the car so you can sit as close as possible to your luggage.
>   Local trains do not have dedicated storage areas but as long as you're not travelling during the rush hour there will be space for your luggage.

available from the train conductor. Trolley services selling ekiben (see box p102), snacks and hot/cold drinks are found on a few services; some trains also have vending machines. However, whichever train you take, it's far better to stock up with food and drink at an ekiben stand, convenience store, or station kiosk, before you travel. There are no dining cars on bullet trains. A more recent design feature is a booth to go to if you want to make a phone call from your mobile/cell phone and also booths for smokers.

The Japan Rail Pass is valid for travel on most shinkansen.

## Limited expresses

Next step down are limited expresses (LEX; called *tokkyu*), which run on the same tracks as the ordinary trains but stop only at major stations.

Most limited expresses are modern and offer almost as smooth a ride as the shinkansen but a few (mainly diesel-powered ones) are not quite as glamorous or hi-tech. The JR companies constantly try to outdo each other by rolling out ever more space-age-style interiors whenever they upgrade their limited express services. Some are called Wide View, which not surprisingly means they have extra large windows.

The seating configuration varies but is usually 2 x 2 (2 x 1 in Green Class) and, as with the shinkansen, all seats can be turned to face the direction of travel, or if in a group so that the seats face each other. Many trains have on-board vending machines and occasionally refreshment trolleys; a complimentary drink may be served in Green Class but in general it is worth buying food and drink in advance. There are usually both Japanese- and Western-style toilets.

## Express, rapid and local trains

Despite their names, **express** (*kyuko*) and **rapid** trains (*kaisoku*) are slower than limited expresses because they stop at more stations. Seating is usually 2 x 2 but seats can't be turned round. Most of these trains have at least one toilet, though this is likely to be Japanese style, but no other facilities.

Slowest of all are **local trains** (*futsu*) as they stop at every station. On these seating is generally long rows of bench-style seats on either side of the train – this leaves plenty of standing room in the middle – but sometimes there are 2 x 2 seats. Trains with just one or two carriages are called 'one-man densha' (one-man trains) because the driver also acts as ticket seller and collector. However, even these have a toilet, though it will almost definitely be Japanese style.

One of the pleasures of a ride on a local train is the chance to stand right at the front next to the driver's compartment; here you'll see close-up how and why the Japanese rail network is so efficient. Wearing a suit, cap and regulation white gloves, the driver of the smallest local train seems just as meticulous as the driver of a 16-carriage shinkansen. Before the train pulls away from each stop the driver points at the clock as if to confirm the train is indeed leaving on time, then points ahead to check the signals have given him (or her) the all clear to go.

## Sleeper trains

The opening of the Hokkaido shinkansen and therefore the end of conventional line services through the Seikan Tunnel means there are now very few sleeper services (see box below) – other than the luxury ones first introduced by JR Kyushu but now being planned by JR East and JR West.

---

### ❏ SLEEPER SERVICES

#### Conventional services
● **Ueno (Tokyo) to/from Aomori (Tohoku, Honshu)**  The **Akebono** (holiday periods; 13 hours) has couchettes, private rooms, and *goron to shito** (see p98), one of which is for women only.
● **Tokyo to/from Takamatsu (Shikoku)**  The **Sunrise-Seto** (1/day; 10 hours) has private rooms and *nobinobi** (see p98).
● **Tokyo to/from Izumoshi (Western Honshu)**  The **Sunrise-Izumo** (1/day; 12 hours) has private rooms and nobinobi* (see p98).

The **Moonlight Nagara*** (Tokyo to/from Ogaki, near Nagoya, Honshu) and **Moonlight Echigo*** (Shinjuku, Tokyo, to/from Niigata, Honshu) services are seasonal and they can be used with the JR Seishun Juhachi Kippu ticket (see box p31).

* Available to rail-pass holders without supplement. However, reservations are essential; see also pp100-1.

#### Luxury 'cruise' trains
In October 2013 JR Kyushu introduced the **Seven Stars** (⌨ www.cruisetrain-seven stars.jp), the first truly luxurious sleeper train in Japan, one aim being to rival trains such as the Venice-Simplon Orient Express and the Blue Train.

The train consists of seven cars: a lounge car, a dining car and 14 guest rooms (2-3 suites per car), each of which is designed differently but all of which are en suite. There are two itineraries: 1 night/2 days (¥150,000-400,000pp) or 3 nights/4 days (¥380,000-950,000pp), depending on triple, twin or single occupancy and level of accommodation.

The service has always been fully booked and it is so popular that tickets are granted through a lottery; applications for October 2016 and beyond opened in April 2016. The Society of International Railway Travelers (IRT; see p38) is the first American company to be able to charter the train.

Hot on JR Kyushu's heels are JR East with their **Train Suite Shiki-shima** luxury sleeper train (⌨ www.jreast.co.jp/shiki-shima) and JR West with their **Twilight Express Mizukaze** (⌨ twilightexpress-mizukaze.jp). Neither service will start till April 2017 but it seems very likely they will be as successful as the Seven Stars.

---

❏ **Sightseeing trains**

It's a sad fact that in Japan, as in other countries, for years many local railway lines have been struggling to survive. To try and find a solution, back in the 1960s, JR East hit on an idea both to boost tourism in rural areas and maintain a transportation service for local communities – they introduced a sightseeing train called a '**Joyful Train**'. This was an old train remodelled inside to have tatami flooring and therefore seem like a Japanese room. Initially this train was mostly for charter services but now all the JR companies have Joyful trains and they compete with each other to have novel and exotic features to entice passengers. JR Kyushu call their sightseeing trains **D&S trains** – Design & Story; this is a good way of summarising the concept as there is always a story behind the design.

Some of the services, such as the Resort Shirakami (see p346) and Ibutama (see pp461-2), operate on lines that are scenic (particularly in good weather!); on others the scenery is not necessarily the highlight but the journey is still likely to be a really enjoyable experience. A benefit for anyone with a Japan Rail Pass is that seat reservations are generally free for JR services. Additional sightseeing trains, particularly those hauled by a steam locomotive, are operated by private companies.

---

In the remaining ordinary sleeper trains the main options are private rooms, couchettes, *goron to shito* (couchettes without bedding but which are categorised as seats), *nobinobi* (carpet cars where you lie on the floor), and reserved seats. For a couchette/private room rail-pass holders have to pay both the limited express charge (around ¥300) and from ¥6500/9500pp for a bed.

## TIMETABLES

This guide contains service frequencies for the main stops on the routes described (see pp504-13). The best option for getting up-to-date timetable information is **online** through 🖳 www.hyperdia.com (see box p94). Note that some station names on Hyperdia are shown without hyphens, even when hyphenated in general use and in this guide. Also, for some private line stations you need to include the name of the private line in the station name.

Twice a year (Mar & Oct) JR publishes a condensed **timetable in English** (*Railway Timetable*) which covers the major shinkansen and limited express services. If you are intending to stick to main rail routes, this is all the information you will need. However, the Railway Timetable is not easy to find. The best place and time to ask for one is where you exchange your rail-pass voucher but if you forget try at any major JR station or the JNTO TIC in Tokyo. Bear in mind, however, that timetables can change monthly so you should not rely on the times; double-check before you travel.

Alternatively, if you can read Japanese, or even if you can't but are up for the challenge of comparing the kanji for stations mentioned in the text with those in the timetable, get a copy of the **Japanese timetable** 時刻表 (*Jikokuhyo*; ¥1183). The huge volume, which lists everything that moves in Japan (trains, buses, ropeways, cable cars, ferry services, chair-lifts) is published monthly. You'll find a well-thumbed copy in every JR ticket office. There is also a version (¥987) that is printed with a larger font making it much easier to use. The easiest to actually carry around is the pocket-sized version (Pocket Jikokuhyo; ¥566), also published monthly; both of these contain details of all the rail services and therefore much more information than the timetable in English, but not as much as the main timetable. All versions of the Japanese timetable are available from any bookstore in Japan.

For a guide to using the Japanese timetable see p504.

## BUYING A TICKET

This is the most expensive way of travelling by shinkansen and is not really recommended if you are planning to take several shinkansen services and are eligible for a rail pass. If your trip is unlikely to include many shinkansen journeys, particularly long ones, having a pass may not be cost effective and therefore you will have to buy tickets.

Fortunately the fare structure in Japan is straightforward. First there is a basic fare which corresponds to the kilometre distance you travel; this is valid only on local and rapid trains. Supplements (see note in box below) have to be paid if using any other train and there are additional charges for seat reservations. The fare for a return trip by rail is discounted by 20% if the one-way distance exceeds 600km.

Tickets can be purchased from ticket machines, or at JR ticket offices. If buying from a machine and unsure of the fare, select the cheapest ticket and then pay the difference to the train conductor, or at a 'fare-adjustment machine' at your arrival station. An easier option, though, is to have an IC (smart) card (see box p66) as that will automatically calculate the fare, but note that this can only be used for the fare, not seat reservations and also not for shinkansen. If you prefer to buy paper tickets a useful feature is that most ticket machines have an option to purchase several for the same journey in one go: simply push the buttons which indicate the number of adults and children in the group.

Ticket counters at major stations accept debit and credit cards issued overseas but at most other places you'll need to pay in cash. Tables of the basic per kilometre fares and limited express/shinkansen supplements are printed in the condensed English language timetable; a few sample fares are provided in the box.

❏ **Sample single fares from Tokyo**

| To | Distance | Fare | Supplement* | Total |
|----|----------|------|-------------|-------|
| Hakata | 1175km | ¥13,820 | ¥8510 | ¥22,330 |
| Hiroshima | 894km | ¥11,660 | ¥6900 | ¥18,560 |
| Kyoto | 514km | ¥8210 | ¥5390 | ¥13,600 |
| Kanazawa | 450km | ¥7340 | ¥6780 | ¥14,120 |
| Nagasaki | 1329km | ¥15,230 | ¥11,020 | ¥26,250 |
| Sapporo | 1163km | ¥14,140 | ¥14,240 | ¥28,380 |
| Shin-Aomori | 714km | ¥10,150 | ¥7400 | ¥17,550 |
| Takayama | 533km | ¥8750 | ¥6260 | ¥15,010 |

* Includes the standard shinkansen (not Nozomi/Mizuho) and limited express surcharges (both increase by ¥200-300 in peak periods and drop by ¥200-300 in the low season) and the seat reservation charge (¥510).

**THE RAIL NETWORK**

## MAKING SEAT RESERVATIONS

Seat reservations are free if you have a JR pass (though for some regional passes you can only make a limited number of reservations) so it's always worth making one, particularly if travelling at peak times. Thanks to JR's computerised system, you can book seats up to the very last minute. Only at peak travel times (see pp14-16) are seats booked weeks in advance. Seat reservations can be made from one month before the date of travel for shinkansen, limited express and express services (rapid & local trains are all non-reserved).

Pass holders are not penalised for not using a seat reservation – if you change your plans hand in your seat-reservation ticket so it can be cancelled. If you sit in a reserved carriage without a seat reservation the conductor will charge you the appropriate supplement, even if you have a rail pass.

**Midori-no-madoguchi**
(Green window reservations office)

At any JR station, find the **reservations office** ('**Midori-no-madoguchi**' or in the JR Tokai/Central area look for 'Shinkansen and JR line tickets'). If there are long queues, try a **Travel Service Center** (TSC); these are JR-run travel agencies which also handle seat reservations; they are found in larger stations. The regional JR companies call their TSCs by different names but they all offer the same service. The names to look out for are JR Tokai Tours (in the JR Central area), View Plaza (JR East), Travel Information Satellite (TiS; JR West), Warp (JR Shikoku), Joyroad (JR Kyushu) and Twinkle Plaza (JR Hokkaido).

You can make a seat reservation at any JR station so at busy periods it may be worth going to a smaller station and/or out of peak hours. If you are planning to book a lot of journeys, it helps staff if you can show them a typed itinerary detailing dates, times and departure & arrival stations: JR Hokkaido (see box p370) and JR Shikoku (see box p466) have **codes** for each station (and by 2020 JR East will) so these can be used instead of the name. Say if you have any special requests regarding window or aisle seats and which side of the train you want to sit; for the classic view of Mt Fuji from the shinkansen, ask for a seat on the right side coming from Tokyo, and on the left side from Kyoto.

---

❏ **Standing in line**
The British may be known for queuing but the Japanese have turned standing in line into an art form. At mainline stations, including all shinkansen stops, locator maps of trains are found on each platform. These show the layout and configuration of your train and indicate precisely where you should wait on the platform. Look along the edge of the platform for numbered signs which indicate the stopping point for each carriage. You can be sure that the train will stop where it should and the doors of each carriage will open opposite the appropriate platform markers. At busy stations the number of signs telling you where to stand can be bewildering. If you've got a seat reservation ticket show it to someone; they are sure to help you. But don't get unduly stressed about standing in the right line: the carriages are interconnected so you can easily find the way to the right compartment once you're on board.

If the Midori-no-madoguchi queue is very long and you have a JR pass and want to make a shinkansen seat reservation for that day, go through the ticket gate and find the ticket window in the shinkansen area – it is usually near the ticket gates – as the queues are generally shorter.

JR East is the only JR company that offers **online reservations** (🖥 www .jreast.co.jp/e/ticket/reservation.html), whether you have a Japan Rail Pass, a JR East Pass or just want to buy a ticket. However, you have to pick up your ticket by 9pm the day before travel at a preselected station/ticket office.

Staff usually print seat-reservation tickets for foreigners in English (as well as Japanese). For details of how to read your seat-reservation ticket if it is just in Japanese, see the sample on p503.

It is essential to have a seat reservation for the Narita Express (N'EX), the Hayabusa, Hayate and Komachi trains (all in the Tohoku region).

## RAILWAY STAFF

JR staff are always impeccably dressed in company uniforms which differ slightly in design from one region to another. Suits are the norm but short-sleeved shirts are worn in summer. Don't expect all JR staff to speak English, though basic questions concerning platform and destination are usually no problem. At the ticket offices in major stations (such as Tokyo, Osaka and Kyoto), you'll find someone who speaks English. Some train conductors on shinkansen also speak some English. All carry pocket timetables – and JR East staff are being equipped with iPad minis – so they can advise on connection times and even tell you from which platform your next train will be departing.

## STATION FACILITIES

Virtually every station has **lockers** (generally called **coin lockers**) in a selection of sizes: small lockers are big enough for day packs only; all but the biggest suitcases or rucksacks should fit into a large locker. The majority of lockers take coins (¥100 or ¥50); but many now accept IC cards (see box p66). The fee is charged on a midnight to midnight basis, so if you store your luggage at 6pm and leave it until the following morning, you have to

❏ **Coin locker dimensions**
Lockers are generally 340mm (13½ins) **wide** and 570mm (22½ ins) **deep**.

| | Height (mm/inches) | Cost (from) |
|---|---|---|
| Small | 200-400/8-15¾ | ¥300 |
| Medium | 550/22 | ¥400 |
| Large | 840/33¼ | ¥500 |
| Extra large | 1030/40½ | ¥600 |

pay the same fee again to retrieve it. If you have a hotel booking it would be cheaper, and probably easier, to leave your luggage there. Every major station has a **Lost and found office**; items handed in are kept for a week; after which they will be sent to a regional Lost and found centre. If you have lost something on a train ensure you know the train's name and number and ideally remember which carriage you were in.

It is easy to find **food** in a station: even the smallest have a kiosk or convenience store, and vending machines; most also have a bakery, coffee shop

❏ **Station melodies**
Several stations around the world play a melody when trains arrive and depart but possibly Japan is the place where this is most popular, particularly for stations on JR East and private railway lines as well as some subways. In 1971 Keihan Railway, in the Kansai area, was the first rail operator in Japan to introduce melodies at their stations but since JR was privatised, and station managers have had more freedom to do what they want, it has become a common feature – especially as passengers complained about the buzzers and bells that were being used.

In many cases the tunes have some association with the area. For example, you will hear *The Third Man* at Ebisu (Tokyo) because the tune was used for an Ebisu beer advert. Kochi station in Shikoku has the Anpanman theme because Takashi Yanase its creator was born there. Railway companies also often have individual melodies for up and down trains; Keihan has taken this to a new level (see box p250).

Listen out as you arrive at and depart from a station!

and/or noodle stall where you can get a filling bowl of udon or soba (¥400-600). Major stations also have restaurant areas with both Western and Japanese food.

The most popular railway food is the ekiben (see box below).

## Facilities for the disabled

In the majority of stations there are lifts/elevators, or stair-lifts, from platform to concourse level as well as accessible toilets. However, if travelling on rural lines it is worth checking in advance what facilities there are. Enquire at the ticket office at least 30 minutes before the departure of your train and staff will bring a ramp and assist with boarding. They will also ring ahead to your destination station and arrange for staff there to help you leave the train. On all shinkansen and some limited express services there is at least one car with space for a wheelchair (reservations are recommended) as well as an accessible toilet. However, on some trains, the aisles are too narrow for wheelchair use and thus it may be necessary to be lifted into a seat; the wheelchair will be left in the luggage area.

Unless facilities are specifically referred to in the route and city guides, seek assistance from station staff.

For further information visit 🖳 www.accessible-japan.com.

❏ **Ekiben (station lunch box)**
'Bento' is a generic term for a packed lunch, but the ekiben is a cut above the rest. There's an ekiben stall (often several) in every station. Ekiben are also sometimes sold on shinkansen and limited express trains, but you will have much more choice if you buy one at the station before you leave. Most cost ¥800-2000.

The boxes feature local ingredients, so the contents vary around the country, and they are all freshly made – some even state by what time of the day they should be eaten. Most ekiben are rice based but it is also possible to get sandwiches and noodles at ekiben stands. A recent development is that some come with a string which, when pulled, heats the food up. Crucial to the success of an ekiben is the shape of the box and whether the contents are pleasing to the eye as the lid is removed.

# TOKYO AND OSAKA

## Tokyo 東京

It will come as no surprise to first-time visitors that Tokyo is one of the most populous cities in the world; over 13 million people are packed within its perimeters. There's no denying this makes Tokyo seriously overcrowded. Rumours that staff are employed at some stations to push passengers on to trains are true, at least during peak times. But if you avoid the morning and evening rush hours, it's possible to travel around Tokyo in comfort. And whatever the time of day, there is a frequent and reliable service on both the JR trains and the subways.

More surprising than the mass of people is the fact that Tokyo became Japan's official capital only in 1868, when Emperor Meiji was restored to the throne (see pp56-7). For centuries before, it was an undiscovered back-water and might have remained so but, in 1603, Ieyasu Tokugawa chose Edo (which was renamed Tokyo in 1868) as the seat of government for the Tokugawa shogunate. Right up until the collapse of the shogunate in 1867, Japan's official capital remained Kyoto but the Emperor who resided there exercised no real power.

In the years since Edo was renamed Tokyo and snatched the capital prize from Kyoto, the small town has become a thriving city of commerce, industry, entertainment and luxury – and in 2020 will host the summer Olympics for the second time; the first time was in 1964. Little of the old Tokyo remains but one area worth seeking out for its atmosphere is Asakusa, home to one of Japan's most vibrant temples and packed with narrow streets which are a world and at least a century away from Tokyo Skytree, the skyscrapers of Shinjuku, and the city-within-a-city in Roppongi.

Some arrive in Tokyo and never leave, captivated by the neon, designer stores and relentless energy of the place. Others arrive and never leave their hotel rooms, terrified of the noise and sheer number of people who fill the streets day and night. The answer is somewhere between these two extremes. Stay just long enough to get a feel for the city but get out in time to make full use of the rail pass and discover how much lies beyond this metropolis.

さまざまの事おもひ出す櫻かな

*Ah! what memories!*
*Myriad thoughts evoked*
*by those cherry trees!*
(MATSUO BASHO)

## WHAT TO SEE AND DO

The number of things to see, do and experience in and around Tokyo would easily fill the whole of this book. Thus this guide focuses mostly on places that are near stops on the Yamanote or other JR lines. See also pp133-44 for details of side trips around Tokyo.

If you plan to visit even just a few museums consider getting the **Tokyo Museum Grutto Pass** 東京・ミュージアムぐるっとパス (🖳 www.rekibun .or.jp/grutto; ¥2000; available Apr-Jan and valid for two months from the date of issue), a booklet with coupons giving free or discounted entry to over 70 museums and galleries. It can be bought at any of the sights as well as at the Tokyo Tourist Information Center (TIC; see p128), Asakusa Culture TIC (see p118) and at branches of Lawson and other convenience stores. Note that it is not available during February and March. See also box p109.

The extremely useful *Tokyo Handy Map* and *Tokyo Handy Guide* (🖳 www .gotokyo.org/book) are available in both a printed (free from TICs) and a digital format as well as a free app for both iPhone (🖳 itunes.apple.com) and Android (🖳 play.google.com) products. The *Handy Guide* has information about the many attractions as well as detailed maps of each area.

### On the Yamanote Line

JR's Yamanote Line 山手線 (Yamanote-sen) runs in a loop around Tokyo; a full circuit takes about an hour. The text below suggests stopping-off points both on and off the line. The route follows an anti-clockwise direction, beginning and ending at Tokyo station. Yamanote Line trains have on-board colour screens above the doors telling you (in Japanese and English) what the next stop is, how long it will take to get there and even which side of the train the exit is going to be, so it's easy to navigate your way around.

**Tokyo station** 東京駅 (Tokyo eki)  This is the terminus for most shinkansen services to the city as well as being a stop on several JR main lines.

The station is divided into **Marunouchi** 丸の内 and **Yaesu** 八重洲 sides; see pp124-5. The Marunouchi side of Tokyo station is the old half and has a traditional red-brick frontage. The landmark Tokyo Station Hotel (see p130) was part of a multi-billion-yen project to restore this side of the station to its early 20th-century heyday but with the benefit of 21st-century technology so that it should now withstand an earthquake, though as a sign outside says, it 'may sway slowly'. The entrance in the middle of this side of the station is for the Emperor so the gateway is likely to be closed.

Kokyo Gaien, the outer area of the **Imperial Palace** 皇居 (Kokyo) is a 10- to 15-minute walk west from the Marunouchi Exit. Home to the Emperor and his family, this is a quiet oasis but is off-limits to the public except if on a guided tour, or on two days of the year (23rd Dec and 2nd Jan), when the Emperor, his wife, and other family members wave from a balcony to thousands of enthusiastic flag-waving patriots and tourists. It is essential to book in advance if you want to join a guided tour of the grounds (🖳 sankan.kunaicho.go.jp; generally Mon-Fri 2/day; 75 mins; English audio guide; free).

The palace is surrounded by a stone-wall moat: **Niju-bashi** 二重橋 is the nickname for two bridges that cross the moat and form the official entrance to the Imperial Palace itself. The stone bridge (Seimon-ishi-bashi) at the front is what can clearly be seen but if you look carefully there is a separate iron bridge (Seimon-tetsu-bashi) behind. However, this entrance is only used on special occasions. The **Imperial Palace East Gardens** 皇居東御苑 (Kokyo Higashi-gyoen; Tue-Thur & Sat-Sun Apr-Aug 9am-5pm, Sep, Oct & Mar to 4.30pm, Nov-Feb to 4pm; free), a park area which includes Ninomaru Teien 二の丸庭園, a Japanese-style garden, are open to the public.

From the East Gardens you can walk to **Kita-no-maru Park** 北の丸公園, home to the **National Museum of Modern Art Tokyo** 東京国立近代美術館 (Tokyo Kokuritsu Kindai Bijutsukan, MOMAT; 🖳 www.momat.go.jp; Tue-Sun 10am-5pm, Fri to 8pm; MOMAT collection ¥430; additional charge for special exhibitions), which showcases contemporary Japanese and Western art and crafts. The closest station is Takebashi (Tozai subway line); take the 1b Exit.

Also in the park is **Nippon Budokan** 日本武道館 (🖳 www.nipponbudo kan.or.jp), a venue for martial arts events and concerts. The park is also a con-venient way to reach **Yasukuni Shrine** 靖國神社 (🖳 www.yasukuni.or.jp; daily Jan-Feb & Nov-Dec 6am-5pm, Mar-Apr & Sep-Oct to 6pm, May-Aug to 7pm; free), where Japan's war dead are remembered. The closest station to these is Kudanshita on the Tozai and Toei Shinjuku subway lines.

Rail fans may like to go to the roof garden on the 6th floor of **Kitte** (**JP Tower** JPタワー; 🖳 jptower-kitte.jp; Mon-Sat 11am-9pm or later, Sun to 8pm) to see trains coming and going. To reach it follow signs to the Marunouchi South Gate Entrance/Exit. Once there turn left and cross the road. The best place for an overall view of the station is the Terrace on the 5th floor of the **Marunouchi Building** 丸の内ビル; the building is opposite the South Gate Entrance/Exit. Both are good places to be in the evening when the station build-ing is lit up (from sunset to 9pm).

**Yurakucho** 有楽町 Alight here for the **JNTO Tourist Information Center** (see pp126-7), which is near **Tokyo International Forum** 東京国際フォーラ ム (🖳 www.t-i-forum.co.jp; daily 8am-11pm). The latter mainly hosts conven-tions but it's worth popping in to see the magnificent architecture. It is about a five-minute walk to the Ginza area (see p116) from Yurakucho (take the Ginza Exit) if you prefer to save the cost of a subway ticket.

**Shimbashi** 新橋 Shimbashi has an important place in Japan's railway histo-ry (see p88) and remains a centre of rail innovation as it is the starting point for a monorail, generally known as the Yurikamome, which whisks passengers to Odaiba (see pp106-8), an island of reclaimed land in Tokyo Bay.

**Hama-Rikyu Garden** 浜離宮庭園 (Hama-Rikyu Teien; 🖳 teien.tokyo-park.or.jp/en/hama-rikyu; daily 9am-5pm; ¥300; free audio guide) is one of Tokyo's best-known landscape gardens; it was originally used by members of the Tokugawa family (see p56) for falconry and wild-duck hunting. The most distinctive feature of the garden is that it has a number of ponds which change level with the tide – the water level is controlled by various gates. Other points of interest are a tea house and a pine tree that was planted in 1709. The garden is a 10- to 15-minute walk from the station. Hama-Rikyu can also be accessed on one of the water-bus services (see box p120) from Asakusa; if you plan to visit the garden from the water-bus you will have to pay for admission to the garden when you get your water-bus ticket. You can pick up a map here to guide you to Kyu-Shiba-Rikyu garden (see p108).

**Shiodome** 汐留, which is a stop on the Yurikamome and also on the Toei Oedo subway line, is called the site of the birthplace of the country's 'first railway system' (see p88). The original Shimbashi station is preserved here, but the surrounding area has been redeveloped into a futuristic office and leisure space. **Caretta Shiodome** カレッダー汐留, a complex with a wide selection of shops and restaurants, is home to **Advertising Museum Tokyo** アドミュージアム東京 (ADMT; 🖳 www.admt.jp; Tue-Fri 11am-6.30pm, Sat & holidays 11am-4.30pm; free). The museum, at the headquarters of Dentsu, Japan's leading advertising company, focuses on the history of advertising from the Edo period (1603-1868) to the modern day; kabuki actors often 'promoted' products in speeches at the end of a performance and signs for a particular face powder were sometimes part of the set. The labels are in Japanese but it is still an interesting place to visit.

### Side trip to Odaiba

The chance to see Tokyo from another angle makes a trip from Shimbashi to Odaiba お台場 worthwhile in itself, but the **Yurikamome** ゆりかもめ (officially New Transit Yurikamome; 🖳 www.yurikamome.co.jp; daily 6am-midnight), a driverless transit system, calls at plenty of tourist attractions along the way. This area and line will become a major focus for the Tokyo Olympics in 2020 as many events are going to be held here.

A one-way journey from Shimbashi to the terminus at Toyosu (¥380) takes around 30 minutes. The **one-day pass** (¥820) is valid for unlimited travel between Shimbashi and Toyosu on the day of purchase, or on one day during the period of validity ie if bought in advance. Some of the attractions offer a discount if you have a one-day pass.

Trains stop at **Shiodome** (see above), **Takeshiba** 竹芝, **Hinode** 日の出, a stop on the water-bus route (see box p120), and **Shibaura-Futo** 芝浦ふ頭, after which the train does a loop and crosses the spectacular **Rainbow Bridge** レインボーブリッジ, so called due to its rainbow-like shape.

If the weather is good it is worth walking across the bridge; there is a 'promenade' プロメナード (Apr-Oct 9am-9pm, Nov-Mar 10am-6pm, closed 3rd Mon of every month), just over a mile (1.7km) long, on either side of the bridge. Take the East Exit from Shibaura-Futo station and then walk straight along the road (about 10 mins) towards Rainbow Bridge. When you get near the bridge turn left and follow the signs to the lift/elevator and take that up to the 7th floor. Turn right to walk on the north 'promenade' (for views of Tokyo Harbour and central Tokyo) and left for the south side (for views of Tokyo Bay and if you are lucky Fuji-san). The noise of the traffic means it isn't really a relaxing walk but the views of Tokyo's cityscape compensate for this. It will take approximately 20 minutes to cross the bridge and reach Odaiba Marine

Park (see below). Get there about an hour before the closing time to be sure you will be allowed to walk across the bridge.

**Odaiba-kaihin-koen** お台場海浜公園 Stop here to visit **Odaiba Marine/ Seaside Park**, a seaside park with a man-made beach, and **Decks Tokyo Beach** デックス東京ビーチ (🖥 www.odaiba-decks.com; daily 11am-9pm), a vast retail space which includes **Tokyo Joypolis** 東京ジョイポリス (🖥 tokyo-joypolis.com; daily 10am-10pm; ¥800, ¥3900/1-day pass, night pass ¥2900), a virtual reality games arcade. The observation deck and beach here are the best places to see Rainbow Bridge illuminated at night.

The space-age metallic building with a sphere suspended in the middle belongs to **Fuji Television** (🖥 www.fujitv.co.jp/en/visit_fujitv.html). In the sphere is **Hachitama** はちたま (Tue-Sun 10am-6pm; ¥550), an observation gallery with a 270˚ view. To reach it take the tube escalator up to the 7th floor and then take the lift/elevator up to Hachitama.

**Daiba** 台場 From here it is an easy walk to two more places offering shops and restaurants. **Aqua City Odaiba** アクアシティお台場 (🖥 www.aquacity .jp; daily 11am-9pm) faces the sea and, in addition to the shops, has **Sony ExploraScience** ソニー・エクスプローラサイエンス (Mediage; daily 11am-7pm; closed every 2nd & 4th Tue; ¥500), an interactive museum focusing on light and sound technology.

**DiverCity Tokyo Plaza** ダイバーシティ東京プラザ (🖥 www.divercity-tokyo.com; daily 11am-9pm), another shopping mall, is also home to **Gundam Front Tokyo** ガンダムフロント東京, with a 18m-high statue of the anime character Gundam.

**Fune-no-kagakukan** 船の科学館 It is a short walk from here to the fascinating Museum of Emerging Science and Innovation commonly called **Miraikan** 未来館 (Nippon Kagaku Miraikan; 🖥 www.miraikan.jst.go.jp; Wed-Mon 10am-5pm but may also be open on Tue in peak periods; ¥620, free with GP), in Tokyo Academic Park. Here you can discover the latest in robot technology such as the kodomoroid®, the world's first news announcer android who has a multitude of voices including a child's, and the therapeutic robot 'Paro' whose purpose is to encourage mental stimulation particularly for the elderly. Alternatively, just lie back and watch the earth revolve with displays of the sea-surface temperature and projections of future global warming and a global chemical weather-forecasting system. Most exhibits are interactive and there are plenty of labels in English.

The museum also has a number of film screenings; they are all free but the 3D ones are popular so it is worth getting a ticket as soon as you arrive. The programme changes every now and then so check the website before you go so you can plan your day. The screens are on the 5th and 6th floors and you need to go to each floor to get the relevant ticket.

**Telecom Center** テレコムセンター Alight here for **Telecom Tower** テレコムタワー which has an observatory 展望台 (Tue-Fri 3-9pm, Sat & Sun 11am-10.30pm; ¥500) offering views of the city but there are better places to go for these. This is also the best stop for **Oedo-onsen Monogatari** 大江戸温泉物語 (🖥 www.ooedoonsen.jp; daily 11am-9am; Mon-Fri ¥2480, Sat & Sun ¥2680, or ¥1980/2180 after 6pm), an enormous hot-spring theme park set in

TOKYO

the Edo period with more baths than you'll be able to visit in a day. The hot water is pumped up from a natural source 1400m below ground. Massages and other spa treatments are available; there are also several restaurants and shops. If you're not expecting to visit another onsen in Japan this will give you a good insight into why the Japanese take the art of bathing so seriously. Note that if you have a tattoo you will not be permitted to enter.

If coming from Toyosu get off here for Miraikan (see p107).

**Aomi** 青海 From here you can visit **Palette Town** パレットタウン, an entertainment complex which includes the **Mega Web** theme park (🖳 www.mega web.gr.jp; daily 11am-9pm, occasional closed days), a showcase for Toyota, where you can see and get in all their latest models and, if you have a driver's licence, go for a spin in one. Palette Town also includes **Venus Fort**, an Italianate shopping centre geared towards women and with plazas and fountains. Also here is **Daikanransha** 大観覧車 (🖳 www.daikanransha.com; daily 10am-10pm, Fri & Sat to 11pm; ¥920; about 15 mins), the tallest (115m-high) ferris wheel in Japan, though the ones in Sakuragicho (see p163) and Osaka (see p150) are not much smaller. Each cabin seats 4-6 people.

**Kokusai-tenjijo-seimon** 国際展示場正門   The stop for **Tokyo International Exhibition Center** 東京国際展示場 at **Tokyo Big Sight** 東京ビッグサイト (🖳 www.bigsight.jp). Shows, such as Tokyo Motor Show and the International Robot Show, are held here. The Conference Tower is probably architecturally the most unusual building in this area as it is based on an inverted pyramid.

Trains then stop at **Ariake** 有明, **Ariake-tennis-no-mori** 有明テニスの森 (where national and international tennis matches are played) and **Shijo-mae** 市場前 (there is a good view of Tokyo Tower from here). Shijo-mae and **Shin-Toyosu** 新豊洲 are the stops closest to the new home for the wholesale part of Tsukiji, Tokyo's fish market (see pp116-17). At the time of research nothing had been finalised regarding seeing auctions at the new site but if anything visitors will only be able to watch from a viewing platform in part of a new shopping and entertainment facility here. For updates check the website (🖳 www.tsukiji-market.or.jp), or ask at a tourist information centre.

The terminus is at **Toyosu** 豊洲, home to Lalaport ららぽーと, a shopping centre/mall. Toyosu links up with the Yurakucho subway line, stops on which include Yurakucho (p105) and Ikebukuro (p112).

**Hamamatsucho** 浜松町  The Tokyo Monorail to **Haneda Airport** (Haneda-kuko; see box p127) starts here. Opposite the North Exit of the station, **Kyu Shiba-Rikyu** 旧芝離宮 (daily 9am-5pm; ¥150) is a landscape garden (see box p86) that was originally built on reclaimed land and is now surrounded by sky-scrapers. It is smaller and less peaceful than Hama-Rikyu (see pp105-6) but quite pleasant in that you can see the whole garden in one view. It is probably not worth making a special trip for, but if combined with the boat trip to Hama-Rikyu you can then walk here and thus make a circuit. You may also like to go up to the Observatory (Seaside Top; daily 10am-8.30pm; ¥620) at the top of the **World Trade Center Building** 世界貿易センタービル. Purchase your ticket on the 1st/ground floor and then take the dedicated lift/elevator to the 40th floor.

The next stop is **Tamachi** 田町.

**Shinagawa** 品川  A useful station as it is also a stop on the Narita Express (see box pp126-7), the Tokaido/Sanyo shinkansen to Shin-Osaka/Kyushu and several main JR lines (Tokaido,

> Places in the text where entry is free, or discounted, with a **Tokyo Museum Grutto Pass** (see p104) are signified with: 'free/discount with GP'.

Keihin-Tohoku, Yokosuka & Sobu). The private Keikyu Line links Shinagawa with Haneda Airport (see box p127). Shinagawa was the starting point of the first rail services in Japan (see p60) and its importance continues as it has been chosen as the terminus in Tokyo for the Maglev (see p92); in fact construction work has already begun, 40 metres below ground level.

The next stops are **Osaki** 大崎, **Gotanda** 五反田, and **Meguro** 目黒.

**Ebisu** 恵比寿  Ebisu is so-named because it used to be the home for a Yebisu beer brewery. This closed some years ago and was replaced by Yebisu Garden Place – a complex of shops, offices, apartments, a cinema, restaurants, a hotel and the **Museum of Yebisu Beer** エビスビール記念館 (🖳 www.sapporo beer.jp/brewery/y_museum; Tue-Sun 11am-7pm; free, tasting of four beers ¥400, guided tour in Japanese and tasting ¥500), where you can learn about the science and history of brewing in Japan and Yebisu's role in it. To get there follow signs for Yebisu Sky Walk.

Fans of the film *The Third Man* may recognise the theme tune used for train departures from and arrivals at this station (see box p102); this is because the music has also been used for Yebisu Beer commercials.

On the roof of Atré Ebisu shopping complex (in front of the East Exit) there is one of JR East's **Soradofarms**. At these people can rent space to grow vegetables and plants. Tools and seeds are provided and expert advice can also be given. It is fun to go up there and see people gardening; it's open 10am-5pm, later in summer.

**Shibuya** 渋谷  Young people come here in droves to visit the many boutiques, bars and nightclubs, but Shibuya is perhaps best known for **Shibuya Ekimae Kosaten** (also known as 'Shibuya Scramble'), the crossing in front of the station, as it is always packed with people. The best view of the crossing is from the branch of *Starbucks* that faces it, but not surprisingly, getting a window seat isn't easy. However, there are other options if you look around as many places have large glass windows. To get there follow signs for the Hachi-ko Exit.

From the crossing walk up Koen-dori to find all the top fashion department stores. The road to the left of Starbucks leads to a pedestrianised area which has plenty of shops and restaurants and the road to the left of that leads to the original branch of **Shibuya 109** 渋谷109, home to over a hundred boutiques with all the latest fashions.

**Hikarie** ヒカリエ (🖳 www.hikarie.jp), on the other side (East Exit) of the station, is a 34-storey complex incorporating a theatre for musicals, galleries (on the 8th floor), shops, restaurants and offices.

TOKYO

❏ **The legend of Hachi-ko**

Hachi-ko ハチ公 was an Akita dog born in Odate (Tohoku) in 1923 and brought to Tokyo the following year by its owner, Eisaburo Ueno. A pet of unflinching loyalty, Hachi-ko bade his master goodbye every morning when he left for work and greeted him at the end of the day at Shibuya station. Such was the dog's devotion, that even after his owner died in 1925 Hachi-ko continued to return to the station every day for the next 11 years and waited patiently for him.

The statue of Hachi-ko which stands today outside the Hachi-ko Exit of Shibuya station is a popular local landmark and meeting place. However, it may be moved due to the major reconstruction work at the station.

Shibuya Station is undergoing a lot of construction work to build a new complex with east, central and west buildings; work is not expected to be fully completed till 2027 so expect some disruption.

**Harajuku 原宿  Meiji Jingu** 明治神宮 (🖥 www.meijijingu.or.jp; daily at least 6.40am-4pm; free), Tokyo's best-known shrine, is in **Yoyogi Park** 代々木公園 (daily Apr-mid Oct 5am-8pm, mid Oct-Mar to 5pm), a 5- to 10-minute walk from the station; turn right out of the exit and then right again. Dedicated to Emperor Meiji and his consort, the shrine is divided into Outer and Inner gardens; the Inner Garden (daily 9am-4/4.30pm, 8am-5/6pm in June; ¥500) is particularly popular in June when the irises are in bloom. Also in the Inner Garden is Kiyomasa's well 清正井 (Kiyomasa no ido), a spring-fed well that is believed to bring good luck.

Harajuku is just as hip as nearby Shibuya and there are plenty of restaurants, cafés and trendy (read: retro/alternative) clothes and music stores in the streets around the station. On Sundays, particularly in the afternoon, crowds of *cosplay* fans take over Harajuku Bridge 原宿の橋, generally referred to as **Jingu Bashi** (Jingu Bridge), and the area leading to Yoyogi Park.

**Yoyogi** 代々木  It's easier to transfer here to the Chuo/Sobu Line for both Tokyo (see p105) and Ryogoku (see pp120-1) than at Shinjuku.

**Shinjuku** 新宿  Probably the busiest station in the world – over three million passengers pass through here every day. Shinjuku is home not only to JR lines (including the Chuo Line for Kawaguchi-ko; see p138) but also other companies, such as the private Odakyu railway (for Hakone, see p141), as well as three subway lines. Even Japanese find it hard to get around but the various rail companies have agreed to ensure they have uniform signs for entrances and exits so it should get easier – at the moment you may see New South Exit, Shin South Gate and Shin-Minami Entrance but they all refer to the same place.

There's a certain Jekyll and Hyde character to the Shinjuku district. While the west side of the station is a sea of grey suits and immaculately turned-out businessmen, conformity is abandoned over on Shinjuku's east side. The streets around **Kabukicho** 歌舞伎町, a few minutes' walk north of the East Exit, fill up as the sun sets and the neon is switched on. Cinemas, clubs, restaurants, pubs and hostess bars compete for business and cater for all tastes. **Golden Gai** 新宿 ゴールデン街 is a particularly atmospheric area of Kabukicho; it comprises six alleyways with about 200 tiny bars. Some bars only welcome people who have been introduced but others are happy to have tourists.

If you were to follow any of the mass of commuters taking the West Exit between 6 and 8.30am, you would probably end up heading directly for the **Tokyo Metropolitan Government Building** 東京都庁, completed in 1991 and the workplace of 13,000 bureaucrats. The best reason for visiting here is the free bird's eye view of Tokyo and even as far as Mt Fuji (Dec-Feb is best for this). To get to the top, take the direct elevator inside the No 1 Building (go down the steps outside so that you enter the building at basement level) up to one of two 202m-high observatories (daily 9.30am-11pm; closed Dec 29-31 & Jan 2-3) on the 45th floor. The South Observatory is generally open during the day and the North at night. On weekdays (10am-3pm) volunteers give **free guided tours** of the observation deck (20 mins; enquire at South Observation Deck Volunteer Desk) and also of the building (40 mins; enquire at the Tokyo TIC, see below).

On your way into, or out of, the building, call in at the **Tokyo Tourist Information Center** 東京観光情報センター on the 1st/ground floor (street level; see p128) for details about Tokyo. Visit the **Japanese Prefectural Tourism Promotion Corner** 全国観光PRコーナー (daily 9.30am-6.30pm), on the 2nd floor, for general information about the rest of Japan.

**Shinjuku Gyoen** 新宿御苑 (🖳 www.env.go.jp/garden/shinjukugyoen; Tue-Sun 9am-4.30pm; daily and extended hours during the cherry blossom season and for the Chrysanthemum Exhibition in early Nov; ¥200) is a complete surprise in amongst Shinjuku's skyscrapers. Built in 1906 as an Imperial Garden, all 58.3 hectares are open to the public and the site includes an English landscape garden, French garden and traditional Japanese garden. People come here to escape the busy city that surrounds the park; though you never quite feel you've left the metropolis, this is a pleasant temporary escape. Take the East Exit from Shinjuku station and walk south-east, following the signs, for about 10 minutes.

To understand more about the samurai spirit and their value of 'honour above life' make time for a visit to the **Samurai Museum** 侍 (サムライミュージアム; 🖳 www.samuraimuseum.jp; daily 10.30am-9pm; ¥1500). All the sets of armour on display here are originals so it is worth remembering that someone once wore them; there is even one with bullet holes. To get a greater understanding try on a helmet and some armoury (¥500). There are also displays of the various forms of samurai weaponry and a room dedicated to Ryoma Sakamoto (1836-67), a prominent figure in the move to overthrow the Tokugawa shogunate (see p56); he was born in Kochi (see pp470-1).

The museum is an 8-minute walk from the East Exit of JR Shinjuku: walk along Yasukuni-dori till you see a small street on your left between a Family Mart convenience store and Matsuya restaurant. Turn left, pass the Robot Restaurant (see box p112), a little way down on the right, and continue to the end of the road, turn right and then first left.

❏ **Robot Restaurant**

The Robot Restaurant ロボットレストラン (☎ 03-3200-5500, 🖳 www.shinjuku-robot.com; daily from 4pm, up to four sittings a day; entrance fee ¥8000, ¥7500 if booked online; bento box meal ¥1000) is not really a restaurant but a show with both humans and robots.

'This place is ridiculous. It's a tourist trap and it's not particularly cheap, but the 90-minute show is brilliant and insanely fun to watch. Everyone is seated very close to what can only be described as live action power rangers. Despite the name, food is not obligatory and many eat beforehand. Book ahead and arrive early (at least 30 minutes before the scheduled time) to ensure you get inside in time. Be aware: it is noisy and there are lots of flashing lights'.                    **Ben Storey & Alex Chambers**

To get to the Robot Restaurant follow the directions for the Samurai Museum (see p111).

The next stops on the Yamanote Line are **Shin-Okubo** 新大久保, and then **Takadanobaba** 高田馬場 where Osamu Tezuka's company, Tezuka Productions, is based. It is the setting for the well-known anime *Astro Boy*; the station uses sounds from the Astro Boy film to signal when trains are departing and some of the characters are painted on the wall that runs under the railway tracks. After this trains stop at **Mejiro** 目白 (see Where to stay p131).

**Ikebukuro** 池袋  On either side of Ikebukuro station are two enormous department stores; **Seibu** is on the east side and its rival **Tobu** is on the west. An underground passageway links both sides of the station. Both Seibu and Tobu have restaurant floors and food halls. See Where to stay p131.

**Otsuka** 大塚  Transfer here for **Toei's Toden Arakawa Line** (see p118), one of two tram/streetcar lines in Tokyo.

The next stop is **Sugamo** 巣鴨.

**Komagome** 駒込  **Rikugien** 六義園 (daily 9am-5pm; ¥300), a large landscaped garden, was constructed in 1702 by Yoshiyasu Yanagisawa, a samurai in the Edo period and an official in the Tokugawa shogunate. It is known for its azaleas so is at its best from April to June but it was also designed as a 'kai-yu' (go-round) garden with features such as a pond, islands, trees, artificial hills and several tea houses so is of interest at any time of the year. Turn left out of the station and cross to the other side of the road. Continue walking to the left and soon on the right is a sign about the garden and in effect the corner of it. However, keep walking to the next junction, turn right and the entrance is soon on the right. Overall it's about a 7-minute walk.

The next stops are **Tabata** 田端 and **Nishi-Nippori** 西日暮里.

**Nippori** 日暮里  Nippori is a point of transfer for the private Keisei Railway Line to Narita Airport and a stop on the JR Keihin-Tohoku Line to Yokohama.

Shimogoinden-bashi, outside the North Gate (East Exit) side of Nippori station is also a great place for **trainspotting**. A poster on the building to the left of the bridge identifies some of the 20 types of train (including the various Tohoku shinkansen) you might see.

If the crowds and noise of Tokyo are getting to you head here to stroll around '**Yanesen**' 谷根千 – a *shitamachi* (old town) area named after the districts of Yanaka 谷中, Nezu 根津 and Sendagi 千駄木 (Ya-Ne-Sen); it is a peaceful residential area but also has a number of temples and art galleries to visit. Start at the North Gate's West Exit and after a few minutes' walk along Goten-zaka you will see signs for **Asakura Museum of Sculpture** 朝倉彫塑館 (💻 www.taitocity.net/zaidan/asakura; Tue, Wed & Fri-Sun 9.30am-4.30pm; ¥500, free with GP). Fumio Asakura (1883-1964), thought of as the father of modern Japanese sculpture, lived and worked here; in fact he designed the buildings and garden and chose all the materials. The house still feels like a home and there is a selection of his work – mostly naked figures and bronze cats – spread around the many rooms and a lovely roof garden, though this is closed if the weather is bad. Return to Goten-zaka and you will soon reach a flight of steps called **Yuyake Dandan** 夕やけだんだん, the top of which is known as a place to watch the sun set. At the bottom is **Yanaka Ginza** 谷中ぎんざ, a traditional shopping street full of places where you can get souvenirs or snacks.

If you don't already have a map of the Yanesen area turn right at the end and walk along to the **Yanesen Tourist Information and Culture Centre** (TICC: 💻 www.ti-yanesen.jp/en; generally daily 10am-6pm); here you can get a map, information about the area and also have a chance to book cultural experiences such as a tea ceremony and wearing a kimono. With a map in hand navigate your way to **Scai the Bathhouse** スカイザバスハウス (💻 www.scaithe bathhouse.com; Tue-Sat noon-6pm). As its name suggests this was originally a bathhouse, but it is now used for a variety of contemporary art exhibitions. A characterful place to have a break is ***Kayaba Coffee*** カヤバ珈琲 (💻 kayaba-coffee.com; Mon-Sat 8am-11pm, Sun to 6pm); this coffee shop first opened in 1938 though the building dates from 1916. During the day there are set menus (¥800-1000) as well as an à la carte menu. The night-time menu (from 6pm) includes dishes such as chicken *kara-age* (¥500) and a *donburi* (rice-bowl; ¥900) the topping for which changes weekly. Walk down the road from Scai; Kayaba is the wooden building on the corner on the right-hand side.

Retrace your steps for a minute or so and walk along Sakura-dori, known in the spring for the cherry blossom. Sakura-dori goes through the middle of **Yanaka Cemetery** 谷中霊園, the resting place for local residents and also many Japanese artists and writers. Pop into **Tenno-ji** 天王寺 to see the Daibutsu, a copper-seated Buddha, created in 1690 by Kyuemon Ota. From there it is only a short walk to the South Gate West Exit of Nippori station.

If you don't have a JR Pass it may be easier to take the subway (Chiyoda Line) to Sendagi as that is closer to the Yanesen TICC. At Sendagi follow signs for Exit 2, cross the road and turn left – Annex Katsutaro Ryokan, see Where to stay (p132), is along the first road on the right. However, keep walking straight till you see a post office. The road on the right after that is Yanaka Ginza but keep walking for a little more until you see Yanesen TICC on your right.

**Uguisudani** 鶯谷  Up until WWII, Uguisudani was a popular geisha quarter but it is now better known as a night-time pleasure area full of love hotels.

**Ueno** 上野  Ueno is a major rail junction: it is a stop on the JR Keihin-Tohoku, Tohoku (Utsunomiya), Takasaki, Joban and Ueno–Tokyo main lines, and the second stop after Tokyo for shinkansen services to the north (see p321).

It is also an access point for Asakusa (see pp118-20) as it is the nearest stop for transferring from the Yamanote Line to the Ginza subway line.

Opposite the Park Exit of the station is **Ueno Park** 上野公園 (Ueno-koen; 5am-11pm), Japan's oldest public park and the largest in Tokyo. During the cherry-blossom season thousands of Tokyo residents come here armed with mats, picnic hampers and crates of beer for *hanami*. The park is also home to a number of museums including: **Tokyo National Museum** 東京国立博物館 (🖳 www.tnm.jp; Tue-Sun 9.30am-5pm, Apr-Dec Fri to 8pm for special exhibitions, Apr-Sep Sat & Sun to 6pm; ¥620, free with GP), the country's oldest and largest, with exhibits on the history and fine arts of Japan, China and India; and the **National Museum of Western Art** 国立西洋美術館 (🖳 www.nmwa.go.jp; Tue-Sun 9.30am-5.30pm, Fri to 8pm; ¥430, free with GP; additional charge for special exhibitions) which displays masterpieces collected by a Japanese business magnate while travelling around Europe in the early 1900s.

Also here is **Ueno Zoo** 上野動物園 (Ueno Doubutsuen; 🖳 www.tokyo-zoo.net/english/ueno; Tue-Sun 9.30am-5pm; ¥600, free with GP), which opened in 1882 and is the oldest zoo in Japan. Visitor number have been boosted dramatically since the arrival in March 2011 of two pandas (RiRi and ShinShin) from China. However, sometimes during the day they are given a rest from the adoring public so may not be on view.

The small but fascinating **Shitamachi Museum** 下町風俗資料館 (🖳 www.taitocity.net/taito/shitamachi; Tue-Sun 9.30am-4.30pm; ¥300; free with GP) features a display of recreated shops and homes from the Edo and Taisho periods. On the 2nd floor there is a chance to play with some children's toys from those periods – several are very challenging! It is on the south-eastern side of Ueno Park near **Shinobazu pond** 不忍池 (Shinobazuno-ike).

Another reason for visiting Ueno is to wander around **Ameyoko Market** アメ横 (Ameyoko). Take the Shinobazu Exit at Ueno station and head for Ameyadori, a long shopping arcade that extends beneath the elevated rail tracks. Stallholders call out loudly to passers-by and this is one of the few places in Japan where you are expected to haggle. You can buy almost anything here, including (fake?) Prada handbags, Rolex watches and clothes as well as food.

It is about a 20-minute walk along Asakusa-dori to Kappabashi Dougu St (see pp119-20).

**Okachimachi** 御徒町  Okachimachi is known for its cheap jewellery stores.

**Akihabara** 秋葉原  For some years Akihabara has been the main discount electrical goods district (Electric Town) of Tokyo and the place to see the latest gadgets months before they hit the worldwide market. (Note: If you're planning to buy, check that the guarantee is valid overseas and that the voltage requirements are compatible.) Akihabara is now also a centre for anime and manga (comics) as well as cosplay and maid cafés.

Whatever your interest a good place to start shopping is **Akihabara Radio Kaikan** 秋葉原ラジオ会館 (daily 10am-8pm), a 12-storey building where you can get electronic goods, anime figures and all kinds of manga. Turn left out of the Electric Town Exit and then walk straight ahead, Radio Kaikan is soon on your left. However, this is only one of many shops so pick up an *Akihabara Guide Map* from the **information office** (daily 9am-7pm) immediately on the left by the manned JR ticket gate.

**Tokyo Anime Center** 東京アニメセンター (🖳 www.animecenter.jp; daily 11am-7pm; free) is on the 4th floor of Akihabara UDX Building. Follow the signs to the Electric Town Exit, turn right out of the station, cross the plaza and go up the escalator. The Anime Center is a short walk along on the left-hand side. The centre is geared to children and to selling anime merchandise, but is worth visiting as, unlike Ghibli Museum (see box below), there is a lot of explanation in English. The 3D Theater here screens new works as well as other anime-related events.

The 1300-year-old **Kanda Shrine** 神田明神 (Kanda Myojin; daily 24hrs) now offers blessings and good-luck charms to protect smart phones and is also

---

### ❏ Animation museums

If Tokyo Anime Center in Akihabara (see above) has whetted your appetite for the cartoon world, there are some other places just outside the city centre you might like to consider visiting.

Best known is **Ghibli Museum** ジブリ美術館 (🖳 www.ghibli-museum.jp; Wed-Mon 10am-6pm; ¥1000), a celebration of the work of Studio Ghibli, in particular leading Japanese animator Hayao Miyazaki. Explanations are only in Japanese, but it's primarily a visual museum, with many of Miyazaki's original drawings on display, and a screening (approx 20 mins) of one of his short films. The nearest station is Mitaka 三鷹 (see map opposite p524), on the JR Chuo line from Shinjuku (frequent service; 20 mins); from Mitaka either take the small community bus from outside the South Exit at bus stop No 9 (2-6/hr; round trip ¥320), or walk 15 minutes along Tamagawa-josui. Entry to the museum is restricted so it is **essential to get tickets in advance** – either from a JTB office in your home country (see pp37-9), or in Japan from a Loppi machine in any branch of Lawson (see box p84). Your ticket will specify the date and time of entry; the latter is either at 10am, noon, 2pm or 4pm. As long as the foreigner allocation of tickets has not been sold for that day you should get in – but **do not** go to the museum until you have a ticket. Note that it is still likely to be crowded so only really worth going if you are a fan.

The tiny **Suginami Animation Museum** 杉並アニメーションミュージアム (🖳 www.sam.or.jp; Tue-Sun 10am-6pm, closed occasional days so check website; free) hosts special exhibitions and has displays on every aspect of animation as well as a theatre showing some anime classics. Take a local/rapid train on the JR Chuo line to Ogikubo 荻窪 station; it's three stops before Mitaka. Follow signs for the North Exit, take a Kanto bus from either stop No 0 or No 1 and get off at Ogikubo Keisatsusho-mae (Ogikubo Police station), a 5-minute journey.

popular with anime/manga fans. It is about a ten-minute walk from Akihabara or seven minutes from JR Ochanomizu station. The shrine is also the location for the Kanda Matsuri (see p130).

Change at Akihabara for the JR Sobu Line to Ryogoku (see pp120-1) and to Kinshicho for the closest JR station to Tokyo Skytree (see p121 & p124).

The next stop is **Kanda** 神田.

**Tokyo Station**   This completes the loop around the Yamanote Line.

### Off the Yamanote Line

**Ginza** 銀座   Ginza is Tokyo's most upmarket shopping district; the main thoroughfare, Chuo-dori, is lined with upmarket department stores and designer-label boutiques. On Saturday and Sunday afternoons the road is closed to traffic.

Apart from shopping, Ginza's best-known entertainment is kabuki (see pp62-3). **Kabuki-za** 歌舞伎座 (🖥 www.kabuki-za.co.jp), the Kabuki theatre, is 10 minutes south-east of central Ginza on a corner of Harumi-dori. The façade of the original building has been retained but considerable building work has updated the interior and the building is also now connected to a multi-storey office block. The Harumi-dori entrance is for the theatre and Showa-dori is the entrance for the office block. The theatre itself is on the 1st/ground floor. The advantage of kabuki is that it is possible just to go to one act. 'Single Act' tickets are only sold on the day; go to the box office on the left side of the main entrance. An English translation is available courtesy of a mini iPad which is plugged into the back of the seat in front of you.

On the 4th floor of Kabuki-za Tower there is a Memories of Kabuki-za Theatre (11am-4.45pm) and on the 5th floor, in Kabuki-za gallery (10am-5pm; ¥500), some videos and an exhibition of kabuki costumes and props but no English labels; there is also a roof-top garden (10am-7pm) here. The main box office, as well as shops and restaurants, is on B2F (the basement 2nd floor); B2F is linked to Higashi-Ginza station on the Toei-Asakusa subway line. Ginza is also one stop on the Marunouchi subway line from Tokyo station,

**Tsukiji** 築地   Tokyo Metropolitan Central Wholesale Market, commonly called **Tsukiji Market** 築地市場 (Tsukiji-shijo; 🖥 www.tsukiji-market.or.jp), is Japan's biggest fish market and where 90% of all fish sold in Tokyo comes. After many years of planning the wholesale part of it will move to a new site in Shin-Toyosu (see p108) in November 2016. This means that one of the most popular tourist attractions for many years – seeing the wholesale auctions take place – will come to an end. If you want to be one of the last visitors to the historic site look at the website for details about visiting. However, since visitor numbers are limited expect it to be even harder to get in. The closest station is Tsukiji-shijo on the Toei Oedo subway line; alternatively Tsukiji station is two stops from Ginza on the Hibiya subway line.

The outer market – an area of shops and restaurants open to anyone – will remain where it is but a new building **Tsukiji Uogashi** 築地魚河岸, a shopping mall, will open, probably by early November before the official move. The atmosphere of the place may be lost but it will still be the best place to go for the very freshest of fish.

**Roppongi** 六本木  A stop on both the Hibiya and Toei Oedo subway lines, Roppongi comes alive at night when the neon goes on and clubs and bars throw open their doors, though it also has plenty to see during the day (see box below).

---

### ❏ Roppongi in the 21st century

For a glimpse of 21st-century urban life, it's worth exploring at least one of the cities-within-a-city that are Roppongi Hills and Tokyo Midtown. In both, shops, cinemas, restaurants, galleries, museums and offices – and some greenery in the form of gardens and parks – all converge on one space. **Art Triangle Roppongi** refers to the National Art Centre, Suntory Museum of Art and Mori Art Museum. If you go to one of these, keep your ticket stub for a discount at the other museums. The galleries are quite far apart but the walking route is well signposted.

**Roppongi Hills** 六本木ヒルズ  Roppongi Hills (🖳 www.roppongihills.com) was the brainchild of construction tycoon Minoru Mori, one of the world's richest men. Crowds of well-heeled Japanese flock to the upmarket design stores and restaurants (shops generally open 11am-9pm, restaurants to 11pm). Make time, though, to visit the landmark **Mori Tower** 森タワー, where you'll find **Mori Art Museum** 森美術館 (Mori Bijutsukan; 🖳 www.mori.art.museum; Wed-Mon 10am-10pm, Tue 10am-5pm; admission price varies; discount with GP), a great contemporary art space on the 53rd floor; check in advance as it may be closed when exhibitions are changing. On the 52nd floor is **Tokyo City View** 東京シティビュー (250m; Mon-Thur & Sun 10am-11pm, Fri, Sat and the day before holidays to 1am; ¥1800, ¥200 discount with GP, or ¥1500 if bought in advance at any convenience store), an indoor observation deck. However, the reason to go up here is for the Sky Deck (270m; 11am-9pm; an additional ¥500) as this provides the highest open-air viewing place in Tokyo and a 360° panorama of the city and surrounding area. Sadly it is closed in bad weather so unless this is your only opportunity for a view of Tokyo check whether the Sky Deck is open before buying a ticket. Take Exit 1C from Hibiya Line's Roppongi station, or it is a 4-minute walk from Exit 3 from Toei Oedo's Roppongi station. Tickets must be bought at the Museum Cone, on the 3rd floor. Pick up a copy of the *Roppongi Hills Town Guide* here for a guide to the many shops and restaurants in the complex.

**Tokyo Midtown** 東京ミッドタウン  Apart from shops, restaurants, offices and residences the Tokyo Midtown site (🖳 www.tokyo-midtown.com) includes a hotel, *The Ritz-Carlton Tokyo* ザ・リッツ・カールトン東京 (☎ 03-3423 8000, 🖳 www.ritz carlton.com; from ¥49,500/D), on the top nine floors of the 53-storey **Midtown Tower** ミッドタウン・タワー, and three exhibition spaces: **Suntory Museum of Art** サントリー美術館 (🖳 www.suntory.com/sma; Wed-Mon 10am-6pm, Fri to 8pm) where the theme is 'Art in Life' and the collection includes painting, ceramics, lacquerware, glass and other items connected to Japanese life; **21_21 Design Sight** 21_21 デザインサイト (🖳 www.2121designsight.jp; Wed-Mon 10am-7pm; ¥1100) also has exhibitions focusing on everyday life but from a design point of view; and the **National Art Center** 国立新美術館 (Kokuritsu Shin-Bijutsukan; 🖳 www.nact.jp; Wed-Mon 10am-6pm, Fri to 8pm; admission cost depends on the exhibition, ¥100 discount with GP), which offers one of the largest exhibition spaces in Japan, but has no permanent exhibition. Exit 6 of the Chiyoda Line's Nogizaka Station leads straight to the centre but it is only a short walk from either of the Roppongi subway stations.

**Tokyo Tower** 東京タワー The 333m-high Tokyo Tower (🖳 www.tokyotow er.co.jp; daily 9am-11pm) opened in 1958 as a symbol of Japan's post-war recovery; its design was inspired by the Eiffel Tower in Paris. Even though since 2011 it has been eclipsed by Tokyo Skytree (see p121 & p124) one thing it offers, if it is not too wet or windy, is the chance to climb 600 steps to the first observatory. Entry to Tokyo Tower's 150m-high observatory costs ¥900 whether you walk or take the lift/elevator; an additional ¥700 gets you up to the 250m 'special observatory', though if the weather is bad this may be closed. Tokyo Tower is a 5- to 6-minute walk from either Akabanebashi on the Toei Oedo subway line, or Kamiyacho on the Hibiya Line.

**Toden Arakawa Line** 都電荒川線 One of Tokyo's two surviving tram/street-car lines runs between Waseda 早稲田 and Minowa-bashi 三ノ輪橋 (29 stops; 6am-11pm; 1-6/hr; approx 57 mins; ¥170/journey, ¥400/1-day pass, see also p129). The line, operated by Toei, passes through some of Tokyo's oldest neigh-bourhoods and the best place to join it is outside **Otsuka station** 大塚駅前 (see p112) on the Yamanote Line. Sadly, the characterful trams dating from 1962 are slowly being replaced and the modern versions aren't as atmospheric. The jour-ney itself also isn't massively exciting, but it does give you a chance to see a different side to Tokyo and it is worth getting off every now and then and just exploring. Take the South Exit at Otsuka station and turn left. Trains to Minowa-bashi leave on the left side but note that some terminate at Arakawa-shakomae 荒川車庫前.

**Asakusa** 浅草 The best-known landmark in Asakusa, the last stop on the Ginza subway line (take Exit 3 from the subway), is lively **Senso-ji** 浅草寺, also known as Asakusa Kannon-ji. The temple is said to have been founded in the 7th century and was named after Kannon, Goddess of Mercy. The main entrance to the temple is **Kaminarimon** 雷門 (Kaminari Gate); from here walk along **Nakamise-dori** 仲見世通り (🖳 www.asakusa-nakamise.jp), a street lined with stalls selling everything from lucky charms to rice crackers, to Hozomon (Hozo Gate). On the left is a **5-storey pagoda** and straight ahead is the main building, **Hon-do**, which was rebuilt in 1958.

Across the street from Kaminarimon (Kaminari Gate) and in a striking 8-storey building is **Asakusa Culture Tourist Information Center** 浅草文化観光センター (daily 9am-8pm). In addition to providing tourist information (1st/ground floor) and information about the local area (7th floor), there is a tea-room and viewing terrace (8th floor); the latter offers great views of Senso-ji.

**Hanayashiki** 花やしき (🖳 hanayashiki.net; daily approx 10am-6pm depending on the season and weather; entry ¥1000, ride tickets ¥100, book of 11 ¥1000, Free Ride Pass ¥2300), just behind Senso-ji, is a theme/amusement park that has operated since 1853 and claims to be the oldest theme park in Japan. Go for the atmosphere rather than thrills. However, a recent addition is a **Ninja Challenge dojo** 忍者体験道場 (¥2000pp; 6 sessions/day, approx 60 mins) where participants can learn stealth walking and ninja escape techniques amongst other things. Visit the Hanayashiki website for more details.

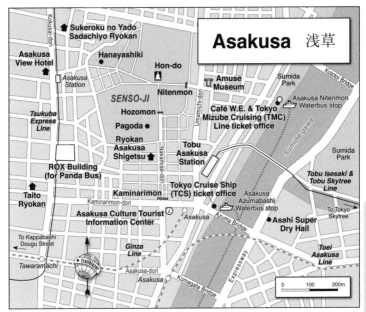

On the east side of Senso-ji, by Nitenmon (Niten Gate), **Amuse Museum** アミューズ ミュージアム (🖳 www.amusemuseum.com; Tue-Sun 10am-6pm; ¥1080, free with GP) has a wonderful collection of traditional clothing worn by farmers and working people but also lots of signs in English explaining about life and traditions in rural areas. Everything is well laid out and you are encouraged to touch the exhibits. On the 1st/ground floor is a shop of Japanese Arts & Crafts. On the 6th floor the Ukiyo-e Theater has digital e-prints from the Spaulding Collection of the Ministry of Fine Arts, Boston, USA. An additional bonus is the wonderful view of Senso-ji from the roof.

**Sumida Park** 墨田公園 (Sumida-koen) is on both sides of the river and is particularly popular at cherry blossom time but is also the site of the Sumida River fireworks (see p130). The unmissable Golden Flame (Flamme d'Or) sculpture, on the top of **Asahi Super Dry Hall** アサヒ ビール スーパードライ ホール, on the opposite side of the river, is often referred to by locals as either *O-gon-no-Unko* or *Kin-no-Unko* 金のうんこ (Golden Poo).

About 15 minutes' walk along the right-hand side of Asakusa-dori takes you to **Kappabashi Dougu Street** かっぱ橋道具街 (🖳 www.kappabashi.or.jp), home to about 170 shops (Mon-Sat 9am-5pm, Sun only some shops open) specialising in everything that the restaurant industry needs, including the plastic/wax food samples so commonly seen outside restaurants all over Japan. You can pick up a fake, but amazingly realistic, bit of sushi for about ¥1000. You will know you have reached the correct street when you see a koban (police office) and blue, white and red cups & saucers above each other on the building next to it with a sign 'Niimi' at the top. Alternatively take the Ginza subway line to Tawaramachi 田原町; Kappabashi is also a stop on the Shitamachi bus route (see p129).

**Ryogoku** 両国 Take the JR Sobu Line from Akihabara and follow signs for the West Exit. The Sumo Stadium is straight ahead and Edo-Tokyo Museum a short walk to the right. The sumo exhibition in the museum at the **Sumo Stadium** 相撲博物館 (Ryogoku Kokugikan; 🖳 www.sumo.or.jp; Mon-Fri 10am-4.30pm except when there's a tournament; free) changes every three months but unless you can read some Japanese it is probably not worth going.

Everything at **Edo-Tokyo Museum** 江戸東京博物館 (Edo-Tokyo Habutsukan; 🖳 www.edo-tokyo-museum.or.jp; daily 9.30am-5.30pm, Sat to 7.30pm; helpful volunteer guides available daily 10am-3pm; ¥600, free with GP; audio rental ¥1000 deposit) is on a grand scale and there are even several

---

**❏ Tokyo from the water**

Two companies operate water-buses 水上バス or sightseeing trips on a variety of routes. All are a great way of seeing Tokyo from the water and a chance to escape the crowds (and walking) and have a feeling of space. There is a recorded English commentary, though other than the former Tsukiji fish market there aren't any sights of particular interest. The fare depends on the distance travelled.

● **Tokyo Cruise Ship** 東京都観光汽船 (🖳 www.suijobus.co.jp) offers two ways of going by boat between Asakusa and Odaiba. The traditional way is to take the **Sumida River Line** 隅田川ライン (daily 10am-6pm; 1-2/hr; 5-40 mins; ¥210-780), which operates between Asakusa Azumabashi and Hinode Pier (near Hinode, a stop on the Yurikamome; see p106) and stops at Hama-rikyu garden (see p105) en route.

For a more hi-tech journey on a futuristic-looking boat take either the *Himiko* or *Hotaluna*. Both operate on the **Asakusa-Odaiba Direct Line** 浅草・お台場直通ライン, though with slightly different routes. The *Himiko* ヒミコ (daily except 2nd Tue and Wed of the month; 2-4/day; 20-75 mins; ¥780-2040) runs in a loop between Asakusa Azumabashi, Odaiba Marine/Seaside Park and Toyosu. It is best to go in the evening when the floor panels on the water-bus are lit up. The *Hotaluna* ホタルナ (3-4/day; 20-60 mins; ¥780-1560) is a similar design but has the advantage of a roof deck so you can go outside. It also runs in a loop but calls at Hinode Pier and Odaiba Marine/Seaside Park before returning to Asakusa Azumabashi.

The **Odaiba Line** operates between Hinode Pier and Odaiba Marine/Seaside Park (¥480; approx 8/day; 20 mins). The **Tokyo Big Sight Palette Town Line** operates from Hinode to Palette Town and Tokyo Big Sight (1/hr; 10-25 mins; ¥210-410).

● **Tokyo Mizube Cruising Line** 東京水辺ライン (🖳 www.tokyo-park.or.jp/water bus; Tue-Sun 2-9/day; ¥310-2160) operates four routes: **Asakusa-Odaiba Cruise** (round trip between Ryogoku and Odaiba Marine/Seaside Park via Asakusa Nitenmon and Hama-Rikyu); **Sumida River Kasai** (Kasai Rinkai Park via Asakusa Nitenmon, Hama-Rikyu and Odaiba); **Sumida River Asakusa** (Kasai Rinkai Park via Asakusa Nitenmon and Odaiba); and **Sea Park Course** (20-60 mins between Kasai Rinkai Park and Odaiba Marine/Seaside Park).

life-size replicas of buildings. The museum focuses on the politics, culture and lifestyle of people in Tokyo over the years; you can learn that in crowded areas newspaper sellers used to sing about the contents of the paper in order to attract sales and farmers came into the city in the morning with *koe-oke* (a set of pails) to collect the human excrement and use it as manure. The ticket booth is on the plaza underneath the museum. A visit here is highly recommended.

To be able to see and go in actual buildings from the Edo, Meiji and Showa eras go to the Edo-Tokyo Open-Air Architectural Museum (see p124).

**Tokyo Skytree** 東京スカイツリー   Opened in 2012, Tokyo Skytree (🖥 www.tokyo-skytree.jp; daily 8am-10pm subject to the weather; Tembo Deck ¥2060, children ¥620-1540; Tembo Galleria additional ¥1030, children ¥310-770), a digital TV broadcasting tower, is the tallest structure (634m/2080ft) in Japan and the tallest broadcast tower in the world. Its construction, though, was influenced by traditional techniques (see box p124). The quality of the view you get will depend on the weather, but also on what time you come; at sunset on a cloudy day you can get almost mystical views with the sun shining through the clouds onto the concrete jungle below you, but you risk not seeing anything clearly. If you are hoping to see Mt Fuji it is best to go in the morning.

The ticket office is on the 4th floor but, because of the crowds, a Fast Skytree Ticket for International Visitors (adults ¥2820, children ¥1240-2260) has been introduced; this enables foreigners to avoid having to queue, which is a huge asset, but does cost more. The ticket is available at a dedicated counter (on the 4th floor), inside the West Hall, on production of a passport or other ID; Japanese people can also go in if accompanying an eligible foreigner.

At the **Tembo Deck** (350m; Floor 350) there are displays showing what to look for and an extremely good view but if you have come this high you may as well go as high as you can so get a ticket for the **Tembo Galleria** (450m), only available at the Tembo Deck. Another lift/elevator takes you to Floor 445 where a 110-metre spiral, sloped 'air walk' takes you to **Sorakara Point** ソラカラポイント the highest spot (451.2m); a photo with this behind you will be proof you went up the tower. There is a separate lift back down to Tembo Deck but this lift goes to a different floor, Floor 340, where you have the option of looking down through a glass floor to the ground and human 'insects' below you.

Back down at street level **Solamachi** 東京ソラマチ (🖥 www.tokyo-sola machi.jp), a complex with over 300 shops and restaurants, should provide anything you fancy. However, to eat with a view head to Solamachi Dining on the 30th and 31st floors, but expect long queues. Before leaving the area walk east along the river on the south side of the tower to **Jikken Bridge** 十間橋 (Jikkenbashi) from where you can get a mirror image photo of the tower.

From Asakusa either take the overground Tobu Isesaki Line to Tokyo Skytree station, or the Toei Asakusa subway line to Oshiage (Skytree) 押上 (スカイツリー) on the B3F (Basement 3rd floor) of the Tower complex. Alternatively, if you have a JR rail pass take the JR Sobu Line from Akihabara to Kinshicho 錦糸町 (one stop beyond Ryogoku) and then find the North Exit.

*(Continued on p124)*

TOKYO

To Mito and Kairaku-en
To Narita Airport
Minami-Senju
JR Joban Line
Keisei Line
Mikawashima
Tohoku Shinkansen
Nippori
UENO
YANESEN
7
6
Nishi-Nippori
To Sendai, Morioka and the north
Tabata
Yamanote Line
Chiyoda Line
Sendagi
Uguisudani
Ueno Park
8
9
Ueno
10
Keisei-Ueno
Shinobazu Pond
11
12
Okachimachi
KAPPABASHI
Kappabashi Dougu-St
13
SEE 'ASAKUSA' MAP
14
15 16
Asakusabashi
Bakurocho
Shin-Nihonbashi
NIHONBASHI
Tokyo Station
Ryogoku
Ryogoku Waterbus Station (TMC)
To Tokyo Skytree and Nikko
To Tokyo Skytree
To Kinshicho (for Tokyo Skytree)
HONGO
29
Kanda
Akihabara
17
Ochanomizu
Ochanomizu
Otemachi
Kudanshita
Suidobashi
28
27
Kita-no-Maru Park
30
31
32
26
25
Iidabashi
JR Sobu Line
Ichigaya
33
34
35
36
Komagome
5
Sugamo
4
Otsuka
Toei/Toden (tram) Arakawa Line
Marunouchi Line
Yurakucho Line
Tozai Line
Toei Shinjuku Line
Waseda
Waseda
Takadanobaba
Toei/Toden (tram) Arakawa Line
Ikebukuro
Seibu Ikebukuro
3
To Kawagoe
Tobu Tojo Line
Shiinamachi
Yamanote Line
Mejiro
2
Shin-Okubo
SHINJUKU
Golden-gai
18
KABUKICHO
19
Sakura-don
24
TIMES SQUARE
Shinjuku
Yasukuni-dori
Marunouchi Line
Yotsuya
Yotsuya
Shinano-machi
Toei Oedo Line
Sendagaya
Yoyogi
Yoyogi
20
21
22
23
Okubo
To Suginami Animation Museum, Ghibli Museum and Edo-Tokyo Open-Air Architectural Museum
Higashi-Nakano
Marunouchi Line
JR Chuo Line
Odakyu Line
Yotsuya
1
To Minowa Bashi
Trailblazer

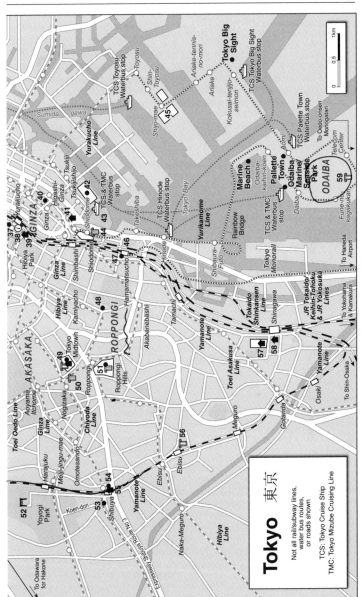

# Tokyo 東京

Not all rail/subway lines,
water bus routes,
or roads shown

TCS: Tokyo Cruise Ship
TMC: Tokyo Mizube Cruising Line

T O K Y O

> ❏ **Earthquake-proof design from the 7th century**
> Tokyo Skytree is definitely a 21st-century structure but its design is heavily influenced by traditional Japanese architecture. The tower shares an unlikely affinity with the construction of Horyu-ji's five-storey pagoda (see pp270-1), which was built in the 7th century. Both have a central column, but the main feature is that this is not attached to the frame of the building. It is believed that if both parts can move independently it protects the structure as a whole. No pagoda has been destroyed as a result of an earthquake, though plenty have by fire.
>
> Tokyo Skytree's ability to withstand an earthquake was tested far sooner than anyone might have imagined. The tower reached its full height a week after the Great East Japan Earthquake in March 2011 but tests showed it had suffered no damage.

*(Continued from p121)* It is a pleasant 10- to 15-minute walk along the road opposite the station exit; you'll see the Skytree in the distance.

**Higashi-Mukojima** 東向島 **Tobu Museum of Transport and Culture** 東武博物館 (🖳 www.tobu.co.jp/museum; Tue-Sun 10am-4.30pm; ¥200; English leaflet available) is compact but interesting. Among its rolling stock are two Manchester-built Beyer-Peacock locomotives (one in the museum and one across the road) dating from the end of the 19th century. The company's type 5700 limited express car 5701 for service to Nikko is resplendent in a beautiful maroon livery. There are also bus and train simulators and model train layouts.

To get here take the Tobu Isesaki Line from Asakusa (¥140).

**Musashi-Koganei** 武蔵小金井 **Edo-Tokyo Open-Air Architectural Museum** 江戸東京たてもの園 (🖳 www.tatemonoen.jp; Tue-Sun Apr-Sep 9.30am-5.30pm, Oct-Mar to 4.30pm; ¥400, free with GP), a branch of the Edo-Tokyo Museum, was set up as a place to relocate and preserve Japanese- and Western-style houses, especially as so many have been destroyed by fire. Some houses, particularly the Western ones, come complete with furnishings; also fun to go in are an old public bath-house, a soy sauce shop and a bar.

Take the JR Chuo Line from Shinjuku to Musashi-Koganei (approx 9/hr; 25 mins; ¥310). Go to the North Exit, then cross the road to bus stand No 2 or 3 and take a Seibu bus (Nos 12, 13, 14, 15 or 21; 5-10 mins; ¥180) to Koganei-koen Nishiguchi 小金井公園西口. Enter the park and walk straight ahead till you reach the fourth turning to the left (after passing some flower beds); turn left and the museum will be in front of you. Alternatively walk diagonally to the left across the grass after the third turning.

### PRACTICAL INFORMATION
#### Station guide
Tokyo station may not officially be as busy as Shinjuku station, but it is just as complicated to navigate.

There are two main sides – Marunouchi on the west and Yaesu on the east – and each has a North, a Central, a South and a Nihombashi ticket gate.

The shinkansen platforms are on the Yaesu side of the station. If arriving by shinkansen you will need to go through the ticket gate for shinkansen lines and then the gates for the normal services before reaching the station concourse. The JR Yokosuka/Sobu Line for Narita Express services is on B5F (the 5th floor of the basement) on the Marunouchi side of the station.

Once here one of the first things you should do is get a map of the station from one of **information counters** on the Central Passage (1st/ground floor).

Alternatively go to JR East's **Travel Service Center** (daily 7.30am-8.30pm) by the Marunouchi North Entrance/Exit. Services here include rail-pass exchange, currency exchange, an ATM and tourist information about Tokyo itself as well as other places in Japan.

There are **shops and restaurants** everywhere, both inside and outside the ticket barriers, but for a huge choice of ekiben go to Nippon no Ekiben ニッポンの駅弁 in Gransta Dining inside the ticket gates. Tokyo Station Hotel (see p130) is by Marunouchi South Gate.

If you need to **store luggage** go to the 'Suica coin-locker search machine' to the side of the Information Centre in the central passage as this enables you to check the location and usage status of coin lockers in the station.

## TOKYO MAP KEY (see map pp122-3)

**Where to stay**
1 Family Inn Saiko
2 Hotel Mets Mejiro
3 Hotel Metropolitan Tokyo Ikebukuro
5 Hotel Mets Komagome
6 Amex Katsutaro Ryokan
7 Hotel Sunny
20 Nishitetsu Inn Shinjuku
21 Hyatt Regency Tokyo
23 Park Hyatt Tokyo
25 Tokyo Central Youth Hostel
34 The Tokyo Station Hotel
35 Hotel Metropolitan Tokyo Marunouchi
39 The Peninsula Tokyo
41 Mitsui Garden Hotel Ginza Premier
49 Ritz Carlton Tokyo
55 Hotel Mets Shibuya
57 Keikyu EX Inn Shinagawa-ekimae
58 Shinagawa Prince Hotel

**What to see and do**
4 Rikugien
8 Tokyo National Museum

**What to see and do** *(cont'd)*
9 National Museum of Western Art
10 Ueno Zoo
11 Shitamachi Museum
12 Ameyoko Market
13 Kappabashi Dougu St
14 Senso-ji
15 Sumo Stadium & Museum
16 Edo-Tokyo Museum
17 Tokyo Anime Center
18 Samurai Museum
19 Robot Restaurant
22 Tokyo Metropolitan Government Building
24 Shinjuku Gyoen
26 Yasukuni Shrine
27 Nippon Budokan
28 National Museum of Modern Art Tokyo
29 Kanda Shrine
30 Imperial Palace East Gardens
31 Imperial Palace
32 Niju-bashi
33 Marunouchi Building
36 Kitte (JP Tower)
40 Kabuki-za
42 Tsukiji Market
43 Hama-Rikyu
44 Advertising Museum Tokyo (Caretta Shiodome)
45 New Tsukiji Market
46 Kyu Shiba-Rikyu
47 World Trade Center Building
48 Tokyo Tower
49 Midtown Tower
50 National Art Center
51 Mori Tower
52 Meiji Jingu
56 Museum of Yebisu Beer
59 Miraikan

**Other**
22 Tokyo Tourist Information Center
36 Central Post Office
37 Tokyo International Forum
38 JNTO Tourist Information Center
53 Shibuya 109
54 Hikarie

TOKYO

**Tourist information**
**JNTO Tourist Information Center** JNTOツ
ーリスト・インフォメーション・センタ
ー (TIC; 🖳 www.jnto.go.jp; daily 9am-5pm

except 1st Jan) is on the 1st/ground floor of
Shin-Tokyo Building, on Marunouchi Naka-
dori facing towards the Imperial Palace. It is
a 5-minute walk from Yurakucho Station

❏ **ARRIVING IN JAPAN**

Tokyo's two main airports are **Narita**, which is 66km south-east of Tokyo and
**Haneda**, which is 19km south of Tokyo.

**Narita Airport** 成田空港
Narita Airport (Narita-kuko; 🖳 www.narita-airport.jp) is Japan's major international
gateway. It has **three terminals** connected by a free shuttle bus.
    In the Arrivals lobby of each is a **hotel reservation desk** (7.30am-9/9.30pm) and
a **currency exchange counter** (daily 6.30am-11pm) as well as mobile (cell) phone
rental (see pp80-1), car hire, baggage delivery and other standard airport services.
Terminals 1 and 2 have a **tourist information desk** (daily 9am-8pm). See also Where
to stay pp132-3.
    Japan Rail and the private Keisei Railway have ticket desks in the Arrivals lob-
bies of Terminals 1 and 2 but to convert a rail-pass Exchange Order you have to go
to a Travel Service Center (daily 8.15am-7/8pm) when they are open. Outside these
times go to the normal JR ticket office (6.30-8.15am & 7/8-9.45pm). Note that the
offices can be very busy at peak times. If you arrive at Terminal 3 you will need to
take the free shuttle bus, or walk along the access corridor (15 mins), to Terminal 2
to pick up any train.
    If planning to use the subway, buy a Tokyo Subway Ticket (see p129) while here
as foreign tourists get a special deal.

**Getting to and from Narita Airport**  The quickest and most efficient way
between Narita and downtown Tokyo is by train (JR or Keisei).
● **JR**  JR East operates the **Narita Express** (N'EX; 🖳 www.jreast.co.jp/e/nex; see
Table 1, p504), which takes about an hour to downtown Tokyo (inc reserved seat
¥3220 to Tokyo Station, ¥3390 to Shinagawa, Shinjuku or Ikebukuro); this is the best
option for those with a rail pass but if you don't have one and are staying no more
than 14 days consider a **N'EX Tokyo Round trip ticket**. This ticket (¥4000) permits
travel to all N'EX stations as well as on JR lines in the designated Tokyo train area.
It also means a saving of at least ¥2000 on the regular price.
    It's better to go to Shinagawa (see p109 and p161), rather than Tokyo station,
particularly if you are planning to transfer onto the shinkansen west to Kyoto/Shin-
Osaka (for Osaka). At Tokyo station, the N'EX services arrive and depart from platforms deep underground, which means a slog through the station to find the
shinkansen/Yamanote Line platforms which are above ground level. The transfer at
Shinagawa is, by contrast, very easy: it's just a short walk from the N'EX platforms
(13-15) to the shinkansen platforms (21-24), or the Yamanote Line (1-2). The station
itself is less chaotic and you avoid endless escalators.
● **Keisei Railway**  The privately operated Keisei Railway is worth considering if you
don't have a rail pass as this is cheaper and faster than the N'EX. **Keisei's Skyliner**
スカイライナー (🖳 www.keisei.co.jp; 2/hr; ¥2470 inc reserved seat, Skyliner e-ticket
¥2200 for non-Japanese citizens) stops at Nippori station (36 mins; see pp112-13) on
the JR Yamanote Line before terminating at Keisei-Ueno station. The Narita Sky
Access Line costs ¥1240 to Nippori (no services to Ueno) and ¥1520 to Shinagawa.

T O K Y O

(take the International Forum Exit), or a slightly longer walk from Tokyo Station's Marunouchi South Exit. The staff are helpful and clued up about travel all over Japan.

In addition to information there is free wi-fi and a PC. They also offer free cultural experiences such as trying on a kimono, making origami, or writing calligraphy.

The **Keisei Skyliner & Tokyo Subway Ticket** (¥2800/3200/3500 for 1-/2-/3-day one-way, ¥4700/5100/5400 for 1-/2-/3-day round trip) includes travel on the Skyliner and unlimited travel on the Tokyo metro for the validity period of the pass.

The main exit for Keisei-Ueno station is located by Ueno Park (see p114). There are passageways from the station to both the Ginza and Hibiya subway (metro) lines but for JR Ueno station you will need to cross the road.

● **Bus** The **Airport Limousine** (⌨ www.limousinebus.co.jp) bus service connects Narita with major hotels in Tokyo in 80-125 minutes (3-4/hr). Tickets (one-way from ¥3100) are available from the Limousine bus counter in the arrival lobby.

● **Taxi** Don't even consider taking a taxi from Narita to Tokyo unless you want to part with about ¥25,000 before you've even really arrived.

### Haneda Airport 羽田空港

Haneda Airport (Haneda-kuko; ⌨ www.haneda-airport.jp), officially called Tokyo International Airport, also has three terminals but is smaller and closer to downtown Tokyo. If possible, it's preferable to fly into Haneda rather than Narita, particularly if you are transferring to a domestic flight; there is a free shuttle bus to the domestic terminals (1 and 2).

On the Arrivals floor (2nd floor) of the International Passenger Terminal there is a **tourist information centre** (daily 24 hours), a **hotel reservation desk** (5am-1am) and a **currency exchange counter** (8.30am-8pm) as well as the usual airport services. The **JR East Travel Service Center** (daily 11am-6.30pm) is to the right of the entrance to the Tokyo Monorail (see below). Go here to convert your rail pass Exchange Order. Departures are on the 3rd floor and there are shops and restaurants on the 4th and 5th floors. However, most restaurants don't open till 10am. See also Where to stay (p133).

### Getting to and from Haneda Airport

The quickest and most efficient way between Narita and downtown Tokyo is by train (Tokyo Monorail, or Keikyu).

● **Tokyo Monorail** The Tokyo Monorail 東京モノレール (⌨ www.tokyo-monorail .co.jp; approx every 3-5 mins; fastest 14 mins; from ¥490 one-way, ¥483 with IC card; free with Japan Rail Pass) operates between Haneda and Hamamatsucho (see p108) on the JR Yamanote line. The journey offers a bird's eye view of the port area of Tokyo and is an interesting experience in its own right. Services are either local, semi local, or express (the latter just stop at the international and domestic terminals).

● **Keikyu Railway** If going to either Shinagawa (4-6/hr; 11 mins; ¥410) or Yokohama (3-6/hr; 23 mins; ¥450) it would be better to take the private Keikyu line. Express trains provide direct connections to Yokohama but if you take a local train you have to change at Keikyu Kamata.

● **Bus** The **Airport Limousine** (⌨ www.limousinebus.co.jp) bus service connects Haneda with major hotels in Tokyo in 25-45 minutes. Tickets (one-way from ¥930) are available from the Limousine bus counters in all the terminals at Haneda.

● **Taxi** A taxi to downtown Tokyo will cost from ¥5600.

---

### ❏ Tokyo online
In addition to Tokyo TIC's official website (see Tourist information) there are dozens of websites dedicated to life in Tokyo.

A few worth checking out for everything from restaurant to art-gallery reviews as well as ideas of what to see and do are: 🖳 metropolis.co.jp, 🖳 www.sunnypages .jp, 🖳 whereintokyo.com, 🖳 100tokyo.jp/listings, 🖳 tokyocheapo.com.

---

**Tokyo Tourist Information Center**
東京観光情報センター (🖳 www.go tokyo.org; daily 9.30am-6.30pm except year end & New Year holiday) is on the 1st/ground floor of Tokyo Metropolitan Government Building No 1. The staff can provide information on accommodation and almost anything else you want to know but they can't make any reservations.

There are also information centres at: Narita & Haneda airports (see box pp126-7), Keisei-Ueno station (daily 9.30am-6.30pm; opposite the ticket gate) and Asakusa (see p118). In addition there are information desks at 150 locations around Tokyo.

### Getting around
The easiest way to get around is with an **IC (smart) card** (see box p66) because, as long as your card is topped up, you don't need to worry about working out the exact fare. If you don't have an IC card and are in doubt about how much to pay, buy a ticket from a machine for the minimum amount and 'fare adjust' when you arrive at your destination. Fare Adjustment machines are located by the exit barriers at all stations. Insert the ticket and the machine calculates how much extra you have to pay; the machines also give change.

Note that fares quoted in the Tokyo text are likely to be at least a few yen less if paid for with an IC (smart) card such as Pasmo or Suica. This does not apply for day passes though.

You can buy a Suica card at Travel Service Centers, ticket offices and multi-function vending machines. Pasmo cards can be bought at the airports, private line ticket offices or ticket vending machines.
● **Rail services** JR East operates the JR rail services (daily 4.30am-1.30am) in and around Tokyo. For JR rail-pass holders the free and most convenient way of getting around is on the various JR lines. The most useful for places included in this guide are: the **Yamanote line** (see pp104-16), which runs in a loop around the city; and the **Chuo/Sobu Line** which goes across Tokyo from Mitaka to Chiba with stops at Shinjuku, Yoyogi and Akihabara. See also box below.

If you don't have a rail pass but plan several journeys on one day on JR East lines (local & rapid services only) consider buying a Tokyo Metropolitan District Pass, commonly called a **Tokunai Pass** 都区内 パス (🖳 www.jreast.co.jp/e/pass/tokunai _pass.html; ¥750/day). Buy it at a purple ticket machine (click on Discount Ticket), or a JR ticket office; the ticket shows the designated area for which the pass is valid. See also **Tokyo Wide Pass**, p33.
● **Subway** There are 13 **subway** 地下鉄 (chikatetsu) lines: nine run by Tokyo Metro 東京メトロ (🖳 www.tokyometro.jp) and

---

### ❏ Ueno–Tokyo line
Since 2015 a 3.8km link between JR's Ueno and Tokyo stations (called the Ueno–Tokyo Line) means it is possible to stay on a main line train from northern/ north-eastern Tokyo and go straight through to stations such as Shinagawa and Yokohama and further south/south-west. This should ease crowding at both Ueno and Tokyo stations and save time crossing Tokyo (north to south); the only downside is that if you fall asleep you may end up miles from where you planned to get off.

❏ **Tokyo by bike**
Forget the railway, if only for a day, and take to the streets of the capital on two wheels. Both Tokyo Great Cycling Tour Company (🖥 tokyocycling.jp) and Tokyo Bike Tour (🖥 www.biketourtokyo.com) offer tours with English-speaking guides.

four by Toei 都営 (🖥 www.kotsu.metro .tokyo.jp). All operate from 5am to shortly after midnight and fares are based on distance (from ¥170, ¥165 with IC card). Each station is identified by a letter (letters) representing what line(s) it is on and a number for each station eg Asakusa subway station is A18 on Toei's Asakusa line and G19 on Tokyo Metro's Ginza Line.

**Tokyo Subway Ticket** (¥800/ 1200/1500 for 1/2/3 days) is a pass that permits travel on all subway lines. Only foreigners (passports will be checked) can buy these at Narita or Haneda Airport but everyone can buy them at travel agencies other than in the Kanto region. Alternatively, the Toei and Tokyo Metro **'Common One-day Ticket'** (¥1000) offers unlimited use of all Toei and Tokyo Metro lines for one day. A **'Tokyo Tour Ticket'** (Tokyo Furii Kippu; ¥1590) can be used on subway lines operated by both Tokyo Metro and Toei, Toei buses, Tokyo's tram line (see p118) and on JR East trains in the Metropolitan District area. However, many of these tickets are not really worth it unless you plan to travel extensively during the day.

● **Bus services** Toei (🖥 tobus.jp; ¥210/ journey, ¥500/one-day pass) operates most of the bus services in Tokyo; see their website for details of the many routes. The one-day pass can be bought from the bus driver; if you have a Pasmo card it will automatically stop deducting fares above ¥500.

● **Sightseeing bus services** Sky Bus's (🖥 www.skybus.jp) **Sky Hop Bus** is a hop-on-hop-off sightseeing bus (¥2500/3500 for a 1-/2-day pass) operating on three routes in central Tokyo.

The open-top **Sky Bus Tokyo** operates on a variety of fixed non-stop routes (from ¥1600) with multi-language guidance systems; see the website for details of the routes as they vary seasonally.

**Hato Bus** はとバス (🖥 www.hatobus .com/en) offers a variety of **sightseeing bus tours** (from ¥5000; multi-language guide system), as well as some walking tours, in and around Tokyo. Most services depart from their bus terminal at Hamamatsucho (see p108); from the JR station head for the World Trade Center Building (South Exit) and then follow signs for the bus terminal. However, the bus will also pick up/drop off at certain hotels. See their website for further details.

**Tokyo Shitamachi Bus** 東京下町バ ス (🖥 www.kotsu.metro.tokyo.jp/bus/shi tamachi; daily 1-3/hr, approx 9.30am-6.45pm) is a hop-on hop-off bus that provides a convenient way to get around the area it covers. During the week services operate between Ueno, Kappabashi, Asakusa, Azumabashi, Narihira (for Tokyo Skytree), Oshiage and Kinshicho. At the weekend a few services start at Tokyo station's Marunouchi North Exit and call at Nihombashi and Kanda before Ueno. See the website for further information.

A rare treat is the **Panda Bus** パンダ バス (🖥 www.pandabus.net; approx 1/hr between 9.50am and 5pm; free!) which operates on a fixed route around the Asakusa area to Tokyo Skytree and back. Services start at the ROX Building ROX ビ ル. It is a great way to see the area but also you can hop on and off. The buses are easily identified as they look like a panda; the eyes can even wink!

### Festivals and events

Senso-ji (see p118) has one of the busiest festival calendars in Japan. One of its more unusual events is the **Asakusa Samba Carnival** (late Aug/early Sep), which combines the Japanese tradition of carrying *mikoshi* (portable shrines) with the rhythm of samba. Dancers from Brazil join in the street party. Other festivals here include **Setsubun** (Feb 3rd; see p18), and **Kiku Kuyo** (Oct), when the temple area is filled with displays of chrysanthemums. **Sanja Matsuri** happens in the Asakusa area in mid May; this is one of the biggest festivals in Tokyo and it features mikoshi processions.

**Kanda Matsuri** is another of the most famous festivals in Tokyo. It is held annually at, and around, Kanda Shrine (see pp115-16) on the Saturday and Sunday closest to May 15th, but on a larger scale in years ending with odd numbers.

**Sumo tournaments** are held at Ryogoku Kokugikan (Jan, May & Sep; see pp120-1). The Sumida River is the location for Tokyo's biggest **fireworks display** (Hanabi Taikai; 🖳 sumidagawa-hanabi .com); it is held on the last Saturday in July.

For a list of the many other festivals and events happening in Tokyo see 🖳 www .gotokyo.org/eventlist/en/list.

## Where to stay

Accommodation (see also box p117) is available all over Tokyo but this guide focuses on places to stay on the Yamanote Line, in the Asakusa district and at the airports. See also pp67-73.

**On the Yamanote Line** There are hotels in the station area at virtually every stop on the Yamanote Line (see pp104-16). A selection is listed below. Rates quoted are for single or double/twin rooms though most hotels have triple/quad rooms as well, or can add a bed to a room. Unless specified the rates generally include a buffet breakfast.

Anyone with a Japan Rail Pass (but not either of the JR East passes) will receive a 10% discount on the rack rate at JR's hotels (see box p71). This is for the room only; discount rates do not include breakfast.

● **Tokyo Station** JR's *Hotel Metropolitan Tokyo Marunouchi* ホテルメトロポリタ ン東京丸の内 (☎ 03-3211 2233, 🖳 www .hm-marunouchi.jp; from ¥22,000/S, ¥26,000/D or Tw) offers the chance to be as close to the station as possible but also to escape the crowds. Reception is on the 27th floor and the stylish, well-equipped rooms with huge windows are above that. Rail fans should ask for a room overlooking the tracks – you won't want to leave the room. You can even book railway tickets at the reception desk. The hotel is in Sapia Tower and is closest to the Nihombashi Exit.

*The Tokyo Station Hotel* 東京ステー ションホテル (☎ 03-5220 1111, 🖳 www .tokyostationhotel.jp; from ¥36,500/S, ¥42,000/D or Tw) first opened in 1915 and has recently been restored to its original European Classical design (but with modern features). It can't match the views at the Marunouchi, but will offer style, luxury and spacious rooms. There is direct access to the hotel from Marunouchi South Gate Exit/Entrance on the 1st/ground floor.

● **Yurakucho** *The Peninsula Tokyo* ザ・ ペニンシュラ東京 (☎ 03-6270 2888, 🖳 to kyo.peninsula.com; from ¥43,000/S, D or Tw), opposite the Imperial Palace, is an elegant hotel with all the facilities and services you would expect at a hotel of this calibre. Take Exit C4 from JR Yurakucho station.

● **Shimbashi** *Mitsui Garden Hotel Ginza Premier* 三井ガーデンホテル銀座プレミ ア (☎ 03-3543 1131, 🖳 www.gardenho tels.co.jp; from ¥20,700/S, ¥21,800/D), a five-minute walk from the Ginza Exit of JR Shimbashi station, is a boutique-style hotel. It's great for watching the shinkansen tracks from the 16th floor open-plan lobby, with fine views from the stunning floor-to-ceiling windows.

● **Shinagawa** *Keikyu EX Inn Shinagawa-ekimae* 京急EXイン品川駅前 (☎ 03-6743

---

❏ **Metropolitan area accommodation tax**

A special accommodation tax is levied on rooms at hotels and ryokan in the Tokyo metropolitan area charging ¥10,000 or more. The tax is ¥100 for rooms costing ¥10,000-14,999 per night; ¥200 for rooms costing ¥15,000 or more.

3910, 🖳 www.shinagawa.keikyu-exinn.co
.jp; from ¥11,000/S, ¥16,000/D, ¥18,000/
Tw) is opposite the Takanawa Exit in a
building called Shinagawa Goos; reception
is on the 3rd floor and the rooms, which are
a good size, are on the 6th-27th floors.

Also opposite the Takanawa Exit is the
vast *Shinagawa Prince Hotel* 品川プリン
スホテル (☎ 03-3440 1111, 🖳 www.prince
hotels.co.jp/shinagawa; from ¥13,068/S,
¥19,602/D or Tw). The rooms are in four
towers; facilities include swimming pools,
bowling alleys, golf/tennis practice facilities, several restaurants and a cinema.

● **Shibuya** *Hotel Mets Shibuya* ホテルメ
ッツ渋谷 (☎ 03-3409 0011, 🖳 www.hotel
mets.jp/shibuya; from ¥15,500/S, ¥25,000/
D or Tw; concept rooms from ¥17,500/S,
¥27,000/Tw) is a JR hotel with standard
well-equipped rooms as well as four 'concept rooms', including a manga-themed
one, designed by local artists. The concept
rooms provide a unique experience and,
since they are all on the top floor, a good
view as well. From the Yamanote Line follow signs for the New South Gate/Exit or
the Saikyo Line. The walk takes several
minutes but there are moving walkways as
well as escalators.

● **Shinjuku** has several world-class hotels.
One of the best value is *Hyatt Regency
Tokyo* ハイアットリージェンシー東京
(☎ 03-3348 1234, 🖳 tokyo.regency.hyatt
.com; rooms from ¥20,700/S, ¥23,700/D or
Tw), nine minutes on foot from the West
Exit of Shinjuku station. Rooms are spacious and facilities include several restaurants and a top-floor pool and spa.

A sleek alternative is *Park Hyatt
Tokyo* パークハイアット東京 (☎ 03-5322
1234, 🖳 tokyo.park.hyatt.com; from
¥47,250/S, D or Tw, check website for
packages), used as the location for Sofia
Coppola's critically acclaimed film *Lost In
Translation*.

Closest to Nishi-Shinjuku station on
the Marunouchi subway line but in walking
distance of Shinjuku station is *Nishitetsu
Inn Shinjuku* 西鉄イン新宿 (☎ 03-3367
5454, 🖳 www.n-inn.jp/hotels/shinjuku;
from ¥10,100/S, ¥16,300/Tw); it offers
standard, clean rooms.

● **Mejiro** *Hotel Mets Mejiro* ホテルメッ
ツ目白 (☎ 03-5985 0011, 🖳 www.hotel
mets.jp/mejiro; from ¥12,500/S, ¥22,000/D
or Tw), a JR hotel, is a minute's walk from
the station – turn right out of the station and
then first right. The rooms are well
equipped but not particularly large.

● **Ikebukuro** *Hotel Metropolitan Tokyo
Ikebukuro* ホテルメトロポリタン東京池
袋 (☎ 03-3980 1111, 🖳 www.hotelmet
ropolitan.jp; from ¥18,000/S, from
¥21,000/D or Tw) is further from the station
than other JR hotels but still conveniently
located and it has a wide range of rooms
and restaurants. Follow signs for South
Exit/Metropolitan Exit and walk through
Metropolitan Plaza between Tobu and
Lumine department stores. The hotel is
diagonally opposite when you emerge onto
the street.

Highly recommended is *Family Inn
Saiko* ファミリーイン西向 (☎ 03-3972
1315, 🖳 www.familyinn-saiko.com; from
¥6900pp, discounts for more than two sharing a room). All the rooms are Japanese
style with a shower and toilet; there is also
a common bathroom. Facilities include:
free wi-fi; a microwave oven, fridge &
washing machine. The staff are very friendly and staying in this residential area provides a chance to feel part of everyday life
in Japan. Take a local train (not an Express)
one stop on the Seibu Ikebukuro line to
Shiinamachi station (approx 8/hr; 2 mins;
¥150). The Inn is a 10-minute walk away
(see the map on the website). Alternatively
take a taxi from the West Exit of Ikebukuro
station (approx ¥1000).

Renting a **Japan Experience** property
(see p73) in Ikebukuro also provides a
chance to feel as if you're living here.

● **Komagome** *Hotel Mets Komagome* ホ
テルメッツ駒込 (☎ 03-5319 0011; 🖳
www.hotelmets.jp/komagome; from
¥12,500/S, from ¥22,000/D or Tw) is
another JR hotel that offers reliably clean
and comfortable accommodation. Follow
the signs for the South Exit; turn left at the
exit and then left again.

● **Nippori** *Hotel Sunny* ホテルサニー (☎
03-3807 3200, 🖳 www.hotelsunny.co.jp;
from ¥7260/S, ¥12,270/D, ¥13,370/Tw)

TOKYO

backs onto the railway tracks and is on the East Exit side of the station between the North and South exits. It offers reasonable accommodation and has a restaurant/café (7am-11pm).

*Annex Katsutaro Ryokan* アネックス勝太郎旅館 (☎ 03-3828 2500, 🖳 www .katsutaro.com/annex_index; from ¥7500 /S, ¥12,400/D), **Yanaka**, is recommended for its friendly staff, location and facilities; up to four people can share a room. Nearby there are plenty of places to eat as well as Yanaka Ginza (see p113), a traditional shopping street. It is a 7-minute walk from the West Exit of Nippori station, though it is only a 2-minute walk from Sendagi station (Chiyoda subway line). The website gives clear details.

**In Asakusa** (see map p119)  Apart from being a very atmospheric area to stay, Asakusa has places to suit all budgets and is handy for exploring the city. Take the Ginza subway line from Ueno (on the Yamanote line) to Asakusa (the last stop).

*Taito Ryokan* 台東旅館 (☎ 03-3843 2822, 🖳 www.libertyhouse.gr.jp/; ¥3000pp; no meals) has only a few tatami rooms (with common bath) in an old building but is central and a great bargain. The manager is extremely friendly and will help you get the most out of your stay in Tokyo. Guests on their own may be asked to share a room. The closest station is Tawaramachi on the Ginza Line.

*Ryokan Asakusa Shigetsu* 旅館浅草指月 (☎ 03-3843 2345, 🖳 www.shiget su.com; Western singles from ¥8000, Japanese-style rooms from ¥9740/S, ¥16,950/Tw; Japanese/Western breakfast from ¥1050 if booked in advance) is a great place just off the arcade which leads up to Senso-ji. The top-floor public bath has a view of the temple's five-storey pagoda.

At the luxury end of the market, and highly recommended, is *Asakusa View Hotel* 浅草ビューホテル (☎ 03-3847 1111, 🖳 www.viewhotels.co.jp/asakusa; from ¥14,500/S, ¥23,000/D). The easiest way to get here is to take a Tsukuba Express line train from Akihabara to Asakusa station as the station is directly connected to

the hotel. Alternatively it is a 7-minute walk from Tawaramachi station on the Ginza subway line.

For an authentic Edo experience try *Sukeroku no Yado Sadachiyo Ryokan* 助六の宿貞千代旅館 (☎ 03-3842 6431, 🖳 www.sadachiyo.co.jp; from ¥14,100/S, ¥9800pp for two sharing, the rooms can sleep up to six people; breakfast ¥1500, evening meal from ¥7200). This ryokan is everything you imagine a Japanese inn to be. The tatami rooms have attached bathrooms and are decorated with antiques from the Edo period. Look for the rickshaw parked outside. The ryokan is a 5-minute walk from Tsukuba Express's Asakusa station or 10 minutes from Tawaramachi on the Ginza Line.

**On the JR Sobu line** (see map pp122-3) *Tokyo Central Youth Hostel* 東京セントラルユースホステル (☎ 03-3235 1107, 🖳 www.jyh.gr.jp/tcyh; member/non member ¥3450/4050pp; buffet breakfast ¥600) has mostly bunk-bed dorms (4-10 beds). It's on the 18th and 19th floors of Iidabashi Central Plaza, right outside the West Exit of **Iidabashi** station on the JR Sobu line (transfer from Yoyogi or Akihabara on the Yamanote line).

**Narita Airport**  There are only two accommodation options in the actual airport but no shortage of hotels in the vicinity; for details see 🖳 www.narita-air port.jp/en/travel/hotel.

*Narita Airport Rest House* 成田エアポートレストハウス (☎ 0476-32 1212, 🖳 www.apo-resthouse.com; ¥9100/S, from ¥6600pp based on two sharing), a somewhat down-at-heel establishment but staying here is convenient, especially if you arrive late at night or are leaving early. Evening meals are available but you may prefer the wider choice in the airport. A shuttle bus (1-3/hr) operates from bus stand No 16 (Terminal 1) and No 32 (Terminal 2).

The other option is *9Hours* (☎ 0476-33 5109, 🖳 ninehours.co.jp/narita; from ¥4900, day rate ¥1500 first hour then ¥500 per hour; shower ¥1000), a capsule hotel in Terminal 2: the hotel is on the first basement level of Car Park No 2. You can either stay the night or just come here for a short break and/or shower. Men's and women's facilities are separate.

**Haneda Airport** *Royal Park Hotel The Haneda* (☎ 03-6830 1111, 🖳 www.rph-the .co.jp/haneda/; from ¥18,100/S, ¥22,000/D or Tw) is directly connected to Haneda Airport International Terminal. The rooms are a good size and the staff are friendly.

### Where to eat and drink
Tokyo has so many good options – for several years it has had more Michelin-starred restaurants than any other in the world – that it is hard to recommend anywhere in particular.

Useful resources include: Gurunavi (🖳 r.gnavi.co.jp/en/tokyo), as you can search according to location, type of food and whether there is a menu in English; and 🖳 www.menu-tokyo.jp.

Tokyo, Shinjuku and Ikebukuro stations have attached department stores with restaurant floors, which are usually open until 10pm. Ginza, Harajuku and Shibuya are good areas to wander around in search of cafés and restaurants. And if you're staying in Asakusa, there are plenty of small, atmospheric restaurants that serve all kinds of Japanese food. Some of the best and most expensive restaurants are in the top hotels.

### Nightlife
Tokyo is very much a 24-hour city, though there are certain areas which really only come alive after dark. You'll never be far from a bar or club in downtown Roppongi (see box p117), or in Shinjuku's Kabukicho (see pp110-11).

In the summer many hotels and department stores open rooftop **beer gardens** (see p77) which offer two-hour all-you-can-eat-and-drink deals for around ¥3500.

# Around Tokyo

### SIDE TRIPS FROM TOKYO
[See map opposite p524]

The incredible rail network around Tokyo means many places can be reached easily for a day trip. For some private line services are more convenient and for the Hakone region, provide the only option, but overall, with a Japan Rail Pass, or a JR East Pass, particularly the Tokyo Wide Pass, you can make Tokyo your base and maximise use of your pass. Also this saves you taking your luggage everywhere, though staying a night (or more) in some places – particularly Hakone, Kawaguchi-ko and Nikko – is recommended.

### Yokohama 横浜
The port city of Yokohama (see pp162-4) makes for an interesting day trip. The JR Tokaido Line, from either Tokyo or Shinagawa station (31/18 mins), provides the quickest service but the JR Keihin-Tohoku Line also goes to Yokohama. From either Shinjuku or Shibuya (34/29 mins) take the JR Shonan-Shinjuku Line. There are frequent services whichever line you take.

### Kamakura 鎌倉  √
[See map p135]

Kamakura, a small town by the sea one hour south of Tokyo, is packed with temples and shrines and makes for a relaxed escape for a day or longer.

Kamakura became the seat of feudal government in the 12th century after the struggle for power between the rival Taira and Minamoto clans was won by Yoritomo Minamoto (see p55).

To reach Kamakura by JR take the JR Yokosuka Line from Tokyo or Shinagawa (4-5/hr; 60/53 mins); some temples are best accessed from Kita-Kamakura which is the stop before Kamakura station. Even if you are not a particular rail fan it is worth changing to the Shonan Monorail at Ofuna (see below). Alternatively, if you are based in Shinjuku and don't have a rail pass consider getting an Enoshima-Kamakura Freepass (see p138).

### An alternative rail experience

An interesting way to make a round trip to Kamakura involves getting off the Yokosuka Line at **Ofuna** 大船 (look for the Kannon statue on the right as you enter the station if coming from Tokyo) and transferring to the 6.6km long Shonan Monorail.

**Shonan Monorail** 湘南モノレール (6/hr; 15 mins; ¥310) is unusual in that the track is 10-15 metres above ground level and the carriages are suspended below it so you get a wonderful bird's eye view of life below you. The line ends at Shonan-Enoshima 湘南江の島; turn right at the bottom of the steps down from the platform and then left out of the station. Walk straight down until you see Enoshima 江ノ島 station on your left. Cross the tracks and buy your ticket and then if going towards Kamakura go back to the platform on the other side of the tracks.

**Enoshima Dentetsu** 江ノ島電鉄 (🖳 www.enoden.co.jp), generally called the **Enoden**, is a single-track railway which runs between Fujisawa and Kamakura (about 10km). The line opened in 1910 and there are both old-fashioned and modern train-sets so it is pot luck what you get; even so the journey is a pleasant one along the coast – at times the track passes so close to houses it almost feels intrusive. If planning to visit the Daibutsu (see p136) it is best to get off at Hase 長谷 (Enoshima to Hase: 5/hr; 20 mins; ¥250), from where it is a 10-minute walk, otherwise stay on till Kamakura (25 mins from Enoshima). Enoden Kamakura station is adjacent to JR Kamakura station.

**Engaku-ji** 円覚寺 (🖳 www.engakuji.or.jp; daily 8am-5pm, Nov-Mar to 4pm; ¥300) is a quiet Zen temple with a 700-year history, set on the wooded hills above Kamakura. The original buildings were either burnt down or destroyed in an earthquake but they have all been replaced. Zen courses are held here in the summer months and are open to the public. Turn right out of Kita-Kamakura station and walk along till you see some steps leading up to the temple.

**Tokei-ji** 東慶寺 (🖳 www.tokeiji.com; daily Mar-Oct 8.30am-5pm, Nov-Feb to 4pm; ¥200) is set in the hillside, up several flights of steps, on the other side of the station. The temple, founded in 1285, was where any Japanese woman wanting a divorce could seek refuge from her husband. It only became legal for women to apply for a divorce in the 1870s so this temple became known as a place where a woman could get a divorce under Temple Law if she lived there for three calendar years. Since 1902 it has been a branch of Engaku-ji. It is a very peaceful place to explore.

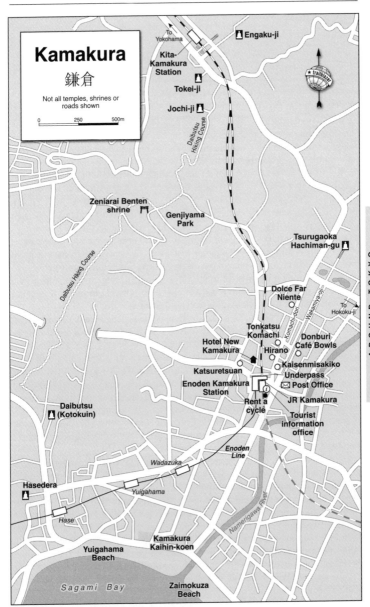

# Kamakura
鎌倉

Not all temples, shrines or roads shown

0 — 250 — 500m

To Yokohama

Engaku-ji

Kita-Kamakura Station

Tokei-ji

Jochi-ji

Daibutsu Hiking Course

Zeniarai Benten shrine

Genjiyama Park

Tsurugaoka Hachiman-gu

Daibutsu Hiking Course

Dolce Far Niente

To Hokoku-ji

Komachi-dori

Wakamiya-ji

Tonkatsu Komachi

Donburi Café Bowls

Hotel New Kamakura

Hirano

Katsuretsuan

Kaisenmisakiko

Underpass

Post Office

Enoden Kamakura Station

Rent a cycle

JR Kamakura

Tourist information office

Daibutsu (Kotokuin)

Enoden Line

Wadazuka

Hasedera

Yuigahama

Hase

Namerigawa River

Kamakura Kaihin-koen

Yuigahama Beach

Zaimokuza Beach

Sagami Bay

The entrance to **Jochi-ji** 浄智寺 (daily 9am-4.30pm; ¥200) is on the right just before the railway line crosses the road. It is one of the five main Zen temples in Kamakura and dates from the 1280s. However, the main reason for walking along here is to join the **Daibutsu Hiking Course** 大仏ハイキングコース (3.5km; 1¼-1¾hrs) as this connects Jochi-ji with the Daibutsu. Follow the road to the left of the entrance to Jochi-ji. Despite this uphill start the walk is mostly downhill. The route is clearly marked but may be a bit muddy after rain.

The big attraction and one of the most popular places in Kamakura is **Zeniarai Benten Shrine** 銭洗弁財天宇賀福神社 (Zeniarai Benten Jinja; daily 8am-5pm; free). At a 'crossroads' on the trail you turn right to stay on the hiking course and cross over to go to this shrine. The entrance is through a tunnel on your right a little way down the hill. In 1185 Yoritomo Minamoto, the first shogun of the Kamakura government, had a dream in which he was told that if he went and found a spring gushing from the rocks in north-west Kamakura, and worshipped the Shinto gods, peace would come. Since he had this dream on the day, month and year of the snake, the shrine is dedicated to the Buddhist goddess associated with snakes. It is now said that any money that has been washed in the spring's water will increase its value (*zeni* means coins and *arai* means wash); nowadays most people wash paper notes rather than coins. If you want to have a go at 'money laundering' put a note in one of the baskets and follow the crowds.

To continue on the official route to the Daibutsu, retrace your steps to the crossroads and then turn left. However, it is also possible to get to Kamakura and the Daibutsu by continuing on downhill from the shrine.

Although its importance as a national power base faded many centuries ago, Kamakura is known for the **Daibutsu** 大仏 (Great Buddha) in Kotoku-in temple 高徳院 (daily Apr-Oct 8am-5.30pm, Oct-Mar to 5pm; ¥200). The Daibutsu (cast in 1252) is a 13.35m-high bronze statue of the Amida Buddha; it is the second largest in Japan after the one in Nara. Originally it was enclosed but the building was destroyed in 1495 and has never been rebuilt. For an additional ¥20 it is possible to go inside (daily 8am-4.30pm) the Daibutsu. Expect it to be looking very shiny as it was closed for cleaning and maintenance in early 2016. If you haven't walked here along the Daibutsu Hiking course the easiest way to get here is by train: Hase 長谷 station is three stops from Kamakura on the Enoden Line. It is then about a 10-minute walk to the Daibutsu.

A temple was first constructed in 736 on the site where **Hasedera** 長谷寺 (🌐 www.hasedera.jp/en; Mar-Sep 8am-5pm, Oct-Feb 8am-4pm; ¥300) now is. The temple is known for its 9m-high 11-headed Kannon statue (the goddess of mercy) in the main building (Kannon-do hall); the statue was carved from the same camphor tree as the Hasedera temple in Nara and is one of the largest such statues in Japan. The temple is built at the base of the side of a hill and is a wonderful place to explore; the garden is known for its hydrangeas (there are about 2000) but has plenty of interest throughout the year. A viewing spot provides excellent views over Kamakura and **Yuigahama Beach** 由比ヶ浜海岸; which, despite its grey volcanic sand, is a pleasant, unspoilt place where you can see fishing boats and surfers.

The main sight in Kamakura itself is **Tsurugaoka Hachiman-gu** 鶴岡八幡宮 (💻 www.tsurugaoka-hachimangu.jp; daily 6am-8.30pm; free); Yoritomo Minamoto (see p55) moved the shrine to this site in the 12th century and then expanded it. However, the current main shrine building, set back in the hills at the top of 60 steps, dates from 1828. There is a pond on each side of the main entrance and on the right-hand side a garden (open seasonally; ¥500), known for its peonies. At the bottom of the steps on the left-hand side was a 1000-year-old ginkgo tree that was blown down in 2010. Part of it was replanted nearby and it seems to be growing; hopefully it will for at least another 1000 years.

**Wakamiya-oji** 若宮大路, the main street leading to the shrine, was built in 1182 to link Tsurugaoka to Yuigahama Beach. In the middle of the street is **Dankazura** 段葛, a raised pedestrian path lined with cherry trees; it has recently undergone major restoration work including replanting many of the cherry blossom trees so hopefully will look spectacular in coming years.

The major attraction at **Hokoku-ji** 報国寺 (💻 www.houkokuji.or.jp; daily 9am-4pm) is the bamboo grove so it is not surprising that this Zen temple – established here in 1334 – is also called Take-dera (Bamboo Temple). Moso bamboo grove (¥200, ¥500 with a cup of matcha tea) has about 2000 trees which you can walk amongst on set paths (in that sense it is more enjoyable to visit than the better-known bamboo forest behind Tenryu-ji in Arashiyama; see pp263-4); Hokoku-ji is a 15- to 20-minute walk along the main road from Tsurugaoka, keep to the right at the Y-junction. You will pass Sugimotodera on the left and then Hokoku-ji is soon after on the right – or take Keikyu bus No 23, 24 or 36 and get off at the Jomyo-ji bus stop from where it is a 3-minute walk.

A torii gate marks the station end entrance to **Komachi-dori** 小町通り, a street which is lined with shops, restaurants and cafés (see Where to eat).

## PRACTICAL INFORMATION
### Station guide
At JR Kamakura station the East Exit is for Tsurugaoka-Hachimangu and the main part of Kamakura, while the West Exit is for the quieter, more residential part of town, but also is from where you can walk to Zeniarai Benten shrine (600m).

One part of the station is for JR services and the other is for the Enoden line (Enoden Kamakura). There are **lockers** (¥300-600) in and around both stations but the ones inside are not available 24 hours/day.

If you don't have a JR rail pass you can use the underpass on the Enoden side of the station, to get to the west side of Kamakura. If coming from the west side walk through the small park with the clock tower and then turn right.

### Tourist information
The tourist information office (💻 www.kamakura-info.jp; Apr-Sep daily 9am-5.30pm, Oct-Mar to 5pm) is on the right, in Ekist shopping centre, on the East Exit side of the station.

### Getting around
Both Kamakura and Kita-Kamakura are easy to walk around though quite far apart, so it is best to take the **train** between them.

Alternatively, and particularly for the Daibutsu if you don't want a long walk, take a **bus** from the East side of Kamakura station. Buses for Hasedera and the Daibutsu go from stand Nos 1 and 6 (bus Nos 1, 2 & 4); from stand No 4 for Hachimangu (bus No 20) and Hokoku-ji. Pasmo and Suica cards are accepted as well as cash.

If you expect to travel a lot in the area it may be worth getting a **Kamakura Enoshima Pass** (¥700/day), which allows unlimited travel on the Shonan Monorail, the Enoden Line (see p134) and JR services in the defined area, or the **Enoshima-Kamakura Freepass** (💻 www.odakyu.jp; ¥1430) which includes a round-trip journey on the Odakyu Line from Shinjuku as well as unlimited use of Enoden trains and the Odakyu line between Fujisawa and Enoshima.

Another option is to **cycle**: Rent a Cycle レンタサイクル (daily 8.30am-5pm; from ¥600/1hr, ¥1600/day) is up the stairs on the right-hand side of the East Exit of the JR station.

### Festivals
Tsurugaoka Hachimangu shrine hosts the **Kamakura Matsuri** in mid April, and in mid September the **Yabusame** festival features archers on horseback, dressed in 12th-century hunting costumes.

### Where to stay and eat
*Hotel New Kamakura* ホテルニューカマクラ (☎ 0467-22 2230, 💻 www.newkamakura.com; ¥4200-10,000/S, ¥6000-16,000/D) has both Japanese- and Western-style rooms; some are en suite but most of the rooms in the original wing, dating from the 1920s, share facilities. Wi-fi is only available in the main building. Turn right out of the West Exit, look for a post box, behind which a small road leads to the road parallel to the railway; walk along for about a minute till you see the sign for the hotel on your left. The rate includes a ¥500 voucher to eat breakfast at one of two local cafés.

On **Komachi-dori** 小町通り there are enough cafés and restaurants to satisfy anyone's taste buds or budget. On the right-hand side near the torii gate is a branch of *Kaisenmisakiko* 海鮮三崎港 (daily 11am-10pm), a kaiten-sushiya which prides itself on using local fish (from ¥110 per dish). A little way down on the left, with a black door, is *Hirano* ひら乃 (daily 11am-8pm; from ¥700) which claims to be the smallest ramen joint in Japan; the owner has served ramen here for over 40 years. Look for the yellow ラメン sign outside the shop.

Further down on the left-hand side look out for *Tonkatsu Komachi* 豚カツ小町 (Wed-Mon 11.30am-7.30pm), serving tonkatsu from ¥1580 and a lunch menu from ¥1000. *Dolce Far Niente* ドルチェファ ールニエンテ (Tue-Sun 11am-9pm) serves pasta and Italian desserts; they also have a set lunch (¥1380) available till 5pm and a happy hour (3-5pm).

An interesting and recommended alternative is *Donburi Café Bowls* どんぶりカ フェBowls (💻 bowls-cafe.jp; daily 11am-10pm, lunch 11am-3pm; from ¥600) on Wakamiya-oji. It is on the right, after Yukinoshita Catholic church, as you walk to Hachiman-gu from the station. Here you get a bowl of rice – you can have either small, medium or large size – and then you choose what you want on top from a huge range of fish, meat and vegetable options. If, when you finish, you see some Japanese characters at the bottom of your bowl you will get a discount! Wi-fi is also available.

On the west side of Kamakura station is *Katsuretsuan* 勝烈庵 (💻 katsuretsuan.co.jp; 11am-8pm) which, despite being in New Building, is a very characterful, somewhat old-fashioned-looking place and the tonkatsu here (from ¥1000) is delicious.

## Kawaguchi-ko 河口湖
Kawaguchi-ko is the second largest of the Fuji Five Lakes (Fuji-goko; 富士五湖) and because it is the most easily accessible from Tokyo and offers majestic views of Mt Fuji it is not surprising that it has developed into a popular resort; Kawaguchi-ko's inclusion in the Cultural Site listing of Fuji-san as a World Heritage site (in 2013) has also helped make the area popular.

● **Getting there** Kawaguchi-ko can be reached in two hours from Shinjuku so could be visited as a day trip but staying the night is recommended. From Shinjuku (see p110) take a Super Azusa (2/day), Azusa (4/day), or Kaiji (12/day) to Otsuki (67 mins; ¥1320 plus ¥930 seat reservation) where you need to change to the Fujikyu Railway (🖳 e.fujikyu-railway.jp).

Fujikyu Railway offers a **Fujisan Express Free Ticket** (¥2250) which permits unlimited travel on the Fujikyuko Line for two days and includes non-reserved seats in the LEX trains; this is therefore only worth getting if you expect to stop at stations en route to Kawaguchi-ko, particularly Shimoyoshida for Chureito Pagoda as the LEX doesn't stop there. (Note that if you have a Tokyo Wide Pass travel on the Fujikyuko Line is included.) The Fujisan LEX (5/day; 45 mins; ¥1440) is more comfortable but the local service (1-2/hr; 57 mins; ¥1140) only takes a little longer. Don't be surprised if a ThomasLand (Thomas the Tank Engine) train turns up as there is a Thomas attraction at Fuji-Q Highland Theme Park (see p140).

Getting to Kawaguchi-ko in the summer months (July-Sep Sat, Sun and public holidays; 1/day each way) is becoming easier as JR East operates a direct rapid service from Shinjuku to Kawaguchiko station with stops at Fujisan and Fujikyu Highland stations amongst others. JR East (🖳 www.jreast.co.jp/e) often offers a seasonal pass at this time; this can be good value if you don't already have a JR pass; see pp32-3 and check their website for details.

● **Otsuki** 大月 From Otsuki it doesn't really matter which side of the train you sit as even though the first views of Fuji-san are on the left they are sometimes on the right; the driver will slow when you get to good sightseeing places.

Otsuki is an access point for the **Yamanashi Prefectural Maglev Exhibition Center** 山梨県立リニア見学センター (🖳 linear-museum.pref .yamanashi.jp; Tue-Sun 9am-5pm; ¥420). The exhibition centre has a shop on the 1st/ground floor as well as the actual Maglev that recorded the fastest train speed in the world. The 2nd floor has exhibits about the development of super-conducting Maglev technology and how it works. Test runs can be seen from the observation room on the 3rd floor – the dates for these are posted on the website when they are announced – and there is a diaroma and a Maglev theatre where you can experience what a journey would be like. A bus (5/day; 15 mins; ¥300) operates from Otsuki station to the centre; it also calls at Tanokura 田野倉 (5 mins), a stop on the FujiKyuko Line (1-2/hr; 6 mins; ¥220); another option is to walk (about 20 mins) from Tanokura.

● **Shimoyoshida** 下吉田 One of the best-known images of Fuji-san is with **Chureito Pagoda** 忠霊塔 on the right-hand side of the iconic mountain. For your chance to have this photo take a train from Otsuki to Shimoyoshida (1-3/hr; 40 mins; ¥960), or from Kawaguchiko (1-3/hr; 13 mins; ¥300).

Turn right out of the station and walk towards the highway (this is obvious when you are there) through rice fields and houses. When you reach the highway turn left (you will see a sign saying Arakurayama Sengen Park 新倉山浅間公園) and then first right under the highway. Walk to the right and you will soon reach Arakura Fuji Sengen shrine 新倉富士浅間神社.

You can either choose to walk up the road to the pagoda or use the steps (approx 400); the whole walk will take 15-30 minutes. The five-storied pagoda is very plain but definitely adds to any photo of Mt Fuji. On your way down when you have gone under the highway make sure you turn second right not first – then follow the small road back to the station.

● **Fujisan** 富士山  The train changes direction here; if the views are good you may like to get off the train here and sit on one of the chairs on the platform until the next train.

● **Fujikyu Highland** 富士急ハイランド  Rollercoaster fans will want to stop at **Fuji-Q Highland** 富士急ハイランド (🖥 www.fujiq.jp; ¥5200/1-day pass) theme park for the chance to have Mt Fuji as a backdrop. Anime fans will be keen to visit the Evangelion:World pavilion, outside which is an actual-size EVA Unit 01 and in which there are exhibits from the world of Neon Genesis Evangelion.

● **Kawaguchiko** 河口湖  **Fuji-Kawaguchiko Tourist Information Centre** (daily 8.30am-5.30pm, to 6pm at peak periods; 🖥 www.fujisan.ne.jp) is to the right as you leave the station.

The retro **Kawaguchiko Sightseeing bus** (🖥 transportation.fujikyu.co.jp; Red Line 3/hr; fares from ¥150-480 depending on stop, ¥1030/1200 1-/2-day pass) operates from outside the station round part of the lake. Stops include various museums (art, herb, music forest), but of most interest if the weather is good are stops No 11 and 14. Stop No 11 is for **Mt Kachi Kachi Ropeway** カチカチ山ロープウェイ (🖥 www.kachikachiyama-ropeway.com; daily Mar-Nov 9am-5pm, Dec-Feb 9.30am-4.40pm; ¥700) which goes up to an observation point near the summit of Mt Tenjo; it is said that if you ring the bell up here whilst looking at Mt Fuji your wish will come true. Stop No 14 is for the **viewpoint of Sakasa-Fuji** where hopefully you can see Mt Fuji reflected in the lake. However, if you can stay the night here you will have much more time to do that. There are plenty of hotels all round the lake but it is only on the northern side that you can see both the lake and Mt Fuji at the same time.

Every room at ***Koraku Onyado Fujiginkei*** 湖楽おんやど富士吟景 (☎ 055-72 0010, 🖥 www.fujiginkei.jp; Japanese-style rooms with beds; from ¥14,000pp inc half board, higher at weekends/holiday periods) looks over the lake and there are wonderful *rotemburo* baths (single sex) on the roof. The whole point about staying in this kind of place is to spend your time in the bath on the roof looking at Mt Fuji so don't be surprised to find it crowded, even if you get up as early as 5am. The food here is absolutely delicious and if you are lucky you will be seated at a table by the window. If booked in advance the hotel staff will pick you up at the station.

Other hotels on this side of the lake include ***Kozantei Ubuya*** 湖山亭うぶや (☎ 055-72 1145, 🖥 www.ubuya.co.jp; from ¥29,000pp inc half board) and ***Kukuna*** 風のテラスくくな (Fujikawaguchiko Resort; ☎ 055-83 3333, 🖥 kukuna.jp; from ¥24,000pp inc half board). Both have onsen and rotemburo as well as rooms with views of the lake.

A budget option is **K's House Mt Fuji** ケイズハウスMt富士 (☎ 0555-83 5556, 🖳 www.kshouse.jp/fuji-e; dorm beds from ¥2500, Japanese room from ¥3600pp); it is a 13-minute walk from the station but if booked guests can be picked up from the station. The staff are friendly and the facilities clean.

See box pp170-1 for details about climbing Fuji-san.

## Hakone 箱根

It's just about possible to visit Hakone (see pp165-8) in a day if you make an early start, but an overnight stay would be far better. The private Odakyu Railway (🖳 www.odakyu.jp) runs services to Odawara (JR passes are not valid; approx 4/hr; 77 mins; ¥1190) from Shinjuku station (connected to JR Shinjuku); at Odawara change to the Hakone Tozan Railway for Hakone-Yumoto (see pp165-6). For an ¥890 supplement each way you can take the more luxurious Romance Car LEX, which runs direct to Hakone-Yumoto (2/hr; 88 mins). JR rail-pass holders can save over ¥1000 by taking a Tokaido shinkansen from Tokyo west to Odawara (see p164).

Rail tickets, accommodation and package tours of the region can be booked at the **Odakyu Sightseeing Service Center** (daily 8am-6pm) on the 1st/ground floor concourse by the West Exit of Odakyu Shinjuku station. Best value is the **Hakone Freepass** (2-/3-day pass ¥5140/5640), which covers virtually all modes of transport in Hakone as well as return travel by regular Odakyu trains from Shinjuku to Hakone-Yumoto (change train in Odawara). If interested in visiting the Kawaguchi-ko area (see p138) as well, consider getting a **Fuji-Hakone Pass** (3-day pass ¥8000) as this includes travel to/from Shinjuku and around both areas; for further details of both see Odakyu's website.

## Narita 成田

Most people land at Narita Airport and head straight into Tokyo but it is really worth making time to visit **Naritasan Shinsho-ji** 成田山新勝寺 (🖳 www.naritasan.or.jp; daily 7am-6pm; free) in Naritasan Park. It is a Shingon Buddhist temple and its history started in 940 when an image of Fudomyo, one of the most important deities in Japanese Buddhism, carved by a Buddhist monk named Kukai, was enshrined here. The oldest building on the site dates from 1701. The extensive complex includes two pagodas and many halls, as well as lovely grounds with waterfalls and a pond. Allow time to see the Goma (Sacred Fire) ceremony which is staged several times every day in **Daihondo** 大本堂. People's prayers are offered to Fudomyo, with the hope that their problems will be solved; the temple is often called Narita-no-Fudo-sama (the God of Fire at Narita).

Shinsho-ji is a 10- to 15-minute walk down Narita's main street, Omotesando-dori 表参道開運通り, which is lined with a variety of shops, including some making and selling crafts, and restaurants.

Narita is about 11 minutes from the airport and can be reached on either the JR (1-2/hr; ¥240) or the Keisei (1-3/hr; ¥260) lines. From the East Exit of the JR station walk straight ahead and then turn left for Omotesando, from the West Exit of Keisei Narita do the same but turn right. There is a small **tourist information office** 成田市観光案内所 (🖳 www.nrtk.jp; daily 8.30am-5.30pm) at JR Narita station. **Narita Tourist Pavilion** 成田観光館 (Tue-Sun Jun-Sep 10am-6pm, Oct-May 9am-5pm), with exhibits about the local area and how it would have been in the Edo period, is on the left as you go down Omotesando-dori.

For a wonderful Japanese experience stay at *Narita-san Monzen Ryokan Wakamatsu Honten* 成田山門前旅館若松本店 (☎ 0476-22-1136, 🖳 www.wakamatsuhonten.jp; from ¥11,880pp inc half board), a 240-year-old inn which has lovely views over the temple grounds. Every room has wi-fi and the public bath is open 24 hours a day. The food is another reason to stay here – the inn's specialities are garlic miso and grilled eel.

*APA Hotel Keisei-Narita-Ekimae* アパホテル京成成田駅前 (☎ 0476-20 3111, 🖳 www.apahotel.com; from ¥7500/S, ¥14,000/Tw; buffet breakfast ¥1100) is right by Keisei Narita station but on a lower level. Walk down the steps at the East Exit and then turn left. The hotel's free shuttle bus to/from the airport only operates every 90 minutes. The rooms are compact but some have views of the rail tracks; there's also a spa. *Mercure Hotel* メルキュールホテル成田 (☎ 0476-23 7000, 🖳 www.mercurehotelnarita.com; from ¥7000/S, ¥10,000/Tw; breakfast ¥1500) is to the left from the West Exit of Keisei Narita station.

Sushi fans, in particular, should head for one of the two branches of *Edokko Sushi* 江戸ッ子寿司 (11.30am-2.30pm & 5-10pm) in Narita. The sushi is thought to be some of the best in Japan and it would be a great place to eat on your last night – or indeed to celebrate your arrival in Japan. From the JR station, walk past McDonald's and down the hill a few yards to the red Japanese-style bridge. Turn left at the street which runs from the bridge and one branch of Edokko (closed Mon) is about 10 metres along the street on your right. The other branch (closed Wed) is along Omotesando; walk along about 200 metres and Edokko is on the right-hand side.

Eel (unagi) is on the menu at many restaurants in Narita town, as it can be fished from the surrounding rivers and lakes year-round. The Unagi Festival (mid Jul-mid Aug) is possibly the best time to try it.

## Tokyo Disney Resort 東京ディズニーリゾート

Only a short journey by train from Tokyo station, but a world away from the commuter belt which surrounds it, is Tokyo Disney Resort (🖳 www.tokyodisneyresort.co.jp; Mon-Fri 9am-10pm, Sat & Sun 8/8.30am-10pm). The main attraction, **Tokyo Disneyland**, opened in 1983 as an almost exact copy of the original in Anaheim, California, which opened in 1955. **Tokyo DisneySea** (theme: the myths and legends of the sea) followed in 2001, the highlight of which – at least for white-knuckle junkies – is the Tower of Terror ride.

A one-day passport to either park costs ¥6900 (12-17 years ¥6000, 4-11 ¥4500). A two-day passport, which allows entry to both parks, costs ¥12,400 (¥10,800/8000). See the website for details of the many other passport options as well as the hotels here. From Tokyo station take a JR Keiyo Line train to Maihama (3-10/hr; 15 mins; ¥220); follow signs for the South Exit and continue left to the Resort Gateway; a monorail (¥260/journey, ¥650/day pass) from here connects all the major destinations within the resort.

## Kairakuen 偕楽園

Kairakuen (daily mid Feb to end Sep 6am-6pm, Oct to mid Feb 7am-6pm; free) is one of the 'three great landscape gardens in Japan'; the other two being Korakuen in Okayama and Kenrokuen in Kanazawa. It is particularly known for its plum trees (there are 100 different types) but it also has a cedar forest and a bamboo grove so is of interest all year. The garden was created by Nariaki Tokugawa and opened in 1842. He also built **Kobuntei** 好文亭 (daily mid Feb to end Sep 9am-5pm, Oct to mid Feb 9am-4.30pm; ¥200), a three-storey building where he held poetry-writing parties; sadly the building is not the original as, like many in Japan, it was destroyed in WWII. However, the top floor provides views of the garden and Lake Senba, though admittedly it is rather spoilt by the modern buildings now seen in the distance.

From Shinagawa, Tokyo or Ueno take either a Hitachi LEX (1/hr; 66 mins) or Tokiwa LEX (approx 1/hr; 80 mins) to **Mito** 水戸, though if visiting during the plum blossom season (mid Feb to end Mar) **Kairakuen station** 偕楽園駅, which is right by the park, is open. At other times from Mito station follow signs for the North Exit and then take a Ibaraki Kotsu bus from stand 4 for Kairakuen-iriguchi (2-3/hr; about 10 mins; ¥240); at the stop walk back to the road junction and turn right and then follow the signs in the road to Kairakuen to the Omotemon (also called Black Gate) entrance.

If planning to continue travelling in the Tohoku area you can avoid backtracking to Tokyo by taking a JR Joban Line train from Mito to Tomobe 友部 (3-5/hr; 13 mins) and then change to the JR Mito Line for Oyama (1/hr; 63 mins), see p323. *Hotel Mets Mito* ホテルメッツ水戸 (☎ 029-22 3100, 🖳 www.hotel mets.jp/mito; from ¥12,500/S, ¥19,000/D, ¥21,000/Tw inc breakfast) provides convenient accommodation right by the station and was refurbished in 2015.

## Nikko 日光

Some 150km by rail north of Tokyo, the temple and shrine town of Nikko (see pp324-5) is well worth an overnight stay but can be seen in a day if necessary. For JR rail-pass holders the best route to Nikko is by shinkansen to Utsunomiya (see pp323-4). Alternatively, take the private Tobu Railway (🖳 www.tobu.co .jp) direct from Asakusa station to Tobu-Nikko (8/day; 131 mins by rapid train; ¥1360). The Kegon LEX (108 mins; ¥2700 inc seat reservation) is faster but only operates once a day in the morning (7.30am).

If staying the night consider the **Nikko Pass** (¥2670; valid for 2 days) which includes the round trip from Asakusa Station to Shimo-Imaichi and unlimited journeys on the train from there to Tobu-Nikko as well as Tobu buses around town. Alternatively, the **All Nikko Pass** (¥4520; valid for 4 days) includes return travel as well as unlimited travel on Tobu buses in and around Nikko. The passes also give some discounts on attractions and permit the holder to get off at Tokyo Skytree and Tochigi station. Passes can be ordered online at least four days in advance, or bought at Tobu Sightseeing Service Center (daily 7.45am-5pm) at Tobu Asakusa station. These passes are available only to foreign visitors.

AROUND TOKYO

## Kawagoe 川越

To step back in time and discover what life was like in Tokyo more than a century ago, make a side trip by rail to the small town of Kawagoe (see pp322-3). It takes around 55 minutes on a rapid train (JR Saikyo Line; 3-4/hr; ¥760, free with JR pass), from Shinjuku (see pp110-11); Kawagoe is the last stop. Alternatively, if you don't have a Japanese passport, or a JR pass, get a **Kawagoe Discount Pass** (¥700; valid for return trip) at Ikebukuro and travel on a Tobu Tojo Line train (frequent service; approx 30 mins; ¥470 one-way). The pass also entitles you to discounts at some shops in Kawagoe.

## Gala Yuzawa ガーラ湯沢

A fantastic day trip in the winter months is to Gala Yuzawa (see box p352), the only shinkansen station directly connected to a ski resort. You don't even need to have any ski-wear as it can all be rented in the station. If the weather is good it is a beautiful place to go, even if you don't plan to ski/snowboard.

# Osaka 大阪

Tokyo may dazzle with size, Kyoto will awe with history, but the centre of Japan's second largest city-region boasts Japan's funniest dialect, gaudiest shop signs and the culture of *kuidaore*: 'eat till you drop'. Culturally, Osakans are friendly, down to earth, and if the stereotype is to believed, greet each other with *mokarimakka* (are you making money?). From the eccentricity of Dotombori to the breakdancing teens outside JR Namba station, Osaka offers the chance to experience the 'other' side of Japan: a thriving, living cityscape far removed from the museums, temples and shrines of its more historic neighbours.

## WHAT TO SEE AND DO

Osaka may be second to Tokyo, but its metropolitan population is still larger than London, Paris or New York. Fortunately, most of the city's draws are located a stone's throw away from the Osaka Loop Line, listed here in an anti-clockwise direction from the 6 o'clock position. If you're considering shuttling

---

❏ **Osaka Amazing Pass (OAP)**
If you're going to spend even just a short time in Osaka, it's worth investing in the Osaka Amazing Pass (🖳 www.osaka-info.jp/osp; ¥2300/3000 1/2 consecutive days). Use of the pass allows you unlimited travel on the Osaka Municipal Subway, the New Tram (a light rail line in the Osaka Port area) and city buses; the 1-day pass also allows you to use private railway lines (Hankyu, Hanshin, Keihan, Kintetsu and Nankai) within the city limits. Both passes get you free admission to 28 attractions, including Osaka Castle and Tsutenkaku tower, and some marginal discounts to selected attractions. The pass can be purchased from tourist information offices in JR Osaka and Nankai Namba, all Municipal Subway station offices, and some hotels.

- EDSON
- WEDNESDAY

100 W TORRANCE

~ PRAIRIE

3440 TO

SUITE 100

**VINEYARD**
B A N K

round multiple attractions, the Osaka Municipal Subway (see p153) is generally faster, particularly for access to Namba and Osaka Port.

Osaka is also an excellent gateway to the Kansai region and offers the most direct way to Koya-san (see pp156-8); also see box opposite.

## Namba 難波

Osaka's neon, eccentric and delicious entertainment district is **Dotombori** 道頓堀 (also known as Dotonbori; 🖥 www.dotonbori.or.jp), a canal-side restaurant and amusement parade flanked with giant illuminated signs and store figurines, most of which have become famous in their own right. From west to east, look out for: Glico Man, Giant Crab, Grandpa Carl, Mother Octopus, Fugu (blowfish), mechanical drummer Kuidaore Taro, gargantuan angry chef Daruma and the Golden Dragon. Come at night to see neon (and increasingly LED) in all its glory. Head behind the restaurants to find Tombori Riverwalk and the 20-minute **Tombori River Cruise** とんぼりリバークルーズ (🖥 www.ipponmatsu.co.jp/cruise/tombori.html; Mon-Fri 1-9pm; Sat & Sun 11am-9pm; approx 2/hr; ¥900, free with OAP).

Running north from Dotombori at Ebisubashi (Ebisu Bridge) is **Shinsaibashi-suji** 心斎橋筋 (🖥 www.shinsaibashi.or.jp), Osaka's busiest covered shopping arcade. Turn left at the TAG Heuer store and cross Mido-suji at the Apple store to find **America-mura** アメリカ村 (America town; 🖥 www.americamura.jp), a haven of independent clothing stores, dessert counters and late-night bars.

Dotombori and the rest of Namba is best accessed by subway (Namba station: Midosuji, Yotsubashi and Sennichimae lines); take Exit No 4 onto Mido-suji, continue straight, and turn right onto Dotombori. If you arrive by JR into JR Namba, which is not on the Loop Line, ignore the immediate exit for Dotombori and instead follow signs for the Subway Midosuji Line for Exit No 4. On your way, level B1 of OCAT, outside JR Namba, is also the home of Osaka's breakdancing battle scene.

## Shin-Sekai 新世界

Originally built in 1912 as part of Luna Park amusement park, Shin-Sekai (🖥 www.shinsekai.net) preserves the spirit of 1950s and '60s downtown Osaka. Plastered with kitsch retro storefront signs and an atmosphere of never-ending festival, the district is also awash with over 100 **Billiken** statues – 'the God of things as they should be' – a curiously American idol that experienced brief popularity in Japan in the early 20th century and supposedly gives good luck to those who rub its feet. There are branches of *Daruma* (🖥 www.kushikatu-daruma.com) all over Osaka but the branch here, *Daruma Shin Sekai* だるま新世界総本店 (11am-10.30pm; look for the angry chef), is the birthplace of *kushikatsu*, deep-fried breaded food on a stick, and an Osakan speciality.

Shin-Sekai's centrepiece is 100m-high **Tsutenkaku** 通天閣 (🖥 tsutenkaku.co.jp; daily 9am-8.30pm; ¥700, ¥600 with Kansai Thru Pass, free with OAP), a famous (albeit ugly) tower that is a landmark of Osaka. Sadly the view is rather lacklustre and the historical exhibition only in Japanese.

Fans of baths may wish to visit **Spa World** スパーワールド (🖥 www.spa world.co.jp; Mon-Sun 10am-8.45am following day; Mon-Fri 3hrs ¥2400, Sat-Sun 3hrs ¥2700; all day ¥300 extra), a gargantuan complex of themed baths with varying fragrances and temperatures, with an attached family water-slide and pool area. Within the nude bathing areas sexes are segregated into European zones and Asian zones, switching each month. It is possible to stay overnight if caught in Osaka without a hotel. From JR Shin-Imamiya station, take the East Exit and follow the left-hand side of the railway above you. Climb the stairs to Spa World on your left and you will descend on the other side into Shin-Sekai. From Dobutsuen-mae station (Midosuji & Sakisuji lines) take Exit No 1 and turn left immediately underneath the railway. Shin-Sekai itself is safe, but be aware that the area immediately south of Shin-Imamiya station has a bad local reputation and is home to Osaka's transient population as well as its red light district.

## Tennoji 天王寺
Completed in 2014 and flanking the South Exit of Tennoji station, **Abeno Harukas** あべのハルカス (🖥 www.abenoharukas-300.jp; daily 10am-10pm; ¥1500) is, at the time of writing in 2016, the tallest *building* in Japan (although only half as high as Tokyo Skytree, the tallest *structure*). Abeno Harukas is also above Osaka-Abenobashi station from where there are direct trains to Yoshino-yama (see p156). A short distance away in Tennoji Park is **Osaka City Museum of Fine Art** 大阪市立美術館 (also known as Osaka Municipal Museum of Fine Art, 🖥 www.osaka-art-museum.jp; Tue-Sun 9.30am-5pm; ¥300, free with OAP), displaying art from Japan, China and around the world. Fifteen minutes north of Tennoji station, or five minutes from Shitennoji-mae subway station, is the expansive **Shitennoji Temple** 四天王寺 (🖥 www.shitennoji.or.jp; daily Apr-Sep 8.30am-4.30pm, Oct-Mar to 4pm; ¥300 each for Chushingaran, the inner prescient, and Honbo, a garden; free with OAP). It was commissioned in 593 by Prince Shotoku (572-622) and is the oldest state-administered temple in Japan, though the buildings you see now are not the originals.

## Osaka Castle Park 大阪城公園
Each spring, Osakans flock to Osaka Castle Park (Osaka-jo koen) to see the plum-, peach- and cherry-blossom. In the grounds, look out for Tako-ishi (Octopus Stone) by Sakura-mon Masugata (Square); it is the largest single block of stone in the castle – 59 sq metres, 90cm thick and weighing about 130 tonnes. **Osaka Castle** 大阪城天守閣 (🖥 osakacastle.net; daily 9am-5pm; ¥600, free with OAP) is the city's proudest landmark, originally built in 1586 by Hideyoshi Toyotomi but destroyed by fire only a few years later in 1615. It was completely reconstructed in 1629, only for the main tower to be struck by lightning and once again burnt to the ground. A further reconstruction in the 1930s suffered aerial bombardment during WWII. The donjon has been fully restored and is worth climbing (thought there is also a lift/elevator) for the views of Osaka but the displays inside are less impressive. The castle is a short walk from Osakajokoen station on the Osaka Loop Line. Taking the Central Exit, you'll see the castle in front of you in the distance.

**Peace Osaka** ピースおおさか (🖥 peace-osaka.or.jp; Tue-Sun 9am-5pm; ¥200, free with OAP; English audio guide available) chronicles the firebombing of Osaka during WWII and the suffering of everyday Osakans under the Imperial Government of Japan. Particularly recommended if also visiting the Hiroshima Peace Memorial Museum. The nearest station is Morinomiya on the JR Osaka Loop Line and subway (Chuo and Nagahori Tsurumi-ryokuchi) lines; follow the elevated highway west to the museum.

## Umeda 梅田

The northern railway hub at Umeda, which includes **JR Osaka Station**, and both Hankyu's and Hanshin's Umeda stations as well as the subway station, is crammed with department stores and shopping malls, as each railway company has scrambled to develop its terminal building into a destination. Notable malls include **Grand Front Osaka** and **HEP5** with its **ferris wheel** 観覧車 (🖥 www .hepfive.jp/ferriswheel; daily 11am-10.45pm; ¥500, free with OAP), while large stores include **Hankyu, Hankyu Mens** and **Yodobashi Camera**.

To the north lies the architecturally distinctive **Umeda Sky Building** 梅田 スカイビル and its **Floating Garden Observatory** 空中庭園展望台 (🖥 www.kuchu-teien.com; 10am-10pm; ¥700, free with OAP), offering a 173m-high, 39th floor 360° view of northern Osaka. The golden sunset over Osaka Bay is particularly stunning. Take the North Central Exit from JR Osaka station, proceed behind Grand Front Osaka and through a lengthy underground walkway.

Two stops east on the Tanimachi subway line is the **Osaka Museum of Housing and Living** 大阪くらしの今昔館 (🖥 www.konjyakukan.com; daily except Tue & 3rd Mon of month 10am-5pm; ¥600, free with OAP; English audio guide available), offering the chance to see what the city was like in the Edo period (see p56) with a reconstructed streetscape and the opportunity to dress up in a kimono (¥200). Take Exit No 3 of Tenjinbashisuji 6-chome station 天神橋筋六丁 and take the nearby lift/elevator to the 8th floor of the Osaka Municipal Housing Information Center.

One stop south on the Yotsubashi subway line, the **National Museum of Art** 国立国際美術館 (🖥 www.nmao.go.jp; Tue-Sun 10am-5pm, Fri to 7pm; ¥420) is housed in a swish, modern underground facility in Osaka's Nakanoshima district and focuses on Japanese and foreign modern and contemporary art. Take Exit No 2 from Higobashi 肥後橋 station, cross the river, turn left and walk west for about 10 minutes.

**Kitashinchi** 北新地, a nightlife district 10 minutes' walk south of Osaka station, bursts into life after 6pm and is packed with restaurants and bars. LGBT travellers may wish to visit nearby **Doyamacho** 堂山町, five minutes' east of Osaka station, with (mostly small and discreet) gay bars and clubs.

## Universal City Walk ユニバーサルシティウォーク

One of Osaka's biggest draws is **Universal Studios Japan** ユニバーサル・ス タジオ・ジャパン (🖥 www.usj.co.jp; variable opening hours; ¥7200/12,110 1-/2-day pass). Modelled on the original Universal Studios theme park in Florida, visitors are offered a similar mix of attractions. *(Continued on p150)*

O S A K A

# Osaka

大阪

Not all rail/subway
lines or roads shown

0  250  500  750m

JR Katamachi Line

JR Line

Osaka Loop Line

Osaka Loop Line

Osakajokoen

Kyobashi

Osaka Castle Park

Peace Osaka

Morinomiya

O-gawa

Sakuranomiya

Osaka Museum of Housing & Living

Osaka Castle

Osaka Castle

Keihan Line

Osakajo Kitazume

Tenjinbashisuji 6-chome

Temma

Osaka Temmangu

Osaka Temma

Temmabashi

Chuo-dori

Doyamacho

Midosuji Line

To Shin-Osaka station

Higashi-Umeda

Umeda (subway)

Umeda (Hankyu)

Hotel Granvia Osaka

Kitashinchi

Yodo-yabashi

Midosuji-dori

Higobashi

Kitashinchi

National Museum of Art

Osaka Station

Nishi-Umeda

Kitashinchi

Umeda (Hanshin)

Hankyu Line

JR Haruka Airport Express Line

Umeda Sky Building

Shin-Fukushima

Dojima-gawa

Tosabori-gawa

Fukushima

Yodo-gawa

Noda-Hanshin

Ebie

Noda

Osaka Loop Line

JR Takarazuka (Fukuchiyama) Line

To Momofuku Ando Instant Ramen Museum & Takarazuka

To Takarazuka

Hanshin Line

Yodogawa

JR Tozai Line

Sakurajima (Yumesaki) Line

Nishi-Kujo

To Universal City Walk for Universal Studios

OSAKA

To Nara
To Yoshino
Kintetsu Line
JR Yamatoji Line
JR Hanwa Line
To Kansai Airport
Tanimachi Line
Osaka-Abenobashi
To Kansai Airport & Koya-san
Tengachaya
Dobotsuen-mae
Imamiya
Shin
Kizu-gawa
Ashiharabashi
Shinmashigawa
To Osaka Port
Bentencho
Osaka Loop Line
Taisho
Hanshin Umeda Line
Yotsubashi
Shinsaibashi
Mido-suji
Shinsaibashi-suji
America-mura
Dotonbori Hotel
Dotonbori
Namba
Osaka Namba (Kintetsu)
JR Namba
Swissotel Nankai Osaka
Namba (Nankai)
Hotel II Cuore Namba
Toyoko Inn Namba Furitsu Taiikukaikan-nishi
Osaka Human Rights Museum (Liberty Osaka)
Toyoko Inn Namba Nihonbashi
Nankai Line
Tsutenkaku
Shin-Sekai
Spa World
Imamiya
Osaka City/Municipal Museum of Fine Art
Shitennoji Temple
Tennoji
Abeno Harukas
Teradacho
Osaka Loop Line
Momodani
Tsuruhashi
Kintetsu Line
Sennichimae-dori
Nagahori-dori
Tamatsukuri

*(Continued from p147)* Expect long queues, though you can buy a 'Universal Express® Pass booklet from ¥3056 which allows you to avoid the queues for major attractions. The park has a working TV studio, and backstage production tours let visitors see behind the scenes of Japanese drama and variety shows. In 2014, the **Wizarding World of Harry Potter** moved in; it is one of only a few places in the world to serve official 'butterbeer'.

Tickets can be purchased at the park entrance but also in advance at JR ticket offices, Lawson convenience stores, and online. The park is about 250m on foot from Universal City station on the JR Sakurajima (Yumesake) Line, which starts from Nishi-Kujo station on the Osaka Loop Line. The journey from Osaka station takes 15 minutes.

### Osaka Port 大阪湖

**Tempozan** 天保山 is an area with several attractions, all of which are within walking distance of Osakako station on the Chuo subway line (change at Bentencho station from the JR Osaka Loop Line).

Tempozan is officially recognised as Japan's lowest 'mountain' with a summit of 4.53 metres above sea level. Take Exit No 1 or 2 from Osakako station and head towards the Ferris wheel. At 112.5m, **Tempozan Giant Ferris Wheel** 天保山大観覧車 (🖳 www.senyo.co.jp/tempozan; daily 10am-10pm; 15 mins; ¥800, free with OAP) was once the world's tallest ferris wheel but it is still high enough to afford a 360-degree view of the city and, in the distance, Mt Rokko (see p296). Two of its cabins are completely transparent, including the floors and seats (it's pot luck if you get to ride in one of them), and the wheel itself boasts the 'world's first transmission of weather information by 100m-diameter illumination'. You can get a next-day forecast for the Osaka region by looking at the wheel in the evening: red means sunny, green means cloudy and blue heralds rain.

Follow the signs to the hugely popular **Kaiyukan (Osaka Aquarium)** 海遊館 (🖳 www.kaiyukan.com; daily 10am-8pm, last entry 7pm; ¥2300, ¥100 discount with OAP; ¥3200 inc *Santa Maria*, see below), which gets more than 2.5 million visitors a year. Start on the 8th floor and begin your journey down to the ocean depths, encountering sharks, seals, sea lions, dolphins, penguins and many more along the way. A particular highlight is the Pacific Ocean tank, which extends down several floors; the fluorescent floating jellyfish at the end are fabulous too.

Directly behind the aquarium, and accessed via a waterfront walkway, is the berth from which the *Santa Maria* サンタマリア (🖳 suijo-bus.jp; daily 11am-4pm, later in summer; hourly; 45 mins; ¥1600 day cruise, free with OAP) departs on tours of the bay area, weather permitting. It's apparently modelled on the ship on which Columbus journeyed to the Americas, but is twice as large. Reservations are needed for a night cruise (from 7pm; 90 mins; ¥2650).

### Ashiharabashi 芦原橋

**Osaka Human Rights Museum** 大阪人権博物館 (🖳 www.liberty.or.jp; daily except Mon & 4th Fri of month, 10am-5pm; ¥500), also known as **Liberty Osaka**, focuses on people who have faced discrimination in Japan, including the country's Korean population and the Ainu (see box p408). One exhibit focuses on those living with HIV/Aids. The museum is 10 minutes on foot south of Ashiharabashi station.

## PRACTICAL INFORMATION
### Arrival and departure
International flights land at **Kansai International Airport** (KIX; 🖳 www.kansai-airport.or.jp), built on a man-made island in the middle of Osaka Bay. KIX is a more impressive gateway to Japan than Narita – the terminal building (designed by Renzo Piano) was at one time the longest airport terminal in the world. Its efficient Wing Shuttle train (every 3 mins) will take you to the main airport building to collect your luggage and complete the formalities.

Staff at **Kansai TIC** (🖳 www.kansai-japan.net; daily 7am-10pm), in the Arrivals lobby, can advise on travel throughout the Kansai region and sell the Kansai Thru Pass (see box p34) for travel on all non-JR rail, subway and bus lines. There are branches of nine banks so there's always at least one open between 6am and 11pm. There are also **ATMs** in the Arrivals lobby that accept foreign-issued debit/credit cards. For somewhere to eat, check out the north side restaurant area on the 2nd floor.

**Rail-pass exchange orders** can be converted at Kansai Airport station in the JR ticket office (daily 5.30am-11pm). Head upstairs for English-speaking staff who can offer better advice on passes, train times and reservations.

### Getting to and from Kansai Airport
The fastest way of accessing Osaka (and Kyoto) is **by rail**; Kansai Airport station is connected to the terminal building. The blue half of the station is run by JR West, the orange half by Nankai Railway (see

---

❏ **Kansai One Pass**
A new IC card option (see box p66), only available to tourists, is the Kansai One Pass. Holders can use it on most transport options in the area and are entitled to discounts at several tourist attractions. For more details see 🖳 kansaionepass.com.

---

below). JR's Haruka LEX (see Table 2, p505) runs every 30 mins to Kyoto (¥3570) and stops on the way at Tennoji (¥2430) and Shin-Osaka (¥3050), but not at Osaka station. Fares listed are for reserved seats, though these are free with a JR Pass. An 'Airport Rapid' service (slower than the Haruka) operates every 20 minutes to Osakajokoen via Osaka station (71 mins; ¥1190). If you don't have a JR Pass consider the **ICOCA & HARUKA**; this includes travel on the Haruka at a discounted price (from ¥1100) and an IC (smart) card topped up with ¥2000. You can buy one for a single (one-way) trip, or for a round trip valid for 14 days. The cost depends on your final destination.

For a slightly more eccentric rail experience (see box p250), **Nankai** (🖳 www.nankai.co.jp), a private line, operates the 'rapi:t' LEX to Osaka Namba station (2/hr; approx 38 mins; ¥1430; reserved only), near Dotombori. The cheapest service is the Nankai express to Namba (1-5/hr; approx 48 mins; ¥920).

Limousine **bus services** (🖳 www.kate.co.jp) run between the airport and various destinations in the Kansai region, including Osaka, Kyoto and Nara. Bus stops are located outside International Arrivals and tickets can be purchased from vending machines outside the terminal building.

### Station guide
● **Shin-Osaka** 新大阪 station marks the western limit of the Tokaido shinkansen and the start of the Sanyo shinkansen. There are restaurants and **lockers** all over the station as well as a **luggage-storage service** on the 1st/ground floor on the West Gate side. However, there is no longer a tourist information centre here. **Exchange vouchers** can be converted for JR rail passes at the JR West Travel Corner on the 3rd floor by the West Gate. Shin-Osaka is located four minutes north of Osaka station on the JR Kyoto Line. The Haruka LEX goes

O S A K A

from here to Kansai Airport via Tennoji. The Midosuji subway line also provides services to Umeda, Namba and Tennoji (see also Getting around). For details of accommodation options in the area see opposite.

● **Osaka** 大阪 station is on the north side of the city and is JR's hub serving the Osaka Loop Line, JR Kobe, Kyoto and Takarazuka lines and most of the long-distance LEX services.

Osaka station (🖳 osakastationcity .com) is branded a 'city'. Certainly it can provide almost anything you are likely to need – a hotel, restaurants, convenience stores, department stores, ATMs, a cinema, a fitness club, even a wedding hall and a garden – let alone the chance to take a train. The new station has a light, spacious and airy feel but it doesn't have the wow factor of Kyoto station. The railway tracks are between the North Gate Building, which houses LUCUA and LUCUA 1100 department stores (daily 10am-9pm), and the South Gate Building, which has Daimaru (Sun-Thur 10am-8.30pm, Fri-Sat 10am-9pm). The **tourist information centre** (daily 8am-8pm) is on the North Side 2nd floor.

A **luggage-storage service** 荷物一時 預かり所 is available for ¥700 per day for up to three days; this is particularly useful for visiting Koya-san where taking suitcases is a hassle. However, the facility is poorly signposted; go to the Midosuji North Gate 1st/ground floor, enter by LUCUA towards the JR lines Central Gate, then take the first left towards the toilets/restrooms.

The bridge on the 4th floor is a good place to view the trains but even better is **Toki-no-Hiroba Plaza** 時空の広場, an open area with a golden clock that connects both buildings and where you can sit and have a drink at *Bar del Sole Café*. The other main areas for **restaurants** and **cafés** are the 10th floor in LUCUA and the 14th floor in Daimaru department store; both generally open daily 11am-11pm.

Take the escalators on the North Gate side up to **Yawaragi-no-niwa** 和らぎの庭 (Yawaragi Garden; 10th floor) for views of Osaka and the Umeda Sky Building. Follow the signs for the 'light hiking course' (a few flights of steps up to the 14th

floor) to **Tenku-no-noen farm** 天空の農園 (vegetable garden) to see a bit of greenery amongst all the concrete.

Don't leave the station without seeing the mesmerising **Water Clock** 水の時計 by the South Central Exit (street level) on the South Gate Building (Daimaru) side. Being a clock the time is of course shown but also 'Welcome' in various languages as well as pictures and patterns that vary with the season. A sign explains that these are shown 'using "Space Printer" technology that can individually control the lengths of each countless strings of water'. In 2014 the American news channel CNN designated it one of the world's 12 most beautiful clocks.

Osaka station is also located adjacent to five other Umeda (and its variant) stations on the Midosuji, Tanimachi and Yotsubashi subway lines, and the Hankyu and Hanshin private lines. It is also a 10-minute, signposted, underground walk from Kitashinchi station on the JR Tozai Line.

● **Namba** 難波 is the private Nankai line's hub to the south of the city, and the terminus for the rapi:t LEX airport trains, as well as for trains to Koya-san (see pp156-8).

● **Tennoji** 天王寺 is Osaka station's southern counterpart on the Loop Line, offering JR trains to Nara, Wakayama and Kansai Airport. It is also opposite Kintetsu's Osaka-Abenobashi 大阪阿部野橋 station, for trains to Yoshino (see p156).

## Tourist information

In addition to the tourist information centre (🖳 www.osaka-info.jp) at Osaka station (see Station guide), there are also TICs at Hankyu Umeda station (daily 8am-8pm; 1st/ground floor), Nankai Namba station (daily 9am-8pm; 1st/ground floor), and Shinsaibashi station (daily 9am-9pm; Exit No 7). Ask for a copy of the 'Explorer Osaka' map, which includes money-saving coupons for certain tourist sights, shops and restaurants. The Osaka Amazing Pass (see box p144) is also available to buy at the aforementioned TICs.

For general background information about Osaka and the area see 🖳 www.osa ka-info.jp.

For a volunteer guide, see box p251.

## Getting around

The main railway junctions are **Shin-Osaka** 新大阪, the shinkansen station to the north of the city; **Osaka** 大阪, further south in Umeda; and **Tennoji** 天王寺.

The JR Kyoto line and Midosuji Subway Line connect Shin-Osaka and Osaka/Umeda. Osaka and Tennoji stations are both on the **Osaka Loop line**. The Osaka Loop line (orange-colour trains; departures from platforms 1 and 2 at JR Osaka station) is the most scenic means of getting around the city as it is above ground; it is also free with a JR rail pass, but it is slow and a change is required to access either Shin-Osaka or JR Namba.

The **Osaka Municipal (City) Subway** is almost always a quicker way around the city, particularly if going to Shin-Osaka, Namba or Osaka Port. Fares around central Osaka range from ¥180 to ¥280.

An '**Enjoy Eco Card**' エンジョイエコカード one-day pass (¥800 weekdays; ¥600 weekends and public holidays) allows unlimited use of the subway and city buses. However, the best deal is with an Osaka Amazing Pass (see box p144) as it also includes the subway and buses.

## Safety

Amongst the Japanese, Osaka has a reputation as being an unsafe city and the home of the *yakuza*, although most actually reside in neighbouring Kobe. While some parts of Osaka may have high crime levels by Japanese standards, it is still a remarkably safe city compared to the likes of London, Paris and New York. The area immediately south of Shin-Imamiya station is a red-light district and its hotels a base for transient manual workers, but in general in Osaka tourists are highly unlikely to experience any problems.

## Festivals

The biggest event in Osaka's busy festival calendar is **Tenjin Matsuri** 天神祭 (24th-25th July). The highlight is a procession of more than a hundred brightly coloured boats down Dojima-gawa on the evening of the 25th. Performances of traditional dance and music are staged on a boat lit by lanterns and moored in the middle of the river. For details of other festivals and events here see 🖳 www.osaka-info.jp.

## Where to stay

Being the business and industrial capital of Western Japan, there is no shortage of accommodation in Osaka. The area around Shin-Osaka station to the north of the city is utilitarian but the most convenient for most travellers with the shinkansen only a short walk away. Hotels near Namba are ideal for walking home from the bright lights of Dotombori and Shinsaibashi.

● **Shin-Osaka** The reception desk for the very clean *Shin-Osaka Youth Hostel* 新大阪ユースホステル (☎ 06-6370 5427, 🖳 osaka-yha.or.jp; ¥3500/dorm bed; ¥9400/ Tw, Japanese-style room ¥4500pp; dinner ¥1080, breakfast ¥500) is on the 10th floor of **Koko Plaza Building**, a short walk from the East Exit of Shin-Osaka station.

*Hotel Shin-Osaka* ホテル新大阪 (☎ 06-6322 8800, 🖳 www.hso.co.jp; from ¥4200/S, ¥10,300/D, ¥10,600/Tw, inc breakfast; good online rates) is conveniently located by the East Exit of the station. The hotel has a floor with rooms called 'sleeping rooms' as the beds in them are meant to offer a more comfortable and relaxing night than most other beds.

There are several branches of Toyoko Inn (🖳 www.toyoko-inn.com) in the area: *Toyoko Inn Shin-Osaka Chuo-guchi Honkan* 東横イン新大阪中央口本館 (☎ 06-6305 1045; from ¥6480/S, ¥7560/D, ¥8640/Tw, inc breakfast) and *Toyoko Inn Shin-Osaka Chuo-guchi Shinkan* 東横イン新大阪中央口新館 (☎ 06-6303 1045; from ¥6480/S, ¥7560/D, ¥8640/Tw, inc breakfast) are next to each other and are both five minutes on foot from the main exit (1st/ground floor of Shomenguchi) of JR Shin-Osaka station; if these are full try *Toyoko Inn Shin-Osaka-eki Higashi-guchi* 東横イン新大阪駅東口 (☎ 06-6160 1045; from ¥5724/S, ¥7344/D, ¥8424/Tw), an 8-minute walk from the East Exit.

Other options with generous discounts through hotel aggregators such as Expedia include: *Hotel Shin-Osaka Conference*

OSAKA

*Center* ホテル新大阪コンファレンスセンター (☎ 06-6302 5571; 🖳 www.shinosaka-conference.com; from ¥5800/S, ¥8000 /D or Tw), a short walk from the Central Gate (1st/ground floor) – see the website for detailed photos of the route; *Shin-Osaka Washington Plaza* 新大阪ワシントンプラザ (☎ 06-6303 8111, 🖳 washington.jp/shinosaka; from ¥9400/S, ¥9610/D; ¥13,180/Tw), also find your way to the Central Gate (1st/ground floor); turn left and find the pedestrian crossing; cross it and walk along and then through the passageway under the overhead road. Cross another pedestrian crossing, follow the path round to the right and go through another small tunnel. You should then see the hotel ahead of you; it is on the left beyond the pedestrian bridge.

*Osaka Garden Palace* 大阪ガーデンパラス (☎ 06-6396 6211, 🖳 hotelgp-osaka.com; from ¥8000/S, ¥12,300/D, ¥14,800/Tw) has a free shuttle bus from Exit No 2 of Shin-Osaka subway station.

● **Umeda** JR-run *Hotel Granvia Osaka* ホテルグランヴィア大阪 (☎ 06-6344 1235, 🖳 www.granvia-osaka.jp; from ¥20,992/S, ¥23,602/D or Tw inc breakfast), in the South Gate building, is directly accessible from the station – the cheapest rooms (mostly for single use) don't have a good view but all others do. Front (reception) is on the 1st/ground floor; the rooms are on the 20th-27th floors.

● **Namba** Touristy and eccentric with Roman columns incorporating facial caricatures of an Asian, African, Arab and a Westerner, *Dotonbori Hotel* 道頓堀ホテル (☎ 06-213 9040, 🖳 www.dotonbori-h.co.jp; from ¥7700/S, ¥9000/D, ¥11,600 /Tw) is perhaps the most photographed hotel in Osaka. For the usual selection, there are two branches of Toyoko Inn nearby (🖳 www.toyoko-inn.com): *Toyoko Inn Namba Furitsu Taiikukaikan-nishi* 東横イン府立体育会館西 (☎ 06-4397 1045; from ¥7344/S; ¥8424/D; ¥10,044/Tw) and the newer *Toyoko Inn Namba Nihonbashi* 東横インなんば日本橋 (☎ 06-7668 1045; from ¥6804/S; ¥7884/D; ¥8964/Tw) are

both within walking distance of Nankai Namba station.

Going upmarket, *Swissotel Nankai Osaka* スイスホテル南海大阪 (☎ 06-6646 1111, 🖳 www.swissotel.com/hotels/nankai-osaka; from ¥24,225/S, D or Tw), directly above Nankai's **Namba station**, is a haven of luxury. Check the website for details of special packages, some of which include treatments at the hotel's top-end Amrita Spa. *Hotel Il Cuore Namba* ホテルイルクオーレなんば (☎ 06-6647 1900, 🖳 www.ilcuore-namba.com; from ¥9500/S, ¥16,000/D, ¥18,000/Tw; breakfast ¥1000) is also conveniently located for Nankai's Namba station. Its design has a bit more flair than your average business hotel. Some rooms are for women only.

● **Kansai Airport** *Hotel Nikko Kansai Airport* ホテル日航 関西空港 (☎ 0724-55 1111, 🖳 www.nikkokix.com; from ¥8750 /S, ¥15,500/Tw; room-only rates also available) is an upmarket place five minutes' walk from the terminal building. Book online and as far in advance as possible for the cheapest deals.

There are also several 'airport hotels' on the mainland, particularly clustered around Hineno (JR), Rinku Town (JR and Nankai) and Izuminosano (Nankai), see box p249.

### Where to eat and drink

Osaka has a reputation as a gastronomic city but mostly at the cheaper end of the market, not fine dining. Dotombori and Shin-Sekai (see p145 for both) specialise in cheap and delicious Osaka specialities, while the top floors of the Umeda (Osaka Station) department stores offer endless choice, particularly for lunch-time deals.

Specialities of Osaka include *okonomiyaki*, *takoyaki*, *kushikatsu* (see p145), *kitsune-udon* and *kaiten sushi*. It is also the city where instant ramen (see box opposite) was invented.

### Nightlife

The two main centres for nightlife are **Dotombori** (see p145) and **Kitashinchi** (see p147).

## ❏ Pot noodle king

Osaka is the undisputed instant-noodle capital of Japan, if not the world. The city's association with this global phenomenon can be traced back to 1958, when Momofuku Ando (1910-2007) launched Chicken Ramen, the world's first instant noodle dish. Generations of students around the world have Ando to thank for inventing the Cup Noodle in 1971, a mass-market product which remains one of the world's most instantly recognisable supermarket-shelf items. Nissin, the company Ando founded in 1948 now sells in excess of 85 billion instant-noodle products in 70 countries each year.

## SIDE TRIPS BY RAIL FROM OSAKA

Osaka is an excellent base for exploring the Kansai region, with great rail connections but still offering an evening's worth of food and entertainment once the sun sets. If you don't have a pass get a Kansai Thru Pass (see box p34).

### Side trip to Ikeda 池田

In 1999 Momofuku Ando (see box above) opened the **Momofuku Ando Instant Ramen Museum** インスタントラーメン発明記念館 (🖥 www.instantramen-museum.jp; Wed-Mon 9.30am-4pm; free but a charge, approx ¥300, for some attractions and ¥2000 deposit for audio guide) in his home city of Ikeda, near Osaka, where noodle fans can wallow shamelessly in chicken-ramen nostalgia. Take a Hankyu Takarazuka Line train (6/hr; 19 mins by express; ¥270). The museum is a 5-minute walk from Ikeda station.

### Side trip to Takarazuka 宝塚

A visit to see the unique all-female song and dance troupe, **Takarazuka Revue** 宝塚歌劇団 (☎ 07-9785 6770, 🖥 kageki.hankyu.co.jp; seat ¥3500-7500, standing ¥1500), at Takarazuka Grand Theatre 大劇場 (Dai Gekijou), is a spectacular experience. The Grand Theatre is the original theatre but there are also shows now in Tokyo. There are five troupes (gumi): Hana- (Flower), Tsuki- (Moon), Yuki- (Snow), Hoshi- (Star), and Sora- (Sky) and each has a different style. The performance is in Japanese (there is an English explanation in the programme) and has at least one large visual musical and dance number.

You can call to reserve a ticket, but an easier option might be to use a machine in a Lawson convenience store (see box p84). Alternatively, if you don't mind getting up early, go to the theatre itself. There are two to three performances a day and separate queues for each so ensure you are in the correct one for what you want. Shows last about three hours.

If you have a Kansai Thru Pass take a train from Hankyu's Umeda station (6/hr; 34 mins by express; ¥280); from Hankyu's Takarazuka station it is an

SIDE TRIPS FROM OSAKA

## ❏ Hankyu – the ultimate railway company business?

The Hankyu corporation is the textbook embodiment of the Japanese railway conglomerate, building not just the lines but reasons to drum up custom along it: commuter towns, department stores, and even owning the Hanshin Tigers professional baseball team. The Takarazuka Revue (see above) was even founded by Hankyu deliberately at the end of the line in order to sell railway tickets!

easy walk to the theatre. JR pass-holders may prefer to use the JR Takarazuka (Fukuchiyama) Line; take a rapid train from Osaka station (2/hr; 25 mins; ¥330) or, if time is not an issue, a local train. Cross to the Hankyu station and follow the signs from there.

### Side trip to Yoshino 吉野

Yoshino-yama 吉野山, together with Koya-san (see below) and Kumano Nachi Taisha (see p242), are part of the World Heritage site called the Sacred sites and pilgrimage routes in the Kii mountain range. Yoshino-yama is particularly well known for its thousands of cherry trees, which are spread over four areas (Shimo Senbon, Naka Senbon, Kami Senbon and Oku Senbon), and also its ancient Buddhist temples and Shinto shrines.

The private Kintetsu Line runs a direct service to Yoshino from Osaka-Abenobashi (adjacent to Tennoji, see p146; LEX 1-2/hr, 76 mins, ¥1480; express 2/hr, 92 mins, ¥970). Note that the Kansai Thru Pass only covers two-thirds of the distance (as far as Tsubosakayama 壺阪山); to continue to Yoshino a supplement of ¥430 in each direction is payable. By JR from either Namba or Tennoji take the Yamatoji Line to Takada and then the Wakayama Line to Yoshino-guchi (sometimes you can stay on the same train; approx 1/hr; 60 mins). At Yoshino-guchi transfer to the Kintetsu Line for the journey to Yoshino (34 mins; ¥380).

At Yoshino you can either walk up the hillside (this first part, Shimo Senbon, is fairly steep), following the pilgrimage trail to Mt Omine, or take **Yoshino Ropeway** 吉野ロープウェイ (cable car; ¥360 one way, ¥610 return) to Yoshino-yama station. Nara Kotsu operates a shuttle bus in the cherry blossom season (April) from the bus stop at Yoshino station to Naka Senbon-koen bus stop near Chikurin-in temple. Also at this time another shuttle bus operates from Chikurin-in-mae bus stop to Oku Senbon-guchi right at the top of the mountain. However, the views of the cherry trees are less good from up here.

From Yoshino-yama ropeway station it is about 10 minutes' walk to **Kinpusen-ji** 金峯山寺 (daily 8.30am-4.30pm; entry to the hall ¥500), a temple with a 7m-high Buddha statue. This area is called Naka Senbon and it is relatively flat; it is also where most of the sights (including the cherry trees) as well as places to stay and eat are. A half-hour walk brings you to **Chikurin-in** 竹林院 (daily 8am to sunset; ¥300), a temple known for its garden but it also has a *ryokan* (☎ 0746-32 8081, 💻 www.chikurin.co.jp; from ¥12,960pp half board). With its open-air bath this would be a wonderful place to spend the night. From the temple it is possible to walk up to Kami Senbon and the Hanayagura viewpoint but the hillside gets steeper again. To walk from Chikurin-in to **Kinbu Shrine** 金峯神社 (Oku Senbon), at the top of the mountain, would take at least an hour.

### Side trip to Koya-san 高野山

A religious centre was founded on Mt Koya, about 850m above sea level, in 815 by the Buddhist monk Kukai (also known as Kobo Daishi) as a place of meditation. Pilgrims and tourists have been flocking here ever since. In 2004 it was added to the UNESCO World Heritage Site list and 2015 marked its 1200th anniversary. Where once the monks of Koya-san earned an income by begging, today they do so by providing accommodation. Don't miss the opportunity to spend a night in a temple, with a superb (vegetarian) dinner and breakfast of *shojin ryori* and the chance to take part in early-morning prayers. Think of a visit to Koya-san as an experience on two levels, namely the journey there and then the place itself.

**The journey** Koya-san is not located on a JR Line and getting there involves the Nankai railway, a cable car/funicular railway, and a local bus. The final part of the route is quite possibly one of the finest rail journeys in Japan.

The quickest and easiest way to get there is using the Nankai railway from Namba or Shin-Imamiya in southern Osaka (from 80 mins to Gokurakubashi); a single journey each way will cost ¥1260 (train ¥870, cable car ¥390); ¥780 supplement for LEX Koya, seat reservations essential. Day trippers can make big savings with a Kansai Thru Pass (see box p34), reducing the travel cost to around ¥1730 on a 3-day pass. Overnighters (though this can also be used for a day trip) may be better off with the **Koyasan-World Heritage Ticket** (🖳 www.nankaikoya.jp; ¥3400); this includes buses, the LEX Koya on the outbound leg, and 20% discount coupons for a few attractions. Whilst it is possible to use JR lines from Osaka to connect further down the line at Hashimoto, the ¥450 saving is poor value for an additional 90 minutes' journey time.

If you can, try to leave large suitcases with the luggage-storage service in Osaka station (see p152) and bring what you need on your back; the buses atop Koya-san have no space for suitcases and are often crowded.

The best part of the journey starts after **Hashimoto** 橋本: the train rattles and squeaks its way slowly upwards until the track becomes surrounded by thick, pine-clad forests. As the train climbs (and your ears pop), the temperature starts to drop. Here it's about 10° cooler than on the plains below (pleasant in the summer but freezing in the winter so come with warm clothing). Each time the train emerges into daylight after a tunnel the scenery becomes more spectacular. Sit on the right-hand side if you can.

The train terminates at **Gokurakubashi** 極楽橋. The last part of the journey is a steep ascent by **cable car** (funicular railway) to **Koyasan station**. From the station buses take about 10 minutes to the centre (2-3/hr). The fare (¥290-410) depends on where you get off; one-day bus passes (¥800) are of more use to day-trippers.

**Koya-san** The central part of Koya-san is small enough to get around on foot. **Koya-san Visitor Information Center** (VIC; ☎ 0736-56 2616, 🖳 www .shukubo.net; 8.30am-5pm), in Daishi Kyokai building in the centre of town, has maps and leaflets about walks in the area. Cycles can be rented from here (¥400/hr, ¥100/each additional 30 mins), as can a portable audio guide (¥500; up to two days). Outside the office there are a few small and large lockers.

Only buy the combination ticket (¥1500), from the tourist office, if you intend to visit most of the sights charging admission. The main one to include is **Kongobu-ji** 金剛峯寺 (🖳 www.koyasan.or.jp/en/kongobuji; daily 8.30am-5pm; ¥500), the central monastery in Koya. This is the residence of the High Abbot of Koya-san, who is responsible for the 3000 monasteries across the country that belong to the Shingon Buddhist sect. Next to the monastery is the 6 o'clock bell, rung by a monk every even hour between 6am and 10pm.

Sooner or later, everyone heads for **Okunoin** 奥の院, part of an enormous cemetery with over 200,000 gravestones and monuments, where the body of Kukai is enshrined. According to tradition, on 21st March 835, he entered into

SIDE TRIPS FROM OSAKA

'eternal meditation'; since then he has been known as Kobo Daishi. It is said he will not wake up until Miroku, the Buddha of the Future, arrives. Okunoin is packed with the tombs and gravestones of Kobo Daishi's followers. The most atmospheric times to visit are early morning or early evening, but at any time it's a long, peaceful walk from Ichinohashi Bridge 一の橋 on the edge of town through the cemetery towards the Hall of Lanterns 燈籠堂 (Torodo), behind which is Kobo Daishi's mausoleum. As you return, take the higher level (right-hand path) for the area with the older graves and the lower level for the tombstones for companies such as UCC (look out for a tea cup), Yakult (look for the Yakult-shaped bottle), Toyota, Komatsu, Panasonic and Nissan.

● **Where to stay and eat**  It's a good idea to book accommodation on Koya-san in advance, especially in spring/autumn: either book directly with a temple – several now have websites in English – or consult **Koyasan Shukubo Association** (🖳 www.shukubo.net), at least a week ahead. Payment is generally in cash though some temples now accept credit cards. However, tourist-office staff will ring around the temples to see what's available if you arrive without a reservation. At all the temples guests are expected to arrive between 2 and 5pm and the evening meal is served at about 5.30/6pm; guests are also invited to attend morning prayers, which usually start at 6 or 6.30am.

The rates quoted below include bed, evening meal and breakfast and are based on two people sharing a room; in peak periods solo travellers may have to pay the full rate. Many temples offer a range of meal options, from standard to luxury, and this also affects the rate.

*Sekishoin* 赤松院 (☎ 0736-56 2734, 🖳 www.sekishoin.jp; ¥9450-18,900pp), founded in 923, is a great place to stay. The temple is next to Ichinohashi Bridge, which makes it very convenient for an early morning/ evening visit to the Okunoin. Rooms in the new building are modern and more like a hotel than temple lodgings, those in the old temple building are more atmospheric; both kinds are available with or without bathrooms. To reach Sekishoin, take a bus heading for the Okunoin from Koya-san station and get off at Ichinohashi-guchi (stop No 10).

Also recommended are Eko-in and Jofuku-in: at *Eko-in* 恵光院 (☎ 0736-56 2514, 🖳 www.ekoin.jp; from ¥10,800pp) guests can attend Ajikan meditation sessions (4.30pm) and practise Buddhist sutra writing. They are also welcome at the morning service and then the goma fire ritual (summer from 6.30am, winter 7am). Only one room is en suite; the rest share a bathroom. Eko-in is between bus stop Nos 9 and 10. At *Jofuku-in* 成福院 (☎ 0736-56 2109, 🖳 homepage3.nifty.com/koya-jfk; ¥10,800-15,120pp) some rooms have en suite toilets and basin, the best also have a massage chair and garden view. Some English is spoken. The entrance to Jofuku-in is to the left of **Konpon Daito** 根本大塔 (the red pagoda) by bus stop No 8 (Rengedani).

Other good choices are *Shojoshin-in* 清浄心院 (☎ 0736-56 2006, 🖳 www.shojoshinin.jp; from ¥9720pp), which is by Okunoin-guchi bus stop (No 11) and has a variety of rooms some with a garden view; and *Muryoko-in* 無量光院 (☎ 0736-56 2104, 🖳 www.muryokoin.org; from ¥10,800pp), though that is in the central part of town (bus stop No 5).

Most temples serve beer and sake; several have wi-fi though this may only be available in public areas. There are also coffee shops, small restaurants and convenience stores around town where you can get lunch and/or snacks.

# HONSHU

## Central Honshu – route guides

Culturally rich and geographically diverse, central Honshu is a vast area stretching from the Pacific Ocean in the south to the Sea of Japan in the north. If this region is Japan's beating heart, the Tokaido Line which runs along the southern coast is the country's transportation artery. It is above all a functional rail line – perhaps the most functional in the world, transporting thousands of people every day between the business and industrial hubs of Tokyo, Nagoya and Osaka.

But it would be a great shame to restrict your travel by rail only to the Tokaido shinkansen. Much of the area along the Tokaido Line is heavily built up and polluted by factories and heavy industry so, in its own way, a journey along this line offers a real taste of Japan. For many visitors who only just have the time to rush between Tokyo and Kyoto, this is all they see of the country. But just a short distance from the industrialised southern coast lie the majestic Japanese Alps and many opportunities to get away from the urban sprawl. The rail network is fast, efficient and even in the winter months of heavy snowfall almost invariably on time.

Highlights of a tour around this region include: **Hakone**, with its wonderful scenery and (in good weather!) views of **Mt Fuji**; **Takayama**, a mini-Kyoto in the mountains; the preserved Edo-period 'post towns' of **Narai** and **Tsumago**; and **Kanazawa** which has one of Japan's most celebrated gardens and is now the terminal station for the Hokuriku shinkansen.

Between April and November the **Tateyama-Kurobe Alpine Route** (see pp184-5) offers an opportunity to appreciate the region's astonishing beauty in a day-long journey from the coast across the Japanese Alps.

For details about using this rail route guide see p12.

---

❏ **Shinkansen services**
The only shinkansen which run all the way from Tokyo to Hakata in Kyushu are the Nozomi for which a Japan Rail Pass is not valid. Thus, if you have a Japan Rail pass, wherever you are going, you will need to take a Hikari or Kodama. Kodama stop at every station so are best for short journeys. If you are going further west than Shin-Osaka you will need to change trains there or at Okayama.

---

*Foggy drizzle!*
*Intriguing is the day*
*we can't see Mt Fuji*
(MATSUO BASHO)

霧雨や富士を見ぬ日ぞ面白き

**Central Honshu**
RAIL ROUTES

To Niigata

Narita Airport ✈
Narita
Chiba

Utsunomiya

Haneda Airport ✈
Ueno
TOKYO
Shinagawa
Shin-Yokohama
YOKOHAMA

Shibukawa
Maebashi
Omiya
KAMAKURA

Minakami
Annaka-Haruna
Takasaki
Kumagaya
Atami
Odawara

Naoetsu
Joetsu-Myoko
Iiyama
Ueda
Sakudaira
Honjowaseda
Otsuki
Hakone-Yumoto
Shin-Fuji
Ito

Itoigawa
Myoko-Kogen
NAGANO
Shinonoi
Karuizawa
Kobuchizawa
Kofu
Mishima
Izukyu-Shimoda
Shuzenji

Kurobe
Unazukionsen
Shinano-Omachi
Okaya
Fuji-san (Mt Fuji)
Fuji
Shin-Fuji

Kurobe
Tateyama
See Alpine Route Map 5a
Hijiri-Kogen
Iida
Igawa
Oigawa Steam Railway
Shizuoka
Kanaya

TOYAMA
MATSUMOTO
Shiojiri
Narai
Kinno

Himi
Johana
Kiso-Fukushima
Nakatsu-gawa
Kakegawa

Takaoka
Hida-Furukawa
TAKAYAMA
Nagiso
Kowada
Chubu-Tenryu
Hamamatsu

Shin-Takaoka
Komatsu
Hida-Kanayama
Gero
Mino-Ota
Tajimi

KANAZAWA
Johana
Gifu
Chikusa
NAGOYA
Toyohashi

Awara-Onsen
Eihei-ji
Omi-Shiotsu
Mikawa-Anjo

Fukui
Takefu
Nagahama
Maibara
Tsu

Sabae
Omi-Imazu
Biwa-ko (Lake Biwa)

Tsuruga
Omi-Maiko
Otsu
NARA

Ayabe
Shin-Osaka
KYOTO
OSAKA
KANSAI

To Wakura-onsen

Hakui

100km
50
0

Shinkansen line
JR line (suggested route)
JR line
Private rail line

HONSHU

## TOKYO TO NAGOYA BY SHINKANSEN
**[Table 3, p505]**

Distances from Tokyo. Fastest journey time (on a Hikari shinkansen): 104 mins.

### Tokyo (Station) to Kakegawa [Map 1]
**Tokyo 東京**      [see pp103-33]

**Shinagawa 品川 (7km)** All the shinkansen services call here. If you are transferring to/from the JR Yamanote Line (see pp104-16), or the Narita Express (N'EX, see box pp126-7) it makes sense to change here as the station is much smaller and easier to navigate your way round than Tokyo Station. If you need sustenance before your journey go to the area called 'ecute', on the platform concourse.

The shinkansen tracks are on the Konan 港南口 (East) Exit side of the station. Also on this side are several places to eat, a branch of Starbucks with a good view over the shinkansen concourse, and on the 3rd floor in Queens Isetan, a supermarket (daily 10am-8pm). Shinagawa is also a very convenient place to stay (see pp130-1) as it is on so many railway lines so provides easy access to lots of places.

A passageway connects the Konan side with the Takanawa 高輪口 (West) Exit where the main line platforms are as well as the private Keikyu Line. There are **lockers** (all sizes) at the back of the platform side of the main JR concourse. Most hotels are on this side of the station.

**Shin-Yokohama 新横浜 (29km)** All the shinkansen services call here. The **tourist information office** (daily 10am-6pm) is by the station's North Exit, opposite the East Exit for the shinkansen tracks. **Lockers** (¥300-600) are available in most parts of the station. The JR Yokohama Line and the Yokohama subway connect Shin-Yokohama with Yokohama Port and areas around there (see pp162-4).

Hotel rates in Shin-Yokohama are often a bit lower than in central Tokyo, so if you have a rail pass you might consider basing yourself here; Shinagawa/Tokyo are only 12/20 minutes

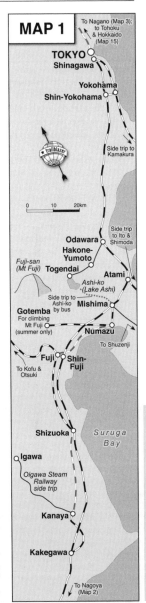

MAP 1

To Nagano (Map 3); to Tohoku & Hokkaido (Map 15)

TOKYO
Shinagawa

Yokohama
Shin-Yokohama

Side trip to Kamakura

★ trailblazer

0   10   20km

Side trip to Ito & Shimoda

Odawara
Hakone-Yumoto
Fuji-san (Mt Fuji)   Togendai
Atami
Ashi-ko (Lake Ashi)
Side trip to Ashi-ko by bus   Mishima
Gotemba
For climbing Mt Fuji (summer only)
Numazu
To Shuzenji

Fuji   Shin-Fuji
To Kofu & Otsuki

Shizuoka   Suruga Bay
Igawa
Oigawa Steam Railway side trip

Kanaya

Kakegawa

To Nagoya (Map 2)

HONSHU

away by shinkansen. Attached to the station is the JR-run *Hotel Associa Shin-Yokohama* ホテルアソシア新横浜 (☎ 045-475 0011, 🖳 www.associa.com/english/syh; from ¥17,000/S, ¥23,000/D or Tw, inc buffet breakfast; small discount for JR rail-pass holders), with smart rooms and compact but stylish bathrooms. *Toyoko Inn* 東横イン (🖳 www.toyoko-inn.com) has two branches, Shin-Yokohama Ekimae Honkan 新横浜駅前本館 (☎ 045-474 1045) and Shin-Yokohama Ekimae Shinkan 新横浜駅前新館 (☎ 045-470 1045), near the North Exit of the station. Both charge from ¥5724/S, ¥7344/D or Tw inc breakfast.

On the North Exit side of the station, **Cubic Plaza** キュービックプラザ (🖳 www.cubicplaza.com) has various restaurants including *Katsukura* 名代とんかつかつくら (daily 11am-10pm) on the 9th floor, which serves delicious tonkatsu, especially *hirekatsu* (80g for ¥1280).

The main tourist sight near the shinkansen station is the unusual **Ramen Museum** ラーメン博物館 (🖳 www.raumen.co.jp/ramen; Mon-Fri 11am-10pm, Sat, Sun & hols 10.30am-10pm; ¥310), five minutes on foot north-east from the North Exit (get a route map from the website or the tourist office). Exhibits on the 1st/ground floor tell the story of how noodles rose from humble beginnings to embrace the global market. But the big attraction is the re-created (1950s) ramen village in the basement, featuring traditional ramen shops from around Japan. Each one has its own machine and you need to order your ramen (¥800-1100) and any drinks and side dishes before going in. Since it may be hard to choose as there are so many options consider ordering a half-size portion so you can try more than one. Note that it can get very crowded so it is worth getting here late afternoon or early evening.

After you've eaten, be sure to walk around the back streets in the museum and look at the very educational shop area.

### Side trip to Yokohama 横浜

The most interesting parts of Yokohama to visit are Sakuragicho, for a taste of the 21st century, and Ishikawa-cho for a bit of history. From Shin-Yokohama take the JR Yokohama Line to Yokohama and Sakuragicho (4-6/hr; 12-16 mins; ¥170); for Ishikawa-cho it is necessary to change at Yokohama or Higashi-Kanagawa and transfer to the JR Keihin-Tohoku/Negishi Line (2-10/hr; about 23 mins in all; ¥220).

There are **tourist information centres** (🖳 www.welcome.city.yokohama .jp; daily 9am-7pm) on the east–west walkway at Yokohama station and in front of the South Gate at Sakuragicho station (daily 9am-6pm). Both have maps and general information in English.

❏ **Yokohama's place in history**
Yokohama was a small fishing village in the Edo period but its place in history came when it was the location for the signing of the Japan-US Treaty of Peace and Amity in February 1854, less than a year after Commodore Perry (see p56) had arrived in the area demanding the Japanese open their ports to trade. Yokohama port was officially opened to foreign trade in 1859 and it was not long before representatives of other nationalities had also moved into the residential area designated for foreigners.

● **Sakuragicho** 桜木町 Home to **Minato Mirai 21** みなとみらい21 (**MM21**), a city within a city featuring hotels, restaurants and shopping complexes, this area all looks very different to how it must have been in 1872, when it opened as a terminus for Japan's first rail line between Shinagawa/Shimbashi and Yokohama.

The Sakuragicho/Ishikawa-cho area is pretty compact so walking is easy but if you prefer to take a bus the **Akai Kutsu** あかいくつ (Red Bus; daily 10am-6pm, weekends to 7/8pm, Chinatown Motomachi route 3-4/hr, Minatomirai route 1-2/hr; ¥100/journey) operates round the main sights from in front of Sakuragicho station. If you plan to travel a lot in the area consider getting the **Minato Burari ticket** ミナトブラリチケット (1/day pass ¥500) as it permits unlimited travel in the designated area on the blue subway line and various buses including the Akai Kutsu.

From Sakuragicho station an escalator and then moving walkway will take you to Landmark Plaza, a shopping complex inside **Landmark Tower** ランドマークタワー; in 40 seconds a lift/elevator (daily 10am-9pm, to 10pm on Sat and in Jul-Aug; ¥1000) will whisk you from the 2nd floor lobby to the **Sky Garden** スカイガーデン, an observatory deck on the 69th floor (273m). *Yokohama Royal Park Hotel* 横浜ロイヤルパークホテル (☎ 045-221 1111, 🖳 www.yrph.com; from ¥23,760/S, ¥34,700/Tw or D inc breakfast), on the 52nd to the 67th floor, is the highest hotel in Japan. Don't leave Landmark Plaza without having a ride up and/or down the curved escalators.

Also in the Minato Mirai 21 area is an amusement park, **Yokohama Cosmo World** よこはまコスモワールド (🖳 cosmoworld.jp; Mar-Nov Fri-Wed 11am-9pm, Dec-Feb weekends only 11am-9pm), with Cosmo Clock 21 (¥800), a 107.5m-high ferris wheel (112.5m on its base). The advantage of this park is that entry is free, you just pay for whatever rides you do (generally ¥300-600 each). At the **Cup Noodles Museum** カップヌードルミュージアム (aka Momofuku Ando Instant Ramen Museum インスタントラーメン発明記念館, 🖳 www.cupnoodles-museum.jp; daily 10am-6pm; ¥500) visitors can make their own cup noodles (additional charge) and learn about Momofuku Ando (see box p155); they may also of course try many of the varieties in the food court. It is aimed at children so expect lots of school groups.

● **Ishikawa-cho** 石川町 This is the best stop for Yokohama's **Chinatown** 中華街; turn left out of the station and follow the signs, which effectively means following the road around, over a bridge and then going straight on. Once in Chinatown proper the street is pedestrianised. Follow the signs to **Yamashita Park** 山下公園 (Yamashita-koen); this is also basically straight on and a 15- to 20-minute walk – you'll know you're there when you see the sea.

On Yamashita-koen-dori, the road running alongside the park, you'll see *Hotel New Grand* ホテルニューグランド (🖳 www.hotel-newgrand.co.jp; from ¥33,264/S, ¥39,204/D or Tw), which is the only original hotel building left in Yokohama and whose facade is virtually unchanged since it was built in 1927, though a modern tower has now been added.

**The Silk Museum** シルク博物館 (🖳 www.silkmuseum.or.jp; Tue-Sun 9am-4.30pm; ¥500) is in English House No 1, the former Jardine Matheson and Company building. The silk production process is explained in a very clear way here and you also see kimonos and other garments made from silk. From here turn back and walk into the park itself.

Yamashita Park is a pleasant place for a rest and to watch the boats and cruise ships coming and going. *Hikawu Maru* 氷川丸 (🖥 www.nyk.com/rek ishi; Tue-Sun 10am-5pm; ¥300) – a former NYK Line passenger liner on the Yokohama to Seattle and Vancouver route – is moored permanently at the other end of the park to commemorate the centenary of the port. A combined ticket with the **NYK Maritime Museum** 日本郵船歴史博物館 (same hours; ¥400) costs ¥500. Not far away is the **Marine Tower** マリンタワー (daily 10am-10pm; ¥750) which has a 106m-high observatory floor.

Soon after the Marine Tower you pass **Yokohama Doll Museum** 横浜人形の家前 (🖥 www.doll-museum.jp; Tue-Sun 9.30am-5pm; ¥400), which houses thousands of dolls from around the world. From here follow signs to **Minato no Mieru Oka Koen** 港の見える丘公園 (Harbour View Park), which is on the other side of Hori-kawa (Hori River). Climb up the steps into the park, walk straight ahead but towards the right side until you see an exit to a road. Walk along that road, away from the park, and you will soon reach **Yokohama Foreigners Cemetery** 横浜外国人墓地 (🖥 www.yfgc-japan .com; Mar-Dec weekends and national holidays only, noon-4pm; donation of ¥200 or more requested). Over 4000 people from about 40 countries are buried here and in return for your donation you will be given a suggested route which shows where notable graves are: Edmund Morel who was the chief architect of the first railroad line in Japan (Shimbashi to Sakuragicho) in 1871 is buried here having died just before the opening ceremony. Even if it is not open it is worth going to look at the inscriptions on the graves you can see from the main entrance (Yamate Gate). From here it is an easy walk down through Motomachi and back to JR Ishikawa-cho station – just follow the signs.

A fireworks display (*Hanabi Taikai*) is held in Yamashita-koen in late July. *Shunsetsu* (Chinese New Year) is celebrated in February.

## Odawara 小田原 (84km) Some Hikari and all Kodama stop here. Once an important castle town, Odawara is now a major junction on both the shinkansen and Tokaido main lines, as well as a terminus for the private Odakyu Line from Shinjuku. It's also the main gateway to **Hakone** (see opposite).

The shinkansen tracks are on the west side of the station; go up the escalators/steps to the main concourse for the Odakyu tracks. The JR main line ticket gates are on the east side of the station. There are **lockers** (¥300-400) on the main east–west concourse including at the top of the escalators from the shinkansen platforms heading to the East Exit.

At **Odakyu Sightseeing Service Center** (daily 8.30am-6pm), on the main concourse, you can get all you need for a trip to Hakone. **Odawara Station Tourist Information Center** (daily 9am-5pm) is also on the concourse; staff here can give you a map and information about Odawara.

There are surprisingly few places to stay around the station and if going to Hakone it is recommended that you continue to Hakone-Yumoto (see opposite). One option on the East Exit side of Odawara station that doesn't really live up to its name, is *Hotel Posh* ホテルポシュ (☎ 0465-22 2155, 🖥 www.hotel-posh .com; from ¥8000/S, ¥11,000/Tw); the rate includes a basic breakfast, which is left in your room. There are lots of restaurants and cafés nearby and along Higashi-dori, the main road to the left of the station, as well as in the station itself, so it won't be hard to find somewhere to eat. For a yakiniku meal (from ¥1850) try *Kai* 快 on Higashi-dori.

**Odawara Castle** 小田原城 (daily 9am-4.30pm; ¥400), a 1960s reconstruction of the 15th-century original, is one of the best in the Tokyo area and has wonderful grounds with cherry blossom in spring, an excellent museum (if you like armoury), and a great view from the top. It is a 10- to 15-minute walk from the station. Recent renovations have included work to make the castle earthquake proof so it should be around for many more years.

### Side trip to Hakone 箱根

The best way to get to Hakone from Odawara is with Odakyu Railway's (💻 www.odakyu.jp) **Hakone Free Pass** 箱根フリーパス (HF Pass; 2/3 days ¥4000/4500), a package ticket which offers incredible value. It includes return rail travel from Odawara (or Shinjuku, see p110) to Hakone-Yumoto and is valid for unlimited travel on: Hakone Tozan Railway, a switchback (mountain) railway; Hakone Tozan Cable Car (funicular); Hakone Ropeway (cable car); Hakone Sightseeing boat trips on Lake Ashi; and also on Hakone Tozan Bus's services within the designated 'Free' area and Numazu Tozan Tokai buses between Mishima and Moto-Hakone. On top of all that it also offers discounts at a number of places of interest and restaurants in the area. At Odawara station, buy the pass from Odakyu Sightseeing Service Center (see opposite). If planning to visit the Kawaguchi-ko area as well consider getting the **Fuji-Hakone Pass** (see p141); it costs ¥5650 from Odawara.

If starting the journey in Odawara the first stage is to take an Odakyu train to Hakone-Yumoto 箱根湯本 (daily 4/hr; 15 mins; ¥310 plus ¥200 to go in the Romance Car).

● **Hakone-Yumoto** 箱根湯本   Hakone-Yumoto station has lockers and an information office but it is better to go to the **tourist information centre** (TIC; daily 9am-5.45pm) across the road from the station; turn left out of the ticket gates, follow signs for the East Exit, walk across the pedestrian bridge and go down the steps. Staff are happy to book accommodation and have a range of leaflets about the many options in the area. Also on this side are the bus stops for Hakone and the ryokan shuttle bus service. A useful website with information about the whole area is 💻 www.hakonenavi.jp and for information about accommodation look at 💻 www.hakone-ryokan.or.jp.

If you are staying the night in the Hakone area and would like to sightsee without being laden go to **Hakone Baggage Delivery Service** 箱根キャリーサービス (daily 8.30am-7pm; ¥800-1100 per bag), behind the stairs on the 1st/ground floor in Hakone-Yumoto station. Luggage must be deposited at their office by 12.30pm and will be delivered to wherever you are staying. On your return luggage can be collected between 1pm and 7pm.

There are though several good options here. *Hakone Suimeisou* 箱根水明荘 (☎ 0460-85-5381, 💻 www.suimeisou.com) is three minutes on foot from the station's West Exit. There is a choice of Japanese accommodation with en suite rooms (from ¥15,120pp half board and based on two sharing), or Western-style single rooms (from ¥7450pp; no meals). There is an onsen, a rotemburo (¥150 bath tax per day; rotemburo hours rotate between men/women) and a private onsen (¥2000/50 mins, reservation required). Alternatively, on the far side of the bridge across the river by the TIC, *Yumoto*

*Fujiya Hotel* 湯本富士屋ホテル (☎ 0460-85-6111, 🖥 www.yumotofujiya.jp; from ¥8640pp inc breakfast, ¥15,120pp inc half board) is a large hotel which also has both Japanese- and Western-style rooms, onsen and rotemburo as well as Japanese, Chinese and French restaurants. For those on a budget *Kappa Tengoku* かっぱ天国 (☎ 0460-85-6121, 🖥 www.kappa1059.co.jp; from ¥5600pp), a short but steep walk up behind the station, offers simple accommodation and also open-air single-sex baths (daily 10am-10pm; residents free, non-residents ¥800, plus ¥150 for towel rental).

For a delicious ramen lunch try *Miharuso* 見晴荘 (daily 11am-2pm; ¥1100); it is on the same road as the information centre but on the other side of the pedestrian bridge.

● Hakone Yumoto to Gora  This stretch of the journey is on the **Hakone Tozan Railway** 箱根登山鉄道線, the only full-scale mountain railway (daily 2-4/hr; 40 mins; ¥400, free with HF Pass) in Japan. The train changes direction three times at switchbacks – so expect a slight delay as the driver and conductor change ends – but in general for the best views sit on the left. The line goes up 550m over 15km of track; some of the sections of track on this railway are the steepest in Japan.

**Miyanoshita** 宮ノ下 is the closest station to the atmospheric *Fujiya Hotel* 富士屋ホテル (☎ 0460-82 2211, 🖥 www.fujiyahotel.jp; from ¥9528pp based on two sharing), which opened in 1878. The hotel has spacious Western-style rooms in five different buildings set in a spacious garden. Each room has natural hot spring water and the hotel is a Registered Cultural Asset of Japan. The many photos of past guests add to the charm of the place. Chaplin's Room (from ¥14,688pp based on two people sharing), where Charlie Chaplin stayed, is only available to foreign guests. Facilities include a swimming pool, hot spring baths and several restaurants. Eating here is not cheap but there are few other options.

**Chokoku-no-Mori** 彫刻の森, the last stop before Gora, is the closest station to **Hakone Open-Air Museum** 箱根彫刻の森美術館 (Hakone Chokoku-no-Mori Bijutsukan; 🖥 www.hakone-oam.or.jp; daily 9am-5pm; ¥1600, ¥1500 if booked online, discount with HF Pass). The museum is spread over 70,000 sq metres and it features works by a range of artists including Henry Moore, 26 of whose works are on show at any one time; there are also over 300 works by Picasso in the Picasso Pavilion and a separate area where the art works are geared to children. It is a glorious place to walk round, especially if the weather is good; if your feet get tired head for the hot spring foot-bath. The museum is only a few minutes' walk from the station and you can see some of the sculptures from the train if you look out on the right-hand side.

At **Gora** 強羅 there is an information office (daily 10am-4.45pm) but the leaflets are mostly in Japanese and the staff don't speak English or book accommodation. There are, however, lots of tourist shops here and some places to eat.

● Gora to Sounzan  **Hakone Tozan Cable Car** 箱根登山ケーブルカー (funicular; 1-4/hr; 10 mins; ¥420, free with HF Pass) operates to Sounzan 早雲山. Most people go straight there but right by **Koenshimo** 公園下 station, the first stop, there is a great place for a special meal. (Alternatively from Gora station walk up parallel to the track; the restaurant is at the end on the left).

*Itoh Dining by Nobu* イトウ ダイニング バイ ノブ (🖳 itoh-dining.co
.jp; daily 11.30am-2.20pm & 5-8.30pm; lunch set menu from ¥3000, Kobe
beef menu from ¥8000, evening set menus from ¥7000) is a teppanyaki restaurant opened in collaboration with revered chef Nobu (Nobuyuki Matsuhisa).
'The lunch menu gives reasonable value for money and the Kobe beef dish is
to die for.' (Ben Storey & Alex Chambers).

● **Sounzan to Togendai** The **Hakone Ropeway** 箱根ロープウェイ (cable
car; 🖳 www.hakoneropeway.co.jp; Mar-Jul & Sep-Nov 8.45am-5.15pm, Aug
to 5.30pm, Dec-Feb 9.15am-4.15pm) service operates continuously but even
so, expect long queues at peak periods. The journey to Togendai takes approximately 24 minutes (¥1370 one-way, ¥2410 return, free with HF Pass).
However, at the time of research the ropeway was closed between Sounzan
and Togendai due to some (invisible) volcanic gas in the Owakudani crater
area; a replacement bus service is operating instead. Also it is not possible to
walk around Owakudani; check the website for updates.

If the weather is good though, just before arriving at the Ropeway's first
stop, Owakudani, look out to the right for views of Mt Fuji. **Owakudani** 大涌
谷 (Hell Valley; 🖳 www.owakudani.com) is an explosion crater that was created about 3000 years ago. It is so called because of the horrible smell coming
from the fumarolic gas with poisonous hydrogen sulphide and sulphur dioxide
which emerges from gaps (vents) in the ground. Don't let the smell put you off
getting out and exploring, though some of the nature trails may be closed
because of concerns about erosion and landslides. If you can, it is worth walking up the main trail (350 metres; approx 10 mins) to Tamago-chaya (8.30am-
5pm) for a *kuro tamago* 黒卵 (¥500 for five); eggs are cooked in the hot spring
ponds and after about an hour the shells turn black due to the reaction of the
hydrogen sulphide and the iron in the water. You may like to know that eating
the eggs is meant to extend your life by seven years. Whilst here look out for
the dedicated ropeway which brings the eggs up to be cooked. If you have
some spare time pop in to **Hakone GeoMuseum** 箱根ジオミュージアム
(daily 9am-4.30pm; ¥300, ¥250 with HF Pass); it has some videos with subtitles in English and exhibits about geo-activity in the area.

Few get out at the next stop, **Ubako** 姥子, but the observation point, a 5-
to 10-minute walk away, is an excellent place for a picnic with views of Lake
Ashi though sadly Fuji-san is obscured here. It also provides a chance to have
a break from the almost inevitable crowds. Take the exit on the right and follow the path. At **Togendai** 桃源台, the final stop, you could rent a swan ped-
alo, but most people join one of the kitsch but fun sightseeing cruise boats;
apart from the scenery this is one of the highlights of the trip.

● **Togendai to Hakone-machi / Moto-Hakone** Hakone Sightseeing
**Ships** 箱根観光船 operates replica 17th-/18th-century ships (🖳 www.hakone-
kankosen.co.jp; mid Mar-Nov 10am-5pm, Dec to mid Mar 10am-4pm; 1-2/hr;
¥1000/1840 one-way/return, first class additional ¥500/770) around Lake
Ashi, a crater lake, providing a scenic, but somewhat incongruous, experience.
Note that the HF Pass is only valid on Hakone Sightseeing's boats, not those
operated by IzuHakone.

The full circuit takes about 100 minutes but most people get off at either
Hakone-machi 箱根町, the first stop, or Moto-Hakone. From Hakone-machi you

can walk along the ancient cedar avenue (see p170) to Moto-Hakone 元箱根. *Moto-Hakone Guest House* 元箱根ゲストハウス (☎ 0460-83-788, 🖳 mo tohakone.com; ¥5250pp) is a friendly place. It is a fairly steep 12- to 15-minute walk along the main road heading inland, or you can take a Hakone Tozan bus heading to Gora/Odawara and get off at Oshiba 大芝 stop (2/hr; ¥170; free with HF Pass). Meals are not available but the proprietor can give you a map showing a pleasant way to walk back to Moto-Hakone. Since most restaurants close early another option is to buy your own provisions from the *7-Eleven* convenience store (at the Moto-Hakone end of the main road) before going to the guesthouse.

If you have a HF Pass you could take a bus from here to Mishima (see opposite) rather than retracing your steps.

**Atami 熱海 (105km)** Kodama and a few Hikari stop here. Atami is a famous onsen town but, due to its proximity to Tokyo, it often gets unpleasantly crowded. Apart from the onsen, the main tourist draw is MOA Museum of Art (see below) but it is also the access point for a side trip to Ito and Shimoda (see below) both of which are of historical interest, particularly to British and Americans. The **tourist information centre** (TIC; daily 9am-5/5.30pm) has maps and information about the local area. There are lots of **lockers** (¥300-400 inside the station, ¥300-500 outside).

**Hot springs** abound, with a choice of seven spas; you can pick up a map at the TIC and stroll around the town visiting them all. There is also a free foot hot spring (*ashi-yu*) just outside the station.

**MOA Museum of Art** MOA美術館 (MOA Bijutsukan; 🖳 www.moaart.or .jp; Fri-Wed 9.30am-4.30pm; ¥1600), on a hillside overlooking Atami, contains a large collection of Japanese and Chinese paintings and ceramics as well as gold and silver lacquerware. Pick up a discount voucher (¥200 per group) from the TIC then either take an IzuTokai bus from Platform 8, or YuYu Loop Bus (13/day; ¥250, ¥800/1-day pass) from the platform designated Platform 0. Another YuYu route covers attractions in central Atami.

### Side trip by train to Ito and Shimoda

Atami is the starting point for the JR Ito Line south to Ito and Shimoda. Both the Odoriko/Super View Odoriko LEX (6/day; about 20/73 mins to Ito/Izukyu-Shimoda from Atami) and local trains (1-2/hr; about 22/66 mins) operate on this line. Japan Rail passes are valid only to Ito. Beyond Ito the line continues to Izukyu-Shimoda, but this section is operated by the private Izukyu Railway 伊豆急行線 (🖳 www.izukyu.jp; ¥1620, ¥2130 inc reserved seat); so JR pass-holders will have to pay at the ticket barrier if not before. Note that the station's name is Izukyu-Shimoda, but the town is Shimoda.

● **Ito 伊東** Ito is where William Adams, the first Englishman to set foot in Japan, spent much of his life after a shipwreck off the coast of Kyushu in 1600. He became known as Anjin-san and his arrival is celebrated during the Anjin Matsuri in August. The William Adams Festival is held here on August 8th-10th; the festival celebrates his success building a Western-style sailing ship, the first such ship in Japan.

● **Shimoda 下田** Shimoda is the southernmost town on the Izu Peninsula and is where Commodore Perry's 'Black Ships' (see p56) landed in 1854. The

Japanese referred to them as 'black ships' because of the black smoke coming from them. Virtually everywhere you walk in Shimoda now has something of historical interest and it would be very easy to fill a day here, let alone enjoying the fact that the town is a fishing port, and also has a canal, several old buildings and some wonderful beaches.

Pick up a walking map from the **tourist information centre** (🖳 www.shi moda-city.info; daily 10am-5pm) at Izukyu-Shimoda 伊豆急下田 station and discover: the **monument** marking where Commodore Perry landed ペリー艦隊来航記念碑; **Perry Rd** ペリーロード where he walked to sign the Treaty of Shimoda at Ryosen-ji; **Gyokusen-ji** 玉泉寺, home first for Commodore Perry and his delegation and later for Townsend Harris and also where Harris opened the first US consulate in 1856. (He lived here until the consulate moved to Edo, now Tokyo, in 1859). Gyokusen-ji's other claim to fame (though it is probably not something it is really proud of) is that this is where the first cow for human consumption was slaughtered in Japan. Also look out for **Hofuku-ji** 宝福寺 where Harris's maid, Okichi, is remembered; sadly she was persecuted for working for a foreigner and eventually she took her own life. **Choraku-ji** 長楽寺 is where Admiral Putyatin of the Imperial Russian Navy signed a treaty in 1855 opening up relations between Japan and Russia.

## Mishima 三島 (121km)
Kodama and a few Hikari stop here. The shinkansen tracks are on the north side of the station and there are **lockers** of all sizes as well as some cafés outside the North Exit. You need to cross to the South Exit for the bus centre and services to the Hakone region (see below) and Kawaguchi-ko (see pp138-41), the latter via an express bus service (daily 6/day; approx 100 mins; ¥2260/one-way, ¥4110/return). Mishima is also an access point for Gotemba if wanting to climb Mt Fuji (see box pp170-1) and for the lovely onsen town of Shuzenji (see pp170-1).

Before moving on from Mishima visit **Rakujuen** 楽寿園 (daily Apr-Oct 9am-5pm, Nov-Mar to 4pm; ¥300), a lovely large stroll garden, across the road from the tourist information centre. Amongst the delights here is a pond which should be filled with water from the sides of Fuji-san but sadly for some years it hasn't been; the locals are always hopeful that will change. The only way you can see **Rakujukan**, a tea ceremony house, is on a tour (hourly 10.30am-3.30pm; free) that is in Japanese only, but it is worth it to see the beautiful screens and also for good views of the garden.

**Mishima Natsu Matsuri** (15th-17th August) is the main festival in Mishima and it includes a procession with floats; yabusame is among the events on the last day.

*Dormy Inn Mishima* ドーミーイン三島 (☎ 055-991 5489, 🖳 www.hote spa.net/hotels/mishima; from ¥8090/S, ¥11,190/D or Tw) is a five-minute walk from the South Exit of the station – turn left and you are likely to see it easily as it stands on its own. Like all branches of this highly recommended chain it has onsen baths (single sex), but from these you may be able to see Mt Fuji.

### Side trip by bus to the Hakone region
Take a Numazu Tozan Tokai bus 沼津登山東海バス from bus stand 5, outside the South Exit of Mishima station, to Moto-Hakone (1-2/hr; 45-50 mins;

H O N S H U

¥1030). From there you could take one of the sightseeing boats on Lake Ashi (see p167), or walk to Hakone-machi along a section of the Ancient Cedar Avenue (cedars were planted to provide shade for travellers on the old Tokaido Highway) passing the Hakone Checkpoint/Exhibition en route. If the weather is good you should be able to see Mt Fuji from the lakeside without taking a boat trip. Buses back to Mishima depart from bus stand 4 (by Hakone-machi pier).

### Side trip by rail to Shuzenji 修善寺

Kobo Daishi (see p156) founded a Shuzen-ji temple here in 807 and is also said to have created a hot spring when he struck a rock with an iron club causing water to flow out; over the intervening years it has developed into a lovely

---

### ❏ Climbing Mt Fuji 富士山 (Fuji-san)

Mt Fuji (3776m) climbing season lasts from mid July to the end of August. There are four trails: the easiest and most popular is the Yoshida Trail (see below) from Mt Fuji Subaru 5th Station (accessed from Kawaguchi-ko). Others are the Gotemba and Subashiri trails (both can be accessed from Gotemba); and the Fujinomiya Trail (from Fujinomiya); for access details see opposite.

Most people climb in the late afternoon and spend the night in one of the huts on the mountain and then get up early in order to go to the summit to see the sunrise. Since the walking season is so limited, expect the mountain to be very crowded.

● **Yoshida Trail from Kawaguchi-ko** (see pp138-41)  For help planning your climb see 🖥 www.fujisan-climb.jp. Here, amongst other useful information, you can find a list of **mountain huts** at the 7th and 8th stations (¥5000-8000 plus ¥1000 for a basic curry dinner & packed breakfast) requiring advance booking by phone. They are very basic affairs set snugly in the side of the mountain over three levels, with two camping barn rows of bunks.

At Kawaguchiko station there is a concierge desk if you need information in English. You can also drop off your luggage in the **baggage store** (daily 6am-10.20pm; ¥700/day), though there are lockers. This will be your last chance to hire essential kit as there is nothing at the 5th station itself (the Japanese see such lack of preparation as near unimaginable hence the lack of serious kit shopping options around Fuji). On exiting the station head across the street to **Sora no Shita** そらのした (daily 9am-7pm) where you can hire boots, an essential head torch, rain gear, walking poles (also vital), backpacks and even thermals: a full 6-piece set will set you back ¥8950 (2 days/1 night) and you must leave a ¥3000-5000 deposit. You can purchase snacks and drinks at some of the huts but if worried about provisions – ensure you have enough **water** as it is understandably expensive to purchase on the mountain – walk down the hill towards the lake to find the Takadaya store 高田屋 on the left. Then, back at the station, hop on the **Fujikyu climbers' bus** from stop No 7 (daily 1-2/hr; 55 mins, ¥1540/2100 one-way/return valid for two days).

Since Mt Fuji was inscribed on the UNESCO World Heritage list as 'a sacred place and source of artistic inspiration' the number of people wanting to climb it has increased massively and a donation of ¥1000 for the Fujisan Preservation Fund is requested for anyone climbing from the 5th Station. The money is used to help preserve the mountain and to provide additional facilities such as toilets and first-aid centres.

At the 5th station, follow the signs for the Yoshida Trail (approx 6½hrs to the summit), but don't rush up as altitude sickness can be a problem. Climbing from late afternoon, three hours will see you to the 7th/8th station mountain huts. It is a well marked but rocky ascent in places.

onsen town. **Shuzenji-onsen** 修善寺温泉 (🖳 www.shuzenji.info) is in a beautiful setting surrounded by hills and with a river flowing through the centre of town; there is also a bamboo grove here and various temples.

Shuzenji 修善寺 station is the last stop on the private Izuhakone railway from Mishima (3-5/hr; 35 mins; ¥510). Two Odoriko LEX services a day (126 mins) also go to Shuzenji from Tokyo; JR rail-pass holders have to pay the fare between Mishima and Shuzenji. Shuzenji-onsen is about 10 minutes (2-5/hr; ¥220) by Tokai Bus from Stop No 1 outside the South Exit of Shuzenji station. Before you get on the bus pick up a map and information from **Izu City Tourist Information Centre** (daily 9am-5.30pm) at the station.

It is also a remarkably convivial affair with many Japanese families sharing their climbing experiences with other tourists.

In the huts, which are very clustered together, the lower bunks get taken first and will be easier to sleep in owing to ambient light. You are encouraged to eat your meal quickly so you can make way for the next batch of hikers. There are no showers and you are asked to leave ¥100 for toilet use. After a very brief sleep (most people have hit the sleeping bags and pillows provided by 7pm), climbers usually begin to make the dawn climb from the huts at about 1am. At this point you will soon discover the uniquely Japanese phenomenon of 'Fuji traffic' as a brightly lit snaked line of head-lamped hikers are corralled into slow and fast lanes by mountain guides, as they hope to make it first to catch the dawn sunrise.

At the **summit**, if the weather allows you will be able to join the camera frenzy although you may also take refuge in the communal food tent, check your wi-fi code works (available at the 5th station information office), or go into the post office (6am-2pm) for a Mt Fuji summit stamp before taking an optional 90-minute circuit of the 'hachi' summit crater (not recommended in foul weather). The three vending machines here add a surreal touch to the proceedings.

The **descent** is on a separate switchback trail and is far more monotonous. Kurosawa filmed scenes from his 1957 Macbeth-inspired *Throne of Blood* on these barren treeless slopes and the soft gravel trail of the descent will continue for what seems an eternity (although it will be quicker than your ascent). Do wear thick socks to avoid your feet rubbing and ensure you deploy walking poles as the sensation is similar to skiing in places.

● **Access to the other trails** For the Gotemba and Subashiri trails change at Mishima (see p169) for a local JR Tokaido line train to **Numazu** 沼津 (2-8/hr; 6 mins). Change at Numazu for the JR Gotemba line to **Gotemba** 御殿場 (1-2/hr; 24-36 mins), the fare for the whole journey costs ¥580, free with a JR pass. From Gotemba you can pick up a Fujikyu bus to Subashiri 5th station 須走五号目 (July to late Sep; 1/hr; 60 mins; ¥1540/2060 one-way/round trip) on Mt Fuji; buses to Gotemba 5th station 御殿場五合目 (40 mins; ¥1110) run less frequently.

For the Fujinomiya Trail take a bus from Fujinomiya station (see p174) to Fujinomiya-guchi 5th station 富士宮口五合目 (Fujinomiya-guchi gogome; 6/day; 2¼hrs; one-way ¥2380, return ticket valid 3 days ¥3100). At weekends and holiday periods the service also operates between May and October (3/day).

For more information on climbing Mt Fuji, see 🖳 mountfujiguide.com and for information about getting around see 🖳 transportation.fujikyu.co.jp.

**Andrew Picknell**

HONSHU

There are hideous smoke stacks everywhere you look as you approach Shin-Fuji, which is a shame since you expect a place with this name to afford picture-postcard views of Japan's most famous natural wonder.

You should start looking out for **views of Mt Fuji** though; on the right side of the train (from Tokyo) or on the left side (to Tokyo). For information about climbing Mt Fuji see box pp170-1.

**Shin-Fuji** 新富士 **(146km)** Only Kodama stop here. If the smoke stacks haven't put you off and the weather is good do stop here as there are several places offering good views of Mt Fuji. **Shin-Fuji Tourist Information Center** (☎ 0545-64 2430; daily 8.45am-5.30pm), almost directly opposite the shinkansen exit gate, provides information about the area and also makes it as easy as possible to get around by offering free bike rental (Apr-Sep daily 9am-5pm, Oct-Mar to 4pm) on a first come first served basis; they have 10 bikes and will accept phone reservations. They will tell you the various options for views of Mt Fuji and provide a route map. In reality if the weather is good you don't need to go anywhere as you can see it from in front of the station. However, cycling just eight minutes to Tadehara Overpass (or walking a little bit longer) will give you a different perspective. Other options include the riverbed of Fujikawa river, Chuo Park, and also Iwamotoyama Park where you can see Mt Fuji through plum and cherry trees in the spring. But possibly the best option is cycling about 20 minutes to Tagonoura Port as then you can see the whole expanse of Fuji-san and have fishing boats at the front of your image. Also your efforts can be rewarded (if you are here between April and December) with a lovely meal of *shirasu-don* しらす丼 (baby whitebait/sardines on a bowl of rice; from ¥650) from *Taganoura Fisheries Cooperative Restaurant* 田子の浦港 漁協食堂 (daily Apr-Dec 10am-1.30pm, or until sold) at the port. Having reached the port you can also ride along the cycle coastal path! If you need to leave luggage at Shin-Fuji station there are lots of **lockers** (¥200-500).

A bus operates between Shin-Fuji and Fuji station (approx 2/hr; 7 mins; ¥170); from Fuji you can pick up the Wide View Fujikawa LEX (see p174).

**Shizuoka** 静岡 **(180km)** Some Hikari stop here and all Kodama. A well-known **tea-producing area**, but another claim to fame is that the city produces more plastic models – such as cars, trains, or popular characters – than anywhere else in Japan. It is also an access point for Nihondaira, deemed one of the top 100 sightseeing spots in Japan, and Kunozan Toshogu, a shrine.

At JR Shizuoka station the main exit for the city is on the north side. There is normally an English speaker on hand at **Shizuoka City Tourist Information Center** (🖳 www.shizuoka-guide.com; daily 9am-5.45pm), by the North Exit. You can pick up maps and information about getting to the various sights. The Bus Terminal is to the right outside the North Exit. There are several restaurants and cafés in Asty in the station building.

For Nihondaira and Kunozan Toshogu take Shizutetsu bus No 42 (Apr-Oct Mon-Fri 6/day, Sat-Sun 8-9/day; 40 mins; ¥580) from bus stand No 11 at Shizuoka station and get off at **Nihondaira** 日本平 (the last stop). Hopefully the weather is good and you can admire the views from this plateau. When you have seen enough take the short **ropeway** ride (🖳 www.shizutetsu.co.jp/park; daily summer 9.10am-5pm, winter to 3pm; 3-6/hr; ¥550 each way, combo ticket inc round trip on the ropeway and entry to the shrine and shrine museum ¥1750) to the shrine; it terminates by the entrance.

**Kunozan Toshogu** 久能山東照宮 (🖳 www.toshogu.or.jp; May-Oct daily 9am-5pm, Nov-Apr to 4pm; ¥500 pavilion, ¥800 inc museum) was built here, on top of Mt Kuno (270m), as requested in Ieyasu Tokugawa's will (1542-1616). He had spent the last years of his life in Shizuoka and wanted to be buried here; his body, however, is now in Nikko. Behind the main shrine, which is surprisingly ornate and colourful, is the simple **mausoleum**, surrounded by trees. Also here is a small but fascinating **museum** (9am-5pm; ¥400) housing a colourful treasure trove of Ieyasu's possessions, including glittering swords, hanging scrolls, samurai armour and an antique table clock from Madrid.

There are two ways back to Shizuoka from the shrine. Either take the ropeway back to Nihondaira and then pick up the bus back to the station, or walk down the 1159 steps from the shrine to the coast. There are several strawberry farms at the bottom of the steps where, most of the year, you can buy strawberries and strawberry juice, ice-cream or jam. Turn left when you reach the foot of the steps (don't go as far as the main road in front of you) and walk 150m to the bus stop, where bus No 14 (approx 1/hr; ¥480) will return you to Shizuoka station. If you really want to climb the 1159 steps up to the shrine you can catch this bus from stop No 22 outside Shizuoka station.

The highlight of **Shizuoka Prefectural Museum of Art** 静岡県立美術館 (Shizuoka Kenritsu Bijutsukan; 🖳 www.spmoa.shizuoka.shizuoka.jp; Tue-Sun 10am-5.30pm; ¥300; additional charge for special exhibitions; English audio guide available) is the Rodin Wing, which boasts an impressive collection of bronze Auguste Rodin casts, including his famous *Thinker* and the *Gates of Hell*. There is also a sculpture garden and the main exhibition includes works by Impressionists such as Monet. Take bus No 44 from stop No 11, which is across the road from Shizuoka station (take the North Exit and cross the road by Hotel Associa Shizuoka) and alight at Kenritsu Bijutsukan (30 mins; ¥350). Alternatively take a train to JR Kusanagi 草薙 station (6/hr; 7 mins; ¥190) and then pick up the bus (about 6 mins; ¥100).

The most convenient place to stay in Shizuoka is the JR-run *Hotel Associa Shizuoka* ホテルアソシア静岡 (☎ 054-254 4141, 🖳 www.associa.com/sth; from ¥12,343/S, ¥16,972/D, ¥22,630/Tw; Japan Rail pass-holders get 10% discount), on your right as you take the North Exit from Shizuoka station. The rooms are a good size. A great place for some sushi is *Numazu Uogashi-zushi Nagare-zushi* 沼津 魚がし鮨 流れ鮨静岡石田店 (daily 11am-10pm) on the 1st/ground floor in Parche at Shizuoka station. TV screens here show fish being unloaded at Numazu port to show you it is really fresh, but also show how to place an order using the iPads by each seat. Depending on where you are sitting your sushi may be delivered on a conveyor belt, or if sitting in the main area the chef will give your order to you, though you still need to order it via the iPad.

HONSHU

### Alternative route back to Tokyo

Even though this is quite a long journey if the weather is good it provides a chance to see some lovely scenery. Take a Wide View Fujikawa LEX to Kofu 甲府 (7/day; 2hrs 21 mins from Shizuoka) via both Fuji and Fujinomiya stations. At Kofu take a Kaiji LEX (10/day; 35 mins), or Azusa/Super Azusa (5/day), to Otsuki where you can change for Kawaguchi-ko (see pp138-41), or stay on the train to return to Shinjuku (Tokyo).

## Kakegawa to Nagoya [Map 2]
## Kakegawa 掛川 (229km) Only Kodama stop here, the nearest point of access for Oigawa Railway (see below), one of Japan's most spectacular steam railway lines. Take the Tokaido line exit from the shinkansen platforms.

### Side trip to Oigawa Steam Railway [see Map 1, p161]

The Oigawa Railway 大井川鐵道 (🖥 www.oigawa-railway.co.jp) began operating in 1926 to transport timber, freight and tea from the mountains along the Oigawa River. During the 1960s revenue from freight began to fall as did the number of people living in the mountainous areas, so the railway turned to tourism. The preserved steam operation (top speed 65kph) runs from Shin-Kanaya to the terminus at Senzu (40km) and really is like stepping back in time. There are four steam engines (including the C12 164), though not all are in use at the same time. Some of the coaches have their original wooden seats and floors, and ceiling fans. The conductor may come through the train playing a harmonica or sing songs over the loudspeaker. To reach the start point for the railway, take a local JR train from Kakegawa two stops east to **Kanaya** 金谷; there are a few lockers (¥300-500) in the station but little else so if you want any souvenirs of the trip buy them at Shin-Kanaya.

The entrance to Oigawa Kanaya station is on your right as you leave JR Kanaya station. You can purchase tickets online through the website or at the station here: the fare from Kanaya to Senzu costs ¥1810, an additional supplement of ¥800 is payable for a journey on the steam locomotive from Shin-Kanaya to Senzu. Thomas the Tank Engine services (liable to be fully booked!) have also operated on this line since 2014. If Thomas or James haul the train the supplement is ¥1000. Senzu to Igawa (Abt Line) costs ¥1320 one-way.

Alternatively get a pass, both of which are valid for two days: **Oigawa Jiyuu Kippu** 大井川 自由きっぷ (¥3620 for Kanaya–Senzu; ¥3440 covering Shin Kanaya–Senzu), or the **Sumatakyo Furii Kippu** 寸又峡フリーキップ (¥4200/5000 Dec-Mar/Mar-Dec) which covers travel between Kanaya and Senzu and also to Sumatakyo-onsen (see opposite). When you have your ticket or pass, board the train (up to 8/day) and go one stop to Shin-Kanaya station, where you transfer on to the steam locomotive for the journey to Senzu (1-3/day). The local train (30 mins) continues all the way to Senzu.

At **Shin-Kanaya** 新金谷 there's a small steam museum (Plaza Loco; daily 9am-5pm) with a few model railways, as well as a gift shop selling Oigawa tea and *ekiben* (railway station lunch box; see box p102); the Kisha (steam train) ekiben (¥1400) is an Oigawa *meibutsu* (speciality). Opposite Shin-Kanaya station is a café called *Warau Neko* 笑うねこ (daily 10am-8pm), easy to find as it's the only place full of good-luck pottery cats, which according to the owner are supposed to bring in customers – if you're there, it's clearly worked. The line passes through the Oigawa tea fields and there are good views on both sides so it doesn't really matter where you sit. However, on the left, look out for the raccoon statues and, later on in the journey, Shiogo suspension bridge. There are also several tunnels – some were built to prevent rock falling on the track and trains – so you may be requested to keep the window closed. There's another small rail museum (10am-4pm; ¥100) at the **Senzu** 千頭 terminus. *Ebisuya* えびすや (daily 11am-4pm), a friendly restaurant just across from Senzu station serves *katsudon* (¥850) and *tendon* (¥900).

From Senzu a narrow-profile railway (partly Abt system cog-and-tooth), the Igawa (Abt) Line (also known as the Minami Alps Abuto Line) travels higher up into the mountains to the very end of the line at **Igawa** 井川 (25km); this is the steepest incline for a railway line in Japan. There are several hot springs near stops en route and the line also passes Nagashima Dam. However, at the time of research, part of the line was out of use following a landslip. Such disruption is not uncommon, so check before travelling.

Places to stay include *Suikoen* 翠紅苑 (☎ 0547-59 3100, 🖥 www.sui koen.jp; from ¥9180/11,880pp Western/Japanese style inc half board) at **Sumatakyo-onsen** 寸又峡温泉, accessible by bus from either Senzu (¥880) or Oku-Izumi on the Igawa Line (¥640). The Furii Kippu pass is valid for this bus.

## Hamamatsu 浜松 (257km)

Some Hikari stop here and all Kodama. Located almost halfway between Tokyo and Osaka, and home to such world-famous companies as Yamaha, Suzuki and Honda. Not surprisingly therefore it is known as the 'Music City': it's said that every piano made in Japan is built here.

The **tourist information centre** (🖥 www .hamamatsu-daisuki.net; daily 9am-7pm) is by the South Exit opposite the shinkansen ticket barrier. **Lockers** of all sizes are slightly hidden down a passageway off the main concourse. Immediately above the station is the May One shopping complex with **restaurants** on the 7th floor and take-out food counters in the basement. There are also fast-food options on and around the station concourse.

The best place to get your bearings is almost directly in front of the North (Act City) Exit of Hamamatsu station and is hard to miss. Standing 212m high, the vast **Act City** complex is home to both the quirky **Museum of Musical Instruments** 浜松市楽器博物館 (🖥 www .gakkihaku.jp; daily except 2nd and 4th Wed of the month Sep-July 9.30am-5pm; ¥400, free audio guide – you can even hear how the instruments sound), which houses more than 2000 instruments from around the world, and the

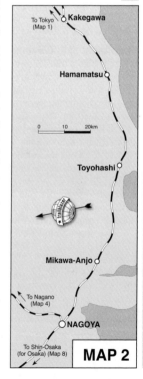

MAP 2

HONSHU

**observatory** (Mon-Fri 10am-6pm; ¥500) on the 45th floor of **Act Tower** アクトタワー, located at a height of 145 metres. The tower is designed to resemble a harmonica and if the weather is good it is well worth the admission fee for the chance to take in the surrounding area including Mt Fuji. The lift/elevator to the observatory is in Okura Act City Hotel. Keep an eye out, too, for the imposing black and white façade of **Hamamatsu-jo** 浜松城 (daily 8.30am-4.30pm; ¥150), a castle originally built over 400 years ago and lived in for 17 years by Japan's most celebrated warlord, Ieyasu Tokugawa (see p56). Anyone hoping for promotion at work should visit the castle: according to legend, Hamamatsu-jo – the present-day incarnation of which dates back to 1958 – gained its nickname 'Castle of Advancement' by virtue of the fact that every feudal lord who lived inside it later went on to enjoy even higher office.

*Okura Act City Hotel* オークラアクトシティホテル (☎ 053-459 0111, 🖳 www.act-okura.co.jp; from ¥12,345/S, ¥25,584/D, ¥22,020/Tw inc breakfast) is conveniently situated right outside the station. The rooms are on the 32nd floor or higher, so you're guaranteed a good view. The hotel plays on the city's musical theme, with associated motifs on everything from the yukatas to the bathroom walls, and even the up/down lift signs are shaped like grand pianos. The hotel can be entered from the walkway from the station but the reception desk is down on the 1st/ground floor.

## Toyohashi 豊橋 (294km)

Some Hikari and all Kodama stop in Toyohashi, which is also a transfer point for the JR Tokaido Line. Tram/streetcar fans may be the keenest to stop here for the chance to experience the sharpest rail bend in Japan, with a radius of just 11m. **Toyohashi Information Plaza** (daily 9am-7pm) on the main concourse has a map which includes sightseeing details and some of the tram stops. Close to the tourist information counter, on your right as you head towards the East Exit, are **lockers** (all sizes, up to ¥600). Take the East Exit for the main part of the city and the tram line; go over the walkway till you see a bus information sign on the left; go down the escalator by that.

A **tram service** has operated in Toyohashi since 1925. The 5.5km line runs through the city (¥150 flat fare) from the Ekimae stop in front of the station to Ihara where it divides: one line goes 'round the bend' to Undokoen-mae and the other continues straight to Akaiwaguchi. The journey to either destination takes about 20 mins (5-7/hr). Another feature is the range of trams used.

The most convenient accommodation is the JR-run *Hotel Associa Toyohashi* ホテルアソシア豊橋 (☎ 0532-57 1010, 🖳 www.associa.com/english/tyh; from ¥9500/S, ¥11,500/D, ¥12,500/Tw; inc breakfast; small discount for rail-pass holders for room-only rate), attached to the station and accessed directly from the 2nd-floor concourse by the East Exit.

After Toyohashi, Kodama call at **Mikawa-Anjo** 三河安城 (336km) but all other services run non-stop to Nagoya.

## Nagoya 名古屋 (366km)      [see pp197-204]

All shinkansen services stop here. If continuing to Kyoto, stay on the shinkansen and connect with the route guide starting on p234.

## TOKYO TO KANAZAWA BY SHINKANSEN [Table 4, p506]

Distances from Tokyo. Fastest journey time: 80 minutes to Nagano, 2hrs 28 mins to Kanazawa.

Asama shinkansen operate to Nagano. Hakutaka and Kagayaki services go through to Kanazawa; Hakutaka services stop everywhere, Kagayaki services are the fastest as they stop at a limited number of stations.

### Tokyo to Nagano [Map 3; Map 4, p180]
**Tokyo 東京 (0km)** [see pp103-33]

**Ueno 上野 (3.6km)** Most trains stop here, though definitely reserve a seat in advance if you're joining the train here.

All shinkansen call at **Omiya** 大宮 (30km; see pp321-2), access point for JR East's Railway Museum and also for Kawagoe (see pp322-3). Some Asama call at **Kumagaya** 熊谷 (65km), change here for the Chichibu Railway (see box p92), and **Honjo-waseda** 本庄早稲田 (86km).

**Takasaki 高崎 (105km)** Most Hakutaka and some Asama call here. Takasaki is a major junction station; it is the point at which the Hokuriku shinkansen line to Nagano/Kanazawa and the Joetsu shinkansen to Niigata diverge. It is also a stop on several JR main lines and is an access point for the rail museum in Yokokawa, a highly recommended onsen in Minakami (for both see p178) and at certain times of the year two steam locomotive services (SL Usui & SL Minakami; see box p92). The town itself is an important production centre for Daruma dolls.

❏ **Daruma dolls**
These are modelled on the founder of Zen Buddhism in China and are popular as lucky charms. The idea is that the purchaser of a Daruma paints in one of the eyes at the time of buying it, then makes a wish. The other eye is only painted in if the wish comes true. Daruma craftsmen receive a rush on orders for the dolls during general election campaigns from candidates trying to buy themselves some luck.

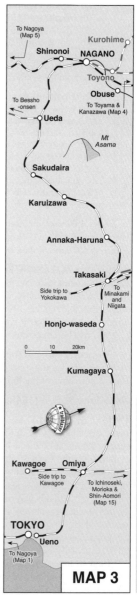

MAP 3

**Side trips by train from Takasaki**

● **To Yokokawa** 横川 **Usui Pass Railway Heritage Park** 碓氷峠鉄道文化
むら (Usuitouge Tetsudo Bunkamura; 🖥 www.usuitouge.com/bunkamura;
Wed-Mon 9am-4.30/5pm; ¥500) is accessible by local train on the **JR
Shinetsu Line** (approx 1/hr; 33 mins). The museum is built on the site of the
old Yokokawa depot and has a good collection of rolling stock. It is a short
walk from the station (ask at the station for directions).

● **To Minakami** 水上 To reach *Takaragawa-onsen Osenkaku* 宝川温泉汪泉
閣 (☎ 0278-75 2611, 🖥 www.takaragawa.com; from ¥11,800pp inc half board
and based on two sharing, sgl occ from ¥14,500) take the **JR Joetsu Line**
(approx 1/hr; 65 mins) to Minakami. A courtesy bus from the station to the
onsen operates once a day (about 3pm; 30 mins) though reservations are
required. The onsen has five *rotemburo* (open-air baths), both mixed and single
sex, and a magnificent setting; it's a world away from city life. If possible book
a room in one of the original wooden buildings rather than East Building which
is a concrete structure. The food is also recommended. Incidentally, Takaragawa
means 'treasure river'. For details of the SL Minakami, see box p92.

After Takasaki, all Asama and some Hakutaka shinkansen call at **Annaka-
Haruna** 安中榛名 (124km). Soon after you start to feel as if you are going
uphill, proof enough that this is now mountain territory.

## Karuizawa 軽井沢 (147km)

All Asama and some Hakutaka shinkansen call
at this mountain resort with top-notch hotels, golf courses and villas for celebri-
ties and wealthy Japanese. Karuizawa is unusual in that events for both the summer (1964) and winter (1998) Olympics have been held here. As well as opportunities to hike and ski it is a pleasant place to escape to in the summer months.

See also box opposite.

The journey from Karuizawa to Sakudaira is either mostly in tunnels or the
vistas are obscured by steep sides or trees but once you reach Sakudaira you
start to get views of the mountains in the distance.

## Sakudaira 佐久平 (164km)

All Asama and some Hakutaka call here.

## Ueda 上田 (189km)

All Asama and some Hakutaka call here. Ueda is a for-
mer castle town but the only thing left of **Ueda Castle** 上田城 (Ueda-jo) is three
turrets; theses are located inside a park about 15 minutes on foot north of the
station (take the Castle Exit, Oshiro-guchi). The castle was completed in 1585
and twice saw off attacks by the Tokugawa clan (see p56). According to a sign
inside the park 'there were many other castles in feudal Japan. But no castle was
attacked twice in this way and none was so brilliantly defended as Ueda Castle',
before revealing – almost as an afterthought – that the castle was indeed 'later
destroyed by the Tokugawa troops', though it was rebuilt in 1626 by the
Sengoku clan and that is what you can see today. The park is a pleasant place to
stroll, especially in the cherry blossom viewing season.

English maps and accommodation details for here and Bessho-onsen (see
opposite) are available at the 1st/ground floor **tourist information counter**
(daily 9am-6pm). Go straight as you leave the shinkansen ticket barrier and it's

at the end of the concourse. The **JR ticket office** (daily 5.40am-10pm) and View Plaza travel agency (Mon-Fri 10am-7pm, Sat & Sun to 5.30pm) are close to the shinkansen ticket barrier. There are **lockers** (including a few ¥500 ones; closed 11pm-6am) to the left as you leave the station.

### Side trip by rail to Bessho-onsen
Bessho-onsen 別所温泉 (🖳 www.bessho-spa.jp), a hot-spring resort where the water is said to have healing properties and to make skin smooth, is a short journey by local train along the Ueda Dentetsu Bessho Line (1-2/hr; 28 mins; ¥590 one-way; JR passes not accepted). To reach the platform at Ueda, head up the stairs by the tourist office and take the Onsen Exit.

There are several **bath-houses** in town; two with a rotemburo are O-yu 大湯 (6am-10pm, closed 1st & 3rd Wed of each month; ¥150) and the more modern Aisome-no-yu あいそめの湯 (10am-10pm, closed 2nd and 4th Mon; ¥500). *Ryokan Hanaya* 旅館花屋 (🖳 hanaya.naganoken.jp; from ¥15,120pp inc half board) is highly recommended; it has both indoor and outdoor hot spring baths and some rooms have their own private hot spring baths.

Soon after leaving Ueda station, the train darts into a long series of tunnels.

### Nagano 長野 (222km)                              [see pp206-10]
All shinkansen call here. Nagano is a major gateway to the Japanese Alps.

### Nagano to Kanazawa                        [Map 4, p180; Map 4a, p186]
**Iiyama 飯山 (252km)** All Hakutaka to Kanazawa call here but only some of the Hakutaka services coming from Kanazawa do. Iiyama is also a stop on the JR Iiyama Line (Toyono to Echigo-Kawaguchi); see box p211.

There is a small Kiosk on the main concourse. The **tourist information centre** (TIC; 🖳 www.iiyama-ouendan.net; daily Apr-Oct 9am-6pm, Nov-Mar to 5pm) and bus stands are on the 1st/ground floor of the main (Chikumagawa) Exit. The TIC has information about the surrounding area but also has a walking map for Iiyama.

Iiyama prides itself on being one of the areas in Japan with the highest snowfall and it calls itself the 'snow country's little Kyoto' because there are so many temples and shrines here. It is also a production centre for Buddhist altars; altars made here are known for their use of gold-leaf which certainly makes

---

### ❏ Nagano to Kanazawa – pre-shinkansen route
The original JR line between Nagano and Naoetsu was transferred to the Echigo-Tokimeki Railway (non JR) and Shinano Railway (change needed at Myoko-Kogen) when the Hokuriku shinkansen opened in March 2015. JR passes are not valid for these stations though the JR East Pass (Nagano, Niigata) is valid from Naoetsu to Arai.

The line between Naoetsu and Toyama is now operated by the Echigo-Tokimeki Railway and the Ainokaze Toyama Railway (change needed at Tomari).

The route from Toyama to Takaoka is operated by the Ainokaze Toyama Railway and from Takaoka to Kanazawa by a combination of the IR Ishikawa Railway and the Ainokaze Toyama Railway (with through trains).

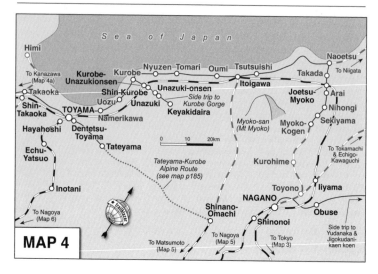

them more striking. To see these head to **Buddhist Altar Street**. Turn right at the end of Altar Street for **Mayumi Takahashi Museum of Doll Art** 高橋まゆみ人形館 (🖥 www.ningyoukan.net; Thur-Tue Apr-Sep & Nov 9am-5pm, Dec-Mar 10am-4pm, Oct daily 9am-5pm; ¥610). This museum features dolls made by Mayumi Takahashi; her designs were based on watching people going about their daily lives in the surrounding countryside. The dolls are very characterful and realistic, particularly those set in a diorama. There is also a film about how the dolls were made. The exhibition changes seasonally. If you think you will have time to see more of the museums here get a Combination Entry Ticket (¥900) at the TIC.

The **Snow Festival** here is held in February (second Sat & Sun).

**Joetsu-Myoko** 上越妙高 **(282km)** All Hakutaka services call here. There is a **tourist information centre** (8.30am-8pm) across from the shinkansen exit with some information in English but the main reason to stop here would be in the winter months to take a bus to the local ski resorts, or for services on the private Echigo Tokimeki railway (Myoko-Haneuma Line), to Naoetsu (see box p179). For this line follow signs for the West Exit.

Between Joetsu-Myoko and Itoigawa there is a long period of tunnels.

**Itoigawa** 糸魚川 **(319km)** All Hakutaka services call here. The shinkansen tracks are on the 3rd floor; the main concourse on the 2nd floor has a 7-Eleven convenience store. The station is also the terminus for the Oito Line from Matsumoto (see pp213-17) and a stop on the private Echigo Tokimeki railway (Nihonkai Hisui Line). Both can be found if you turn left out of the shinkansen exit going towards the North Gate.

> ❏ **The Fossa Magna**
> The Fossa Magna (a 'great rift/depression') appeared when the Japanese islands were
> wrenched apart dividing Japan between the North American Plate to the east and the
> Eurasian Plate to the west; on the western side the rock is 400 million years old and
> on the eastern side only 16 million years old. The Itoigawa–Shizuoka Tectonic line,
> which runs for about 250km to Shizuoka, marks the western border of the Fossa
> Magna. The Fossa Magna Museum and Park can be reached by taking the Loop Bus
> from Itoigawa station at weekends and in holiday periods.

In 2009 Itoigawa was recognised as Japan's first global GeoPark because of
its 'exceptional geological heritage'; you can learn a lot about this without even
leaving the station area. Follow signs for the South Gate for the tourist information centre. First on the right is the **Model Kiha 52 Waiting room** (8.30am-
7pm) where you can go in the train carriage but next door to this in **Itoigawa
Geostation Geopal** 糸魚川ジオステーション ジオパル (🖳 www.geo-itoi
gawa.com; Mon-Fri 10am-6pm, Sat & Sun 9am-6.30pm) is an information centre about the geology of the area and the 24 geosites that can be visited. Also
here is a **Diaroma and Model Railroad Gallery** ジオラマ鉄道模型ステーシ
ョン where you can either observe the various trains on their circuits, or choose
one and control it yourself (¥500/30 mins); the instructions are in Japanese but
the staff will help.

Cross back over to the other side of the station for the **Jade Kingdom
Center** ヒスイ王国館 (Hisui Okokukan; daily 8.30am-11pm; free) where you
can see samples of jade rock and also a polished stone showing the fault of the
Fossa Magna. Most labels are in Japanese but it is definitely worth a visit. Also
here is a tourist information centre (to 5pm), a product centre/souvenir shop, a
*coffee shop* (*kare raisu* ¥600), *soba bar* and some lockers (¥200-300).

After Itoigawa the scenery is rather industrial but the Japanese Alps provide
a lovely backdrop. After yet another tunnel the scenery improves with farmland
before reaching Kurobe-Unazukionsen.

### Kurobe-Unazukionsen 黒部宇奈月温泉 (358km)
All Hakutaka services
call here. The main reason to come here is for the side trip by private railway to
**Kurobe Gorge** 黒部峡谷 (Kurobe-kyokoku). There are lockers on the station
concourse. Follow the East Exit for the Tourist Information Gallery (daily 9am-
7pm) and the South Exit for Shin-Kurobe station (see p182). For additional
information see 🖳 www.kurobe-unazuki.jp.

### Side trip by rail through Kurobe Gorge
This journey offers a chance to travel on a narrow-gauge railway which affords
sweeping views of the northern Japanese Alps. And anyone into Japan's *onsen*
culture should consider taking this side trip as the line passes a number of open-
air hot springs. The line was originally built to carry construction materials for
the Kurobe Dam. An unusual feature of this line is that it is rebuilt every year
– the bridges are dismantled before the winter so that they are not destroyed

H O N S H U

by the snow or avalanches and they are stored in the tunnels. On the journey you will pass through 41 tunnels and over 21 bridges, the latter each a different design.

Note that the Kurobe Kyokoku railway is very busy during the summer and also in late October/early November when many come to see the autumn leaves. Tickets can be booked online but in Japanese only; if going at a peak time it is therefore best to book through JTB or another travel agent. At other times it is fine just to turn up. In some respects the views are best in spring when the leaves aren't fully open, or in autumn when they have fallen as otherwise the many trees block the views.

From the South Exit of Kurobe-Unzaukionsen station walk across the road to **Shin-Kurobe** 新黒部 station for services on the private Toyama Chiho railway line to **Unazuki-onsen** 宇奈月温泉 (Unazuki LEX 2/day, 17 mins, ¥630 seat fee ¥110; local train 1-2/hr, 30 mins, ¥630). Go down the steps at the main exit from the station and turn left, you will soon see a tourist information centre on your left. Pick up a map of Unazuki and then continue on uphill (follow the crowds) for about five minutes to **Unazuki** 宇奈月 station, starting point for the private Kurobe Kyokoku (🖥 www.kurotetu.co.jp; mid Apr to late Nov 11-20/day; approx 78 mins) railway line through the gorge to the terminus at Keyakidaira. The basic fare is ¥1710/2740 (one-way/return) in a *torokko* open-air carriage. However, a seat in a car with windows, in other words protection from the elements, costs an extra ¥360-530 depending on the kind of seat. Not all services have a torokko so you may find you have to pay extra if you don't want to hang around for a later train.

From either **Kuronagi** 黒薙 or **Kanetsuri** 鐘釣 stations it is a short walk to some open-air riverside baths. At Kuronagi the bath is part of a ryokan but it is open to daytime visitors (¥500).

At **Keyakidaira** 欅平 station there is an observation deck on the roof and a restaurant (curry rice ¥800, udon/ramen ¥700) and on the concourse level a coffee stand. There are lockers (¥200-500) in the toilet block to the left of the station exit. Outside the station there is a large map showing the way to an observatory, foot-baths, open-air onsen and also the hiking paths. Note that some routes are only suitable if properly equipped for hiking.

It is likely that you rushed straight to the train when arriving at **Unazuki-onsen** but on your return it is worth spending time in the town. At the **Yamabiko Promenade and Observatory**, a short walk from Unazuki station, you can take a photo of the torokko crossing the red suspension bridge.

**Kurobe River Memorial Museum** 黒部川電気記念館 (daily mid Apr to Nov 7.30am-6pm, Dec-mid Apr Wed-Mon 10am-4pm; free), also called the Hydropower Museum, is worth a visit. The labels are in Japanese but there are fascinating videos showing how the dams and power plants along the river were constructed as well as the building of the railway line and these have an English soundtrack or subtitles.

There is then more of the same with tunnels interspersed with lovely scenery until you reach the urban sprawl of Toyama.

**Toyama** 富山 **(392km)** All Kagayaki, Hakutaka and Tsurugi services call here. Toyama connects with the JR Takayama main line (Gifu to

Nagano/Tokyo), and the private Ainokaze Toyama Line (Kanazawa to Naoetsu). The local line tracks are on the right side as you go through the shinkansen ticket gates. The Toyama Light Rail Toyomako Line (see box below) is on the North Gate side of the station. An underground passageway connects both sides; this is useful if you don't have a rail pass.

If you go through the ticket gates at the Central (South) Gate the Centram tram, which covers the central part of town, is straight opposite, right in the station; this is the first time a tram/streetcar line has been connected to a shinkansen station. To the right of the tram stop is a JR Information Center and beyond that a passageway to the West Gate with a **tourist information centre** (daily Mar-Nov 8.30am-8pm, Dec-Feb 8.30am-7pm) on the left-hand side. On the right-hand side of the shinkansen exit is a Midori-no-madoguchi.

Toyama is a major business city so the main reason for stopping here is to begin the **Tateyama-Kurobe Alpine Route** (see pp184-5), or if you don't have a JR Pass, the Kurobe Gorge (see p181; 2-5/hr to Unazaki-onsen; ¥1840, limited express additional ¥210). Services for both are operated by the Toyama Chiho Railway: turn left out of the Central Exit on the south side. There is a branch of *Starbucks* on the left side but go up the escalator for Dentetsu Toyama 電鉄富山 station, from where services depart to Tateyama (for the start of the Alpine Route) and to Unazuki-onsen (see opposite). Tickets are available from the Toyama Chitetsu Ticket Center 富山地鉄乗車券センター (daily 7am-7pm) on the left by the ticket gates.

If beginning the Alpine Route early in the morning it may be necessary to overnight in Toyama. There are several hotels around the station but two of the most convenient are *Toyama Chitetsu Hotel* 富山地鉄ホテル (☎ 076-442 6611, 🖳 chitetsu-hotel.com; from ¥5200pp), right in Dentetsu Toyama station, and *Excel Hotel Tokyu* 富山エクセルホテル東急 (☎ 076-441 0109, 🖳 www .toyama-e.tokyuhotels.co.jp; from ¥8300/S, ¥12,000/Tw) which is directly across the street on the left side of the main road heading away from the station. Rather than crossing the road take a lift/elevator down to the underpass.

The 6th floor of **Marier** マリエ (🖳 www.marier-toyama.co.jp) by the station has a selection of restaurants: *Tonkatsu Saboten* とんかつ新宿さぼてん (daily 11am-9.30pm) offers tonkatsu (from ¥745). Other options for a meal include a soba/udon and Italian.

---

❏ **A light-railway experiment**
Rail fans might like to consider riding **Portram** ポートラム, the private **Toyamako Light Rail Line** 富山港線 (🖳 www.t-lr.co.jp) from Toyama north up to the coast at Iwasehama 岩瀬浜, a journey of 7.6km (25 mins; ¥210).

This short stretch of line is unique in Japan since it marks the first time that a conventional rail track was discontinued and converted for use by a light-rail operator. The Toyamako Line, previously operated by JR West, was shut down in 2006 and reopened a month later in its new guise as a light railway. The main reason for this conversion was to make it easy for elderly people to get around without a car.

HONSHU

## Tateyama–Kurobe Alpine Route 立山黒部アルペンルート

Toyama is a gateway for the 90km Tateyama–Kurobe Alpine Route (🖥 www
.alpen-route.com) through the Japanese Alps and Kurobe Dam to Shinano-
Omachi. More than a million people every year follow this route, which
involves a combination of train, cable car (funicular), bus, ropeway (cable car)
and a bit of legwork. Note that if the weather is bad the bus and ropeway may
not operate.

If any journey in Japan is proof of the Japanese desire to conquer the elements, it must be this one. The route is impassable in winter, when Siberian
winds sweep south across the Japan Sea, dumping snow in blizzards across the
Tateyama mountain range that doesn't melt away until well into July. It is open
from around mid April to the end of November (heavy snowfall can delay the
opening). The journey can be completed in a day (6-8 hours) in either direction.

A one-way package ticket covering all stages between Dentetsu-Toyama
and Shinano-Omachi costs ¥10,850 (¥18,260 return). However, if you prefer
to go straight back to Nagano there is an express bus (🖥 www.alpico.co.jp/
access/express/nagano_omachi; 4/day; 100 mins; ¥2600) from Ogizawa in
which case you should just buy a ticket to Ogizawa (¥9490 one-way); before
you plan this check the time of the last bus from Ogizawa as it may be as early
as 4.30pm. When you buy your package ticket you should be given an itinerary showing connection times for the different modes of transport on the route
– if not, ask for one. The Tateyama Kurobe Option Ticket (🖥 www.jrtateya
ma.com; ¥9000 one-way, valid for 5 days) is the best option for anyone with a
JR Pass who also has Temporary Visitor status. The ticket covers the route
from Dentetsu-Toyama to Shinano-Omachi/Nagano, or vice-versa, and saves
about ¥3000 on the full price of the route. It include the local bus from
Shinano-Omachi to Nagano (not the express from Ogizawa), though if going
to Matsumoto you can pick up a JR train at Shinano-Omachi.

A baggage-forwarding service (¥1500-1900 per bag) is available from
certain hotels in Toyama, or at Dentetsu-Toyama station, to JR Shinano-Omachi
(Alps Roman Kan); bags must be delivered by 9.30am and will arrive between
3 and 6pm. Charges to other places and hotels in the region vary. There are various places where you can get a meal though it is also worth taking food especially if the weather is good, so that you can sit outside and enjoy the scenery.

**The journey**  The route from Toyama is accessed by taking a train on the
Tateyama Line of the private Toyama Chiho Railway 富山地方鉄道 – from
Dentetsu-Toyama 電鉄富山 to Tateyama 立山 (approx 1/hr; 62-70 mins;
¥1200). From Tateyama the cable car (funicular; 7 mins) operates to
Bijodaira 美女平.

The first of two spectacular sections on the route is the 23km bus journey
(50 mins) from Bijodaira 美女平 to Murodo 室堂 (2450m); the scenery is fantastic on both sides at different times so it doesn't really matter where you sit.
There are announcements in English about what you are seeing. The final part
of the journey is through the snow wall (corridor). It used to take nearly two
months of bulldozing to carve out this corridor and remove a depth of around
20m of snow. However, now they can use GPS so the process takes only 7-10
days. You will be able to walk on the road here but you have to stay on the bus
until it reaches Murodo Terminal. The yuki no otani walk 雪の大谷ウォーク
(snow wall walk) is one of the many highlights of this trip. Assuming you are

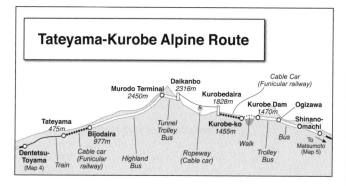

here when there is still snow look out for all the 'graffiti' and feel free to add your own.

It is worth spending time at Murodo and walking to **Mikuriga-ike** みくりが池 (Mikuriga Pond, a volcanic crater lake; about 30 mins return) though if it is still snowy it is quite hard work as the snow is likely to be soft. From here it is not far to **Mikurigaike-onsen** みくりが池温泉 (🖳 www .mikuri.com; 9am-4pm; ¥700), the highest-altitude national hot springs in Japan; the baths are single sex. For the path to the pond/onsen go up to the viewpoint on the top floor of the terminal building. Turn left out of the door, go up the steps and when the path divides take the left one.

From Murodo you take the first **trolleybus** (10 mins) through the tunnel to Daikanbo 大観峰. Then the second most spectacular section is the **ropeway** (cable car; 7 mins) down to Kurobedaira 黒部平. From there take Kurobe **cable car** (funicular; 5 mins) to Kurobeko 黒部湖. The only section of the entire route which requires any footwork is the 20-minute walk here across **Kurobe Dam** 黒部ダム, completed in 1963 and the highest dam in Japan.

Apart from when you take the Kanden Tunnel **trolleybus** from the dam to **Ogizawa** 扇沢, individual travellers have a different entrance queuing point from the many groups that do this trip so ensure you are in the correct place. Generally individuals get priority though sometimes groups are allowed in at the same time. Be prepared for there to be lots of groups everywhere.

If your ticket is only valid to Ogizawa you can either take an express bus (see opposite) from here to Nagano station or pay extra for the **bus journey** to **Shinano-Omachi** 信濃大町 (¥1360) from where you can pick up a limited express (35 mins) or local train (65 mins) on the JR Oito Line to Matsumoto (see pp213-17).

Since the last train to Matsumoto leaves Shinano-Omachi at 9.50pm and takes about an hour you may prefer to stay there. *Ryokan Nanakuraso* 旅館七倉荘 (☎ 0261-22 1564, 🖳 www.nanakuraso.co.jp; ¥4700/5700/7300pp room only/inc breakfast/inc half board) is a short walk from the station; turn left out of the station and walk past the bus ticket booth for Ogizawa. Cross the first road to the left but then take the second road. The ryokan is the white building at the end of the road. The roof garden here is a pleasant place to sit and admire the view.

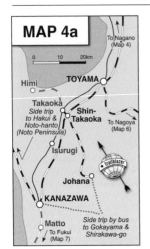

❑ **The Belles Montagnes et Mer**
The Belles Montagnes et Mer is a **sightseeing train** (JR passes valid; seat reservations essential) which runs at weekends and in the main holiday periods on both the Johana Line to Johana and on the Himi Line to Himi (approx 2/day). The line to Himi is the more scenic of the two.

**Shin-Takaoka 新高岡 (411km)** All Hakutaka and Tsurugi services call here. Shin-Takaoka connects with the Johana Line and thus services to Takaoka (see below; 1-2/hr; 3 mins), one mile (1.5km) away, and to Johana 城端 for buses to Gokayama and Shirakawa-go (see pp224-6). Trains operate daily (1-2/hr) to Johana (approx 14 mins) and to Takaoka (3 mins; see below) and Himi (approx 27 mins). Shin-Takaoka is also a stop on some Belles montanges et mer services (see box above). There is a **tourist exchange centre** (daily 9am-8pm) in the station.

**Side trip to Takaoka 高岡** Takaoka has the distinction of being the smallest city in Japan to boast its own light rail (tram) line; the Man'yo light railway operates to Imizu on the coast. Takaoka is also on the JR Johana and Himi lines (see above) as well as the private Ainokaze Toyama Railway. There's a **tourist information centre** (🖳 www.takaoka.or.jp; daily 9am-7pm) in the station. A covered passageway on the 2nd floor connects the station to **Wing Wing Takaoka** ウイング・ウイング高岡, a facility that includes a café, bakery, convenience store, and a *yakitori* restaurant as well as shops selling local products.

Doraemon fans should go to the waiting room on the 1st/ground floor to see the **Doraemon postbox** ドラえもんポスト; it was made, using Takaoka bronze, to celebrate the 80th anniversary of Fujiko F Fujio who was born in Takaoka and created the famous anime/manga character. Letters or cards posted here (collected daily at 10am) will have a Doraemon postmark. The **Man'yo Line** 万葉線 (🖳 www.manyosen.co .jp; 2-4/hr; ¥150-350/journey, 1-day pass ¥800) also has Doraemon decorated trams.

Takaoka is known as a centre for bronze production; the biggest bit of bronze in town is the **Daibutsu** 大仏, a 15.85m-high Buddha statue weighing 65 tonnes, the third largest in Japan. The statue is in Daibutsu-ji (daily 6am-6pm) 5-10 minutes on foot from the station's North Exit.

**Kanazawa 金沢 (450km)** [see pp226-32]
Kanazawa has long been famous for Kenrokuen, a spectacular garden, and for its former geisha district; it's now also the terminus for the Hokuriku shinkansen.

## NAGANO TO NAGOYA VIA MATSUMOTO
### [Table 5, p506]

Distances by JR from Nagano. Fastest journey time: 3 hours.

### Nagano to Nagoya [Map 5]
**Nagano 長野 (0km)** From Nagano, pick up the Wide-View Shinano LEX, which runs along the Shinonoi Line towards Nagoya. The Shinano has large panoramic windows, hence the name.

**Shinonoi 篠ノ井 (9km)** The first stop after Nagano by limited express.

After Shinonoi there are views, to the left, of the valley and towns below the rail line. A few limited expresses call at **Hijiri-Kogen** 聖高原 (31km). There's one very long tunnel shortly before arriving in Matsumoto.

**Matsumoto 松本 (63km)** [see pp213-17]
Matsumoto is a historic castle town set amid fine mountain scenery and a terminus for the JR Oito Line to Itoigawa (see pp180-1).

Should you wish to return to Tokyo pick up the Azusa/Super Azusa LEX (1/hr), which takes just under three hours to Shinjuku (see p111).

**Shiojiri 塩尻 (76km)** If planning to visit Narai (see below), you'll need to change from a limited express to a local train here.

Follow signs for the East Exit and take the escalator down to street level for lockers (¥300-600) and the **tourist information office** (🖳 www.city.shiojiri.nagano.jp; daily 9am-5pm) which has information in English. There is a kiosk and soba stand (soba from ¥290), as well as a *café* (Midori) in the station; the café also offers take-away coffee and bento (lunchboxes).

From Shiojiri, the Shinonoi Line becomes the Chuo West Line, though there's no need to change trains as limited expresses run direct to Nagoya. The line runs through the beautiful Kiso Valley, surrounded by the Central Alps to the east and the Northern Alps to the west.

**♦ Narai 奈良井 (97km)** Narai is the first in a series of '**post towns**' along this route that were

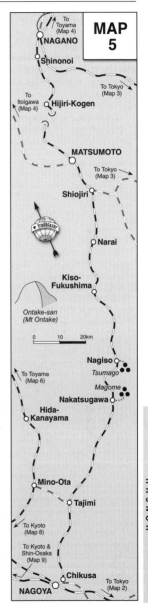

MAP 5

HONSHU

once used as stepping stones on the journey to Edo (Tokyo). In the days before the railway, a total of 69 post stations lined the Nakasendo highway, a trunk road connecting Edo with Kyoto; Narai was 34th overall. Not all have survived but a handful, including the one here in Narai and two more further down the line, have been preserved. Here you'll find a 1km stretch of road lined with Edo-period houses. With its traditional atmosphere, the town was used in 2011

---

### ❏ Tsumago and Magome – Edo highlights in two days

The opening of the Chuo railway line in 1911 along Kiso-gawa effectively robbed the post towns of their purpose, as the old highway was abandoned in favour of the locomotive. For decades Tsumago stood forgotten, left behind by the age of the train. But in 1968, a century after the beginning of the Meiji era, a renovation programme began on Tsumago's houses, which had by then fallen into disrepair. Now the old post town has been reconstructed and survives, as it did before, thanks to a steady influx of visitors. Most of the houses are now craft shops, minshuku and restaurants. This doesn't mean that the area is tacky or full of souvenir kitsch but it is more commercial than nearby Narai (see p187) and can feel like you've walked onto an Edo-period film set.

A great way to fully experience post-town life is to do what those who once travelled the road between Edo (Tokyo) and Kyoto did – stay overnight at a minshuku. A possible 2-day itinerary might be: on the first day, leave Matsumoto and travel by local train to Narai. Spend the morning there before picking up another local train to Nagiso. Then take a bus to nearby Tsumago (see below). After a night in Tsumago, you could return the same way to Nagiso or, better still, hike through the Kiso Valley to Magome (2½-3hrs), the southernmost post town, and then pick up a bus to Nakatsugawa for a train to Nagoya.

**Tsumago** 妻籠  Buses from Nagiso pull in at the terminal just below Tsumago's main street, from where you head up a path to a side entrance. In the early evening, once the day crowds have gone, Tsumago 妻籠 feels much less like a Universal Studios Edo theme park. The minshuku here offer similar rates (¥7500-9300pp inc half board); ask at the tourist office (daily 8.30am-5pm; in a traditional building with steep steps) along the main street about which have vacancies.

Attractions in Tsumago include **Wakihonjin Okuya** 脇本陣奥, which is a three-storied building made of Japanese cypress, behind which is a local history museum (daily 9am-5pm; ¥600). On the opposite side of the road is the **Tsumago Juku Honjin** 妻籠宿本陣 (same days/hours; ¥300, or combined ticket ¥700). Associated with the Shimazaki family, its appearance belies the fact that it is a re-creation. There are many places to eat offering local soba or *oyaki* (vegetable buns). *Fujioto Ryokan* 藤乙旅館 (🖳 www.tsumago-fujioto.jp; from ¥10,800pp inc half board) is 'an absolutely fantastic place to stay – beautiful location, very friendly staff but the best aspect is the food. Breakfast is incredibly good, but it's the extravagant dinners freshly cooked by the owner's wife that makes this such a memorable place. You can relax in their warm baths, dress in a yukata and then sit down for dinner, work through 7-8 courses – with the staff talking you through each dish and explaining what local ingredients were used' (Ben Storey & Alex Chambers). If you need further convincing you should note that it has even attracted ambassadorial praise; both US and Italian ambassadors have stayed here. Apart from overnight stays, Fujioto offers attractive lunches (10am-3pm), including a local trout sashimi set (¥1100) and a Shinshu beef set cooked at the table on a 'hoba' magnolia leaf (¥1700).

as the location of *Ohisama*, one of NHK's popular morning dramas; each season NHK chooses a place in a different prefecture and in general this becomes a huge tourist boost for that place. Narai was the most prosperous post town in the Kiso Valley; steep slopes and thick forest made this section challenging (it took three days to cross the valley), so it became an important stop for weary travellers to rest and stock up on supplies.

Annual events include the **Fuzoku Emaki Parade** in Tsumago on 23rd November every year. Every year since the preservation of Tsumago started in 1968, locals dress up in Edo-period costumes.

**Tsumago to Magome** The 2½- to 3-hour (7.7km) walk between these two historic towns, reaching a maximum height of 801 metres, is not particularly strenuous, though you'd need proper hiking boots in winter when snow can be deep. A **luggage-delivery service** (daily 20th Mar to 30th Nov; ¥500 per piece) is available at the tourist information office (and also at the tourist information office in Magome). Drop off your luggage between 8.30am and 11am and it will be waiting for you at the other end.

The walk first takes you past **O-Tsumago** 大妻籠, where some of the local minshuku are located before heading into countryside. You will then pass the **Gyutou Kannon** 牛頭観音 commemorating black cattle once used to carry loads on this route. Periodically you will also see bells which you are encouraged to ring to deter bears; 3.1km from Tsumago you will come to a map which indicates the slight deviation you need to make to see the **Odaki** 男滝 and **Medaki** 女滝, literally male and female waterfalls which are located close to each other. Then, either walk back to the hiking route or walk briefly along the road to rejoin it. In the next section, you will soon come across notable local trees, two cypress trees which are now joined as one and a weeping cherry tree. Soon after the latter, you will see a rest house with tea on your right. A shop follows, but like many amenities in this area it closes early. You will then cross the border between Nagano and Gifu prefectures. Just before reaching Magome, a lookout offers good views, including of Mt Ena (2191m).

**Magome** 馬籠 The main street in Magome is both more pedestrian friendly and more hilly than Tsumago. There are two tourist offices, with the one on this main street (daily 8.30am-5pm) next to the best toilets in the area. At the coach parking area at the bottom of the hill is the other tourist office; this is the one which offers the luggage-delivery service. The historic **Magome Tea House** 馬籠茶屋 only offers meals for those staying at the associated lodgings. Attractions in Magome include **Toson Memorial Museum** 藤村記念館 (Apr-Nov daily 9am-5pm, Mar daily 9am-4pm, Dec-Feb Thur-Tue 9am-4pm; ¥600), commemorating noted novelist Tōson Shimazaki (1872-1943).

To rejoin the rail route take a bus (11-12/day; 25 mins; ¥560) from Magome to Nakatsugawa, the next limited express stop along the Chuo Line to Nagoya.

If your limbs are feeling tired after the walk, **Kua Resort Yubunezawa** クアリゾート湯舟沢 offers soft water in its indoor and outdoor baths (daily except 4th Thur of month; 10am-8.30pm; ¥800; use your own towel or rent for ¥100). To find it get off the bus at Nakagiri 中切 (¥240), then continue a bit further along the road which the bus stop is on and it is on the right. From there, the resort offers a free bus to Nakatsugawa in the daytime, or rejoin the local bus (¥520).

The local train service from Shiojiri to Narai (20 mins) operates irregularly, with intervals of between an hour and 2½ hours. The trains, which have two cars, are called 'One-man densha' because the driver also checks (and sells) tickets; you will only be able to leave the train from his car.

The old wooden station at Narai sets the tone for what to expect along the main road. Even the benches in the waiting room are fitted with mini tatami mats. More unusually, the station is run not by JR staff but by a local senior citizens' club – members take it in turns to be at the station to meet trains. There are no lockers at Narai station but you can leave your luggage with whoever is on duty until 4pm (¥300).

Turn left out of the station and the main street is straight in front of you. Look out for the odd sake shop (a hangover from the drinking houses that provided Edo-era travellers with some liquid relief) and craft shops, many of which sell locally made *nurigushi* (lacquered combs). Two former residences are open to the public; both are on the right as you walk along from the station. You reach **Kamidonya Shiryokan** 上間屋資料館 (daily Apr-Nov 9am-5pm, Dec to 4pm; ¥300) first and then **Nakamura Residence** 中村邸 (same hours; ¥300).

Several of the old buildings contain small restaurants serving soba. Alternatively, at the far end of the street on the right is **Kokorone** こころ音 (daily 11am-2.30pm), which does hearty portions of delicious *toji soba* (noodles with vegetables; ¥1400) that will fill you up for the rest of the day. If you order this you will be brought all you need to cook the noodles yourself. There are also cafés, including **Matsuya Sabo** 松屋茶房 (daily 9am-5pm), where the friendly owners offer delicious items including siphon coffee, green tea roll and local apple pie. There is an English menu, a guest book to sign and poodles to stroke! Just before that, coming from the station, you can try tasty pork *nikkuman* (¥200) or *oyaki* (¥180), their vegetable equivalent, made with local ingredients.

Return to the station and pick up a local train to Kiso-Fukushima (20 mins) from where you can rejoin the main route. There is one very long tunnel just after leaving Narai.

**Kiso-Fukushima** 木曽福島 **(118km)**  Kiso-Fukushima was once a checkpoint on the highway between Edo and Kyoto.

**Nagiso** 南木曽 **(152km)**  Only a few limited expresses stop here, the nearest station to **Tsumago** (see box p188) so you may need to take a local train. Buses run from outside the station to Tsumago (9-10/day; 7 mins; ¥300), or take a taxi (about ¥1350). Luggage can be left in lockers outside the station for ¥300. In the station the **tourist information counter** (🖳 www.town.nagiso.nagano.jp; summer daily 8.30am-5.30pm) has guides to Tsumago.

If you have time to spare turn right out of the station and walk downhill for a few minutes. Soon on your left you will see a **double-span wooden suspension bridge** 桃介橋 (Momosuke-bashi; 247.76m long and 13m high), which you can walk across. This impressive pedestrian bridge was built in 1922 by Momosuke Fukuzawa in order to make it easier to access the nearby sites where hydro-electric power stations were being constructed.

**Nakatsugawa** 中津川 **(171km)** Nakatsugawa is only 10 minutes down the line by limited express from Nagiso but it feels much further away. Business hotels, concrete, the odd factory smoke stack … here are the realities of post-Edo life, an unpleasant warning that you are less than an hour from the industrial heartland of Nagoya.

The **tourist information counter** (daily 8.30am-6pm), on the left as you leave the station, has a guide map to this region (Nakasendo) in English. There are **lockers** (mostly ¥300-500) and there's a kiosk, as well as a coffee bar and udon/soba stand in the station waiting room. The udon and soba stand (from ¥300) can also be accessed from the platform. **Buses to Magome** (see box p189; 12/day; 25 mins; ¥560) depart from stop No 3 outside the station.

**Tajimi** 多治見 **(215km)** Tajimi is a terminus for the local Taita Line to Mino-Ota on the Takayama Line (2/hour; 30 mins). If planning to visit Takayama (see pp218-24), instead of going all the way to Nagoya to change lines, cross via the Taita Line here to Mino-Ota (see p193) and pick up the route (in reverse) to Takayama.

The Japanese Alps are a distant memory. Instead there are chimney stacks and pachinko parlours for the last 20 minutes into Nagoya. **Chikusa** 千種 (244km) is the final stop on the limited express, just a few minutes before Nagoya station.

**Nagoya** 名古屋 **(251km)**                                        **[see pp197-204]**
From Nagoya, connect up with the Kansai route guide beginning on p234.

**TOYAMA TO NAGOYA VIA TAKAYAMA** [Map 6, p192; Table 6, pp506-7]
Distances quoted are from Toyama. Fastest journey time to Nagoya: 3hrs 50 mins.

**Toyama** 富山 **(0km)** Take the Wide-View Hida LEX (4/day; Takayama Line). The panoramic windows are great but tunnels frequently block out the mountainous scenery. All the same, the line to Takayama remains one of the great rail journeys in Japan, as the train runs south from the coast deep into the Hida mountain range.

The train calls at **Hayahoshi** 速星 (8km), **Echu-Yatsuo** 越中八尾 (17km) and **Inotani** 猪谷 (37km). If on a local train from Takayama to Toyama you may have to change at Inotani but the connecting times are good.

**Hida-Furukawa** 飛騨古川 **(75km)** If nearby Takayama is a miniature Kyoto, Hida-Furukawa is an even smaller version of Takayama and is certainly less crowded; it is also a very pleasant place to walk around.

Pick up a map and guide from **Hida-Furukawa Tourist Information Center** (TIC; 🖳 www.hida-kankou.jp; daily 9am-5pm) to the right of the station in the building beyond the large map. There are **lockers** in the station and also outside the TIC.

Every April (19th-20th) the peace of Hida-Furukawa is shattered by the town's annual festival, the highlight of which is a parade of floats and a big

HONSHU

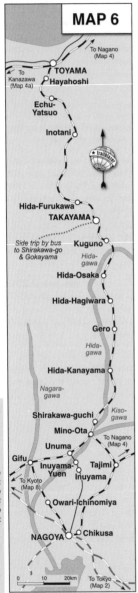

**MAP 6**

To Nagano
(Map 4)

To
Kanazawa
(Map 4a)

**TOYAMA**
**Hayahoshi**

**Echu-
Yatsuo**

**Inotani**

*trailblazer*

**Hida-Furukawa**
**TAKAYAMA**

*Side trip by bus
to Shirakawa-go
& Gokayama*

**Kuguno**
*Hida-
gawa*

**Hida-Osaka**

**Hida-Hagiwara**

**Gero**
*Hida-
gawa*

**Hida-Kanayama**

*Nagara-
gawa*
*Kiso-
gawa*

**Shirakawa-guchi**
**Mino-Ota**

**Unuma**
To Nagano
(Map 4)

**Gifu**
**Tajimi**
**Inuyama-
Yuen**
**Inuyama**
To Kyoto
(Map 8)

**Owari-Ichinomiya**

**NAGOYA**
**Chikusa**

0    10    20km

To Tokyo
(Map 2)

HONSHU

*okoshi daiko* drum, carried by a team of men dressed in white loincloths. Throughout the year, a few of the floats are on display at **Hida-Furukawa Matsuri Kaikan** 飛騨古川祭り会館 (daily 9am-5pm, to 4.30pm in winter; ¥800, or ¥1000 inc the Crafts Museum), a 10-minute walk from the station. In addition to seeing the festivals as well as displays showing how the marionettes on the floats work, you can watch an amazing 3D film of the festival parade; it really brings the event to life.

Across the street is **Hida Crafts Museum** 飛騨の匠文化館 (Hida-no-Takumi Bunkakan; daily 9am-5pm in summer, Wed-Mon 9am-4.30pm until end Feb, to 5pm in March; ¥300, or ¥1000 inc Festival Hall), a heritage centre which displays techniques and tools used by local craftsmen, particularly carpenters. From there it is a short walk to the **canal area** lined with old houses, breweries and storehouses.

**Takayama** 高山 **(89km)**    **[see pp218-24]**
From Takayama, the line continues to follow roughly the course of Hida-gawa. The best part of the journey is the next 50km to Gero, with stunning river and mountain scenery on both sides of the track.

Some of the Wide-View Hida services that start in Takayama also stop at **Kuguno** 久々野 (103km), **Hida-Osaka** 飛騨小坂 (117km), and **Hida-Hagiwara** 飛騨萩原 (129km).

**Gero** 下呂 **(138km)**    Gero-onsen 下呂温泉 (🖥 www.gero-spa.or.jp) is one of the best-known spa towns in Japan. This onsen resort dates back over 1000 years and is mainly popular with elderly Japanese holidaymakers. The town is also known for its tomato juice, considered to be a healthy tonic after a day wallowing in a hot tub.

Turn right out of the station for the **tourist information centre** (daily 8.30am-5.30pm); the staff there can give you a map of town and if it is raining will lend you an umbrella. From there take the passage under the railway tracks to the main part of town. There are several places where you can sit down at an *ashi-yu* (foot-bath) and Charlie Chaplin fans will be pleased to see the statue of him by Shirasagi Bridge; see also box p194.

*Sumeikan* 水明館 (☎ 0576-25 2801, 🖳 www.suimeikan.co.jp; from ¥11,840pp inc half board), a vast onsen hotel near the station, has everything you could possibly want – and some things you might not want: indoor/outdoor onsen (one panorama bath on the 9th floor, one rotemburo – the men's is definitely the best – and one with a wood bath), a swimming pool, gym, disco, karaoke, dining/banquet rooms, souvenir shops, a slot machine area and a café in the lobby. Despite its size it is a great place to stay. Staff wait at the station for LEX trains and will take guests to the hotel (and back the next day), even though it is only a few minutes' walk away.

A few limited expresses call at **Hida-Kanayama** 飛騨金山 (159km) and **Shirakawa-guchi** 白川口 (193km); despite the name this is not an access point for Shirakawa-go (see pp224-6).

**Mino-Ota** 美濃太田 **(199km)** Situated on Kiso-gawa, Mino-Ota is the junction for the local Taita Line to Tajimi on the Chuo Line (30 mins). There is a Kiosk in the station but nothing else.

If planning to visit Matsumoto (see pp213-17), instead of going all the way to Nagoya to change lines, cross via the Taita Line here to Tajimi and pick up the route to Matsumoto from p191 (though it is described in reverse).

**Unuma** 鵜沼 **(209km)** A few limited expresses stop here, the nearest JR station to Inuyama (see pp204-5). Trains to Inuyama-Yuen (5-7/hr; 4 mins; ¥170) for Inuyama Castle can be caught from the private Meitetsu Railway's Shin-Unuma 新鵜沼 station, which is adjacent to the JR station.

**Gifu** 岐阜 **(226km)** Gifu is more of a political and administrative centre than a tourist destination. The city suffered heavy air raids during WWII. The main reason to stop here is to see the cormorant fishing.

Gifu station is a terminus for the Takayama Line and a stop on the Tokaido main line. The main exit is the Nagara 長良 side, outside which the main road heads north towards Nagara-gawa, and where you can also see a gold statue of famed warlord Nobunaga Oda (1534-82).

There are a few **lockers** in a corner of the 2nd floor, the same level as the ticket barrier. **Gifu City Tourist Information Office** (🖳 www.gifucvb.or.jp/en; daily Mar-Nov 9am-7pm, Dec-Feb to 6pm) is also on this floor. Maps are available and staff will help book accommodation. For further information see 🖳 travel.kankou-gifu.jp.

**Cormorant fishing** 鵜飼 (*ukai*; daily mid May to mid Oct 6.15pm ¥3400pp; 6.45 or 7.15pm ¥3100pp) takes place on Nagara-gawa, 2km north of the station. Fishermen dressed in traditional costume of straw skirt, sandals and black kimono use cormorants to fish for *ayu* (sweetfish). The birds, tied to reins and steered by fishermen standing inside the boats, dive down and catch the fish in their beaks. The rein around each bird's neck prevents it from swallowing any of the catch. Today, the event is geared towards the tourist trade, but when the river is lit up by fire and the cormorants set to work, it's an impressive sight. If you don't want to pay to watch from a boat, there's no charge for standing along the riverbank.

For fishing schedules and ticket information, contact the tourist information office in Gifu station, or the cormorant fishing viewing boat shipyard 岐阜市 鵜飼観覧船 (☎ 058-262 0104; 🖳 www.ukai-gifucity.jp/ukai) by Nagara-gawa. Walk south-west of the office to **Kawara-machi** 川原町, where there are some traditional wooden houses which date from the Meiji period and earlier, as well as shops selling local crafts and cafés and restaurants.

To reach these areas either walk, or take a N32, N80 or N86 (Gifu Bus), or the City Loopline bus in the coun-

> ❏ **Chaplin and Basho**
> Comedian Charlie Chaplin fell in love with Japan as a result of reading books by Lafcadio Hearn (see p312). Chaplin visited Japan four times and one thing he became a particular fan of was cormorant fishing; apparently he was 'so enchanted that he came to Gifu to witness the sight a second time'. Locals recall with pride that Chaplin described the activity as 'the greatest art Japan has to offer'.
>
> He was not alone in admiring the skills of the fishermen. The celebrated Japanese poet Matsuo Basho composed a haiku on the subject (just as he did on many other topics):
>
> *'Cormorant boat, where*
> *Before long, what looks like fun*
> *Perhaps ends in sorrow.'*

terclockwise direction (15 mins; ¥210) from outside the Nagara (North Side) Exit of Gifu station to Nagara-bashi (bridge). Services also stop at Meitetsu Gifu station.

A good place to stay the night is *Comfort Hotel Gifu* コンフォートホテル岐阜 (☎ 058-267 1311, 🖳 www.choice-hotels.jp/cfgifu; from ¥9500/S, ¥16,000/Tw inc continental breakfast), across the street from the station.

There are many **places to eat** both in and around the station, but rail fans would probably prefer to go to *Train Café Haruka* 鉄道 CAFE はるか (🖳 traincafe-haruka.com; spaghetti bolognaise ¥680, curry rice from ¥700). In the middle of the café is a diorama with model trains running around. Customers can either just watch or rent a train (around ¥100 for 10 mins). The café is generally open Thursday to Tuesday 11am-6pm but hours do vary and it is also closed at times for private events. Walk along Kinkabashi-dori 金華橋通り from the station and turn right onto Yanagase 柳ヶ瀬 shopping street (the third turning after Kogane Park). The café is on the left (on the 2nd floor) between the first and second set of traffic lights.

After Gifu (note that the train changes direction here), some services stop at **Owari-Ichinomiya** 尾張一宮 (239km).

## Nagoya 名古屋 (256km)  [see pp197-204]
To link with the Kansai route guide, see p234 (shinkansen route), or p237 (Kii peninsula route).

HONSHU

## KANAZAWA TO KYOTO, OSAKA OR NAGOYA

### Kanazawa to Fukui [Map 7; Table 7, p507]

### Kanazawa 金沢 (0km)  [see pp226-32]

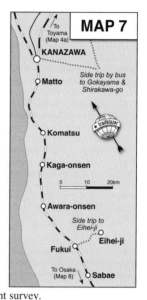

Distances quoted are from Kanazawa. Fastest journey time to Osaka 2hrs 34 mins.

Now that the shinkansen line to Kanazawa is open construction work is focusing on the extension to Tsuruga, expected to be completed in 2022. There are already shinkansen tracks in view as you leave Kanazawa. However, one compensation is that you can still see the Alps in the distance.

A few services stop at **Matto** 橋上 (9km) and most, but not all, stop at **Komatsu** 小松 (28km) and **Kaga-onsen** 加賀温泉 (42km). Some limited expresses stop at **Awara-onsen** 芦原温泉 (59km).

**Fukui 福井 (77km)** History has not been kind to Fukui; the city has been completely destroyed twice, once by war and soon after by an earthquake. However, the prefecture now prides itself on being ranked Japan's happiest in a recent survey.

The main reason for stopping here is to take a side trip to Eihei-ji (see below). The **tourist information booth** (daily 8.30am-7pm) is by the East Gate Exit; here you can pick up information about getting to Eihei-ji and maps of Fukui city. For online information visit 🖳 www.fuku-e.com. **Lockers** (all sizes) are available all around the station.

*Hotel Riverge Akebono* ホテルリバージュアケボノ (☎ 0776-22 1000, 🖳 www.riverge.com; from ¥6800/S, ¥12,600/Tw) has rooms in two buildings; those in the East (new) building are more expensive and are both Western- and Japanese style. Ask for a room with a view of the river. The hotel is a 10-minute walk from the station, has good-value rooms, a good breakfast buffet and a hot spring bath on the roof.

### Side trip to Eihei-ji 永平寺

Eihei-ji (daily summer 5am-5pm, winter 5.30am-4.30pm, except on festival and ceremony days; ¥500; a booklet in English is available in the temple, not at the ticket booth), built onto a mountainside to the east of Fukui, was founded in 1244 by the Buddhist monk Dogen as a centre for Zen training. The name means 'Temple of Eternal Peace', though with so many tour groups piling through it's best to arrive early to appreciate the tranquillity.

The site includes over 70 buildings connected by corridors and thus it is one of the largest temple complexes in Japan. The most sacred building inside the compound is the **Joyoden** (Founder's Hall), in which Dogen's ashes are kept along with those of his successors. **Sanshokaku Hall** is known for the

230 paintings on its ceiling; of these only five are not of a bird or flower and it is said that if you can see these a wish you make will come true. Cooks should look for the *surikogibo* (large wooden pestle) by the **Daikuin** (kitchen); it is said that if you touch this your cooking skills will improve. **Sodo** (the monks' hall) is where they practise zazen meditation; each monk has one tatami mat (approx 1x2 metres) on which to meditate, sleep and eat. In July/August the lotus flowers here should be in bloom; they are known as a symbol of purity and holiness as they are so clean and beautiful but grow in muddy water.

Just as impressive as the fine buildings and beautiful setting is the feeling of how busy and alive the temple remains so many years after its foundation. As you walk around you'll almost certainly see monks at work, perhaps practising how to move sacred objects, or trainee monks reciting a sutra. Visitors are requested to dress modestly, walk quietly along the corridors, and not take photos of the trainee monks.

Rail services towards Eihei-ji start from the private Echizen Railway station outside the East Exit of JR Fukui station. Take the train as far as Eiheiji-guchi 永平寺口 (2/hr; 24 mins; ¥450; no rail passes), then change on to a Keifuku bus (🖳 bus.keifuku.co.jp; 6-8/day; 15 mins; ¥410) for Eihei-ji. More practical and cheaper but less frequent is the direct Keifuku bus (6-8/day; approx 33 mins; ¥720) from the East Gate Exit at Fukui station to Eihei-ji.

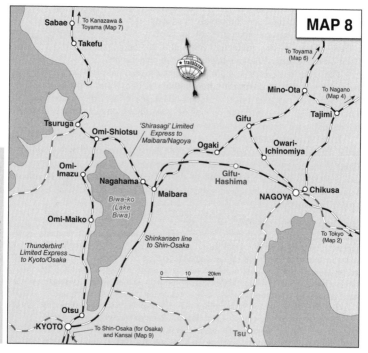

### Fukui to Tsuruga [Map 8; Table 7, p507]

The route from Fukui heading south has a number of tunnels. Some limited expresses make a brief stop at **Sabae** 鯖江 (90km).

After Sabae, some trains also call at **Takefu** 武生 (96km). There's one very long tunnel that lasts around 10 minutes shortly before Tsuruga, just north of Lake Biwa, the largest lake in Japan.

### Tsuruga 敦賀 (131km)

Tsuruga is a major rail junction, marking the end of the Hokuriku Line. This is the last chance to change between the Shirasagi LEX for Nagoya and the Thunderbird LEX for Osaka and Kyoto, but note that the Thunderbird does not always stop at Tsuruga.

### Moving on from Tsuruga: to Kyoto, Osaka or Nagoya [Map 8]

Fifteen kilometres after Tsuruga the track divides into two lines which run down either side of Lake Biwa. The **Thunderbird LEX** heads down the west side of the lake, before joining the Tokaido Line westbound to Kyoto (225km), Shin-Osaka (264km) and Osaka (268km).

The **Shirasagi LEX** (8/day) runs down the east side of the lake to Nagahama (169km), Maibara (177km; p234), then joins the Tokaido Line eastbound to Ogaki (212.5km), Gifu (226km), Owari-Ichinomiya (239km) and Nagoya (256km). If you are on a Shirasagi LEX don't worry when the train seems to double back on itself between Tsuruga and Maibara; there is a spiral section on the line so it's part of the route.

There are better views of the lake (on the left) on the journey to Kyoto/Osaka but even so trees and tunnels often block the view.

# Central Honshu – city guides

### NAGOYA 名古屋

Just over a century ago, Nagoya had a population of 157,000. Today, over 2.2 million people live in what has become the fourth largest city in Japan. Much of the city was flattened by WWII air raids and, in 1959, the Ise Bay typhoon struck the southern part of Nagoya, flooding the entire area and destroying over 100,000 buildings. But the city has bounced back to become a major industrial centre with the headquarters of various companies including Brother and Toyota, as well as production plants of Toyota, Honda and Mitsubishi, in the immediate area.

Nagoya has several places of interest but also functions as a rail gateway to the Japanese Alps and to Kansai, so most travellers will pass through at some stage. Tokyo and Osaka may be better known but Nagoya feels more relaxed and easier to manage.

### What to see and do

Glance up as you leave the station: the skyscraper across the street from the Sakura-dori Exit is **Midland Square** ミッドランドスクエア (🖳 www.midland-square .com), the headquarters for Toyota and the *Mainichi Shimbun* newspaper. The building, completed in 2007, is just under 2m higher than the JR Central Towers (246.9m vs 245m) building which looms above the station itself. Midland Square is home to a host of retail and restaurant outlets as well as the multiplex Midland Square Cinema (see 🖳 www.midland-sq-cinema.jp for film listings) on the 5th floor. You'll know the anchor tenant of the building is Toyota because of the gleaming white car showrooms on the 1st/ground and 2nd floors. Look out for the Toyota staff who spend most of their day cleaning and polishing the cars. The best (and highest) place in Nagoya to see the city is from the 46th-floor Sky Promenade (220m high; daily 11am-10pm; tickets ¥750, from the 42nd floor) inside Midland Square.

**Nagoya Castle** 名古屋城 (🖳 www .nagoyajo.city.nagoya.jp; daily 9am-4.30pm; ¥500) was built in 1612, on the orders of Ieyasu Tokugawa, to be a secure base along the main Tokaido Highway. The castle was razed to the ground during a WWII air raid and only three corner towers and gates survived. The donjon was reconstructed in 1959 and is known for the pair of gold mythical sea creatures (*kinshachi*), which are often described as dolphins, on the roof (very occasionally these are brought down and put on display). Though hard to tell from the ground, the dolphin on the north side is male and the one on the south side is female. It's worth climbing up the tower to reach the 7th-floor observatory and the grounds provide a pleasant respite from built-up Nagoya.

In the grounds is the **Honmaru Palace** 本丸御殿; it was destroyed in wartime bombing but is currently being restored using original construction materials and methods. The Genkan (Entrance hall) and Omote Shoin (Audience hall) are already open for visitors (who should enter by 4pm); the Taimenjo (Reception hall) will be completed in 2016 and the rest of the work by 2018.

The 15m-high *ishigaki* (stone walls) around Nagoya Castle are also being renovated – for the first time in 300 years. That work started in 2004 and will take until at least 2019. **Ninomaru Garden** 二之丸庭園 was originally designed at the same time as the castle was constructed. However, in 1716 it was changed into a landscape garden

that could be walked through. The tea house here was made using hinoki cypress from the Kiso region. **Ninomaru East Garden** 二之丸東庭園 was rebuilt after the war based on an illustration. It has some ponds and an area of lawn.

To reach the castle either take the Meijo subway line to Shiyakusho, or Me-Guru, the Nagoya Sightseeing Route Bus (see p203).

After visiting the castle and gardens, look in on the 630-seat **Nagoya Noh Theater** 名古屋能楽堂 (same times as castle; free), built in 1997. It's open to the public when there are no performances.

**Tokugawa Art Museum** 徳川美術館 (🖳 www.tokugawa-art-museum.jp; Tue-Sun 10am-5pm, closed mid Dec to New Year; ¥1200) exhibits gorgeous treasures that belonged to the Owari branch of the ruling Tokugawa family as well as sections of a 12th-century illustrated scroll of *The Tale of Genji* – though the pieces are too fragile to be kept on permanent display. Take a local train from JR Nagoya station along the Chuo Line four stops to Ozone 大曽根 station. The museum is 10 minutes on foot from the South Exit.

In the former headquarters of the Toyoda Spinning & Weaving Company is **Toyota Commemorative Museum of Industry and Technology** 産業技術記念館 (🖳 www.tcmit.org; Tue-Sun 9.30am-5pm; ¥500); this is much more interesting than it sounds. The Toyota Group was founded by Sakichi Toyoda, inventor of the automatic loom. Automobiles were only added later, by Kiichiro, Sakichi's eldest son. In the Museum of Industry and Technology, the Textile and Automobile pavilions are interactive in parts, and exhibits are informative about how prototype ideas are turned into reality.

The name 'Toyoda', incidentally, did not change to 'Toyota' until 1935, when it was used as a brand name for export cars. It was thought that Toyota would be easier for foreigners to pronounce. The new spelling also brought the number of katakana strokes in the word to eight, which is considered lucky in Japan; Toyoda had 10 strokes. The museum is a 15-minute walk north from the Sakura-dori Exit of JR Nagoya station. See also p205.

Just before the Toyota Museum, on the same side of the road, is **Noritake Garden** ノリタケの森, whose free-to-enter open-plan grounds are home to the **Noritake Craft Center** ノリタケクラフトセンター (🖥 www.noritake.co.jp/mori; Tue-Sun 10am-5pm; ¥500). This world-renowned porcelain company gives visitors the opportunity to follow the manufacturing process from creation and decoration to final inspection. There's also a museum where some of the company's special-order vases, many with price tags of up to ¥10 million, are on display. If those are beyond your budget, there are several shops where mere mortals can purchase more affordable pieces of porcelain.

**Toyota Automobile Museum** トヨタ博物館 (🖥 www.toyota.co.jp/Museum/english; Tue-Sun 9.30am-5pm; ¥1000), an ideal place for car fans, is divided into two parts: the main building, which exhibits 120 cars from some of the earliest models to the present day, and the annex, which traces the history of the motor car in Japan. Take the Higashiyama subway line to Fujigaoka and then the Linimo maglev line to Geidai-dori station (¥290). This was the first commercial maglev line in Japan and was built for the 2005 Aichi Expo. However, it is not especially fast unlike the planned Linear Shinkansen due to open between Tokyo and Nagoya in 2027. In general, there is no driver on the Linimo.

The Linimo can also be used to reach two further attractions: Aichi Expo Commemorative Park 地球博記念公園 (Aichi Kyuhakukinenkoen) is the stop for Studio Ghibli fans, who will enjoy the replica of **Satsukei and Mei's house** サツキとメイの家 (Tue-Sun 10am-4.30pm, from 9.30am in winter; ¥510; booking is necessary at 🖥 1-tike.com/event/satsukito mei) from my *My Neighbour Totoro*. Toujishiryokanminami is the stop for **Aichi Prefectural Ceramic Museum** 愛知県陶磁美術館 (🖥 www.pref.aichi.jp/touji; Tue-Sun 9.30am-4.30pm, to 5pm in summer; ¥400), whose location reflects the nearby ceramics hub of Seto.

**Sakae area** The beating heart of the city may be shifting ever more towards the JR station area, but that doesn't mean that downtown Sakae is giving up without a fight.

Aside from the many shops, bars and restaurants, it's also home to the 180m-high **Nagoya TV Tower** 名古屋テレビ塔 (🖥 www.nagoya-tv-tower.co.jp). Now dwarfed by the JR Towers and Toyota headquarters, the tower was deemed a skyscraper when it was built in 1954 as the first television tower in Japan. Climb the 435 steps to the 100m-high Sky Balcony (daily 10am-9/10pm; ¥700) for a panoramic view of life from the centre of city. With the digitalisation of Japanese TV in 2011, the tower's future is uncertain.

● **Fushimi** Reached from Exit 5 at Fushimi station (Higashiyama Line; midway between Sakae and Nagoya stations), and in Shirakawa Park, is **Nagoya City Science Museum** 名古屋市科学館 (🖥 www.ncsm.city.nagoya.jp; Tue-Sun exc 3rd Fri of month 9.30am-5pm; ¥400, or ¥800 with planetarium).

As well as hands-on demonstrations, it also features the world's largest planetarium with a diameter of 35m.

**Osu area** For fans of Japanese technology, the Osu 大須 area is Nagoya's equivalent to Akihabara in Tokyo. It's also good for restaurants serving different ethnic cuisines. It is within walking distance of Sakae station, or take the subway to Osu-Kannon, or Kamimaezu.

**Nagoya Port area** South of the centre of Nagoya city, Nagoya Port 名古屋港 has been redeveloped as a 'Leisure Zone'. Attractions in one area of the port include **Fuji Antarctic Museum** 南極観測船ふじ (Tue-Sun 9.30am-5pm, daily Jul-Sep; ¥300), on board the *Fuji*. *Fuji* was used for 18 Antarctic expeditions until its retirement to Nagoya Port in 1983. Inside are crew quarters, including a kitchen, dentist's surgery and barber shop, as well as operation rooms. On the top deck is a small museum about the Antarctic expeditions.

*(Continued on p202)*

HONSHU

0    250    500m  Not all roads shown

To Inuyama
and Meiji Mura

Kikunoo-dori

Sengen-cho

**Toyota Commemorative
Museum of Industry
and Technology**

Noritake
Garden

★ trailblazer

● **Noritake Craft
Center**

Kamejima

Kikui-dori

Egawa-dori

**Super Hotel
Nagoya Ekimae**

**Mercure
Nagoya Cypress**

*JR Tokaido
Shinkansen
Line*

**Central
Post Office**

**Hotel Resol
Nagoya**

Kokusai
Center

Sakura-dori

**JR Gate
Tower**
(open in 2017)

Nagoya

**Escalators
to ESCA**

**Enoteca
Pinchiorri**

Horikawa

**Toyoko Inn
Nagoya-eki
Shinkansen-guchi**

**Nagoya
Station**

**Towers
Plaza**

Midland
Square

**Nagoya Marriott
Associa Hotel,
Mikuni Nagoya, Ka-Un,
Sky Lounge Zenith**

*Aonami
(Blue Wave)
Line*

**Latin Bar
São Luis**

ⓘ

**Maruya
Honten**

Meitetsu
Dept Store

Nishiki-dori

To Nagoya Port Area
(Fuji Antarctic Museum,
Nagoya Public Aquarium
& Linear Railway Hall)

Taiko-dori

**Meitetsu &
Kintetsu
stations**

Hirokoji-dori

HONSHU

# Nagoya

名古屋

To Centrair (Chubu Centrair
International Airport, Nagoya)

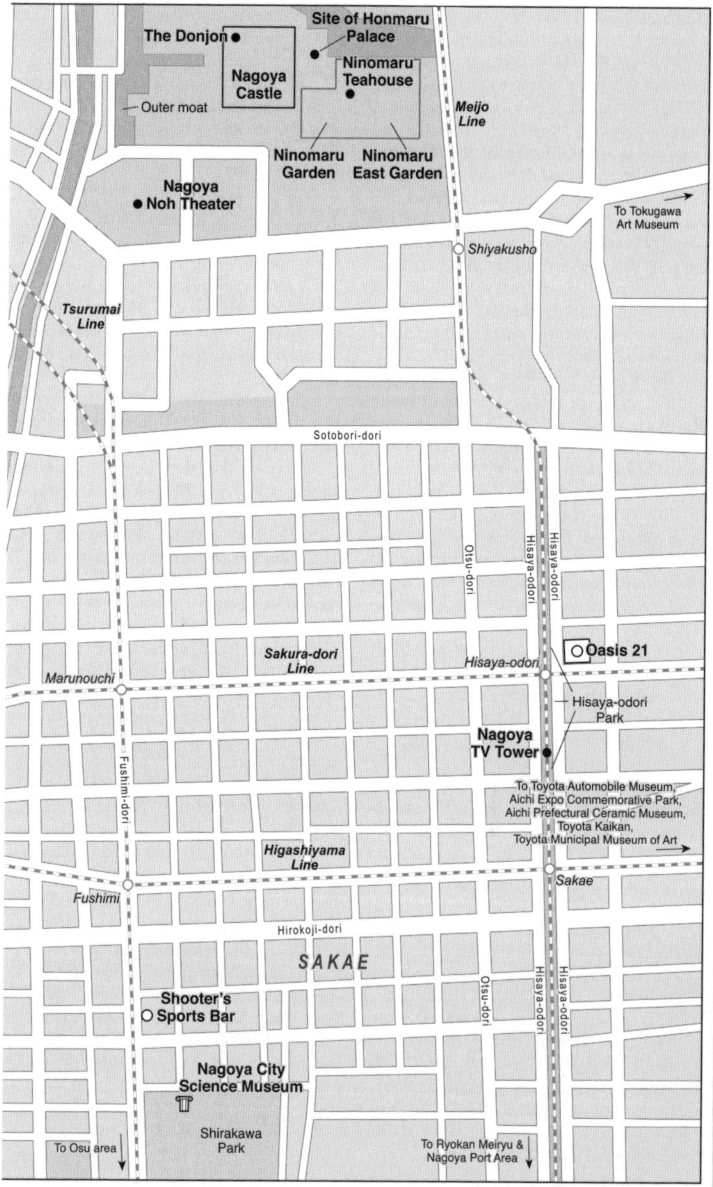

The Donjon ●

Site of Honmaru Palace

Nagoya Castle

Ninomaru Teahouse ●

Outer moat

*Meijo Line*

Ninomaru Garden

Ninomaru East Garden

**Nagoya ● Noh Theater**

To Tokugawa Art Museum →

○ *Shiyakusho*

*Tsurumai Line*

Sotobori-dori

*Otsu-dori*

*Hisaya-odori*

*Hisaya-odori*

*Sakura-dori Line*

*Marunouchi* ○

*Hisaya-odori*

○ **Oasis 21**

*Fushimi-dori*

Hisaya-odori Park

**Nagoya TV Tower** ●

To Toyota Automobile Museum, Aichi Expo Commemorative Park, Aichi Prefectural Ceramic Museum, Toyota Kaikan, Toyota Municipal Museum of Art →

*Higashiyama Line*

*Fushimi* ○

*Sakae* ○

Hirokoji-dori

*SAKAE*

*Otsu-dori*

*Hisaya-odori*

*Hisaya-odori*

**Shooter's ○ Sports Bar**

**Nagoya City Science Museum** ⛩

To Osu area ↓

Shirakawa Park

To Ryokan Meiryu & Nagoya Port Area ↓

HONSHU

*(Continued from p199)* The Antarctic theme continues at **Nagoya Public Aquarium** 名古屋港水族館 (🖳 www.nagoyaaqua.jp; Tue-Sun 9.30am-5.30pm, to 5pm in winter; ¥2000), where the penguin tank recreates extreme weather conditions to make the birds feel at home. Next to the aquarium is a stadium for shark and dolphin shows.

If you have a JR rail pass, to save a few yen on the subway fare to Nagoya Port for these attractions, first take a local train from JR Nagoya one stop on the Chuo Line to Kanayama station, from where you can connect up with the Meiko subway line (branch of the Meijo Line) to the terminus at Nagoyako (Nagoya Port; ¥230).

JR Central's railway museum is in another area of Nagoya Port. **Linear Railway Hall** リニア鉄道館 (Linear Tetsudo Kan; 🖳 museum.jr-central.co.jp; Wed-Mon 10am-5.30pm; ¥1000) but you'll also see signs in English calling the place 'SCMAGLEV and Railway Park'. As well as a prototype linear 'maglev' car (see pp91-2), there are various bullet trains and other more historic rolling stock including a C62 steam locomotive. It is a type that holds the world record of 129km/hr for non-standard-gauge steam. Access from JR Nagoya station (shinkansen side) is by the private Aonami (Blue Wave) Line to its terminus at Kinjo-Futo (¥350).

See pp204-6 for details of side trips.

## Practical information
**Station guide** Nagoya Station's Towers (Central, Office and Hotel) are a city landmark and home to the city's top hotel and the JR Takashimaya department store. They will be joined by JR Gate Tower, with a hotel, mall and offices in April 2017.

For the city centre take the Sakura-dori Exit. Sakura-dori is the main road heading away from the station towards Sakae. Within the station, there are plenty of **lockers** (¥300-¥700).

On the main concourse you'll find a JR ticket office and branch of the JR Tokai Tours travel agency. To exchange your Exchange Order for your rail pass, or to get any other rail-related information in English, head for the **JR Information Centre** (daily 10am-7pm), in the middle of the concourse on the Taiko-dori side of the station.

Several JR lines run through or terminate at Nagoya: the **Tokaido Line** (main line trains; platforms 1-6), which heads east to Toyohashi and west to Gifu; the **Chuo Line** (platforms 7-10) for Nakatsugawa and Matsumoto; and the **Kansai Line** (platforms 11-13) for Matsusaka, Ise and Toba. The **shinkansen tracks** (platforms 14-17) have an entrance near the Taiko-dori side of the station. Nagoya is also a hub for two private railways, **Meitetsu** and **Kintetsu**. The stations (first Meitetsu, then Kintetsu) are a couple of minutes' walk to the right from the Sakura-dori side of JR Nagoya. Finally, the **Aonami Line** (see column opposite), a third-sector railway, also operates from here.

**Tourist information** The tourist information office (🖳 www.ncvb.or.jp; daily 9am-7pm) is on the 1st-/ground-floor concourse

---

### ❏ Nagoya station – Guinness World Record holder
Shinjuku station in Tokyo may be deemed the busiest in the world but Nagoya station is the biggest and therefore is a Guinness World Record holder. There is even a plaque proclaiming this: 'The JR Central Towers is the world's largest station building, with: 410,000 sq metres (4,413,000 sq feet) of floor space and a height of 245 metres (803.8ft)'. **Central Towers** comprises Office Tower, which has 51 stories (the observation deck on top of it now has a café, wine bar and beauty spa) and **Hotel Tower**, which has 53 stories including six floors below ground. **Sky Street**, on the 15th floor, spans both towers and offers wonderful views of Nagoya through glass windows. It can be accessed from the lifts/elevators to the left as you enter the main (non-shinkansen) side of the station.

of the Sakura-dori side of the station. The English-speaking staff can give you an accommodation list but can't make bookings. Ask also for a copy of the English *JR Nagoya Station Guide*, which details all the shops and restaurants in the vast station complex.

**Getting around** Nagoya has an efficient **subway system** with six lines: Higashiyama (yellow), Meijo (purple), Tsurumai (blue), Sakura-dori (red), Meiko (purple and white) and Kamiida (pink). Nagoya station is connected with the Higashiyama and Sakura-dori lines. Operating hours are 5.30am to 12.30am, with a further 45 minutes of operation on the Higashiyama Line on Friday nights or nights before a public holiday.

A one-day subway **pass** costs ¥740, a one-day bus pass is ¥600 and a combined pass is ¥850. On weekends and on weekdays which fall on the 8th of the month, the price of the combined pass (called on these days the Do-Nichi Eco Ticket) is reduced to ¥600.

**Nagoya Sightseeing Route Bus** (🖥 www.nagoya-info.jp/en/routebus; Tue-Sun; ¥200/journey, ¥500 one-day pass inc discounts for some sights), called **Me-Guru**, runs on a circular route to several of the main sights including the castle, several of the museums and also the TV Tower. It departs from stop 8 outside the Sakura-dori side of Nagoya station.

**Central Japan International Airport**, known as **Centrair** (🖥 www.centrair.jp), is on a man-made island off the coast of Tokoname, a suburb of Nagoya. The private Meitetsu Railway operates a direct service (Sky LEX 2/hr, LEX 4/hr; 28 mins; ¥870, ¥1230 inc reserved seat; no rail passes) between the airport and Meitetsu-Nagoya station (next to the JR station).

**Festivals** The biggest festival of the year is **Nagoya Festival**, a three-day event in mid October.

**Nagoya Port Festival** in July is also worth visiting; it has a high number of participants and spectators (around 380,000 in 2015) plus impressive fireworks.

**Where to stay** Towering above JR Takashimaya in the station is the luxurious *Nagoya Marriott Associa Hotel* 名古屋マリオットアソシアホテル (☎ 052-584 1111, 🖥 www.associa.com/english/nma; from ¥21,500/S, ¥29,500/D, ¥34,000/Tw). This world-class hotel certainly can't be beaten for location – from the station concourse a lift/elevator whisks you up the twin towers to the gleaming 15th-floor lobby. The rooms are beautifully furnished and have spacious bathrooms. Facilities include a fitness club with an indoor pool and a state-of-the-art gym.

Another good upscale choice close to the station is *Mercure Nagoya Cypress* メルキュール名古屋サイプレス (☎ 052-571 0111, 🖥 www.thecypress.co.jp; from ¥21,000/S, ¥27,000/D), which sometimes has good online rates.

In the station area, a good bet is another chain hotel, *Toyoko Inn Nagoya-eki Shinkansen-guchi* 東横イン名古屋駅新幹線口(☎ 052-453 1047, 🖥 www.toyoko-inn.com; from ¥7344/S, ¥9504/D, ¥10,5840/Tw inc breakfast). Take the Taiko-dori Exit (shinkansen-side) and walk up the main road which leads off from there. The hotel is on the first road on your left after Bic Camera. Also near the station, on the shinkansen side, is *Super Hotel Nagoya Ekimae* スーパーホテル名古屋駅前 (☎ 052-451 9000, 🖥 www.superhoteljapan.com; from ¥6480/S, ¥8980/D, inc breakfast) which has the usual functional rooms.

A five-minute walk up Sakura-dori from the station is *Hotel Resol Nagoya* ホテルリソル名古屋 (☎ 052-563 9269, 🖥 www.resol-nagoya.com; ¥10,000/S, ¥15,000/Tw or D), which has compact but modern rooms.

*Ryokan Meiryu* 旅館名龍 (☎ 052-331 8686, 🖥 www.japan-net.ne.jp/~meiryu; ¥5350/S, ¥9000/Tw, ¥11,400/Tr; breakfast ¥650, dinner exc Sun ¥2300) is a homely Japanese inn with tatami rooms (none en suite). Services include free internet access and coin-operated laundry. The ryokan is a 3-minute walk south-east of Kamimaezu station (Exit 3) on the Meijo/Tsurumai subway lines.

HONSHU

If you want to stay the night at **Centrair Airport**, your best bet is the on-site *Comfort Hotel Central International Airport* コンフォートホテル中部国際空港 (☎ 0569-38 7211, 🖥 www.choice-ho tels.jp/centrair; from ¥8800/S, ¥14,600/D, ¥14,600/Tw), which is adjacent to the terminal building.

See also pp67-73.

**Where to eat and drink** Inside the station, head for **Towers Plaza** タワープラザ on the 12th and 13th floors of the JR Takashimaya JR-高島屋 department store, where you'll find nearly every kind of Japanese food as well as Italian and Chinese. The two basement floors are also crammed with food and outlets selling freshly made take-away lunch boxes.

For more upmarket dining, **Nagoya Marriott Associa Hotel** (see p203) has a wide range of restaurants including: *Mikuni Nagoya* ミクニナゴヤ (daily 11.30am-2.30pm & 5.30-10pm), a top-class French restaurant on the 52nd floor with views over the city; and *Ka-Un* 華雲, the hotel's best Japanese restaurant with sushi and tempura bars, as well as table and tatami seating. If you just want to enjoy an elevated view for the price of a drink, try the hotel's 52nd-floor *Sky Lounge Zenith* スカイラウンジジーニス, where they do cocktails from 5pm to midnight, as well as a lunch buffet (11.30am-3pm; Mon-Fri ¥3500, Sat & Sun ¥4000).

Across the road from JR Nagoya station at **Midland Square** you'll get the cheapest deals in the restaurants on the basement and 4th floors. But for a splurge, why not book a table with a floor-to-ceiling window view at the upscale modern Italian restaurant *Enoteca Pinchiorri* エノテーカピンキオーリ (🖥 ep-nagoya.jp; daily 11am-3pm & 5-11pm). Lunch courses start from ¥4320 + 10% service, but the spectacular views more than repay the expense.

On the 9th floor of **Meitetsu department store** 名鉄百貨店, next to JR Nagoya station, is *Maruya Honten* まるや 本店 (daily 11am-11pm), where the speciality is delicious pieces of grilled eel in soy sauce (from ¥2035).

*Yabaton* 矢場とん (daily 11am-10pm), a Nagoya-based restaurant chain famous for its *misokatsu* (deep-fried pork cutlet dipped in a delicious miso-based sauce), has several branches around the city. Downtown branches often have long queues – a better bet is to visit the Nagoya station branch in the basement (northernmost part) of the **Esca shopping mall**, the entrance to which is down an escalator right outside the Taiko-dori Exit. Dishes include tonkatsu sets with the two main cuts of meat: *rosukatsu* (¥1188) and *hirekatsu* (¥1728). Also in the Esca shopping mall is *Kishimen Yoshida* きしめん 吉田 (daily 11am-9.30pm), where you can try the Nagoya speciality *kishimen* noodles, with a variety of toppings, including *kaki-age getoji* (deep fried vegetable and egg; ¥830), or tempura (¥910).

Also on the Taiko-dori side of Nagoya Station is *Latin Bar São Luis* ラテンバルサンルイス (Tue-Sat 5pm to midnight, Sun 3-11pm). Reflecting the large Brazilian population and influence in Aichi and Nagoya, it offers filling items including half a chicken (¥1080) and feijão bean stew and rice (¥880), a wide selection of drinks and occasional live music.

In the **Fushimi** district just west of Sakae and popular with foreign residents is *Shooter's Sports Bar* シューターズスポーツバー, which has draught beer, pool tables and a variety of lunch menus (¥893-998) as well as Shooter's Classic Burger (¥1350). **Oasis 21** オアシス２１ in Sakae has a good range of cafés and restaurants; attractions include skating on an artificial rink in the winter.

### Side trips by rail from Nagoya

● **Inuyama Castle** 犬山城 A popular side trip is to nearby Inuyama Castle (daily 9am-4.30pm; ¥550), perched on a hill overlooking Kiso-gawa. Built in 1537, it was partly destroyed during the division of Japan into prefectures at the beginning of the Meiji era in 1871 and then again after an earthquake in

1891. Four years later, what was left of the castle was handed back to the Naruse family who had originally owned it – this act of charity was, however, tempered by a condition: the castle had to be repaired. Restoration work on the donjon was completed in 1965. However, the central keep and stone wall are the originals and it is the oldest standing castle in Japan. Note that like most castles in Japan the steps inside are very steep and also there is little to see inside so the best bit is the view from the top. A free English volunteer guide is available if you want.

Take the private Meitetsu Inuyama Line (3-5/hr; 30-43 mins; ¥600, ¥960 inc seat reservation) from Meitetsu-Nagoya and get off at either Inuyama 犬山, or one stop after at **Inuyama-Yuen** 犬山遊園. The advantage of getting off at Inuyama-Yuen is that it is a pleasant walk (from the West Exit) following the river and then the road up to the castle; pick up a map at the station.

If you want to save money and have a JR rail pass, the closest JR station to Inuyama-Yuen is Unuma (see p193) on the Takayama Line. From Nagoya, take a Hida LEX, or Tokaido Line train, to Gifu and change there for a Takayama Line train to Unuma (total journey approx 46 mins). At Unuma transfer to Meitetsu's adjoining Shin-Unuma station. From Shin-Unuma, Inuyama-Yuen is the first stop.

● **Meiji Mura** 明治村  The other big sight near Inuyama is Meiji Mura (🖳 www.meijimura.com; Mar-Oct daily 9.30am-5pm, Nov-Feb daily to 4pm; ¥1700), an open-air collection of Western-style buildings from the Meiji era, including the 1898 Sapporo Telephone Exchange, St John's Anglican Church from Kyoto, as well as part of Frank Lloyd Wright's Taisho-era Imperial Hotel. Two steam locomotives chug the short distance between 'Tokyo' and 'Nagoya' stations while there are also historic trams and more modern buses. Rides on those are ¥500, but a free pass is available for ¥2700 covering entrance and unlimited rides. Make sure that you allow the best part of a day to see Meiji Mura as its combination of park and many historic buildings takes time to cover. There are several places to eat and drink, with retro snacks such as *curry pan* (¥260). Sometimes, meal sets include items associated with historic figures such as writer, Natsume Soseki. On one visit, this included 'Marie' biscuits, apparently the only food he liked when he stayed in Britain!

For Meiji Mura see the route for getting to Inuyama Castle but stay on the Meitetsu Line train to Inuyama. Pick up a bus (2-3/hr; 20 mins; ¥420) there.

● **Toyota City** 豊田市  East of Nagoya is Toyota City, once known as Koromo, but now indicating that it is the headquarters of the company. With a population of more than 422,000, it is actually larger by area than Nagoya. The plant tour (11am-1pm), which needs to be booked in advance (🖳 www.toyota.co.jp/en/about_toyota/facility/toyota_kaikan), includes the production line. The tour leaves from **Toyota Kaikan** トヨタ会. Before or after that you can wander around Toyota Kaikan Museum (Mon-Sat 9.30am-5pm; free) which explains the history of Toyota (Toyoda) and has displays of most models.

The most direct way to Toyota City is by subway (Tsurumai Line) connecting into Meitetsu's Toyota Line. You then need to change to the Aichi Loop Line two stops to Mikawa-Toyota 三河豊田 (the nearest station to the Kaikan which is 20 minutes away on foot). Mikawa Toyota can also be reached by taking a JR Tokaido Line Rapid to Okazaki and then Aichi Loop

Line (approx 60-70 mins in all), or via the JR Chuo Line (Rapid) to Kozoji 高蔵寺 and then Aichi Loop Line (similar journey length).

En route between Toyota City and Mikawa Toyota, **Toyota Municipal Museum of Art** 豊田市美術館 (🖥 www.museum.toyota.aichi.jp; Tue-Sun 10am-5.30pm, to 5pm in winter; ¥300) can be seen. It features a tranquil setting with design by famed architect, Yoshio Taniguchi.

## NAGANO 長野

Situated in the centre of Honshu, Nagano is the junction of the northern, central and southern Japanese Alps, and is often referred to as the 'roof of Japan'.

### What to see and do

The main sight within Nagano is Zenko-ji but a highlight is seeing the snow monkeys at Jigokudani Monkey Park. For details of this and other side trips from Nagano, see pp210-13.

According to the Nagano tourist literature, **Zenko-ji** 善光寺 (🖥 www.zenkoji.jp; daily 5am-4.30pm; free) is regarded as a special temple which one 'must visit at least once even if a great distance must be travelled'. Judging by the number of tour buses that pull up outside, this instruction continues to be followed to this day.

To avoid the inevitable crowds, arrive in the early evening, or better still at dawn, when the abbot and abbotess make an appearance to pray for the salvation of visiting pilgrims. The starting time of this daily ceremony depends on the season – in the summer it's as early as 5.30am, in December at 7am; check with the tourist office. You can find a guide in English at the **information office** 善光寺案内所 on the left side of the approach to the temple.

The temple is said to have been founded in the 7th century as a place to house the **golden triad**, a sacred image of the Buddha. It is never displayed in public but every seven years an exact copy is brought out as part of the Gokaicho ceremony – the next will be in 2022. Inside the **main hall** (Hondo), people gather around the statue of Binzuru, considered to be Buddha's most intelligent follower; by rubbing the statue, they hope their own aches and pains will be rubbed away. Access to the pitch-black passage containing the 'Key to Paradise' is by ticket from vending machines (daily 9am-4/4.30pm; ¥500, ¥1000 with Sanmon Gate ticket, see below) inside the main hall. Anyone who touches the key is assured eternal salvation. Anyone who doesn't can buy another ticket and try again. Don't go in if you're claustrophobic or afraid of the dark.

The 20m-tall **Sanmon Gate**, the main gateway to the temple precinct, was constructed in 1750 but extensive restoration work was completed in 2007. Visitors can climb the steep stairs (¥500) inside the gate

---

### ❏ From princess to perfume

The story of Nagano would not be complete without mention of the legendary Nyoze Hime (Princess Nyoze) whose bronze statue (atop a fountain) stands proudly on the plaza directly outside the Zenkoji Exit of the station. To cut a long and rather convoluted story to its bare bones, Princess Nyoze became gravely ill and was granted a miraculous recovery by the triad now housed in Zenko-ji. As a mark of respect and thanks, the statue of Nyoze offering incense is positioned looking towards the temple to the north.

As if to prove that a legend is nothing if it cannot be commercialised, visitors to Nagano can now purchase Princess Nyoze Eau de Parfum (¥3000 a bottle) which is promoted locally as having a 'fresh floral fragrance to evoke the healthy and elegant figure of Princess Nyoze and the refreshing weather of Nagano'.

to the top, for a view down the long street leading to the temple.

Though it's possible to take a bus to the temple from the station (bus No 6, from stop No 1 outside Zenkoji Exit; ¥150), it's easy to walk the 30 minutes north along Chuo-dori, though it is gently uphill all the way. For a slightly shorter walk take a train (2-3/hr; ¥170) from Nagaden's Nagano station to either Gondo 権堂 (2 mins), and walk through Gondo-dori shopping arcade to Chuo-dori, or stay on the train to the next stop, Zenkojishita 善光寺下 (4 mins) and walk west from there.

If walking along Chuo-dori look out on the right for **Saiko-ji** 西光寺, a small temple founded in 1199; a leaflet is available. You'll know you've reached the start of the main path towards Zenko-ji because it's lined with shops, soba restaurants and stalls. Legend has it that 7777 stones were used to pave the final 450m leading to the temple's main hall.

Just to the east of Zenko-ji, **Nagano Prefectural Shinano Art Museum** 長野県信濃美術館 and the adjacent **Higashiyama Kaii Gallery** 東山魁夷館 (🖳 www .npsam.com; both Thur-Tue 9am-5pm; ¥500) are both worth popping into. The former showcases the work of local artists, mainly landscapes of the surrounding mountains and countryside. The latter houses the work of Yokohama-born painter Higashiyama Kaii, who died in 1999. Between the museum and the gallery is *Café Kaii*, with outdoor seating in the summer – a good place to grab a coffee away from the bustle.

The **Nagano Olympic Memorial M-Wave Arena** 長野市オリンピック記念アリーナ　エムウェーブ is now home to **Nagano Olympic Exhibition Corner** (🖳 www.nagano-mwave.co.jp; Sat & Sun only 10am-5pm; free). The M-Wave Arena was the speed-skating venue during the Olympics and displays include the Japanese Olympic team uniforms, the Olympic torch and the skates used by Hiroyasu Shimizu, who became a national hero when he took gold in the 500m speed-skating event and bronze in the 1000m in the M-Wave Arena. The vast arena has the world's largest

wooden suspension roof, which is supposed to resemble ocean waves. In summer the arena is used for a variety of events including a sumo tournament. The skating rink is open from early October to the end of March (daily 10am-6pm). To reach the M-Wave Arena take bus No 8 from stop No 1 outside the station's East Exit and get out at M-Wave-mae (20 mins; ¥350).

## Practical information

**Station guide**  Although rebuilt for the Olympics, Nagano Station, was rebuilt again in 2015 for the opening of the Hokuriku Shinkansen. It has two sides: East and Zenko-ji. Take the latter for the city centre and Zenko-ji itself. **Lockers** (a few ¥600, plenty of ¥300 and ¥500) are near both exits.

Shinkansen services depart from platforms 11-14 and have a separate entrance to other JR lines. There are lifts/elevators between the shinkansen platforms and main concourse. There is a transfer area at the top of the escalator from the shinkansen platforms for connecting services: JR East's Iiyama Line for Nozawa-onsen and Shinano Railway's Kita Shinano Line for Myoko-Kogen.

There are several cafés and restaurants in the station (see Where to eat, p208).

**Tourist information**  Nagano City TIC (🖳 www.go-nagano.net; daily 9am-6pm) is on the station concourse, opposite the shinkansen ticket barrier. There are maps and brochures about Nagano and the surrounding area and staff will book accommodation for you (Nagano city only); they can also advise on the best places to ski and hike and have bus timetables and information on late-season skiing. They will provide English leaflets on request.

**Getting around**  The private **Nagano Dentetsu Railway** (🖳 www.nagaden-net .co.jp), known as '**Nagaden**', operates in the Nagano area. The entrance is outside the Zenkoji Exit of JR Nagano station; the station itself is underground.

The main **bus terminal** バスターミナル is at street level outside the Zenkoji Exit.

Stop No 1 is for buses to Zenko-ji. The **Gururin-go city area bus** (Stop No 4; daily 8.35am-7.20pm; 4/hr; flat fare ¥150) operates on a circular route round the city. Buses to Jigokudani Monkey Park (see p212) depart from the East Exit.

**Where to stay** The JR-operated *Hotel Metropolitan Nagano* ホテルメトロポリタン長野 (☎ 026-291 7000, 🖳 www.hotel metropolitan-nagano.jp; from ¥13,500/S, ¥17,500/D or Tw; rail-pass holders and early reservations get a small discount), one of the most luxurious places in town, is located to the left as you take the Zenkoji Exit. Even if you aren't staying here it is worth popping in to see the model railway diorama in the lobby area.

*Mielparque Nagano* メルパルク長野 (☎ 026-225 7800, 🖳 www.mielparque.jp/ nagano; from ¥8800/S, ¥12,800/Tw; tatami rooms from ¥13,000/2 people, ¥18,000/5 people) is less than five minutes on foot from the station's East Exit. It is in a sleek modern building with glass lifts/elevators that whisk you from the lobby to your room. The singles are nothing special, twins are roomy with larger bathrooms but best of all are the Japanese tatami rooms which can sleep up to five people.

*Hotel Chisun Grand Nagano* ホテルチサングランド長野 (☎ 026-264 6000, 🖳 www.solarehotels.com; from ¥6500/S, ¥11,300/Tw) offers spacious rooms and a plentiful buffet breakfast. The restaurant and some rooms offer a good view of Nagano city centre, including the station.

*Island Hotel* アイランドホテル (☎ 026-226 3388, 🖳 www.island-hotel.co.jp; ¥6500/S, ¥11,500/Tw) is a typical business hotel, with a simple inclusive Japanese-style breakfast. All rooms are en suite, but there is also a hot-spring-style common bath. The twins are reasonably spacious with relatively large bathrooms.

*Comfort Hotel Nagano* コンフォートホテル長野 (☎ 026-268 1611, 🖳 www .comfortinn.com; ¥5800/S, ¥10,200/Tw) has compact rooms with bright and cheerful common areas.

For something a little more upmarket try *Hotel JAL City Nagano* ホテルＪＡＬ

シティ長野 (☎ 026-225 1131, 🖳 www.jal hotels.com; ¥7700/S, ¥13,600/D, ¥16,600/ Tw), which is closer to Zenko-ji.

A good budget business hotel choice is *Smile Hotel Nagano* スマイルホテル長野 (☎ 026-226 3211, 🖳 www.smile-hotels .com/nagano; ¥4900/S, ¥8100/D or Tw), with standard facilities including laundry facilities and an in-house café.

*Zenko-ji Kyojuin Youth Hostel* 善光寺教授院ユースホステル (☎ 026-232 2768, 🖳 www.jyh.or.jp; dorm bed from ¥3360pp, private room ¥4000pp; additional ¥600 for non members; no meals) is just outside the main temple compound. A stay must be reserved in advance and the hostel is closed from 10am to 3pm. Bags must be left in the entrance hall lockers so as not to damage the specially hand-made tatami in all the dormitory rooms (the building is over 100 years old). It's 20 minutes on foot from the station up Chuo-dori.

*Shimizuya Ryokan* 清水屋旅館 (☎ 026-232 2580, 🖳 www.chuoukan-shimi zuya.com; from ¥6600pp inc breakfast, dinner ¥2200), on the road leading up to Zenko-ji, is a convenient place to stay for early-morning access to the temple and it has free internet. Tatami bedrooms can sleep up to four people; the price per person is the same whether you are in a single or sharing. There are no en suite bathrooms: as usual in ryokan, the large common bathrooms are shared. Look for the white sign on the street outside the entrance – with the name written in English and kanji.

Another option for Japanese-style accommodation, and with a great location, is *Matsuya Ryokan* 松屋旅館 (☎ 026-232 2811, 🖳 matsuyaryokan.server-shared .com; from ¥6480pp, or ¥10,800pp half board). It is a small traditional inn within the precinct which leads up to the main gate of Zenko-ji.

**Where to eat and drink** While places to eat at the station were formerly sparse, the new station offers a great selection. For something lighter, there is *Becks Coffee Shop* ベックスコーヒーショップ (daily 7am-8pm) next to the information centre and *Kobeya Kitchen Bakery* 神戸屋キッチ

# Nagano

← NORTH

SOUTH →

長野

Nagano Dentetsu Line

Shiyakusho-mae

Showa-dori

To Nagano North map

Smile Hotel Nagano

Hotel JAL City Nagano

Saiko-ji

Chuo-dori

Hotel Chisun Grand Nagano

Island Hotel

Comfort Hotel

Mielparque Nagano

Ginya Shokudo

Nagano-dori

Nagano Shinkansen Line

To Kanazawa

To Nagano Olympic Memorial Arena M-Wave

Bus stops

Nagano Station

Beck's Coffee Shop, Kōbeya Kitchen Bakery, Karuizawa Kobo & Meiji-tei (in MI DO RI)

Nagano (Dentetsu)

Sobatei Aburaya

Post office

Hotel Metropolitan Nagano

Shin-etsu Line

Higashiyama Kaii Gallery

Nagano Prefectural Shinano Art Museum

Zenko-ji Kyojuin Youth Hostel

Zenko-ji Hondo

Sanmon Gate

Zenko-ji (Information) ⓘ

Matsuya Ryokan

Suyakame Miso

Niomon Gate

To Zenkojishita (station)

Fujiya Gohonjin

Fujikian

Rakucha Rengakan

Patio Daimon

Post office

Shimizuya Ryokan

Yanagimachi-dori

Chuo-dori

To Obuse & Yudanaka

Nagano-dori

Gondo

Gondo-dori

Covered arcade

To Nagano South map

0    100    200m

HONSHU

ン (daily 7.30am-8pm) reached by turning right at the Zenkoji Exit and continuing downstairs. Soba (from ¥310) is available from traditional noodle bars in the waiting room and on platforms. A good selection is also available in the new MI DO RI building (Zenkoji Exit), with lighter items on the 2nd floor, including local Shinshu hot dogs and ham at *Karuizawa Kobo* 軽井沢工房 (daily 9am-8pm). For full meals, the 3rd floor Ogosso dining area (11am-10pm) has a wide range of restaurants: *Meiji-tei* 明治亭 (🖥 www.meijitei.com; daily 11am-9pm) offers a variety of rice bowls including katsudon; the chain also has its own special dipping sauce. Expect to pay around ¥1500. There is also a branch of Meiji-tei on the 2nd floor (11am-8pm) when you can get take-out meals.

For a more formal place to eat soba, try *Sobatei Aburaya* そば亭油や (daily 11am-11pm), right across the street as you take the Zenkoji Exit. Bowls of soba noodles start from ¥750, or for ¥1430 you get a filling soba and tempura set menu. Take the zebra crossing from the station, and the entrance is to the left of the escalator leading up to the Heiando bookshop. Look for the blue 'Soba' sign in hiragana hanging over the food display window.

Convenient for some of the hotels featured above is the *Ginya Shokudo* 吟屋食堂 (Tue-Sun 11am-2pm & 5.30pm to midnight) featuring economical dishes, such as *gyoza teishoku* (¥705) and *karaage teishoku* (¥820), with add-on mini soba (¥300) or ramen (¥350).

On the right approaching Zenko-ji itself you can see a group of traditional buildings making up **Patio Daimon** ぱていお大門, an area where former merchant houses and warehouses have been transformed into a variety of attractive shops, cafés and restaurants in a traditional style, but most are not open in the evening.

There are also plenty of soba restaurants on the approach to Zenko-ji, including *Fujikian* 藤木庵, along Chuo-dori opposite a small branch post office. Seating is on tatami or at wooden tables. The tempura and soba (from ¥1140) are delicious.

*Rakucha Rengakan* 楽茶レンガ館 (daily 11am-8pm), whose building evokes the site's former post station, is in a brick building with a small red awning above the door; it is to the right as you face the entrance to Fujikian. They serve soba set meals (¥1150 for a meal with all the trimmings, including an ice-cream dessert) as well as Western-style meals such as pasta. The lunch set costs ¥1480.

*Suyakame Miso* すやかめみそ (daily 10am-5.30pm) does grilled rice balls with miso (soybean paste) for ¥250, and miso-flavoured ice-cream (¥300), which sounds awful but tastes good. Also worth trying is the *amazake* (¥200), a sweet form of sake usually served warm. It's on a corner as you approach the temple and has a sign in English.

With a history dating back to 1648 and occupying an impressive old building that used to house one of Nagano's most upmarket ryokan, *The Fujiya Gohonjin* 藤屋御本陣 (🖥 www.thefujiyagohonjin.com; Mon-Fri 11.30am-3pm & 6-10.30pm, Sat & Sun 7-10.30pm) is now a café, bar and wedding hall. The menu includes 'main plate' lunches for ¥1500, chef's special-course lunches for ¥2400, and afternoon tea and cake sets for ¥1100. A 10% service charge is added.

### Side trips from Nagano

Possible trips by private Nagano Dentetsu 長野電鉄 (Nagaden) railway are to the small town of Obuse, or to the rail terminus and gateway to the Japanese Alps at Yudanaka. The 'snow' monkeys at Jigokudani Monkey Park (Jigokudani Yaen-koen) can be reached on a local bus from Yudanaka station, but if starting from Nagano it is easier to take the direct express bus (see p212).

For a day trip to Jigokudani Monkey Park, and/or Yudanaka, the **Snow Monkey One-day Pass** (¥2900) provides the best value. It is valid for unlimited use of the Nagaden railway; the express bus to the Monkey Park; local buses between Yudanaka and Kanbayashi-onsen/the Monkey Park; and free admission to the park itself. Passes are available from the ticket office in Nagano Dentetsu's Nagano station (underground); if no one is there ask at the ticket counter.

● **Obuse** 小布施 Obuse was a stop on the old highway linking the Japan Sea with Edo (Tokyo) and now boasts a number of museums, temples and gardens. The biggest draw is **Ganshoin Temple** 岩松院 (🖳 www.gansho-in.or.jp; daily Apr-Oct 9am-5pm, Nov 9am-4.30pm, Dec-Mar 9.30am-4pm; ¥300), which belongs to the same Zen Buddhist sect as Eihei-ji (see pp195-6), near Fukui. The temple is renowned for its ceiling painting of a phoenix 'staring in eight directions' by the artist Katsushika Hokusai (1760-1849). The impressive **Hokusai Museum** 北斎館 (🖳 www.hokusai-kan.com; daily May-Aug 9am-6pm, Sep-Nov 9am-5.30pm, Nov-Apr 9am-5pm; ¥500), a 10-minute walk from the station, houses some of the artist's best works of art.

Download a map and guide for Obuse from 🖳 www.obusekanko.jp, or pick one up from the tourist information office at Nagano station. Trains (1-3/hr; 33/22 mins local/express train; ¥670, ¥770 on express with seat reservation) depart from Nagano Dentetsu's Nagano station. The **lockers** (¥300) at Obuse station are suitable for day packs. The town is manageable on foot but at the weekend (and on weekdays in high season) a **shuttle bus** (9.50am-5pm; 1/hr; ¥300/one-day pass) runs from the station in a loop and stops at all the main sights, including Ganshoin Temple and the Hokusai Museum.

● **Yudanaka** Yudanaka 湯田中 is an onsen town and a good base for a visit to Jigokudani Monkey Park (see p212). *Yorozuya Annex Yurakuan* よろづや アネックス湯楽庵 (☎ 0263-33 2117, 🖳 www.yurakuan.com; from ¥9000pp inc breakfast; extra ¥1000 for a room with a view) is highly recommended for its baths and its meals. The main indoor bath (Momoyamo-buro) is a registered National Cultural Treasure, the rotemburo is wonderful, and there is also a

---

❏ **Sightseeing trains in the Nagano area**
Nagano has its share of the new and ever-increasing variety of sightseeing trains (see box p98) which provide a comfortable and relaxing way to travel on local lines, mainly at weekends and holidays.

The '**OYKOT**' (¥1740, reserved seat ¥520) operates on the Iiyama Line between Nagano and Tokamachi (Apr-Nov); in winter (Dec-Mar) it operates only as far as Togarinozawa-onsen. Its name (Tokyo spelled backwards) symbolises its traditional and leisurely image; the trains were designed to make Japanese feel nostalgic and that they were back in their grandmother's house. JR pass-holders have to pay the basic fare (¥250) between Nagano and Toyono; seat reservations must be made in advance.

The **Koshino Shu*Kura**, which goes from Tokamachi to Joetsu-Myoko (Mar-Sep weekends 1/day), promotes sake and local products from the Niigata area.

Shinano Railway's **Rokumon restaurant train** (🖳 www.shinanorailway.co.jp/rokumon; approx 75 mins; 3/day; ¥1640; return fare & a full meal ¥12,800) operates between Nagano and Karuizawa (see p178). From Nagano to Karuizawa Japanese food is served and from Karuizawa to Nagano the food is Western. There are two cars: one has private dining cabins and the other is a normal car so it is not essential to book a meal. However, if you do want one it must be booked through a travel agency.

HONSHU

Jacuzzi (men can use the former in the morning and the two latter in the evening; women at other times). Evening meals must be booked in advance (*kaiseki ryori* costs from ¥3000). However, the rooms (Japanese- and Western-style) are getting rather old, though they are spacious and en suite. Station pick-up is provided if you reserve ahead. Trains (1-2/hr; approx 46/63 mins express/local train; fare ¥1160, ¥1260 inc seat reservation on express train) depart from Nagano Dentetsu's Nagano station. Local buses (winter 18/day, summer approx 4/day; ¥210) to Kanbayashi-onsen for the Monkey Park depart from outside Yudanaka station. Alternatively a taxi costs about ¥1500.

● **Jigokudani Monkey Park** The most popular side trip from either Yudanaka, or from Nagano, and well worth the visit is to Jigokudani Monkey Park 地獄谷野猿公苑 (Jigokudani Yaen-koen; 🖥 www.jigokudaniyaen koen.co.jp; daily Apr-Oct 8.30am-5pm, Nov-Mar 9am-4pm; ¥500) to see the **wild 'snow' monkeys**. The park is 7km from Yudanaka and 850m above sea level. The species (*Macaca fuscata*) of monkeys here is native to Japan and is the only non-human primate species living so far north and in areas covered by snow for several months of the year.

The best time to go is in the winter months as the monkeys are more likely to be bathing in the natural hot spring pools allocated to them – Jigokudani means 'Hell Valley' in English as the water the monkeys bathe in is far too hot for humans. They are often referred to as 'snow monkeys' because of photos taken in the bath with snow on them. But at any time of the year you can watch them posing, grooming each other and playing games and there is always the chance one or more will decide to take a bath. It is hard to leave as you never know what will happen next.

The easiest way to get to the park from Nagano is to take the express bus (Dec-Apr 9/day, Apr-Dec 4/day; 55 mins) which departs from stand No 3 on the East side of JR Nagano station; its final destination is Shiga-Kogen, a ski/hiking area. (If you have bought the One-Day Pass at the Nagaden ticket office in the railway station you can use the underground east–west passage to reach the bus stop). The bus stops on the main road at Kanbayashi-onsen guchi (bus stop C). Walk downhill a little bit and then take the first right going uphill to **Kanbayashi-onsen** 上林温泉. Note that the local bus from Yudanaka (15 mins) stops in Kanbayashi-onsen either at bus stop A (Dec-Apr 6/day, Apr-Dec approx 4/day) or at bus stop B (Dec-Apr 12/day, Apr-Dec approx 4/day), not on the main road.

The park is about a 30-minute walk from the bus stop. The walk is mostly flat but is a bit uphill at the beginning and at the end. Be aware that the monkeys will pounce on you very quickly if you bring out any food; there are lots of notices warning you not to eat or drink anything. If you are hungry stop at *Enza Café* (daily 9.30am-5pm), in Kanbayashi-onsen. They have an extensive menu, but their speciality is ramen: chicken broth ramen costs ¥860/980 (normal/large), special spicy chicken, or Zenkoji-miso chicken, ramen is ¥1050.

Also be aware that your feet can get very cold in the winter months and on wet days, or after rain, it can be very muddy. If you aren't prepared, at **Snow Monkey Resorts Information and Gift shop** (🖥 www.snowmonkey resorts.com; daily 9am-5pm), by the entrance to the actual park, you can rent jackets or boots (¥500), or buy gloves, socks or hats (from ¥500). From here it is a 1.6m walk to the snow monkeys.

The closest accommodation option is **Kourakukan** 後楽館 (☎ 0269-33 4376, 🖳 www.kanbayashi-onsen.com/kourakukan.htm; from ¥12,000pp inc half board) as it is about a 5-minute walk from the monkey's hot springs. Staying here means you can have the monkeys to yourself in the morning – for a bit! The other advantage is that there is a rotemburo you can get into; the downside is that there is no road access from the bus stop/car park so you have to carry your luggage to the ryokan.

A very helpful English-speaking guide who lives in **Shibu-onsen** 渋温泉, a spa resort two kilometres from Yudanaka station, is Zeno Kubicek. He is a Slovakian expatriate and runs his own website (🖳 www.yudanaka-shibuonsen .com), which is a one-stop-shop for local hotel/ryokan reservations and sightseeing tours off the beaten track.

## MATSUMOTO 松本

Surrounded by mountains, Matsumoto is an ancient castle town and a gateway to the north-western corner of Nagano prefecture. The 3000m peaks of the Japanese Alps form a backdrop to the west of the city. Locals like to think of Matsumoto as not the heart but the 'navel' of Japan. Whichever it is, thousands visit to see one of the country's best-preserved castles.

### What to see and do

Matsumoto is easy to walk around but if you prefer a bus see p216 for details of the **Town Sneaker bus and pass (TS Pass)**.

Fifteen minutes on foot north of the station is **Matsumoto Castle** 松本城 (Matsumoto-jo; 🖳 www.matsumoto-castle .jp; 8.30am-5pm; ¥610 inc Castle Museum, or ¥550 with TS Pass, inc City Museum) considered to be one of the finest castles in Japan. A small fortress was first built here in 1504 but this was remodelled and expanded in 1593 to become what still stands today. The fortification once dominated the city skyline but the view is now obscured by office blocks and the castle remains invisible until the final approach.

The 5-storey donjon is one of several in Japan known as a 'Crow Castle' because the outside walls are mainly black. The design is unusual because although the castle is built on a plain, rather than a hill, it still contains traditional defensive elements: the hidden floor, sunken passageways, specially constructed holes in the wall to drop stones on the enemy below and incredibly steep stairs to make an attack on the castle difficult for intruders. Tacked on

to the side is the moon-viewing room, where guests could stare up at the moon while enjoying a cup or two of sake. This was a later addition and was only possible to add in a time of peace as anyone sitting there is very exposed.

If on a Town Sneaker Northern Course bus get off at Matsumotojo-Shiyakushomae. The only entrance to the castle is at Kuromon Gate; Uzumibashi, the red bridge, on the west side of the castle is not an entry point.

The nearby **Matsumoto City Museum** 松本市立博物館 (🖳 matsu-haku.com; daily 8.30am-5pm; ¥300, or ¥250 with TS Pass, ¥610 inc castle), also known as the Japan Folk Crafts Museum, focuses on the history of the city from ancient times through to the Meiji era. Exhibits include a very uncomfortable-looking box-shaped pillow used by geisha to protect their hair when sleeping and some weapons used by the police which most people would want to stay well away from. Everything is well labelled and it is definitely worth a visit.

If you walk to the castle along Daimyo-cho-dori, look out for **Seikando** 青翰堂, a second-hand bookshop whose roof is shaped like the castle. It is actually best seen from the right-hand side of the road as it is squeezed between two buildings. Also worth looking out for all over town are the **wells** where you can have a drink of clear spring water.

The large frog sculpture at the entrance to **Nawate-dori** 縄手通り, on the Daimyo-cho-dori side, makes the street hard to miss.

In the early years horse carriages weren't allowed down this road so Yohashira Shrine 四柱神社, a small shinto shrine here, and the businesses that had opened up on the street decided to promote it by saying people can buy frogs (*kaeru*) here but also go home safely (kaeru also means 'to return'); the kanji for these are different but if written in hiragana かえる, they are the same. Not surprisingly Nawate-dori is often now called Frog Street, but aside from this it is a characterful Edo period stone-paved street with a variety of shops including several selling *sembei* (snacks) – but also models of frogs.

**Nakamachi-dori** 中町通り (🖥 nakamachi-street.com) is another stone-paved street with several old buildings including some originally used as warehouses (*kura*); these are now converted to cafés, craft and antique shops as well as places to stay (see Where to stay). Also on this street is the unusual **Matsumoto City Scale Museum** 松本市はかり資料館 (Tue-Sun 9am-5pm; ¥200, or ¥150 with TS Pass). There are few labels in English but ask for the leaflet in English when you buy your ticket. It is a fascinating chance to see the wide variety of instruments used to weigh and measure things including a device to separate male and female cocoons; Matsumoto was a major centre for silk production in the Meiji era. Behind the museum are some kura (former warehouses) which you can also wander around.

Ten minutes on foot north of the castle, but also a stop on the Town Sneaker Northern Course bus, is **Kyu-Kaichi Gakko** 旧開智学校 (Tue-Sun 8.30am-5pm; ¥300, or ¥250 with TS Pass), a former elementary school that was built in 1876. The oldest Western-style school building in Japan, it remained open for 90 years and is now open to all.

Proving that, contrary to popular belief, the education system in Japan was not all work, the school has a room dedicated to extra-curricular activities, which included ice-skating (note the 'geta-skates' that look uncomfortable and dangerous to wear). There are few labels in English but you should be given an explanatory leaflet when you buy your ticket.

**Matsumoto Timepiece Museum** 松本市時計博物館 (Matsumoto Tokei Hakubutsukan; Tue-Sun 9am-5pm; ¥300, or ¥250 with TS Pass; English pamphlet available) is by the river and features a large pendulum clock (supposedly the biggest in Japan) outside. If possible, get here on the hour when you can see many of the clocks on display swing into action and chime. It's a small museum but watch- and clock-lovers will be in heaven. You'll find everything from tiny intricate pocket watches to enormous clocks – look out for the 19th-century cannon-shaped sundial from England. Inexplicably there is also a small selection of antique gramophones. The museum is on the Town Sneaker Eastern Course route.

See also pp217-18 for details of side trips from Matsumoto.

### Practical information
**Station guide** As trains pull into Matsumoto station, a female voice virtually sings the station's name to arriving passengers. The JR Shinonoi Line (also known as JR Chuo East), for services to Shinjuku in Tokyo, JR Chuo West (for services to Shiojiri and Nakatsugawa), JR Oito Line

---

## MATSUMOTO – MAP KEY

| **Where to stay** | **Where to stay** (*cont'd*) | **Where to eat and drink** |
|---|---|---|
| 1 Hotel New Station | 10 Toyoko Inn Matsumoto | 2 Kobayashi |
| 3 Hotel Mor-Schein | Ekimae Honmachi | 5 Ario department store |
| 4 Ace Inn Matsumoto | 12 Dormy Inn Matsumoto | 7 Toritetsu |
| 6 Toko City Hotel | 14 Marumo Ryokan | 8 Gusto |
| Matsumoto | 15 Nunoya Ryokan | 9 5 Horn |
| 8 Richmond Hotel | | 11 Shinmiyoshi |
| Matsumoto | | 13 Kobayashi |

KyuKaichi
Gakko ●

Uzumibashi ●    Matsumoto
      ● Castle

Kuromon ●
Gate

Matsumoto 🛕
City Museum

ℹ️

Daimyo-cho-dori

Seikando 🏛️

Spring water ●    ○ 13
well       ● Spring water
          well

Nawate-dori     Matsumoto
          Scale Museum

Frog ●
statue

Metoba-gawa

To Nagano

Matsumoto       14 🛕 🛕
Timepiece     Nakamachi-dori    ● Spring water
Museum 🛕             well
          🛕
Ise-machi-dori    Parco   15
         Department
         Store    NAKAMACHI
   2          DISTRICT
1 🛕 ○ 3    🛕🛕
       8 🛕 9         ● Spring water
To    Koen-dori              well
Itoigawa         10 🛕 ⊠ Post Office

Hommachi-dori

      ○ 7    ○ 11
     Agatanomori-dori    ● K Conbini         Agatanomori-dori
Matsumoto           (convenience)
Station    6 🛕       12    store
ℹ️      5 🛕🚌 Alpico Bus        Fukashi Park
    4     Terminal
      Ario          🛕
      Dept    Tenjin-dori
      Store

Matsumoto
Dentetsu Line
(to Oniwa for Japan
Ukiyo-e Museum &
Matsumoto City Open-Air
Architectural Museum)

Hommachi-dori

To Shinjuku
(Tokyo) &
Nagoya

## Matsumoto
松本

0   100   200m

★ trailblazer

Ima-machi-dori

(for Shinano-Omachi) and the private Matsumoto Dentetsu Kamikochi Line (for Kamikochi) call here. The latter is on the Alps Exit (West Exit) side of the station.

Follow the signs for the Castle (Oshiro; East) Exit. On the station concourse is a branch of JR East's View Plaza travel agency. There are **lockers** (daily 5.15am-12.30am; ¥300-500) in the waiting room to your right as well as opposite the entrance to MI DO RI department store before you take the escalator down to street level and by the East Exit. There are also cafés such as *Vie de France* (1st/ground floor) and *Starbucks* (3rd floor) in the station.

**Tourist information** The **tourist information centre** (TIC; ⌨ welcome.city.mat sumoto.nagano.jp; daily 9am-5.45pm) is in front of you as you exit the ticket barrier. Friendly, English-speaking staff can assist with same-day reservations and will provide sightseeing information. There is also a **tourism information centre** (TIC; daily 9am-5.45pm), on the way to the castle, with basically the same information.

**Getting around** Matsumoto is compact enough to visit **on foot**. Another option is to **rent a bicycle** (9am-5pm; free) from either Sui Sui Town (available at eight sites around town including the City Museum and Clock Museum), or Rikisha (available at 32 shops/hotels in the centre of the city. For further details ask at either TIC.

However, if you really need it the **Town Sneaker bus** (TS; ⌨ www.alpico.co .jp/traffic/matsumoto/townsneaker; ¥200 flat fare, ¥500 1-day pass) runs on four different loops (Northern, Eastern, Southern & Western; approx 9am-5pm; 1-2/hr) from outside Matsumoto station. Note that the Western Course leaves from the West (Alps) side of the station but the other routes depart from the Castle (Oshiro) side. The 1-day pass also gives reduced-price entry to many of the city's attractions.

Other local and long-distance buses depart from the **Alpico bus terminal** アル ピコバスターミナル beneath Ario department store, across the street from the station. Pick up the English-language *Town*

*Sneaker Timetable and Bus Route Map* from the tourist information counter at Matsumoto station.

**Festivals** An annual outdoor performance of **Noh** is held in the grounds of Matsumoto Castle on the evening of 8th August. The show is illuminated by bonfires, with the brooding presence of the castle as a backdrop. On 3rd November, **Matsumoto Castle Festival** features a samurai parade and puppet shows.

In October (usually over a long weekend), the annual **Soba Noodle Festival** is marked with over a hundred soba stalls setting up inside Matsumoto Castle Park.

The **Taiko Drum Festival** (last Sat & Sun in July) also takes place next to Matsumoto Castle and attracts some of the country's best taiko drummers.

**Where to stay** *Ace Inn Matsumoto* エー スイン松本 (☎ 0263-35 1188, ⌨ www .ace-inn.net; from ¥6900/S, ¥11,500/D, ¥13,500/Tw inc breakfast) is a standard business hotel conveniently located right outside the station. Take the Castle Exit from the station and it's on the corner on your right.

*Toko City Hotel Matsumoto* トーコー シティホテル松本 (☎ 0263-38 0123, ⌨ www.tokocityhotel.co.jp/matsumoto; from ¥7500/S, ¥12,000/D, ¥14,000/Tw; breakfast ¥900) is across the street from the station. Reception ('Front') is on the 10th floor; this is also where guests have breakfast as there are wonderful views of the Alps. The rooms are on the 4th-9th floors.

A good alternative is *Dormy Inn Matsumoto* ドーミーイン松本 (☎ 0263-33 5489, ⌨ www.hotespa.net/hotels/mat sumoto; from ¥8590/S, ¥11,090/Tw or D); this chain offers an onsen and rotemburo on the roof, an excellent buffet breakfast and free noodles in the evening. It is conveniently located between the station and the main sights.

*Toyoko Inn Matsumoto Ekimae Honmachi* 東横イン松本駅前本町 (☎ 0263-36 1045, ⌨ www.toyoko-inn.com; from ¥5724/S, ¥7884/D, ¥8964/Tw inc breakfast) is also conveniently located.

From the station go over the pedestrian crossing and along the bricked road till you reach a plaza. The hotel is on the far side of the plaza.

*Richmond Hotel Matsumoto* リッチモンドホテル松本 (☎ 0263-37 5000, 🖥 richmondhotel.jp/matsumoto; from ¥10,500/S, ¥13,000/D, ¥17,000/Tw) is also only a few minutes on foot from the station and is next to Parco department store. It's a hyper-efficient place with automatic check-in, clean, compact rooms and a coin laundry. A more economical option is *Hotel New Station* ホテルニューステーション (☎ 0263-35 3850, 🖥 www.hotel-ns.com; from ¥5800/S, ¥8300/D, ¥11,800/Tw, exc breakfast), two minutes on foot from the station. The rooms are basic but all have en suite facilities. Just across the street is *Hotel Mor-Schein* ホテルモルシヤン (☎ 0263-32 0031, 🖥 www.mor-schein.co.jp; ¥7560/S, ¥12,900/D, ¥15,120/Tw; breakfast ¥650), another standard business hotel.

*Marumo Ryokan* まるも旅館 (☎ 0263-32 0115, 🖥 www.avis.ne.jp/~marumo; from ¥5000pp, breakfast ¥1000), a traditional inn in the Nakamachi district by Metoba-gawa, has tatami rooms (none en suite) with a fantastic wooden bath and great breakfast. It gets booked up fast. The entrance is on the narrow road between Nakamachi-dori and Nawate-dori.

An alternative is the small and friendly *Nunoya Ryokan* ぬのや旅館 (☎ 0263-32 0545, 🖥 www.mcci.or.jp/www/nunoya; from ¥4500pp, no meals), one block back from the river. It's a small, traditional Japanese inn with the usual creaking wooden floors and communal (lockable) bathrooms. The owner speaks a little English.

## Where to eat and drink
One of Matsumoto's specialities is *basashi*, raw horse-meat (which is also popular in Kumamoto, see box p451). A good place to try it is *Shinmiyoshi* 新三よし (Mon-Sat 11.50am-2pm & 5-11pm), a short walk from the station. The restaurant is known for its *sakura nabe* (horse-meat hotpot; ¥2580) as well as basashi, and the décor includes harnesses, saddles, whips and horse-themed calligraphy. Set menus start at ¥1500.

For yakitori go to *Toritetsu* とり鉄 (🖥 www.tori-tetsu.com; 11.30am-2pm & 5.30pm to midnight); there is an English menu and even though they specialise in chicken there are vegetarian and other options. A 'skewer' costs from ¥130 and there are some interesting combinations.

*Kobayashi* こばやし (daily 11.30am-6pm) serves delicious hand-made soba noodles. It's a quaint, traditional place on a quiet street just set back from the river. They serve a wide variety of soba dishes from ¥1100; tempura soba costs ¥1500. Look for the small display of plastic food in the window. There is another **branch** outside Matsumoto station with similar opening hours.

*Gusto* ガスト, a 24-hour family restaurant on the 1st/ground floor of Hotel Richmond Matsumoto, is open to anyone (not just hotel guests). *5 Horn* ファイブホルン (🖥 5horn.jp; daily 10am-10pm, lunch 11.30am-2.30pm, teatime 3-6pm; evening meals from 6pm), an Italian café on the ground floor of Parco department store, specialises in cakes and desserts – look out for their 'Sacher Torte of Blonde Chocolate' (¥440) – but also does main meals: a lunch set menu costs from ¥1300, spaghetti dishes from ¥950. A branch in the basement of **Ario** (10am-9pm) sells their cakes. On Ario's 7th floor there is a branch of *Saizeriya* サイゼリヤ (daily 10am-10pm; spaghetti from ¥399), the pasta chain, which has great views of the Alps. However, they may close the blinds in the afternoon as the sun can be very bright.

## Side trip by rail to Oniwa 大庭
On the outskirts of Matsumoto, in Oniwa, is the **Japan Ukiyo-e Museum** 日本浮世絵博物館 (🖥 www.japan-ukiyoe-museum.com; Tue-Sun 10am-5pm; ¥1200), a private museum built by the Sakai Family which houses over 100,000 Japanese woodblock prints, though only a fraction are on display at any one time. Take the private Alpico Kamikochi railway line from Matsumoto

station to tiny Oniwa station 大庭 (1-2/hr; 6 mins; ¥170). Ask at Oniwa ticket office for a map with directions to the museum, about 15 minutes' walk away.

While here, stop by the **Matsumoto City Open-air Architectural Museum** 歴史の里 (Rekishi-no-Sato; Tue-Sun 9am-5pm; ¥400), which is next door. The main building is an old wooden court house, the only one of its kind still standing in Japan today. Displays focus on the history of Japanese law and court proceedings, and on items used by the police, including *shuriken*, the small but lethal handheld weapon known as a 'ninja star'. One of the other buildings is a reconstructed prison block.

## TAKAYAMA 高山

Deep in the mountains, in the region known traditionally as Hida, Takayama is deservedly one of the most popular destinations in central Honshu, combining as it does ancient traditions with a stunning natural setting. Often referred to as 'Little Kyoto', Takayama boasts temples, shrines, small museums, traditional shops and inns. As a result it gets very busy, particularly during the spring and autumn festivals, when 300,000 people come to watch the parade of floats. The greatest pleasure, however, comes from the chance to wander round the old, narrow streets of wooden houses and discover a side of Japan that has been largely airbrushed out of the big cities. Set aside enough time to simply enjoy the atmosphere; two or three days would be ideal. Takayama is also a good place to hunt for souvenirs, particularly lacquerware, woodcraft and pottery.

### What to see and do

Takayama has many highlights, not least of which are its festivals (see p220). It is also a convenient base for a trip to Shirakawa-go and Gokayama (see pp224-6).

If you're not here at festival time, you can see some of the large floats at **Takayama Yatai Kaikan** 高山屋台会館 (Float Exhibition Hall; daily Mar-Nov 8.30am-5pm, Dec-Feb 9am-4.30pm; ¥820). In all there are 23 floats: 12 are used for the spring festival and 11 in the autumn. The 11 floats kept here are changed three times a year (Mar, July and Nov), and there are four on display in the Yatai Kaikan at any one time. The rest are stored in special buildings around town; as you walk around the preservation areas look out for signs about them. Most of the floats were built over 200 years ago though they have been repaired since then. The original **mikoshi** (portable shrines) used in the festivals weighed 2½ tons and needed 42 people to carry each one; since it is hard to get enough people the same height they now use smaller ones that can be carried by four people. The short film (every 10 mins) about the festival has some English subtitles but is not as evocative as the 3D film in Hida-Furukawa (see pp191-2).

The yatai kaikan is part of **Sakurayama Hachimangu Shrine** 桜山八

---

❏ **Sukyo Mahikari – a new religious movement**

From the higher floors of hotel rooms looking south, or on the bus to/from Hida Folk Village, it is hard not to see a structure with an elaborate gold roof and a red sphere perched on top. This is the Main World Shrine of Sukyo Mahikari 崇教真光 (🖳 www.sukyomahikari.or.jp), one of Japan's 'new religions' that sprung up in the post-war years. Mahikari is described as 'true light, a cleansing energy sent by the Creator God that both spiritually awakens and tunes the soul to its divine purpose'.

You are unlikely to find this place on any official maps of Takayama, but if you are anywhere in the surrounding area it is hard to miss, particularly if the sun is shining on it.

幡宮 (24hrs/day; free), and if you have the time and climb up the steps to see it. However, top priority should be a visit to **Sakurayama Nikko-kan** 桜山日光館. Here you will see models (at a one-tenth scale) of the main buildings at Toshogu shrine in Nikko; a team of 33 carpenters took 15 years to build them. The craftsmanship is incredible and there are interesting labels in English.

The nearby **Yoshijima Heritage House** 吉島家住宅 (Yoshijima-ke Jutaku; summer daily 8.30am-5pm, winter Wed-Mon 9am-4.30/5pm; ¥500), built in the Meiji period for a sake-brewing family, is worth popping into if it is the only preserved house you will see, but a visit to Hida Folk Village is a better option.

During the Edo period, **Takayama Jinya** 高山陣屋 (Mar-Jul & Sep-Oct daily 8.45am-5pm, Aug to 6pm, Dec-Feb to 4.30pm; ¥430; a 40-minute tour in English may be available) was used as the government building for Gifu prefecture. It's now open to the public and everyone can use the same entrance – in the past where you entered depended on your status.

Many of the rooms have interesting displays and there are now labels in English for most things but if you have the time and a guide is available it would be worth having one. Look out for the rabbit-shaped 'ornaments' (there are 152), which were used to conceal the nails in the building. It was thought that rabbits were guardians against fire, but also that their long ears symbolised good governance because they were listening to human voices. In the rice storeroom there are straw rice sacks; each could contain 60kg of unpolished rice and were how people paid their taxes to the shogun. The torture room tells its own story.

A visit to a **morning market** 朝市 (*asaichi*; daily 7am-noon, from 8am in winter) is on many itineraries. **Jinya-mae** 陣屋前朝市 market is right by Takayama Jinya; every morning women from the surrounding area come here to sell vegetables, flowers and locally made crafts. However, the weather and other factors can affect how many stalls there are. **Miyagawa** 宮川朝市店), on the banks of Miya-gawa (Miya river) that flows west to east across town, is more gift orientated.

**Hida-Kokubun-ji** 飛騨国分寺 (🖳 hidakokubunji.jp; daily 9am-4pm; ¥300) is the oldest temple in Takayama; it was first founded in 764, though the oldest building here now is the main hall which dates from the 16th century. In the grounds is a gingko tree that is over a thousand years old. The 22m-high three-storied pagoda here is said to be unique in the Hida region.

If you pick up the *Higashiyama Walking Map* you will see how in the 17th century virtually everyone lived north of the river. This area is now being preserved and you can see many streets with **traditional houses** as well as businesses such as breweries and shops. The best known is **San-machi Suji** 三町筋 on the east side. It is about a 15-minute walk from the station and consists of three narrow streets. In addition to the houses there are lots of souvenir shops and cafés/restaurants.

Takayama's **Museum of History and Art** 飛騨高山まちの博物館 (daily 9am-7pm, garden until 9pm; free) is housed in traditional warehouse-type buildings (*kura*). Each of the 14 rooms focuses on a different theme including the town's history, the festival, local handicrafts and traditional houses.

The main temple district, **Higashiyama** 東山, is north of Miya-gawa river and east of Enako-gawa. The area is a little hilly but still a great place to explore on foot and easy to do if you picked up *Higashiyama Walking Map* from one of the TICs here. The youth hostel (see p223) is part of Tensho-ji.

For more recent history, try **Takayama Showa Kan** 高山昭和館 (daily Apr-Oct 9am-6pm, Nov-Mar to 5pm; ¥500). One of a number of places in Japan catering to nostalgia for the Showa period (1926-89), it features a wide selection of memorabilia, a small cinema shows historic newsreels, and there are recreated rooms such as a classroom, toy shop, café, home, a chemist and much more.

## Hida Folk Village (Hida-no-Sato) area

Ten minutes out of town along Highway 158, scenically situated in the hills overlooking Takayama, is **Hida Folk Village** 飛騨高山民族村 (🖳 www.hidanosato-tpo.jp; daily 8.30am-5pm; ¥700, Hida no Sato combination ticket ¥930 inc bus journey). Over 30 traditional farmhouses and merchant cottages from rural areas have been moved here and restored; most have artefacts used by the former inhabitants. It's a fascinating place and is well labelled in English. As well as the buildings, traditional crafts such as woodcarving and weaving can be observed. To reach the Folk Village take a Sarubobo route bus (2/hr) from stop No 1 at the Nohi Bus Center.

Teddy bear fans and young children might like the **Teddy Bear Eco Village** テディベアエコビレッジ (🖳 www.teddyeco .jp; daily 10am-6pm, closed some days Jan-Mar; ¥600), a museum full of bears from all over the world, the oldest of which dates back to 1903. In the ecology corner there's a display of how real bears are suffering as a result of environmental destruction. It's a short walk down the hill from the Folk Village.

**Hida-Takayama Museum of Art** 飛騨高山美術館 (🖳 www.htm-museum.co .jp; daily 9am-5pm, closed some days Dec-Mar; ¥1300, ¥200 discount voucher from TICs) has a large collection of European Art Nouveau and Art Deco glassware and furniture. In addition to a Mackintosh room exhibiting some of the Scottish architect's (CR Mackintosh) work there is a café and restaurant with furniture in the Mackintosh style. It's in a modern building two minutes further down the road from the Teddy Bear Eco Village. Alternatively take the Sarubobo route bus (see Getting around) but only one an hour calls here.

## Practical information

**Station guide** At the time of research the station was being rebuilt; work is scheduled to be completed by November 2016. Expect to find a beautiful station with lots of wood. There is also going to be a walkway between the west and east gates; the main exit is the East Gate.

**Tourist information**  **Hida Takayama Tourist Information Center** 飛騨高山観光案内所 (TIC; 🖳 kankou.city.takayama .lg.jp; daily May-Oct 8.30am-6.30pm, Nov-Apr to 5pm) is in a wooden booth outside the station but will probably be in the station when the rebuilding work is finished. The staff have a range of information about the area and will help book same-day accommodation.

**iSite Takayama** (🖳 www.isitetakaya ma.com; daily 11am-6pm) provides similar information and can also help with accommodation; in addition they offer a variety of tours including to Shirakawa-go (see p226).

Also worth looking at is 🖳 www .takayama-guide.com.

**Getting around**  Takayama is best negotiated on foot, though since there is a lot to see and if you have limited time consider renting a **bicycle** from the shop (daily 8.30am-10pm; ¥300/hour, ¥1200 for 4-24 hours) on the corner beyond Takayama Nohi Bus Center 高山濃飛バスセンター. They also offer luggage storage (small ¥300, large ¥500). The shop doesn't have a name but look for the sign outside. However, many of the accommodation options in Takayama also offer bike rental and are probably more convenient.

Nohi Bus (🖳 www.nouhibus.co.jp; ¥100-210 per journey; ¥600/day pass with discounted entry to certain places) operates two circular routes from Takayama Nohi Bus Center: the **Machinami Bus** (2/hr; from stand No 2) route operates around the central part of town. The **Sarubobo Bus** route goes to the Hida-no-Sato area (see opposite column; 2/hr; from stand No 1). For details of services to Shirakawa-go and Kanazawa see pp224-6.

**Tourist rickshaws** (*jinrikisha*; two/three people ¥4000/6000 for 15 mins, ¥14,000/20,000 for 60 mins) are an emergency standby.

**Festivals**  Takayama is known for its two annual **float festivals**, when 300-year-old floats are paraded through the streets. One is in spring (14th-15th Apr) and the other in autumn (9th-10th Oct).

HONSHU

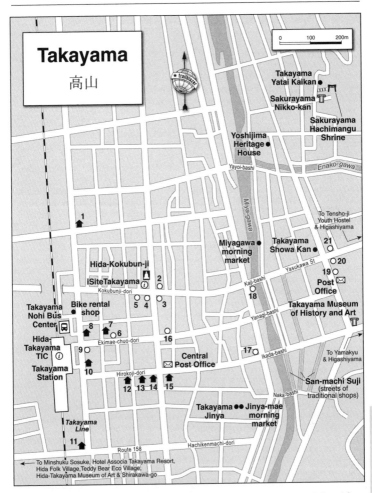

# Takayama

高山

Takayama Yatai Kaikan

Sakurayama Nikko-kan

Sakurayama Hachimangu Shrine

Yoshijima Heritage House

Yayoi-bashi

Enako-gawa

Miya-gawa

To Tensho-ji Youth Hostel & Higashiyama

Miyagawa morning market

Takayama Showa Kan

21

20

Yasukawa St

Hida-Kokubun-ji

iSiteTakayama

Kokubunji-dori

2

5 4 3

Kaji-bashi

18

19

Post Office

Takayama Museum of History and Art

Takayama Nohi Bus Center

Bike rental shop

8 7 6

Ekimae-chuo-dori

16

Yanagi-bashi

Hida-Takayama TIC

9

Central Post Office

17

Ikada-bashi

To Yamakyu & Higashiyama

Takayama Station

10

Hirokoji-dori

12 13 14 15

San-machi Suji (streets of traditional shops)

Naka-bashi

Takayama Line

Takayama Jinya

Takayama Jinya-mae morning market

11

Route 158

Hachikenmachi-dori

← To Minshuku Sosuke, Hotel Associa Takayama Resort, Hida Folk Village,Teddy Bear Eco Village, Hida-Takayama Museum of Art & Shirakawa-go

0 100 200m

HONSHU

## Where to stay
1 Hida Hotel Plaza
7 Best Western Hotel Takayama
8 Country Hotel Takayama
10 Hida-Takayama Washington Hotel Plaza
11 Takayamaouan
12 Super Hotel Hida Takayama

## Where to stay (cont'd)
13 K's House Takayama
14 Spa Hotel Alpina
15 J-Hoppers Hida-Takayama

## Where to eat and drink
2 Bistro Mieux
3 Mieux's Bar
4 Maruaki

## Where to eat (cont'd)
5 Heianraku
6 Hidaki Soba
9 Black Sea Café and Bar
16 Hida Komeya
17 Le Midi
18 Hanamizuki
19 Center4Hamburgers
20 Masakatsu Tonkatsu
21 Alice

**Where to stay** Note that rates for all accommodation options are higher at peak times such as during the festivals.

*Takayamaouan* 高山桜庵 (☎ 0577-37 2230, 🖳 www.hotespa.net/hotels/takayama; from ¥10,700/S, ¥15,800/D or Tw inc buffet-style breakfast), part of the excellent Dormy Inn chain, is a 5-minute walk to the right from the station. The onsen and rotemburo on the 13th floor (rooftop) are wonderful and provide amazing views. The hotel has standard business hotel Western-style rooms but also some Western-style rooms with a tatami-mat sitting area.

Also conveniently located is *Hida Hotel Plaza* ひだホテルプラザ (☎ 0577-33 4600, 🖳 www.hida-hotelplaza.co.jp; from ¥9654/S, ¥19,308/D or Tw; breakfast ¥1665). It is a large hotel with three interconnecting buildings and it offers spacious Western- and Japanese-style rooms. Facilities include a range of restaurants, a heated swimming pool, and onsen baths. The bath in the basement has a dry sauna and the one on the roof has a rotemburo, a Jacuzzi, and a mist sauna. There is an entrance on the main road if walking from the station but you need to walk through the hotel to reach the main lobby.

*Best Western Hotel Takayama* ベストウエスタンホテル高山 (☎ 0577-37 2000, 🖳 www.bestwestern.co.jp/english/takayama; from ¥8700/S, ¥16,400/D, ¥18,400/Tw, inc a buffet breakfast) is a 5-minute walk east of the station and has the rooms and facilities you would expect from an international chain. The standard twins are comfortable if not overly large.

The name *Spa Hotel Alpina* スパホテルアルピナ (☎ 0577-33 0033, 🖳 www.spa-hotel-alpina.com/english; ¥10,080/S, ¥15,020/D or Tw inc buffet breakfast) is a giveaway that this hotel, like several in Takayama, has hot spring facilities; the onsen bath, including outside rotemburo, is on the roof. The rooms are clean and tidy and a reasonable size.

*Hida Takayama Washington Hotel Plaza* 飛騨高山ワシントンホテルプラザ (☎ 0577-37 0410, 🖳 washington.jp/takayama; from ¥6290/S, ¥9000/Tw; breakfast ¥1080) is convenient for the rail tracks: it's across the street from the station and is popular with tour groups. Close by is *Country Hotel Takayama* カントリーホテル高山 (☎ 0577-35 3900, 🖳 www.country-hotel.jp; ¥6500/S, ¥8000/D, ¥9000/Tw; breakfast ¥860), with fairly compact but clean rooms. The budget *Super Hotel Hida Takayama* スーパーホテル飛騨高山 (☎ 0577-32 9000, 🖳 www.superhoteljapan.com; ¥5640/S, ¥8200/Tw inc breakfast) chain has a conveniently located branch but with a more subdued appearance than usual. However, there is an onsen and the breakfast ingredients are organic and preservative free where possible.

The best ryokan in Takayama can set you back up to ¥25,000pp (inc half board) but minshuku are a much more affordable option. *Minshuku Sosuke* 民宿惣助 (☎ 0577-32 0818, 🖳 www.irori-sosuke.com; ¥5184pp room only, Japanese/Western breakfast ¥756, dinner from ¥2200; special rates at festival/holiday periods), a short walk behind the station, is a friendly and homely 13-room minshuku where you will be given delicious meals. However, the walls between the rooms are quite thin and those facing the road can be noisy. *Yamakyu* 山久 (☎ 0577-32-3756, 🖳 www.takayama-yamakyu.com; from ¥8000pp inc half board) is in a quiet neighbourhood in the Higashiyama part of town; the charm of the place is enhanced by the antiques everywhere. Its Japanese-style rooms have a toilet and there is an onsen with a waterwheel and a rotemburo. The meals here are also wonderful. See their website for details of their shuttle bus service from the station.

Centrally located and converted from a former ryokan to a backpackers' hostel is *J-Hoppers Hida-Takayama* J-Hoppers 飛騨高山 (☎ 0577-32 3278, 🖳 takayama.j-hoppers.com; dorm beds from ¥2700pp, private rooms ¥3000-3200pp, en suite ¥3500-3800pp). Two dorms (6- and 8-bed) are mixed; there is also a female 6-bed dorm. Private rooms (Japanese style) sleep up to four people. Bicycle rental (¥500/day) is available except when it is snowy. Another option for budget accommodation is *K's House Takayama* ケイズハウス高山 (☎ 0577-34-4410, 🖳 kshouse.jp/takayama-e;

dorm beds from ¥2900pp, rooms sleeping 2/3/4 people from ¥3400pp). Apart from the single and double rooms most rooms have bunk beds. However, the staff are friendly and facilities include a lounge, kitchen, washing machine and dryer (¥300) as well as bike rental (¥300/hour).

Possibly the most atmospheric budget option is the 95-bed *Tensho-ji Youth Hostel* 天照寺ユースホステル (☎ 0577-32 6345, 🖥 www.hihostels.com; dorm bed ¥2808pp, private room sleeping 2/3/4 ¥6480/ ¥9288/12,096; Mar-Dec). Lights go out at 10pm in the single-sex dorms. Meals are not provided but there is a kitchen and lounge area. The hostel is 20 minutes' walk east from the station across the Miya-gawa and Enaka-gawa rivers, at Tensho-ji in Higashiyama.

The JR-operated *Hotel Associa Takayama Resort* ホテルアソシア高山リゾート (☎ 0577-36 0001, 🖥 www.associa .com/tky; from ¥13,110/S, ¥22,980/D or Tw inc buffet breakfast; 10% discount with JR rail pass) is the place to head for first-class luxury in the hills overlooking the town. Expect spacious en suite rooms, two high-quality restaurants and impeccable service. The best reason for staying here is the chance to use the extensive in-house spa and hot-spring facilities. The baths are on two separate floors and are open either to men or women on a daily rotating basis. A free shuttle bus service runs between Takayama station and the hotel (10 mins).

**Where to eat and drink** Hida beef is on many menus here. It comes in different qualities: Hida-gyu 飛騨牛, the best, is ranked on a scale of 3 to 5: '5' means the beef comes from a black-haired breed of Japanese cattle and has been raised in the prefecture for at least 14 months. The main feature of the beef is its marble-patterned appearance because of the large amount of fat. However, this does make eating it a melt-in-the-mouth experience. Hida Wagyu 飛騨和牛 comes from different breeds; some is premium quality but it does vary.

*Center4Hamburgers* (☎ 0577-36 4527, 🖥 tiger-center4.com; Thur-Tue 11am-2.30pm & 6-9.30pm) prides itself on being the only hamburger restaurant in Takayama; that is true but hamburgers are on the menu of most restaurants here. Their menu includes a range of hamburgers (from ¥760) but if you are going to come here you should have the best, their Hida burger (¥2300 inc French fries). Not only is the food good but the restaurant itself is very characterful. However, expect to have to queue and be aware that only about 30-40 Hida burgers are available each day so it is first come first served. Reservations by phone are accepted except for lunch on Saturdays, Sundays and holidays.

Restaurants combining Hida beef and French cuisine are popular in Takayama. At *Le Midi* ルミディ (🖥 www.le-midi.jp; Mon-Wed & Fri 11.30am-3pm & 6-9.30pm, Sat & Sun 11.30am-3.30pm & 5-9.30pm), the cheapest option is a 135g burger (¥2100); a 150g fillet steak costs ¥6090. For an additional ¥600 it is served with soup and bread or for ¥2000 with starter, dessert, bread or rice, and coffee.

Another choice is *Bistro Mieux* ビストロミュー (Thur-Tue 11.30am-2pm & 5.30-10pm), a 5-minute walk from the station along Kokubunji-dori. Creative food is presented with flair and there's a good selection of wines. A Hida Beef hamburger set costs ¥1800, but there is much more to the menu including daily specials. Across the street the newer *Mieux's Bar* ミューズバー (Thur-Tue 11.30am-2pm & 5-11pm) serves Hida beef set meals from ¥3400 at lunch, ¥3900 in the evening. However, the service here seems variable.

*Hida Komeya* 飛騨米屋 (11am-8pm) specialises in Hida beef (meals from ¥1750) but also serves tonkatsu (¥1300) and *ebi-fri* (deep-fried prawns; ¥1400). On the 2nd floor they have a **coffee shop** (8am-8pm) and claim it was the first coffee shop to open in Takayama – that was in 1948. *Maruaki* 丸明, which also specialises in Hida beef, has both a restaurant (daily 11am-9pm) and a butcher's shop where you can see some very marbled meat at up to ¥2000 for 100 grams. The shop faces Kokubunji-dori but the restaurant entrance is round the corner. Shabushabu costs from ¥1380 but expect to pay ¥4980 for a sirloin steak. Alternatively a plate of premium Hida beef to cook yourself (*yakiniku*) and serving 2-3 people costs ¥5980.

For an economical taste of Hida beef, *Hanamizuki* ハナミズキ (daily 9am-9pm) offers burgers from ¥690 (set meal ¥990; takeaway available); they also offer a selection of cakes (from ¥400) and pancakes such as chocolate and banana (¥850).

*Masakatsu Tonkatsu* 政かつとんか つ (Wed-Mon 11am-2pm & 5-8pm), on Yasugawa-dori, is a small place that serves large portions of melt-in-the-mouth tonkatsu (sets from ¥1060). Almost directly opposite is *The Alice* ザ・アリス (Thur-Tue 11am-1.50pm & 4.30-7.50pm), also a wedding hall, which serves a variety of set meals from ¥1300 as well as more expensive options such as a steak set (¥4050).

*Hidaki Soba* 飛騨そば 小舟 (Hida Soba Kofune; 11am-8pm) on the left-hand side of Ekimae Chuo-dori, serves delicious soba; options include: 'Hida cow' (¥1300) and Sansai (wild vegetable; ¥780).

Vegetarians in particular will want to head to *Heianraku* 平安楽 (Thur-Tue 11am-2pm & 5-9.30pm) as there is a vegetarian menu, though meat is also served. The food is tasty and the staff are used to foreigners, but the restaurant only has 12 seats so you need to get here very early. There are two set meals (¥750/1100 for one/two dishes plus rice and soup), or an à la carte menu including dishes such as tofu teriyaki (¥750) and sweet and sour chicken (¥900).

For a quick caffeine fix, try *Black Sea Café and Bar* (café daily 11.30am-6pm, bar open to midnight), across the street from the station. It also serves ramen (from ¥750). Look for the sign written in English.

### Side trip to Shirakawa-go and/or Gokayama

● **Shirakawa-go** 白川郷 (🖳 shirakawa-go.org/english), a World Heritage Site, is known for its *gassho zukuri* 掌造り (constructed like 'hands in prayer') houses, some of which are over 250 years old. The houses have steep thatched roofs to help protect them from the heavy snowfall in this area; the thatch can be up to a metre thick and a feature of the roofs is that they were built without using any nails. Their location also optimises wind resistance and sunlight.

The bus stop in Shirakawa-go is located right by the main information centre (daily 9am-5pm) in **Ogimachi village** 荻町; pick up a map here and then cross the sturdy suspension bridge over the Shokawa River to reach the main part of Shirakawa-go.

Many of the houses here are now cafés, minshuku or souvenir shops. Some – **Kanda**, **Nagase** and **Wada** – are open to the public most days (9am-5pm; ¥300 each) and give you a chance to understand a bit what life was like here. Also worth visiting is **Myozen-ji** (8.30am-5pm, to 4pm in winter; closed some days; ¥300), a temple that is also a 5-storied home and one of the biggest buildings in the village; it is also unusual as a temple because it has a thatched roof. **Doburoku Festival Museum** どぶろく祭りの館 (daily Apr-Nov 9am-5pm; ¥300) showcases the festival associated with the local white unrefined sake. A fairly steep walk (about 15 minutes) after passing Wada House brings you to a **viewpoint** and a great panoramic view of the village.

Near the tourist information centre is **Gassho Zukuri Minka-en** 合掌造 り民家園 (🖳 www.shirakawago-minkaen.jp; Apr-Nov daily 8.40am-5pm, Dec-Mar Fri-Wed 9am-4pm; ¥600), a collection of buildings (family homes, storehouses etc), some of which were rebuilt after being relocated from Kazura, a more remote part of Shirakawa, which its inhabitants abandoned in the 1960s. The buildings contain artefacts illustrating life in the area in the past and are fascinating. However, if you have been to Hida no Sato in Takayama you may not feel the need to go here.

If you are here in Shirakawa-go in May your visit may coincide with the annual **rice-planting festival**. Rice is generally planted by machine now but one paddy a year is chosen and women (what a surprise!) plant the rice in the traditional way, watched by a mass of photographers. Another event you might be lucky to see is a building being rethatched; this is done every 30-40 years and traditionally involved the whole community but now sometimes has to be done by professional companies as so many people have left the village to work in towns and cities.

The crowds here most of the time can spoil the experience. For this reason staying the night in one of the minshuku is highly recommended as the atmosphere is very different when the coachloads have gone. *Furusato* ふるさと (☎ 0576-96 1033; from ¥8900pp inc half board) is both characterful and conveniently located. The rooms, as in all minshuku here, are downstairs as the buildings are all a fire risk so it is considered unsafe for guests to be upstairs. The *shoji* (sliding screens) that divide the rooms also mean you can hear everything if there are guests in the next-door room. But on the plus side the food is filling and very tasty and there is a mass of memorabilia on the walls including photos of when Crown Prince Naruhito and his security officers stayed here. To get here walk straight up the road from the suspension bridge, cross over the main road and then Furusato is the first house on the right by the road.

Note that there are no rubbish (trash) bins in the village so if you are just on a day trip please take any rubbish home with you.

● **Gokayama** 五箇山 (🖳 www.gokayama-info.jp) is the other World Heritage Site with gassho-zukuri houses, though on a smaller scale and also much less touristy. The main villages to visit are Ainokura and Suganuma. There are 23 gassho-zukuri houses in **Ainokura** 相倉, all of which are over 100 years old; the bus stop is a short walk from the village. **Suganuma** 菅沼 has nine houses and the bus stop is also a short walk from the village; you can either walk all the way or take the lift/elevator. For both villages you can pick up a map and there are some lockers near the bus stop. Both also have houses that you can visit and folklore museums where you can learn about life in the villages (approx ¥300 for each). Some places in Ainokura provide accommodation (from ¥8800pp; see the website for details).

● **Getting to and from Shirakawa-go/Gokayama** There are various options and your decision will depend on whether you are returning to Takayama (and if so, whether you want a guided tour or not, see p226), staying the night in Shirakawa-go/Gokayama, or continuing on to Kanazawa, or Takaoka/Shin-Takaoka.

Nohi Bus operate 10 services a day (from stop No 4) to Shirakawa-go (¥2470/4420 one-way/return); 4/day continue on to Kanazawa (¥3390/6070 one-way/return). Note that most services require advance reservation either at the Reservation Center in Nohi Bus Center, or by phone (☎ 0577-32 1688; 9am-6pm; English is spoken). To get from Shirakawa-go to Gokayama take one of Kaetsuno's buses (6/day) to Suganuma (¥860), or Ainokaru (¥1300).

The **Shirakawa-go Gokayama World Heritage Bus Ticket** (¥3700) is valid for a one-way journey between Takayama and Shirakawa-go (operated by Nohi) and then on a hop-on and hop-off basis between Shirakawa-go and Johana including Gokayama (operated by Kaetsunou Bus; 6/day). From

HONSHU

Johana JR pass holders can pick up a train back to Takaoka (see p186), or Shin-Takaoka on the Hokuriku shinkansen line. This ticket can be bought at Nohi Bus Center.

There are also **round-trip sightseeing services** with an English-speaking guide. A half-day tour to Shirakawa-go (2/day; 4/hrs; ¥4400) can be booked through iSite Takayama, see p220. Nohi Bus operates tours to both Shirakawa-go and Gokayama. The tour departing at 8.30am goes to Gokayama Ainokura village, then stops for lunch and continues to Shirakawa-go. The tour departing at 10.30am is the same but goes to Gokayama Suganuma village. Both cost ¥6690.

## KANAZAWA 金沢

Even before the start of Hokuriku shinkansen services to Kanazawa the variety of sights here more than repaid the effort of the journey; now with the ease of getting here from Tokyo it should be part of any itinerary.

In 1580 the Maedas, the second largest clan in feudal-era Japan, settled here. Peace and stability followed and Kanazawa quickly became a prosperous centre for the silk and gold-lacquer industries. As its citizens became wealthy, Kanazawa's arts and culture scene began to flourish. Even today Kanazawa has a reputation for its patronage of 'high-class' arts such as Noh and the tea ceremony.

The city is also curiously proud of another claim to fame: it is allegedly one of the wettest places in the country, with an average of 178 rainy days per year. A local proverb translates as 'Even if you forget your packed lunch, don't forget your umbrella'. The station's design (see p230) picks up on this theme.

### What to see and do

Apart from the much-hyped Kenrokuen garden there are other surprises, such as well-preserved geisha and samurai districts, art and gold-leaf museums as well as a working Noh theatre and an indoor market.

The city also functions as a gateway to the Noto Peninsula, a knuckle of land that juts out into the Japan Sea north of the city. And just for good measure, a short train ride away is the intriguing UFO town of Hakui; another side trip from Kanazawa is to Gokayama and/or Shirakawa-go (see pp232-3).

**Kenrokuen and around** On most people's itineraries is **Kenrokuen** 兼六園 (🖵 www.pref.ishikawa.jp/siro-niwa/kenrokuen; Mar to mid Oct daily 7am-6pm, mid Oct to Feb 8am-5pm; ¥310), rated as one of the top three gardens in Japan. Constructed 200 years ago as the garden for Kanazawa Castle, it is spread over 11.4 hectares and contains about 12,000 trees. The number six 六 (*roku*) in the garden's name refers to the six attributes of a perfect garden: vastness, seclusion, careful arrangement, antiquity, water and panoramic views. Water features in particular are everywhere, including the first fountain (Funsui) ever placed in a Japanese garden. Inside, professional photographers wait around for the tour groups but if you can find some space away from the crowds, a couple of hours can easily be spent wandering round the grounds.

Apart from **Ishikawa-mon gate** 石川門 most of the buildings in **Kanazawa Castle Park** 金沢城公園 (daily Mar-Oct 7am-6pm, Oct-Feb 8am-5pm; free) burnt down but some have been reconstructed and Ishikawa-mon was also renovated recently. The park is a pleasant area to explore but not necessarily top priority. Kanazawa Goodwill Guide Network (🖵 kggn.sakura.ne.jp) has an information booth (Apr-Nov daily 9.30am-3.30pm) by Ishikawa-mon gate and guides will take you around the park and Kenrokuen for free. Alternatively just pick up a map.

The best stop on the Loop Bus (see p230) for Kenrokuen is either RL8, S7 or S9; for the Castle Park the best stop is LL9 though it is also possible to cross the road and walk up to Kenrokuen.

**Kanazawa 21st Century Museum of Contemporary Art** 金沢21世紀美術館 (🖥 www.kanazawa21.jp; Mon-Thur & Sun 10am-6pm, Fri & Sat 10am-8pm, closed occasionally to hang new exhibitions) opened in 2004 and was billed as the 'world's most advanced art museum'. The design of the building – gleaming white, circular and set in its own landscaped gardens – threatens to overshadow its permanent collection, an eclectic mix of Japanese and foreign contemporary art.

The entry charge depends on the exhibition; expect to pay ¥800-1000 for the main exhibition but this may include entry to any additional exhibitions at the museum. Even if you don't want to go into an exhibition it is still worth visiting the museum as there is a lot to explore that is free. There's also a well-stocked contemporary art library and one of Kanazawa's swankiest *cafés* (Tue-Sun 10am-8pm), just to the right of the main entrance.

If you would like more art **Ishikawa Prefectural Museum of Art** 石川県立美術館 (🖥 www.ishibi.pref.ishikawa.jp; daily 9.30am-5pm; ¥360) focuses on works made by local artists or with a local connection and it is full of cosmetics' boxes, decorated plates, hanging scrolls and *shoji* screens. The closest stop is S6; it is also near the Noh Theatre (see p232).

Unless you know about Buddhism you may not have heard of Daisetsu T Suzuki but he was born in Kanazawa and became a noted (Zen) Buddhist philosopher. At the **D T Suzuki Museum** 鈴木大拙館 (🖥 kanazawa-museum.jp/daisetz; Tue-Sun 9.30am-5pm; ¥300) there are some touch screens where you can learn about his life and then go into the main rooms where there are a variety of exhibits; these have Japanese labels but if you go to the far end of the rooms you can pick up English translations. Most people though come to sit and look at the Water Mirror Garden – an ideal place for some contemplation – or to stroll around the other wonderful garden areas.

From the RL10 bus stop walk on a bit and turn left after the branch of Lawson; follow the road round and if the gate ahead of you is open go through it, across a car

park, then turn left and the museum is soon on your left. If the gate is closed stay on the road and turn left at the first junction.

**Higashichaya district** More than 90% of Japan's gold-leaf is produced in Kanazawa and in Higashichaya ひがし茶屋, or 東茶屋街 at the small but interesting **Kanazawa Yasue Gold Leaf Museum** 金沢市立安江金箔工芸館 (🖥 www.kanazawa-museum.jp/kinpaku; daily 9.30am-5pm; ¥300, ¥50 discount with bus pass) you can learn about the process of making gold leaf, the tools used, and the different kinds of gold leaf. At the end of the exhibition there are some stunning products with gold-leaf on including porcelain, a Buddhist altar and lacquer work. Most signs are in Japanese but there is a video screen explaining everything in English.

Get off at the RL5 bus stop; the museum is a short walk back along the road. Alternatively from the LLl1 stop just cross the road.

From the museum walk back towards the river and turn left at the first junction and then left again for **Sakuda Gold and Silver Leaf Shop** 株式会社金銀箔工芸さくだ本社本店 (☎ 076-251-6777, 🖥 www.goldleaf-sakuda.jp; daily 9am-6pm); it is a little way down on the left. You will be offered a cup of tea in which there are some pieces of gold-leaf. Suitably refreshed have a look around: the most expensive item for sale is a pair of gold-leaf screens for ¥3 million. At the other end of the scale are gold-leaf boiled sweets (around ¥350) and tattoos (body stickers; ¥800) that will last a week. There's no charge at all for visiting the gold-leafed toilets on the 2nd floor, though sadly the actual toilets are normal.

If booked in advance through the website or by phone, you can learn how to apply gold-leaf to small objects; each session (4/day) lasts 60-90 minutes. You can choose from a variety of products: chopsticks are ¥600 and a small box from ¥1100.

Retrace your steps to the concrete paved street and turn left to reach the former **geisha quarter** which still retains a traditional charm. Here you'll find a few streets lined with old geisha houses, instantly recognisable by their wooden latticed windows. If there is a crowd of people on the right-hand corner of the square when you enter it, it is probably because they are queuing for, or eating, some gold-leaf ice-cream (¥891). If you get one, eat it here as it is not considered polite to walk around the area eating.

At **Shima** 志摩 (🖳 www.ochaya-shima.com; daily 9am-6pm; ¥500), on the left as you go down the main street, you can see the rooms where guests used to wait for their entertainment and where the geisha prepared as well as some of the traditional instruments they played. Many of the other houses are now tea and coffee shops but several are still privately owned so please respect this. If you are here in the early evening there's the chance of spotting a geisha but during the day you are more likely to see people dressed up in a kimono.

**Teramachi district** Temple lovers should head south of Sai-gawa to the Teramachi 寺町 district. Even if you think you are tired of visiting temples in Japan do visit **Myoryu-ji** 妙立寺, better known as the **Ninja Temple** (Ninja-dera; 🖳 www .myouryuji.or.jp; reservations required for the compulsory tour: call ☎ 076-241 0888; Mar-Oct daily 9am-4.30pm, Nov-Feb to 4pm; 2/hr; ¥800). A defensive stronghold as well as a temple, it was originally built near the castle but was moved here in 1643. Its architecture is incredibly complex – it was constructed to look like a 2-storey temple as at that time no building could be higher

than three storeys. In reality it has four storeys though within the building there are seven tiers. There are also 29 staircases. Its rooms contain trick doors, false exits, secret tunnels and pits – no wonder you have to go on a guided tour (in Japanese only, but you will be given notes in English). Visit the website to see the questions you will be asked when making a tour reservation by phone. However, if you turn up without making one and there is space on a tour you may be able to join it.

Visitors are requested to be suitably dressed to visit a temple; babies and young children are not allowed.

The closest Loop Bus stop is LL5 (Hirokoji); from here walk back to the main road and turn left. Turn left again, just after a branch of Lawsons, and walk along the narrow lane. The back entrance to the temple is straight ahead of you at the end when the lane turns to the right.

If you're in Teramachi at 6pm on a Saturday, listen out for the bells of six temples ringing together – rated as one of the '100 best soundscapes in Japan'.

**Nagamachi district** It's a pleasant surprise to stumble upon Nagamachi 長町 – an area of narrow, cobbled streets with a few preserved **samurai houses** – just a few minutes' walk from the Korinbo shopping district.

The **Nomura family's house** 武家屋敷野村家 (🖳 www.nomurake.com; daily Apr-Sep 8.30am-5.30pm; Oct-Mar to 4.30pm; ¥550, ¥500 with bus pass; ¥800 with tea) contains a shrine, a tea ceremony

## KANAZAWA – MAP KEY

| Where to stay | Where to stay (cont'd) | Where to eat and drink |
|---|---|---|
| 1  Kanazawa Manten Hotel Ekimae | 7  Kanazawa Central Hotel | 3  MoriMori Sushi, Tomikinton (Forus) |
| 2  Hotel My Stays Kanazawa | 8  Hotel Nikko Kanazawa | 5  La Veranda, Seattle's Best Coffee |
| 5  APA Hotel Kanazawa Eki-mae | 9  Toyoko Inn Kanazawa Eki Higashi-guchi | 8  Hacchouya, Menza, The Olive Oil Kitchen (Porte Kanazawa) |
| 4  Via Inn Kanazawa | 11  Toyoko Inn Kanazawa Kenrokuen Korinbo | 10  Omi-cho Market |
| 6  Dormy Inn Kanazawa | 12  Ryokan Murataya | |

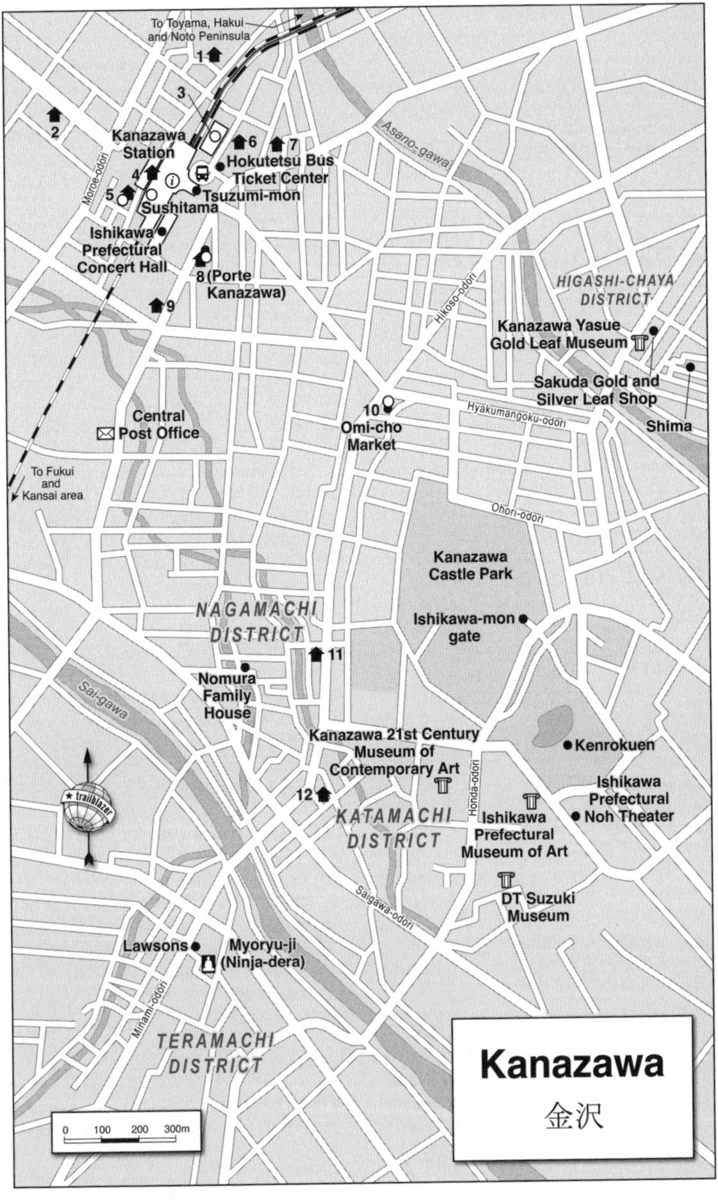

To Toyama, Hakui and Noto Peninsula
1
3
2
Kanazawa Station
4
5
6 7
Hokutetsu Bus Ticket Center
Sushitama
Tsuzumi-mon
Ishikawa Prefectural Concert Hall
8 (Porte Kanazawa)
9
Asano-gawa
HIGASHI-CHAYA DISTRICT
Hikoso-odori
Kanazawa Yasue Gold Leaf Museum
Sakuda Gold and Silver Leaf Shop
Shima
Hyakumangoku-odori
Central Post Office
To Fukui and Kansai area
10
Omi-cho Market
Ohori-odori
Kanazawa Castle Park
NAGAMACHI DISTRICT
Ishikawa-mon gate
11
Nomura Family House
Saigawa
Kanazawa 21st Century Museum of Contemporary Art
12
KATAMACHI DISTRICT
Honda-odori
Kenrokuen
Ishikawa Prefectural Noh Theater
Ishikawa Prefectural Museum of Art
Saigawa-odori
DT Suzuki Museum
Lawsons
Myoryu-ji (Ninja-dera)
Minami-odori
trailblazer
TERAMACHI DISTRICT

0    100   200   300m

**Kanazawa**

金沢

HONSHU

room (upstairs), a small but immaculate Japanese garden and a museum area with a collection of samurai armour and swords as well as a beautiful gold-lacquered box. There are also some original letters which are translated into English.

From the RL14 stop walk back to Tokyu Excel Hotel and turn right down the hill, then right and first left. When you reach the canal turn right for Nomura House.

### Station area  Omi-cho 近江町 (🖳 ohmi cho-ichiba.com; market 7am-6pm, restaurant area daily 11am-8pm) is a daily indoor market with around 170 stalls selling fresh fish, fruit and vegetables. A market is said to have existed here for more than 280 years.

The market is about a 10-minute walk from the station. Alternatively, the closest bus stops are LL1 (from Kanazawa station) and RL16; you can enter the market by going through the glass doors to the right of *Mister Donut*, by the LL bus stop.

### Practical information
**Station guide**  Kanazawa is the terminus for the Hokuriku shinkansen and Hokuriku main line, as well as the Nanao, Hokutetsu and IR Ishikawa lines.

There are **lockers** (all sizes; ¥300-600) in various locations, including in the corridors off the main concourse. Kanazawa Station Baggage Center (daily 10am-8pm) charges ¥500 per item.

Kenrokuen (East) Gate – with its enormous steel and glass **Motenashi (Welcome) Dome**, and stunning wooden gate (**Tsuzumi-mon**) – has become a symbolic gateway to the city. The dome was designed to look like an umbrella and keep new arrivals from getting wet in notoriously rainy Kanazawa; the wooden gate symbolises a traditional Japanese drum. The sightseeing buses and city centre are on this side. The other main exit is Port (West) Gate.

### Tourist information  The **tourist information centre** (🖳 www.kanazawa-tourism.com; daily 9am-7pm) is opposite the shinkansen ticket gates. Staff can give you maps and information about the city.

### Getting around  The city centre is a 10-minute bus ride from the station. As its name suggests, **Kanazawa Loop Bus** (4/hr; ¥200/ride or ¥500 for a one-day pass, purchased from the driver) does a circular tour of the main city sights and thus is a great way for tourists to get around. There are two bus routes: the Left Loop (LL) and Right Loop (RL).

The prime destination for **Kenrokuen Garden Shuttle** (weekends and holidays only; 3/hr; ¥100/ride) is Kenrokuen, but it does stop at other places. Its stops are signified by the letter 'S'.

**Kanazawa Flat Bus** (4/hr; ¥100/ride) operates on four routes and also goes to the main tourist sights but it is more for locals. All services run daily (8.30am-6pm) and the buses leave from stops outside the East Exit of the station.

JR pass-holders may like to take the **JR bus** (1-3/hr) though the pass is not valid on all services. Buses depart from the JR bus stop (stop No 4) outside Kanazawa station's Kenrokuen (East) Gate exit. The bus stops at most of the main sights.

Kanazawa also has a useful **bicycle-rental service** called Machi-nori まちのり (🖳 www.machi-nori.jp; basic access fee ¥200/day, first 30 mins free then ¥200 per 30 mins). Bicycles can be rented from any of the 19 docking stations around town, including two near Kanazawa station, between 7.30am and 10.30pm but can be returned 24 hours a day.

### Festivals  Hyakumangoku Festival takes place over three days every year around the first Saturday in June. The event celebrates the arrival of Lord Maeda into the city and begins at dusk with a procession of floating lanterns down Asano-gawa. Public tea ceremonies are also held in Kenrokuen, but the highlight of the day is a parade through the streets which mixes acrobatics, horse-riding, period costume and even a 'Miss Hyakumangoku' beauty contest.

### Where to stay  Right in the station, on the Port (West) Gate side is *Via Inn Kanazawa* ヴィアイン金沢 (☎ 076-222 5489, 🖳 www.viainn.com/en/kanazawa; from ¥6400

HONSHU

/S, ¥6800/D or Tw exc breakfast). The hotel re-opened recently after refurbishment. The rooms (5th-8th floors) are fairly standard but breakfast is not provided; either buy a voucher (¥700) here to use at a designated local restaurant/café in the station, or find somewhere of your own choosing.

For top-class luxury, choose **Hotel Nikko Kanazawa** ホテル日航金沢 (☎ 076-234 1111, 🖳 www.hnkanazawa.jp; from ¥12,700/S, ¥19,600/D or Tw inc buffet breakfast). It's outside the station's East Gate exit and can hardly be beaten for its friendly staff and service. It is 30 storeys high and all rooms are on the 17th floor or higher so it also offers wonderful views.

Less than a 5-minute walk east of the East Gate exit is **Kanazawa Central Hotel** 金沢セントラルホテル (☎ 076-263 5311, 🖳 www.centralh.co.jp/english; from ¥4800/S, ¥8400/Tw; Japanese-style rooms from ¥4800pp), a good, standard business hotel with clean, comfortable rooms spread over two buildings: the East Building has only Western-style rooms and an onsen spa on the 2nd floor. The Main Building has both Western- and Japanese-style rooms and (a buffet) breakfast is served here on the 3rd floor.

Like all branches of this excellent chain **Dormy Inn Kanazawa** ドーミーイン 金沢 (☎ 076-263 9888, 🖳 www.hotespa .net/hotels/kanazawa; from ¥7990/S, ¥11,990/D or T) has a natural onsen and rotemburo on the roof. It also provides a wonderful buffet breakfast with eggs cooked to order and their Yonaki free soba (9.30-11pm) is served every evening. It is also only a short walk from the station.

**Hotel My Stays Kanazawa** ホテルマイ ステイズ 金沢 (☎ 076-290 5255, 🖳 www .mystays.com/e/location/kanazawa (from ¥7200/S, ¥10,200/D or Tw inc Western/ Japanese buffet breakfast) is on the Port (West) Gate side of Kanazawa station. Turn left out of the Port (West) Gate exit and go down the underpass and then straight as far as you can go. When you come back up to street level the hotel is a short walk along on the left. The rooms are a very good size, though the walls seem thin; there is a free coin laundry.

**Toyoko Inn** 東横イン (🖳 www .toyoko-inn.com) has two branches here: **Kanazawa Eki Higashi-guchi** 金沢駅東口 (☎ 076-224 1045; ¥5184/S, ¥6804/D, ¥8424/Tw inc breakfast, and curry rice supper on weekdays) is very convenient for the station. An older branch, **Kanazawa Kenrokuen Korinbo** 金沢香林坊 (☎ 076-232-1045; ¥4860/S, ¥6480/D, ¥9180/Tw inc breakfast) is in the Korinbo district, closer to the shopping, restaurants and bars. However, there is a free shuttle bus service (3-9pm; 1-2/hr) to and from the Port (West) Gate exit of the station; follow signs for the taxi stand タクシーノリバ. Then look for the 'Group Bus' parking area sign.

A 3-minute walk from the station's Port (West) Gate exit is **Kanazawa Manten Hotel Ekimae** 金沢マンテンホテル駅前 (☎ 076-265 0100, 🖳 kanazawa.mantenhot el.com; ¥6800/S, ¥12,600/Tw). The rooms are small but well furnished; all rooms feature semi-double beds. **APA Hotel Kanazawa Eki-mae** アパホテル金沢駅前 (☎ 076-231 8111, 🖳 www.apahotel.com; from ¥15,000 /S, ¥18,000/D or Tw; buffet breakfast ¥1600 if booked), right outside the Port (West) Gate exit. It's an upmarket place with reasonable rooms, a selection of restaurants, and Eki Spa (a hot spring with rotemburo) on the 2nd floor. The spa is open to non residents (6am-midnight; ¥1000/3hrs, ¥2000/day).

If you prefer Japanese-style accommodation, a great choice is **Ryokan Murataya** 旅館村田屋 (☎ 076-263 0455, 🖳 murata ya-ryokan.com/eng; from ¥4900/S, ¥9400 /Tw, ¥14,100/Tr; Western breakfast ¥550, Japanese ¥850). This traditional inn is just set back from the Katamachi district. Some of the rooms overlook a small garden and all are simply decorated with Japanese paper screens and hanging scrolls. The bath and toilet facilities are shared.

See p73 for details of **Japan Experience**'s apartments/houses here which can be rented.

**Where to eat and drink** Kanazawa is known as a good place to have sushi so it is not surprising that there are several options. A great place to stop for lunch is one of the sushi restaurants inside **Omi-cho market** 近江町市場 (see p230) as the fish is guaranteed to be fresh.

Closer to the station in **Kuugo Dining Resort** on the 6th floor of Forus department store, there are several very good places to eat. *MoriMori Sushi* もりもり寿し (daily 11am-10pm) is a kaiten-sushi place. The sushi that you order using the touchpad at your table/seat (English option available) is delivered on a shinkansen. Their automated way to count the dishes you have had, and therefore establish your bill, is rather fun. Be prepared to wait at busy times; prices are reasonable – expect to pay about ¥2000pp. If sushi doesn't appeal also on this floor is *Tomikinton* 富金豚 (daily 11am-11pm), where you can get delicious tonkatsu and croquettes; expect to pay about ¥1500.

*Sushitama* すし玉 (daily 11am-9.30pm; dishes from ¥130), another kaiten sushi-ya, is on the 2nd floor of Kutsurogi-kan in Hyakubangai Anto on the Port (West) Gate side of the station. Expect to queue at peak hours and, as in all such places, you can either take sushi from the conveyor belt or order. There is also a supermarket on this floor. The **Gourmet Floor**, on the 3rd floor, also has a range of restaurants including two izakayas, a shabu-shabu restaurant and a place serving ramen.

In the basement (B1F) of **Porte Kanazawa** ポルテ金沢, a 30-storey building, there are several Japanese restaurants including *Hacchouya* 八兆屋 (daily 11am-midnight) which serves soba (from ¥830) and a selection of *teishoku* (set meals) from ¥1500 and *Menza* 麺座 (daily 11am-10pm, lunch 11am-2pm) where you can get ramen

(from ¥780) and gyoza (five for ¥200). However, if you fancy tapas or paella head to *The Olive Oil Kitchen* オリーブオイルキッチン (daily noon-2pm & 5.30-10.30pm); three tapas and a beer is ¥1000 and paella costs from ¥2100 but the menu also includes fresh oysters (six for ¥2100).

*La Veranda* ラ・ベランダ at APA Hotel (see Where to stay) serves buffet meals at breakfast, lunch and in the evening (around ¥1600 for breakfast/lunch and ¥3300 in the evening) with a mixture of Japanese and Western dishes. Also on the 1st/ground floor here is a branch of *Seattle's Best Coffee* シアトルズベストコーヒー (7am-10pm), where pasta and pizza cost from ¥720.

For further ideas visit 🖳 gourmet.hot-ishikawa.jp.

**Entertainment** **Ishikawa Prefectural Concert Hall** 石川県立音楽堂 (Ishikawa Ongakudo; 🖳 www.ongakudo.jp) is the large modern building to your right as you leave the station's East Gate exit, next to the ANA Hotel. It's the home of Kanazawa Orchestra Ensemble but also attracts orchestras from across Japan and abroad. The main hall seats 1500 and is a tremendous concert space. Ask for a performance schedule at the tourist information centre (see p230) or check the website – with luck there will be something on while you're in town.

Performances (some free) at **Ishikawa Prefectural Noh Theatre** 石川県立能楽堂 (Nogakudo; Tue-Sun 9am-4.30pm; free) are held throughout the year. In July and August performances are held on Saturday evening. If there are no performances or rehearsals it's possible to take a look inside.

### Side trips from Kanazawa
● **To Gokayama and Shirakawa-go** (see pp224-6) Hokutetsu Bus (☎ 076-234 0123, 🖳 www.hokutetsu.co.jp/en) operates services to **Gokayama** (see 3-4/day; 60 mins; ¥1540/2780 one way/round trip) and **Shirakawa-go** (8/day; 75-85 mins; ¥1850/¥3290 one way/round trip) from outside Kanazawa Station's East Exit. Four services a day continue to **Takayama** (2¼hrs; ¥2470/4420). Tickets include a seat reservation and for most services should be reserved in advance (English speakers are available if you call) but it is sometimes possible to turn up and get on a bus. Hokutetsu Ticket Office is opposite Bus Stop No 2 on the Kenrokuen (East) Gate side of the station. Don't presume

the bus journey from here will be scenic; an awful lot of the latter part of the journey is in tunnels.

● **To Hakui** 羽咋 The JR Nanao Line heads north from Kanazawa towards the **Noto Peninsula** 能登半島 (Noto-hanto). An intriguing place to visit lies 40km (LEX 6/day, 32 mins; local 1-2/hr, 63 mins) along the line at **Hakui**, a self-proclaimed 'UFO town'. **Cosmo Isle Hakui** 宇宙科学博物館 コスモア イル羽咋 (🖥 www.hakui.ne.jp/ufo; Wed-Mon 9am-5pm; ¥350 admission, ¥500 for Cosmo (Dome) Theater) is an enormous dome containing a space and UFO Museum. On display are assorted spacecraft, astronaut suits and genuine moon dust. A few of the exhibits (all signed in English), including the Soviet Union's Vostok capsule and a NASA space suit with 24-carat gold helmet, are real. Video booths show interviews with sober and eccentric professors and scientists connected with SETI (Search for Extra Terrestrial Intelligence); there's also an extensive UFO database. Cosmo Isle Hakui is 10 minutes' walk north of Hakui station's East Exit. It's easy to spot as it's the only building with a 26m-high American rocket parked outside.

● **To Wakura-onsen** 和倉温泉 The **Hanayome Noren**, a luxurious sight-seeing train runs on the same line (Nanao Line) but continues beyond Hakui to Wakura-onsen (2/day weekends & holidays; 87 mins); from Nanao to Wakura-onsen it operates on the private Noto Railway. Hanayome Noren literally means 'bride's curtain' – noren are commonly used in front of restaurants to show they are open – and one is hung on the platform (No 4) to differentiate between ordinary trains and this one. This magnificent train is decorated with images based on local Wajima-nuri lacquerware and Kaga-yuzen textile dyeing with gold-leaf highlights. To add to the experience the staff are dressed in kimonos. All seats are reserved (free with JR pass) and if ordered in advance (from a Midori-no-madoguchi office) passengers can buy: a 'wakeishoku set' (Japanese-style light meal), made with food produced in the Noto region; a 'Horoyoi set' with local sake and delicacies; or a 'sweets set,' created by a patissier. The opulence of the train outclasses the scenery on the journey, but it is worth it just to have been on the train.

# Kansai – route guides

All roads lead to Kyoto, at least that's what most tourist brochures and travel documentaries on Japan let you assume. The ancient capital does indeed lie at the heart of the Kansai region, but it would be a shame to restrict your travel solely to the well-beaten track. Japan's even more ancient capital, Nara, is less than an hour away by rail and it's easily worth having a day or two there. Further south, the landscape becomes more rural, the crowds thin out and the views are worth seeking out. Kansai has one of the most extensive networks of rail lines in the country (operated by both JR and private railways), which means it's easy to go exploring.

The first part of this route guide follows the shinkansen line **from Nagoya to Osaka** via Kyoto – there is relatively little to see en route but it's useful if you're in a hurry. With more time, consider a much longer route to Kyoto **via the rural Kii Peninsula**, easily accessed from Nagoya but very much off the tradi-tional tourist trail. Limited expresses operate around the peninsula so the journey needn't be too time-consuming; the countryside and coastline certainly repay the effort. Taking this longer route also gives you the opportunity to go to **Ise**, home of the Grand Shrine and spiritual centre of Japan's indigenous religion, Shinto, but also to walk on some of the **Kumano Kodo pilgrimage routes**.

Another spiritual centre, the mountain retreat of **Koya-san**, offers a wholly unexpected change of pace. It is best accessed from Osaka but can also be reached from Wakayama as part of a longer journey around the Kii Peninsula, and also of course from Kyoto and Nara. The final stage, whichever route you take, is a hair-raising cable car (funicular) journey.

If you've arrived in Japan without a rail pass, the Kansai Thru Pass (see box p34) is likely to be worth getting. JR West (see box p30), which operates serv-ices throughout the Kansai area, also sells regional passes over the counter though these can be more expensive than if arranged before arriving in Japan.

For up-to-date information on events throughout the Kansai region, check ⌨ www.kansai.gr.jp.

## NAGOYA TO SHIN-OSAKA (OSAKA) BY SHINKANSEN

For the route from Tokyo to Nagoya (366km) see pp161-76.

Distances from Tokyo. Fastest journey time on a Hikari to Shin-Osaka: (from Tokyo) 173 mins; (from Nagoya) 52 mins.

Some Hikari and all Nozomi run non-stop from Nagoya to Kyoto.

### Nagoya to Shin-Osaka       [Map 9, p239; Table 3, p505]

### Nagoya 名古屋 (366km)       [see pp197-204]
All shinkansen stop here. Look out for Sanyo's huge **Solar Ark** ソーラーアーク (315m wide, 31.6-37.1m high) on the right soon after leaving Nagoya. There are 5046 solar panels generating up to 530,000kw/h of green electricity.

**Gifu-Hashima 岐阜羽島駅 (396km)** Some Hikari and all Kodama stop here. Despite its name, this station is not close to Gifu city at all; Gifu is on the Takayama Line on the route from Toyama (or Kanazawa) to Nagoya.

**Maibara 米原 (446km)** Some Hikari and all Kodama stop here. Maibara is a major rail junction: in addition to being a stop on the Tokaido shinkansen, trains on the Tokaido main line (Tokyo to Kobe), Biwa-ko Line (Maibara to Kyoto) and Hokuriku main line (Nagoya to Kanazawa) call here.

#### Side trips by rail from Maibara
● **On SL Kita-Biwako** SL北びわこ On some Saturdays and Sundays, typi-cally around Golden Week and in the autumn, the SL Kita-Biwako (see box p92) runs 22km (approx 55 mins) north along Lake Biwa 琵琶湖 (Biwa-ko) between Maibara and **Kinomoto** 木ノ本 on the Hokuriku Line.

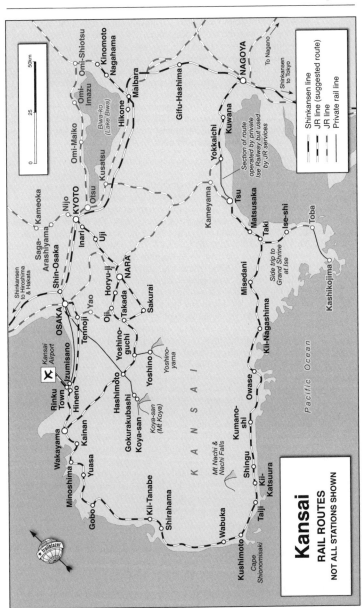

**Kansai**

**RAIL ROUTES**

NOT ALL STATIONS SHOWN

Shinkansen line

JR line (suggested route)

JR line

Private rail line

Section of route operated by private Ise Railway but used by JR services

Pacific Ocean

KANSAI

H O N S H U

A ride on this steam locomotive is enjoyable in its own right, but it's also worth stopping along the way at **Nagahama** 長浜 where you'll find the oldest station building in Japan; at that time goods were transferred from the Pacific (Tsuruga) to the Japan Sea (Kobe) via Nagahama and Otsu. The original station, built in 1882, is now a museum, **Nagahama Railway Square** 長浜鉄道 スクエア (daily 9.30am-5pm; ¥300). Even though the labels are mostly in Japanese it has some interesting exhibits and rail enthusiasts will be pleased to see the D51 model No 793 steam locomotive and the only ED70 model No 1 AC electric locomotive in Japan. The Railway Square is a short walk from the West Exit; pick up a map from the **tourist information office** (Mon-Fri 10am-4.45pm, Sat, Sun & hols 9.15am-5pm) in the station.

● **To Hikone** 彦根 Maibara is one stop east from the castle town of Hikone (Biwa-ko Line; 2-6/hr; 6 mins; ¥190), situated on Lake Biwa, Japan's largest lake. Hikone Castle is not quite as dramatic as the one at Himeji (see p272 & p274) but it benefits from the superb natural backdrop of Lake Biwa.

There are **lockers** (¥300-600) to the right of the ticket gate exit and also at the castle by the entrance and after the ticket desk. The **tourist information centre** (🖳 www.hikoneshi.com; daily 9am-6pm) is to your left at the foot of the stairs leading down from the Castle (West) Exit of the station. The castle is a 10-minute walk up the main street from the station.

**Hikone Castle** 彦根城 (Hikone-jo; daily 8.30am-5pm; ¥600 inc castle and garden, ¥1000 inc castle, garden & museum) is one of the few original castles left in Japan. Naotsugu Ii built the castle as his father Naomasa Ii, who had intended to build it, was killed in a battle in 1601. Construction began in 1603 and took almost 20 years; subsequent members of the family added more buildings and the garden; the castle was used until the Meiji Restoration in 1868 when it was under threat of demolition because it was seen as a symbol of the feudal era. However, Emperor Meiji visited the area and was persuaded by some of his staff to keep it. The ticket includes access to many of these buildings, most of which now have some form of exhibition. Note that as in many castles the steps inside are often very steep.

**Hikone Castle Museum** 彦根城博物館 (daily 8.30am-5pm; ¥500), by the main gate, exhibits artefacts from all aspects of the Ii family's history, including wonderful Noh costumes, and there are plenty of labels in English. There is also a reconstructed Noh stage and tea ceremony room.

**Genkyu-en** 玄宮園 (daily 8.30am-5pm; ¥200), a Japanese landscape garden dating back to 1677, is at the foot of the castle. It is a pleasant place to stroll around and has ponds and nine bridges connecting the islands.

From Hikone either backtrack to Maibara and pick up the shinkansen to Kyoto, or continue directly along the Tokaido Line from Hikone station (the fastest trains take 50 minutes to Kyoto; 3-9/hr).

## Kyoto 京都 (514km)  [see pp250-62]

As you leave Kyoto, you might catch sight of Tojo-ji's pagoda on the left-hand side. If sitting on the right look out for the shinkansen 'car park' (*torikai* yard) between Kyoto and Shin-Osaka.

## Shin-Osaka 新大阪 (553km)  [Osaka – see pp144-54]

## NAGOYA TO OSAKA (SHIN-OSAKA) VIA THE KII PENINSULA

Fastest journey time from Nagoya via Shingu to Tennoji (for Osaka) is 7¼ hours), or to Shin-Osaka 7½ hours.

**Nagoya to Shingu**                [Map 9, p239; Map 10, p243; Table 8, p507]
Distances by JR from Nagoya.

### Nagoya 名古屋 (0km)                [see pp197-204]

From Nagoya board a Wide-View Nanki LEX (4/day), or the slower Mie Rapid train (1/hr), heading towards Tsu and Shingu. The Nanki has lovely big windows and raised seats with foot rests. If planning to visit the Ise Grand Shrine (see p240) take the Mie train as it runs direct from Nagoya to Ise-shi. Both the Nanki and the Mie have reserved and non-reserved cars; see also box below. The Ise-Kumano Area Tourist Pass (see box p35) would be worth considering if you don't already have a pass.

The private Kintetsu Railway also runs services (6-7/hr) from Kintetsu-Nagoya to IseNakagawa (59-77 mins; ¥1140, reserved seat ¥900) where you need to change to Ise-shi station (19-22 mins; ¥490, reserved seat ¥510).

The journey as far as **Kuwana** 桑名 (24km) is not particularly scenic, but after leaving **Yokkaichi** 四日市 (37km) the industrial landscape starts to clear.

Unless you are on a Mie Rapid Train, you won't notice **Kawarada** 河原田 (44km); see box below. Some trains stop at **Suzuka** 鈴鹿 (48km); change to a local train here for Suzuka Circuit Ino station 鈴鹿サーキット稲生駅 and access to one of the oldest tracks on the Formula One circuit and location of the Japanese Grand Prix (🖥 www.suzukacircuit.jp).

**Tsu** 津 (66km) is also a stop on the Kintetsu and Ise railway lines; its main claim to fame is having the shortest station name in Japan, though it is not the only station with one 'kana'. After Tsu the ride starts to get more interesting as you can see hills in the distance on the right.

**Matsusaka** 松阪 **(85km)**  Matsusaka is known for its beef, the best of which is so tender it can be eaten with chopsticks. The locally bred cows receive meticulous care: their unusual diet includes beer and they are given gentle, full-body massages. Some shops here do a brisk trade in beef sushi, though in restaurants the most popular dish is either steak or *shabu-shabu*.

---

❏ **Ise Railway supplement**
The section of track between Kawarada and Tsu is owned by Ise Railway 伊勢線 (Ise-Tetsudo). If you have bought a ticket, the fare will include the supplement for this. However, JR rail-pass holders are supposed to pay the conductor on board the train. If travelling on the Nanki LEX this means paying both the standard fare (¥510) and limited express fare (¥310) just for that section (whatever your total journey is). On the Mie Rapid Train, only the standard fare has to be paid. You could get away without paying the supplement if you are in a non-reserved seat and if the conductor checks tickets only when the train has left Tsu, since there is no way of telling from the rail pass where you joined the train.

HONSHU

Matsusaka is a stop on both the JR and the Kintetsu lines. A guide map to Matsusaka is available from the **tourist information office** (🖥 www.city.matsu saka.mie.jp; daily 9am-6pm), in the glass building next to the police box 交番 (*koban*), on the right as you leave the South Exit (JR side) of the station.

The main sights are in or around the castle ruins of **Matsusaka Park** 松阪 公園, a 10- to 15-minute walk north-east of the station. Only a few stone walls are left of Matsusaka Castle, so head to **Gojoban Yashiki** 御城番屋敷 (Tue-Sun 10am-4pm; free), a preserved street with 19 wooden houses which used to be where local samurai lived. A few of the people who still live on this street are descendants of the samurai.

There are also several business hotels near the station; one of the closest is *Toyoko Inn Ise Matsusaka Ekimae* 東横イン伊勢松阪駅前 (☎ 0598-22 1045, 🖥 www.toyoko-inn.com; from ¥5300/S, ¥6300/D or Tw), a minute's walk from the South Exit of the station. For more character try *Taiya Ryokan* 鯛屋旅館 (☎ 0598-23 1200, 🖥 www.taiyaryokan.com; from ¥11,340pp), which is about a 10-minute walk from the station's South Exit en route to Matsusaka Park: turn right at the second traffic lights and it is soon on your right.

To try some of Matsusaka's famous beef, head up the main road that runs straight ahead from the station. On the corner at the first set of traffic lights, and on the right, is *Kameya* かめや (daily 11am-8pm; set lunch 11am-12.30pm), a casual restaurant that serves up good-value set meals, including shabu-shabu. The cheapest meal with **Matsusaka beef** is a truly delicious *gyudon* (from ¥2600); the most expensive steak costs ¥19,000. The entrance is next to a butcher's counter, so you can guarantee that the meat is fresh. However, make sure you get here early as they close when they sell out of meat and this may be before the evening especially on a Sunday. If they are closed non-residents can also have a delicious meal with Matsusaka beef (kaiseki lunch box ¥2700; evening meal from ¥3780pp) at *Taiya Ryokan* (see above). If you haven't eaten Matsusaka beef while here get a *gyuniku ekiben* at the station (from ¥1350).

**Ujisato Festival** (3rd Nov) takes place near the station and the castle ruins; highlights include a parade around the city by about 200 people dressed as fully armoured samurai warriors.

**Taki** 多気 **(93km)**  In the Edo Period, Taki was a stop along the pilgrim path to Ise Grand Shrine.

▲ Taki is a tiny rather rundown station with nothing other than a waiting area but it is an important rail junction as the track divides here. The route described follows the Kisei Line south towards Shingu and the Kii Peninsula (see p241).

However, if you took the Nanki LEX from Nagoya but are planning to do the side trip to visit the Grand Shrine at Ise (see p240) change to the JR Sangu Line here. This goes to **Ise-shi** 伊勢市駅 (12 mins by Mie rapid train approx 1/hr, 20 mins by local train also approx 1/hr).

Beyond Ise-shi, JR trains run as far as **Toba** 鳥羽, famous for Mikimoto pearls, but the only way of moving on from Ise to continue the rail route described below is to backtrack to Taki.

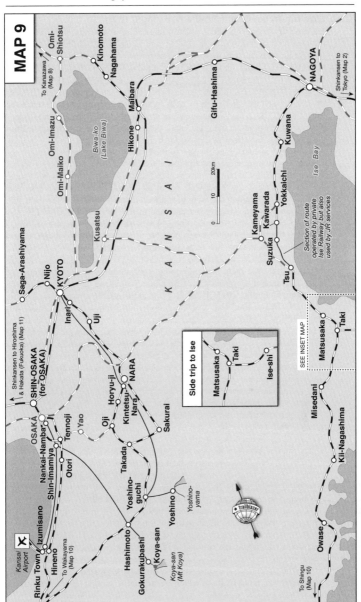

**MAP 9**

To Kanazawa (Map 8)

Omi-Shiotsu

Kinomoto

Nagahama

Maibara

Gifu-Hashima

NAGOYA

Shinkansen to Tokyo (Map 2)

Omi-Imazu

Biwa-ko (Lake Biwa)

Hikone

Kuwana

Omi-Maiko

Ise Bay

Kusatsu

K A N S A I

Yokkaichi

Kameyama

Kawarada

Saga-Arashiyama

Nijo

KYOTO

Suzuka

Section of route operated by private Ise Railway but also used by JR services

Inari

Uji

Tsu

Shinkansen to Hiroshima & Hakata (Fukuoka) (Map 11)

SHIN-OSAKA (for OSAKA)

Horyu-ji

NARA

0   10   20km

Side trip to Ise

Matsusaka

Taki

Ise-shi

SEE INSET MAP

Matsusaka

Taki

OSAKA

Nankai-Namba

Shin-imamiya

Tennoji

Yao

Oji

Kintetsu Nara

Takada

Sakurai

Misedani

Kansai Airport

Izumisano

Rinku Town

Hineno

Otori

Yoshino-guchi

Yoshino

Yoshino-yama

Kii-Nagashima

To Wakayama (Map 10)

Hashimoto

Gokurakubashi

Koya-san

Koya-san (Mt Koya)

Owase

To Shingu (Map 10)

trailblazer

HONSHU

### Side trip to Ise Grand Shrine (Ise Jingu) 伊勢神宮

**Ise town** 伊勢 receives about seven million visitors annually, many of whom are making a once-in-a-lifetime pilgrimage to Ise Grand Shrine (🖥 www.ise jingu.or.jp; daily dawn to dusk; free). The shrine is the home of Japan's indigenous religion, Shinto, and it is considered to be the most spiritually important shrine for the Japanese.

The complex comprises Outer 外宮 (**Geku**) and Inner 内宮 (**Naiku**) shrines, as well as **Uji Bridge** 宇治橋, which you have to cross to reach the Inner Shrine. Since the two shrine areas are 2¼ miles (3.7km) apart most people catch a bus between them but Geku shrine is an easy (8-minute) walk from the JR side of **Ise-shi** 伊勢市 station. Before you leave the station (used by both JR and Kintetsu) go to the **tourist information centre** (daily 9am-5.30pm) to pick up a map of the town and shrine areas as well as a useful explanatory leaflet about the shrines. There are also **lockers** (¥300-600) here.

To reach the Geku shrine walk out of the JR side of the station, cross over the road and walk along the main paved road directly ahead. On the right side before you cross the road to the entrance to the shrine is **Ise City TIC** (🖥 www.ise-kanko.jp; daily 8am-5.30pm), which has basically the same information as in the station TIC, but it is possible to rent a bicycle here (¥500/4hrs, ¥800/1 day). On the left side is the **bus stop** for Naiku shrine.

There are 125 shinto shrines altogether at Ise Grand Shrine. One of the key features is that the main ones are completely rebuilt on a neighbouring site every 20 years in a process called Shiniken Sengu; the 62nd rebuilding was completed in autumn 2013. Thus the wood at the rebuilt shrines looks beautifully new. **Sengu-kan** せんぐう館 (daily 9am-4.30pm but closed every 4th Tue; ¥300) is an information centre where you can learn about the rebuilding, the craftsmanship involved, and the ceremony for transferring the deities to the new shrines. When you buy your ticket you should be given an English explanation. Sengu-kan is on the left side at the entrance to the Geku shrine. The main shrine at **Geku** is Shogu; twice a day sacred food is offered here to Amaterasu Omikami, the supreme deity. Toyouke Omikami, the guardian of food and industry, is enshrined at Taka-no-miya. Devoid of gaudy decorations, the shrines are simple to the point of austerity.

To get to **Naiku**, the Inner Shrine, either take bus No 51 or 55 (10-15 mins; 1-5/hr; ¥430), or hop on a CAN bus (Mie Transit Bus; 🖥 tourismmie japan.com/travel/michikusa.html; 1/hr; ¥430, or ¥1000/1600 1-/2-day pass), which shuttles between the station, the shrines, Toba (see p238) and other sights in the area. There is also a fleet of taxis (approx ¥2000 for up to four people) waiting for the many pilgrims and visitors. The sun goddess Amaterasu Omikami, the Imperial family's ancestral *kami* (deity), is enshrined at Naiku. A sacred mirror, symbol of the kami, is carefully wrapped up and hidden away in the inner sanctuary and never shown in public. Indeed, there's not a great deal to see at all, since the interior of both shrines is off limits.

Before you leave Naiku walk down **Oharai-machi** おはらい町, a 800m-long street which was the original way pilgrims approached Naiku; 'oharai' also refers to the purification ritual pilgrims perform before entering a Shinto shrine. The street is on the right after you cross Uji Bridge; it is now lined with shops and restaurants, many of which are still in Edo-period style and is a great place to get a snack or meal.

When leaving Taki, sit on the left side of the train for the best views of the small mountain ranges and rivers, as well as the rice fields and then tea fields. Some trains stop at **Misedani** 三瀬谷 (118km). From Misedani the track shadows the Pacific coast, albeit at a slight distance.

Around **Kii-Nagashima** 紀伊長島 (127km) there are great but brief views of clusters of rock and small islands. A few minutes from **Owase** 尾鷲 (151km) there are also some glimpses of lovely bays with fishing villages but also a number of tunnels, some of which are pretty long. The next stop is **Kumano-shi** 熊野市 (186km), which is on the Iseji pilgrimage route (see box p242).

**Shingu** 新宮 **(209km)** Shingu serves as a useful transport hub as JR Central's services from Nagoya terminate here and JR West's services to Shin-Osaka start here. It is also an access point for one of the three Kumano Sanzan (see box p242) shrines.

The **tourist information office** (🖥 kumano-shingu.com; Fri-Wed 9am-5.30pm), on the left as you exit the ticket barrier, has friendly staff, a good map, information about the area and bus timetables. You can **rent a bicycle** here for ¥500/day. There are a few **lockers** (mostly ¥300) to the right as you exit the ticket barrier and also an ekiben stand.

Shingu has a small number of reasonably priced business hotels. Not surprisingly the closest to the station is *Station Hotel* ステーションホテル新宮 (☎ 0735-21 2200, 🖥 www.rifnet.or.jp/~station; from ¥4900/S, ¥8000/D or Tw, ¥16,500/Tr); turn right out of the station and then first right and the hotel is a couple of minutes' walk along on the right-hand side.

## Shingu to Shin-Osaka/Kyoto [Map 10, p243; Table 9, p507]
Distances by JR from Shingu.

**Shingu** 新宮 **(0km)** The Kuroshio LEX operates from here along the JR Kisei (Kinokuni) Line to Shin-Osaka/Kyoto.

For the most part, the line from Shingu to Nachi follows the coast, though the view is sometimes obscured by tunnels and trees. There are several fishing villages but also industrial areas.

♦ **Nachi** 那智 **(13km)** Limited expresses don't stop here, so take a local train from Shingu (11/day; 18 mins), or from Kii-Katsuura (see p243) which is actually closer. Nachi station does not have a ticket barrier so you will have to walk to the front of the train so the driver can check your ticket. Nor does the station have any services and there are no places to eat in the immediate station area. But you may well see lots of flags suspended from the ceiling on the platform; these are for football teams and are here because Kakunosuke Nakamura, the founding father of football in Japan, was born in Shingu.

To the right of the main exit is the entrance to Nishiki-no-yu, the station's own onsen and in the same building a small **Kumano World Heritage Information Center** (Tue-Sun 9am-5pm; free; the general area is open till 9pm), both of which are definitely worth visiting. The information centre has several boards with explanations in English about the Kumano pilgrimage routes and sacred sites;

HONSHU

there is also a video about Nachi Fire Festival (see opposite) but that is in Japanese only. From the bath at **Nishiki-no-Yu** 丹敷の湯 (Tue-Sun 1-9pm; ¥600 plus ¥200 towel rental) there are great views out over Nachi Bay and also of the train tracks below, so rail enthusiasts can enjoy the unusual experience of trainspotting from the comfort of a bathtub. If here in the summer months you could also go and sit on Nachi's lovely sandy beach.

Bus No 8 runs from Katsuura station via Nachi station (1-2/hr; 17 mins; ¥480) to **Nachi-san** 那智山. A short walk uphill from Nachi-san bus stop leads to **Kumano Nachi Taisha** 熊野那智大社, the head shrine of 4000 Kumano shrines in Japan and part of Kumano Sanzan (see box below). The shrine is dedicated to the 'god of desires fulfilled'. In the sacred area is **Karasu-ishi**, the stone of Yatagarasu (the three-legged crow); according to legend the crow guided the first Emperor, Jimmu (also known as Jinmu), and was transformed into stone when it returned from this task. It is believed that anyone who can walk through the hole in the 850-year-old camphor tree here will have good health.

The harmonious relationship between Shinto and Buddhism means that temples and shrines are often found on the same site. This is the case here: **Seiganto-ji** 青岸渡寺, a Buddhist temple, is actually the oldest structure in Kumano and the giant bell here is the biggest in Japan (450kg and 1.4m wide).

From the temple you can walk down on some of the cedar-tree-lined pilgrimage paths to Nachi waterfall; the paths are atmospheric, even if it is pouring with rain and very misty. After passing some souvenir shops – some of which have areas where they serve meals such as soba and curry rice – walk under the *torii* (shrine gate) and down a flight of stone steps towards the 133m-high, 13m-wide waterfall, **Nachi-no-Otaki** 那智滝. If you pay ¥300 you can walk up to the worship altar and get a closer view of the waterfall. Legend has it that Emperor Jimmu arrived here in the 7th century, having seen the cascading water from the seashore, and pronounced it the spiritual embodiment of a *kami* (deity).

From Nachi-no-Otaki either pick up a bus to Nachi station, or walk down **Daimonzaka** 大門坂, one of the ancient pilgrimage routes, to the Chushajo-mae bus stop 駐車場 and pick up the bus there.

---

### ❏ Kumano Sanzan

Kumano Nachi Taisha (see above) is one of the three **grand shrines** in this area which have great significance in the Shinto religion; the others are Kumano Hongu Taisha 熊野本宮大社 and Kumano Hayatama Taisha 熊野速玉大社. Indeed, they are so important that they are known as Kumano Sanzan (🖳 www.tb-kumano.jp) and these, along with Koya-san (see pp156-8) and Yoshino-yama (see p156) and the pilgrimage paths 参詣道 (sankeimichi) between them, have been declared part of the World Heritage listed 'Sacred sites and pilgrimage routes in the Kii Mountain Range'.

The **pilgrimage routes** are: Iseji, which runs along the east coast from Ise-shi to near Shingu; Omine Okugakemichi goes from Yoshino-yama, and Kohechi goes from Koya-san, to Kumano Hongu Taisha; the Nakahechi path crosses from Kii Tanabe to Nachi and Shingu (this is the most popular route); Kiiji from Osaka to Kii-Tanabe, and Ohechi south from Kii-Tanabe around the peninsula to Kii-Katsura/Nachi. Details about all the walks can be obtained from the Kumano Sanzan website.

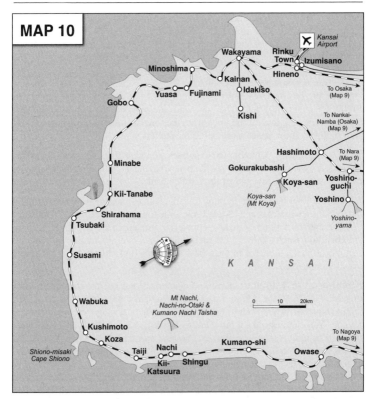

**Nachi Fire Festival** (Nachi-no-Hi matsuri), one of the three largest fire festivals in Japan, is held here on 14th July; 6m-high portable shrines that represent the spirits associated with the waterfall are purified with the fires from large torches that men dressed in white carry up from the waterfall to the shrine.

For more information about the area visit 🖥 www.nachikan.jp.

**Kii-Katsuura** 紀伊勝浦 **(15km)** The town, called Katsuura 勝浦, is a fishing port which boasts Japan's largest catches of tuna.

There are also several onsen here, the best known of which is **Boki-do spa** 忘帰洞, inside a cave but with views out to sea. The cave is one of six kinds of bath at *Hotel Urashima* ホテル浦島 (☎ 0735-52 1011, 🖥 www.hotelurashima .co.jp; from ¥11,200pp inc half board). Another feature of this hotel is that it has Japan's longest escalator (a 6-minute journey). To reach the hotel walk along Ekimae-Hondori, the road heading straight ahead from the station, till you reach the sea and then round to the left to the Tourist Pier at the harbour; this is where the free ferry to the hotel departs (a 5- to 10-minute walk in all). Check where

H O N S H U

the boat is going as in addition to sightseeing trips of the local islands there's a ferry service from here to **Hotel Nakanoshima** ホテル中の島 (☎ 0735-52 1111, 🖳 www.hotel-nakanoshima.jp; from ¥12,000pp inc half board); Hotel Nakanoshima is on a small island and it also offers open-air baths facing the sea but not in a cave.

Katsuura is another access point for Kumano Nachi Taisha and Nachi-no-Otaki as the bus operates between Shingu and Kii Katsuura (¥620, round trip ¥1000; 25 mins) via Nachi. The bus stands are opposite the station to the left. You can pick up a map of the town from the **tourist information centre** (daily 8am-6.30pm) at the street level exit to the station.

**Taiji 太地 (20km)** Some limited expresses stop here. Taiji is known for whaling and, despite calls for a worldwide ban, whale meat still sometimes turns up on the menu around this part of the Kii Peninsula.

For the final part of the journey towards Kushimoto, the train heads inland but the journey is still scenic. After Taiji, some trains stop at **Koza** 古座 (35km).

The impressive line of rocks on the left as you approach Kushimoto station are **Hashigui Rocks** 橋杭岩: the rocks are spread over 850m and are lined up seeming to make a bridge to the island here, called **O-shima** 大島, but aren't actually connected.

**Kushimoto 串本 (42km)** Kushimoto station is the nearest stop to **Shiono-misaki** 潮岬灯 (Cape Shiono), the most southerly point on Honshu, a 16-minute bus ride away (10/day; ¥380); note that the buses say they are bound for Shingu. You can also take a bus (9/day; 4 mins; ¥150), or walk in 25-30 minutes to Hashigui Rocks (see above). The area around here is known as '**Taifu Ginza**' because 'taifu' (typhoons) are common in the summer months; 'ginza' means silver street ie the main street in a town.

The staff at the **tourist information office** (daily 9am-5pm) in the station have leaflets in English about the sights in the area and a bus timetable; the bus stop is right outside the station. There's a small locker area in the station.

You'll probably only notice **Wabuka** 和深 (56km) if on a local train but it's a good vantage point for views of the Pacific Ocean. The latter half of the journey towards the next major stop at Shirahama is mostly inland.

All trains stop at **Susami** 周参見 (73km); if sitting on the left-hand side as you pull into the station look for a mural depicting a windsurfer and two divers – one seeming to be posting a card in a postbox in the sea and the other to be collecting it. This is because since 1999 there has been a postbox in the sea here (10 metres, approx 33ft, down); this holds the record in the *Guinness Book of Records* for the deepest underwater postbox 海中郵便ポスト (Kaichu Yubin-Posto) in the world. Not surprisingly the cast-iron postbox rusts in the sea water so it has to be changed twice a year. Any diver wanting to send a (waterproof) postcard must prearrange a dive to the postbox through Club Noah Susami クラブノアすさみ (🖳 www.susami.club-noah.net/post.html). Any post is then collected by the diving shop and taken to an official postbox on land. There is no tourist information office at Susami station but the ticket office has a map of the town in Japanese. The station also has an exhibition about katsuo fishing and showcases products made in the area.

After Susami some trains call at **Tsubaki** 椿 (87km).

**Shirahama** 白浜 **(95km)** Shirahama is an onsen town and a very popular summer vacation destination but out of season it is a very pleasant place to visit. The highlights are the historic rotemburo with views of the Pacific Ocean and the lovely white sand beach here. However, the soft toy panda by the ticket barrier, the panda-painted windows in the station and at the Midori-no-madoguchi counters, let alone the panda seats in some of the carriages of Kuroshio trains, are a clue to one of the other attractions here: **Adventure World** アドベンチャーワールド (🖥 www.aws-s.com; Mar-Nov daily 9.30am-5pm, to 8.30pm in holiday periods, Dec-Feb 10am-5pm, closed approx two Wed/month but check website; ¥4100/1-day pass), a theme park and zoo in one. The park is divided into zones, including Safari World, Marine World and Panda Land. Twin panda cubs, Ouhin and Touhin, were born here in 2014; at the time of research their mother Rauhin had given birth to seven pandas. Meiko Bus No 2 runs non-stop from Stand 3 to Adventure World from Shirahama station; other buses that stop there are Nos 6 and 102. Overall there are 1-2 buses an hour.

To reach the main resort area and the beach from Shirahama station it is best to take a bus. Before you leave visit the **tourist information centre** (🖥 www .nanki-shirahama.net; daily 9.30am-6pm) which is beyond the waiting room in the station. Staff have a map of the main area, bus timetables and accommodation lists but they are unable to make reservations. In the station there are **lockers** (¥300/400) and a food kiosk. You need to buy a ticket for the bus before you board so go to **Meiko bus** 明光バス (🖥 meikobus.jp; daily 10am-5pm) ticket office to the left of the station. Bus Nos 12 and 30 (1-3/hr; 15 mins) go to **Shirahama Bus Center** 白浜バスセンター the access point for the beach area; the fare is ¥340 but Meiko Bus's Shirahama-onsen 1-day Pass (¥1100 inc some discount coupons) is best if you expect to see several sights.

The beach, **Shirarahama** 白良浜, is known for its white sand which contains 90% crystal and was created from weathered sandstone. The additional 'ra' is to distinguish this beach from others of the same name in Japan. However, the original sand eroded so what you see now is sand imported from Australia.

Top priority should be having a bath at **Saki-no-yu** 崎の湯 (daily Apr-June & Sep 8am-6pm, July & Aug 7am-7pm, rest of year 8am-5pm; ¥420); the water here has been flowing into the rock baths by the Pacific Ocean for over 1300 years and it is believed that several emperors (in the Asuka and Nara periods) bathed here. Since there are no shower facilities, nor is there soap or shampoo (it is best to bring your own towel), the usual protocol for having a bath in Japan is not possible. But when you have undressed fill one of the bowls with water from the bath and pour it over yourself before getting in. The women's side has three baths; the men's side has only two and is more exposed. To get here walk along the path or road by the beach and when the road starts going up hill take the road that stays at coast level. If you have a swimming costume another option is **Shirasuna** 浜露天 (daily 10am-3pm, July-Sep to 7pm; ¥100 for locker and ¥200 for shower and access to change room), on the main beach. If you visit out of the main season you can use it just as an *ashi-yu* (foot-bath). There are also several other foot-baths around town.

A great place for a meal is ***Fishermans Wharf*** フィッシャーマンズワーフ白浜 (🖳 fw-sh.com; 8.30am-6pm, lunch 11am-3pm) on the beach front. Choose some fish from the display, say how you want it prepared ie sashimi (no extra charge) or grilled (¥50), then pay for it at the counter; a bowl of rice costs ¥200 and miso soup ¥100. Choose a table and the staff will bring your meal.

Pick up Bus No 101, 102, or 105 for the wider route round Shirahama to see **Engetsuto** 円月島, a small island where the rock has eroded leaving a hole that looks like the shape of a full moon. The best time to be here is at sunset, but it is scenic at any time of the day. Get off at Rinkai りんかい stop.

**Kii-Tanabe** 紀伊田辺 **(105km)** Right in front of the station is an area, **Ajikoji** 味光路, of narrow alleys full of bars, restaurants, love hotels and pachinko parlours. However, there's much more to the town, called **Tanabe** 伊田辺.

The founder of aikido, Morihei Ueshiba (1883-1969), was born here; a memorial statue to him stands close to the ocean and he is buried on the other side of town in **Kozan-ji** 高山寺. This is a pleasant and peaceful temple to visit even if you are not an aikido fan. To get there walk along Ekimae-Shin-dori, the one-way street that heads right from the station, turn first right then left after crossing the railway line and walk along till you reach the pedestrian bridge which crosses the river. Cross the bridge and walk up the steps to the temple. There are a few cherry trees here so it is especially nice in spring.

Tanabe is also the junction of the Kiiji, Ohechi and Nakahechi paths on the **Kumano Kodo pilgrimage route** (see box p242). Two companies – Ryujin and Meiku – operate bus services from here to Kumano Hongu Taisha-mae (90-120 mins; 7/day; ¥2060).

**Tanabe Tourist Information Center** (daily 9am-6pm) is to the left as you exit the station. There are plenty of leaflets in English about the Kumano Kodo pilgrimage routes and the staff will give you a map of Tanabe as well as bus timetables. They have information about accommodation but can't make any bookings – for Tanabe, or for the pilgrimage routes. There is always at least one English speaker in the office. There are **lockers** (¥300-700) on the station concourse and there is a **Kiosk** here as well as a *bakery/café* (Café Noix).

*Hotel Hanaya* ホテル花屋 (☎ 0739-22 3877, 🖳 www.hotel-hanaya.com; from ¥5200pp, breakfast ¥700) is a nice place to stay and the rooms are a good size, but the baths are tiny. It is on the left-hand side near the end of Ekimae-shin-dori; reception (Front) is on the 2nd floor. Breakfast (either Western or Japanese) is served in the café on the 1st/ground floor. Alternatively, consider *Altier Hotel* アルティエホテル (☎ 0739-81 1111, 🖳 www.altierhotel.com; from ¥5775/S, ¥8400/D, ¥11,550/Tw, inc breakfast). The rooms are small but have attached bathrooms and wide beds. It's five minutes from the station; walk along Ekimae-dori, the main street that runs away from the station; the hotel is on the right-hand side, soon after the road becomes Aoi-dori.

Finding somewhere to eat is easy in Ajikoji: *Ginchiro Honten* 銀ちろ 本店 (🖥 www.ginchiro.jp; 11am-9pm but closed some days) is a great place for a meal; the menu, available in English, includes a wide range of dishes. Expect to pay about ¥3000 for a meal. There are two other branches nearby. *Tokkuri* とっくり (Mon-Sat 5-10.30pm), an izakaya, also has a range of dishes including delicious roast garlic 焼きニンニク. For other places in the area see 🖥 www.tb-kumano.jp/en/dining/gourmet-map.

About 10 minutes out of Kii-Tanabe, there are views of the Pacific as the train runs along an elevated track. Some trains stop at **Minabe** みなべ (114km). From Minabe the line goes by the coast for about 15 minutes then inland.

### Gobo 御坊 (146km)

Rail enthusiasts may want to take a ride on the **Kishu Railway** 紀州鉄道線 which runs between Gobo and Nishi-Gobo 西御坊; this is the second shortest railway line (2.7km; 1-2/hr; 8 mins; ¥180) in Japan. Trains depart from Track 0 at JR Gobo station; pay the driver on the train. If you return immediately you may be given a discount on the return fare. This may not be the best-maintained line in Japan, but it clearly provides a useful service for the local community and for the rail enthusiasts who come to travel on it.

Gobo Station has a Kiosk, vending machines and **lockers** (¥300-600) as well as a display of the products made locally.

After Gobo the train passes through a number of tunnels.

### Yuasa 湯浅 (164km)

A few limited expresses stop here. Yuasa is notable as the place where soy sauce was created. The method of making soy-bean paste (miso paste) had reached Japan from China but it was here, in the 12th century, that the liquid version we know today was first made. In the early 19th century there were as many as 92 shoyu breweries here but there are now only a few. However, the area where the breweries was has been made into a preservation district and you can still see some of the old breweries. For a leaflet in English (with a map of the area) go to the **information centre** (daily 9am-5pm) in the town office 湯浅町役場 about 10 metres from the station; turn right out of the station and the building is on your left set back from the road. There are some **lockers** in the station (¥300-600) and a Soyjoy vending machine selling – of course – some of the Soyjoy snacks made from whole soy beans.

The stop after Yuasa is **Fujinami** 藤並 (166.5km). After that the scenery is just a line of identikit towns and industrial plants. Some limited expresses stop at **Minoshima** 箕島 (175km), part of Arida city, which is known for its oranges and for cormorant fishing (June to early Sep) on the Arida-gawa. Just before the train pulls in at **Kainan** 海南 (190km) there's a big area of industrial plants out to the left, drawing a final line under the rural part of the peninsula.

### Wakayama 和歌山 (201km)

The two main reasons for getting out of the train here are to transfer to the JR Wakayama Line to Hashimoto, for Koya-san (see pp156-8) and to have a journey on Wakayama Dentetsu railway line made famous because a cat was made a station master (see box p248) here in 2007.

There is a **tourist information office** (🖳 www.wakayamakanko.com; Mon-Sat 8.30am-7pm, Sun 8.30am-5.15pm) by the Central Exit to the JR side of the station. To find **lockers** (all sizes; ¥300-500) turn left out of the station and look for the locker room on the side of the station building.

Within the station building there are **restaurants** on the basement level of VIVO department store and a small bakery on ground level. Another place to look is Dining Street in the basement of Mio on the left of the station concourse.

**Wakayama Castle** 和歌山城 (daily 9am-5.30pm; ¥410) was originally constructed in 1585 but parts of it were destroyed by bombing in WWII. The reconstructed parts date from 1958 but some of the gates, stone walls, keep and bell tower are original. The 600 cherry trees in the grounds mean it is a popular place in the spring. It's a 10-minute bus ride (¥220; frequent services) from stop No 2 right outside the station; get off at Koen-mae 公園前.

If you need a place to stay, the JR-run *Hotel Granvia Wakayama* ホテルグランヴィア和歌山 (☎ 073-425 3333, 🖳 www.granvia-wakayama.co.jp; from ¥11,642/S, ¥20,790/D, ¥26,037/Tw) is connected to the station. *Dormy Inn Premium Wakayama* ドーミーインPremium 和歌山 (☎ 073-402 5489, 🖳 www .hotespa.net/hotels/wakayama; ¥7490/S, ¥11,490; inc buffet breakfast), a branch of the highly recommended Dormy Inn chain, is on the left after the second set of traffic lights along the road heading straight from the station; a 5- to 10-minute walk. *Okonomiyaki-gu* お好み焼き偶 (🖳 www.okonomiyaki-gu .co.jp/store_wakayama.htm; 11am-11pm; from ¥660), an okonomiyaki restaurant on the left after the first set of traffic lights, is a great place for a meal.

### Side trip by rail to Kishi (on the TamaDen)

Even if you aren't a cat fan a trip on the TamaDen, officially known as the Wakayama Dentetsu Kishigawa Line 和歌山電鐵貴志川線 (🖳 www.wakaya ma-dentetsu.co.jp), is an enjoyable experience. The trains operating on this

---

### ❏ Tama – the world's first cat to be a Super Station Master

Tama was a stray cat whose life changed, in 2004, when Toshiko Koyama adopted her; coincidentally at about the same time as the decision was made to close the private Wakayama Dentetsu Kishigawa Line. Locals protested and won their case but in 2006 all station masters on the line were made redundant and replacements were found from employees of local companies. Luckily, as it turns out, Koyama san was chosen for Kishi station and in 2007 he nominated Tama for the role of station master; not surprisingly word got around that a cat was now in charge and people started to visit. Such was Tama's fame that in 2009 a Tama densha (Tama train) started and in 2010 Kishi station was rebuilt to look like her head.

By now Tama was getting old so Nitama (Tama II) was recruited in 2012 to help share the workload; Tama was then promoted to Super Station Master. Tama's death in June 2015 at the age of 16 was even flashed up as breaking news on the LED on Tokaido shinkansen services. Her funeral was attended by about 3000 people and posthumously she was granted the status of a Shinto goddess; she is also a kind of guardian deity of Wakayama Dentetsu. After 50 days of mourning, Nitama was appointed to replace Tama, but at the time of research it wasn't certain that an assistant would be appointed to help Nitama.

line are: Tama Densha, which is covered in cat images; the Ichigo train which promotes strawberry-picking (Feb to mid May) at a farm near Kishi station; the Omocha train which has toys for children to play with and a vending machine selling capsules containing a selection of things such as metal badges; and the latest, starting in 2016, is the Umeboshi train as *umeboshi* (pickled plum) is a well-known product in the area. All have a variety of seating and wooden floors. The timetable varies so check the website first.

Officially Nitama is on duty 10am-4pm (Fri-Tue), but you have to be prepared for the fact that she is likely to be in her glass 'office' and may be asleep. However, you can pop into *Tama's Café* (daily 9.15am-5.15pm), at Kishi, for a Tama's 'tale' cookie and coffee (¥470), or next door to the souvenir shop where there are now also some Nitama products. Despite its fame at the time of research there was no actual ticket office at Kishi station so if you are starting your journey here you don't need to pay till you get to your destination.

The fare between Wakayama and Kishi is ¥400 but a day pass costs ¥780. Trains (2-3hr; 30 mins to Kishi) depart from Platform 9 at Wakayama station; to reach this you need to take the underground passageway from the JR tracks.

From Wakayama, trains continue along the JR Hanwa Line towards Tennoji and Shin-Osaka.

**Hineno** 日根野 **(227km)**  A few LEX stop here (mostly services that started in Shirahama). Change here for the short journey on the Kansai Airport Line to Kansai International Airport.

A few trains then stop at **Otori** 鳳 (247km).

**Tennoji** 天王寺 **(262km)**  Tennoji is a station on the JR Osaka Loop Line (see p146) so if going to Osaka station change here rather than at Shin-Osaka.

**Shin-Osaka** 新大阪 **(277km)**                    **[Osaka – see pp144-54]**
Change here for the shinkansen for the route around Western Honshu (see p272) and also for Osaka if you are going there but didn't change at Tennoji.

A few limited expresses continue to **Kyoto** (316km; see pp250-62).

---

❏ **'Airport' hotels**
Unless you are booked to stay at Hotel Nikko Kansai Airport (see p154), the only hotel on the airport island, you will find that the shuttle buses for so-called 'airport' hotels will bring you back to the mainland. Since most services operate fairly infrequently it would save time to get off at **Hineno**, especially if you are booked to stay at the *Kanku Joytel Hotel* 関空ジョイテルホテル (☎ 072-460 1900, 🖳 www.joytel hotels.com/kanku; from ¥6060/S, ¥9500/D or Tw), formerly a Best Western hotel.

Other options are going to: **Izumisano** 泉佐野 (Nankai Line only) which is about five minutes' walk from *Bellevue Garden Hotel* ベルビューガーデンホテル 関西 空港 (☎ 072-469 1112, 🖳 www.bellevue-kix.com; from ¥6500/S, ¥11,000/D or Tw); or to **Rinku Town** りんくうタウン (one stop away on both the JR and Nankai lines), which is convenient for *Kansai Airport Washington Hotel* 関西エアポートワシン トンホテル (☎ 072-461 2222, 🖳 kansai-ap.washington-hotels.jp; from ¥8400/S, ¥16,000/D or Tw).

# Kansai – city guides

## KYOTO 京都

Kyoto may have lost its status as national capital and Imperial home in 1868, at the time of the Meiji Restoration (see pp56-7), but nobody could dispute its title of modern-day tourist capital. The temples here, many of which are on the World Heritage Site List, let alone the other attractions, make it an essential place to visit on even the briefest of visits to Japan. Arriving by bullet train, the impression is more of a city like so many others: Kyoto has office-blocks as well as shrines, Starbucks as well as wooden tea houses. But you only need to walk a few minutes north, or south, from the station to reach the first temple and instantly leave the city behind.

Kyoto is also known for its geisha population but nowadays you're more likely to see a Japanese (or a foreigner) who has paid to be dressed up as a geisha for a day than catch a glimpse of a real one (see box p255).

With a superb network of trains radiating out from the city, Kyoto is an excellent base for rail travel around Kansai and beyond; it's also the perfect place to return to, as there's always somewhere else waiting to be discovered.

## What to see and do

When planning an itinerary for Kyoto it is important to remember that even though the public transport service is excellent it can take quite a long time to get from one temple, or sight, to another as many are spread out over the city. To help plan your sight-seeing this guide arranges the attractions geographically but also suggests some 'must sees' (see box below).

Bear in mind that the temples/shrines will be particularly crowded in spring when people pour in to see the cherry blossom and in autumn for the crimson leaves.

If you've already started your rail pass before arriving in Kyoto and are planning to stay in the city for more than a couple of days, you'll probably want to use it as much as possible rather than 'waste' days of rail

> ❏ **Must sees**
> Kinkaku-ji, opposite; Ryoan-ji, p252; Nijo-jo, p252; Ginkaku-ji, p254; Kiyomizu-dera, p255; Fushimi-Inari, p256; To-ji, p256; Arashiyama, p263.

> ❏ **Kansai's private lines**
> Kansai has a dense network of private lines that criss-cross the region, often with multiple competing routes that penetrate deep into city centres and with competitive journey times. For rail fans, these lines offer endless quirky differences.
>
> The train-departure melodies at **Keihan Line** (Osaka–Kyoto) stations join together to form melodies (see box p102) that reflect the destination (upbeat towards cosmopolitan Osaka, understated towards historical Kyoto); ride the train from one end to the other and you will hear the whole tune.
>
> **Hankyu**, also running between Osaka and Kyoto, operates the retro 'Kyo-train' with elegant interiors and tatami seat covers.
>
> **Nankai**'s *rapi:t* Airport Express has a design theme of 'outdated future', features portholes for windows and sports a stylised blade extruding from the train front.
>
> Limited express services on the Hankyu, Hanshin, Keihan & Nankai railways (non-reserved coaches only) do not require a surcharge; those on the Kintetsu lines do.

HONSHU

❏ **Volunteer guides**
Having a volunteer guide is a great way of seeing Kyoto with someone who knows the place better than anyone else: a local. There are various groups that organise tours, but **Visit Kansai** (🖥 www.visitkansai.com/volunteerguide) is worth recommending; they also offer tours of Kobe, Osaka and Nara. You need to pay transportation costs, entrance fees and meals for the guide.

travel you've paid for. With this in mind some suggestions for excursions by rail are also included (see pp263-5).

**Kyoto station area** (see map p253) The top of **Kyoto station** 京都駅 is a good vantage point for views of the city, since it's free. **Kyoto Tower Observatory** 京都タワ ー古都展望 (🖥 www.kyoto-tower.co.jp; daily 9am-9pm; ¥770 or ¥700 with tickets from the TIC and some hotels), the eyesore across the street built in 1964, offers 360° views for a fee, but contains high-power telescopes, annotations on the windows pointing out major landmarks, and a view of Osaka on a clear day.

A 5-minute walk north of the station, the vast and opulent temples of Higashi Hongan-ji and Nishi Hongan-ji serve as the headquarters of two factions of the Jodo-Shin (True Pure Land) sect of Buddhism. **Higashi Hongan-ji** 東本願寺 (🖥 www .higashihonganji.or.jp; daily Mar-Oct 5.50am-5.30pm, Nov-Feb 6.20am-4.30pm; free) has an enormous Goei-do (Founder's Hall) that boasts 175,000 roof tiles, 90 wooden pillars and 927 tatami mats. Look for the rope on display made of followers' hair; 53 ropes of this kind were used to transport and hang the enormous wooden beams of the two main halls when they were rebuilt in 1895. Conventional ropes were not strong enough for the task, so human hair was used instead. The Amida-do (Amida Hall) is almost as big, with 108,000 roof tiles, 401 tatami mats and 66 wooden pillars. It is worth getting here by 4pm as the screens in front of the main statues in Goei-do and Amida-do are closed then.

**Shosei-en** 渉成園 (daily Mar-Oct 9am-5pm Nov-Feb 9am-4pm; ¥500), a small, well-maintained garden belonging to the temple, is a short walk to the east; it is a great place to go for some peace and quiet.

Nearby, the equally impressive **Nishi Hongan-ji** 西本願寺 (☎ 075-371 5181, 🖥 www.hongwanji.or.jp; Mar-Oct 5.50am-5.30pm Nov-Feb, 6.20am-4.30pm; free) is a World Heritage site. Even though you can see a lot of the stunning temple on your own it is worth joining a tour (free but donation appreciated; bookable by phone; English ability depends on guide) as it gives a chance to see the inside of the temple. The walls of one room depict written documents and since the scent in them is said to attract mice, cats have been painted on the ceiling as a deterrent. There are also two outdoor Noh stages, one of which is the oldest in Japan; plays (¥5000) are staged here on 21st May.

See p256 for details of other places of interest near Kyoto station, but which are not on the Station area map.

**Western Kyoto** (see map p258) **Kinkaku-ji** 金閣寺 (daily 9am-5pm; ¥400) literally means Temple of the Golden Pavilion but it is generally known as the **Golden Temple**, though its proper name is Rokuon-ji 鹿苑寺. The pavilion, its reflection glittering in Kyoko-chi, the Mirror Pond, is deservedly one of Japan's most-photographed buildings; not surprisingly the temple is a World Heritage site. The façade was regilded in 1987 and the roof restored in spring 2003 so it looks magnificent even on an overcast, or rainy, day. The building was originally a retirement villa for a shogun, Yoshimitsu Ashikaga, but on his death (in 1408) he instructed that it should become a Zen temple. To get here from Kyoto station take Raku Bus No 101 (see p257).

As you exit Kinkaku-ji, turn right on to the street and go straight. From here it's a

HONSHU

15- to 20-minute walk south-west to Ryoan-ji, or a ride on bus No 59 from outside the temple (rather than on the main road). Midway, if you walk, look out for a sign pointing towards the 'Museum for World Peace' – not an essential stop but interesting if you have time. Ritsumeikan University's **Museum for World Peace** 立命館大学国際平和ミュージアム (🖳 www.ritsumei.ac .jp/mng/er/wp-museum; Tue-Sun 9.30am-4.30pm; ¥400) tackles with astonishing candour the subject of Japan's military aggression during WWII and the country's 'unresolved war responsibilities'. It's unlikely you'd find anywhere else a picture of 'schoolchildren beating the portraits of Roosevelt and Churchill with large sticks in 1943'. The displays are well thought-out and informative; they also include images of what Kyoto might have looked like had it suffered the fate of Hiroshima and Nagasaki. Originally on the list of possible A-Bomb targets – the planned epicentre was about 1km west of Kyoto station – Kyoto was later removed as a target for nuclear attack because the US Secretary of War knew it was the ancient capital of Japan, that it was very important for the Japanese, and that it was too beautiful to destroy.

**Ryoan-ji** 龍安寺 (🖳 www.ryoanji.jp; Mar-Nov daily 8am-5pm, Dec-Feb 8.30am-4.30pm; ¥500), a World Heritage site, provides a complete contrast to the showy opulence of the Golden Pavilion and is soundproofed by the mountains from the rest of Kyoto. Come here to sit and gaze out over Kyoto's (and probably the world's) best-known rock garden. Assembled sometime between 1499 and 1507 and measuring about 200 square metres, the garden consists of raked white sand and 15 rocks. The focus here is on the rock garden but a walk round the pond, Kyoyo-chi, and the rest of the grounds is recommended.

**Toei Kyoto Studio Park** 東映太秦映画村 (🖳 www.toei-eigamura.com; Mon-Fri 9am-5pm, Sat & Sun 9am-4.30pm, closes half-an-hour earlier in winter; ¥2200, or ¥3600 inc the 3D attractions) is about 15 minutes on foot from Hanozono 花園 station on the JR Sagano Line. This very in-your-face thrills and spills entertainment

park may be a good antidote for anyone tiring of Kyoto's temples. The park owners stress that it is a working film set, so there's a chance to see a real samurai film in production, actors running around in full costume, and special effects such as collapsing mountains. You can even dress up and be photographed in Edo-period clothes from ¥4000.

Also on the western side of Kyoto, and another of the must sees, is **Arashiyama** (see p263).

**Central Kyoto** (see map pp258-9) **Nijo-jo** 二条城 (Nijo Castle; 🖳 www2.city .kyoto.lg.jp/bunshi/nijojo; daily except Tue in Dec, Jan, July & Aug 8.45am-4pm; ¥600), another World Heritage site, was originally built in 1603 as an official residence of the first Tokugawa shogun, Ieyasu. It is well preserved and, unlike the former Imperial Palace (see below), visitors are allowed inside. The residential part of the castle was **Ninomaru Palace** 二の丸御殿; an unusual feature in the palace is the 'nightingale floor', so called because the floorboards that run along the side of the building 'squeak and creak' when you tread on them. This is an intended feature as it means no one can appear unexpectedly. On your way out through the gardens, look out for the *koi* (carp) in the central pond. Nijojo-mae station on the Tozai subway line is the closest station, or take Raku Bus No 101 or bus Nos 9, 12 or 50 from Kyoto station; these services stop outside the castle. Alternatively, Nijo station, on the JR Sagano Line, is 15 minutes' walk away.

**Kyoto Imperial Palace** 京都御所 (🖳 sankan.kunaicho.go.jp; Mon-Fri tours 10am all year & at 1.30pm Sep to July 20th; free) can only be visited on a tour with an official guide. Apply online at least one day in advance. To reach the palace, take the subway to Imadegawa (Karasuma Line); the entrance is on Karasuma-dori. The grounds, which include some picture-postcard Japanese gardens, are interesting enough to make the effort of applying to join a tour worthwhile. Rooms have to be viewed from a distance but it's just possible to make out the inside of the throne room. When the

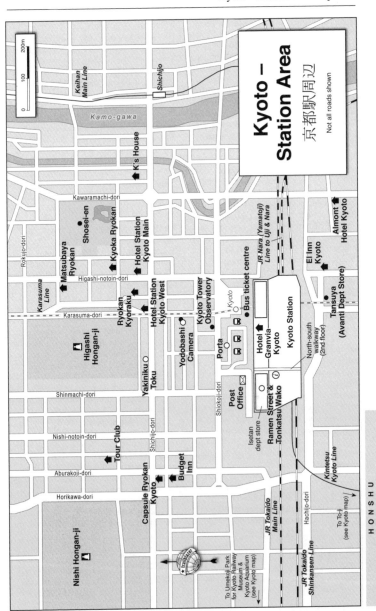

Kyoto –
Station Area
京都駅周辺

Not all roads shown

HONSHU

present Emperor was crowned in Tokyo, the thrones were taken from here and flown by helicopter to the capital. Even though the palace is no longer home to the Imperial Family, tight security remains; an official carrying a walkie-talkie follows the tour group around to make sure nobody sneaks away. The impression is not so much of grandeur but of how much the grounds feel like a prison – or must have done for the Emperor, who hardly ever left the palace.

A short walk north of the Imperial Palace is **Shimogamo Shrine** 下鴨神社; Shimogamo and **Kamigamo Shrine** 上賀茂神社 are two of the oldest shrines in Kyoto. Both have lovely grounds, are on the World Heritage list, and they also provide the setting for the Aoi Festival (see p260).

The **Museum of Kyoto** 京都府京都文化博物館 (🖳 www.bunpaku.or.jp; daily except 3rd Wed 10am-6pm, Fri to 7.30pm; free, ¥500 for special exhibition), on Sanjo-dori, a 3-minute walk from Karasuma-oike subway station, traces the history of Kyoto, focusing on its glory days as the nation's capital and then moving on to the period of modernisation after power shifted to Edo (Tokyo). There are good model displays that let you see what Kyoto once looked like but otherwise not much of a permanent collection. The redeeming factor is an excellent English volunteer guide service; this is very useful as most of the displays are only in Japanese. There is also an audio guide (¥100), but it is an extremely limited alternative at just 11 minutes' worth of audio. On the 1st/ground floor is a recreated Kyoto street from the Edo period with shops selling traditional crafts, and a couple of restaurants.

**Nishiki Food Market** (see p262) is best visited when you are feeling hungry but is fascinating at any time.

Fans of Japanese animation should fit in a visit to **Kyoto International Manga**

**Museum** 京都国際マンガミュージアム (🖳 www.kyotomm.jp; Thur-Tue 10am-6pm; ¥800). As much a research facility as a museum, the building is home to 50,000 volumes of Japanese manga and a smaller number of foreign comics. On a fine day, you'll find people sitting on the grass outside, devouring comic books borrowed from the museum's shelves. Inside the adjacent museum café, manga artists have signed their names and left sketches on the walls. The museum is housed in a former primary school, with a number of preserved rooms with English explanations and textbooks from WWII. Jump on a subway train to Karasuma-oike (Karasuma & Tozai lines) and take Exit No 2.

**Eastern Kyoto** (see map p259) **Ginkaku-ji** 銀閣寺 (daily Mar-Nov 8.30am-5pm, Dec-Feb 9am-4.30pm; ¥500, audio rental ¥500), a World Heritage site, is better known as the **Silver Pavilion**. Like its golden counterpart it was built as a retirement villa and then became a Zen temple, but the plan to cover its outer walls in silver were never carried out. Despite the lack of silver there is much to see: the dry sand garden, with the flawless Mt Fuji-like sand cone ('Ginshadan'), and the impressive moss garden, let alone the views of Kyoto from the garden. Either take bus No 5 or 17 to Ginkakuji-michi, or Raku Bus No 100 to Ginkakuji-mae (the closest stop) from where it is a 5-minute walk.

The **Philosopher's Way** 哲学の道 (Tetsugaku-no-michi) is a walk of about 2km along a section of canal, passing cafés, boutiques and craft shops as well as a number of shrines and temples. The Way is pleasant at any time of the year but particularly in the spring and autumn; however, then it is likely to be very crowded. Ginkaku-ji (see above) is easily reached from the northern end of the Way and the

❏ **Seeing red**
Some parts of Kyoto are considered to be of such historical importance that they are protected by laws which prohibit the use of brightly coloured signs. If they are too close to temples, signs for McDonald's and Coca Cola cannot be coloured red.

## ❏ Getting to know geisha

Unless you have contacts in extremely high places (no amount of money will do unless you know someone) you are unlikely to meet a geisha while in Japan. The best option is to look for *maiko-san* (apprentice geisha) around 5-6.30pm, along Hanami-koji in Gion and also, on the other side of the river, along the narrow street called Pontocho (see map p259).

Kyoto City Tourist Information Center (see p257) can provide a list of shops which will dress you up as a maiko or geisha if that appeals; most places require reservations and the cheapest makeovers start at around ¥9975. One good option, with English-speaking staff, is **Studio Shiki** スタジオ四季 (☎ 075-531 2777, 🖳 www.maiko-henshin.com); it has two branches in Kyoto and also offers men the opportunity to dress up as a samurai swordsman.

If all else fails, Peter MacIntosh, a Canadian expat married to a former geisha, runs guided walking lectures (☎ 090-5169 1654, 🖳 www.kyotosightsandnights.com; ¥3000) of Kyoto's geisha districts.

---

southern end is near **Nanzen-ji** 南禅寺 (🖳 www.nanzen.net; daily 8.40am-5pm, to 4.30pm in winter; grounds free, temple buildings ¥300-500), one of the most important Zen temples in Japan. As with many temples in Kyoto it started its life as a retirement villa. None of the buildings is the original but it is still an impressive place; there is a rock garden in Hojo Hall as well as a brick aqueduct in the grounds. Also here is **Konchi-in Teien** 金地院庭園 (daily 8.30am-4.30/5pm; ¥400), a tea ceremony garden.

Even though **Heian Jingu** 平安神宮 (🖳 www.heianjingu.or.jp; daily 8.30am-5.30pm; free, but gardens ¥600) is not particularly old it is notable because it is the site of the Jidai Festival (see p260). Also, the entrance is marked by one of the biggest torii gates in Japan – 24 metres high and with a top rail that's almost 34 metres wide. The gardens here are a popular place to see the cherry blossom in spring.

**Gion** 祇園 (🖳 www.gion.or.jp) is known as Kyoto's geisha quarter (see box above), but it is also the home of **Yasaka Jinja** 八坂神社 (🖳 www.yasaka-jinja .or.jp; open 24 hours; free), a Shinto shrine dating back to 656, in Maruyama Park. It becomes the focus of the city for the entire month of July during the Gion Festival (see p260). As you stand at the entrance to the shrine, Shijo-dori runs west towards the centre of Gion; look out just before Shijo

Bridge, for **Minami-za** 南座, Kyoto's famous kabuki theatre. There are no tours of the theatre building so to see inside you have to buy a ticket for a performance (see p262). The biggest annual event is in December when some of the country's best-known kabuki actors come here to perform.

**Kyoto National Museum** 京都国立博物館 (🖳 www.kyohaku.go.jp; Tue-Sun 9.30am-5pm, Fri to 8pm), opened in 1897, specialises in fine arts and handicrafts, including rare examples of Heian-period pottery and lacquerware but also has special exhibitions. From bus stop D2 outside Kyoto station, take City Bus No 206 or 208 to Hakubutsukan Sanjusangendo-mae, from where the museum is a minute's walk.

**Kiyomizu-dera** 清水寺 (🖳 www.kiyo mizudera.or.jp; daily 6am-6pm; ¥300) temple, a World Heritage Site, is known for its incredible observation platform. The wooden structure juts up and out from the hillside and was built without using any nails. The view out over the cherry and maple trees below and beyond to Kyoto is spectacular. Visit early in the day, or be prepared for the crowds. Note that renovation work here is being done in stages so there will always be something to see but work is likely to take most of the decade.

From Kyoto station take Raku Bus No 100 or city bus No 206 to Kiyomizu-michi 清水道 bus stop and then walk uphill for about 10 minutes following everyone else.

HONSHU

**South of Kyoto station** (see map p259)
**To-ji** 東寺 (🖳 toji.or.jp; daily mid Mar to mid Sep 8.30am-5.30pm, mid Sep to mid Mar 8.30am-4.30pm; ¥500) contains one of Kyoto's most famous landmarks: a 5-storied, 57m-high pagoda that is the tallest in Japan. It was first built in 826 but has burnt down four times since then; the current pagoda dates from 1644. The temple, a World Heritage Site, is a 15-minute walk from the station; turn right out of the Hachijo Exit and walk along Hachijo-dori until you get to the junction with Aburanokoji-dori. Turn left and walk along till the road meets Toji-michi at some traffic lights. Turn right here and walk along until you reach the temple grounds. Alternatively, if you are coming from Nishi Hongan-ji all you need to do is walk along Omiya-dori.

An **antiques market** is held in the grounds by To-ji temple on the first Sunday of every month and a general market on the 21st of every month.

Just one stop along the JR Nara Line, and barely out of Kyoto station, it's a few minutes' walk south-east of Tofukuji station to **Tofuku-ji** 東福寺 (🖳 www.tofukuji .jp; daily Apr-Oct 9am-4pm, Nov-Dec 8.30am-4pm, Jan-Mar 9am-3.30pm; grounds free, Tsutenkyo and Kaisando Hall ¥400, Hojo and gardens ¥400), one of Kyoto's largest Zen monasteries and also known for its stunning foliage in autumn. Tsuten-kyo (Tsuten Bridge) is one of the most popular viewing spots. The Hojo is where the head abbot used to live and around it are some gardens. For Kansai Thru Pass users, Keihan's Tofukuji station is adjacent.

Right outside **Inari** 稲荷 station, the second stop on the JR Nara Line from Kyoto station, is the first orange-lacquered *torii* (shrine gate) marking the entrance to Fushimi-Inari. The station itself is bright orange, giving you a taste of what to expect in the shrine. (For Kansai Thru Pass users, Fushimi-Inari station is adjacent on the Keihan Line.) **Fushimi-Inari Shrine** 伏見稲荷大社 (🖳 www.inari.jp; daily dawn to dusk; free) is a huge complex and contained within the grounds is a long series of tunnels

of torii, about 10,000 in all, which you might recognise from the film *Memoirs of a Geisha*. Pilgrims dressed in white are a common sight here. It's only a short walk to the main shrine, behind which paths lead off through the torii tunnels which snake up Mt Inari. Though the walkways are surrounded by trees and mostly in the shade, it's a step up from a gentle stroll, so wear comfortable shoes.

There are a few tea houses along the way, where you can sit on tatami mats by the window and enjoy views of the mountain on which the shrine complex is built. You are rewarded for your effort when you reach an observation point offering a great view of Kyoto, though from here it's a further walk up to the highest point of 233m (where there are no great views). In all it is about a 4km walk from the station and you should reach the top within an hour.

**West of Kyoto station** (see map p258)
**Kyoto Railway Museum** 京都鉄道博物館 (🖳 www.kyotorailwaymuseum.jp; daily 10am-5.30pm; ¥1200) opened in spring 2016 and merged the former Kyoto Umekoji Steam Locomotive Museum and Osaka Modern Transportation Museum into Japan's largest railway museum. The procession of steam locomotives from Japan's Golden Age are now joined by much younger counterparts, including the original 0-series bullet train, and the more modern and streamlined 500 series. Simulators offer the chance to drive both commuter and shinkansen services; there is also a huge railway diorama. The museum is 20 minutes' walk west of Kyoto station, or take a city bus No 208 from outside the station to Umekoji koen-mae.

**Kyoto Aquarium** 京都水族館 (🖳 www.kyoto-aquarium.com; daily 10am-8pm; ¥2050), in Umekoji Park 梅小路公園, is full of environmentally friendly features and has all the standard aquarium attractions, such as dolphins and penguins, but being an inland aquarium – one of the largest in the world – it also has a section focusing on the eco-systems in Kyoto's rivers.

## Practical information

**Station guide** Kyoto station (💻 www.kyoto-station-building.co.jp), rebuilt in 1997, is one of Japan's most eye-catching modern buildings. Japanese architect Hiroshi Hara suggests that the 27m-wide, 60m-high and 470m-long concourse lets you feel what it's like 'travelling down the side of a mountain into the valley basin'. Certainly it's an impressive sight whether looking up from the main concourse or down from the 12th-floor Sky Garden on to the station atrium.

The shinkansen and Kintetsu Line tracks are on the Hachi-jo (south) side of the station. To reach the Karasuma-dori (north) side, for JR's main line tracks and the Central Gate Exit, for central Kyoto, follow signs for the pedestrian walkway or for the Central Concourse.

The station has plenty of **lockers** (all sizes; ¥300-600), with most on the Hachi-jo side; on a busy day empty lockers can be found in the Porta underground shopping centre on the Karasuma-dori side. There's a **meeting point** 時の灯 (*toki-no-akari*) opposite the west ticket gate on the 2nd floor pedestrian walkway and **ATM corners** on the 1st/ground floor: there is one on the left of the bottom of the steps up to the main station concourse and another by the Central Gate for JR main lines.

Isetan, the big in-station **department store**, stretches up both sides of the escalators that run up from the main concourse.

## Tourist information

**Kyoto City Tourist Information Center** (TIC; 💻 www.kyoto-magonote.jp; daily 8.30am-7pm) is on the north–south pedestrian walkway on the 2nd floor of the station. Staff can provide you with a general map of Kyoto, a *Kyoto City Bus Travel Map* and 1-day bus pass (see Getting around), a hotel and ryokan list, a restaurant guide, details of walking and cycling tours as well as information about the many sights.

Useful websites are: 💻 www.kyoto.travel and 💻 www.city.kyoto.lg.jp. The best guide to what's on in Kyoto is the monthly *Kyoto Visitor's Guide* (💻 www.kyotoguide.com), available free at the TIC as well as at major hotels. Another good guide to Kyoto and the Kansai region as a whole is 💻 www.kansaiscene.com.

**Getting around** Since Kyoto is so spread out, the best plan is to take buses or subways to the different areas and then explore on foot. There's a flat rate of ¥230 on buses within the city but it's almost always worth investing in the **1-day city bus pass** (¥500) which is valid for buses to all the 'must-sees' and optional sights, as well as some of the side trips mentioned in this guide. Alternatively, a **combined subway/city bus ticket** costs ¥1200, or a **2-day ticket** is ¥2000. All passes are available from the **bus ticket centre** バスチケットセンター (💻 www2.city.kyoto.lg.jp/koho/eng/access) in front of Kyoto station near bus stop D1, or from the TIC. One-day bus passes can also be bought from the driver when you get off the bus.

Be sure to pick up a *Kyoto City Bus Travel Map*, which details how to get from the station and between the main sights by bus; a useful online resource is 💻 www.arukumachikyoto.jp.

If you're following the familiar tourist trail, it's worth considering the **Raku Bus Kyoto Easy Sightseeing bus service** (signed in English), which are special city bus routes with the standard fares and pass acceptances but stop announcements are made in English. The *Bus Travel Map* gives full details of routes and stops.

Another option for getting around is by **bicycle**: visit 💻 www.cyclekyoto.com for information about where to rent a cycle and suggested routes. There are very strict rules about parking bicycles so be very careful and do not park downtown – the Shijo/Sanjo area – unless in an official cycle park; expect to pay at least ¥150 for a space.

Although Kyoto's municipal tramways were dug up in 1978, you can still ride a surviving piece on the way to Arashiyama (see p263). Take the **Randen tram** 嵐電 (💻 randen.keifuku.co.jp/en; ¥210, free with Kansai Thru Pass but not JR rail passes; 22 mins; approx 6/hr during the day) from Shijo-Omiya on the Keifuku-Arashiyama Line. (Cont'd on p260)

HONSHU

0      0.5      1km

Not all roads shown

Kinkaku-ji

Ryoan-ji

Ritsumeikan University's
Museum for World Peace

Kita-oji-dori

Imadegawa-dori

Takaoguchi   Omuro   Ryoanjimichi   Tojiin

Narutaki

Myoshinji

Kitano-
Hakubaicho

**Keifuku
Kitano
Line**

Hanazono

**JR Sagano Line**
(also known
as San-in Line)

Marutamachi-dori

To Saga-Arashiyama

Uzumasa

Katabiranotsuji

To Arashiyama

Uzamasa-
Koryuji

**Toei Kyoto
Studio Park**

Uzumasa-
Tenjingawa

Oike-dori

Nishioji-Oike

Nijo

**Tozai
Line**

Nishi-oji-dori

Nijo-jo ●

Oike-dori

Yamanouchi

Kaikonoyashiro

**Keifuku
Arashiyama
Line**

Nishioji Sanjo

Shijo-dori

Saiin

Omiya

Sai

Shijo-
Omiya

**Hankyu
Kyoto
Line**

Gojo-dori

Tanbaguchi

Nishikyogoku

Omiya-dori

**Umekoji
Park**

**Kyoto Railway
Museum**

●

**Kyoto
Aquarium**

Katsura

Nishioji

**JR Kyoto
(Tokaido)
Line**

Kujo-dori

To Umeda (Osaka)

To Shin Osaka
& Osaka

**JR Tokaido
Shinkansen Line**

HONSHU

**Kyoto**

京都

To Kamigamo Shrine

Kuramaguchi

Shimogamo-dori

Kamo-gawa

Chayama

Eizan Line

Shimogamo Shrine

Mototanaka

Demachiyanagi

★ trailblazer

Gingaku-ji

Imadegawa

Keihan Main Line

Kyoto Imperial Palace

Kawaramachi-dori

Kamo-gawa

Kawabata-dori

Philosopher's Way (Tetsugaku-no-michi)

Karasuma-dori

Jingu-marutamachi

Marutamachi-dori

Marutamachi

Heian Jingu

Higashi-oji-dori

Nijojo-mae

Karasuma-oike

Kyoto-shiyakusho-mae

Nanzen-ji

Horikawa-dori

Museum of Kyoto

Chao Chao

Sanjo-Keihan

Westin Miyako Hotel Kyoto

Kyoto International Manga Museum

Teramachi-dori

Kiyamachi-dori

Pontocho

Sanjo

Higashiyama

Keage

Nishiki Food Market

Kawaramachi

Agotsuyu Shabu Shabu Yamafuku

Shijo-dori

Shijo

Karasuma

Minami-za

Yasaka Jinja

Maruyama-koen

Gion-Shijo

Hanami-koji

Yasaka Hall Gion Corner

Daiwa Roynet Hotel Shijo-Karasuma

Karasuma Line

GION

Studio Shiki

Gojo-dori

Kiyomizu-Gojo

Studio Shiki

Kiyomizu-dera

Gojo

SEE 'STATION AREA' MAP

Kyoto National Museum

Hyatt Regency Kyoto

To Nagoya & Tokyo

Shichijo

JR Tokaido Line

Kyoto

Kyoto Station

HONSHU

Tofukuji

JR Tokaido Shinkansen Line

To Nagoya & Tokyo

To-ji

Toji

Kinetsu Kyoto Line

Kujo

Tofukuji

Tofuku-ji

To Fushimi Inari, Uji & Nara

*(Cont'd from p257)* To get **to/from Kansai Airport** take the Haruka LEX. If your rail pass has yet to begin or has expired, a bargain route for ¥1200 is to take the Hankyu train from Kawaramachi, or Karasuma, in downtown Kyoto, change at Awaji to the Hankyu/Osaka City subway joint service to Tengachaya, and then to the Nankai Line to Kansai Airport. Discounted tickets must be bought at station office counters at either Kyoto or Kansai Airport; the journey takes 110 minutes.

**Festivals** In a city packed with temples there's nearly always a festival (matsuri) going on somewhere. For details, enquire at any tourist office, or check the *Kyoto Visitor's Guide*.

The most famous festival is the **Gion Matsuri**, the main annual celebration is at Yasaka Jinja (see p255) and around downtown Kyoto. The festival runs throughout July, with the principal events between the 17th and 20th, when there's a huge procession of floats. If you're in Kansai, don't miss the eve-of-festival celebrations on the 14th-16th July around Shijo-Karasuma, where even non-Japanese turn up in large numbers in traditional dress.

Another of Japan's biggest and most vibrant festivals is **Jidai Matsuri** (Festival of the Ages), which takes place on 22nd October. The highlight is a huge street procession from the Imperial Palace to Heian Shrine. Participants dress in costumes from different periods in Kyoto's history, starting with 1868 (the Meiji era) and going back in time to the Heian period and the founding of Kyoto in 781.

At the **Aoi Matsuri**, held in mid May, participants dressed in costumes from the Heian period parade north from the Imperial Palace first to Shimogamo Shrine and then on to Kamigamo Shrine.

**Where to stay** There is accommodation in Kyoto to suit all budgets. However, it's worth booking ahead for peak periods such as cherry-blossom time (late Mar/early Apr) and autumn-leaves viewing (late Oct/early Nov). For convenience this guide focuses on places that are near the station; the TIC can provide a list of accommodation options for the whole of the city. See also pp67-73.

● **Kyoto station area** Undoubtedly the best bargain, and conveniently close to the

---

❏ **Bargain hunt**

Many visitors to Kyoto have at least one item on their souvenir-shopping list: a kimono. But with top-end garments selling for hundreds of thousands of yen, it's not something that falls within most budgets.

A good option for bargain-conscious shoppers is a small store called **Tansuya** たんす屋 (see Station Area map, p253; ☐ tansuya.jp; daily 10am-9pm), in a corner of the 1st/ground floor of the Avanti department store across the street from the shinkansen side of Kyoto station. This shop (which has other branches in Kyoto and elsewhere) is one of the few kimono outlets in Kyoto which won't burn your credit card. You can pick up new and second-hand kimonos in a range of colours and fabrics from ¥10,000, and *obi* (sashes) from ¥5000.

Alternatively, consider buying a yukata, a similar-looking but casual and more affordable traditional Japanese robe, that is still sported by young and old alike at festivals and onsen. Several shops on **Teramachi-dori** 寺町通 (the westerly of the two downtown covered arcades) offer new or used yukata, *obi* (belt) and *geta* (wooden shoes) from ¥6000; a good starting point is **Chicago** 原宿シカゴ (☐ www.chicago .co.jp/store_kyt.html; daily 11am-8pm). Chicago is on the left-hand side of the northern part of Teramachi-dori, if walking up from Shijo-dori. The second-hand clothes are on the 2nd floor.

station, are three places under the same ownership: *Capsule Ryokan Kyoto* カプセル旅館京都 (☎ 075-344 1510, 💻 www.capsule-ryokan-kyoto.com; from ¥5980/S, ¥7980/D or Tw; capsule ¥3500pp) combines the style of a ryokan with the chance to experience the infamous capsule accommodation. The **capsules** are in mixed dorms that sleep up to eight people. However, each capsule is private, air conditioned and has a 16" TV. There is lockable storage and a shared bathroom. There are also 32 compact but fantastically well-designed **rooms** each with a monsoon shower, toilet, 32" TV, and clever luggage storage. Everyone can use the lounge area, kitchenette, laundry facilities, internet access and look at the very useful file with information about sightseeing and local restaurants. Book early. Nearby is the spotless *Tour Club* ツアークラブ (☎ 075-353 6968, 💻 www.kyotojp.com; dorms ¥2450pp; ¥6980/D or Tw, ¥8880/Tr), a small place with four-bed bunk dorms set around a small rock garden as well as a selection of well-maintained Western- and Japanese-style rooms. The third place, *Budget Inn* バジェットイン (☎ 075-344 1510, 💻 www.budgetinnjp.com; ¥10,980/Tr, ¥12,980/quad, ¥14,980/5 beds) also offers clean, Japanese-style rooms, all with private bathrooms. As for Capsule Ryokan Kyoto these places offer internet access (¥100/20 mins) and have coin laundries and files with information about Kyoto.

Further away, but part of a chain of places offering budget accommodation, *K's House* ケイズハウス (☎ 075-342 2444, 💻 www.kshouse.jp/kyoto-e; from ¥2400pp/dorm; ¥3800/S, ¥6200/Tw or D) offers a variety of rooms and facilities. There are sitting areas and a roof-top terrace, a kitchen, wi-fi, as well as a café (daily 8am to midnight).

On Higashi Notoin-dori, four minutes' walk from the station on the Karasuma (north) side, is *Hotel Station Kyoto Main* ホテルステーション京都本店 (☎ 075-365 9000, 💻 www.hotel-st-kyoto.com; from ¥5000/S, ¥9000/Tw, ¥12,000/Tr), with en suite Japanese- and Western-style accommodation, free internet access and nice communal baths. *Hotel Station Kyoto*

*West* ホテルステーション京都西店 (☎ 075-343 5000; same website and prices), another branch, is very similar but, being on Shichijo-dori, is even nearer the station. Breakfast is available at both branches for an additional ¥800 (buffet).

There's a variety of Western-style business accommodation, mostly on the south (Hachi-jo) side of Kyoto station; good online rates can be found by booking in advance. *El Inn Kyoto* エルイン京都 (☎ 075-672 1100, 💻 www.elinn-kyoto.com; ¥7800/S, ¥12,000/Tw) is just a couple of minutes' walk south-east of Kyoto station. Most rooms are (wide-bedded) singles, though there are a few twins and doubles, and there's a coin laundry and a restaurant. *Almont Hotel Kyoto* アルモントホテル京都 (☎ 075-681 2301, 💻 www.almont.jp; marked price ¥20,800 but often reduced online to ¥5300/S, ¥8400/D) is a newly built offering, with a communal bath for guests and wi-fi.

Good-value Japanese inns in this area include the friendly *Matsubaya Ryokan* 松葉家旅館 (☎ 075-351 3727, 💻 www.matsubayainn.com; from ¥4400/S, ¥8100/D or Tw, ¥17,700/Tr, ¥22,000/quad), about a 10-minute walk from the station. It has spacious tatami rooms, some of which overlook a small garden.

*Kyoka Ryokan* 京花旅館 (☎ 075-371 2709; from ¥3500pp) is a bit faded but has tatami rooms with and without en suite bathrooms. Just around the corner is *Ryokan Kyoraku* 旅館京らく (☎ 075-371 1260, 💻 www.ryokankyoraku.jp; ¥6270-7790/S, ¥10,640-14,630/Tw, ¥15,960-18,620/Tr), a rambling but efficiently run place that also offers rooms with and without en suite facilities. If none of these ryokan has a vacancy, try the **Kyoto Ryokan** website (💻 www.kyoto-ryokan.com).

At the top end of the market and built into JR Kyoto station is *Hotel Granvia Kyoto* ホテルグランヴィア京都 (☎ 075-344 8888, 💻 www.granvia-kyoto.co.jp; from ¥21,132/S, ¥29,700/D, ¥33,264/Tw; discounts and special packages available online), where all the rooms are tastefully furnished, have large bathrooms and free wi-fi. It's a luxurious haven and an ideal

HONSHU

base if you're travelling a lot by rail. The indoor pool (for anyone aged 20 and above) has excellent views of the station's atrium and there are 13 restaurants and bars.

● **Other areas** A good luxury choice in the **Higashiyama temple district** (north-east of Kyoto station) is *Westin Miyako Hotel Kyoto* ウェスティン都ホテル京都 (☎ 075-771 7111, 🖥 www.miyakohotels.ne .jp/westinkyoto; from ¥31,104/S, ¥44,000 /D, often heavily discounted online), which has all the facilities you would expect in a top-class hotel.

*Hyatt Regency Kyoto* ハイアット リージェンシー 京都 (☎ 075-541 1234, 🖥 kyoto.regency.hyatt.com; from ¥29,000/D) is east of Kyoto station. It might look very uninspiring from the outside and it is minimalist inside but it has everything you would expect and prices to match.

A well-located **central choice** is *Daiwa Roynet Hotel Shijo-Karasuma* ダイワロイネット四条烏丸 (☎ 075-342 1166, 🖥 www.daiwaroynet.jp/kyoto-shijo; from ¥7430/S, ¥9300/D, ¥12,800/Tw; breakfast ¥600pp), a solid business hotel minutes away from downtown Kyoto's shopping, restaurants and bars.

If you prefer **self-catering** in a house or apartment, consider Japan Experience (see p73); they have a number of properties in the city.

**Where to eat and drink** Around Kyoto station, there are plenty of places to eat and drink. **Ramen Street** ラーメン小路 (daily 11am-10pm), on the 10th floor of Isetan in the station building, boasts Hakata, Tokyo and Sapporo ramen, to name only a few varieties; expect to pay ¥730-1150 for a large bowl, or ¥1000 for a lunch set. On the 11th floor, Eat Paradise offers a wide range of restaurants including *Tonkatsu Wako* とんかつ和幸 (daily 11am-10pm) which serves delicious tonkatsu; expect to pay ¥1728 for *rosukatsu*, ¥1512 for a 150g *hirekatsu* set.

A stone's throw from the station, consider the restaurants in the attached **Porta** ポルタ (11am-10pm) mall and **Yodobashi Camera** ヨドバシカメラ (6th floor; daily 11am-11pm) electronics store, offering unlimited choice of Japanese and Western cuisines.

For more authentic fare, a few *yakiniku* restaurants such as *Yakiniku Toku* 焼肉とく (5pm to midnight) are clustered a 5-minute walk to the north, at the intersection of Shichijo-dori and Shinmachi-dori; turn left at the third set of traffic lights after leaving Kyoto station from the Karasuma-dori Exit.

If you're in Kyoto's downtown area during the daytime, **Nishiki Food Market** 錦市場商店街 (🖥 www.kyoto-nishiki .or.jp; daily 9am-6pm; most stalls close one day a week, usually Wed or Sun) is a covered arcade known as 'Kyoto's kitchen': look out for *Nishiki Soya* 錦そや, a shop which sells delicious soy-milk (*tonyu*) ice-cream and doughnuts. In the evening, head to **Kiyamachi-dori**, a narrow lane packed with restaurants and bars between busy Kawaramachi-dori and the Kamo River; *Chao-Chao* チャオチャオ (Mon-Fri 5pm to late; Sat & Sun 2pm to late) offers unusual and delicious *gyoza* (from matcha to ice-cream) and *Agotsuyu Shabu Shabu Yamafuku* あごつゆしゃぶしゃぶ山福 (Tue-Sun 5pm to midnight) does authentic *shabu-shabu*.

**Evening entertainment** Kabuki is sometimes staged at **Minami-za** 南座 in Gion; reserved seats start from ¥3000. A list of upcoming performances can be found at 🖥 www.kabuki-bito.jp/eng.

*Yasaka Hall Gion Corner* 三条高倉 ギオンコーナー (☎ 075-561 1119, 🖥 www.kyoto-gioncorner.com; Mar-Nov nightly 6pm & 7pm; Dec-Feb weekends only; ¥3150 from the box office and major travel agencies) is a tourist-oriented performance of **traditional Japanese arts** featuring an abbreviated tea ceremony, *ike-bana* (flower arranging), traditional dances, and excerpts from *kyogen* (traditional comic plays) and *bunraku* (puppetry). They're staged on the 1st/ground floor of Yasaka Hall in Gion.

The main nightlife district is located around Kiyamachi-dori between Kawaramachi-dori and the Kamo river in downtown Kyoto.

## Side trips by rail from Kyoto

The first of the two sample excursions described below can be easily done as a day trip, while the second is convenient as part of a trip to Nara (see p265).

**To Arashiyama** 嵐山  Arashiyama may be touristy but it offers a complete change of pace, has a lot worth seeing, and offers spectacular scenery particularly in the spring and autumn. It is easily reached by train (2-4/hr; 14-17 mins) on the JR Sagano Line; the station for Arashiyama is called Saga-Arashiyama. Stops before reaching Saga-Arashiyama include **Nijo** 二条 (4.2km; for Nijojo; see p252) and **Hanozono** 花園 (6.9km) for Toei Kyoto Studio Park (see p252). If you don't have a JR pass consider taking the Randen tram; see p257.

● **Saga-Arashiyama** 嵯峨嵐山  There are ¥300 lockers in JR Saga-Arashiyama station. Take the North Exit for Daikaku-ji (see p264) and the South Exit for the river area.

**Torokko Sagano** トロッコ嵯峨 railway station is on the right by the South Exit; the **tourist information centre** here is open (8.30am-5pm) when the Torokko Romantic car (see box below) is operating. A Rental Bicycle shop (daily 9am-5.30pm; ¥300/hr, ¥700/day) is on the right as you walk to the river.

Walk (or cycle) straight down the road from the station until you get to the river. Turn right and walk along until you reach **Togetsu-kyo** 渡月橋 (Moon Crossing Bridge) on the left, a traditional-style bridge first built in 836 though the current bridge dates from 1934. Togetsu-kyo is a famous spot for viewing both cherry blossom and autumn leaves. Cross the bridge and at the end either turn left to explore the area of cherry trees, or turn right to either walk along the path by the river or jump into a boat upriver with **Yakatabune** 屋形船 (🖳 www.arashiyama-yakatabune.com). You can take a **boat tour** (daily 9am-4.30pm, Dec-mid Mar 10am-3.30pm; from ¥3500 for 30 mins, discounts for groups of 3+), or hire a **rowing boat** (¥1500 per hour, up to 3 people). Whether walking or in a boat it is not long before you escape the sights and sounds of

---

❏ **Riding the Romantic Train – and returning by boat**

Expensive but fun is a ride on the **Torokko open-air carriage 'Romantic Train'** 嵯峨野ロマンチックトレイン (🖳 www.sagano-kanko.co.jp; Mar-Dec daily in peak/holiday periods, Wed-Mon at other times; hourly; 25 mins; ¥620 one-way, neither JR rail passes nor Kansai Thru Passes accepted), which runs along the scenic Hozu River from Torokko-Sagano station (adjacent to JR Saga-Arashiyama) to Torokko-Kameoka トロッコ亀岡 (from where it is a 10-minute walk to JR's Umahori 馬堀 station). It gets completely booked out in the autumn when crowds descend on Arashiyama to see the leaves fall, but it's wise to reserve ahead at any time; book at JR West ticket counters or at the TiS travel agency in Kyoto station.

As an alternative to returning by train, consider taking a **boat trip** (🖳 www.hozugawakudari.jp/en; Mar-Nov hourly 9am-3pm, rest of year every 90 mins; 2hrs; ¥4100) on the Hozugawa (Hozu River) to Arashiyama. The course from the starting point in Kameoka – shuttle buses (¥310) run between Torokko-Kameoka and the river – back down to Arashiyama is 16km. Accept as hyperbole the description of the journey down the rapids as being the 'most exciting experience not only in Japan but also throughout the world'. It's not the Zambezi but the scenery is still spectacular. And, being Japan, the boat is heated in the winter!

the city. If walking, about 1km along the river you will come to **Arashiyama Daihikaku Senkou-ji** 嵐山大悲閣千光寺 (daily 10am-4pm; ¥400), a Zen temple which was built in 1614 as a memorial to people who had died in river-control projects. There is a haiku here by Matsuo Basho, the famous Edo-period poet, celebrating the cherry blossom. Signs along the path rightly mention a 'Great View': the final climb to the temple is worth the effort for the panorama over the river, with Kyoto in the distance. If in need of a rest en route there are a few *cafés* by the river.

On your way back, if the prospect of **Iwatayama Monkey Park** モンキーパークくいわたやま (⌨ www.monkeypark.jp; daily 9am-5.30pm, Nov to mid Mar to 4.30pm, closed in bad weather; ¥550) appeals, follow the signs up the hill. Then cross back over the bridge and keep heading straight, along the road lined with tourist shops and restaurants. Turn first left after passing Keifuku-Arashiyama station and follow the signs to Tenryu-ji.

**Tenryu-ji** 天龍寺 (⌨ www.tenryuji.com; daily 8.30am-5.30pm, Nov to mid Mar to 5pm; garden ¥500, garden and temple ¥600), originally built in 1255 as a palace with a view of Mt Arashiyama, was converted into a Zen temple in 1339 and is now a World Heritage site. The focal point of the garden is a pond behind which the rest of the garden is spread out on the hillside. When you have seen enough, take the exit behind the temple leading to the **bamboo grove path** 竹林の道. Cool and shady in the summer, the forest offers a number of paths: head left to walk back to the river through Kameyama Park, or right for the small **Nonomiya Shrine** 野宮神社 (⌨ www.nonomiya.com), where Imperial princesses underwent purification rites for three years as part of their training before being sent to the Grand Shrine at Ise (see p240). From the shrine go back to the main road and turn left. A 10-minute walk brings you to **Seiryo-ji** 清涼寺 (⌨ www.seiryoji.or.jp; daily 9am-4pm; grounds free, temple ¥400), once a country villa and a good place for a special lunch as there's a tiny restaurant, to the right of the main building, called *Chikusen* 竹仙 (⌨ www.kyoto-chikusen.com; 10am-7pm; reservation necessary after 5pm). The ¥3500 (¥3780 inc tax) lunch served on a tray is a visual delight.

Just north-east of Seiryo-ji is **Daikaku-ji** 大覚寺 (⌨ www.daikakuji.or.jp; daily 9am-5pm; ¥500), which has a viewing platform over the adjacent Osawa Pond. Originally part of the country villa of Emperor Saga, the complex became a temple after his death in 876. To get there turn left out of Seiryo-ji, go straight over at the crossroads, walk along till you come to a petrol station on the left, then follow the signs.

A great place for a sit down after all this walking is the **foot onsen** 足湯 (*ashi-yu*; ¥200) at the Arashiyama terminus of the Randem tram (see p257); the signs recommend 10 minutes in the spa for pedi-health.

**To Uji and Nara** A rapid service on the JR Nara Line takes 17 minutes to Uji (approx 3/hr) and 45 minutes to Nara though the line becomes the JR Yamatoji Line at Kizu. Local services (approx 2/hr) take proportionately longer.

Kansai Thru Pass holders, or anyone without a JR pass who is only going to Nara, can pick up a direct train to Kintetsu-Nara from the Kintetsu tracks at Kyoto station (2/hr; 34-48 mins; ¥620, reserved seat ¥510), or from any Kyoto Karasuma subway line station to Takeda and then pick up a Kintetsu Line train. Going to Kintetsu-Nara is recommended as it is more centrally located in Nara. Distances quoted below are on the JR line.

● **Uji** 宇治 **(14.9km)** Uji has been a well-known tea-producing area since the Kamakura era (1185-1333) and features in the last 10 chapters of one of Japan's most famous novels, *The Tale of Genji*. Uji Bridge, mentioned in the book, was first built by a Buddhist monk in 646, though the present construction dates from the 1990s. (For Kansai Thru Pass users, change at Chushojima on the Keihan Line for Uji, as it is more central than the JR station.)

At the JR station, there are lockers (¥300-400) to the left of the exit on the 2nd floor to the right of the exit at street level. There is a **tourist information booth** (Mar-Nov Mon-Fri 9am-5pm, Sat & Sun to 6pm, Dec-Feb daily to 5pm) in the building opposite the station.

**Byodo-in** 平等院 (🖥 www.byodoin.or.jp; daily 8.30am-5.30pm; ¥600, plus ¥300 to enter Phoenix Hall by timed tickets), a 10-minute walk down the hill from the JR station, is a peaceful temple set back from the west bank of Uji-gawa. It's a World Heritage site and is known for the large Buddha statue in its main building, the Phoenix Hall. The shape of the hall, with annexes stretching out either side, is said to 'resemble a phoenix spreading its wings' and is depicted on the ¥10 coin. The main ticket includes entry to **Hosho-kan** 鳳翔館, a museum which displays a wide variety of objects associated with the temple. An additional ¥300 will grant you a guided group tour of the Phoenix Hall itself; an English written translation is provided.

As Japan's most famous 'tea town', there is no shortage of tea, whether in leaf, cup or ice-cream form. Behind Byodo-in is **Taiho-an** 対鳳庵 (🖥 www .kyoto-uji-kankou.or.jp; daily 10am-4pm), Uji's municipal tea house, with offerings from matcha tea and a sweet (¥500) to a fully personalised tea ceremony experience (¥1200; reserve three days in advance); check the website for a useful guide to Japanese tea ceremony etiquette. For food over ceremony, *Nakamura Tokichi* 中村藤吉 (🖥 www.tokichi.jp; daily café 11am-5.30pm, shop 10am-5.30pm) offers matcha soba, matcha ice-cream, matcha jelly, or simply a cup of pure concentrated matcha. From JR Uji, cross the road and continue down the street ahead; the shop and restaurant are identified by a large cross in a circle on a canvas. Expect to put your name on a queue list and for lengthy waits due to high demand!

● **Nara** 奈良 **(41.7km)** Rapid services from Kyoto stop at Uji, so you can pick the train up here and continue directly to Nara (25 mins).

## NARA 奈良

Some 40km south of Kyoto, Nara boasts a longer history than its nearby rival. It became Japan's first permanent capital in 710 and, even though its time at the top was short-lived (the Imperial court had decamped to Kyoto by 794), the period was marked by the influence of Buddhism from mainland China.

Nara's tremendous collection of temples, particularly enormous Todai-ji, which houses Japan's largest statue of the Buddha, still stand today as proof of that influence and of the great wealth that once poured into the city. Just outside the centre of Nara, Horyu-ji contains the world's oldest surviving wooden structures (particularly impressive when you consider how frequently wooden temples burn to the ground in Japan).

Nara's compact size makes it much more manageable than Kyoto and its vast park is more attractive than Kyoto's urban sprawl. A lightning-fast day excursion can be made from Kyoto but an overnight stay in Nara would allow you time to enjoy the sights at a more leisurely pace.

HONSHU

Kansai Thru Pass holders can access Nara from both Kyoto and Osaka on the Kintetsu railway to Kintetsu-Nara station, adjacent to Nara Park which saves 13 minutes walking; change at Yamato-Saidaiji if necessary.

**What to see and do**  With just one day here, focus on Nara Park. With more time you could also take in the Naramachi quarter, visit one or two of the museums, or do one of the suggested side trips (see pp270-1). Though it's easy enough to tour Nara Park on your own, it may be worth organising a guided tour of the museum with one of the volunteer guide groups mentioned in the box on p251. Kofuku-ji, Todai-ji and Kasuga Taisha are all World Heritage sites.

Approaching Nara Park from JR Nara station along Sanjo-dori, look out on your left for the three- and five-storeyed pagodas which belong to **Kofuku-ji** 興福寺 (🖵 www.kohfukuji.com; daily 9am-5pm). Moved here in 710 when Nara became the capital, at the height of its prosperity, this temple boasted as many as 175 buildings but most of them have since burnt down. The three-storeyed pagoda dates from 1143 and the five-storeyed one from 1426. The latter is at its most spectacular when lit up at night (summer only). The Tokondo 東金堂 (Eastern Main Hall; ¥300) and impressive Treasure Museum 国宝館 (¥600), renovated in 2011, display a variety of Buddhist sculptures, although there are no English explanations inside. Performances of Noh take place in the temple precincts in May. The Central Golden Hall, the main hall, is being rebuilt and work will take until 2018.

The biggest draw in the park is **Todai-ji** 東大寺 (🖵 www.todaiji.or.jp; Apr-Sep daily 7.30am-5.30pm, Oct 7.30am-5pm, Nov-Feb 8am-4.30pm, Mar 8am-5pm; ¥500 to visit the Daibutsuden, ¥800 inc museum). Its main building, the Daibutsuden 大仏殿 (Great Buddha Hall), is the world's largest wooden structure and houses a 16.2m-high, 15-tonne bronze statue known as the 'Great Buddha of Nara'. The adjacent **Todai-ji Museum** 東大寺ミュージアム (🖵 culturecenter.todaiji.or.jp; from 9am but closing hours same as Todai-ji; ¥500, ¥500 audio guide) displays the temple's priceless collection of Buddha statues and other historic art, and chronicles the history of Buddhism in Japan. The audio guide is particularly recommended.

Nara's most important shrine is **Kasuga Taisha** 春日大社 (Apr-Sep daily 6am-6pm, Nov-Mar 6.30am-5pm; inner area ¥500), the pathway to which is lined with lanterns – there are said to be 3000 in the shrine precincts. Founded in 768 at the foot of Mt Mikasa, this shrine of the Fujiwara family remained influential throughout the Heian Period (794-1185), after the capital had moved to Kyoto. Inside the compound, fortune sticks are available in English for ¥200, or ¥500-600 if bundled with a cute toy souvenir. There are also 12 attached small shrines behind the main compound, including **Fufu Daikokusha** 夫婦大國社 (Married Couples' Shrine) that offers heart-shaped *ema* (wooden prayer plaques) and water fortunes. Also in the grounds is **Shinen Manyo botanical garden** 萬葉植物園 (Mar-Nov daily 9am-5pm, Dec-Feb to 4pm; ¥500), probably at its best

---

**❏ Harmonious co-habitation**

Apart from its rich cultural heritage, Nara is known for the harmonious co-habitation of humans and deer. It won't be long before you spot one (they tend to wander into souvenir shops in search of food), and it's often not up to you how close you want to get to them. At least this means a picnic in Nara Park will never be lonely, although be sure only to feed them **shika sembei** (deer crackers), sold widely. The deer are protected because they are believed to be messengers from the gods (at one point they were even considered to be higher in status than humans). Today the deer population stands at around 1100, a figure which has remained more or less stable for many years; around 200 die and 200 are born every year, and it is an offence to kill one.

in April and May when the wisteria is in bloom, and a **Treasure House** 宝物殿 (daily 9am-5pm; ¥400). The main shrine's annual festival, Kasugasai 春日祭, is held on 13th March; other festivals are held here in early February and mid August.

**Nara National Museum** 奈良国立博物館 (🖳 www.narahaku.go.jp; Tue-Sun 9.30am-5pm, to 7pm on Fri from late Apr to late Oct; ¥520), in the park, opened in 1895 as one of three Imperial museums (the other two were in Kyoto and Tokyo). Nearly all exhibits have brief explanations in English but it's difficult to get a perspective on the wealth of ceremonial objects, paintings, scrolls, statues and sutras without an English-speaking guide. There are two parts to the permanent collection: 'Masterpieces of Buddhist Sculpture' is in the original building (the Sculpture Hall) and 'Masterpieces of Buddhist Art' is in the New West wing. There's a pleasant *café* on the lower-level passageway between the old and new buildings, which does coffee-and-cake sets in the afternoon.

An unexpected attraction in central Nara is **Okumura Commemorative Museum** 奥村記念館 (Okumura Kinenkan; 🖳 www.okumuragumi.co.jp/en/ commemorative; daily exc 3rd Tue 10am-5pm; free), run by the Okumura Corporation, which designs earthquake-prevention systems for buildings and was founded in Nara in 1907. The star attraction is the rather grandly named 'Earthquake and Seismic Isolation Experience Device' – essentially a special chair into which you can be strapped before feeling the full force of a quake. Don't leave the building without visiting the open-air terrace and its great views of Todai-ji. Few tour groups stop here, so it's a welcome break from the hordes. Feel free to linger here, as the museum promotes itself as a 'place to rest while strolling around this historic city'. They even offer free tea and coffee. The entrance is on the left soon after the road junction to the left for Daibutsudenmae Parking Lot.

Fans of Japanese gardens should make a beeline for **Isui-en** 依水園 (daily Apr-May & Oct-Nov, Wed-Mon rest of year, 9.30am-4.30pm; ¥900), a stroll garden divided into two sections, each of which has its own pagoda and assorted tea houses. In the classic way of Japanese gardens, Isui-en makes full use of the 'borrowed scenery' of nearby temples and mountains. If you're on a budget, try the adjacent, smaller garden at **Yoshiki-en** 吉城園 (mid Mar-Dec daily 9am-5pm; ¥250, free to passport-bearing foreign visitors) instead, from where there are views out onto Isui-en, which it overlooks. Yoshiki-en seems less popular than its larger neighbour and is often more peaceful.

Another area of interest is the **Naramachi** 奈良町 district, a very atmospheric old quarter with traditional houses, narrow streets, craft shops, mini museums and cafés. Both **Gango-ji** 元興寺 (daily 9am-5pm), also known as Gokuraku-bo (Paradise Temple) and dating from the 13th century, and **Naramachi Koshi-no-Ie** ならまち格子の家 (Naramachi Lattice House; Tue-Sun 9am-5pm; free), a typical private house, are worth visiting.

## Practical information

**Station guide** Rail-pass holders are likely to arrive at **JR Nara station**. The two principal JR lines are the Yamatoji Line (to/from Horyu-ji, Tennoji and Osaka) and the Nara Line (to/from Uji and Kyoto). JR Nara station has been rebuilt; the old station building, with a temple-style roof, is a listed building and is to the left as you leave the new station.

To the right of the station ticket barrier at the East Exit is the JR ticket office, a branch of Nippon Travel Agency and the tourist information counter (see below). Lockers of all sizes are in a building next to the station, to your left as you exit.

The other main station in Nara is **Kintetsu-Nara** with through services onto the Kyoto Karasuma Line to Kyoto and to Namba station in Osaka.

**Tourist information** There are **information counters** in both JR Nara (daily 8.30am-5pm) and Kintetsu-Nara (daily 9am-9pm) stations. Staff can assist with accommodation bookings.

HONSHU

The main **Nara City Information Center** 奈良市観光案内所 (📟 narashi kanko.or.jp; daily 9am-9pm) is along Sanjo-dori, five minutes from JR Nara station, and can provide maps of suggested walking tours. Nara Prefecture also publish leaflets detailing the ties between the city and various regions around the world (📟 www.pref.nara.jp/nara_e).

**Tours & goodwill guides** Nara YMCA organises free **English-speaking guides** for tours of Nara. Reservations are preferred (📟 sites.google.com/site/eggnaragg) or enquire at the tourist information counters in JR/Kintetsu-Nara stations. A similar service is provided by Nara Student Guides (📟 www.narastudentguide.org). See also box p251.

Nara Walk (📟 www.narawalk.com) offers guided **walking tours** in English around the city, park and temples including Nara Park Classic Tour (3½hrs; ¥2000pp), Great Buddha Tour to Todai-ji (2hrs; ¥1500pp), and tours of Naramachi and Horyu-ji. Prices do not include entrance fees; reserve ahead, online, particularly between 21st December and 28th February when tours run only if pre-booked.

**Getting around** The best way to see central Nara is on foot. If you're pressed for time rent a **bicycle** from the Eki Rent-A-Car 駅レンタカー booth (daily 8am-6pm; ¥700), to your right as you exit JR Nara station. If a bus appeals, the **Gurutto Bus** ぐるっとバス (daily 9am-5pm; ¥100/journey) Nara Park Route (red colour; 4/hr) runs round Todaiji and Kasuga Taisha. Both JR Nara and Kintetsu-Nara stations are a stop on the route.

**Festivals** As one of Japan's ancient capitals, Nara has many festivals, though one you may wish to avoid is the annual deer antler-cutting ceremony in the autumn. A more appealing event may be **Shikayose** 鹿寄せ (Jan/Feb/Mar Tue-Sun 10am for about 15 mins) when the deer are attracted to an area near Kasuga Taisha by the sound of a horn (playing a Beethoven symphony) and are rewarded with lots of acorns.

July to October is the **'light-up' season**, when some of Nara's best-known sights, including Kofuku-ji and Todai-ji, are lit up nightly until 10pm.

The thousands of lanterns at Kasuga Taisha are only lit twice a year: once on February 3rd at **Setsubon Mantoro** 節分万灯籠 to welcome in the spring, and again at **Chugen Mantoro** 中元万灯籠 on the 14th-15th August. **Kasuga Wakamiya On-matsuri** 春日若宮おん祭り (15th-18th Dec) has been held since the 12th century and is one of the largest festivals in the area. The highlight is a procession on the 17th featuring costumes from the Heian period to the Edo.

**Where to stay** One of the cheapest options, and just across the street from JR Nara, is **Super Hotel JR Nara Ekimae Sanjo-dori** スーパーホテルJR奈良駅前・三条通り (☎ 0742-27-9000, 📟 www.super hotel.co.jp; ¥6740/S, ¥9780/D), with the usual functional rooms and a free continental breakfast. Right outside the station is **Super Hotel Lohas JR Nara Ekimae** スーパーホテルLohas JR奈良駅前 (☎ 0742-27-9000, 📟 www.superhotel.co.jp; ¥6740 /S, ¥9780/D, ¥13,500/Tr), which has a natural hot-spring spa.

An excellent mid-range business hotel is **Nara Washington Hotel Plaza** 奈良ワシントンホテルプラザ (☎ 0742-27 0410, 📟 www.washington.jp/nara; from ¥6750/S, ¥12,770/D or Tw), five minutes from JR Nara station along Sanjo-dori.

The plushest modern place in town, **Hotel Nikko Nara** ホテル日航奈良 (☎ 0742-35 8831, 📟 www.nikkonara.jp; ¥12,700/S, ¥22,000/D or Tw), looms up behind JR Nara station (take the West Exit). It's a haven of luxury with spacious Western-style rooms and a choice of places to eat, including a swish Chinese restaurant *Shuko*. The buffet breakfast is ¥1800; some packages include this.

**Hotel Fujita Nara** ホテルフジタ奈良 (☎ 0742-23 8111, 📟 www.fujita-nara.com; from ¥6200/S, ¥8100/D or Tw) is a little old-fashioned but all right for the price and well located; the hotel offers a number of packages so check the website.

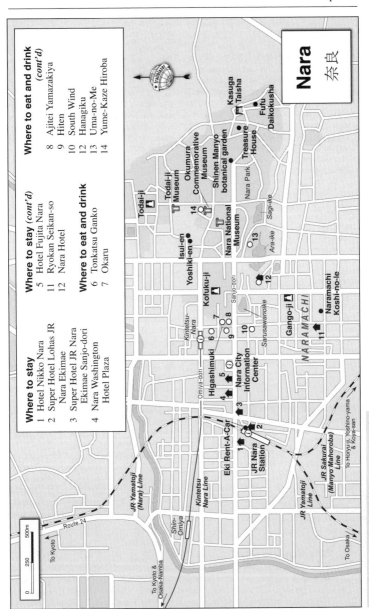

Where to stay
1 Hotel Nikko Nara
2 Super Hotel Lohas JR Nara Ekimae
3 Super Hotel JR Nara Ekimae Sanjo-dori
4 Nara Washington Hotel Plaza

Where to stay (cont'd)
5 Hotel Fujita Nara
11 Ryokan Seikan-so
12 Nara Hotel

Where to eat and drink
6 Tonkatsu Ganko
7 Okaru

Where to eat and drink (cont'd)
8 Ajitei Yamazakiya
9 Hiten
10 South Wind
12 Hanagiku
13 Uma-no-Me
14 Yume-Kaze Hiroba

**Nara**
奈良

A more appealing area is the historic **Naramachi district**, with its small lanes and traditional houses. Here you'll find *Ryokan Seikan-so* 旅館静観荘 (☎ 0742-22 2670, 🖳 www.nara-ryokanseikanso.com; ¥4320pp; Western breakfast ¥486, Japanese ¥756), an old inn built around a traditional Japanese garden. None of the tatami rooms has an attached bathroom but this is a popular, very reasonably priced place that fills up quickly. It's 15 minutes on foot south of Kintetsu-Nara station (part of the way is along a covered arcade) or 25 minutes from JR Nara station.

By far the most atmospheric place to stay is *Nara Hotel* 奈良ホテル (☎ 0742-26 3300, 🖳 www.narahotel.co.jp; ¥16,000/S, ¥29,700/D or Tw, exc breakfast, ¥1000 discount on D/Tw for rail-pass holders), opened in 1909 and designed by the architect responsible for the famous red-brick Tokyo Station Hotel (see p130). The old wing has enormous rooms with high roofs and spacious bathrooms. Rooms in the new wing lack the history but are just as comfortable. The bar is the perfect place to sip a gin and tonic after a hard day's sightseeing and maybe flick through the guest book. Members of the Imperial Family always stay here when visiting Nara (snapshots of their visits line a wall near reception). You too could try the Imperial Suite: a snip at ¥356,500 a night.

**Where to eat and drink** For restaurants, head to the area around Kintetsu-Nara station, in particular **Higashimuki** – a covered arcade leading away from Exit No 2 of the station. Along Higashimuki, *Hiten* 飛天 (Mon-Fri 11am-3pm & 5-10pm; Sat & Sun 11am-10pm) serves a wide range of Chinese dishes such as dim sum, spicy pork, chicken, shrimps and beef. Lunch sets start at ¥980 but it's still good value in the evening when small plates cost from

around ¥500. *Okaru* おかる (daily 11am-9.30pm) is a great okonomiyaki place with both tatami and table seating where you choose the ingredients for your pancakes (from ¥750), which are then cooked and served in front of you. *Tonkatsu Ganko* とんかつがんこ (daily 11am-10pm), next to a branch of Mister Donut, serves delicious tonkatsu and does lunch sets which cost from around ¥1000; an English menu is available. They also do take-outs. *Ajitei Yamazakiya* 味亭山崎屋 (Tue-Sun 11.15am-9pm), the entrance to which is behind a shop in the arcade selling pickled vegetables, is a traditional Japanese place where you can order from the plastic models of sample dishes outside; lunch costs from ¥880. For lighter bites, look out for *South Wind* 南風 (daily 9am-8pm) serving coffee, sandwiches and *omu-rice* (omelette filled with fried rice), a home-cooked staple.

To really empty your pocket pay a visit to *Uma-no-Me* 馬の目 (☎ 0742-23 7784; Fri-Wed 11.30am-3pm & 5.30-8.30pm), close to Nara Hotel and about as traditional a Japanese place as you are likely to find. It's a very small restaurant decorated with Japanese *yakimono* (pottery), some of which dates from the early Meiji period. Seating is on tatami mats in the main part of the restaurant or in private rooms with a view over the garden. Lunch costs from ¥3500 and an evening meal (reservation only) from ¥8000. *Hanagiku* 花菊 (daily 11.30am-2pm & 5.30-9.30pm), in Nara Hotel, serves skilfully prepared (and multi-layered!) box-style lunches (*manyo bento*) for about ¥3800.

If none of these appeals, try one of the regional-produce restaurants in **Yume-Kaze Hiroba** 夢風ひろば (Yume-Kaze Plaza; 🖳 www.yume-kaze.com; complex open daily 9am-7pm though restaurant hours vary), opposite Nara National Museum.

### Side trips from Nara
● **To Horyu-ji** 法隆寺  Some 12km south-west of Nara lies the temple of **Horyu-ji** 法隆寺 (🖳 www.horyuji.or.jp; daily mid Feb-Oct 8am-5pm, Nov-mid Feb 9am-4.30pm; ¥1500), founded in 607 and now a World Heritage site. Highlights of its western compound are the Five-storeyed Pagoda and the

Main Hall, believed to be the world's oldest surviving wooden structure. In the eastern compound, the Hall of Dreams (built in 739) houses a statue of the temple's founder, Prince Shotoku (see also p146). Its octagonal shape is auspicious since the number eight is considered lucky in Japan.

To reach Horyu-ji, take a train from JR Nara station on the JR Yamatoji Line (towards Osaka) to Horyuji (11 mins). It's a 20-minute walk, or bus No 72 (3/hr; 5 mins; ¥190) runs from Stop No 2 outside Horyuji station, to the temple; get off at Horyujimon-mae.

● **To Yoshino-yama** 吉野山 (See p156)   Take the JR Sakurai (Manyo Mahoroba) Line, which becomes the JR Wakayama Line at Takada, to Yoshino-guchi (1/hr; approx 60 mins). If you take the JR Yamatoji Line you will have to change at Oji and possibly also Takada. At Yoshino-guchi transfer to the Kintetsu Line for the journey to Yoshino (34 mins; ¥380).

● **To Koya-san** 高野山 (see pp156-8)   Take the JR Sakurai (Manyo Mahoroba) Line, which becomes the JR Wakayama Line at Takada, to Hashimoto (1/hr; approx 100 mins). Additional services may require a change at Oji and/or Takada. The remaining fare through to Koyasan is ¥830 (train ¥440, cable car ¥390; ¥510 supplement for the all-reserved LEX Koya).

From Kintetsu-Nara you will need to change at Yamato-Saidaiji on the edge of Nara and again at Kashiharajingu-mae (from 80 mins; ¥850, seat reservation ¥900).

# Western Honshu – route guides

Many visitors to Japan take the shinkansen west along the Sanyo coast from Shin-Osaka to Hiroshima, perhaps en route to Kyushu. But western Honshu, also known as **Chugoku** ('the Middle Lands'), has much more to offer than a hurried stop in Hiroshima.

The Sanyo (southern) coast may have the fastest rail connections and the best-known sights but the less-developed Sanin (northern) coast provides a complete change of pace but still plenty to see and do. The journey along the Sanin coast offers spectacular mountain and river scenery and the chance to see a part of Japan that has not been bulldozed into the industrial revolution. The route leads to: **Tsuwano**, a picturesque town with an interesting history; **Matsue**, justly famous for the sunsets over its splendid lake, Shinji-ko, and for being the former home of writer Lafcadio Hearn; **Izumo-Taisha**, Japan's oldest shrine, and **Tottori** with its expanse of desert-like sand dunes.

Two stations on this route are connection points for other rail journeys: Okayama is the starting point for the Shikoku route guide, and from Shin-Yamaguchi it's only 20 minutes by shinkansen to Kokura, the starting point for the Kyushu route guide.

---

❏ **Hikari Rail Star**
Green Class pass-holders should be aware that the Hikari Rail Star, used for the
Kodama service between Shin-Osaka and Hakata, **doesn't have a Green Car**, but the
seating in the reserved cars is 2 x 2 so there is more space than in most shinkansen.

---

## SHIN-OSAKA (OSAKA) TO SHIN-YAMAGUCHI BY SHINKANSEN

Distances from Shin-Osaka. Fastest journey time: 2 hours.

This route follows the shinkansen line; regular JR trains go on the Sanyo
Line which roughly parallels the route described but stops at more stations and
takes longer.

### Shin-Osaka to Okayama           [Map 11, p274; Table 3, p505]

All shinkansen stop at Shin-Osaka. For **Osaka** see pp144-54 and for notes
about the Hikari Rail Star see box above.

### Shin-Kobe 新神戸 (37km)           [Kobe, see pp289-96]

All shinkansen stop here.

Some Hikari/Sakura and all Kodama call at **Nishi-Akashi** 西明石 (60km),
the next station along the line. As the train pulls in to Himeji (see below), look
out on the right and you'll see Himeji Castle on a hill in the distance.

### Himeji 姫路 (92km)   All kinds of shinkansen stop here but not all services.

Himeji is also a stop on the JR Sanyo (Kobe) Line.

You have to go through both the shinkansen and the local line ticket gates
before you reach the main concourse. At the **tourist information centre** (Himeji
Kanko Navi Port; 🖳 www.himeji-kanko.jp; daily 9am-7pm) on the left by the
Central Exit, pick up a map and leaflets and ask there if you fancy renting a bicycle (9am-4pm, must be returned by 5.30pm; free); these are available on a first
come first served basis. There are stacks of **lockers** of all sizes; some (¥300-700)
on the shinkansen concourse and more just outside the station's Himeji Castle
Exit, on the right. However, the station gets so busy that they may all be taken.

The picture-postcard perfect Himeji Castle is about a 20-minute walk from
the station and once at the castle there is a lot more walking if you want to see
everything. So, if you prefer a more relaxing start, and haven't rented a bicycle,
take **Himeji Castle Loop Bus** (Mar-Nov daily 9am-5pm, Dec-Feb weekends
and holidays only; 20 mins per loop; 2-4/hr; ¥100/trip, one-day pass ¥300); buses
depart from stop No 6 outside the station. The pass entitles you to a 20% discount
on a ticket for the castle and Koko-en. If the Loop Bus isn't operating take a bus
from stops 7-10 and get off at Himeji-jo Otemon-mae 姫路城大手門前.

**Himeji Castle** 姫路城 (Himeji-jo; 🖳 www.himejicastle.jp; daily May-Aug
9am-6pm, Sep-Apr to 5pm, last entry one hour earlier; ¥1000, ¥1040 inc Koko-
en) is truly one of the most stunning buildings in Japan, even more so since a
four-year restoration programme of the main keep (Daitenshu) was finally completed in 2015. Separate to that, what makes it so special is that it has never been

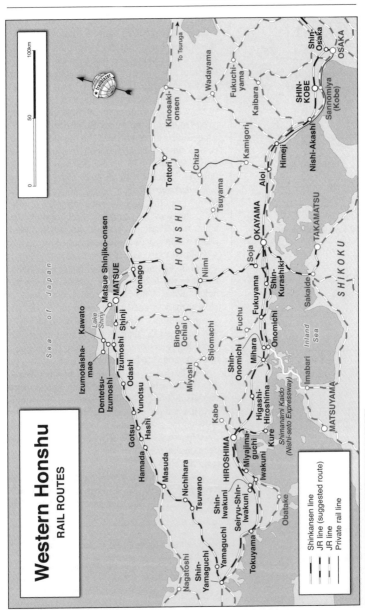

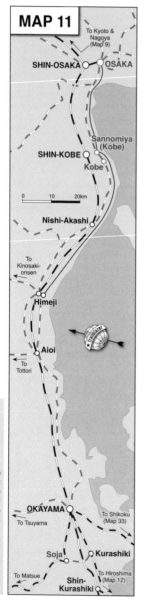

MAP 11

To Kyoto &
Nagoya
(Map 9)

SHIN-OSAKA ○ ○ OSAKA

Sannomiya
(Kobe)

SHIN-KOBE ○
Kobe

0    10    20km

Nishi-Akashi

To
Kinosaki-
onsen

Himeji

Aioi

To
Tottori

OKAYAMA ○
To Tsuyama          To Shikoku
(Map 33)

Soja ○    ○ Kurashiki

To Matsue          To Hiroshima
(Map 12)
Shin-
Kurashiki ○

bombed or reduced to rubble from either a fire or an earthquake. Originally a 14th-century fort, it was rebuilt in its present style at the beginning of the 17th century and has been on the World Heritage list since 1933. It is also known as Hakuro-jo (White Heron Castle) as it resembles a heron with its wings spread out. It is frequently used as a backdrop in samurai movies and even features in the James Bond film *You Only Live Twice* (see p485). The castle's clever design adds to its attraction. There are: endless twists and turns; 21 gates; doorways that are doubly protected with an inner and outer door; *mushakukushi* (warrior hiding places); as well as 997 'shooting holes' – either circular, square, or triangular for gunshots, rectangular for arrows, and lattice windows with holes underneath where stones could be dropped on anyone who dared to try to attack.

From Otemon Gate, the main gate, walk round to the left of the big grassy area for the ticket office. The route around the castle is clearly marked and even though the rooms are generally empty (apart from the weapon racks still on the walls) there is lots to read in English about all aspect of the castle, even if you don't have the app (see box below).

At the end of several flights of steep steps, you reach the 6th floor of the Main Keep, where there is a shrine. Also here you can see Himeji city, the station and surrounding area but since no windows were installed in the corners of this floor the views are limited. However, most will be more interested in the views of the castle from the city.

From the outside the main keep appears to have five layers (floors), but in reality inside there are six: the 3rd and 4th floors seem to be

❏ **Himeji Castle Great Discovery App**
Anyone with a smart phone (Apple or Android Version 4 or later) may like to download the free Himeji Castle Great Discovery App; see 🖵 www.himejicastle.jp/sp/en/ar.html for more details.

HONSHU

one floor; this was partly so the ceiling round the outside could be higher and therefore any gun smoke could escape. The bamboo sticks you can see in these high ceilings were to hold bags of gunfire. There is also a basement; an unusual feature of this is that two toilets were installed here but there is no sign they were ever used.

The 240m-long **Nagatsubone** 長局 (Hyakken Roka) connecting corridor, in the West Bailey, is where Princess Sen, the grand-daughter of Ieyasu Tokugawa (see p56) is said to have lived. There are now exhibitions in many of the rooms along this corridor, but make sure you don't miss the video about the restoration work; even though it is in Japanese it is easy to understand what was happening and the craftsmanship and attention to detail is incredible.

It will take at least 90 minutes to explore the castle and the grounds. There are a few English-speaking **volunteer guides** at the castle (call ☎ 079-285-1146 if you want to be certain you have a guide), and their enthusiasm and ability to point out bits you may miss makes a visit to Himeji even more rewarding. However, if you have a guide you may not have time to read the many signs and labels on each floor.

Even though the garden, **Koko-en** 好古園 (🖳 www.himeji-machishin .jp/ryokka/kokoen; daily 9am-6pm, Sep-Apr to 5pm; ¥300, ¥1040 inc castle) behind the castle was created in 1992, techniques from the Edo period were used in its construction. It has nine different gardens and, rather like the castle, it can seem that you have seen everything but then suddenly you discover another area. In **Souju-an** (10am-4pm; ¥500), the tea ceremony house, you can have some green tea. And if you prefer a proper (Japanese) meal with a view of the garden try **Kassui-ken** 活水軒 (10am-4.30pm); they serve a variety of *teishoku* (set meals); a tempura teishoku costs ¥2570.

If udon or soba appeal look out on the right as you walk back to the station for **Menme** めんめ, where you can get a filling bowl of tempura udon (¥850).

Himeji is a great place for a day trip but if you would like to stay the night most hotel chains (Via Inn, Toyoko Inn, Dormy Inn, APA Hotel, Comfort Hotel; see box p70) have a branch here. There are hotels on both sides of the station.

Note: If you have a Kansai Thru Pass (see box p34) use the Sanyo Electric Railway; its Himeji station is in Sanyo department store, near the JR station so the walk to the castle is very similar.

Some Hikari/Sakura and all Kodama stop at **Aioi** 相生 (112km).

## Okayama 岡山 (180km) [see pp297-301]
All shinkansen stop at this castle town, famous for it stroll garden, Korakuen.

## Okayama to Hiroshima [Map 12, p277; Table 3, p505]
**Shin-Kurashiki** 新倉敷 (206km)  Only Kodama stop here. For Kurashiki (see below) transfer to the JR Sanyo Line (4/hr; 10 mins).

### Side trip by rail to Kurashiki 倉敷
The main sight here is the preserved **Bikan Historical Quarter** 倉敷美観地区 with its quaint old buildings, narrow lanes, small museums and canal.

HONSHU

At the **tourist information centre** (💻 www.kurashiki-tabi.jp; daily Apr-Sep 9am-7pm, Oct-Mar to 6pm) on the station concourse you can pick up a map and leaflets about the area; staff speak English and can help book accommodation. There are **lockers** to the right after the ticket barrier (all sizes; ¥300-600).

From Kurashiki station take the South Exit for the Bikan Historical Quarter; it is less than 1km along Chuo-dori, the main road heading away from the station. Once in the quarter, find your way to the canal and continue to **Nakahashi** 中橋 bridge. On the corner there is another tourist information centre, **Kurashiki-Kan** (daily Apr-Oct 9am-6pm, Nov-Mar to 5pm); it is a European-style building dating from 1917 and, apart from getting any information you don't already have, is a good place for a sit down.

There are several museums and galleries in Bikan. Top priority should be given to **Ohara Museum of Art** 大原美術館 (Ohara Bijutsukan; 💻 www.ohara.or.jp; Tue-Sun 9am-5pm; ¥1300 inc entry to Kojima Memorial Hall; audio guide available). The museum was established in 1930 by Keisaburo Ohara, the then president of Kurashiki Spinning Corporation, to display the works of Western art that his friend Torajiro Kojima had collected on visits to Europe. Since then, the museum has expanded to house not only Western art but also a gallery of Asiatic art and a Craft Art gallery of ceramics and woodblock prints. The biggest draws are still the works by Monet, Gauguin, Matisse, Picasso and Modigliani though the museum is now also trying to promote contemporary Japanese art. **Kojima Torajiro Memorial Hall** 児島虎次郎記念館 (Tue-Sun 9am-5pm), in Ivy Square, is where Kojima's own paintings are exhibited.

**Japan Rural Toy Museum** 日本郷土玩具館 (Nihon Kyodo Gangu-kan; 💻 gangukan.jp; Mar-Nov 9am-5pm, Dec-Feb from 10am; ¥400) contains a private collection, curated by Mr Ooga, with more than 200 Japanese kites from all over Japan, including many which are antique. Also here, as the name suggests, is a wonderful selection of traditional Japanese toys – the museum has over 40,000. It is on the right-hand side of the canal as you walk down from the Ohara Museum.

One of the town's many quirky museums is **Kurashiki Sanyo-do** 倉敷貯金箱博物館 (also known as **Chokinbako** or **Character Banks Museum**; 💻 www.sanyo-do.com; Fri-Wed 10.30am-5pm; ¥200), a character bank (piggy bank) museum above an antiques shop. It's on Shirakabe-dori, opposite Kurashiki Ivy Square, which is on the far side of the Historical Quarter – look out for the Nipper statues on the roof. Nipper was the dog who was in a painting entitled His Master's Voice; he was shown listening carefully to a phonograph and this image was then used in HMV adverts. In Japan Nipper is also known as Victor's dog and is mostly associated with Victor and JVC.

Also not in the Historical Quarter, is **O-Hashi House** 大橋家住宅 (💻 www.ohashi-ke.com; Tue-Sun 9am-5pm, to 6pm Sat Apr-Oct; ¥500), the home of a wealthy rice and salt merchant, which dates from about 1796. A bamboo water bucket hangs by the entrance in case there is a fire, though luckily it has never had to be used partly because the walls are clay not wood, but the architecture is still Japanese in style. It is a lovely house with a small garden and gives an understanding of how the inhabitants lived. To reach it turn right at the first set of lights at a crossroads on Chuo-dori (before you reach the official entrance to the Historical Quarter); the house is a short walk along on the left.

HONSHU

There are branches of business hotel chains near Kurashiki station (such as APA and Toyoko Inn; see box p70) but this is a place where it would be good to stay in a ryokan. ***Ryokan Kurashiki*** 旅館くらしき (🖳 www.ryokan-kurashiki.jp; from ¥23,000pp, sgl occ from ¥38,000, inc half board) has five characterful rooms with both Japanese- and Western-style accommodation. The evening meal is kaiseki (the menu focuses on seafood dishes) and breakfast can be Japanese or Western. It is located in the centre of the Historical Quarter by Kurashiki-Kan. Their **restaurant** is open for lunch (11am-2.30pm) and the menu includes a sushi bowl (¥1700) and a seasonal lunch box (from ¥1850).

On the left-hand side by the entrance to the Historical Quarter is ***Restaurant Kiyutei*** レストラン亀遊亭 ( daily 11am-9pm). The lunch menu (11am-3pm) includes curry rice (from ¥1100) and a hamburger set (¥1400) as well as some weekly specials; expect to pay ¥3400 for a meal with steak in the evening. ***Restaurant Swan*** レストラン Swan (🖳 www.kurashiki.co.jp/swan; Thur-Tue 11am-10pm) serves an excellent soup, salad, spaghetti and coffee lunch for ¥1280 and also coffee and cake from ¥700. It is on the right by the canal, just past the entrance to **Senichi Hoshino Memorial Museum** 星野仙一記念館 (10am-5pm; ¥500). However, this museum is likely to be of limited interest unless you are a baseball fan.

If continuing west it is best to pick up a JR Sanyo Line train to Fukuyama rather than returning to Shin-Kurashiki.

**Fukuyama** 福山 **(239km)** All kinds of shinkansen stop here but not all services. As the train arrives look out on the right for a glimpse of Fukuyama Castle.

This former castle town suffered extensive damage from WWII bombing raids. The view of concrete blocks as far as the eye can see is not an encouragement to linger but Fukuyama is worth a half-day stop; it is also an access point for two very different side trips.

MAP 12

OKAYAMA
To Shin-Osaka & Tokyo (Map 11)
To Shikoku (Map 33)
Kurashiki
To Matsue    Soja
Shin-Kurashiki
0    10    20km
Fukuyama
Fuchu    Matsunaga
Higashi-Onomichi
Shin-Onomichi    Onomichi
Shimanami Kaido (Nishi-seto Expressway)    Itozaki
Mihara
Takehara
Higashi-Hiroshima
Kabe
Hiro
Kure
HIROSHIMA
Yokokawa
Miyajima
Miyajima-guchi    Iwakuni
Shin-Iwakuni
Seiryu-Shin-Iwakuni
To Shin-Yamaguchi (Map 13)

HONSHU

There are two sides to Fukuyama station. Take the North Exit for the main sights. **Lockers** (¥300-500 plus a few ¥600 ones) are outside and to the right as you take the North Exit. Staff at the **tourist information counter** (🖳 www.fukuyama-kanko.com; daily 9am-5pm) on the main concourse give out maps but don't deal with hotel reservations. Within the station is a shopping and restaurant mall, where you'll find a range of eat-in/take-away restaurants and cafés.

**Fukuyama Castle** 福山城 (Fukuyama-jo), built in 1619 and situated in a park by the North Exit of the station, has a reconstructed castle tower and museum (Tue-Sun 9am-6pm; ¥200); exhibits include weapons and artefacts symbolic of the surrounding area, such as farming tools. However, there are no labels in English. Much more fun is **Fukuyama Automobile and Clock Museum** 福山自動車時計博物館 (🖳 www.facm.net; daily 9am-6pm; ¥900, ¥700 for foreigners) as you're encouraged to get in all the cars on display; these include a 1915 Ford, a 1954 Mercedes Benz and some original 1960s Mazdas. The nostalgia continues with the range of gramophones, early TV sets, electric organs, horse-drawn carriages, light aircraft and rather bizarrely some waxworks including Abraham Lincoln and Bill Clinton. The museum is a 15-minute walk north of the station: turn right out of the North Exit and walk along till you see a Family Mart on the left-hand corner. Cross over and walk north along this road; eventually it gets narrower and curls round to the right behind a large building. Follow it round then turn first left. Walk along till you come to the junction with the main road. FACM is to the left on the far side of the road. You will know you are in the correct place if you see some battered-looking vehicles.

There are several hotels near the station but one of the cheapest is *Fukuyama Terminal Hotel* 福山ターミナルホテル (☎ 0849-32 3311, 🖳 www.fukuyama-t-hotel.jp; from ¥5250/S, ¥10,000/D or Tw), a 5-minute walk to the left from the south side of the station.

### Side trip to Matsunaga – the 'sole' of Japan

Matsunaga 松永, one of Japan's top production centres of traditional *geta* (wooden clogs). Its importance in terms of making footwear means it is not surprising that the town is home to the unique **Fukuyama City Matsunaga Footwear Museum** 福山市松永きも資料館 (🖳 www.city.fukuyama.hiroshima.jp/soshiki/matsunaga-hakimono; Fri-Sun and holidays 10am-4pm; ¥300). The museum is five minutes on foot (how else?) from the South Exit of Matsunaga station. Laid out inside in pairs is a sweeping history of footwear, from the earliest straw sandals to a pair of lunar boots (worn in space).

The footwear from all over the world is displayed in only two of the eight exhibition rooms; the rest of the space is for the display of traditional toys, dolls, kites and talismans, most of which are connected with religious festivals.

The museum is in an area called **Ashi-ato Square** あしあとスクエア (Footprint Square). Here there are pavilions with displays about the traditional industry of the Matsunaga area and also the house of a geta craftsman which was built in 1919; the finishing touches to geta, which had been made in a factory, were done by hand. There is no charge to visit any of these.

Matsunaga is between Fukuyama and the next shinkansen station at Shin-Onomichi. To reach it, take a local train two stops (3-4/hr; about 10 mins) from

Fukuyama along the JR Sanyo Line. From Matsunaga, rejoin the route by taking a train on the Sanyo Line four stops to Mihara (approx 20 mins), which is on the shinkansen line.

**Side trip by bicycle to Shikoku** Nishi-Seto Expressway 西瀬戸自動車道 connects Onomichi 尾道, on Honshu, to Imabari 今治 (see pp477-8), on Shikoku, via six islands. The Expressway, also known as **Shimanami Kaido** しまなみ海道, is a trail for cyclists or pedestrians. This follows the same road route over a distance of about 37 miles (59km) on the Expressway and about 43 miles (70km) on the cycling road on the islands; here cyclists and pedestrians take a different route to vehicles. The route has become extremely popular largely because of the scenery and views of the Seto Inland Sea but also because it is easy to do in a day and is well signposted; there are no major hills – it was designed with cyclists in mind – but a bicycle with gears is recommended.

To reach **Onomichi Station** 尾道駅 you can take a local JR Sanyo Line train from Fukuyama (1-4/hr; approx 20 mins), or from Mihara (1-4/hr; approx 12 mins). There is a small **tourist information office** (daily 9am-6pm) in Onomichi station and the station itself is near the port. Staff can give you a map of Onomichi and also provide information about the Shimanami Kaido. If cycling doesn't appeal Onomichi is a very pleasant place to walk around and has a lot of temples to see as well as a castle on the hilltop behind town.

The better quality, but also more expensive, bicycles are available from **Giant** (☎ 0848-21 0068, ⌨ giant-store.jp/onomichi; Mon & Wed-Fri 10am-7pm, Sat, Sun and public hols 9am-7pm; ¥3000-9000/5hrs; ¥4000-13,000/day to 6pm; ¥5000-20,000/2 days) in **Onomichi U2**, a former maritime warehouse that is a 5-minute walk to the right from Onomichi station. If you want to return a bike to the Imabari store you need to let them know in advance and also will have to pay ¥3000. The bicycle-rental places at **Onomichi Port** (7am-6pm) and on Mukaishima (see below) are considerably cheaper (bicycle/tandem bicycle ¥1000/day; electric bicycle ¥1500/6hrs) but also much less-good quality. A deposit of ¥1000 is required and will be refunded if you return your bike to the place where you rented it. Note that tandem and electric bicycles **must be** returned to where you rented them. Also note that wherever you rent a bicycle you are likely to have to provide a phone number so they can contact you if necessary and also have proof of identity such as a passport.

Onomichi U2 also now houses places to eat; a great place to stay before you start your trip is: *Hotel Cycle* ホテルサイクル (⌨ www.onomichi-u2 .com; 8 rooms; from ¥9720pp inc breakfast). It was designed with cyclists in mind: the rooms have hooks so your bike can be lifted up out of the way.

The official route starts on **Mukaishima** 向島 (Mukai Island) so you need to take a ferry (daily 6am-11.10pm; 5/hr; 5 mins; ¥110 adult and bicycle) from Onomichi port. Cyclists need to pay some tolls to cross the bridges (¥50-200 per bridge usually), but sometimes there is no charge for foreigners.

For further information visit: ⌨ cycling-shimanami.jp, ⌨ www.go-shima nami.jp, or ⌨ www.city.onomichi.hiroshima.jp.

**Shin-Onomichi** 新尾道 **(259km)** Only Kodama stop here. There is an **information office** (daily 7am-6pm) on the 1st/ground floor where you can pick up a bus timetable; services operate (approx 3/hr; about 12 mins; ¥190) from here to Onomichi Station (see above).

**Mihara** 三原 **(270km)** Only Kodama stop here. Mihara is also on the JR Sanyo (for Onomichi; see p279) and JR Kure (for Takehara; see below) main lines. The **tourist information centre** ('Ukishiro Lobby'; Mon-Sat 8am-7pm, Sun and holidays 10am-6pm) is by the South Exit; in addition to information on the Mihara area, you can rent a bike there. However, you can only get a map for Takehara in Takehara.

> ### Side trip to Takehara 竹原
> Takehara (🖳 www.city.takehara.lg.jp) is a former samurai town which can be accessed by local train (approx 4/hr; 34 mins) from Mihara. The town prospered late in the Edo era due to the salt manufacturing and brewing businesses in the area.
>
> The **historic preservation area** is a 15-minute walk from Takehara station and it has been designated one of Japan's 109 most scenic towns (Important Preservation District for Groups of Traditional Buildings). The main sight is **Saihou-ji** 西方寺; this temple is on top of a small hill and has good views over the old part of town and the Seto Inland Sea. Many of the original houses, with their tiled roofs, plastered walls and lattice windows, still remain. It is almost as if time has stood still. Pick up a map from the **tourist information centre** (daily 8.30am-5pm) to the right outside the station.
>
> From Takehara consider continuing on the JR Kure Line as the route, particularly from Mihara to Hiro, is very scenic; see p312.

**Higashi-Hiroshima** 東広島 **(310km)** Only Kodama stop here.

**Hiroshima** 広島 **(342km)**                  **[see pp301-8]**
All shinkansen stop here. Hiroshima is best known for its **Peace Memorial Park** but it is also the access point for the unmissable island, **Miyajima** (see pp308-11).

**Hiroshima to Shin-Yamaguchi**     **[Map 13, p283; Table 3, p505]**
**Shin-Iwakuni** 新岩国 **(383km)** Only Kodama stop here. Note that there is no lift/elevator, or downward escalator, from the tracks. There are **lockers** (¥300-600) on the station concourse but very few large ones. The bus stand for services to Iwakuni is to the right of the station exit.

> **Side trip to Iwakuni** Iwakuni 岩国 is known for **Kintai-kyo** 錦帯橋, a five-arched bridge which spans Nishiki-gawa. When Hiroyoshi Kikkawa, a feudal lord of Iwakuni, constructed Kintai-kyo in 1673 his aim was to ensure that it could never be washed away, but unfortunately it has been twice. The bridge is now rebuilt every 20 years one arch at a time to keep it strong and also to keep the traditional craftsmanship skills alive.
>
> The bridge is worth seeing in itself but whilst here walk over it to **Kikko Park** 吉香公園 where Kikkawa's residence used to be. There are now several attractions including a ride by ropeway up to Iwakuni Castle. A package ticket which includes the bridge, ropeway and castle costs ¥940 and is sold daily between 9am and 3.30pm, to give you time to get up and down by 5pm. Alternatively to walk across the bridge to Kikko Park and back costs ¥300. At the **information office**, about 10 metres beyond the bridge opposite the car park, you can pick up a leaflet in English – if it is closed there will be some outside.

Even if it seems there are lots of people around, a stroll around Kikko Park feels relaxing and an escape from concrete life; the range of plants and trees adds to the interest and it is also wonderful to hear the sound of birds. A visit to see the **white snakes** 岩国の白蛇 (daily 9am-5pm; ¥100) is worth doing as much to get a copy of the textured pamphlet about them as it is to see the albino snakes themselves; they are designated a natural monument as they are unique to Iwakuni city.

The base of the **ropeway** ロープウェイ (¥320/550 one-way/return trip) for the journey up to Iwakuni Castle is nearby. Destroyed in 1615 at the time of the Tokugawa shogunate **Iwakuni Castle** 岩国城 (¥260) was rebuilt in 1962 and moved to the top of the hill – not for reasons of military defence but to improve the view. There's little of interest inside but, in good weather, the top-floor lookout commands excellent views of Nishiki-gawa, the bridge and the Inland Sea in the distance. In the summer it's a little cooler up here and there are some walking trails.

Kintai-kyo and Kikko Park are roughly equidistant between Shin-Iwakuni, the shinkansen station, and Iwakuni, which is on the JR Sanyo Line: **buses** between Shin-Iwakuni station and Iwakuni station stop at Kintai-kyo bus stop (2-6/hr; about 15 mins from either direction; ¥250 from Iwakuni, ¥290 from Shin-Iwakuni).

**Tokuyama** 徳山 **(430km)** All kinds of shinkansen stop here but not all services. It is also a stop on the Sanyo main line.

**Shin-Yamaguchi** 新山口 **(474km)** All kinds of shinkansen stop here but not all services. Transfer here to the JR Yamaguchi Line for the route to Tsuwano and Matsue (see pp312-16) and for the Lady of Rank steam train (see box below). If heading for **Kyushu**, continue on the shinkansen; see p414.

---

❏ **The Lady of Rank – a grand steam experience**
At weekends from March to November, and daily during Golden Week (late Apr to early May) and throughout most of August, the SL Yamaguchi-go SLやまぐち号 (🖳 c571.jp; 1/day; 130 mins) runs between Shin-Yamaguchi and Tsuwano (see pp284-5). The train's nickname is 'Lady of Rank' in railway pamphlets but those produced by the local government tend to just say 'Lady' or 'The Lady'. All seats are reserved but there are no additional charges for JR rail-pass holders. Without the pass, the fare from Shin-Yamaguchi to Tsuwano is ¥1660.

The train departs in the morning from the old-fashioned platform No 1 at Shin-Yamaguchi and steams along on its 63km journey through the countryside to Tsuwano; it then returns to Shin-Yamaguchi in the afternoon. Rail fans might like to know that the Yamaguchi Line was the first in Japan to witness a steam renaissance, when JNR (see p90) introduced the SL Yamaguchi in 1979. Scheduled steam trains had only been retired from the same stretch of railway line in 1973.

Apart from the steam locomotive itself, the highlight is a ride in one of the five carefully preserved carriages, some dating from 1937 and each designed to recall different eras of Japan's railway history. The best place to sit, however, is at the back of the train, where there's an observation car with (non-reserved) armchairs facing the window. Staff dress up in old railway uniforms and a huge crowd lines up to take photographs as the train pulls out of the station.

HONSHU

The **tourist information office** (daily 8.30am-5pm) is on the 2nd floor to the right of the shinkansen exit and to the left of the local exit. The JR ticket office and a waiting room are also on this floor; *Levain Bakery Café* and a soba bar/stand are at the back of the waiting room. There are **lockers** (¥300-700) behind the waiting room. The **JR bus info counter** is on the 1st/ground floor as is a branch of *Vie de France*. If you need to stay here a convenient option is *Toyoko Inn Shin-Yamaguchi Eki Shinkansen-guchi* 東横イン新山口駅新幹線口 (☎ 083-973 1045, 🖳 www.toyoko-inn.com; from ¥5184/S, ¥7344/D, ¥7884 /Tw, inc breakfast and a curry rice supper). It is a short walk to the right from the shinkansen exit side of the station – and is on the opposite side of the road.

## SHIN-YAMAGUCHI TO MASUDA
[Map 13; Map 14, p287; Table 10, p508]

Distances by JR from Shin-Yamaguchi. Fastest journey time: 95 minutes.

**Shin-Yamaguchi** 新山口 **(0km)** Take a Super Oki LEX (3/day), or a local train on the JR Yamaguchi Line though you are likely to have to change at Yamaguchi if on a local train. From here Bocho bus (8-9/day; approx 45 mins; ¥1170) operates services to Akiyoshi-do (see opposite).

**Yuda-onsen** 湯田温泉 **(10km)** This small hot-spring resort is favoured by Japanese looking for a cure for arthritis and other aches and pains. According to legend, 600 years ago a wounded white fox bathed in the hot spring here and was miraculously healed. A 26ft-high statue of a white fox now stands in front of the station and there are many more fox statues around town as well as a mass of colourful **manhole covers** (see box p522) to look out for; many show scenes depicting the legend of the white fox as well as other scenes symbolic of the town.

It is a very pleasant place to walk around and has six *ashi-yu* (foot-baths) that you can visit – starting with the one at the station. Walk straight down the main road from the station passing Inoue-koen (Inoue Park) on your left. Turn right when you reach a road called Yu-no-machi; soon on your right is **Yuda Onsen Tourism/Ryokan Center** (🖳 www.yudaonsen.com; daily 9.30am-7pm) with a foot-bath outside. In addition to picking up information and maps you can pay ¥200 for a small sake-size cup and then go and drink as much hot spring water as you like before sitting down for a rest in the foot-bath.

To feel part of Japanese history have a night at *Matsudaya Hotel* 松田屋ホテル (🖳 www.matsudayahotel.co.jp; from ¥21,000pp inc half board). The hotel is over 300 years old and is notable as being a place where Meiji Restoration leaders, such as Takamori Saigo (see box p458), met to discuss the future of Japan. There is also a lovely garden here as well as onsen baths. The rooms are Japanese style but there are two single bedrooms. The older rooms are in the main building. The hotel is on the corner of San-In Road and Motoyu-dori, not far from the Tourism/Ryokan Center.

**Yamaguchi** 山口 **(13km)** Off the shinkansen track, if not quite off the beaten track, Yamaguchi must be one of the smallest prefectural capitals in Japan. The

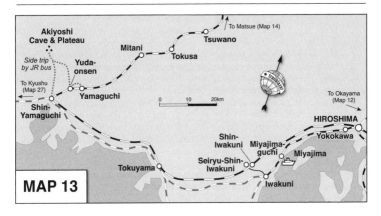

main reasons for pausing here are to visit Ruriko-ji, one of the oldest 5-storied pagodas in Japan, and also Akiyoshi cave and plateau (see below).

**Yamaguchi Tourist Association Information Office** (🖳 yamaguchi-city .jp; daily 9am-6pm) is on the 2nd floor of the station; the map of Yamaguchi also includes Yuda-onsen (see opposite).

**Ruriko-ji** 瑠璃光寺 (daily 24hrs; free) is a Buddhist temple known for its 31m-high 5-storied pagoda which was built in 1442. The pagoda's setting in front of a wooded hill makes it very photogenic. The temple is about 2km north-east of the station so the easiest way to get there is to take the yellow community bus (daily 1/hr; about 10 mins; flat fare ¥200) from bus stand 4 outside the station; Ruriko-ji is the last stop on the route.

About a 15-minute walk from the station is the modern **St Francis Xavier Memorial Church** サビエル記念聖堂 (Sabieru Kinen Seido; daily 9am-5pm; ¥100). The original church, built in 1952 to commemorate the 400th anniversary of Xavier's stay in Yamaguchi, burnt down in 1991. It was rebuilt in 1998 and now has a modern, pyramid design with two 53m-high square towers. The church is on top of the hill in Kameyama Park; to get there walk along the road going straight ahead from the station and, after crossing the river, turn left on to San-In Road, then first right and right again uphill to the church.

### Side trip by JR bus to Akiyoshi cave and plateau

Though not accessible by rail, it's worth considering a trip to Akiyoshi cave 秋芳洞 (Akiyoshi-do) and plateau 秋吉台 (Akiyoshi-dai; daily 8.30am-4.30pm; ¥1200) since the route from Yamaguchi (also from Yuda-onsen) is operated by JR Bus and rail-pass holders can travel for free. The cave is 100m below Akiyoshi plateau and is the largest limestone cave either in Japan or in the Orient – depending on who you talk to, or which leaflet you read. For further information visit 🖳 english.karusuto.com.

From Yamaguchi station, JR buses (8/day; 55 mins; ¥1210) run via Yuda-onsen (40 mins) to Akiyoshi-do Bus Center 秋芳洞バスセンター which is close to the cave entrance. You can pick up a guide to the cave and plateau from the **tourist information desk** (daily 8.30am-4.30pm) in the bus centre. From here, follow the signs to the cave entrance; it is a 10-minute walk through a parade of shops. After buying an entrance ticket, you enter an area that resembles a rainforest; it's an unexpected scene, especially after the man-made shopping arcade just outside. The entrance to the **cave** is no less impressive. The path (about 1km; approx 30-minute walk) is obvious so there's no danger of disappearing down a dark tunnel. You wind your way past various impressive rock formations, some of which have been given unusual names such as 'large mushroom' and 'pumpkin rock' as well as pools and waterfalls. There's no denying that the interior is breathtaking. If visiting in the winter it's advisable to put on several layers as the temperature drops considerably inside the cave. In the summer, the temperature is a good reason for heading on in, to beat the humidity.

At the end of the trail inside the cave, you can either take a lift/elevator to within an easy 300m walk of **Akiyoshi plateau** or walk through tunnels, decorated with images of the plateau, to the Kurotani Exit. The plateau measures some 130 sq km and dates back 300,000,000 years to the time when a coral reef formed in the sea; the karst pinnacles (rocky boulders) that you can see spread over the plateau were once lumps of coral reef. Only 500,000 years ago, rhinoceros, giant deer and elephants roamed around the tree-covered plateau. The plateau even boasts its own 'Akiyoshi thistle'. At the top, there's a look-out observatory, shop and drinks outlet.

To return to Akiyoshi-do Bus Center you can retrace your steps (¥100 to take the lift back down) and walk back through the cave; alternatively, you can walk, or catch a bus down from the plateau.

The Super Oki calls at **Mitani** 三谷 (39km) and **Tokusa** 徳佐 (50km). The final approach to Tsuwano used to have some amazing views of the countryside as the track is quite high on the east side of the valley but since the landslides in July 2013, following very heavy rain, a lot of construction work has been going on to strengthen the track and at the time of research this was spoiling the views. However, looking across the valley you can see the orange of the torii gates at Taikodani Inari Shrine (see opposite).

## Tsuwano 津和野 (63km)

Tsuwano is not the only town in Japan to hanker after the name 'Little Kyoto' but it is certainly one of the most picturesque stops on a journey through Western Honshu. A former castle town of samurai lodgings and small canals filled with plump *koi* (carp), Tsuwano can trace its foundation back over 700 years. During the Edo period (1600-1868), a number of persecuted Christians were banished to Tsuwano, a place presumed to be sufficiently out of the way for the troublemakers to be forgotten about.

The steam locomotive from Shin-Yamaguchi (see box p281) terminates here. **Lockers** (including a couple of large ¥600 ones) are on the left side of the station as you exit. There's a **tourist information office** (🖳 tsuwano-kanko.net; daily 9am-5pm) in a small building to the right as you leave the station; the staff can give you a pamphlet with a map and suggestions of what to see.

Even though it is possible to get everywhere on foot, cycling is easy and particularly enjoyable on the narrow road alongside the river; conveniently there's a **Rent a Cycle** (¥500/2hrs, ¥800/day) across the road from the station.

The colourful **Taikodani Inari Shrine** 太鼓谷稲荷神社 is known for its tunnel of 1000 *torii* gates; these are spread along the path leading uphill to the shrine. It is also considered one of Japan's five greatest Inari shrines. From the top you can walk along to the **ruins of Tsuwano Castle** 津和野城 (Tsuwanojo-seki). At certain places on the walk there are excellent views over the valley and if you are lucky you will be able to see the Lady of Rank steam engine en route to Tsuwano. However, an enjoyable and less energetic way to reach the ruins is to take the **'sightseeing' lift** 観光リフト (Mar-Nov daily 9am-4.30pm, Dec-Feb weekends and hols only; ¥450 round trip), a chair-lift which ascends the hill to near the castle ruins. To reach the lift take the road cars use to reach the shrine and after walking uphill a bit you will see the base of the chair-lift on your left. Walking in Tsuwano's many wooded hills is one of the attractions here but a sign at the top of the chair-lift warns that it is bear country! Another sign gives the days and times the 'Lady' (see box p281) operates so you can watch it steam past; expect the chair-lift to be very popular on these days.

**Tsuwano Catholic Church** 津和野カトリック教会 is on Tonomachi Street in the centre of town. The original was built at the end of the 19th century but then burnt down in 1931; it was rebuilt in 1932 and has some lovely stained-glass as well as tatami-mat 'seating' instead of pews. Tsuwano is unusual in that it has two Catholic churches: the **Chapel of Santa Maria** 乙女峠マリア聖堂 (Otome Toge Maria Seido), which was built in 1951 in memory of 36 Japanese Catholics who were martyred here in the late 19th century, is hidden in the hills behind the station but is worth making the effort to visit; it also has some lovely stained-glass windows.

Virtually all accommodation in Tsuwano is in a ryokan or minshuku. *Hoshi Ryokan* 民宿星旅館 (☎ 0856-72 0136, 🖳 www.sun-net.jp/~hoshi; from ¥7500pp) is near the station and the rooms are spacious and full of interesting objects. The owner is also very friendly and helpful. Follow the road by the rent-a-cycle shop to the right; Hoshi Ryokan is very soon on your right-hand side. Book early if planning to come to the yabusame and also when the steam train operates. For details of other places to stay look at the Tsuwano website.

There is no shortage of restaurants or cafés where you can go for lunch; however, since virtually all the ryokan/minshuku in Tsuwano include an evening meal in the rate, most shut by 7pm.

Festivals are held in Tsuwano throughout the year but it is well worth planning a trip here for the annual display of **yabusame** (Japanese horseback archery; 2nd Sun in Apr) on Japan's only remaining mounted archery course (270m long) at **Washibara-Hachimangu Shrine** 鷲原八幡宮. The shrine is about 2km from the centre of town so a bicycle is recommended.

After Tsuwano, the Super Oki LEX stops at **Nichihara** 日原 (73km). The train then continues north towards the Sanin coast, roughly following Takatsu-gawa (Takatsu River) all the way out to the Japan Sea. If you've already travelled around Shikoku, you might notice the similarity of the landscape – lush and green, with rivers, forests and the occasional village and rice field.

A couple of minutes before arriving in Masuda, the scenery changes dramatically. After a slow journey through the rural spine of Western Honshu, it's a rude awakening to emerge into a sea of smokestacks and factory buildings.

**Masuda** 益田 **(94km)** Masuda is an important railway junction as it marks the end of the line from Shin-Yamaguchi and is the connecting point for lines running along the Sanin coast. There's no need to change trains here for the next part of the route if you're on the Super Oki LEX.

## MASUDA TO MATSUE                [Map 14; Table 10, p508]

Distances by JR from Masuda. Fastest journey time: 2 hours.

**Masuda** 益田 **(0km)** From here two of the three Super Oki a day continue to Yonago, while the other continues to Tottori (see pp317-18). Another LEX, the Super Matsukaze, starts here and also goes to Tottori.

A few minutes out of Masuda, the train finally reaches the Japan Sea, which is dotted with rock formations. The sea here is rough and much less inviting than the calm water of the Inland Sea. For coastal views, sit on the left side.

Some services stop at **Mihomisumi** 三保三隅 (22km), all stop at **Hamada** 浜田 (41km), beyond which the train heads slightly inland, so views of the Japan Sea are less frequent. Some services then stop at **Hashi** 波子 (51km).

**Gotsu** 江津 **(60km)** All services stop here. Change to a local/rapid train if planning to visit Nima (see opposite; approx 1/hr; 23/35 mins) as not all limited expresses stop at Yunotsu.

**Yunotsu** 温泉津 **(77km)** Yunotsu-onsen is part of the Iwami Ginzan Silver Mine and its Cultural Landscape World Heritage site because in the past the mined silver was shipped from nearby ports. It is also a spa town and is popular with elderly holidaymakers. The hot spring here is believed to have been established 1300 years ago as a result of a monk seeing a raccoon use the water to heal some injuries it had sustained. The waters are supposed to help rheumatism, neuralgia, gout, dermatitis and – of all things – whiplash. The onsen part of town is a 15- to 20-minute walk from the station.

---

❏ **The 'singing sand' beach of Kotogahama**
Kotogahama 琴が浜 is named after Princess Koto, a member of the Heike clan who fled north to the Sanin coast after the Heike were defeated by the rival Genji clan in the 12th century. To thank the people who lived by the beach for offering her protection, she played the *koto* (Japanese zither) every day. According to legend, after her death the sand itself began to make a noise similar to that of the koto.

To this day it's said that whoever walks along the beach will hear the sound of the sand 'singing' to them. The science behind this is that the fineness of the sand means it makes a hollow sound when walked on. However, don't bother to go if it is, or has been, raining as you won't hear anything. The closest station to the beach is at **Maji** 馬路, 3km from Nima. Some local trains call there before reaching Nima.

Forest surrounds both sides of the track along this section of the route but you might catch the odd glimpse of the sea.

♦ **Nima** 仁摩 **(86km)**  Just before the (local/rapid) train arrives at this small station, look to the right and you might catch sight of some glass-pyramid buildings, the largest of which is 21m-high and looks a bit like the entrance to the Louvre in Paris. This is **Nima Sand Museum** 仁摩サンドミュージアム (🖳 www.sandmuseum.jp; daily except 1st Wed of month, 9am-5pm; ¥700). The main attraction is a 5m-high hourglass which towers above the central atrium. It is filled with a ton of sand that has been sifted so that no grain is more than 0.13mm and it lasts for one year before needing to be turned over again. As the flow of sand is affected by the outside temperature, a computer is required to regulate the flow and ensure that the year does not end too quickly. Every year at midnight on 31st December, about a hundred people help to turn the hour-glass round and welcome in the new year. It's an 8-minute walk from the station to the Sand Museum; sand fans though may prefer to go to Tottori Sand Museum (see p317).

Nima is also an access point for Iwami Ginzan (see below).

**Odashi** 大田市 **(97km)**  A stop on the limited express and an access point for Iwami Ginzan (see below).

### Side trip by bus to Iwami Ginzan (from Nima or Odashi)

Iwami Ginzan 石見銀山 was a silver mine for around 400 years. A large proportion of the silver mined here contributed to the fact that at one time Japan produced a third of the world's silver thanks to the 200,000 or so miners who worked there. The mines and surrounding area were designated a World Heritage Site in 2008.

The area can be accessed by bus from either Odashi (1-2/hr; 25 mins; ¥670) or Nima (4-5/day; 15 mins; ¥480). Buses go to Omori Town 大森 and the first stop is

MAP 14

Omori-Daikansho 大森代官所跡. Attractions near this include: **Iwami Ginzan Museum** 石見銀山資料館 (daily 9.30am-5pm; ¥500, ¥1000 inc the residences and Sekai-Isan) in the former Government Office; **Kumagai Residence** 熊谷家住宅 (daily 9.30am-5pm except last Mon of every month; ¥500), a former merchant's house; and **Kawashima Residence** 旧河島家 武家屋敷 (daily 9am-4.30pm; ¥200), a former samurai house. You can then either stroll along the road (1km) popping into some of the shrines, temples and shops along the way, or hop back on the bus (1-4/hr; 5 mins; ¥210) to Omori Town bus stop. **Gohyakurakan** 五百羅漢 (daily 9am-5pm but irregular closing days; ¥500), a series of man-made caves with about 500 stone statues of Buddha's disciples, is near Omori Town bus stop.

There is no vehicle access beyond Omori Town bus stop to the mining area (about 2km away) so you must either walk (30-45 mins) or rent a cycle (¥500-700 for 2hrs; additional charge for extra hours). Two of the approximately 600 mineshafts in the area are open to the public. One of them is **Ryugenji Mabu Mine Shaft** 龍源寺間歩 (Apr-Nov 9am-5pm; Dec-Mar to 4pm; ¥410), a 273m long tunnel.

Some of the buses go from Omori to Sekai-Isan Center (7 mins; ¥230). **Sekai-Isan Center** also known as **Iwami Ginzan World Heritage Center** 石見銀山世界遺産センター (🖳 ginzan.city.ohda.lg.jp; daily Mar-Nov 8.30am-6pm, Dec-Feb 8.30am-5.30pm; closed on last Tue of month; fee-payable exhibition rooms 9am-5/5.30pm; ¥300) is the best place to get an overview of the history of the mines and the area.

The entry charges quoted are the standard rates for an adult; foreigners receive a discount of up to 50% on production of a passport.

There are great views of the Japan Sea on the approach to Izumoshi as the train runs on an elevated track.

## Izumoshi 出雲市 (130km)

Izumoshi is the nearest JR station to **Izumo Taisha** (see below), one of the most important Shinto shrines in Japan. Staff at the **tourist information centre** (daily 8.30am-5.15pm) in the station can give you maps and timetables. There are some **lockers** by the north entrance.

Izumo Taisha can be reached by private Ichibata Railway (JR rail passes not valid): Dentetsu-Izumoshi station is a short walk from Izumoshi station and from there services go to Kawato (1-2/hr; 8 mins) where you have to change for services to Izumotaisha-mae (1-2/hr; 11 mins). The whole journey costs ¥490. However, it is far easier to take the bus (2/hr; 28 mins; ¥520) direct from outside the North Exit of Izumoshi station.

Izumoshi is the last stop on the Yakumo LEX (1/hr) from Okayama.

### Side trip to Izumo Taisha

Izumo Taisha 出雲大社, also known as Izumo Ohashiro, is Japan's oldest shrine and at 24m-high the **Honden** 本殿 (main hall) is the tallest wooden shrine building in Japan. Okuninushi, the God of Relationships, is enshrined in the honden so you can expect to see lots of happy couples, but also unhappy ones trying for a spiritual repair job; Lafcadio Hearn (see p312), who himself found love in Matsue, visited Izumo Taisha twice and became the first foreigner to be allowed to enter the *honden*.

Like Ise Jingu (see p240), the main buildings are rebuilt periodically. The fourth rebuilding (*sengu*) in the shrine's history was completed in 2013. As you walk to the main buildings from the shrine entrance you will reach an area with pine trees on either side. The gods are said to go down the middle so worshippers and other visitors should walk on the other side of the pine trees.

It is believed that Okuninushi summons all the deities to Izumo Taisha in the 10th month of the lunar calendar (October) to decide the fate of all people in terms of relationships for the next year. Thus elsewhere in Japan October is called *Kannazuki* ie the 'month of no gods' whereas at Izumo it is *Kamiarizuki* 'the month of gods'. The gods are said to stay in **Jukusha** 十九舎, the buildings on either side of the Main Hall, so in October the doors there are kept open; the rest of the year they are closed. The 13m-long *shimenawa* 注連縄 in front of **Kagura-den** 神楽殿, the Sacred Dance Hall, is the one of the largest in Japan and it is one of the main features of Izumo Taisha.

The whole complex is spread out so be prepared for a lot of walking, particularly if you came by train. However, don't leave Izumo without going down to the **former Taisha railway station** 旧大社駅, now open as a museum (daily 9am-5pm; free); it was built in 1912 but its useful life came to an end in 1990 when the then JNR line here was closed. The Japanese-style wooden building is pretty much as it would have been when it was first built so is very atmospheric and gives an idea how rail travel used to be.

**Shinji** 宍道 **(146km)**  This station is right on the edge of Lake Shinji (Shinji-ko) but trees block all views until just before the train reaches Matsue.

**Tamatsukuri-onsen** 玉造温泉 **(156km)**  This popular hot-spring resort, where it is claimed the gods once enjoyed bathing, is on the shore of Lake Shinji.

During the last few minutes of the journey towards Matsue, there are views of Lake Shinji on the left.

**Matsue** 松江 **(163km)**  **[see pp312-16]**

**Moving on from Matsue**  Rather than retracing your steps take a Yakumo LEX **to Okayama** (approx 1/hr; fastest journey time just over 2½ hours), see pp297-301. Alternatively, the Super Matsukaze LEX (4/day) and Super Oki (1/day) continue east **to Tottori** (122km), which is particularly worth visiting for its sand dunes (see pp317-18); the fastest journey time to Tottori is 90 minutes.

# Western Honshu – city guides

### KOBE 神戸
Kobe is a good place to break a journey along the Sanyo coast. Like Nagasaki, it developed as an international port city and is today a popular tourist spot for Japanese interested in seeing the foreign settlements and Western-style houses that lent the city an 'exotic' feel in the decades following the Meiji Restoration (see pp56-7) in 1868.

The biggest event of the more recent past took place at 5.46am on 17th January

1995, when Kobe was struck by the Great Hanshin Earthquake. Over 6000 people were killed, more than 100,000 buildings destroyed, and much of the city and surrounding area reduced to rubble. But few outward signs of this tragedy remain.

## What to see and do

The attractions in Kobe are quite spread out so, other than in the downtown Kobe area, you probably need to take a train or subway. See pp296-7 for details of side trips from Kobe.

### Around Shin-Kobe  Shin-Kobe station

新神戸駅 is the only shinkansen station in a city from where in a few minutes' walk you can be in the countryside. It is built over the Ikuta River and about 400m behind and above the station is **Nunobiki Falls** 布引の滝 (Nunobiki no otaki); actually they comprise a set of four falls including Mendaki (the 'female' waterfall) and Ondaki ('male' waterfall)! To reach the path go down to the 1st/ground floor; turn left out of the exit and then left again and walk under the station. Within minutes you will be surrounded by greenery. Turn left for the Mendaki falls but continue on up for the much-bigger Ondaki falls. The **Miharashi Observation Platform** 港みはらし台 is a short walk further on and on a clear day is a great place to take in Kobe's geography. If you are enjoying the walk continue on to Nunobiki Dam, one of Japan's oldest but also one that was made earthquake resistant after the Hanshin-Awaji Earthquake. The water in **Nunobiki Reservoir** 布引貯水池 here is what you may end up drinking while in Kobe. There are paths all over the hillside so you can walk for hours, even up to the entrance to the Herb Gardens.

If the weather is good, a ride on **Shin-Kobe Ropeway** 新神戸ロープウェー (cable car; daily 9.30am-4.45pm, till 8.15pm at weekends, holidays and mid July to Aug; one-way/return trip ¥900/1400 inc herb park, ¥800 return trip after 5pm) to **Kobe Nunobiki Herb Gardens** 神戸布引ハーブ園 (🖳 www.kobeherb.com; daily 10am-5pm, to 8.30pm at weekends, holidays and

mid July to Aug), up behind the station, gives you the chance for a spectacular aerial view of the waterfalls and surrounding area. To get the best of both worlds take the ropeway one-way and then walk the other way. The herb gardens have less to see in the winter months, but even so may be of interest to plant lovers. The ropeway is a few minutes on foot from Shin-Kobe station: take the covered walkway from the 2nd floor of the station to Shin-Kobe Oriental City; walk through the building to the other side and then follow the signs.

The **Kitano district** 北野町, about a 10-minute walk west of the ropeway, is known for its Western-style buildings (Kitano Ijinkan-gai; 🖳 www.kobeijinkan.com) from the early 20th century, though many of them had to be reconstructed after the 1995 earthquake. Even though they are probably of more interest to the domestic tourist it is worth popping in to at least one and anyhow it is an enjoyable area to walk around. **Weathercock House** 風見鶏の館 (Kazamidori-no-Yakata; ¥500) is unusual for the houses in this area as part of the exterior is brick. The house was built in 1909 for a German merchant, Mr Godfried Thomas. Sadly the butler's pantry and the kitchen aren't open to the public, but all the other rooms have furniture and you still feel a family could be living here. There is also a good view from the 2nd floor. The house is known because of the metal rooster weathercock on the roof; in addition to showing the direction of the wind it is believed that it wards off evil spirits. Since a ticket to see both this and Moegi House only costs ¥150 more (ie ¥650 for both) it is worth popping in to **Moegi House** 萌黄の館 (Moegi-no-Yakata; ¥350), built in 1903 for Mr Hunter Sharp, a former US Consul General. The red-brick chimney on the top provides a strange contrast with the green clapboard (wood-covered) house. Both are open daily (Apr-Nov 9am-6pm, Dec-Mar to 5pm) apart from about two days a year, usually in February.

On the hill above these Western-style houses is **Kitano Tenman Shrine** 北野天満神社; the shrine dates from the late Heian period (794-1185), so it predates all the other buildings, though the main building here dates from the 18th century. It is worth the effort of climbing up the steps on the right-hand side of Weathercock House (the torii gate marks the entrance) as the shrine provides the best views – unless you have climbed up to the observation platform behind Shin-Kobe station (see opposite).

The Kitano area is full of boutiques, cafés and souvenir shops and **Kitano-cho Plaza** 北野町広場 is a fun place to sit and have an ice-cream surrounded by some of the statues of jazz musicians.

**Sannomiya area** JR's Sannomiya station 三ノ宮駅 is one stop (¥210) on the Seishin-Yamate subway line from Shin-Kobe. (Note that JR uses the katakana ノ for 'n' in the station name though the pronunciation is still Sannomiya).

Sannomiya 三宮 is downtown Kobe and is a great area for shopping, eating and nightlife. A short walk south of Sannomiya station, down the right-hand (west) side of Flower Road, brings you to a flower clock and then to **Kobe City Hall** 神戸市役所. There are great views from the observation deck (Mon-Fri 8.15am-10pm, Sat & Sun 10am-10pm; free) on the 24th floor; it's accessed by lifts/elevators from the glassed-in area to the left of the main entrance. The deck becomes particularly popular during the Luminarie festival (see p294) as it is a great vantage point for seeing the lights.

North of Sannomiya is **Ikuta Shrine** 生田神社 (🖳 www.ikutajinja.or.jp; daily 7am to sunset); it is believed to have been founded in AD201 so is one of the oldest Shinto shrines in Japan. Even though some of the buildings have been damaged, in general it has managed to survive both natural and man-made disasters and the park here is a haven of peace.

**East of Sannomiya** To see for yourself what happened to Kobe in January 1995, head for the **Disaster Reduction and Human Renovation Institution** 人と防災未来センター (🖳 www.dri.ne.jp/english; Tue-Sun 9.30am-5.30pm, Jul-Sep to 6pm, Fri & Sat to 7pm; ¥600). The **Disaster Reduction Museum** (West Building) uses video, dioramas and interactive exhibits to great effect to depict and re-enact the destruction wrought by the earthquake. After seeing the film about the earthquake, and a very moving personal experience of a woman who lost her sister in it, you go to the main exhibition area. If a volunteer approaches you here do accept their offer to guide you round. However, don't go down to the 3rd floor with them until you feel you have seen everything on this floor properly (the main exhibition) as sadly there is no way back up other than on the staff staircase. Even though everything is really geared up for school groups, and if not part of one you are likely to be in a minority, there are lots of labels in English and plenty to look at and learn about, particularly in terms of disaster recovery. Kobe's experience has benefited many others unlucky enough to be part of a similar event.

The **Human Renovation Museum** (East Building), whose theme is the 'preciousness of life', is less effective and could easily be skipped.

From JR Sannomiya station, take a local train one stop east to Nada station (5-10/hr; 3 mins; ¥120). The building is about a 10-minute walk from the station along Museum Road; the road goes straight ahead from the South Exit and under the Hanshin Expressway. Turn right when you reach Hyogo Prefectural Museum of Art (see below); the Institution is a little way along on the left-hand side. It is also about a 10-minute walk from Iwaya or Kasuganomichi stations on the Hanshin Railway.

The vast **Hyogo Prefectural Museum of Art** 兵庫県立美術館 (🖳 www.artm .pref.hyogo.jp; Tue-Fri & Sun 10am-6pm, Fri & Sat to 8pm; permanent exhibition ¥510; additional charge for special exhibitions). Billed as the largest museum in western Japan, the vast space houses an impressive collection of modern art and sculpture, both Japanese and Western. Highlights include print art by Goya, Picasso, Manet, Ernst and Ensor.

Sake has been brewed in the Kobe area for many years and several of the breweries now have museums describing the process. The best is **Hakutsuru Sake Brewery**

**Museum** 白鶴酒造資料館 (🖳 www.hakutsu ru-sake.com; Tue-Sun 9am-4.30pm, closed over New Year and O-bon; free) as it has useful English-language explanations as well as interesting videos on the 2nd floor, where you can compare the modern brewing process with that of 1928.

To reach the museum take a train from JR Sannomiya along the Tokaido Line two stops east to Sumiyoshi station. Turn left out of the station and walk round till you join the main road. Continue left (east) and walk along till the Rokko Liner goes overhead. Cross the road and walk south along the river. Turn right when you meet the private railway line and then left to go under that (through a tunnel), then turn right and keep walking till you see the brewery on your left. It should take 15-20 minutes from Sumiyoshi. If you feel lost, look up: the brewery building has a symbol of a crane on it (Hakutsuru means 'white crane'). Alternatively take a Hanshin Line local train from Kobe-Sannomiya to Hanshin's Sumiyoshi station (3-5/hr; 17 mins; ¥190).

If you are running out of time and want to visit a sake brewery consider **Kobe Shu-Shin-Kan** 神戸酒心館 (🖳 www.shushin kan.co.jp; daily 10am-6pm; free) as it opens till 6pm and has award-winning sake. To get there take a train on the Hanshin Line from Kobe-Sannomiya to Ishiyagawa 石屋川 (3-5/hr; 10 mins) from where it is a 5-minute walk.

**West of Sannomiya** Two stops west along the Sanyo Line by local train from JR Sannomiya station is JR Kobe station, access point for **Harborland** ハーバーランド (🖳 www.harborland.co.jp) and its shopping malls, department stores and small amusement park with Ferris wheel. Head either underground as you exit the station, or overground, walking under the elevated expressway, towards the main shopping and entertainment area.

For a good walk, follow the bay around from Harborland all the way to **Meriken Park** メリケンパーク, a waterside park with some interesting architecture and sculptures and which is popular with young couples searching for a romantic bay view. Meriken Park is also home to the **Earthquake Memorial Park** 港震災メモリアルパーク, an area that has been left as it was on the day to act as a permanent reminder of what happened, since most of the city has been rebuilt.

About a 5-minute walk north of the park, or south from Motomachi station, is a small **Chinatown** 南京町 (Nankinmachi; 🖳 www.nankinmachi.or.jp), a good place to eat and shop. The area is the centre of celebrations during Chinese New Year.

All these places are also stops on the City Loop Bus (see p294).

## Practical information

**Station guide** The main JR stations in Kobe city are **Shin-Kobe** (for shinkansen services), and **Sannomiya** (for main line services) in the city centre. There is also a station called **Kobe** on the JR Kobe Line, which is useful for access to the Harborland District (see West of Sannomiya).

● **Shin-Kobe** At Shin-Kobe the entrances/ exits are only on one side as the station is built into the hillside. You'll find **lockers** (all sizes) straight ahead after the ticket barrier; there are some at the end of the concourse (¥300-500), but go around the corner near the toilets for large ones (¥300-700). On the main station concourse are a few **cafés** and **restaurants** (see Where to eat) and stalls selling the city's best-known souvenir, Kobe beef.

---

### ❏ Shinkansen viewing spot

Shinkansen fans should note that Shin-Kobe is a good place to view the bullet trains speeding past. The station is unusual in that it has only two tracks (no middle track for trains not stopping at the station), so the services that don't stop at Shin-Kobe shoot straight past along the platform edge. A barrier on the platform closes automatically whenever a train approaches so it is not possible to fall onto the tracks.

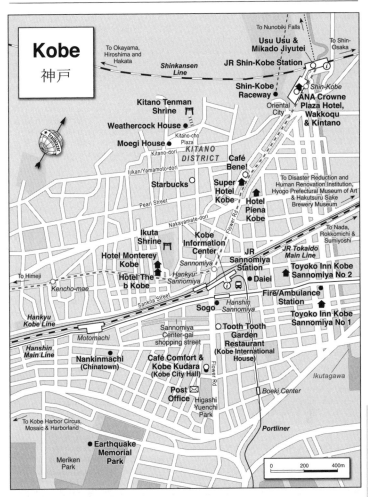

# Kobe

神戸

To Okayama,
Hiroshima and
Hakata

*Shinkansen
Line*

To Nunobiki Falls

**Usu Usu &
Mikado Jiyutei**

To Shin-
Osaka

**JR Shin-Kobe Station**

**Shin-Kobe
Raceway** ●

*Shin-Kobe*

**ANA Crowne
Plaza Hotel,
Wakkoqu
& Kintano**

Oriental
City

**Kitano Tenman
Shrine** 卍

**Weathercock House** ●

**Moegi House** ●

*Kitano-cho
Plaza*

*Kitano-dori*

**KITANO
DISTRICT**

*Ijikan/Yamamoto-dori*

**Café
Bene!**

To Disaster Reduction and
Human Renovation Institution,
Hyogo Prefectural Museum of Art
& Hakutsuru Sake
Brewery Museum

**Starbucks** ○

**Super
Hotel
Kobe**

**Hotel
Piena
Kobe**

*Pearl Street*

*Nakayamate-dori*

*Flower Rd*

To Nada,
Rokkomichi &
Sumiyoshi

**Ikuta
Shrine** 卍

**Kobe
Information
Center**

**JR
Sannomiya
Station**

**JR Tokaido
Main Line**

**Toyoko Inn Kobe
Sannomiya No 2**

**Hotel Monterey
Kobe**

*Sannomiya*

*Hankyu
Sannomiya*

● **Daiei**

To Himeji

**Hotel The
b Kobe**

*Kencho-mae*

*Sankita Street*

**Fire/Ambulance
Station**

*Hanshin
Sannomiya*

**Toyoko Inn Kobe
Sannomiya No 1**

**Hankyu
Kobe Line**

**Sogo** ●

*Motomachi*

*Sannomiya
Center-gai
shopping street*

○ **Tooth Tooth
Garden
Restaurant
(Kobe International
House)**

**Hanshin
Main Line**

**Nankinmachi
(Chinatown)**

**Café Comfort &
Kobe Kudara**
(Kobe City Hall)

*Flower Rd*

*Ikutagawa*

**Post
Office** ✉

*Higashi
Yuenchi
Park*

● *Boeki Center*

To Kobe Harbor Circus,
Mosaic & Harborland

*Portliner*

● **Earthquake
Memorial
Park**

*Meriken
Park*

0    200    400m

HONSHU

The entrance to the **subway** (one stop to Sannomiya station for central Kobe; see below) is downstairs on the 1st/ground floor. The Loop Bus also departs from outside the station here.

● **Sannomiya**  Sannomiya is a major rail junction, with the private Hanshin and Hankyu railways, subway, Port Liner and

JR stations all passing through here. This means that Sannomiya, far more than Shin-Kobe, is the centre for commerce, shopping and entertainment. There are **lockers** (¥500-700) under the railway tracks near the main road and also on either side of the information centre (¥300-700) and plenty of fast-food restaurants, cafés and convenience stores in the area. However, at the time of research the station was undergoing major reconstruction; work is not expected to be completed until 2017. It is then possible there will be a hot spring onsen here as, whilst digging, natural hot water was discovered deep underground on the south side of the station.

**Tourist information** Kobe Information Center (🖳 www.feel-kobe.jp; daily 9am-7pm) is on street level under the tracks for JR Sannomiya station (on the East Gate side). You can pick up maps, leaflets and information about the city and the Loop Bus; there are also restaurant guides for both Kobe beef and patisserie in Kobe, though these are in Japanese. The staff are also happy to assist with accommodation. The **information counter** at Shin-Kobe station (daily 10am-6pm), on the left after the ticket barrier, doesn't have as much information but you can pick up a map for the Loop Bus.

See box p251 for details about volunteer guides.

**Getting around** Kobe has a modern and efficient two-line **subway** (daily 6am-11pm), with signs in English. The Seishin-Yamate Line goes west to east and provides a useful link from Shin-Kobe to Sannomiya (one stop; ¥210). The Kaigan Line loops south from Sannomiya and back round to connect with Shin-Nagata, also on the Seishin-Yamate Line.

The **City Loop bus** シティー・ループバス (🖳 www.kctp.co.jp/outline/car/city loop; daily 9am-5/6pm; 3-4/hr; ¥260/journey, ¥660/day pass) is a tourist bus which does a circuit from Shin-Kobe to Sannomiya, Meriken Park and the Kitano area in around an hour. Route maps are available from the tourist information offices as well as on the bus. Pass-holders get small discounts to some attractions. Show your pass, or pay, the guide/ticket person who stands in the middle of the bus. They may only speak Japanese but announcements and signs are in English. JR-pass holders may prefer to use JR services as JR stations are conveniently placed for many of the sights.

The 1-day **city bus and subway pass** (¥1030) permits unlimited travel on the two subway lines and all Kobe city buses.

Rokko Island and Port Island are man-made land masses off the coast and are accessible from the centre of Kobe via unmanned **light-transit railways**.

Roads are named on most of Kobe's maps but sadly these are not always clear on the actual streets which makes it harder if you are walking around. However, the 'sightseeing maps' on street corners in the tourist areas mean you shouldn't get lost.

**Festivals** As with most cities there are festivals throughout the year.

The biggest annual event is **Kobe Matsuri**, which is held mid to late May and lasts for about 10 days. On the last weekend there's a big fireworks display and a parade of floats through the city.

In late July there is a **Samba Festa** in the Harborland area and in August **Minato Kobe Fireworks Festival** is held in Meriken Park.

The **Kobe Luminarie** has been held every December (4th-13th) since the Great Hanshin Awaji Earthquake in 1995. The decorative lights used in the festival were donated by the Italian government; they are turned on for 3-5 hours every evening and for the first time in 2015 were LED lights making them more environmentally friendly. The event is free but there are donation boxes at various places; there are also stalls where you can buy food and drinks.

**Where to stay** Connected to **Shin-Kobe** station via a covered walkway is the skyscraper *ANA Crowne Plaza Hotel* (☎ 078-291 1121, 🖳 www.anacrowneplaza-kobe.jp; from ¥13,860/S, ¥17,100/D or Tw; buffet breakfast ¥2800, ¥2000 if prebooked), where rooms start on the 14th floor and the best are on the Club Floor (30th-32nd and 37th floors); guests who are staying in a Club Floor room have exclusive access to the Club Lounge (37th floor) where breakfast, afternoon tea and cocktails are served. Facilities include an indoor swimming pool, several restaurants and internet access. Reception is on the 4th floor.

There are two options almost equidistant (about a 10-minute walk) between Shin-Kobe and Sannomiya. *Hotel Piena Kobe* ホテルピエナ神戸 (☎ 078-241 1010, 🖥 www.piena.co.jp; from ¥8500/S, ¥13,300/D inc breakfast), a European-style hotel, with a range of accommodation. The reason most people stay here is for its breakfast: it 'serves a really delicious breakfast including steak, mussels, wing prawns and the biggest range of petit fours and gateaux, all of which are gorgeous' (Georgie Tongue). A cheaper option but basically only with single rooms, is *Super Hotel Kobe* スーパーホテル神戸 (☎ 078-261 9000, 🖥 www.superhoteljapan.com; from ¥5900/S inc breakfast). For both hotels take either the Central Exit of JR Sannomiya station, the East Exit of Hankyu Sannomiya, or the North Exit of Hanshin Sannomiya.

Other budget choices are two branches of the Toyoko Inn chain (🖥 www.toyoko-inn.com): *Toyoko Inn Kobe Sannomiya No 2* 東横イン　神戸三ノ宮2 (☎ 078-232 1045; ¥6264/S, ¥7344/D, ¥8964/Tw), five minutes' walk south from the East Exit of any of the Sannomiya railway stations, and *Toyoko Inn Kobe Sannomiya No 1* 東横イン　神戸三ノ宮1 (☎ 078-271 1045; from ¥5076/S, ¥6480/D, ¥8640/Tw inc breakfast), about another five minutes' walk from the No 2 branch.

There are two hotels a short walk from the north side of any of the Sannomiya stations. At *Hotel Monterey Kobe* ホテルモントレア神戸 (☎ 078-392 7111, 🖥 www .hotelmonterey.co.jp/en/htl/kobe; from ¥12,000/S, ¥14,000/Tw; buffet breakfast ¥1944) the design theme is medieval-era Italy, with whitewashed walls, patio courtyards and fountains. The en suite guest rooms are less ambitious but pleasant enough and have wide beds, free wi-fi and LAN cables. The Italian theme continues at *Hotel The b Kobe* ホテル　ザ・ビー　神戸 (☎ 078-333-4880, 🖥 kobe.theb-hotels .com; from ¥7300/S, ¥10,300/D or Tw) as an Italian-style breakfast buffet is served at Il Alberta Kobe, on the 1st/ground floor. The rooms are stylish and comfortable and the staff friendly.

**Where to eat and drink** Plenty of restaurants serve the famous Kobe beef. This comes from Tajima-gyu, one of the few remaining domestic breeds of black cattle. Each cow has a 10-digit ID number so you can check exactly where your beef came from. The beef is known for its marbling (partly a result of the cows being massaged) as well as its taste and tenderness.

The *Kobe Beef Official Restaurant Guide* (available from Kobe Information Center) usefully points out that 'no cow comes into this world and begins its life as Kobe beef'; only the best Tajima-gyu cows get this designation.

One of the best-known places for Kobe beef is *Wakkoqu* 和黒 (🖥 www.wakkoqu .com; daily 11.45am-9pm; lunch noon-3pm), on the 3rd floor of Oriental Avenue in **Shin-Kobe Oriental City** 新神戸オリエンタルシティ, adjacent to Shin-Kobe station. An evening meal here doesn't come cheap, with set menus starting from ¥8000pp (at lunchtime from ¥3480), though expect to pay ¥14,500 for a meal with Kobe beef. (If this seems too much there are some other restaurants and cafés in Oriental City including places specialising in ramen, teppanyaki and tonkatsu.) Another option is *Kitano* (daily 11.30am-2.30pm & 5.30-9pm), in ANA Crowne Plaza hotel; at lunch time expect to pay ¥5000 and in the evening about ¥13,000.

The area in, around and underneath the railway station in Sannomiya is packed with places to eat. *Tooth Tooth Garden Restaurant* トゥーストゥースガーデンレストラン (🖥 www.toothtooth.com; daily 11am-10pm; lunch 11am-3pm around ¥1500; dinner courses around ¥2750) is a café with a relaxing roof-top garden. It is on the 11th floor of **Kobe International House** 神戸国際会館, Flower Road; to get there take the lift/elevator at street level by the escalator to Kokusai Bldg; don't go up the escalator. There are also other restaurants in the building.

*Café Comfort* フェコンフォート (daily 10am-5pm, lunch menu 11am-2pm), on the Observation Deck floor in Kobe City Hall, serves pasta dishes as well as waffles and ice-creams with the added advantage of a great view; set lunches cost from ¥800. Also on this floor is **Kudara Kobe**百済神戸 (lunch menu 11am-5pm, evening 5-10pm), a Korean restaurant with dishes from ¥1000 and an English menu.

The **Harborland** district around JR Kobe station also has countless dining possibilities (🖳 www.harborland.co.jp). Two big shopping and restaurant complexes close to Kobe station are **Kobe Harbor Circus** and **Mosaic**. The latter is the busiest and also has a cinema complex. Sogo Department Store and Daiei supermarket are also worth visiting if you are self catering.

In Shin-Kobe station try *Usu Usu* 臼臼 for soba and udon, or *Mikado Jiyutei* みかど自由亭, for Western options such as burgers. Both are open all day.

Kobe is a great place for anyone with a sweet tooth: *Kashi's Patri* 菓子sパトリー本 (カシスパトリ) (daily 10am-6pm), at Hotel Piena (see Where to stay), serves cakes (from ¥350) as well as a range of teas and coffees, biscuits (cookies), breads and jams, including 'milkish jam'.

*Café Bene!* カフェ ベーネ (café 10.30am-7pm, shop to 7.30pm) is part of Kobe College of Patisserie so whilst eating a delicious cake you can see the kitchen and future patisserie chefs learning their trade – or tidying up after cooking if you get there later in the day.You can either buy cakes (around ¥360 each) to take away or choose one and sit down and then order a drink; a coffee costs ¥399.

**Kitano Monogatari-kan** was first built in 1907 as a home for some Americans living in Kobe at the time. The building was taken down after being damaged in the Great Hanshin Earthquake but was rebuilt here in 2001 and then opened as a branch of *Starbucks* スターバックス神戸北野異人館店 (daily 8am-10pm) in 2009. It is distinctive as it has the same colours as the Starbucks logo; green and white.

The menu is the same as in all branches, but the advantage here is that you have a range of rooms to choose to sit in including the dining room, living room, guest room or sun parlour.

### Side trips from Kobe

Probably the most popular side trip from Kobe is to the 931m-high **Mt Rokko** 六甲山 (Rokko-san; 🖳 www.rokkosan.com). As with many natural escapes that lie so close to densely populated areas in Japan, the Rokko area has its charms – gentle hikes and views of the Inland Sea – but also shameless tourist traps, such as a museum of music boxes, Mt Rokko pasture and a 'Kobe Cheese Castle' and Japan's first golf course as well as restaurants and shops.

A trip to Mt Rokko can be combined with a visit to **Arima-onsen** 有馬温泉 (🖳 www.visit.arima-onsen.com). Arima-onsen is one of the 'three most famous springs' in Japan, along with Kusatsu (accessible from Shibukawa in Central Honshu) and Dogo-onsen (see pp494-5). The water quality is meant to be excellent and it has a long history of being visited by the Imperial Family and other members of the élite, but the modern hotels that cater to tourists have rather spoiled the atmosphere.

The options for **getting to Mt Rokko/Arima-onsen** depend in part on whether you have a JR rail pass. If you do, take a local train from JR Sannomiya two stops east to JR Rokkomichi, then Kobe City Bus No 16 (¥210) to Rokko Cable-Shita station, the starting point for a 10-minute cable car/funicular ride (daily from 7.10am-9.10pm; ¥590 one-way) to Rokko Sanjo Station from where you can take the mountaintop bus (9-13 mins; ¥260) to Rokko Arima Ropeway Sancho station (approx 12 mins; 1010 one-way) for a ropeway/cable car journey to Rokko Arima-onsen Ropeway station. If you don't have a JR rail pass take the Hankyu Kobe Line from Sannomiya to Rokko station (7 mins; ¥190) and then take Kobe City bus No 16 (as above).

To go direct to Arima-onsen from either Sannomiya or Shin-Kobe take the Hokushinkyujo Railway to Tanigami station (¥540/360); then transfer to the Shintetsu Arima/Sanda Line to Arimaguchi station (4-8/hr; 11 mins; ¥350) and transfer again to the Shintetsu Arima Line (5 mins; 4-5/hr; ¥240) to Arima Hot Springs station. Alternatively take the JR bus (6-8/day; 30 mins; ¥770) directly there from Sannomiya bus terminal – 4/day start from Shin-Kobe – though JR rail passes are not valid.

## OKAYAMA 岡山
One of the largest cities in western Japan, Okayama faces the Inland Sea, enjoys a mild climate and is particularly known for its large stroll garden, Korakuen.

The city expanded politically and economically during the Edo period (1603-1867) but suffered a devastating air raid on 29th June 1945. The extensive damage from the bombing of Okayama has been largely forgotten because it happened just a few weeks before the atomic bomb was dropped on Hiroshima.

### What to see and do
Korakuen garden is the city's star attraction but making time for a side trip to Kurashiki (see pp275-7) is recommended; to get there take a JR Sanyo (Habuki) Line local train (2-4/hr; 14 mins), or a Yakumo LEX (1/hr; 11 mins).

Constructed on an island on Asahigawa, **Korakuen** 後楽園 (🖳 www.okayama-korakuen.jp; daily mid Mar-Sep 7.30am-6pm, Oct to mid Mar 8am-5pm; ¥400) was commissioned in 1700 by Tsunamasa Ikeda, feudal lord of Okayama, and was one of the first gardens in Japan to include grass lawns. It is also one of the 'three great landscape gardens' in Japan – the other two are Kenrokuen (see p226) and Kairaku-en (see p143). The garden is very spacious and includes a large pond, streams, tea and rice fields, shrubs as well as plum, cherry and maple trees. However, the highlight of a stroll around the landscaped gardens is the 'borrowed' view – the

---

❏ **Momotaro – the Peach Boy**
You can't wander around Okayama for long without coming across one of Japan's most celebrated folk heroes: Momotaro, the legendary Peach Boy. A well-known fairy tale begins with an old woman washing her clothes in a river, when she discovers an enormous peach floating by. She fishes it out and drags it home to her husband. Salivating at the prospect of tucking into a juicy peach, the old man takes a knife and is about to cut it when the fruit suddenly breaks in half and a baby boy jumps out. The 'Peach Boy' grows up with superhuman strength and soon leaves his adoptive parents to sail off to the Demon's Isle, where, in the best tradition of good against evil, he defeats the Demon King – with the help of a spotted dog, a monkey and a pheasant he picks up along the way.

Okayama claims the heroic figure of Momotaro for its own, partly because the prefecture is known for peaches but also because the legendary Demon's Isle is thought to be the island of Megijima (see p486), in the Inland Sea between Okayama and Shikoku.

A statue of Momotaro and his entourage on their way to fight the demon stands on the plaza outside the East Exit of Okayama station, and Momotaro's face appears on many of the city's manholes and souvenir products. There's also a road and a tourist information centre named after him and a naked Peach Boy statue (holding a peach) near the South Gate Exit at Korakuen. And every year the town hosts a Momotaro Matsuri (see p300).

HONSHU

❏ **Combination tickets**

Combination tickets offer modest reductions on individual entrance fees: for example Korakuen plus Okayama Castle costs ¥560, and Korakuen plus Okayama Prefectural Museum costs ¥520. However, the latter does not include entry to any special exhibitions at the museum.

black façade of Okayama Castle's donjon looming down from the hill above. An audio guide can be rented at the main gate information centre (¥500; ID or a ¥2000 deposit required). *Fukuda Teahouse* 福田 茶屋, suitably located by the tea plantation in Korakuen, serves matcha (¥500) as well as a variety of ice-creams (peach or matcha soft ice-cream ¥300). The best way to get to Korakuen is to take Bus No 18 (10 mins; ¥140) to Korakuen-mae bus stop.

When you leave Korakuen, the easiest access to Okayama Castle is via the smaller South Gate Exit. For the castle turn to the right and then first left and cross Tsukimi Bridge. However, there are two nice places for a meal here (see Where to eat) and from one of them, Hekisuien, you can **rent rowing boats** (¥800; 20 mins; up to two people) or swan pedalos (¥1800; 20 mins; up to four people).

If you turn left out of the gate a short walk leads you to the **statue of Momotaro** 水辺のももくん (Mizube no Momokun), naked and holding a peach above his head; the statue also benefits from the 'borrowed' view of the castle as a backdrop.

**Okayama Castle** 岡山城 (Okayama-jo; ❏ okayama-kanko.net/ujo/english; daily 9am-5.30pm; ¥300) is known as *Ujo*, or 'Crow Castle', after its black exterior. The original donjon was built by Hideie Ukita, the daimyo of Okayama at the time, but it was destroyed during a heavy WWII air raid; the present reconstruction, using reinforced concrete, dates from 1966. The donjon is an irregular pentagon and the interior is unlike many other castles because it has a lift/elevator and modern flooring. Nevertheless, the castle is an impressive sight as you approach the donjon, with gold glittering from its roof.

The route starts at the top (the 6th floor), with the first two floors covering the

history of the castle, then the final days of the Tokugawa shogunate and finally life in a castle town. Sadly, the labels are virtually all in Japanese.

On the 2nd floor there are some lovely scrolls and screens and the chance to be photographed in a kimono for free (10am-noon & 2-4pm) or in a palanquin, though you can take photos of that yourself. The 1st/ground floor has an exhibition of household utensils as well as a Bizenyaki studio (¥1230 for 60 mins, hourly 10am-3pm) where you can make some pottery.

Take the Okaden bus No 8 to Kencho-mae (approx 3/hr) from bus stop No 1; the castle is a 5-minute walk away. By tram take the Higashiyama Line from the terminus outside the station all the way down Momotaro-dori to Shiroshita (¥100; 8 mins). From there walk along to the right and then first left, following the signs, to the castle; it's about a 10-minute walk.

From Shiroshita tram stop turn left and walk north for a minute to find **Okayama Orient Museum** 岡山オリエント美術館 (❏ www.orientmuseum.jp; Tue-Sun 9am-5pm; ¥300); the collection includes ceramics and glassware mainly from Syria, Egypt and Iran though there are also temporary exhibitions. The displays are well lit and there is some English signage.

A bit beyond the Orient Museum is **Okayama Prefectural Museum of Art** 岡山県立美術館 (❏ www.pref.okayama.jp/seikatsu/kenbi; Tue-Sun 9am-5pm, to 7pm in summer for special exhibitions; ¥350, additional charge for special exhibitions), which focuses on art or artists associated with Okayama; the main exhibition includes both modern and traditional works.

**Okayama Prefectural Museum** 岡山県立博物館 (Apr-Sep Tue-Sun 9am-6pm, Oct-Mar to 5pm; ¥250; additional charge

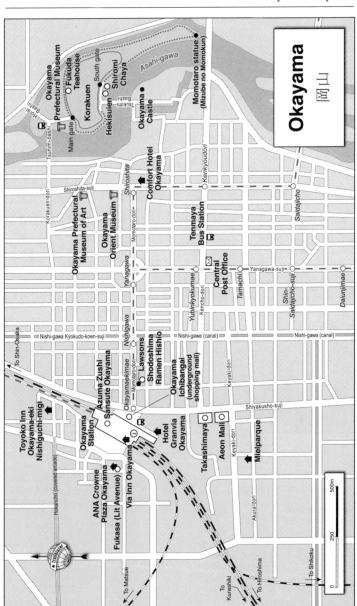

## Okayama 岡山

Okayama Prefectural Museum
Fukuda Teahouse
Shirōmi Chaya
Korakuen
Hekisuien
South gate
Main gate
Hōrai-bashi
Tsurumi-bashi
Asahi-gawa
Tsukimi-bashi
Okayama Castle
Momotaro statue (Mizube no Momokun)

Comfort Hotel Okayama
Shiroshita
Kenkyoudon
Saidaijcho
Shiroshita-suji
Korakuen-dōri
Okayama Prefectural Museum of Art
Okayama Orient Museum
Momotaro-dōri
Tennaya Bus Station
Yanagawa
Central Post Office
Yanagawa-suji
Yubinkyokumae
Kencho-dōri
Tamachi
Shin-Saidaijicho-suji
Daiunjimae
To Shin-Osaka
Nishi-gawa Kyokudo-koen-suji
Nishigawa
Nishi-gawa (canal)
Nishi-gawa (canal)
Azuma Zushi
Sansute Okayama
Shodoshima Ramen Hishio
Lawsons
Okayama Ichibangai (underground shopping mall)
Okayamaekimae
Momotaro-dōri
Keyaki-dōri
Shiyakusho-suji
Toyoko Inn Okayama-eki Nishiguchi-migi
Okayama Station
Hotel Granvia Okayama
Takashimaya
Aeon Mall
Keyaki-dōri
Mielparque
ANA Crowne Plaza Okayama
Fukasa (Lit Avenue)
Via Inn Okayama
Hokancho (covered arcade)
Akura-dōri
To Matsue
To Kurashiki
To Hiroshima
To Shikoku

0   250   500m

HONSHU

for special exhibitions) focuses on the history of the Okayama region with exhibits dating back to the Paleolithic period but also works of art and crafts through the ages including Bizen pottery which is the traditional pottery for this area. To get here take the bus to Korakuen.

## Practical information

**Station guide** Okayama station's **East Exit** (Higashi-guchi) is the main exit for Momotaro-dori, Korakuen and Okayama Castle; the **West Exit** (Nishi-guchi) is the exit for the ANA Hotel and Toyoko Inn.

Okayama is a major junction station with lines from here in all directions. The Seto-Ohashi Line goes to Shikoku, both the Sanyo main line and the shinkansen line have services to west and east. It is also possible to take the Yakumo LEX (on the Hakubi Line) north to Matsue (see pp312-16) and Izumoshi (see pp288-9).

Most **lockers** (all sizes) are on the east side in the far left-hand corner of the station concourse (on the 1st/ground floor). See also Where to eat opposite.

**Tourist information** Staff at the **Okayama City Tourist Information Center** (daily 9am-6pm), on the left as you walk towards the East Exit, can provide an accommodation list but will direct you to Nippon Travel Agency opposite to make bookings. **Momotaro Tourist Information Center** (🖳 www.okayama-kanko.net; daily 9am-8pm) at the end of Blue St in the Ichibangai underground shopping mall, has English-speaking staff and information about hotels in Okayama as well as places of interest in the city and surrounding area but a lot of the brochures are in Japanese. Also worth looking at is 🖳 okayama-japan.jp.

**Getting around** Okayama's **tram/streetcar** network has a terminus in front of Okayama station. Journeys cost ¥100 within the central area, ¥140 to go further afield; a 1-day pass is ¥400. **Buses** also provide a convenient way of reaching the main sights particularly Korakuen; services depart from the East Gate side of the station but also call at Tenmaya Bus Station. Okayama is

also easy to walk around **on foot**; it takes about half-an-hour from the station to reach the main sights.

**Festivals** Various events are held in Korakuen throughout the year. On the third Sunday in May there is a **tea-picking festival**; the new tea leaves are picked and a dance is performed. From late July to the middle of August the garden is also the location for various illuminations.

**Momotaro Matsuri** (see box p297) in early August includes a fireworks display in the area by Asahi-gawa river and people dress up in costumes and parade along the streets performing a variety of dances.

**Where to stay** The JR-run *Hotel Granvia Okayama* ホテルグランヴィア 岡山 (☎ 086-234 7000, 🖳 granvia-oka.co .jp; from ¥14,437/S, ¥18,249/D, ¥22,720 /Tw; 10% discount for JR pass holders) is an upmarket place right outside the East Exit of the station, though it possible to reach the hotel from the 2nd floor of the station without going outside. There is a huge range of rooms, including some Japanese style, as well as restaurants.

More luxurious still is *ANA Crowne Plaza Okayama* ANAクラウンプラザホ テル岡山 (☎ 086-898 1111, 🖳 www.anac pokayama.com; from ¥12,000/S, ¥15,000 /D or Tw; breakfast ¥1800pp), on the west side of the station; the entrance is at street level. It has plush rooms, facilities galore and a stylish ground-floor café/restaurant.

Those on a more limited budget but wanting a convenient location should try *Via Inn Okayama* ヴィアイン岡山 (☎ 086-251 5489, 🖳 www.viainn.com/en/oka yama; from ¥8610/S, ¥10,100/D, ¥13,400 /Tw inc buffet breakfast); it opened in 2012 and offers excellent-value accommodation. The entrance is close to the Central Exit and the reception desk is on the 5th floor (Sansute Western Building).

About a 7-minute walk from the East Exit side of the station is *Mielparque* メル パルク (☎ 086-223 8101, 🖳 www.mielpar que.jp/okayama; Western style from ¥9000/S, ¥12,000/Tw, ¥19,000/Tr; Japanese style ¥12,000/S, ¥16,000/21,000 two/three sharing); there are both Western- and Japanese-style rooms and the rate includes a buffet breakfast. The hotel promotes itself as a place for weddings, so don't be surprised if you see its 'happy bus' outside.

Turn right out of the West Exit and walk parallel to the railway lines to reach a branch of the reliable Toyoko Inn chain: *Toyoko Inn Okayama-eki Nishiguchi-migi* 東横イン岡山駅西口右 (☎ 086-253 1045, 🖥 www.toyoko-inn.com/hotel/00143; from ¥5724/S, ¥7884/D, ¥8964/Tw, inc breakfast). Some rooms have views of the tracks.

Another good choice for the budget traveller is *Comfort Hotel Okayama* コンフォートホテル岡山 (☎ 086-801 9411, 🖥 www.choice-hotels.jp/cfoka; from ¥5200/S, ¥6600/D, ¥9000/Tw, inc continental breakfast), especially as it is close to Korakuen.

**Where to eat and drink** The local speciality in Okayama is *barazushi* (a platter of fresh local vegetables with seafood). One place to try this is at the station: *Azuma Zushi Sansute Okayama* 吾妻寿司さんすて岡山店 (🖥 azumazushi.ecgo.jp; daily 11am-10pm, lunch 11am-2pm; from ¥280 per plate) is a branch of a popular sushi restaurant (with take-out) in Sun Station Terrace (Sansute) off the main concourse of the station.

*Shodoshima Ramen Hishio* 小豆島ラーメンHishio (🖥 www.hishiosoba.com; daily 11am-midnight) serves ramen with an unusual but delicious broth made with Shima shoyu (soy sauce made on Shodoshima) and anchovies. For some reason they call the noodles soba but that is not important. The chef's speciality, Hishio soba, costs ¥700 and a roasted pork fillet soba with a very generous amount of pork is ¥880; they also offer *kaedama* (unlimited soba refills) for any 'soba' meal. To reach it walk along Momotaro-dori and turn right down the road when you see a branch of

Lawsons on the corner; then first left for Hishio. There is also a branch (daily 11am-11pm) on the 6th floor in Aeon Mall.

Outside the West Exit of the station, the 2nd floor of the complex which houses the ANA Hotel has a section called **Lit Avenue** where you'll find a few restaurants. One of the nicest is *Fukusa* 四季菜 (Wed-Sat 11am-2.30pm & 5.30-10pm, often closed on Sun, Mon or Tue), a modern Japanese restaurant where set lunches start at ¥1500 and evening set meals from ¥2100; a Washoku Halal set menu costs ¥5000.

There are two convenient places for lunch after visiting the castle and en route to the South Gate of Korakuen; both offer tasty food and have menus in English. At *Shiromi Chaya* 城見茶屋 (daily 9am-5pm) both tempura and oyster udon cost ¥850 but for something rather unusual try the white peach and grape curry for ¥750. You can either sit inside, or by the river. Next to it is *Hekisuien* 碧水園 (🖥 www.hekisuien.jp; Apr-Sep 10.30am-6pm, Oct-Mar to 5pm; café 9am-6pm, to 5pm in winter) where a kara-age set meal costs ¥900 or a set meal with green-tea buckwheat soba is ¥1200. Hekisuien has an interesting history in that it was built using parts of ships that used to moor here.

There is a selection of cafés, take-out bakeries and restaurants, in **Okayama Ichibangai** 岡山一番街 (10am-9pm), an underground shopping mall on the East Gate side of the station. **Aeon Mall** イオンモール also has a wide range of restaurants (6th & 7th floors; generally 11am-11pm), including a branch of Shodoshima Ramen Hishio (see column opposite). There is a huge supermarket on the 1st/ground floor of the mall as well as next door in the 'Food Maison' at **Takashimaya** 高島屋 (daily 10am-8pm); both provide excellent options if you want to self-cater.

## HIROSHIMA 広島

For many visitors, the story of Hiroshima begins and ends with the dropping of the world's first atomic bomb at 8.15am on 6th August 1945. But it was the city's historical

importance that made Hiroshima an obvious target to the American military.

Hiroshima was the largest castle town in the Chugoku region throughout the Edo period, and it continued to be a centre of political and economic affairs right up to and beyond the Meiji Restoration (see pp56-7), when the city became the seat of the prefectural government. In the decades following the Meiji Restoration the city grew as a centre for heavy industry, while the nearby port of Ujina expanded to become a base for the Imperial Army.

The atomic bomb wiped out the military garrison in an instant but what is remembered is the human devastation – it's estimated that 140,000 had died as a direct result of the bombing by the end of 1945. Some feared it would be decades before grass would grow again, while others believed the scorched land would remain desolate for ever. Clocks and watches froze at 8.15am but time did not stand still after the blast. It took only 17 days to rebuild the railway between Hiroshima and Ujina, and just three for the first tram line to restart. Many survivors took heart in seeing the trams back in service so soon after the blast. In the decades since 1945, Hiroshima has reinvented itself as a centre for world peace and now, as you pull into the station by shinkansen, what you see is a thriving city.

### What to see and do

Most people come to see the Peace Memorial Park but Hiroshima has additional attractions; the side trip to Miyajima (see pp308-11) is particularly recommended.

### The Peace Memorial Park 広島平和記念公園

The park is on the west side of the city, sandwiched between the Honkawa and Motoyasu-gawa rivers. Before the A-bomb razed the city to the ground, this area was Hiroshima's main shopping and entertainment district. The Peace Park contains over 50 memorial statues and peace monuments; details are given of the main sights but it is worth allowing at least a day to explore the park properly. To reach the park take a No 2 or 6 tram from Hiroshima station to Genbaku Dome-mae, or a No 1 tram to Chuden-mae.

The **Peace Memorial Museum** 平和記念資料館 (Heiwa Kinen Shiryokan; 🖳 www.pcf.city.hiroshima.jp; daily Mar-Jul & Sep-Nov 8.30am-6pm, Aug to 7pm, Dec-Feb to 5pm; ¥200) is the one place everybody should visit. Exhibits are in two buildings: the Main Building, which is in front of you as you walk from the Cenotaph (the arch-shaped structure; see opposite), and the East Building, which is to the left. However, the Main Building is closed as renovation work there is expected to last till spring 2018.

Enter the museum on the 1st/ground floor of the East Building – there is a video theatre here, a museum shop and some special exhibits. Take the escalator to the 3rd floor where there is an introductory area and then a section called 'the dangers of nuclear weapons'. There is also an area where you can see video testimonies recorded by some of the A-Bomb survivors – known as *hibakusha* – about the day Hiroshima's sky turned black. Descend to the 2nd floor where you can learn about Hiroshima during the war and how it has recovered and developed since then into a city of peace. The most powerful exhibits are personal objects, such as a twisted pair of spectacles and a mangled tricycle frame but these are exhibited in the main building.

When the Main Building reopens exhibits will focus on the reality of the atomic bomb – the horrors suffered by those who experienced it and the appalling aftermath. For the Main Building audio guides are available.

**Hiroshima National Peace Memorial Hall for Atomic Bomb Victims** 国立広島原爆死没者追悼平和祈念館 (Kokuritsu Hiroshima Genbaku Shibotsusha Tsuito Kinenkan; 🖳 www.hiro-tsuitokinenkan.go.jp; same hours as the Peace Memorial Museum; free) is a national memorial for those who either perished in the blast or who died subsequently from the effects of radiation.

Just across the river, and clearly visible from the tourist office, is the **A-Bomb (Genbaku) Dome** 原爆ドーム, the burned-out shell of what was once the Hiroshima Prefectural Industrial Promotion Hall. A car park close by marks the actual hypocentre but the A-Bomb Dome is the only monument to be preserved as a reminder of the devastation. It was added to the UNESCO World Heritage Site list in 1996.

The **Children's Peace Monument** 原爆の子の像 (Genbaku-no-ko-no-zo) is easily identifiable by the colourful paper cranes draped over it. The monument was erected in memory of Hanako Sasaki, a young girl who contracted leukaemia a decade after the bomb and who sadly died in hospital before she could achieve her goal of making 1000 paper cranes. An ancient Japanese legend holds that a person's wish will be granted if they make 1000 paper cranes.

The annual peace ceremony takes place in front of the **Cenotaph** 原爆慰霊碑, underneath which is a chest containing the names of all those claimed by the city as atomic-bomb victims. By 6th August 2015 the list of names stood at 292,325.

Some of the monuments in the park are more unexpected. Near the tourist information centre lies a large stone, cut from Ben Nevis in Scotland, which was presented to the city as a symbol of goodwill and of the wish for reconciliation and world peace. The base of the **Korean A-Bomb Victims Monument** 韓国人原爆犠牲者慰霊碑 is a turtle because in Korean legend dead souls are carried to heaven on the back of a turtle. There are 2527 registered Korean victims but it's thought that as many as 20,000 were killed. For years the monument was only permitted to stand outside the Peace Park, on the other side of the river. It was finally allowed into the park in 1999.

Other places of interest in the Peace Park (but not marked on the map on p305) are: the **Peace Bell** 平和の鐘, which is rung on August 6th; the **Peace Clock Tower** 平和の時計塔 which rings every day at 8.15am to commemorate the time the bomb exploded; the **Atomic Bomb Memorial Mound** 原爆供養塔, which contains the ashes of those who were killed but whose remains were not able to be identified; the **Peace Fountain** 平和の泉, which symbolises compassion for those who were unable to get water to drink; and the **Flame of Peace** 平和の灯, which has burned continuously since 1st August 1964.

**Away from the Peace Park** Try to fit in a visit to **Shukkei-en** 縮景園 (🖳 shukkeien.jp; daily Apr-Sep 9am-6pm, Oct-Mar to 5pm; ¥260), a beautiful Edo-period garden originally designed in 1620 but destroyed by the atomic bomb. The garden, located on the banks of Kyobashi River, has been fully restored. At the centre of the garden is a pond in which there are some islets and around which there are miniature mountains, valleys, bridges and tea cottages. The closest tram stop is Shukkeienmae (line No 9).

**Numaji Transportation Museum** ヌマジ交通ミュージアム (Numaji Kotsu Myujiamu; 🖳 www.vehicle.city.hiroshima.jp; Tue-Sun 9am-5pm; ¥510), formerly Hiroshima City Transportation Museum but renamed when Numata Driving School (nickname 'Numaji') acquired the naming right (until 31st Mar 2018). The museum has interactive exhibits geared mostly towards children – the train simulator is the most popular – so serious trainspotters will find the place a bit gimmicky. However, there's just about enough here – old train posters, tickets, model engines and the like – to make the visit worthwhile. Pride of place goes to a huge model city, which is either a dream-like vision of how we will all be moving around in the future, or a futuristic urban nightmare, where the quaint idea of walking on foot has long since been abandoned. Outside, there are *omoshiro-jitensha* ('interesting bikes') and battery-powered cars (chargeable).

Rail enthusiasts will enjoy the journey to the museum, by **Astram Line** アストラムライン (🖳 astramline.co.jp), Hiroshima's automated (driverless) transit system, as much as the place itself; take the Astram Line (daily 6am to midnight) from Hondori 本通 station in the city centre north to Chorakuji 長楽寺 (¥400). The museum is next to the large Astram Line office outside Chorakuji station.

**Hiroshima Castle** 広島城 (🖳 www.rijo-castle.jp/rijo/main.html; main keep daily 9am-6pm, Dec-Feb to 5pm; ¥370) is a rather unremarkable 1958 concrete reconstruction of the 1589 original. In the main keep there is a museum about the history of the castle and Hiroshima and an observation platform on the 5th floor with good views. The grounds are free and a pleasant place for a stroll.

## Practical information

**Station guide** Hiroshima is a stop on the Sanyo shinkansen line, the Sanyo main line (for Miyajima-guchi) and the terminus for the Kure Line (to Kure).

There are two sides to the station: the south side for the city centre and the north also known as the 'Hotel Granvia', side for the shinkansen; an underground passageway connects them. The reconstruction work on the north side of the station should be completed in 2017; then the station's layout should be the same as at Okayama!

On the south side, you'll find Asse department store, with **restaurants** on the 2nd and 6th floors and a food hall in the basement. The **tram/streetcar terminus** is outside the South Exit.

For **lockers** (all sizes) on the shinkansen side, head for the far right-hand corner (as you face the exit). At the South Exit, the main bank of lockers (all sizes) is opposite the taxi rank outside: turn left as you exit the station and walk along the station building.

**Tourist information** There are **tourist information offices** on both sides of Hiroshima station. The one on the shinkansen side (daily 9am-5.30pm) is clearly signed on the 2nd floor by the ticket barrier. Staff will help with same-day bookings for hotels in Hiroshima. On the south side, the office (daily 9am-5.30pm) is on street level in a corner of the main JR ticket office. Ask for the *Get Hiroshima* English maps.

The main tourist office in the central part of the city is **Hiroshima City Tourist Information Center** 広島市観光案内所 (🖳 www.hiroshima-navi.or.jp/en; daily Mar-Jul & Sep-Nov 8.30am-6pm, Aug 8.30am-7pm, Dec-Feb 8.30am-5pm); it's in the Rest House on the edge of the Peace Park, just after you cross over Motoyasu Bridge.

**Getting around** Hiroshima is one of Japan's best-known **tram/streetcar** cities; provided the trams don't get stuck in traffic, they are by far the best way of getting from the station to the downtown area. Fares are ¥160 per journey in the city centre but it's probably more economical to get a pass (¥600 1-day, ¥840 1/day Streetcar and Ferry Pass) from the **Hiroshima Electric Railway** 広島電鉄株式会社 (Hiroden) terminal outside the South Exit.

Pick up a map of the tram network either from one of the tourist offices or from Hiroden's ticket booth outside the station. Even if you have a tram pass you will need to put it in the ticket machine when you enter and leave the tram.

The tram routes are numbered 1 to 9 but actually there is no No 4, possibly because the kanji for '4' can mean death). The most useful routes are: Nos 1, 2 and 6 from Hiroshima station for the Genbaku (Atomic Bomb) Dome; the stop is Genbaku Dome-mae. Route No 2 goes to Hiroden Miyajima-guchi for the ferry to Miyajima. For Shukkei-en take Route No 9 from Hatchobori (a stop on routes Nos 1, 2 and 6) and get off at Shukkei-en-mae. For further information see 🖳 www.hiroden.co.jp.

Also worth considering is **Hiroshima Meipuru-pu** (sightseeing loop bus; 🖳 www.chugoku-jrbus.co.jp; ¥200, ¥400 1-day pass, free with Japan Rail Pass; 9am-5.30pm; daily 2/hr). Buses go to all the main sights and with a one-day pass you can hop on and off as much as you want. Pick up the bus from the shinkansen side of Hiroshima station and enter at the front.

A **river cruise** offers an alternative perspective on the city. Subject to the weather, Aquanet Service アクアネットサービス (🖳 mariho-miyajima.com/page20) offers a variety of cruises from its terminal near Motoyasu Bridge, including a daytime cruise (7/day; Mar-Nov Thur-Tue, Dec-Mar Thur-Mon; ¥1200). Aquanet Hiroshima アクアネット広島 🖳 www.aqua-net-h .co.jp/en) offers a World Heritage Cruise incorporating Miyajima (¥2000 one way, ¥3600 return trip).

The **Astram Line** (see p303) goes north to Koiki-koen-mae; Shin-Hakushima

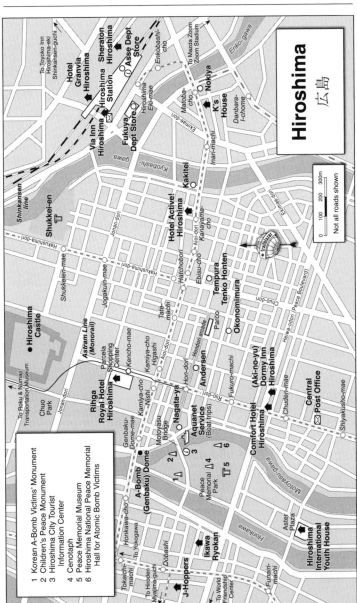

# Hiroshima
広島

**To Toyoko Inn Hiroshima-eki Shinkansen-guchi**

Hotel Granvia Hiroshima

Sheraton Hiroshima

Asse Dept Store

Hiroshima Station

Via Inn Hiroshima

Enkobashi-cho

To Mazda Zoom Zoom Stadium

Nokiya

Fukuya Dept Store

Hiroshima Eki-mae

Ekimae-dori

Matoba-cho

K's House

Kyobashi-gawa

Inari-machi

Danbara-1-chome

Shukkei-en

Shinkansen line

Kakitei

Hakushima-dori

Jonan-dori

Hotel Active! Hiroshima

Aioi-dori

Kanayama-cho

Shukkeien-mae

Jogakuin-mae

Hakushima-dori

Hatchobori

Ebisu-cho

Tempura Tenko Honten

0   100   200   300m
Not all roads shown

Hiroshima Castle

Astram Line (Monorail)

Parcela Shopping Center

Kencho-mae

Tate-machi

Aioi-cho

Parco

Hondori arcade

Okonomimura

Chuo-dori

To Roku & Numaji Transportation Museum

Chuo Park

Jonan-dori

Rihga Royal Hotel Hiroshima

Kamiya-cho Nishi

Kamiya-cho Higashi

Hon-dori

Andersen

Fukuro-machi

Rijo-dori

Heiwa-dori (Peace Boulevard)

(Aki-no-yu) Dormy Inn Hiroshima

Genbaku-Dome-mae

Motoyasu Bridge

Nagata-ya

Aquanet Service (Boat trips)

Chuden-mae

Comfort Hotel Hiroshima

Central Post Office

Shiyakusho-mae

A-Bomb (Genbaku) Dome

Honkawa-cho

Motoyasu-gawa

1

2

3

Peace Memorial Park

4

6

5

Ebisu-dori

To Yokogawa

Tokaichi-machi

Honkawa

Aster Plaza

Hiroshima International Youth House

Ikawa Ryokan

Dobashi

J-Hoppers

To Hiroden / Miyajima-guchi

To World Friendship Center

Funairi-machi

1 Korean A-Bomb Victims' Monument
2 Children's Peace Monument
3 Hiroshima City Tourist Information Center
4 Cenotaph
5 Peace Memorial Museum
6 Hiroshima National Peace Memorial Hall for Atomic Bomb Victims

Enko-gawa

HONSHU

新白島 station connects with Shin-Hakushima on the JR Sanyo main line.

**Festivals** The annual **Peace Ceremony** is held on 6th August inside the Peace Park. In the evening, thousands of paper boats containing lighted candles are set afloat on the rivers and left to drift towards the sea. Also in August is **Miyajima Water Firework Festival**, see p309.

**Where to stay** Book well in advance if planning to visit Hiroshima for the annual Peace Ceremony on 6th August.

Outside the shinkansen (north) side of Hiroshima station is *Hotel Granvia Hiroshima* ホテルグランヴィア広島 (☎ 082-262 1111, 🖳 www.hgh.co.jp; from ¥11,511/S, ¥16,036/D, ¥21,086/Tw inc buffet breakfast), an upmarket member of the JR Hotel group (see also box p71). Despite being right next to the station it's a peaceful place with an impressive lobby, spacious rooms and a choice of restaurants. Also on

this side of the station is the highly recommended *Sheraton Hiroshima* シェラトンホテル広島 (082-262 7111, 🖳 www.sheraton-hiroshima.jp; from 12,750/S, ¥14,250/D, ¥15,750/Tw). The rooms are a good size and, because they are on the 9th-21st floors, offer a great view, especially if you are facing towards central Hiroshima.

*Toyoko Inn Hiroshima-eki Shinkansen-guchi* 東横イン広島駅新幹線口 (☎ 082-506 1045, 🖳 www.toyoko-inn.com; ¥6264/S, ¥8964/D or Tw, inc breakfast) is a 4-minute walk from the North Exit (shinkansen side) of the station.

*Via Inn Hiroshima* ヴィアイン広島 (☎ 082-264 5489, 🖳 hiroshima.viainn.com; ¥6825/S, ¥10,500/Tw, inc breakfast) is a business hotel bolted on to the end of the station building. It's accessed by turning right out of the South Exit: the entrance to the hotel is down an alley between *Café Di Espresso* (where you will go if you want a Western-style breakfast) and *Eki-zen* (which serves a Japanese-style breakfast).

---

### ❏ Hiroshima Carp baseball game

If in Hiroshima during the baseball season (Mar-Oct) consider going to a Hiroshima Carp (🖳 www.carp.co.jp) game at Mazda Zoom-Zoom Stadium. Georgie Tongue describes it as: 'a really fun experience of another side of Japanese culture'.

Hiroshima Carp belongs to the Central League (see pp61-2) though sadly, at the time of research, the last time Carp had won the League championship was in 1991. Hiroshima Carp is unusual in Japan in that it is not sponsored by any company. How fans support teams in Japan is also different compared to elsewhere in the world and this style was started by Carp fans. They form a cheering party and compose theme songs for each player. They also play trumpets and some other music instruments as part of their support whilst a match is happening. Even though Carp isn't a particularly successful team its fanbase is said to be the most enthusiastic, probably because locals feel the team is theirs rather than belonging to a large company.

**Mazda Zoom-Zoom Stadium** MAZDA Zoom-Zoom スタジアム (🖳 www.mazdastadium.jp), where Hiroshima Carp play home games, is the newest home stadium of the professional baseball team in Japan. Its design concept was that anyone can enjoy being there and it seems to be succeeding as the number of female Carp fans, who are called 'Carp girls', is increasing. The stadium is about a 10-minute walk from the South Exit of Hiroshima station.

Tickets (¥1700-4700) can either be bought: at the stadium from 1st March up to the day before a match (11am-4pm on non match days, 11am to 30 mins after a day game and up to 10pm on evening match days); at a convenience store (see box p84) up to just before a match; or from a JR West Midori-no-madoguchi ticket office up to two days before a match. For further information visit 🖳 gethiroshima.com/carp-ticket-guide.

About an 8-minute walk from the station (or two minutes from Matoba-cho 的場町 tram stop) is a branch of *K's House* ケイズハウス (☎ 082-568 7244; 🖥 kshouse .jp/hiroshima-e; dorm from ¥2600pp, Japanese room from ¥2800pp, double en suite from ¥3950pp; sgl occ rates from ¥4800). It has a well-equipped kitchen and a rooftop terrace.

*Hotel Active! Hiroshima* ホテルアクティブ！広島 (☎ 082-212 0001, 🖥 www .hotel-active.com/hiroshima; from ¥6000/S, ¥9000/D or Tw, inc breakfast) is a gem of a place – a stylish hotel at budget prices. You'll even find the words 'Welcome home' on the bedspread! Check out the plasma-screen fire in the lobby. The rooms are small but nicely furnished with flat-screen TVs. Nescafé coffee machines on each floor are a nice touch, as are the trouser presses. It's ideally located near Kanayama-cho tram stop and midway between the station and the Peace Park. The entrance is on the side road, not on Aioi-dori.

*(Aki-no-yu) Dormy Inn Hiroshima* (安芸の湯) ドーミーイン広島 (☎ 082-240 1177, 🖥 www.hotespa.net/hotels/hiroshima; from ¥8990/S, ¥13,990/D) is close to the Peace Park and a cut above the usual business hotel. A bonus is the hotel's own hot spring on the 8th floor. Breakfast is served at the café/restaurant on the 1st/ground floor and in the evening free Yonaki soba (9.30-11pm). Close by is *Comfort Hotel Hiroshima* コンフォートホテル広島 (☎ 082-541 5555, 🖥 www .comfortinn.com; ¥6800/S, ¥8400/Tw), another good budget/mid-range choice.

An upmarket and recommended choice in the downtown area is *Rihga Royal Hotel Hiroshima* リーガロイヤルホテル広島 (☎ 082-502 1121, 🖥 www .rihga.com/hiroshima; from ¥11,500/S, ¥14,500/D, ¥15,000/Tw, exc breakfast). The hotel is in **Parcela**, a shopping and restaurant complex; the entrance is at street level but the rooms are on the 14th-31st floors; some have good views of the castle.

*Ikawa Ryokan* いかわ旅館 (☎ 082-231 5058, 🖥 www.ikawaryokan.net/en; Japanese-/Western-style rooms from ¥4725pp, en suite from ¥4860pp), a 5- to

10-minute walk west of the Peace Park, is a small, modern Japanese inn with friendly owners. Meals (breakfast ¥735, dinner ¥1365) are available if requested in advance.

The *World Friendship Center* ワールドフレンドシップセンター (☎ 082-503 3191, 🖥 www.wfchiroshima.net; Japanese-style room ¥3900pp, inc Western breakfast) is a small house run by a very welcoming American couple. The not-for-profit centre, founded in 1965 to promote world peace, has a couple of tatami rooms as well as a living room where guests may sleep if desperate. It's a clean and tidy place with lots of maps and information. There's no curfew and a ¥1000 key deposit gives you the freedom to come and go as you please. See the website for directions.

*J-Hoppers* ジェイホッパーズ (☎ 082-233 1360, 🖥 hiroshima.j-hoppers .com; dorm beds ¥2500pp, Japanese-style rooms sgl occ ¥3500, ¥3000pp in Tw/D or Tr) has mixed dorms, a female only one and some private rooms. They offer free wi-fi and internet access and also have bicycles for rent (¥700/day or ¥500 if you are staying here).

*Hiroshima International Youth House (Aster Plaza)* 広島国際青年会館 (アステールプラザ) (☎ 082-247 8700, 🖥 hiyh.pr.arena.ne.jp; discounted rates for foreigners: from ¥3720/S, ¥6420/Tw) is just south of the Peace Park in Aster Plaza. The rooms are spacious, brightly decorated and an absolute steal for foreign guests. Facilities include a coin laundry; the only downside is a midnight curfew. Take bus No 24 from stop No 3 (6.30am-10pm; 7-10/hr; ¥220) outside the south side of Hiroshima station and get off at Kakomachi 加古町, from where it's one minute on foot to Aster Plaza.

*Roku* 碌 (☎ 082-221 6789, 🖥 roku-hostel.com/english; dorm beds ¥2800pp, Japanese-style rooms ¥7000/S or D; breakfast ¥400) has mixed dorms, a female-only dorm and private rooms. They offer free wi-fi and internet access and also have bicycles for rent (¥300/6hrs or ¥500/day). It is a 5-minute walk from JR/Astram Line Shin-Hakushima station. Walk to the east along the north side of the road parallel to the JR line; Roku is behind 7-Eleven at the intersection of Hakushima-dori.

See also pp67-73. For accommodation on Miyajima see pp310-11.

**Where to eat and drink** Hiroshima is known for *kaki* (oysters) and also for *okonomiyaki* (savoury pancakes). The best place to try the latter, and possibly also one with kaki, is at **Okonomimura** お好み村 (🖳 www.okonomimura.jp), a building packed with three floors (2nd-4th) of small okonomiyaki places; some have menus in English. Most are open for lunch (daily 11.30am-2pm) and again in the evening (about 5-11pm). Expect to pay ¥700-1600. Okonomimura is about a 3-minute walk from Hatchobori tram stop. The entrance is opposite the underground car park on the paved plaza behind Hiroshima Parco department store.

If you're in or around Hiroshima station, head for the 2nd floor of **Asse** アッセ, a department store, where you'll find a row of okonomiyaki places, the best of which (and hence the one with the longest queues at lunchtime) and with a menu in English is **Reichan** 麗ちゃん. Alternatively, try **Oimatsu** 老松; at either expect to pay around ¥1350.

Another recommended place by the station is **Goemon** 五エ門 (🖳 www.goe mon.in/menu/index; 11am-10pm); it is on the 10th floor of **Fukuya** 福屋 department store in front of Hiroshima station. Okonomiyaki 'Powerful' (with soba or udon noodles, pork and egg) costs ¥700; the 'special' (¥1000) or 'de luxe' (¥1200) versions have a variety of ingredients but you can also choose your own toppings (from ¥100 per topping).

*Nagata-ya* 長田屋 (🖳 nagataya-oko nomi.com/en; Wed-Fri & Mon 11am-8.30pm, Sat 11am-9pm, Sun 10.30am-8.30pm, closed Tue and 4th Wed of month) serves great okonomiyaki (from ¥810) including vegetarian options and has an English menu. It's on the left before you cross Motoyasu Bridge.

There are plenty of places along the covered **Hondori** 本通 shopping arcade, including the enormous branch of *Andersen* アンデルセン (daily except 3rd Wed 11am-9.30pm), which has a bakery and deli on the 1st/ground floor and a 2nd-floor restaurant serving a hearty kitchen buffet (Mon-Fri 6-9.30pm, Sat & Sun 5-9.30pm; ¥4720).

For fantastic tempura go to *Tempura Tenko Honten* 天冨良天甲本店 (daily 11.30am-2pm & 5.30-9.30pm; closed in peak periods such as Golden Week and mid August); the set lunch/tasting menu (from ¥3500) includes a selection of vegetables and fish which are cooked in front of you; you will be shown which seasoning sauce to have for each piece you are given. Note that the restaurant is on the 2nd floor. If your budget is more limited *Nokiya* 乃きや (11am-9pm), on the left-hand side by Matoba-cho 的場町 tram stop, serves delicious tempura udon.

By Kanayama-cho 銀山町 tram stop are some riverside bistros including *Kakitei* 牡蠣亭 (🖳 www.kakitei.jp; Wed-Mon 11am-2.30pm & 5-9.30pm), where you can try Hiroshima's oysters served in a myriad of ways including: grilled ¥600; quiche of oysters with seasonal vegetables ¥800; in a seafood salad ¥1000; and fried ¥1200.

For further information about places to eat in Hiroshima visit 🖳 visithiroshima .net/dining.

## Side trips from Hiroshima
Hiroshima is a good base for several side trips. The one that should be on everyone's itinerary is to Miyajima.

**To Miyajima** Famous for its iconic *o-torii* 大鳥居 (shrine gate) that rises out of the sea, **Itsuku-shima Shrine** 厳島神社 is considered one of the top three scenic spots in Japan and is the main attraction on the island of Miyajima 宮島; officially called Itsuku-shima 厳島 (Itsuku Island). Other good reasons to make this side trip are the opportunity to hike to the top of Mt Misen (see p310), a free ferry ride if you have a JR Pass or Hiroden Streetcar and Ferry pass, and the chance to visit somewhere that has no traffic lights or convenience stores.

Since Miyajima Island is regarded as an object of worship, childbirth and burial have never been permitted on the island as both are seen as being unclean. Although few think like that now it is still not possible to give birth or be buried here.

From Hiroshima, JR rail-pass holders should take a local train eight stops westbound along the JR Sanyo Line to Miyajima-guchi 宮島口 (2-7/hr; 30 mins). Alternatively, if you have a Hiroden Pass take tram/streetcar No 2 to Hiroden Miyajima-guchi (3-9/hr; 70 mins; ¥260).

At Miyajima-guchi, walk straight down the road from the station to the **ferry terminal**. From here, JR West ferry services (🖳 www.jr-miyajima ferry.co.jp; daily 6am-11pm; 2-4/hr; ¥360 return, free to JR rail-pass holders) take 10 minutes to Miyajima. JR shares the terminal with Matsudai Ferry, which runs an identical service; the Hiroden Streetcar and Ferry Pass (see Getting around, p304) is valid for this ferry.

The **tourist information desk** 観光案内所 (🖳 www.miyajima.or.jp; daily 9am-6pm) inside Miyajima ferry terminal can help book accommodation and also has a tide timetable (useful for working out when to see the torii gate at high and also low tide). There are **lockers** (¥200-500) outside the ferry terminal. **A free shuttle bus** 無料送迎バス (3/hr; 10am-5pm) runs to the base of the ropeway (see p310). **Aquanet Hiroshima** アクアネット広島 (🖳 www .aqua-net-h.co.jp) offers a 'Light up' cruise (six per evening from about 6pm; 30 mins; ¥1600) from No 3 pier to the O-torii and if the tide is right you can go through the torii gate. Reservations are essential and can be done by email through the website. Another option is to take the train/tram and ferry here and return to Hiroshima by boat on one of Aquanet's services.

Expect to see **deer** everywhere when you get off the ferry; you may be chased if you are carrying food. Gluttons for punishment can even pay ¥200 for deer food and watch the ensuing chaos.

According to legend, **Itsuku-shima Shrine** 厳島神社 (6.30am-5.30/6pm; ¥300) was founded in 593 when three goddesses were led to Miyajima by a crow. It was remodelled in its present structure, with long corridors connecting the main shrine halls, in 1168 and is now a World Heritage Site. Noh performances are occasionally staged at the shrine, which has even seen the occasional fashion show – the 202m-long corridors doubling as the perfect catwalk. Be aware that the route through the shrine is one-way only. The real attraction of the shrine is the o-torii gate rising out of the sea (or, depending on the tide, sticking out of the silt) 200m from the main shrine. At high tide the gate (16m high) appears to float in the water. The first gate here was built in 1168; the current one was constructed in 1875. It is made of camphor wood and covered with vermilion lacquer as that helps protect it from corrosion; the vermilion colour is also believed to keep evil spirits away. It's worth planning several hours on the island so you have a chance to see the gate at both high and low tide. The o-torii gate is the focal point for the spectacular **Miyajima Water Fireworks Festival** held offshore here on August 11th (7.40-8.40pm).

The Buddha of Medicine is enshrined in **Gojunoto** 五重塔, a 5-storied 27m-high pagoda that is easily visible from the shrine. **Daisho-in Temple** 大聖院, at the bottom of Mt Misen, dates from the 12th century and had close

HONSHU

links with the Imperial Family until the 19th century. As you walk up to the temple you pass 500 small statues with unique facial expressions. The temple is also the site of an impressive **Fire-Walking Ceremony** (Hiwatarishiki) held twice a year (15th Apr & 15th Nov from 11am).

At 530m, **Mt Misen** 弥山 is the highest peak on Miyajima and there are excellent hiking trails (see below) to its summit as well as a **ropeway/cable car** ロープウエー (🖳 miyajima-ropeway.info/en; daily Mar-Oct 9am-5pm, 8.30am-5.30pm in Golden Week and Obon; Nov 8am-5pm; Dec-Feb 9am-4.30pm; ¥1000/1800 one-way/return; closed for safety checks twice a year, usually for about five days in June & Dec) from Momijidani-koen 紅葉谷公園. It is an easy walk up from Itsuku-shima shrine to the base of the ropeway.

Each of the three main **hiking trails** takes about 1½-2 hours to the top of Mt Misen; the routes are outlined on a map available from the tourist information desk at the ferry terminal. The **Momiji-dani** 紅葉谷 **(Maple Valley) route** is the shortest but steepest; it is lovely at any time of the year but particularly recommended in the autumn. It starts from near the base of the ropeway. The **Daisho-in route** starts at Daisho-in Temple; it is the least steep route and also offers good views. The other route, the **Omoto Route** starts from Omoto Shrine 大元神社, which is beyond Itsuku-shima Shrine, but meets the Daisho-in route before you reach the top. The paths are generally easy to follow and not really challenging. However, make sure you stick to them to avoid treading on any snakes and carry water in the summer as it can get very hot.

As you near the top follow signs to **Shishi-iwa observatory** 獅子岩展望台 (it is near the top of the ropeway) for great views over the Inland Sea. If you are lucky you might also see wild monkeys grooming the deer, especially if the latter are resting. There is a *café* (open during ropeway hours) under the viewing platform as well as a vending machine. Then head to the summit of Mt Misen.

Even if you take the ropeway (in fact a gondola journey followed by a cable car) you still need to walk for about half an hour to reach the very top of Mt Misen; the path descends first before climbing uphill so don't worry that you have taken the wrong turn.

If you haven't hiked all the way up, do consider making the descent on foot. The Momiji-dani route (45-60 mins) takes you through Momiji-dani-koen where there are places to eat and stay. The menu at *Momiji-chaya*, a café belonging to Momiji-so, includes a variety of *udon* (¥700) as well as curry rice (¥650); place your order and then sit at one of the tables outside and admire the view. If the thought of leaving this spot is too much a stay at *Momiji-so* もみぢ荘 (☎ 0829-44 0077, 🖳 www.gambo-ad.com; ¥8640pp room only, ¥17,280pp inc half board) is highly recommended; if booked in advance they will pick you up from the port.

Also in Momiji-dani-koen and with an onsen, is a ryokan called *Iwaso* 岩惣 (☎ 0829-44 2233, 🖳 www.iwaso.com; from ¥22,680pp for half board and two sharing). The rooms are in a variety of buildings and not all are en suite. Both these places are close to the ropeway/cable car which runs up to Mt Misen.

*Watanabe Inn* 四季の宿 わたなべ (☎ 0829-44 0234, 🖳 www.auberge-watanabe.com; from ¥17,280pp inc half board) as far as Georgie Tongue is concerned is 'superb'. The Inn only has four rooms but each has its own cypress wood bath. It is near Daisho-In Temple, about a 30-minute walk from the port.

If you prefer to be by the sea, *Miyajima Seaside Hotel* 宮島シーサイド
ホテル (☎ 0829-44 0118, 💻 www.gambo-ad.com; from ¥12,000pp inc half
board) is recommended though it is a little way from the main sights; if
requested in advance they can pick you up from the ferry terminal.

Right by the ferry terminal, and a place that also comes highly recommended, is *Kinsui Villa* 錦水別荘 (toll free in Japan ☎ 0120-44 2193, ☎ 0829-
44 2191, 💻 www.kinsui-villa.jp/en; from ¥15,000pp inc half board). There are
some single rooms in the loft but the stairs are steep. Online reservation in
Japanese only.

There are plenty of other accommodation options on Miyajima; ask at the
tourist information office. However, at peak times (autumn and spring) it is
worth booking well in advance.

The cheapest place to stay is back **on the mainland** at *Backpackers
Miyajima* バックパッカーズ宮島 (☎ 0829-56 3650; 💻 www.backpackers-
miyajima.com; Western-/Japanese-style dorm ¥2900pp). The hostel has cooking facilities, free wi-fi as well as free internet access. Walk down the road
from Miyajima-guchi station and keep walking past the ferry terminal. Take
the second road to the right and the hostel is on the left.

**To Yokogawa**  Yokogawa is a minor place of pilgrimage for omnibus fans.
It is the second stop along the Sanyo Line (to Iwakuni) from Hiroshima; alternatively take a tram (Hiroden Yokogawa Line).

The first omnibus to operate in Japan started service in Kyoto in 1903 but
it only had five seats. Thus people who live in Yokogawa claim that the first
omnibus service was the one that started here on February 5th 1905 since that
bus had 12 seats amd the current law defines that an omnibus should be a vehicle that more than 11 people can ride. The 15km route was between Yokogawa
and nearby Kabe. The bus was manufactured in Japan using an American
engine and parts, and passengers were charged a fare of 24 *sen* (by comparison, a horse-drawn carriage cost 15 *sen*). Sadly, the tyres could not cope with
the bumpy road conditions and the service was halted after just nine months.
A replica of the original bus, painstakingly put together by a local club of
omnibus enthusiasts from the only surviving photo of the original vehicle, is
on display – encased in glass – in front of Yokogawa station. Unlike many old
steam engines, which are left to gather dust on sidings in many parts of the
country, this replica is kept gleaming.

A sign by the replica suggests that 'we intend to preserve this monument
eternally as a symbol of the birthplace of Japan's first omnibus and as a force
to breathe new life into the Yokogawa area in future'.

**To Kure**  Another possible side trip by rail is to the seaside town of Kure, just
over 30 minutes south-east of Hiroshima on a rapid train (2/hr; local train also
2/hr, 46 mins) on the JR Kure Line. The journey is very scenic as the line runs
near the sea and you can see many of the islands in the Seto Inland Sea.

A 5-minute walk from Kure station towards the coast is the **Yamato
Museum** 大和ミュージアム (also known as Kure Maritime Museum and
Kure City Naval History & Science Museum; 💻 www.yamato-museum.com;
daily mid July to end Aug 9am-6pm; rest of year Wed-Mon 9am-6pm; ¥500,
free audio guide), which displays a 1/10th reproduction of what was at one
time the world's largest battleship.

The *Yamato* was launched from Kure in 1941 but sank four years later during a suicide mission to attack the United States fleet on American-held Okinawa. On display are the handwritten wills of some of the 2475 sailors who perished on board.

To add a bit of luxury take the **Setouchi Marine View** (⌨ www.jr-odekake.net/train/marineview; 44 mins; 1/day Sat & Sun Mar to late Sep, daily in Aug; ¥500, free with JR Pass; reserved seat ¥520) sightseeing train from Hiroshima all the way to Mihara. The round windows are to make it seem like being in a ship. The scenery, though, is the same on a local train and they operate more frequently (1-2/hr; 2hrs 48 mins from Hiroshima), but you will have to change at Hiro.

## MATSUE 松江

*'There seems to be a sense of divine magic in the very atmosphere, through all the luminous day, brooding over the vapoury land, over the ghostly blue of the flood – a sense of Shinto'.*

Thus wrote **Lafcadio Hearn** of Matsue's Lake Shinji, which glistens to your left as the train pulls into Matsue station from Masuda. The seventh largest lake in Japan is unusual in that it's a combination of fresh and sea water, depending on the tide.

Divided by Ohashi-gawa (Ohashi river), on the shores of Lake Shinji, with a moat around the castle and with one of the highest rainfalls in Japan, Matsue well deserves its title 'City of Water'. It is an old castle town and the perfect place to break a journey along the Sanin coast. Lafcadio Hearn (1850-1904) took up an English-teaching appointment here in 1890; though he only lived in Matsue for 15 months, his former residence is now one of the city's big draws.

In his time here he met and married Setsu Koizumi, the daughter of a local samurai family, and he also became Japanese (his Japanese name is Yakumo Koizumi). He was unusual enough just being a foreigner in Japan at this time let alone marrying a Japanese. In his books Hearn often voiced his regret that Meiji-era Japan, in its rush to catch up on centuries of isolation from the outside world, was abandoning many of its ancient traditions. He would probably have been dismayed at the tourist industry that has grown up around his name. As well as the usual postcards, souvenir trinkets and T-shirts, more unusual Matsue souvenirs include Hearn chocolates and bottles of locally brewed Lafcadio Hearn beer.

### What to see and do

Matsue has a lot to see and do; it is also a good base for day trips to several notable places: to the east are **Adachi Museum of**

---

### ❏ Matsue – City of love as well as City of water?

Izumo Taisha Shrine (see pp288-9) has always been known as a place for people to go if looking for luck in love. Matsue's main association has been as a 'city of water' (see p314) but it is now developing *enmusubi* ('good fortune in love') tourism and has created some places for young women and couples to go to in search of romantic reassurance – often places that have had no particular romantic associations in the past. Look out for heart shapes as you go around Matsue Castle – one has also been cut into one of the 100-year-old pine trees along Shiomi Nawate, the street by the north moat of the castle. And a normal postbox in Karakoro Kobo (see opposite) has been painted pink. By the time you reach Matsue there may be many more symbols of love to look for. Given the city's scenic location and its reputation for beautiful sunsets it is not surprising Matsue is developing an association with romance.

**Art** (see pp316-17) and **Tottori's sand dunes** (see pp317-18), and 30km to the west is **Izumo-Taisha** (see pp288-9).

**Station area** To get orientated in Matsue itself and – on a clear day – enjoy a stunning view of Lake Shinji and the castle, take the express lift/elevator up to the 14th floor of the **San-In Godo Bank** 山陰合同銀行 headquarters (the tallest building in town), at 10 Uo-Machi, a 10- to 15-minute walk from the station. The lift is hidden in a corner of the 1st/ground floor and there are no signs in English, but bank staff will point you in the direction of the observation gallery (daily 9am-5pm). On a bright day you can see as far as Mt Daisen (1711m), over 50km away.

If you can't be in Matsue for the drum festival (see p315) you can still see some of the drums in the **Drum Display** 鼕伝承館 on the right-hand side as you walk towards the lake; press the button for an explanation in English (8am-8pm).

**Shimane Art Museum** 島根県立美術館 (Shimane Kenritsu Bijutsukan; 🖥 www1.pref.shimane.lg.jp/contents/sam; Mar-Sep Wed-Mon 10am to 30 mins after sunset, Oct-Feb 10am-6.30pm; ¥1000, or ¥500 for foreign visitors) is in a modern glass building on the banks of Lake Shinji. Come here just before dusk to watch the sun set over the tiny tree-studded island in the lake. The museum contains both Japanese- and Western-style paintings and prints. There are also several **sculptures** outside the museum – look out for the rabbits and the monument to Lafcadio Hearn, who loved observing the sunset here.

The best time to come to this area is for the sunset; walk along the lakeshore from the museum to the official **sunset viewpoint** 宍道湖夕日スポット.

**Matsue Castle area** From Matsue station, take the Lakeline Bus (see p314) to the castle and then walk between the sights described below, all of which are open daily (Apr-Sep 8.30am-6.30pm, Oct-Mar to 5pm).

**Matsue Castle** 松江城 (Matsue-jo; ¥560, or ¥280 for foreign visitors) was built by the feudal lord Yoshiharu Horio in 1611. In 1875 all the buildings here other than the donjon and the castle wall were destroyed. The fact that the donjon (castle keep/tower) was kept means the castle is deemed one of 12 original castles in Japan and it was designated as a National Treasure in 2015. The other buildings were reconstructed in the 1950s. Hearn often climbed the donjon, which he described as 'grotesquely complex in detail, looking somewhat like a huge pagoda'. Exhibits inside include the original dolphin- and gargoyle-shaped roof tiles and scale models of the castle and city over which it once presided. But the best part is the tremendous view from the top-floor observation gallery. For a different perspective take the **Horikawa Sightseeing Boat** (see p314).

**Shiomi Nawate** 塩見縄手, a stop on the Lakeline Bus, is a street where some samurai houses 武家屋敷 (buke-yashiki), built in the 18th century, are preserved. One, the home of a middle-ranking samurai family, is open (daily 9am-4.30pm; ¥300, or ¥150 for foreign visitors) and contains domestic items from the Edo period giving an idea about life here at that time. See also Where to eat, p316.

The **Lafcadio Hearn Memorial Museum** 小泉八雲記念館 (daily Apr-Sep 8.30am-6.30pm, Oct-Mar to 5pm; ¥300, or ¥150 for foreign visitors) exhibits objects from Hearn's house and his stay in Matsue. Unusual items include a pair of iron dumbbells and a trumpet shell which Hearn 'blew half for fun when he wanted his maid to bring him a light for his tobacco'. Look out also for the high desk Hearn used to compensate for his poor eyesight. Next door, **Lafcadio Hearn Former Residence** 小泉八雲旧居 (daily Apr-Sep 8.30am-6.30pm, Oct-Mar to 5pm; ¥300, or ¥150 for foreign visitors) is now bare but there's a useful leaflet that describes how the rooms would have looked in Hearn's day. The small house looks out onto an even-smaller Japanese garden that's similar to the one Hearn enjoyed when he lived in Kumamoto (see p452).

**Karakoro Kobo** カラコロ工房 (daily 9.30am-6.30pm), in the former Bank of

HONSHU

Japan building on the north side of Ohashi-gawa, houses temporary art exhibitions, a café, restaurant as well as art and craft shops and a pink post box (see box p312). The word 'karakoro' comes from Lafcadio Hearn; it's said that when Hearn woke up after his first night in Matsue, he heard the noise of wooden geta shoes in the street outside his ryokan. To Hearn's ears, the noise each footstep made was 'kara, koro, kara, koro'.

### Matsue Shinjiko-onsen area

Matsue Shinjiko-onsen 松江しんじ湖温泉 is the city's hot-spring resort; it is on the banks of Lake Shinji close to Ichibata Railway's Matsue Shinjiko-onsen station. The source of the spring is 1250m underground, near the lakeshore. At source, the water temperature is around 77°C, though it's cooled down by the time it reaches the bath-houses of the lakeside hotels and ryokan. The best way to enjoy the area is to stay at one of these hotels (see p316), most of which have their own hot spring with a lakeside view.

If this isn't an option you can always soak your feet in the **foot-bath** (*ashi-yu*) outside Matsue Shinjiko-onsen station. It's open all hours and has a cover to protect both you and the water if it's raining. To reach the resort, take the Lakeline Bus from outside Matsue station.

### Practical information

**Station guide** Matsue station has two exits; the North Exit is the one for tourist information and the bus platforms. You'll find **lockers** of all sizes in a corner of the station concourse. As you leave the ticket barrier, on your left is the **JR ticket office** (daily 5.15am-10.30pm).

The branch of the *Little Mermaid bakery*, beyond *Starbucks* as you walk left out of the station, offers everything from cakes and buns to slices of pizza – perfect for a lakeside picnic. A variety of **ekiben** are sold in the stand on the right-hand side of the North Exit on the main concourse; the *kanizushi* (strips of crab meat on a bed of rice) is recommended. For details of other restaurants in and around the station see Where to eat.

### Tourist information

Matsue International Tourist Information Office (💻 www.visit-matsue.com; daily 9am-6pm) is in the modern glass building to the right outside the North Exit of the station. Staff can provide a walking map and a map in English showing the City/Lakeline bus route (but passes for travel on the buses have to be bought on the bus) as well as details about the various boat tours. They can also assist with accommodation booking and sell various passes and tours (see Getting around).

### Getting around

Matsue is a lovely place to walk around and the central area is very compact, but if you prefer four wheels hop on the retro tourist **Lakeline Bus** レイクライン (daily Mar-Nov 8.40am-5.55pm, Dec-Feb 8.40am-5.10pm; 3-4/hr; ¥200/journey, ¥500 one-day pass, ¥1000 2-day pass inc city buses), which departs from bus stop No 7 at the station and runs in a loop around the city. In some cases it may be quicker to walk between the attractions rather than wait for the bus and also to get back to the station from the castle area as the bus route from there goes a long way around the city and only in one direction.

As the 'City of Water', Matsue naturally enough offers opportunities for enjoyable boat rides. **Horikawa Sightseeing Boat** 堀川めぐり (💻 www.matsue-horika wameguri.jp; daily Mar-June & Sep-Oct 9am-5pm, Jul-Aug to 6pm, Dec-Feb to 4pm; 3-4/hr; ¥1640, or ¥820 for foreign visitors) does a 50-minute cruise around the moat of Matsue Castle. The boats have to pass under some very low bridges but this is Japan so a flick of the switch lowers the boat canopy and allows a safe passage underneath. There are three boarding points (see map opposite) so it is easy to pick up a boat. **Lake Shinji Pleasure Cruise** 宍道湖観光遊覧船 (💻 www.hakuchougo.jp; daily Mar-Nov 11am-5pm, Dec to Feb weekends and national holidays; 6-7/day; ¥1300) offers one-hour rides and a daily sunset cruise; boarding point No 2 is a 5-minute walk from Matsue station.

If you're expecting to stay here for three days, especially if you don't have a JR

## Matsue

松江

Not all roads shown

1 Yakumo-an
2 Be-d'oro
3 Hotel Route Inn Matsue
4 Hotel Ichibata
5 WaraWara
6 Dormy Inn Express Matsue
7 Toyoko Inn Matsue Ekimae
8 Yakitori Bankichi
9 Waraku
10 Matsue Excel Hotel Tokyu
11 Cappricciosa
   (Matsue Terrsa)

Pass, consider the **Enmusubi Perfect Ticket** (¥3000); this includes travel on buses and trains in the Matsue and Izumo areas as well as discounts for 23 attractions.

**Festivals** At the end of July/beginning of August is the **Suigo-sai Festival**, the highlight of which is a massive fireworks display over Lake Shinji.

The most raucous annual event is the **Drum Festival** (Do-gyoretsu) on 3rd November.

**Where to stay** Directly opposite the station is *Matsue Excel Hotel Tokyu* 松江 エクセルホテル東急 (☎ 0852-27 0109, 🖳 www.matsue-e.tokyuhotels.co.jp/ja; from ¥6700/S, ¥10,600/D, ¥12,600/Tw exc breakfast), a mid-range business hotel with two non-smoking floors. Also in the station area is *Toyoko Inn Matsue Ekimae* 東横イン 松江駅前 (☎ 0852-60 1045, 🖳 www.toyoko-inn.com; from ¥5184/S, ¥6804/D, ¥8424/Tw inc breakfast), to the left on the main road which runs parallel to the station. The rooms at this chain hotel are as spotless as in most branches of this chain.

*Dormy Inn Express Matsue* ドーミーインEXPRESS松江 (☎ 0852-59-5489, 🖳 www.hotespa.net/hotels/matsue; from ¥5490/S, ¥6990/D, ¥8490/Tw), next door, also has good clean rooms. The free noodles are provided as at other branches of Dormy Inn (see box p70).

*Hotel Route Inn Matsue* ホテルルートイン松江 (☎ 0852-20 6211, 🖳 www.route-inn.co.jp; ¥5900/S, ¥9850/D, ¥11,600/Tw) is a smart place a short walk north of the station across Ohashi-gawa.

**Terazuya Ryokan** 旅館寺津屋 (☎ 0852-21 3480, 🖳 www.mable.ne.jp/~tera zuya; tatami rooms ¥4500pp, ¥5000 inc breakfast, or ¥8900pp inc half board) is a small family-run inn. The rooms are a good size and there's a very homely atmosphere. Turn left out of the station and follow the train tracks round for about 10 minutes until you see the ryokan on the left side. Or call for a lift from the station.

At **Matsue-Shinjiki-onsen** the top place to stay is **Hotel Ichibata** ホテル一畑 (☎ 0852-22 0188, 🖳 www.ichibata.co .jp/hotel; from ¥9100/S, ¥11,300/Tw inc breakfast; half board also available). Ask for a room in the new annex (many of the rooms in the original building are dated and not worth the money) and with a view over Lake Shinji, but expect to pay quite a bit more than the rates quoted above.

See also pp67-73 for general information about accommodation.

**Where to eat and drink** Matsue is known in Japan for 'seven delicacies of Lake Shinji' 宍道湖七珍. Since the lake is a combination of fresh and sea water, the seven fish are an unusual mix: carp, eel, shrimp, *shijimi* clams, whitebait, sea bass and smelt. The fish don't all appear in the same season so there are usually only two or three on one plate but it's occasionally possible (for a lot of money) to eat all seven in one sitting. The best place to go for this is **Waraku** 和らく (🖳 wa-ra-ku.net; daily 11.30am-2pm & 5.30-10pm), but booking is recommended and expect to pay at least ¥3000. It is on the left-hand side as you walk down the road ahead from the station towards the river.

On your left as you leave the north side of the station is **Matsue Terrsa** 松江テル

サ, a glass building in which there is an impressive atrium and a clock with characters that emerge on the hour. On the 2nd floor is **Capricciosa** カプリチョーザ (daily 11am-9.30pm), a branch of the popular Italian pizza and pasta chain; most main dishes cost around ¥1200.

On the right-hand side of Station-dori is the atmospheric **Yakitori Bankichi** やきとり番吉 (daily 5pm-midnight; expect to pay ¥2000), which serves yakitori. You can either sit in a cubicle, at a normal table, or at the bar and watch the chef in action. The menu is in Japanese but includes several photos, though if you sit at the bar you can point to what you want. The *shisomaki* しそ巻 (chicken wrapped in shiso) are particularly recommended as well as the baked potato ベイクドポテト.

A few minutes up the main road past Toyoko Inn you will come to a branch of **WaraWara** 笑笑 (daily 5pm-3am), an izakaya chain. It serves everything – from kara-age (¥428) to yakitori (from ¥298), a sashimi platter (¥1288) and salads (¥498) – plus a good selection of beer and sake. The food is good and since Wara means 'smile' you should be warmly welcomed.

The French café/restaurant **Be-d'oro** びぃどろ (daily 11.30am-2pm & 5.30-10pm) is in **Karakoro Kobo** (see pp313-14). The lunchtime set menu (from ¥1100) usually includes soup and a choice of fish or meat; the dinner is more pricey (from ¥3000).

A highly recommended place for lunch is **Yakumo-an** 八雲庵 (🖳 www.yakumoan .jp; daily 10am-3pm), a small soba shop on Shiomi-Nawate. The soba and udon are delicious – expect to pay about ¥1000 – and there is a lovely garden to look at while you are eating.

### Side trips from Matsue

**To Adachi Museum of Art** A short train and bus ride away is Adachi Museum of Art 足立美術館 (Adachi Bijutsukan; 🖳 www.adachi-museum .or.jp; daily Apr-Sep 9am-5.30pm, Oct-Mar to 5pm; ¥2300, or ¥1150 for foreign visitors; audio guide ¥500), rightly considered one of the top cultural attractions in Japan. It is as famous for its stunning and immaculate landscaped gardens (which have won several awards and are frequently named the best in Japan) as for its collection of contemporary Japanese art.

The museum and garden are integrated and everyone follows the same route, in parts seeing the gardens (dry landscape; white sand and pine trees; moss; and pond) and at other times seeing the works of art ending up with several by Taikan Yokoyama including his fabulous image of Mt Fuji on one folding screen and on another mountains and the rising sun. Even though it is disappointing that you often have to look at the gardens through glass (and can't walk in them), they are still likely to take your breath away. A highlight is the 'living hanging scrolls' where the wall in an alcove was cut so that the garden can be seen; unlike most hanging scrolls this changes by the season so never needs to be replaced.

To reach the museum, take a local or LEX train (1-3/hr; 25/15 mins) east towards Yonago and get off at **Yasugi** 安来. A free shuttle bus (about 9/day; 20 mins) to the museum runs from bus stop No 2 outside Yasugi station; see the website for the timetable.

## To Tottori's sand dunes

Tottori 鳥取 is known for its **sand-dunes** 砂丘 (*sakyu*) which extend east to west along the coast for some 16km, and for its unique **Sand Museum** 砂の 美術館 (Apr-Jan 9am-8pm; ¥600) where stunning and highly detailed sand sculptures, based on a theme that changes every year, are exhibited. Most are in the main exhibition hall but a few are outside and beyond those is a sand-dune viewing square where you get a great view of the dunes themselves.

Leave the museum by the secondary exit and you can then take a **chair-lift** (¥200/300 one-way/return) down to the main sand-dune area. It's hard to believe unless you actually make the effort to travel out here that Japan really does have its own mini desert. Just in case you hadn't realised this, non-native camels wait on the edge of the dunes for a classic Japanese photo opportunity (¥500 on a camel, ¥100 beside one), or to take you for a short ride (Mar-Nov 9.30am-4.30pm, Dec-Feb to 10am-2pm; ¥1300 for one person, ¥2500 for two). You can walk all over the dunes, but if you plan to do this think ahead in terms of your footwear!

The **tourist information centre** (🖳 www.city.tottori.lg.jp; daily 8.30am-5.30pm) at Tottori station has English-speaking staff as well as maps, pamphlets and a bus timetable. (For additional information about what to do in the area see 🖳 tottrip.jp.) There are also **lockers** should you want to leave your bags at the station. Then take a **bus** (¥370; 1-2/hr) from stand 0 outside the North Exit – the last stop is the main sand-dune area but it is worth getting off at the stop before and going to the Sand Museum first.

Buses run infrequently so be sure to check the timetable for the last bus back. Alternatively, take the Loop Kirinjishi bus ループ麒麟獅子バス (from bus stand 6; daily July/Aug; weekends only rest of year; full circuit 80 mins; ¥300 per journey, ¥600 1-day pass) which goes to other places of interest in Tottori as well as the sand-dunes area.

It is easy to visit Tottori as a day trip from Matsue. However, there are several options if you want to stay the night here. ***Tottori Washington Hotel Plaza*** 鳥取 ワシントン ホテル プラザ (🖳 washington.jp/tottori; from ¥4400/S, ¥8300/D or Tw) is to the right of the North Exit of the station and comes recommended. An added advantage is a convenience store on the 1st/ground floor. Failing that there are branches of several business hotel chains here (see box p70). There's a *café* in the station and a basement **food hall** in Daimaru department store, just beyond the North Exit.

**Moving on from Tottori** Tottori is easily visited as a day trip from Matsue, but it is also possible to go to Okayama, Himeji, Osaka and Kyoto from here. The only downside is you will have to go on the track between Chizu and Kamigori, which is operated by the **private Chizu Kyuko railway**; this means JR rail-pass holders must pay a ¥1300 supplement (payable on board), or ¥1820 if travelling on a LEX in a reserved seat (¥2340 in a Green Car). Services that use this route are the Super Inaba LEX (6/day) to Okayama; the Super Hakuto LEX (7/day) to Himeji, Osaka and Kyoto; and the Hamakaze LEX (1/day) to Osaka via Himeji. For anyone with a JR Pass it would be better to go back to Matsue and travel from there.

Another option is to take a local Sanin Line train to Hamasaka and then change to a train to Kinosaki-onsen from where the Kinosaki-onsen LEX (10/day; 65 mins) goes to Kyoto, with no additional charge.

**To Izumo Taisha** Izumo Taisha (see pp288-9) is accessible from Matsue Shinjiko-onsen station via the private Ichibata Railway and this route is best if you don't have a JR Pass. Take a train to Kawato 川跡 (1-2/hr; 48 mins) and change there for the final leg to Izumo-Taisha-mae (1-2/hr; 11 mins). The whole journey costs ¥810. JR pass-holders need to backtrack to Izumoshi (see p288) and from there take a bus (daily 2/hr; 28 mins; ¥520).

# Tohoku (North-eastern Honshu) route guides

This region came to the world's attention on 11th March 2011 as a result of the devastating Great East Japan Earthquake and ensuing tsunami (see box p329). Undoubtedly there are parts of Tohoku where life will never be the same again (as attested by the many signs placed in impacted areas showing the height the tsunami water reached), but it is still possible to visit almost everywhere in this region and you are likely to get a warm welcome and have an extremely rewarding visit.

A trip around the Tohoku region offers a rare chance in an overcrowded island to go off the beaten track. When Japanese TV programmes poke fun at rural life and local accents, more often than not their targets are the 'country folk' of Tohoku. Some Japanese will only reluctantly venture into the region, fearing that the dialects they encounter will be so strong that they might as well be speaking a different language!

In contrast to other parts of the country, Tohoku offers little in the way of famous castles, temples or shrines. Volcanoes, lakes, mountains and rivers predominate, a geography which explains why north-eastern Honshu lagged behind in the industrial race of the late 20th century. But, the region is not without its

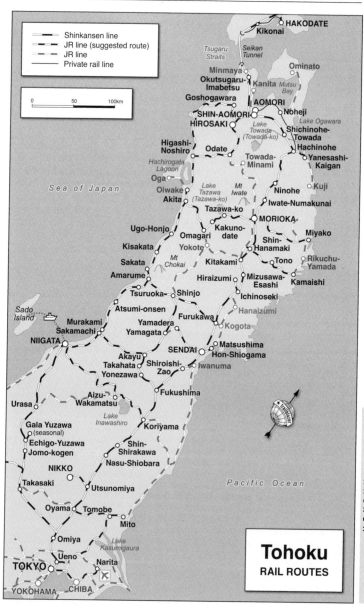

**Tohoku**
**RAIL ROUTES**

attractions: **Kakunodate** and **Hirosaki** are known for their cherry blossoms in spring; in summer the festivals here, particularly in **Aomori** and Hirosaki, are some of the best in Japan; and **Nikko** is a must whenever you visit.

Rail access to this region is fast and efficient, thanks in particular to the number of shinkansen routes. Beyond these is a network of ordinary lines served by both limited express, rapid

❏ **JR East Infoline**
For information in English on all JR East services call the JR East Infoline (☎ 050-2016 1603; daily except year-end/new-year holiday period, 10am-6pm). Operators can provide information on timetables and fares, and advise on routes. Seat reservations are not accepted by phone.

and local trains; these are the best means of seeing Tohoku close up – the shinkansen is fast but due to the proliferation of tunnels the views are nearly always fleeting. The following route loops around the region, starting with the journey north from Tokyo, along the eastern side of Tohoku, to Shin-Aomori (Aomori) at the northern tip of Honshu and the rail gateway to Hokkaido; then back down the less-travelled western side. Several side trips either to the coast, or heading inland from either coast, are suggested; the latter make it possible to crisscross the region easily and ensure you never need to double back on yourself.

## TOKYO TO SHIN-AOMORI BY SHINKANSEN

The fastest shinkansen service from Tokyo to Shin-Aomori is the **Hayabusa** (see box below); since March 2016 some services also operate to Shin-Hakodate-Hokuto in Hokkaido (see p368). **Yamabiko** services operate frequently to Sendai, some continue to Morioka; **Komachi** services (often coupled

❏ **Hayabusa – a Gran(d) experience**
Whatever shinkansen journey you take you are almost guaranteed a smooth, comfortable ride; for anyone from Britain at least that is an exciting prospect. However, **Gran Class**, available on the Hayabusa (and now the Kagayaki to Kanazawa), has taken shinkansen travel into a new league.

There are only 18 seats (2 x 1) so you immediately feel special. The car attendant will greet you and show you through the space-age carriage, done out in a tastefully understated livery, to your leather seat. Slip off your shoes (slippers are provided) and use the various buttons to shape the seat to whatever suits you best. You will be given an *oshibori* (hot towel) and served a light meal (a *bento* lunch box or sandwiches, both of which will include local products) and a drink of your choice. Then it's time to relax and enjoy the feeling of being cocooned from the world – with the attendant only a button's press away.

Anyone with a JR Ordinary/Green Pass can reserve a seat for free, but for Gran Class, even with a pass, you must pay the full express supplement as well as the reserved seat ticket cost. Since the complimentary meal and a drink is provided whatever the length of your journey the best-value way to have a taste of this luxury is to do a short stretch, such as from Morioka to Shin-Aomori (¥9790).

with the Hayabusa) operate to Morioka but then head west to Akita; **Nasuno** services terminate at Koriyama. **Hayate** services operate to Shin-Morioka/Aomori but mostly only in holiday periods; the first stop is always Sendai.

Seat reservations are essential for Hayabusa, Hayate and Komachi services.

### Tokyo to Sendai [Map 15; Map 16, p327; Table 11, p508]

Distances from Tokyo. Fastest journey time by Hayabusa shinkansen: 91 minutes.

### Tokyo 東京 (0km) [see pp103-33]

**Ueno** 上野 **(4km)** Most trains call here (see p114). If joining the train here rather than at Tokyo, it's worth reserving seats because at certain times the non-reserved cars are full by the time the train leaves Tokyo. The shinkansen tracks start underground (allow at least 10 minutes if transferring from the Yamanote Line) but you soon get good views of Tokyo – and if you are lucky Mt Fuji (ensure you are sitting on the left-hand side).

Until they reach Omiya, shinkansen don't go at full speed because there are noise restrictions due to the residential neighbourhoods; the bonus is that it is easier to see what you are passing.

**Omiya** 大宮 **(30km)** Every service stops here, located in Saitama city and prefecture. Saitama is so close to Tokyo it's impossible to see where one ends and the other begins.

Even though some of the exhibits are geared to children, a visit to the **Railway Museum** 鉄道博物館 (Tetsudo Hakubutsukan; 🖳 www.railway-museum.jp; Wed-Mon 10am-6pm; ¥1000) is recommended. The museum, operated by JR East, focuses in particular on the history of Japanese railways. The history zone has 37 real train cars including two of the first shinkansen from 1964 – even these had seats that could be changed to face the direction of travel, a chilled water dispenser and a bottle opener – as well as royal cars used by former

emperors. Some labels have QR barcodes that can be scanned with smartphones for English translations. Don't miss the railway model diorama on the upper floor, with 80 sets of trains, 1002 cars, and plenty of seating for spectators. There are also two train-driving options: if the overcrowded Tokyo rail network hasn't put you off, you can climb into and drive a mini variant of your favourite unit around a tiny network (¥200) – complete with signals, stations, and the Narita Express. For a more full-size experience, there are mocked-up driving simulators near the entrance (the SL requires a ¥500 reservation, other simulators are free).

There is a ***restaurant*** on the 1st/ground floor but it is much more interesting to have a picnic in the **View Deck** on the 3rd floor. Here you can watch real shinkansen speed past – there is a special timetable showing which train will pass by and when. To get to the museum, take a **New Shuttle** ニューシャトル (6/hr; 2 mins; ¥190; rail passes not valid) train to Tetsudo-Hakubutsukan station.

If railways are getting a bit much, consider the **Omiya Bonsai Museum** 大宮盆栽医術間 (🖥 www.omiyabonsai.jp, Fri-Wed Mar-Oct 9am-4.30pm, Nov-Feb 9am-4pm; ¥300 entry, ¥300 audio guide), an excellent place that explains how bonsai are sculpted, displayed, and how to view and appreciate a specimen. The audio guide in English is particularly recommended for the collection outdoors, where the qualities of each masterpiece are discussed in detail. The museum is located in the middle of Omiya Bonsai Village, a hub of bonsai nurseries. Take the JR Utsunomiya Line one stop north from Omiya to **Toro** 土呂, where it is a signposted 5-minute walk.

Omiya is the last chance to change to the Nagano and Hokuriku shinkansen for Nagano (see pp206-10) and Kanazawa (see p226-32) respectively. It is also possible to access Kawagoe (see below) from here; take the JR Saikyo Line (rapid train; 3/hr; 20 mins).

### Side trip to Kawagoe 川越
The streets of Kawagoe (🖥 www.koedo.or.jp), sometimes called Little Edo (Ko-edo), are lined with historic *kura* (warehouses) that double as traditional confectionery shops, noodle houses and private homes.

The **tourist information counter** (daily 9am-4.30pm; no English spoken but English map available) is by the ticket gates for the Tobu Toju Railway. With a map in hand it is an easy (20- to 30-minute) walk from the East Exit of the station to the main sights. If you prefer take the **Tobu Koedo Famous Locations Loop Bus** (🖥 www.koedo.or.jp; 1-2/hr; ¥180/journey, ¥300/one-day pass, purchase from the driver) from stop No 3 outside the station's East Exit. Alternatively, the **Koedo Loop Bus** (2/hr; ¥180/journey, ¥500/one-day pass) operates round a wider area. Both operate daily (approx 9am-4pm).

On and around the main street are 30 *kurazukuri* 蔵造り (clay-walled residences and stores from the Edo period); their main purpose was to be fireproof and they are so solid-looking it is not surprising each one took 2-3 years to build. However, Kawagoe's most famous sight is the 16m-high **Toki-no-kane** 時の鐘 (Bell Tower). First constructed in 1624, the tower that stands today was rebuilt after a fire in 1893. Sadly, there are no campanologists on hand to ring the bell, but a recording is played four times a day (6am, noon, 3pm and 6pm).

**Kashiya Yokocho** 菓子屋横丁 is a small street famous for its traditional sweet shops. If the streets elsewhere in Kawagoe are deserted, it will be because the hordes of elderly Japanese tourists have made a beeline for the candy stores here, where you'll find them in fits of nostalgia buying bags and boxes of traditional sweets.

Pick up the Loop Bus for **Kita Temple** 喜多院 (Kita-in; daily 8.50am-4pm; ¥400); the temple dates from 830 but the original buildings and Tosyogu Shrine were destroyed in a fire in 1638; in 1640 Iemitsu Tokugawa (third shogun in the Tokugawa clan) ordered them to be rebuilt and as part of this several buildings were moved here from Edo Castle (now the Imperial Palace) in Tokyo. They are the only parts of Edo Castle that still exist as the rest were destroyed by the earthquake in 1923 and in WWII. In a corner of the temple grounds are **Gohyaku-Rakan** 五百羅漢; this literally means 500 stone statues of Buddhist monks, but actually there are 540. They are in a variety of quirky poses and states of emotion, from happy to furious, and are very entertaining. The entry charge for Gohyaku-Rakan is included in the ticket for Kita Temple; in fact you have to go to the main building of the temple to get the ticket so do make time to look around as it is worth it. The entrance to Gohyaku-Rakan is by the souvenir store; the staff there will check you have a ticket.

The best time to visit Kawagoe is on the third weekend of October for **Kawagoe Matsuri** (🖳 www.kawagoematsuri.jp), the highlight of which is a parade through town with huge, colourful floats.

After Omiya, all Nasunos and some Yamabikos call at **Oyama** 小山 (81km). Transfer at Oyama for the JR Mito Line to Shimodate and then to Mooka to see its steam-engine-shaped station building (see box p92). The JR Mito Line also, of course, goes to Mito, access point for Kairakuen (see p143).

**Utsunomiya 宇都宮 (110km)** All Nasunos and most Yamabikos stop here. If going to **Nikko** (see p324) you need to change trains here.

Look to the right after you walk out of the shinkansen part of the station for the *ekiben* (see box p102) cart; this station was where ekiben were first sold at the end of the 19th century and is one of the few stations that still sell them from a cart rather than from a kiosk, or on the train.

**Utsunomiya City Information Centre** (daily 8.30am-8pm), on the left as you exit the shinkansen tracks, has information about Nikko and can advise about accommodation, but to book a hotel you need to go to View Travel Agency (Mon-Fri 10.30am-6.30pm, Sat to 5.30pm) nearby. **Lockers** (¥300-500) are down the corridor by the North Exit to the right of the stairs, and also by the South Exit.

If you have time to spare, head out of the West Exit and walk straight down the main road for about 15 minutes to **Futaarayama Shrine** 二荒山神社, on the right-hand side; a giant set of torii make it hard to miss. The shrine is 1600 years old and it is believed that its original name, Shimotsuke-ichinomiya, is the origin of the name Utsunomiya. Many students visit with the hope that it will assist with entrance examinations.

A comfortable and stylish place to stay the night is *Hotel R-Mets* ホテルアーメッツ宇都宮 (☎ 028-600 3300, 🖳 www.hotelmets.jp/utsunomiya; from

¥13,000/S, ¥21,000/D or Tw inc Japanese or Western breakfast). It is also convenient as it is linked to the West Exit of the station. They have a range of packages and rates depend on when you check-in and how long you stay so you can save money by arriving late and leaving early.

### Side trip by train to Nikko 日光

The Japanese have a saying: 'don't say *kekko* [magnificent] until you have seen Nikko'. Nikko is at its most stunning in the autumn, but at any time of the year, even in the rain, the colourful opulence of the shrine complex makes this an unforgettable place.

For anyone with a JR pass the easiest way to reach Nikko is to transfer at Utsunomiya onto a JR Nikko Line train (1-2/hr; 50 mins). Follow signs from the shinkansen tracks to platform 5; there is no need to exit Utsunomiya station first. Note that not all trains from platform 5 go to Nikko. (See p143 for details about reaching Nikko from Tokyo if you don't have a JR pass.) Don't rush to leave JR Nikko Station as it is an interesting place in its own right; it was designed by Frank Lloyd Wright and opened in 1890 and thus is one of JR East's oldest wooden station buildings. The White Room upstairs is the former waiting room for first-class passengers.

If arriving at JR Nikko you will need to go to the main **tourist information centre** (⌨ www.nikko-jp.org; daily 9am-5pm, English-language speaker Apr-Nov 10am-2pm) for comprehensive information. It is on the left-hand side about a 30-minute walk uphill from the station and about midway to the shrine area. It has very useful maps and accommodation leaflets but staff are unable to make bookings. If you have arrived at Tobu Nikko Station (a short walk from the JR station) you can pick up similar information at the tourist information office (daily 8.30am-5pm) there. If you have luggage and are staying near the shrine area it is worth taking a **taxi** (about ¥710) or a **bus** (3-4/hr; 10 mins; ¥200) to Shinkyo Bridge. If you expect to use a bus quite a bit consider getting a **Sekai-isan-meguri pass** (¥500/day) from Tobu Nikko station. This pass is valid for unlimited travel on Tobu buses in central Nikko.

● **What to see and do** The main sights are in the vast area known as **Nikko Sannai**, which has been on the World Heritage Site list since 1999. The original gateway to the Nikko Sannai area was the red-lacquered **Shinkyo Bridge** 神橋 across the Daiya River. It is still possible to cross this bridge (daily Apr-mid Nov 8am-5pm, mid Nov-Mar 9am-4pm; ¥300) but it is free to use the road and that way you can admire the bridge properly.

From there be prepared to climb lots of steps to reach the temples and shrines as they are all spread over the hillside. There are various paths but the first major site you are likely to reach is the **five-storied pagoda** 五重塔. From there you go through **Omote Gate** 表門 (Omote-mon) to the star attraction: the grand **Toshogu Shrine** 東照宮 (Apr-Oct 8am-5pm, Nov-Mar to 4pm; ¥1300), originally built in 1616 as a mausoleum for Ieyasu Tokugawa, founder of the Tokugawa shogunate. The first shrine was rebuilt a few years later in 1636 on the orders of Iemitsu, who wanted an even more majestic and everlasting memorial to his grandfather. There are over 5000 engraved works on the various buildings in this shrine – look out for dragons, elephants, monkeys, cats, flowers and birds. Also here is the **Sacred Stable** 神厩舎 (*Shinkyusha*) and some storehouses on which you will see the famous monkeys, carved in relief, which show the various stages in life and are best known for the depiction of the belief that children should 'See no evil, Speak no evil, Hear no evil'; the monkeys were meant to protect the horses from harm. Nearby is **Yomei Gate** 陽明門 (Yomei-mon) which is likely to be under wraps as renovation work is expected to continue until 2019. Ieyasu's tomb (¥520) is at the top of a flight of steps (207 to be precise); at the bottom of the steps look up at the famous **sleeping cat** 眠り猫 (nemurineko) carving.

The beautiful **Rinno-ji** 輪王寺 (🖳 rinnoji.or.jp; Apr-Oct 8am-5pm, Nov-Mar to 4pm; Sanbutsudo ¥400, treasure house and Shoyo-en ¥300), one of the three main temples in the Tendai sect of Buddhism, dates back to 766. Since the temple is also being renovated it may not be possible to see all of the buildings properly but Shoyo-en 逍遥園 garden should be visited, especially in autumn. **Futarasan-jinja** 二荒山神社 (¥200), a shrine, is home to the patron god of Nikko (god of matchmaking) and is dedicated to Mt Nantai, a nearby mountain, but otherwise is far simpler than the opulent Toshogu Shrine and if time is tight could probably be missed; it also is undergoing renovation work.

Navigate your way back to the main road and if you turn right you will soon reach **Tamozawa Imperial Villa Memorial Park** 日光田母沢御用邸記念公園 (🖳 www.park-tochigi.com/tamozawa; Wed-Mon 9am-4.30pm; ¥510, audio guidance ¥200). This was built in 1899 as a holiday residence for Prince Yoshihito, later the Taisho Emperor; since then it has been expanded and it is now the largest wooden structure at any of the Imperial villas, though only about a quarter of it can be visited.

The current Emperor, Akihito, lived here for about a year during WWII (look out for the air-raid shelters in the magnificent garden) and it was opened to the public in 2000. As you walk round you will see an Imperial toilet, a billiard table and an Imperial throne – the latter seeming a bit surprising as it is on an Axminster carpet.

**Kanaya Hotel History House** 金谷ホテル歴史館 (🖳 nikko-kanaya-history.jp/en/house; Apr-Nov 9.30am-4.30pm, Dec-Mar 10am-3pm; ¥400) started life as a samurai warrior's residence in the Edo period, hence also being called Kanaya Samurai House, but then was converted to a hotel called Kanaya Cottage Inn in 1873. Five years later, Isabella Bird, a 19th-century British explorer, stayed here for 10 days and wrote that she almost wished 'that the rooms were a little less exquisite, for I am in constant dread of spilling the ink, indenting the mats, or tearing the paper windows'.

This house has been preserved for over 140 years and opened to the public in 2015; amongst other things you can see the room where Bird stayed in 1878. Kanaya Hotel still exists but in 1893 it was moved to a different site.

● **Festivals** Yayoi Festival (13th-17th Apr) is based around Futarasan-jinja and involves portable shrines being carried around the area as well as dance performances. **Toshogu Grand Spring Festival** (Shunki Reitaisai) is held on 17th-18th May as well as in October (Shuki Taisai; 17th Oct). Both these events feature a procession of men dressed in samurai costumes.

● **Where to stay and eat** There are several options but closest to the JR station – just across the road – is *Nikko Station Hotel Classic* 日光駅ホテルスクラシック (☎ 0288-53 1000, 🖳 www.nikko-stationhotel.jp; from ¥11,500pp; buffet breakfast); it has good-sized rooms, an onsen as well as a rotemburo. *Tsurukame Daikichi* 鶴亀大吉 (☎ 0288-54 1550, 🖥 www.nikko-turukame.jp; from ¥11,500pp inc half board), near Toshogu Shrine, has river and mountain views; it also has indoor and outdoor baths and delicious meals. *Johsyu-ya Ryokan* 上州屋旅館 (☎ 0288-54 0155, 🖥 www.johsyu-ya.co.jp; from ¥4500pp; dinner from ¥2160, Japanese/Western breakfast ¥864/1080) is on the right-hand side near the top of the road to Toshogu Shrine. The rooms are large (some sleep up to four) but can be noisy as the main road is busy. It also has a (single-sex) hot-spring bath. Meals must be booked in advance.

On the same side of the road as Johsyu-ya but downhill is a branch of the *Skylark-Gusto* すかいらーくガスト restaurant chain serving both Western and Japanese dishes; a soba and ramen noodle place; and *Hi no Kuruma* ひの車 which serves vegetable okonomiyaki. On the opposite side and up the hill, *Hippari Tako* ひっぱり凧 serves a wide range of dishes including yakisoba (¥480) and yakitori (¥320). Most of the restaurants open daily from around 11am to 7/8pm, although Skylark-Gusto is open until midnight.

## Nasu-Shiobara 那須塩原 (158km)

All Nasunos and some Yamabikos call here. The main reason to stop here is to visit Shiobara-onsen. The best part, if you have a Japan Rail Pass (JR East passes are not valid), is that it can be reached on a JR bus (1/hr; 60 mins; ¥1170 for non pass-holders) and you can use the bus to get around town as it is quite spread out.

### Side trip to Shiobara-onsen

Shiobara-onsen 塩原温泉 (🖥 www.siobara.or.jp/vc) is spread along a wooded valley and the hot spring water here comes from 11 different sources so it is not surprising that there are lots of baths to soak in. However, if you tire of this there is also plenty to see. The Taisho Emperor (1879-1926) had health problems and because the air quality and climate in Shiobara was meant to be very good a villa was built for him here: **Emperor's Room Memorial Park** 天皇の間記念公園 (Tenno-no-ma-kinen-koen; daily 9am-5pm; ¥200) has not been used by the Imperial family since 1948 but is now open to the public. The striking feature of this villa, though not unique in Japan, is that it was built with no nails. One place you mustn't miss, particularly if you are here in the azalea season (May), is **Myoun-ji** 妙雲寺 (daily 8.30am-4.30pm; ¥400). The grounds are spread over the hillside and are lovely to wander around.

At the bottom of the town and a walk of about 15 minutes from the road is the 60m-high **Ryuka Waterfall** 龍化の滝 (Ryuka no taki; daily 8.30am-5pm); the waterfall is said to resemble a flying dragon.

There's a great **foot-bath** in Shiobara but several onsen hotels in this area are also open to the public if you want to pop in during the day. Most also have rotemburo and there are quite a few 'mixed onsen'. Highly recommended is *Yumori Tanakaya* 湯守　田中屋 (☎ 0287-32 3232, 🖥 www.tnky.jp; from ¥13,000pp inc half board, from ¥25,000pp with private rotemburo), though it is 300 steps down to the river. The men's bath is mixed (ladies are allowed to wear a towel), but the ladies' is separate. You can pick up a map and information at the **Visitor Center** (Wed-Mon 9am-4.30pm) in the centre of town.

The next stop is **Shin-Shirakawa** 新白河 (185km). Soon after Shin-Shirakawa a brief succession of tunnels blocks out the view before opening up again as the train approaches Koriyama.

**Koriyama** 郡山 **(227km)** Almost all Nasuno and Yamabiko services stop here – mainly useful as an interchange for the samurai-castle and sake-brewing town of Aizu-Wakamatsu (see below), which is on the Ban-etsu West Line that runs some 190km across Honshu from Koriyama to Niigata. There is also the chance to ride the SL Banetsu Monogatari (see pp328-9) from Aizu-Wakamatsu to Niigata.

At Koriyama station there is a **Travel Service Center** (daily 9am-5.30pm) where staff can provide both tourist and rail service information and have a map of Koriyama. On this floor there is a **restaurant zone** and at street level there is a *Food Bazaar* with a selection of fast-food stands sharing an eating area. In the morning they do coffee and breakfast sets here.

If you decide to stay in Koriyama, *Washington Hotel* 郡山ワシントンホテル (☎ 024-923 1311, 🖥 www.washington-k.co.jp; from ¥6588/S, ¥13,068/D, ¥14,256/Tw; breakfast ¥1080) is a good choice as it is only a short walk from the Central Exit of the station, though the rooms are rather dated. Alternatively, *Toyoko Inn Koriyama* 東横イン郡山 (🖥 www .toyoko-inn.com; ¥5184/S, ¥6804/D, ¥7884/Tw, inc breakfast) is about a 7-minute walk (parallel to the railway tracks) heading west from the station's West Exit.

### Side trip by rail to Aizu-Wakamatsu
Aizu-Wakamatsu 会津若松 is known for its castle and as a place where sake is brewed, but it was also one of the samurai's last strongholds in Japan; it only lost its influence when the Meiji government took over and ended the feudal era.

Trains to Aizu Wakamatsu from Koriyama depart from platform No 1. Local trains operate (approx hourly) on the Ban-etsu West Line. On some weekends, as part of JR East's strategy to revitalise tourism after the Fukushima disaster (see box p329), the new 2-car **FruiTea** フルーティ ア (pronounced 'Furuutia') train, described as a travelling café, runs between Koriyama and Aizu-Wakamatsu (2/day). On other

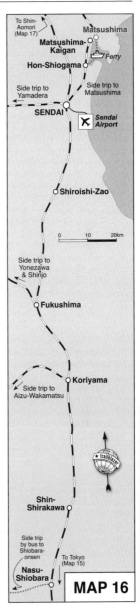

MAP 16

HONSHU

weekends it runs to Fukushima (and it occasionally operates on a Monday or Tuesday). One of the cars is a café which serves cakes/tarts made using locally grown fruit; the other has seats for up to 36 people. Staff also serve 'Sweet Sets'. Tickets must be bought at a View Plaza Travel Service Center.

There is an **information centre** (💻 www.city.aizuwakamatsu.fukushima.jp; daily 9am-5.30pm) on the right by Aizu-Wakamatsu station exit. From there walk straight out to the **bus ticket centre** on the left; buses stop to the right of that. **Aizu Loop Bus** ハイカラさん まちなか観光バス (daily 8am-6.30pm; ¥200, day pass ¥500) is the best way to get round town as the attractions are spread out. The green bus (daily 2/hr) operates the full route, the red bus (6/day) takes a more limited route. Show your pass as you leave the bus. You will be given a timetable when you buy the pass.

Your first stop should be **Aizu Buke-Yashiki** 会津武家屋敷 (Aizu Samurai Residence; daily Apr-Nov 8.30am-5pm, Dec-Mar to 4.30pm; ¥850). Even though all the buildings are reconstructions everything has been recreated to look as it would have done in the Edo era. The residence includes areas for the samurai and his family and staff as well as guest rooms, gardens, a tea house, an archery range and a rice mill. Mannequins in the rooms bring it all to life. Back on the bus and en route to the castle you may like to stop at **Oyakuen** 御薬園 (daily 8.30am-5pm; ¥320), a landscape garden with a pond and a medicinal-herb garden.

**Wakamatsu Castle** 会津若松城 (Wakamatsu-jo also known as Tsuruga-jo 鶴ヶ城; daily 8.30am-5pm; castle ¥410, castle and tea house ¥510) was first built in 1384 and the original building lasted until 1868. This reconstruction dates from the 1960s and for non-Japanese speakers is chiefly of interest for its unique, 'original-style' red roof. From the castle bus stop, cross the road, take the narrow path to the right of the souvenir shop and then follow the signs.

Sake requires good-quality rice, pure water and a cold climate, and as Aizu-Wakamatsu has all three it is not surprising that there are several sake breweries here. **Aizu Sake Museum** 會津酒造歴史館 (daily 9am-4.30pm; ¥200), a short walk from the castle, exhibits both modern and traditional brewing methods. **Suehiro Sake Brewery** 末廣酒造嘉永蔵 (daily 9am-5pm) was founded in 1850 and produces not only some of the best sake in Japan but also sparkling sake, sake jelly, sake cakes and a sake bath extract. The hourly tours take in the brewing area and a sake museum as well as a museum of film cameras (¥300) that houses over 500 cameras. The scientist Hideyo Noguchi, whose portrait is on the ¥1000 note, was born in Aizu-Wakamatsu and knew the Suehiro family well so some of his letters and pictures can be seen at the brewery. He became famous as a result of his medical research, particularly into syphilis.

If planning to stay the night, try *Toyoko Inn Aizu-Wakamatsu Ekimae* 東横イン会津若松駅前 (☎ 0242-32 1045, 💻 www.toyoko-inn.com; from ¥5724 /S, ¥7884/D, ¥8424/Tw, inc breakfast), to the left of the station, or *Hotel Alpha 1* ホテルアルファーワン会津若松 (☎ 0242-32 6868, 💻 www.alpha-1.co.jp/aizuwakamatsu; from ¥5400/S, ¥10,100/D, ¥10,600/Tw) to the right.

Instead of returning to Koriyama and assuming you are here at the right time of the year, it is worth taking the **SL Banetsu Monogatari** SLばんえつ物語 (Apr-Nov weekends only; 3hrs 50 mins) from here to Niigata. All seats on this steam train are reserved so you'll need to book ahead at any JR travel agency (reservations are free to JR pass holders). Tickets go on sale one month in advance and are often sold out within the day. A good part of the route follows the Agano river, making for a scenic journey (especially on the left going towards Niigata), with 10-minute long photo stops included. Train staff will let you hold a sign with the date of your journey and they will take your photo in front of the steam engine. The train also has an observation car.

It's only after Koriyama, over 200km from Tokyo, that the scenery starts to improve as the landscape becomes more rural, offering the first glimpses of what Tohoku has to offer. The view, however, is frequently blocked by tunnels.

**Fukushima 福島 (273km)** All the Yamabiko services stop here. It is worth noting that Fukushima City, and thus the shinkansen station, is 62km (about 38 miles) from the Fukushima Daiichi nuclear power plant.

❏ **The Great East Japan Earthquake**
Few outside Japan had heard of Fukushima before a 9.0-magnitude quake struck off Tohoku's Pacific coast on the afternoon of 11th March 2011. But within minutes this rural backwater of north-eastern Japan became the epicentre of a tragedy that continues to unfold to this day.

The quake was the most powerful ever to have hit Japan, dwarfing the 1995 Great Hanshin Earthquake which flattened the city of Kobe (see pp289-90). Tsunami waves more than 10m in height powered inland along 530km of the coastline, destroying villages, communities and at least 20,000 lives.

The worst affected areas were north from Choshi, in Chiba, up to and including the southern and eastern coastline of Hokkaido. The tremors were felt west of Tokyo and as far north as Sapporo in Hokkaido. Regional railway services were paralysed, and JR East – the company which manages the rail network in Tohoku – was left with a bill of more than ¥100 billion to repair seven damaged rail sections along a combined total of 325km of track.

But the lasting legacy of the earthquake and tsunami – beyond the tragic loss of life – remains the damage inflicted on the Fukushima Daiichi nuclear power plant. Its cooling systems were knocked out, which led to a series of explosions and meltdowns, and Fukushima prefecture became the scene of the world's worst nuclear accident in 25 years. Tokyo Electric Power Company, operator of the nuclear plant, struggled for months to contain the disaster, before achieving a state of cold shutdown. It is likely to be several decades before the stricken plant is fully decommissioned. The accident rekindled a debate – which some said was long overdue – about Japan's reliance on nuclear energy, and about the safety of nuclear plants built along earthquake fault lines. All nuclear power stations were shut down after the earthquake, but in August 2015, in the face of considerable public opposition, Japan restarted its first nuclear power reactor – largely due to a lack of viable alternatives.

Following the quake, tens of thousands of residents who lived within what became known as the exclusion zone around the nuclear plant were evacuated; many are still living in temporary residences. The long-term impact on the regional economy continues to be felt. Local industries and farmers say their livelihoods have been destroyed because of the association of the name Fukushima with nuclear contamination. However, reconstruction has been progressing steadily – in particular town centres that were destroyed are being rebuilt a few metres higher to make them less prone to flooding and in the Miyagi prefecture a 400km-long 12-metre-high seawall dubbed the 'Great Wall of Japan' is being constructed (controversially blocking the ocean view).

HONSHU

Since the Yamagata Line branches off here some trains divide: the Tsubasa shinkansen heads to **Yonezawa** (313km; see below).

### Side trip on the Yamagata shinkansen and to the west coast

The Yamagata shinkansen offers some spectacular scenery, pine forests, rivers (and a few tunnels) but it does make you wonder why a shinkansen was built here, since it's not exactly a teeming metropolis. However, if you are travelling at the weekend, or on a national holiday, plan a trip on the **Tsubasa Toreiyu** (1/day; seat reservation essential, free with a JR pass), the only shinkansen with a foot-bath (¥350/15 mins); tickets for the foot-bath, which is in Car 16, are sold as part of a package but if there is space you can buy a ticket on the train. Cars 12-14 have tatami seating, and Car 15 has a bar.

If feeling hungry get off at **Yonezawa** 米沢 (approx hourly; 35 mins) and have a meal with Yonezawa beef, one of the three major beef 'brands' in Japan. Every Yonezawa beef cow is reared and fattened over a period of 32 months; during this time its diet may include rice straw, the resulting meat is marbled and finely textured. Not surprisingly it comes at a premium price – upwards of ¥10,000 for a full-course meal. One place that's not too expensive, and where Yonezawa beef is the only thing on the menu, is *Toyokan* 東洋館, across the street from the station. The restaurant name is written in black kanji on the side of the building (on the right-hand corner of the main street which runs away from the station). Look for the picture of a black bull. Its cheapest set menu is ¥2900. A map showing the various restaurants is available at the **tourist information desk** (daily 8am-6pm), but it is in Japanese so ask staff to point out the best ones. A cheaper option is the delicious beef *doman-naka* (¥1150) ekiben which you can buy at the station.

Rail fans might like a further side trip from Yonezawa along the scenic JR Yonesaka Line to **Sakamachi** 坂町 on the west coast (from where you can connect with the route guide on p352). The trains are mostly local services, but once a day there is a rapid service called Benibana べにばな which runs all the way to Niigata (see pp359-62). This is a scenic journey, particularly when the weather is good and in late autumn when the snow is new; towards the end of the winter it can look rather dirty which spoils the view. It is probably best to sit on the right-hand side if you can, but there are good views on both sides.

Alternatively, pick up the Tsubasa for **Takahata** 高畠 (322km) and then **Yamagata** 山形 (360km), change here for the pilgrimage site of Yamadera (1/hr; 16 mins; ¥240; see p358), which can also be accessed as a side trip from Sendai. The Tsubasa terminates at **Shinjo** 新庄 (421km), from where you can take a JR Rikuu West Line train to Amarume (see p350; 11/day; 46 mins) to cross to the west coast.

There are several tunnels on the route between Fukushima and Sendai. After Fukushima some shinkansen stop at **Shiroishi-Zao** 白石蔵王 (307km).

## Sendai 仙台 (352km)　　　　　　　　　　　　[see pp353-8]

All services stop here. Change here for a side trip to the extremely scenic Matsushima Bay (see below).

### Side trip by rail to Matsushima 松島

Over 260 islands are scattered around Matsushima Bay; collectively they count as one of the top three scenic spots in Japan, along with Miyajima (see pp308-11) and Amanohashidate. For centuries, poets have journeyed here in search of inspiration – indeed, the islands themselves are sometimes compared to verses of a poem. In the station there is even a small haiku box where travelling poets can deposit their own work. Matsuo Basho visited on his epic journey through the region and wrote that Matsushima was the 'most beautiful spot in the whole country of Japan'. He was reportedly left speechless by the beautiful scenery and abandoned plans to write a haiku in honour of his visit in 1689.

The mainland was protected from the worst of the March 2011 tsunami by the islands. However, signs across the bay highlight how high the tsunami waters came, and photos inside the ferry dock show pictures from after the disaster.

From Sendai, take the JR Senseki Line from either Aoba-dori in the city centre or Sendai station platform No 9 (approx 2/hr; 40 mins) to Matsushima-Kaigan. Note that the rapid trains from Sendai run to Matsushima (without the -Kaigan suffix), which is a different station (see p333).

There is enough to see and do in Matsushima, but if the idea of going by boat one way appeals leave the train at **Hon-Shiogama** 本塩釜 (16km). The tourist information office (daily 10am-4pm) is just outside the Jinja-sando Exit of the station on the left. If you have 75 minutes to spare before the ferry, follow signs for a short walk up the hill to **Shiogama Shrine** 塩竈神社, where the magnificent Zuishinmon Gate is your prize for ascending the 202 steps.

For the ferry, take the Aqua Gate Exit from the station, turn left and walk past a branch of *Baskin Robbins* and then Aeon department store. If you keep going straight you will reach Marine Gate Terminal. Here you'll find seafood restaurants with harbour views and an observation platform. **Marubun Matsushima Kisen** 丸文松島汽船 offers a cruise (🖳 www.marubun-kisen .com; daily 9am-3pm; 1/hr; 50 mins; ¥1500, ¥1350 if bought at Hon-Shiogama station or a TIC) between Hon-Shiogama and

MAP 17

To Shin-Aomori (Map 28)

MORIOKA

Side trip to Tazawa-ko & Kakunodate

To Jodogohama (Pure Land) Beach

Hanamaki — Shin-Hanamaki

To Kamaishi →

Kitakami

0    10km

Mizusawa-Esashi

Hiraizumi

Side trip

Ichinoseki

Kurikoma-Kogen

Hanaizumi

To Naruko-onsen & Shinjo

Kogota

Furukawa

Matsushima

Matsushima-Kaigan

Hon-Shiogama

Side trip to Yamadera

Matsushima Bay

SENDAI

To Tokyo (Map 16)

Sendai Airport

HONSHU

Matsushima as well as round-trip cruises from both Shiogama and Matsushima. All go past some of the many tiny islands that are a familiar sight along this coastline. There's a tourist information desk (daily 8am-5pm) at the boat pier in Matsushima, but the staff here don't speak English.

If you stay on the train you will get your first proper view of the islands – and will understand why you have come here – after **Higashi-Shiogama** 東塩釜 station, but the view is fleeting and after that it's tunnels for most of the journey to **Matsushima-Kaigan** 松島海岸. **Matsushima Information Center** (🖳 www.matsushima-kanko.com; Mon-Fri 9.30am-4.30pm, Sat, Sun and holidays 9am-5pm) is in a booth to the right as you exit the station. With a map in hand it is an easy walk to the main sights.

A few of the islands just off the shore are linked by bridges to the mainland. The most popular is tiny **Godaidojima** 五大堂島, on which stands a hall containing five Buddhist statues which are put on view only once every 33 years (the last time was in 2006, so the next viewing won't be until 2039). Try not to trip on the bridge across – this is said to deem you unworthy of entering! Pleasant though it is, the tranquillity is spoilt by the souvenir stalls set up along the approach to it. Much more relaxing is nearby **Fukuurajima** 福浦島, connected to the mainland via a long, red footbridge (¥200 to cross). This island has wooded paths free from souvenir stands and (almost) out of sight of any vending machines. From here, there are views to some of the other islands.

Also pleasant to visit is **Oshima** 雄島 – the bridge to which is free to cross and is a new construction after the previous bridge was destroyed in the 2011 tsunami. It originally had over 100 caves, although there are now around 50. These served as places for monks to meditate. Set slightly further south along the coast from Godaidojima, it is effectively opposite a car park. Many people either do not realise it is there, or do not know that the bridge has reopened so it is relatively quiet.

Set just back from the port area is **Zuigan-ji** 瑞巌寺 (daily 8am-6pm, to 5pm in winter, art museum to 5pm, or 3.30/4.30pm in winter; ¥700), a Zen Buddhist temple built in 828 and later reconstructed by Masamune Date (see p353). On the right as you walk through the pine trees towards the temple entrance are some caves inside which monks used to train before the temple was built. Look out for the rail monument near the caves, a tall column flanked by railway wheels on pieces of track. It was built to remember those who died during the construction of the railways or in rail accidents. The main hall is closed for restoration work until March 2018 but some others are open. At the weekends, English guides in green jackets will show you around for free (10am-3pm). However, next door, **Entsuin** 円通院 (Mar-Nov daily 8.30am-5pm; ¥300) includes a rock garden, a moss and maple garden, a rose garden (best Jun-Sep) and Sankeiden, the mausoleum for Mitsumune Date, the grandson of Masamune Date, who died aged 19. The mausoleum is unusual because it has Western as well as Buddhist symbols as the family was interested in Western technology.

For an overnight stay right up against the coast head to *Matsushima Century Hotel* 松島センチュリーホテル (☎ 022-345 4111, 🖳 www.century hotel.co.jp; from ¥9126/S or Tw). The rooms in this hotel are in either Japanese- or Western-style, but only Japanese-style rooms face the ocean. The hotel is between Godaidojima and Fukuurajima.

HONSHU

When returning from Matsushima, **Aoba-dori** あおば通, the stop after Sendai station and the terminus for the Senseki Line, is slightly closer to the city centre and offers a direct transfer to the Namboku subway line.

**Alternative route to Ichinoseki** If going to Ichinoseki rather than backtracking to Sendai, and for a change of scenery, take the JR Tohoku Line from **Matsushima** 松島 (not Matsushima-Kaigan) station. The Tohoku Line suffered major damage in the 2011 earthquake but it is now open again and operates roughly once an hour (through trains 74 mins; ¥1140), though you may have to change at Kogota 小牛田. Matsushima station is 30 minutes on foot from Matsushima-Kaigan, or take a taxi (5 mins).

## Sendai to Shin-Aomori [Map 17, p331; Map 18, p337; Table 11, p508]
Note: distances are from Tokyo. Fastest journey time: 87 minutes.

If you are joining the shinkansen at Sendai and wish to travel direct to Shin-Aomori, you will have to take a Hayabusa. For stops en route to Morioka you can also take a Komachi, Yamabiko or Hayate.

Look out for the shinkansen 'car park' on the right about 3-5 minutes after leaving Sendai. Soon after that the train dips into several tunnels, but otherwise the view of rural Japan to the left and right is superb.

**Furukawa** 古川 **(395km)** All Yamabiko and some other services stop here.

**Optional route from Furukawa to the west coast** From Furukawa you can take the JR Rikuu-to Line 陸羽東線 (approx 1/hr; 46 mins) to **Naruko-onsen** 鳴子温泉 (look out for the foot-baths outside the station and around town). Between here and the station for **Nakayamadaira-onsen** 中山平温泉 is the **Naruko Gorge** 鳴子峡 which is a popular destination from late October to early November. At this time a sightseeing bus operates between the two stations. From Nakayamadaira-onsen you can continue on the Rikuu-to Line to **Shinjo** 新庄 (see p330; 9/day; 56 mins).

The Rapid Resort Minori, a Joyful train, operates on this route (between Sendai and Shinjo) seasonally at weekends (1/day).

Yamabiko services then stop at **Kurikoma-Kogen** くりこま高原 (416km).

**Ichinoseki** 一ノ関 **(445km)** All Yamabiko and some Hayabusa services call here; Tohoku main line services also stop here. Ichinoseki, divided by the Iwai river, developed as a castle town in the Edo period; the name means 'first gate' and it symbolises that this is the start of the rural north-east. The main reason to stop here is for a side trip to the temple town of Hiraizumi (see pp334-5). An overhead passageway connects the shinkansen (east) side of the station with the west side for the local JR lines. The **tourist information office** (daily 9am-5.30pm) is to the left of the station's West Exit. There are **lockers** outside the station and on the shinkansen concourse.

A convenient place to stay is *Toyoko Inn Ichinoseki Ekimae* 東横イン一ノ関駅前 (☎ 0191-31 1045, 🖥 www.toyoko-inn.com; ¥5724/S, ¥7344/D, ¥8964/Tw, inc breakfast); it is modern and has clean, comfortable Western-style rooms. To reach the hotel walk out of the station's West Exit and turn first right. The Inn is soon on the left.

HONSHU

For **food** there are several izakaya-style restaurants in the station area but otherwise little choice other than a bakery (daily 7.30am-7pm) and a soba/ramen/curry rice stand in the station's waiting room near the West Exit; buy a ticket from the machine (¥310-610).

## Side trip by rail to Hiraizumi [see Map 17, p331]

Hiraizumi 平泉 (8km north of Ichinoseki) is reached in less than 10 minutes by hourly local train along the JR Tohoku Line. At first glance it's hard to believe that this rural town once boasted a population of over 100,000. In the 12th century it was a major centre of politics and culture, a period dominated by the wealthy Fujiwara family, who ruled for four generations. Today, a couple of historic temples remain as a reminder of the place that once rivalled Kyoto in wealth and national influence. These were granted World Heritage Site status in 2011.

Hiraizumi station is small with a few ¥300 **lockers** (there are some ¥600 lockers hidden just off to the right from the exit). The **tourist information office** (🖳 hiraizumi.or.jp; daily 9am-5pm, to 4.30pm in winter) is in the small house with wooden doors to the right as you leave the station. Next door is a small **Rent-a-Cycle booth** (¥500/3 hours, ¥1000/day) which provides maps of a recommended 3-hour cycling route, including stops at both the temples described below. However, the area is hilly so you may prefer to take the **Hiraizumi Run Run Loop bus** 平泉巡回バスるんるん (Hiraizumi Jyunkai Basu Run Run; mid Apr-early Nov daily 1-4/hr; ¥150, ¥400 day pass), which goes to all the main sites from the station (bus stand No 1). There is also a local bus service which operates year-round but less frequently.

Even though it doesn't make sense in terms of the bus route, it is worth going to **Hiraizumi Cultural Heritage Center** 平泉文化遺産センター (daily 9am-5pm; free) first to get an overview of the history of the area.

**Chuson-ji** 中尊寺 (all buildings daily Mar-early Nov 8.30am-5pm, Nov-Feb 8.30am-4.30pm; grounds and many buildings free, ¥800 for Konjiki-do, Sankozo and a few other temples) was established in 850 and once comprised over 300 buildings. Not all have made it into the 21st century but those that have are impressive sights.

You can rent an informative and innovative audio guide (¥500) at the entrance to the compound near the bus stop. Rather than typing numbers into a keypad, you simply tap the nib of the pen-shaped player on the number for the recording you want to hear (unfortunately the technology struggles in the sun, so you might need to hold your hand around the player). This guide can be taken all the way up to the top including into the modern **Sankozo** 讃衡蔵, a treasure house featuring many impressive Buddhist statues.

The most important surviving building is the **Konjiki-do** 金色堂 (Golden Hall), which was completed in 1124. The theme here is light (as that is believed to drive evil away) and everything, apart from the roof, is covered with gold-leaf and filled with gold, silver and mother of pearl. Hiraizumi is the northernmost place that Basho (see p331) visited. After visiting Konjiki-do he wrote a haiku (see box).

If you walk as far as is possible along the tree-lined avenue through the temple

> *Early summer rains*
> *Fall not here*
> *Temple of light.*
> Matsuo Basho (1644-94)

compound and then take a path off to the right, you'll reach **Hakusan Shrine** 白山神社. After the opulence of Konjiki-do, the austerity of this Shinto shrine is a pleasant surprise. From a corner of the shrine area there are great views down below of plains typical of the Tohoku region. Also here is the temple's thatched-roof **Noh stage** (Noh is performed here on the evening of 14th August, but other events are also held here throughout the year).

Hop back on the Loop Bus for **Motsu-ji** 毛越寺 (daily 8.30am-5pm, to 4.30pm in winter; ¥500); the temple was founded in 850 and is known today for its 'Pure Land garden' (see box p86) centred around a pond, Oizumiga-ike 大泉が池. Few of its 40 buildings have survived but it is still an impressive place, particularly for the feeling of space. Look out for the winding stream which every May is the site of a poetry festival, Motsuji Gokusui no En 毛越寺曲水の宴. Participants, dressed in traditional costumes, have to create a short poem while a sake cup is floating down the stream towards them. Once their poem has been read out by the master of the ceremony they can drink the sake.

*Maizuruso* 旅館舞鶴荘 (☎ 0191-46 3375; from ¥3500pp, plus 10% for single occupancy; half board also possible) offers Japanese-style accommodation and is a short walk from the station. Head straight out of the station and take the turning on the right as the buildings turn into grassy ground. The minshuku is a short way along on the right.

Soba fans in particular should not leave Hiraizumi without going to the very popular *Basho-kan* 芭蕉館 (daily 10am-5pm, Dec-Mar closed Thur); *zaru soba* costs ¥580 and *wanko soba* (see p336) is from ¥1850. It's at the railway station by the bus stand for the Loop Bus.

If visiting in either early May or early November, be sure to see the Spring 春の藤原まつり or Autumn Fujiwara **festivals** 秋の藤原まつり respectively. Both include a parade of children in elaborate costumes and local performing arts spread across a few days.

After Ichinoseki all Yamabiko and some Hayabusa services stop at **Mizusawa-Esashi** 水沢江刺 (470km) and **Kitakami** 北上 (487km).

## Shin-Hanamaki 新花巻 (500km)

All Yamabiko and some Hayabusa call here. **Hanamaki** 花巻 is a small city known for its hot springs and as the birthplace of the poet Kenji Miyazawa, who achieved popularity as a writer of children's stories such as *Night on the Milky Way Train*. The major annual event is the 3-day **Hanamaki Festival** held on the second weekend of September, when large floats and portable shrines are carried through the streets in time to music. On February 11th, Hanamaki is also the location for the '**All Japan Wanko Soba Contest**', where contestants gorge on as many bowls of soba as they can for five minutes; the record at the time of research was 188 bowls.

Since 2014, a steam locomotive called **SL Ginga** SL銀河 (🖳 www.sl-ginga.com) has been operating on the JR Kamaishi Line 釜石線 between Hanamaki and Kamaishi 釜石. The design for the four carriages is based on Miyazawa's fairy tale *Ginga Tetsudo no Yoru* or *Night on the Galactic Railroad*; the interiors are luxurious and one car includes a small planetarium. The train operates seasonally (Apr-June weekends & holiday periods; free with JR pass but seat reservations essential); since the journey takes 4½ hours each way it goes to Kamaishi one day and returns the next. Unless planning to stay the night (there are several hotels near the station), take a local train (10/day; approx 2hrs) back to Hanamaki; there are usually good connections.

To reach Hanamaki city take a local train two stops west along the Kamaishi Line (10/day; 7 mins).

**Morioka 盛岡 (535km)** Yamabiko services terminate here; all Hayabusa and Hayate services stop here before continuing to Shin-Aomori/Shin-Hakodate-Hokuto (a few Hayate services also start here). Consider indulging yourself and going Gran Class in the Hayabusa from here to Shin-Aomori (see box p320). Komachi services run west from here to Akita.

Shinkansen services depart from the 2nd floor of the station. Also on this floor is the **Northern Tohoku TIC** (daily 9am-5.30pm); staff can help with accommodation bookings in Morioka. There are **lockers** in various corners of the station including large ¥500 ones in the passage between the north and south sides of the station. The entrance to the private **Iwate Galaxy Railway** いわて 銀河鉄道 (IGR; 🖳 www.igr.jp), also known as Iwate Ginga Railway, is in a corner of the 1st/ground floor of the station. This operates from Morioka 盛岡 to Metoki 目時, on the former Tohoku main line.

Morioka calls itself the 'Castle town of northern Japan' but only the ruined stone walls remain. The main reason for stopping here is to take one of the suggested side trips (see pp338-40), or if passing through between August 1st and 4th, when **Sansa-odori** さんさ踊り (🖳 www.sansaodori.jp) is held. Groups dressed in traditional costumes dance down the main street to the accompaniment of taiko drums and flutes. Festival stalls line the streets and there's a real street-party atmosphere. The festival is in the *Guinness Book of Records* for having the largest number of Japanese drums being played at the same time.

For Japanese-style **accommodation** try the friendly *Ryokan Kumagai* 熊ヶ 井旅館 (☎ 0196-51 3019, 🖳 kumagairyokan.com; ¥5000/S, ¥4500/Tw; breakfast ¥1000pp, dinner ¥1500pp). It is an 8-minute walk from the station across Kitakami-gawa. For a Western-style hotel, *Toyoko Inn Morioka Ekimae* 東横 イン盛岡駅前 (☎ 0196-25 1045, 🖳 www.toyoko-inn.com; ¥5292/S, ¥6804/D, ¥8964/Tw) is two minutes on foot from the station's Central Exit: look for the tall building with 'HOTEL' written above '東横イン'.

More upmarket is the JR-run *Hotel Metropolitan Morioka* ホテルメトロ ポリタン盛岡 (☎ 0196-25 1211, 🖳 www.metro-morioka.co.jp; from ¥9504/S, ¥18,770/D or Tw, breakfast ¥1782; JR rail-pass holders get a discount), which also has a New Wing (not actually that new), with more spacious – and more expensive rooms – and access to the Central Fitness Club next door (¥540/day).

In terms of **food** Morioka's most famous culinary export is *wanko soba*, bowls of good-quality soba, served with side dishes and traditionally eaten in a competition where diners race to scoff the most noodles. Try it at *Yabuya* やぶ 屋 (10am-10pm) in the Gourmet Town section of the basement of Fesan フェ ザン department store (🖳 www.fesan-jp.com), on the left of the main station exit. Here you can get 10 bowls for ¥1500; they also serve tempura soba (¥1000). Alternatively, if you prefer ramen, head to *Iwate no Ramen* 岩手のら ーめん (daily 9am-10pm) in the Menkoi Yokocho part of Fesan.

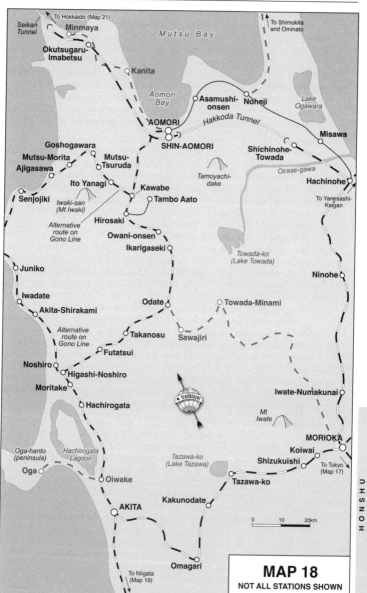

MAP 18

NOT ALL STATIONS SHOWN

## Side trips by shinkansen from Morioka [see Map 18, p337]

The Komachi shinkansen (to Akita; 1/hr) makes it easy to do day trips from Morioka to either **Tazawa-ko** (34 mins) or **Kakunodate** (about 47 mins), though it would be hard to see both in one day. Alternatively, you could create a circular route around the northern part of Honshu by continuing on the line to **Akita** (pp347-8; 99 mins) and from there proceed to **Aomori** by doing the Aomori to Akita route (see pp344-7) in reverse, and finally return to Morioka (or Tokyo). Local trains (3/day to Omagari, frequent services Omagari to Akita) also run on this route. An added attraction to this side trip is that for the first part of the journey there are good views of the volcanic peak of **Mt Iwate** 岩手山.

**Tazawa-ko (Lake Tazawa)** 田沢湖 This is the deepest lake in Japan (423.4m) and is renowned for being a nearly perfect circle. It also attracts more than its fair share of legends, such as the following: 'Once upon a time, a village girl named Tatsuko drank the water of Lake Tazawa as instructed by the goddess Kannon, in order to make her wish of perpetual beauty come true. In the end, she was transformed into a dragon, whereupon she sank into the depths of the lake and was never seen again.' Though she does live on in a way as there is now a statue of her in the lake.

The **tourist information centre** (🖳 www.tazawako.org; daily 8.30am-6.30pm) is on your right after going through the ticket gate. Staff have bus timetables for the lake, and there's a huge topographical model of the area. The bus ticket counter is to the right of the exit. There are lockers in front of the station. Several **buses** go to the lake area; services operating year-round include the Nyuto Line 乳頭線 (approx 1/hr; 15 mins; ¥360), which continues to Nyuto-onsen 乳頭温泉, and the Tazawako Isshu Line 田沢湖一周線 (1-3/hr; ¥360), which operates a circular route around the lake. Additional lines operate in the summer months.

Conveniently the bus stops right by the ticket counter for the **round-trip cruises**, operated by Tazawa-ko Yuran-sen 田沢湖遊覧船 (Apr-Nov 4-8/day; 40 mins; ¥1200), on the lake. The main highlight is getting close to the **statue of Tatsuko** たつこ像 though if the weather is good the trip can be very scenic. If you prefer something more energetic there are plenty of swan, duck, panda or other pedalos for hire (¥1500/30 mins for 2-3 people).

**Kakunodate** 角館 A former samurai town, this makes an interesting destination at any time but is especially worthwhile in mid April to early May when hundreds of *shidarezakura* (weeping cherry trees) are in blossom along the river bank, or in late October to mid November when the foliage turns crimson. Its scenic charms are why several films, including *The Twilight Samurai* (2002) and *The Hidden Blade* (2004) have used Kakunodate as a backdrop.

The town comprises **Uchimachi** 内町, samurai village, in the north, and **Tomachi** 外町, merchant village, to the south. Allow around three hours to do a loop including both. Pick up a map from the **tourist information centre** (TIC; 🖳 kakunodate-kanko.jp; daily late Apr-Nov 9am-6pm, Oct to late Apr to 5.30pm), the white building with a wooden base to the right of the exit. There are lockers around the station but the staff here will keep luggage (¥300 per bag) until 30 minutes before closing.

Kakunodate is a small town and the sights can all be reached on foot. Walk into town and turn right at the post office for **Uchimachi** (also signposted as

Bukeya-shiki 武家屋敷); this begins properly with the trees after the next set of traffic lights. About 80 families used to live here; several descendants still reside here and now sell souvenirs. On the right-hand side, there are three family houses – **Odano-ke** 小田野家, **Kawarada-ke** 河原田家 and **Iwahashi-ke** 岩橋家 (all daily 9am-4.30pm) – where you may enter the grounds without charge, but not step into the buildings. In the absence of English, compare the wooden signs on the gate with the characters printed above.

At the next crossroads on the corner, **Kakunodate Denshokan** 角館樺細工伝承館 (daily Apr-Nov 9am-5pm, Dec-Mar to 4.30pm; ¥300, or ¥200 with discount coupon from TIC) has demonstrations of the traditional local art of *kabazaiku* (products made from the bark of the cherry trees) as well as displaying various samurai artefacts. If you visit the town on the 11th of the month (the characters for 1 一 and 10 十 can be overlaid to form the character for samurai 士), costumed samurai will be standing outside the Denshokan.

After the crossroads, there are two samurai houses on the right worth paying to enter. The first, **Aoyanagi Samurai Manor Museum** 青柳家 (Aoyanagi-ke; 🖳 www.samuraiworld.com; Apr-Oct 9am-5pm, Nov-Mar to 4.30pm; ¥500) has a wide variety of exhibits including armoury, household objects such as sake cups, miso and rice bowls, and dolls (to see these, take the steep stairs on the right as you leave the armoury). There's also a display of military uniforms and a Folk Gallery containing Edison voice-recording machines and record players as well as masses of records – everything from Duke Ellington to *La Traviata*. The second, **Ishiguro-ke** 石黒家 (daily 9am-5pm; ¥300) is smaller but the descendants will give you a brief guided and informative (albeit scripted) tour, explaining the function and layout of the house, as well as some of the architectural details. At the end of the road, there is the small **Hirafuku Memorial Art Museum** 平福記念美術館 (Apr-Oct daily 9am-5pm, Nov-Mar Tue-Sun to 4.30pm; ¥500), dedicated to two Hirafuku generations of Kakunodate-born artists. The second room contains works of other artists with a local connection. Turn left after the museum to reach the river; returning left and back into town, there is a 2km **tunnel of sakura** (cherry blossom) trees alongside the Hinokinai River 絵木内川 that look beautiful in any season, but particularly when in bloom.

For contrast, do visit the **To-machi** 外町 (Merchant District) in the lower half of the town. On your way back and just before the post office, drop into **Tatetsu** たてつ (daily 10am-5pm; free) on your right (no English exterior signage; look for the red banner), a former storehouse and historical museum. From the post office in the centre of town, walk back towards the station and turn right at the first set of traffic lights. On your left is **Nishinomiya-ke** 西宮家 (daily 10am-5pm), a former warehouse for rice and pickles that is now a museum, shop and restaurant. The museum displays household objects in glass cabinets, including a radio and sewing machine. Don't leave without looking around the former warehouses or trying the truly delicious sushi containing home-made pickles. At the bottom of the road on the right is **Ando-jozo** 安藤醸造 (daily 8.30am-6pm), a miso and soy-sauce brick storehouse and shop; visit the warehouse with its wonderful screens and then go to the back of the shop where you will be able to try some pickles, tea and *dashi* (soup) for free.

The most convenient place to stay is *Folkloro Kakunodate* ホテルフォルクローロ (☎ 0187-53 2070, 🖳 www.folkloro-kakunodate.com; ¥12,020/Tw, inc buffet breakfast; discounts for JR rail-pass holders); it is to your left as you leave the station. Some of the hotel's twin rooms can sleep up to four people. Book early in peak seasons (spring and autumn), when rates usually rise.

**Omagari** 大曲 Omagari's claim to fame is that the Omagari National Japan Fireworks Competition is held here, by Omono River, on the fourth Saturday in August; it takes 20-25 minutes to walk there from the station. Pick up a map of the town from the **tourist information centre** (daily 9am-6pm) to the right of the stairs to the West Exit as you leave the ticket barrier.

**Side trip to Jodogohama (Pure Land) beach** Jodogohama beach 浄土ヶ浜 is a stunning place of natural beauty including a deep blue sea, pale white sand and rich greenery. The water is clean and perfect for swimming in, in the summer. Nearby and accessible only via the small **Sappa Boats** サッパ船 (🖳 www.j-marine.com; Mar-Nov 8.30am-5pm; ¥1500) is the impressive **Blue Cave** 青の洞窟, which contains bright blue water and vividly coloured rock walls. Getting to the beach is a 2½-hour train journey on the JR Yamada Line to Miyako 宮古 (4/day) followed by a bus from the station at stand No 3 to Oku-Jodogahama (10/day; 20 mins; ¥220).

After Morioka, some Hayabusa services stop at **Iwate-Numakunai** いわて沼宮内 (121km). You don't take this route for the views. It is almost exclusively tunnels so there is little to report in the way of sights.

**Ninohe** 二戸 **(601km)** Some Hayabusa stop here. 'Ichinohe' means the 'first door'. In medieval times, the northern part of Iwate and southern part of Aomori prefectures were divided into different political districts. Each district was known as a 'door', meaning the door or gateway to that district. So, in this case, 'Ninohe' means the 'second door'. The next 'door' to be found on the shinkansen line is at Hachinohe (the eighth door).

**Hachinohe** 八戸 **(632km)** Most Hayabusa stop here. Hachinohe is an industrial and port city; the main reason to stop here is for the Sansha Taisai festival (see opposite), but it does make a good base if planning to go to the Tanesashi Coast (see p342), or for an unusual side trip into the mountains to a small village where it's claimed Jesus Christ is buried (see box opposite).

The 'South Bridge' waiting area as you come up from the shinkansen platforms overlooks the tracks. The **JR ticket office** (daily 6am-11.15pm) and **View Plaza travel agency** are on the 3rd-floor main concourse. **Hachinohe Tourism Information Plaza** (daily 9am-7pm) is on the 2nd floor by the East Exit. **Lockers** (with a few large ¥600 ones) are behind you on your right.

The most convenient place to stay, since it's built into the station, is the JR-operated *Hotel Mets Hachinohe* ホテルメッツ八戸 (☎ 0178-70 7700, 🖳 www.hotelmets.jp/hachinohe; ¥6500/S, ¥12,900/Tw; ¥500 breakfast, discount for JR rail-pass holders). The entrance is to the left of the escalators down to the East Exit.

There is a **soba/udon** counter on the main concourse (to the right as you exit the ticket barrier). Alternatively there's a reasonably cheap revolving **sushi restaurant** opposite the lift/elevator which takes you to Hotel Mets. And if you take the escalator down to the East Exit and turn left, you'll see a line of **yatai/izakaya-style places**; these get packed out with businessmen at the end of the working day but are recommended for the atmosphere.

It is well worth trying to be in Hachinohe for the **Sansha Taisai festival** 三社大祭 (31st July to 3rd Aug). This is about 300 years old and the festival is designated one of Japan's National Important Intangible Folk Cultural Assets. There are parades of 27 floats, each of which is made by a different area of the city, and three *mikoshi* (portable shrines). One mikoshi comes from each of the three shrines (san-sha), Ogami, Shinra and Shinmei, taking part in the festival.

If you can't be here for the festival you can still see at least one of the enormous floats in **Yew Tree Plaza** ユートリープラザ (daily 9am-7pm); turn right as you leave the station and you will see the large building straight ahead. Regional products are sold here and there are more large lockers (cheaper at ¥400). There's a restaurant on the 2nd floor, which tends to be less busy than those in and immediately outside the station.

---

### ❏ Jesus in Japan?

The journey to the remote village of **Shingo** 新郷, deep in the mountains west of Hachinohe, certainly feels like a pilgrimage. There is no rail line and the only way of reaching the village is to take two buses. Your destination is the Christ Park キリストの里公園, so called because locals claim that it contains the grave of none other than Jesus Christ. The story goes that instead of dying on the cross, Jesus escaped at the last minute, fled to Siberia, made his way to Alaska and finally boarded a boat bound for Japan, where he landed at the port of Hachinohe. He quickly found his way to the village of Herai (now called Shingo) where he married a Japanese woman called Miyuko, had three daughters and lived to 106. In his latter years, Christ is said to have travelled around Japan, 'endeavouring to save the common people, while observing the language, customs and manners of the various regions'. He is described in village records as being 'grey haired and rather bald with a ruddy complexion and high nose and [he] wore a coat with many folds, causing people to hold him in awe as a long-nosed goblin.'

The extraordinary story only came to light in 1935 when two graves were found in a bamboo thicket at the top of a small hill in the village. It wasn't until May 1936, when Christ's 'last will and testament' mysteriously turned up in the village, that the significance of these graves was revealed: one of the graves was Christ's, the other belonged to his brother, called Isukiri. Or rather, just his brother's ear. Supposedly Jesus managed to avoid crucifixion thanks to his brother who 'casually took Christ's place and died on his cross', allowing him to escape to Japan clutching one of Isukiri's ears along with some 'hair of the Virgin Mary'. Further 'proof' can be found down in the village: Herai, the ancient name of the village, is said to be a corruption of 'Hebrew' and a villager who died some years ago 'looked not like a Japanese, his eyes were blue like those of a foreigner'. Curiously, there has been little attempt to cash in on the story by turning the park into a tacky tourist trap. Indeed, there's so little publicity that it's almost as if the village is embarrassed by the legend and doesn't quite know what to do with its two graves up on the hill.

The Tourist Information Plaza at Hachinohe station (see opposite) can advise on bus times and connections to/from Shingo; they also have an information sheet in English.

HONSHU

### Side trip by rail to the Tanesashi Coast [see map p319]

Hachinohe may be an industrial centre, but the Tanesashi Coast (Tanesashi Kaigan), a nationally designated Place of Scenic Beauty, is only a short train ride away and offers a scenic hike (approx 3½hrs) and a chance to swim. The coastline was hit rather badly by the 2011 tsunami and in an effort to promote tourism here, the hiking trails and maps are usually marked well in English.

Jump on a JR Hachinohe Line train to **Tanesashi Kaigan** 種差海岸 station (9/day; 33 mins; ¥320); the line is one of the few left in Japan that, at the time of research, still has trains without air-conditioning and offers a unique chance to feel the summer breeze in your hair coming in through the open windows. Walk out towards the main road and turn left, where you will find **Tanesashi Coast Information Centre** 種差海岸インフォメーションセンター (daily Apr-Nov 9am-5pm, Dec-Mar to 4pm). On the other side of the road lies **Tanesashi Natural Lawn** 種差天然芝生地, a fact of life for rainsoaked Europeans but a rare botanical phenomenon in the Japanese climate, particularly next to the sea. Turn left and follow the lawn up the coast and through the campsite to join the **promenade** towards Shirahama Fishing Port, a trail path up the cliff that periodically burrows into pine forests before presenting stunning views of the cliff edge and ocean. After passing through a little port and up another small cliff, take a dip at **Shirahama Swimming Beach** 白浜海水浴場, designated as one of the top 100 beaches by the Ministry of the Environment. Continue along **Osuka Beach** 大須賀海岸, known as a beach of squeaking sand, and climb up to **Ashigezaki Lookout** 葦毛崎展望台. A final 40-minute hike and you'll arrive at **Kabujima Island** 蕪島 and its temple, a famous breeding ground for black-tailed gulls (*umineko*) who gather between February and late July, swelling to a population of over 40,000 birds. Do visit the adjacent Information Centre (daily 9am-5pm), providing not just information about (and refuge from) the gulls, but also images of the devastation of the 2011 tsunami. To return to Hachinohe, walk another 15 minutes to **Same** 鮫 station (1-2/hr; 24 mins; ¥240). If hiking gets tiring, a ¥100 bus (7/day) operates along the coastal road, and **Mutsu-Shirahama** 陸奥白浜 station on the Hachinohe Line is a short walk up the hill from Shirahama Swimming Beach.

The luxury **Tohoku Emotion** (🖥 www.jreast.co.jp/tohokuemotion) restaurant train operates on this line (Apr-Sep 1/day; lunch/dessert buffet outward/return journey ¥7900/¥4500; round trip ¥11,900). JR passes are not valid; tickets must be bought at a View Plaza Travel Service Center (see p100). The promotional video on the website is worth watching even if you can't travel on this.

### Alternative route by rail to Aomori

The shinkansen line is undoubtedly the quickest way to reach Aomori from Hachinohe but the original Aoimori Line 青い森鉄道線 offers better scenery and if you have a Japan Rail Pass (see box opposite) you can do this journey (1-2/hr; about 90 mins) for free if you stay on the train, other than at Noheji. If you don't have a pass it will cost ¥2280. **Noheji** 野辺地 (51km) is a point of interchange for the JR Ominato Line 大湊線 that runs part of the way up the Shimokita Peninsula. Sadly, it's not until just before the train approaches Aomori that the track gets close enough to the shore for a sweeping view of **Mutsu Bay** 陸奥湾. Look out for a beautiful pine-clad island that is impressive enough to make people look up from their newspapers. If you fancy an onsen and are prepared to pay if you have a Japan Rail Pass, stop at **Asamushi-onsen**

❏ **Changes for the Japan Rail Pass and Seishun Juhachi Kippu**
With the completion of the Tohoku Shinkansen, JR East transferred the original rail-way tracks between Hachinohe and Aomori to Aoimori Railways, a non-JR compa-ny. This results in the unique situation where the JR Ominato Line (from Noheji to Ominato on the Shimokita Peninsula) is now completely isolated from the rest of the JR network and the JR Hachinohe Line remains connected to the JR network only through a shinkansen line. In order to keep these two lines accessible to holders of the Japan Rail Pass, JR East Tohoku Pass, and Seishun Juhachi Kippu (see pp29-32), a special rule was introduced, allowing pass holders to ride the Aoimori Railway 'for free' if they only get on or off at Aomori, Noheji or Hachinohe stations. If getting on or off at any other station along the line the regular fare has to be paid.

浅虫温泉 (79km). Right outside the station is **Yusa Asamushi** ゆさ浅虫, a modern building which contains a great hot spring (🖳 www.yu-sa.jp; daily 7am-9pm; ¥350 to/from Aomori) with views over Mutsu Bay. Small towels are sold but bring your own soap. It's a shame after the brief views of Mutsu Bay that the final approach into **Aomori** 青森 (96km) is less impressive.

Some Hayabusa services stop at **Shichinohe-Towada** 七戸十和田 (668km).

## Shin-Aomori 新青森 (714km)          [see pp363-6 for Aomori]
Shin-Aomori is the final station on the Tohoku shinkansen and, since March 2016, the start of the Hokkaido Shinkansen. For Aomori you will need to trans-fer from the shinkansen part of the station to the platforms for the JR Ou Line 奥 羽線 and take either a local line train or a Hakucho LEX to JR Aomori (6 mins).

**Aomori TIC** (daily 8.30am-7pm), on the left on the general concourse, pri-marily has information on Aomori prefecture rather than the city. In the station, there is also a View Plaza Travel Service Center (daily 10am-5.30pm) and a Midori-no-madoguchi reservation window (daily 5.20am-10.30pm). Even if you aren't hungry, head downstairs on the left of the shinkansen exit to **Aomori Shunmi-kan** あおもり旬味館 (daily 9am-9pm); this is designed to resemble a typical traditional street with stands selling local foods as well as restaurants offering sushi, yakisoba and ramen. *Café de Tsugaru* (7am-5.30pm), in the tick-et area on the main concourse, serves sandwiches and cakes (¥300-600).

❏ **The difference a shinkansen line makes**
The fastest journey between Hachinohe and Aomori before the shinkansen line opened was 58 minutes; with the shinkansen the journey takes about 28 minutes (to Shin-Aomori). The considerable time saving is possible because of the large number of tunnels on this section – in fact one-third of the journey is in tunnels, the majority being in the **Hakkoda Tunnel** 八甲田トンネル between Shichinohe-Towada and Shin-Aomori. This tunnel took 6½ years to construct and at 26.5km was for a brief period the world's longest tunnel. But its claim to fame was short lived, since it was soon eclipsed by the 34.6-km long Lötschberg Tunnel in Switzerland. However, Hakkoda Tunnel can still claim to be the longest land-based tunnel if the specifica-tion 'double-track' is added.

HONSHU

## AOMORI / SHIN-AOMORI TO AKITA AND NIIGATA

The route described below goes across Tohoku and then down the western side. In addition to this a predominantly coastal route (see p346) from Aomori/Shin-Aomori, or Hirosaki, to Akita is included as it offers magnificent views and at weekends and national holidays an enjoyable rail experience.

### Aomori to Akita                                    [Map 18, p337; Table 12, p509]

Distances by JR from Aomori. Fastest journey time: 2 hours 40 minutes.

### Aomori 青森 (0km)                                              [see pp363-6]

From Aomori, take a train on the JR Ou Line 奥羽線 towards Akita.

The first stop is **Shin-Aomori** (3.9km). Gradually the residential scenery recedes and the landscape opens up.

The main sight from the train is **Mt Iwaki** 岩木山, spiritual symbol of the area. It has three peaks and many different profiles, which means everyone claims their region has the best view. Look out for it in the distance to the right about 20 minutes after leaving Aomori.

### Hirosaki 弘前 (37km)  All trains stop here. If on a Tsugaru LEX change here

for the JR Gono Line and the coastal route to Akita described on p346.

Hirosaki flourished from the early 17th century as a castle town of the Tsugaru feudal lords. It is now known as an area of apple production; 20% of the apples grown in Japan come from this area. It won't be hard to find apple products: the sparkling apple wine (*cidre*) is very refreshing.

Follow signs for the Central Exit, turn immediately left as you leave the station and walk to the end of the building to find **lockers** (up to ¥600 size). At the **tourist information office** 弘前市観光案内所 (🖳 www.hirosaki.co.jp; daily 8.45am-6pm), to the right as you go out of the station, staff will help book same-day accommodation. **Hirosaki Sightseeing Information Center** 弘前観光コンベンション協会 (daily 9am-6pm), in a modern building opposite Hirosaki Park, offers similar services.

The best way to get around is the **Dotemachi ¥100 Loop bus** 土手町循環100円バス (daily 6/hr; ¥100/journey, ¥500 1-day pass). The bus stops at or near all the main sights and can be identified by the '100円' on the front of the bus. It's worth noting that you are unlikely to get value from the day pass as most people simply take the bus to the park and then back again.

Top priority on a visit to Hirosaki should be **Fujita Memorial Japanese Garden** 藤田記念庭園 (Fujita Kinen Teien; daily mid Apr to late Nov 9am-5pm; ¥310, combined ticket inc the castle and arboretum ¥510), a typical Edo-period stroll garden but with a difference because it is built on two levels. From the upper level, Mt Iwaki can be seen in the distance.

Across the street from the garden is **Hirosaki Park** 弘前公園 which has over 2500 cherry trees and is one of Japan's most popular cherry blossom-viewing spots (late Apr to early May). Inside the park is the site of **Hirosaki Castle** 弘前女 (Apr-Nov daily 9am-5pm; ¥310), completed in 1611. The original 5-storey castle tower was struck by lightning in 1627 and burnt to the

HONSHU

ground, so what stands today is a replacement 3-storey tower (built in 1810) which usually houses a museum of samurai artefacts. However, the castle is currently closed as part of a 10-year long reconstruction of its underlying stone walls. This entails physically moving the castle tower to a different location, reconstructing the stone walls and then moving it back again – a process that will finish in 2024. The grounds are still open to enter for the admission fee and worth walking around even without being able to enter the castle. The gardens at **Hirosaki Castle Arboretum (Botanical Gardens)** 弘前城植物園 (Hirosaki-jo Shokubutsu-en; daily early April to late Nov 9am-5pm; ¥310) seem fairly unkempt and are only worth seeing in spring, but the cheapness of the combined ticket means even only visiting two of the attractions still saves money.

From Hirosaki Park it is a short walk to the **Sightseeing Information Center** (see opposite), at O-temon Square, and in a separate building an exhibition (daily 9am-6pm; free) of floats used in the Neputa as well as the old library and missionaries' house plus a display of miniature models of original buildings in the city. **Neputa Mura** ねぷた村 (daily 9am-5pm; ¥550) also contains some of the festival floats as well as other symbols of Hirosaki. Get off at Shiyakusho-mae bus stop. Get off here also, or at Bunka Center-mae, for the Ishiba Residence 石場家, a **merchant's house** (daily 9am-5pm, closed irregular days; free except central area ¥100) and three **samurai residences**: Ito 旧伊東家 & Umeda 旧梅田家 (July-Oct Mon, Wed-Thur, Sat & Sun 10am-4pm); Iwata 旧岩田家 (July-Oct Tue-Wed, Fri-Sun 10am-4pm, Nov-June all houses Sat-Sun 10am-4pm; free).

The big festival of the year, **Neputa Matsuri** 弘前ねぷた祭り, rivals Aomori's Nebuta Matsuri (see p364) and takes place at the same time (1st-7th Aug). There is a nightly procession through the town of colourful floats.

For accommodation, right outside Hirosaki station try *Route Inn Hirosaki Ekimae* ホテルルートイン弘前駅前 (☎ 0172-31 0010, 🖳 route-inn.co.jp; ¥6200/S, ¥9050/D, ¥10,550/Tw, inc buffet breakfast). Rooms are compact but quite stylish and include a fridge. The only downside is that the beds are firm – almost hard. The hotel also has an onsen and massage chairs (¥100/10 mins). On the left side in front of the station is *Hotel Naqua City Hirosaki* ホテルナクアシティ弘前 (☎ 0172-37 0700, 🖳 www.naquacity-hirosaki.com; from ¥20,520/D, ¥28,080/Tw, exc buffet breakfast), an upmarket hotel with a wide variety of rooms and restaurants.

### Side trip to Inakadate Rice Paddy Art

An unusual trip in the summer is to go and see the Inakadate Rice Paddy Art 田舎館村田んぼアート (Inakadate-mura Tambo Aato; daily June & Sep to mid Oct 9am-5pm, Jul-Aug 8.30am-6pm; ¥200). Every year two rice fields in the area are planted such that, from a high vantage point, the crops resemble a work of art or image. Previous works include *Star Wars*, the *Mona Lisa* and *Gone with the Wind*, along with famous works of Japanese art. The two fields are reached by differing routes, but the easiest to reach is the second (Dai Ni Tambo Aato 第2田んぼアート). Pick up a map and timetable from the information office in Hirosaki station and then take a Konan Railroad 弘南線 (1-2/hr; approx 20 mins; ¥430) train to **Tambo Aato** 田んぼアート; note the station is open only between April and November. You'll need to get off at the front of the train here; once you do, the lime-green observation tower is hard to miss. The ticket cost is to get the lift/elevator to the top and look down on the art. A free shuttle bus will take you to field No 1 and back if you want. On the return train journey, get on at the front and take a numbered ticket. You don't pay until you reach Hirosaki again – where you can just give your money to the ticket inspector at the gate.

### Alternative route: by Resort Shirakami from Aomori / Shin-Aomori or Hirosaki to Akita via Senjojiki  [Map 18, p337]

JR East's (🖳 www.jreast.co.jp/railway/joyful) original Joyful Train (see box p98) on the JR Gono Line went into service in 1997 under the name **Resort Shirakami** リゾートしらかみ, though these days there are actually three tourist trains operating on this line: the orange Kumagera (Woodpecker), the green Buna (Beech Tree), and the blue Aoike (Blue Pond). In general the trains have four carriages with a variety of seating areas, the main features being large windows and lounge areas. At least one of the carriages has a number of compartments seating four people in each. The seats in these can be pulled out so that passengers can sit as if sitting on the floor.

On all Resort Shirakami trains, passengers get the chance to see some wonderful scenery and are also treated to live *shamisen* (see pp63-4) music and traditional Japanese storytelling as they travel. Sadly these trains only operate on the Gono Line at weekends and in holiday periods (New Year; Golden Week in late Apr/early May; and late July to end Sep). The journey from Aomori to Akita (or vice versa; 3-4/day) takes about 5 hours 10 minutes. Rail-pass holders can travel for free but you must have a **seat reservation**; ask for Seat A if you would like a sea-side view. Without a rail pass, the Aomori to Akita (or vice-versa) fare costs ¥5560 and ¥520 for a seat reservation.

The train runs first from Aomori to **Hirosaki**, where it changes direction and heads for the coast via **Kawabe** 川部, where the traditional storyteller gets on and stays until **Mutsu-Tsuruda** 陸奥鶴田. The shamisen players get on at **Goshogawara** 五所川原 and leave at **Mutsu-Morita** 陸奥森田. They sing and play in Car 3 (occasionally Car 4), but the TV monitors in each car also broadcast the entertainment, and you can walk along to Car 3 whenever you like. When the entertainers are not playing the monitors are used to show the driver's view – straight tunnels become much more fun when you can see a small circle of light ahead which slowly gets larger and larger.

The route is inland until just after **Ajigasawa** 鰺ヶ沢 and then mostly runs parallel to the coast (with the possibility of seeing a great sunset) until Higashi-Noshiro. Between these two stations, the train stops for about 15 minutes at **Senjojiki** 千畳敷 so that everyone can get out and take photos. Senjojiki ('Thousand Tatami Mats') is so named because the flatness of the beach around here made a former emperor think it was as big as a thousand tatami mats. Steam fans should look out on the right at **Wespa-Tsubakiyama** ウェスパ椿山 (not on Map 18) to see a SL78653. The train slows down when you are passing places of scenic interest such as between **Juniko** 十二湖 and **Akita-Shirakami** あきた白神.

At **Higashi-Noshiro** 東能代駅 (technically the end of the JR Gono Line) the train changes direction; you then pass Hachirogata Lagoon en route to **Akita**, but scenically this is not as interesting as the coast line already passed.

**Owani-onsen** 大鰐温泉 **(49km)** Only 10 minutes down the line by limited express, this is a popular stop for skiers in winter as there is a ski resort here.

It's apple-tree, rice fields and pine-tree territory on both sides of the line between Owani-onsen and Odate. A few trains stop at **Ikarigaseki** 碇ヶ関 (57km). **Odate** 大館 (82km) is the terminus for the JR Hanawa Line from Towada-Minami and Morioka. The train may then stop at **Takanosu** 鷹ノ巣 (100km) and **Futatsui** 二ツ井 (112km). The track, which has been roughly following Yoneshiro-gawa towards the coast, turns south at **Higashi-Noshiro** 東 能代 (129km) on its way to Akita. The scenery around **Moritake** 森岳 (139km) is mostly rice fields with pine trees in the distance.

**Hachirogata** 八郎潟 **(157km)** There is a major land reclamation area out to the right (west) along this stretch of the journey. Although there's not a great deal to see, it's an amazing project on paper: Hachirogata Lagoon, once the second largest lake in Japan, was reclaimed and is now a vast expanse of rice paddies – an area equal in size to the space inside Tokyo's Yamanote Line.

**Akita** 秋田 **(1186km)** Akita is a large industrial city with a bright, modern station which was rebuilt when the Komachi 'mini-shinkansen' service opened along the conventional-speed Tazawa-ko Line, linking Akita with Morioka. The station has several exits (including Topico and Metropolitan), but it is easiest to follow signs for the Central Exit and once through the ticket barrier head for the West Gate. **Lockers** (including a few ¥500) are in the waiting room adjacent to the JR ticket office on your right as you exit the main ticket barrier. There's a **View Plaza Travel Service Center** (Mon-Fri 10.30am-6pm, Sat & Sun to 5pm) opposite the JR ticket office. The **tourist information office** 秋田市観光案内 所 (daily Apr-Oct 9am-7pm, Nov-Mar to 6pm) is directly opposite the ticket barrier. Topico department store is built into the west side of the station.

The highlight of the year in Akita is **Kanto Matsuri** 竿燈まつり (early Aug), when men parade through the streets balancing bamboo poles topped with heavy lanterns (weighing 5-30kg) on their foreheads, shoulders, chins, heads and other parts of the body. During the rest of the year, drop by **Akita City Folklore and Performing Arts Center** 秋田市民俗芸能伝承館 (Akita-shi Minzoku Geino Densho-kan; daily 9.30am-4.30pm; ¥100, ¥250 inc Akarenga-kyodo-kan) to see a film of the action and a display of some of the weighty lanterns and poles. Volunteers demonstrate the astonishing pole-balancing act and will help visitors attempt this feat themselves. The lack of labels in English make this museum less interesting than it might otherwise be. More appealing is the preserved **mud-walled storehouse**, home and shop for the Kameko family – go out through the door next to the lift/elevator, not the door you came in by. The museum is 20 minutes on foot west from the station.

**Akarenga-kyodo-kan Museum** 赤れんが郷土館 (daily 9.30am-4.30pm; ¥200), a striking white-and-red brick building, served as the headquarters of Akita Bank from 1912 to 1969; the teller windows on the 1st/ground floor are still there. Inside are some fine examples of Akita *hachijo* (naturally dyed silk fabric), lacquerware and dolls. It's a 20-minute walk across town.

HONSHU

**Akita Museum of Art** 秋田県立美術館 (daily 10am-6pm; ¥310 but may change for special exhibitions) opened in 2013 and was designed by renowned Japanese architect, Tadao Ando. The museum is small but its main feature is a mural by Tsuguharu Foujita called *The Events of Akita*; at more than 20 metres wide this is worth the admission price alone. An English leaflet is available at the ticket office. The museum is in the centre of Akita by Senshu Park 千秋公園.

A convenient choice for an overnight stay is the JR-run *Hotel Metropolitan Akita* ホテルメトロポリタン秋田 (☎ 018-831 2222, 🖥 www.metro-akita.jp; ¥11,500/S, ¥23,000/D, ¥21,500/Tw, right outside the West Exit of the station – take the stairs down to the right at the start of the covered walkway. The rooms are stylish and have 42" TV screens; the premium rooms have a chaise longue so you can recline and look down on life around the station area. A cheaper option is *Toyoko Inn Akita-eki Higashi-guchi* 東横イン秋田駅東口 (☎ 018-889 1045, 🖥 www.toyoko-inn.com; ¥5724/S, ¥6804/D, ¥8964/Tw). Turn left as you exit the main ticket barrier and then follow signs for the East Exit. Take the lift/elevator or stairs to M2F and enter AL*VE (sic) building; the Toyoko Inn is on the right. Reception is on the 2nd floor but the rooms are on the 8th to 19th floors. Offering a similar deal is *Hotel Alpha 1* ホテルアルファーワン秋田 (☎ 018-836 5800, 🖥 www.alpha-1.co.jp/akita; from ¥4500/S, ¥7600/D, ¥9800/Tw; buffet-style breakfast ¥950), on your left as you take the West Exit – look for the 'α-1' sign on the roof.

For **food**, the local specialities are *inaniwa udon* and *kiritanpo nabe*, made with seasonal ingredients. You can try both at *Sato Yasuke* 佐藤養助 (daily 11am-8.30pm) on the basement floor of Seibu department store outside the West Exit; set meals cost from ¥1000. *Doden Shita* どでん舌 (daily 5pm-12am) does a range of meat dishes and yakisoba but is best visited to try the Adult Banana Parfait アダルトばななパフェ which at just ¥200 is worth paying for simply for the ensuing giggles (it certainly earns its name). The restaurant is a bit tricky to find – it's above a Sunkus convenience store. Look for a lobby just to the left of the store with a lift/elevator that will take you up to the restaurant. On the same floor as the Toyoko Inn, *Nonbe-Kube* のんべえくうべえ (daily 11am-2.30pm & 5.30-11pm) does set meals including tonkatsu (¥1018) and soba (from ¥1000).

If in a hurry to return to Tokyo take the all-reserved Komachi shinkansen that runs east to Morioka – effectively the side trip from Morioka (see pp338-40) in reverse – and from there on to Tokyo. Alternatively, it would be easy to visit either Omagari or Kakunodate and also possibly Tazawa-ko as a day trip from Akita. The train travels 'backwards' as far as Omagari, the first stop after Akita – don't bother to turn the seats around, though, because the direction of the train reverses after leaving Omagari.

## Akita to Niigata                  [Map 19; Map 20, p351; Table 13, p509]
Distances by JR from Akita. Fastest journey time: 3½ hours.

**Akita** 秋田 **(0km)** This part of the route continues south towards Niigata along the Uetsu Line on the Inaho LEX. Fifteen minutes after leaving Akita there are glimpses of the Japan Sea out to the right. These views last for another 15 minutes, before the line heads back towards more rice fields.

Limited expresses stop at both **Ugo-Honjo** 羽後本荘 (43km) and **Nikaho** 仁賀保 (57km) but the surrounding area is not particularly noteworthy.

Some trains stop at **Kisakata** 象潟 (68km). The coastline round here is very dramatic in parts and until the beginning of the 19th century it was similar to Matsushima (see pp330-3), with tiny islands scattered along the coast. The islands disappeared forever after a huge earthquake in 1804 pushed up the sea floor. For the next 40km or so there are great views to the left of the mountains in Chokai Quasi-National Park 鳥海国定公園.

The railway line skirts around the park, at the centre of which is **Mt Chokai** 鳥海山 (2236m), a semi-dormant volcano known as the Mt Fuji of Akita. Gradually the focus shifts towards the coast, with views out to sea on the right side. The train stops then at **Yuza** 遊佐 (93km).

## Sakata 酒田 (105km)

Sakata is a large port town at the mouth of Mogami-gawa 最上川. The area around the station is rather drab and depressing but Sakata does boast a good example of the classic Japanese stroll garden.

Only small **lockers** (¥300) are available at the station. The **tourist information office** (daily 9am-5pm) is on the right after passing the ticket barrier.

The highlight at **Homma Museum of Art** 本間美術館 (🖳 www.homma-museum.or.jp; Mar-Oct daily 9am-5pm, Nov-Feb Tue-Sun 9am-4.30pm; ¥900) is the small Japanese garden, **Kakubuen** 鶴舞園, even though the 'borrowed' view of Mt Chokai has now been blocked out by buildings. Tea is served at the wooden guest house but go up to the 2nd floor for better views and for an optical illusion: at the top of the stairs turn right and look at the blank screens on the left. Then walk to the window and turn back and see if they are still blank.

The Homma family were one of the wealthiest in Japan thanks to rice production on their

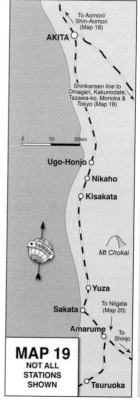

MAP 19
NOT ALL
STATIONS
SHOWN

HONSHU

---

❑ **Kirakira Uetsu Joyful train**
This 4-car train operates between Sakata and Niigata generally at the weekends. Car 2 has a kiosk where you can buy ekiben, beer and sake. There are observation areas in the other cars. Rail passes are valid; seat reservations essential.

land, and they remained the most influential family in the area until WWII brought an end to their power. The museum houses some of their treasures but labels are in Japanese. It is a 5-minute walk from the station.

**Amarume 余目 (117km)** Amarume is a stop on the Uetsu Line and also a terminus for the Riku Saisen Line running east to Shinjo. A quick way of returning to Tokyo from here would be to take a local train to Shinjo (50 mins; see p333), from where you can pick up the Yamagata shinkansen (see p330).

**Tsuruoka 鶴岡 (132km)** Tsuruoka station has ¥400 and ¥600 **lockers** (in the waiting room). The staff at the **tourist information office** (daily Mar-Oct 9.30am-5.30pm, Nov-Feb 10am-5pm), to the right as you go out of the station, don't speak English but will help book accommodation.

The primary reason people stop in Tsuruoka city (🖳 www.tsuruokakan ko.com) is to go to Dewa Sanzan (see below). The main tourist sight in Tsuruoka city is the **Chido Hakubutsukan** 致道博物館 (Chido Museum; 🖳 www.chido.jp; daily Mar-Nov 9am-5pm, Dec-Feb to 4.30pm; ¥700). There's an odd architectural mix of buildings here, including the former Tsuruoka police station, a Western-style building from the late 19th century, the retirement residence of the former ruling Sakai lords, and a feudal-era 3-storey home that you can walk around. There's also a small Japanese garden. All signs inside are in Japanese, though a leaflet in English is available. It's a half-hour walk from the station, or take a bus and get off at the Shiyakusho-mae stop (12 mins; ¥270), then keep following the road past the park and look for the entrance on the right.

For accommodation, immediately opposite the station is *Tsuruoka Washington Hotel* 鶴岡ワシントンホテル (☎ 0235-25 0111, 🖳 www.washing ton-hotels.jp/tsuruoka; from ¥7128/S, ¥11,286/Tw, ¥11,880/D). Alternatively, *Hotel Route-Inn Tsuruoka Ekimae* ホテルルートイン鶴岡駅前 (☎ 0235-28 2055, 🖳 www.route-inn.co.jp/en/pref/yamagata.html; from ¥6900/S, ¥10,350/D) is a few minutes' walk to the right after leaving the station and has a complimentary breakfast and public bath.

### Side trip by bus to Dewa Sanzan 出羽三山

Most people who stop at Tsuruoka are on their way to **Haguro-san** 羽黒山 (Mt Haguro; 🖳 www.hagurokanko.jp), part of a chain known as Dewa Sanzan (Three Mountains of Dewa). These mountains are considered to be the home of the *kami* (spirits) and pilgrims visit year-round to undertake spiritual cleansing: first to be climbed is Haguro-san (414m), which represents birth, followed by **Gas-san** 月山 (1984m), which represents death, and finally **Yudono-san** 湯殿山 (1504m), representing the future or re-birth.

The easiest to climb as it is accessible year-round, and possible as a day trip from Tsuruoka, is Haguro-san. Shonai-Kotsu operate buses (from stand No 2 to the left of the station exit) to the base of Haguro-san (7-10/day; 40 mins; ¥820) and to the top 羽黒山頂 (up to 8/day; 55 mins; ¥1180). Get off at the base in the centre of town – Zuishin-mon 隋神門 if you want to follow the pilgrim's route to the top through a cedar forest with 2446 stone steps; the walk takes about an hour. It is possible to stay on the bus all the way to the top, but the walk is highly recommended. Near the start of the walk and on the left stands the almost 30m-high **5-storied pagoda** 羽黒山五重塔 – a wooden structure built in the 14th century and designated a National Treasure. The cedar trees along the path are up to 500 years old. Near to the top (and with a fantastic view towards the sea) is a tea house serving *mochi*. Staff there will write certificates which state that you have climbed all 2446 steps despite the fact that it is before the summit. Finally, at the top is the **Sanjin Gosaiden** 山神合祭殿 (daily 8am-5pm) – a shrine dedicated to the deities of the three mountains. The pond here is revered as holy and a place to cleanse oneself holistically.

It is possible to stay on the mountain in temple lodgings in *Saikan* 斎館 (☎ 0235-62 2357; ¥7560pp inc half board), but bookings must be made by phone; the staff at the information office in Tsuruoka will help with this.

**Atsumi-onsen** あつみ温泉 **(162km)** More than a thousand years ago, Atsumi served as a border checkpoint for travellers entering Tohoku. Sandwiched between mountains and the coast, it is nowadays a busy hot spring resort. According to legend, the spring in question was discovered by none other than Kobo Daishi, the monk who founded the Shingon sect of Buddhism and established its headquarters on Koya-san (see pp156-8). The hot spring water flows from the river into the sea.

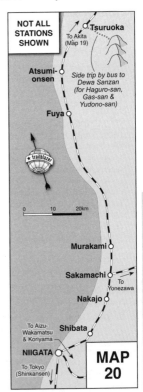

The main onsen area (🖥 www.atsumi-spa .or.jp) is wedged between mountains 2km inland from the station; it is a bus ride (2/hr 6am to noon & 3.30-6.30pm, infrequent at other times; 6 mins; ¥240) from the station. Alight at Shonai Ginko-mae 庄内銀行前 (the stop after NTT-mae NTT前) for the tourist information centre. It is on the other side of the road (light blue sign marked as 観光案内, no English writing), and has helpful staff who will store bags for free; particularly useful as there are no lockers at the station. There are nine onsen, of which three have *rotemburo* (open-air baths), and a further three foot-baths in the town. There is even a foot-bath café, *ChittoMotché* チットモッシェ (Mon-Fri 10am-6.30pm, Sat & Sun to 10pm).

After Atsumi-onsen, some limited expresses call at **Fuya** 府屋 (176km). From here to Murakami the railway line runs along the coast, though views are limited due to the proliferation of tunnels. From **Murakami** 村上 (212km) the train heads inland and after 15 minutes passes a major industrial complex. The views gradually deteriorate as the surrounding area becomes more built up on the final approach into Niigata.

Before arriving in Niigata, there are stops at **Sakamachi** 坂町 (224km), the junction with the JR Yonezawa Line from Yonezawa (see p330), **Nakajo** 中条 (233km) and **Shibata** 新発田 (246km).

## Niigata 新潟 (273km)                                  [see pp359-62]

If not returning to Tokyo from here, Niigata also has rail connections with Joetsu-Myoko (Shirayuki LEX 5/day; approx 120 mins), though note that the section between Naoetsu and Joetsu-Myoko is operated by a private line so not free for JR rail-pass holders (fare ¥240; LEX supplement ¥210). From Joetsu-Myoko the Hokuriku shinkansen goes south to Nagano and then Tokyo, or west to Kanazawa. Pick up the route guide from Joetsu-Myoko (see p180).

## Niigata to Tokyo

The fastest, though least scenic, way of returning to Tokyo from Niigata is by Joetsu shinkansen (1-3/hr; 125 mins).

If you have more time and are prepared to change trains you might consider the local Ban-etsu West Line that runs inland from Niigata, via the castle town of **Aizu-Wakamatsu** (see pp327-9), to **Koriyama** (see p327) on the Tohoku shinkansen line; from Koriyama you can take a shinkansen back to Tokyo.

---

### ❏ From a shinkansen to the ski slopes

The Joetsu shinkansen provides access to several ski resorts but **Gala Yuzawa** ガーラ湯沢 is the only shinkansen station (open mid Dec to early May) actually attached to a resort – Gala Resort (🖳 www.galaresort.jp). JR East owns the ski slopes here – possibly the only ones anywhere owned by a railway company.

At **Cowabunga Ski Center** in the station you can rent everything you need for a day's skiing or snowboarding; see the website for details. Even if you don't want to ski, if the weather is good it is an easy way to get into the mountains and see some breathtaking views. A **gondola** leaves from the station building and goes up to 800 metres. From the top station other lifts spread over the large skiing area (and during the season there is a play area for children here), though it is also possible to ski right down to Gala Yuzawa station. A round trip on the gondola costs ¥1300, but if you have a JR Tokyo Wide Pass (see p33) you can also get a free rental sled, boots and gloves; see the JR East website for additional offers. Note the gondola doesn't operate if it is too windy.

If going **from Niigata** it is essential to change train at **Echigo-Yuzawa** 越後湯沢 (1-2/hr; 48 mins); some connections to Gala Yuzawa (3 mins) are good but not all; another option is to take the free shuttle bus from Echigo-Yuzawa to Gala Yuzawa. If coming **from Tokyo** some trains (3/day in the morning; 80 mins) go direct to Gala Yuzawa; overall there are 11/day from Tokyo but most are in the morning for skiers having a day trip. At peak times book a seat as the trains get very crowded.

If you have time at Echigo-Yuzawa station find your way to the sake centre at the back of CoCoLo Yuzawa Gangi-dori street, a retro Showa-era shopping street. For ¥500 you will be given a cup and you can then try five sakes (there are 93 to choose from). There are notes in English to help you choose ones that are likely to appeal to you. You can then, of course, buy any you like.

Additional ski resorts on the Joetsu shinkansen line can also be accessed from **Echigo-Yuzawa** (🖳 www.e-yuzawa.gr.jp) and **Jomo-Kogen** 上毛高原 stations.

❏ **The world's first art gallery on a shinkansen**
The **Genbi shinkansen** (🖥 www.jreast.co.jp/genbi/en), which started in April 2016, is probably the first moving art gallery in a train. Cars 12-16 each have works of contemporary art by a different artist. Car 11 has a café which anyone on the train can visit. Services operate at weekends and holiday periods (6/day) between Echigo-Yuzawa and Niigata. Seats must be reserved but JR rail passes are valid.

A good reason for taking the Ban-etsu West Line is the chance to take the **SL Banetsu Monogatari** ばんえつ物語 (see pp328-9) to Aizu-Wakamatsu. From Koriyama, you can complete the journey by jumping on a southbound shinkansen to Tokyo.

# Tohoku (North-eastern Honshu) – city guides

## SENDAI 仙台

Tohoku's largest city, Sendai, lived in relative peace in the centuries when other regions were fighting civil wars, but the city and its castle were razed to the ground during WWII and consequently it has few preserved sights of historical interest. Sendai's history is dominated by the figure of Masamune Date (1567-1636), a feudal lord who earned the nickname 'one-eyed dragon' after he contracted smallpox during infancy and lost the sight in his right eye.

### What to see and do

There are several places of interest in Sendai itself but many visitors stop here briefly before heading to Matsushima (see pp330-3). Another option for a day trip is Yamadera (see p358).

The best way of seeing the main sights in Sendai is to have a Loople Pass and take the **Loople Sendai** (see p357) bus. The following is a guide to the most interesting places along the way. A map at each bus stop shows the route to the place of interest.

At stop No 4, **Zuihoden** 瑞鳳殿 (daily Feb-Oct 9am-4.30pm, Dec-Jan to 4pm; ¥550, ¥450 with Loople Pass) is a temple-style mausoleum of the Date family reconstructed in 1985. There's a pleasant wooded area you can wander around and a museum

with statues, artefacts and video. There is an English audio explanation in front of the mausoleum and also in the guide pamphlet.

**Sendai City Museum** 仙台市博物館 (Sendai-shi Hakubutsukan; 🖥 www.city .sendai.jp/kyouiku/museum; Tue-Sun 9am-4.45pm; ¥400, ¥320 with Loople Pass), at stop No 5, offers a comprehensive overview of Sendai and its history from prehistoric times through to the present day. The scale model of the former castle is impressive. Explanations are translated into English with further detail in the comprehensive audio guide (free). There is a good *restaurant* offering reasonably priced Japanese/Western lunch sets for ¥800.

Stop No 6 is for the site of the **former Sendai Castle** 仙台城 (Sendai-jo), known locally as Aoba Castle 青葉城 (Aoba-jo), built on top of the 132m-high Aoba Hill in 1602 by Masamune Date (this also offers an impressive panoramic view out over Sendai). Destroyed in 1945, it has never been rebuilt, although a diagram of where the rooms once stood is printed onto the ground. **Sendai Castle Guidance Facility** 仙台城見聞館 (daily 9am-5pm; free), a small air-conditioned lodge next to the ruins offers a brief exhibition of the castle history with an English pamphlet. (Cont'd on p356)

HONSHU

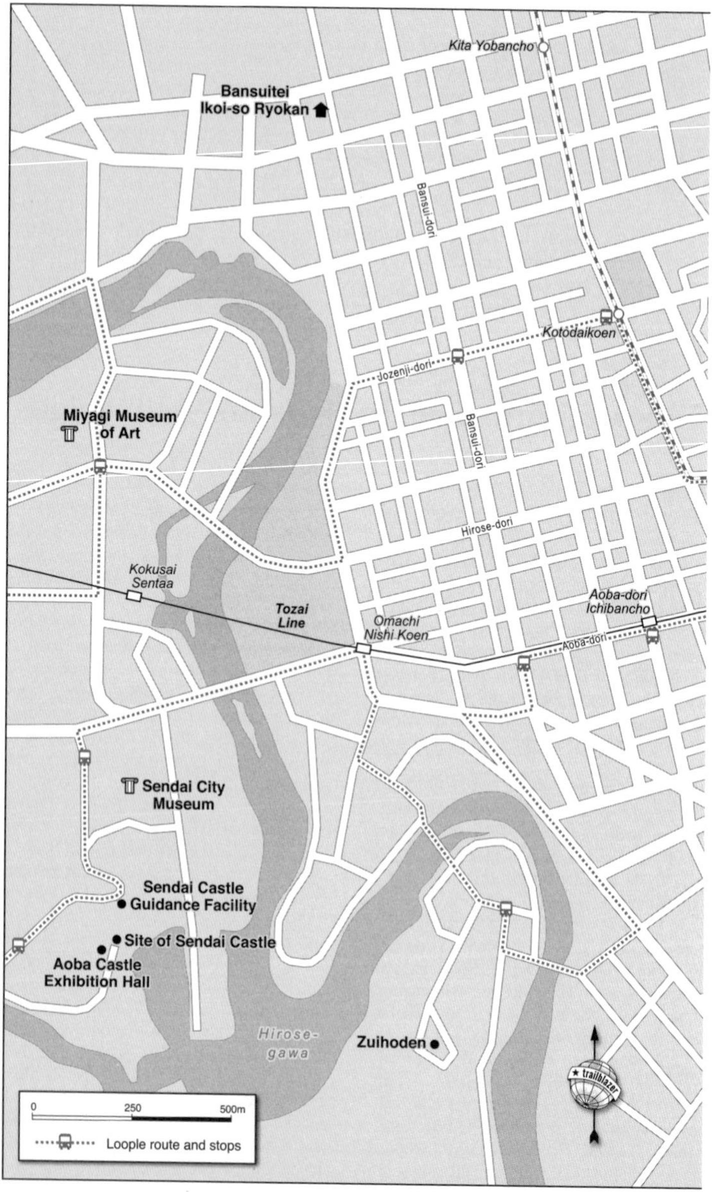

Kita Yobancho

Bansuitei
Ikoi-so Ryokan

Bansui-dori

Kotodaikoen

Jozenji-dori

Miyagi Museum
of Art

Bansui-dori

Hirose-dori

Kokusai
Sentaa

Tozai
Line

Omachi
Nishi Koen

Aoba-dori
Ichibancho

Aoba-dori

Sendai City
Museum

Sendai Castle
● Guidance Facility
● Site of Sendai Castle
Aoba Castle
Exhibition Hall

Hirose-
gawa

Zuihoden ●

```
0        250        500m
```

······ Loople route and stops

HONSHU

Ekimae-dori

Richmond Hotel Sendai

Toyoko Inn Nishiguchi Hirose-dori

Hirose-dori

Hirose-dori

AER building

Comfort Hotel Sendai Higashi-guchi

Covered arcade

Chuo-dori

Clis Road

Hapina Nakakecho

Parco

Daiei dept store

Aoba-dori

Aoba-dori

Gyutan-dori & Sushi-dori

Sendai Station

Richmond Hotel Premier Sendai Eki-mae & Hana

S-Pal

Minamimachi-dori

Miyagino-dori

Hotel Metropolitan Sendai

Senseki Line

Miyagino Dori

Hotel Monterey Sendai

To Matsushima-Kaigan & Sendai Umino-mori Aquarium

Higashihachenba-dori

Tanagimachi-dori

Tozai Line

ANA Holiday Inn Sendai

Central Post Office

Itsutsu-bashi

Sendai

仙台

To Sendai Yagiyama Zoological Park & Sendai Shiden Hozonkan (Streetcar) Museum

HONSHU

(Cont'd from p353) Also within the hilltop shopping centre, **Aoba Castle Exhibition Hall** 青葉城資料展示館 (Aoba-jo Shiryo Denjikan; daily Apr-Oct 9am-5pm, Nov-Mar to 4pm; ¥700, ¥500 with Loople Pass), offers a small exhibition and a child-oriented 16-minute CGI video of the former castle in Japanese only.

**Miyagi Museum of Art** 宮城県美術館 (Miyagi-ken Bijutsukan; 🖳 www.pref.miyagi.jp/site/museum-en; Tue-Sun 9.30am-5pm; ¥300, ¥240 with Loople Pass) is 500m north of Sendai City Museum, but if you prefer to take the bus get off at stop No 10. The main gallery exhibits the work of 20th-century local artists and some minor works by foreign artists, including three early figurative paintings by Kandinsky. There's also a pleasant modern sculpture garden and café.

For views of the city and the Pacific Ocean in the distance take a visit to the **Observation Terrace** 展望テラス (daily 10am-8pm; free) on the 31st floor of the office (not the shopping) part of the **AER building**.

Families might enjoy a trip to **Sendai Yagiyama Zoological Park** 仙台市八木山動物公園 (🖳 www.city.sendai.jp/kensetsu/yagiyama; Mar-Oct Tue-Sun 9am-4.45pm, Nov-Feb Tue-Sun to 4pm; ¥400), home to more than 145 species including the African lion, Sumatran tiger, polar bears and a hippo. In the winter months there is also the unusual sight of elephants playing in the snow. The zoo is a 5-minute walk

from Yagiyama Zoological Park 八木山公園 station on the Namboku subway line (¥300). Alternatively, take a trip to **Sendai Umino-mori Aquarium** 仙台うみの杜水族館 (🖳 www.uminomori.jp; daily 9am-6pm; ¥2100), featuring bottlenose dolphin performances and Humboldt penguins. Take the JR Senseki Line 仙石線 to Nakanosakae station 中野栄 (4-7/hr; 19 mins; ¥200), where there is a free shuttle bus or a signposted 15-minute walk to the Aquarium.

## Practical information

**Station guide** There are both east and west sides to Sendai station. The main exits into the city are on the west side.

On the 3rd floor is the central shinkansen entrance and main JR ticket office (daily 5.30am-10.30pm). On the 2nd floor is the central entrance for all other JR lines, including the Tohoku, Senseki (for Matsushima), Senzan for Yamadera and Sendai Airport lines. Also on this floor is the JR-operated View Plaza Travel Service Center (daily 10am-7pm), where rail-pass vouchers can be exchanged.

There are **lockers** all around the station as well as large ones on the 1st/ground floor (street level) right outside the station building. See Where to eat for details of restaurants and cafés in the station.

Heading out of the station from the 2nd floor brings you to the overhead walkways that run above the central streets in front of the station.

---

❏ **Sendai Streetcar Museum** 仙台市電保存館

Rail fans might like to pay a visit to this museum (Shiden Hozonkan; 🖳 www.kotsu.city.sendai.jp/shiden; Tue-Sun 10am-4pm; free), located a 12-minute walk from Tomizawa 富沢 subway station, the southern terminus of the Namboku subway line. The museum traces the history of streetcars/trams in Sendai, which for half a century were the main form of public transport in the city. The first four-wheeled wooden streetcar went into service in 1926 and at the height of its popularity the system was carrying more than 100,000 passengers a day. But the age of the automobile heralded the demise of the streetcar, which was finally taken out of service on March 31st, 1976, almost exactly 50 years after it was inaugurated.

The museum exhibits some of the original carriages as well as a collection of mechanical parts, period photographs, tickets and signs. A free shuttle bus operates from outside the West Exit No 1 of Tomizawa station to the museum.

## Tourist information

The **tourist information office** (🖥 www.city.sendai.jp/kanko; Apr-Mar daily 9am-7pm, Jan-Feb to 5pm) is in a large booth one floor down from the shinkansen level at Sendai station, by the exit. Staff will not book accommodation (although they will call the youth hostel) but will direct you to the View Plaza Travel Service Center (see Station guide).

## Getting around

The **Loople Sendai** るーぷる仙台 (daily 9am-4pm; 3-4/hr; ¥260/journey, 1-day pass ¥620 inc small discounts at some attractions) is a retro-style tourist bus service that departs from platform No 15-3 of the bus pool outside the West Exit of the station. Buy tickets from the driver or at the bus terminal. The buses run one way around the city, with 12 stops (displayed and announced in English) en route.

Sendai also has a network of **buses** (from ¥180) and two **subway lines** (¥200-360). The Namboku Line runs from Izumi city in the north through the city centre to the southern suburbs, while the brand-new Tozai crosses the city from east to west. For details see 🖥 www.kotsu.city.sendai.jp.

## Festivals

Sendai's biggest annual bash, and one of the largest summer events in Tohoku, is the **Tanabata Matsuri** (6th-8th Aug). This attracts around two million visitors (so book early if coming then). Colourful paper streamers and decorations are hung from bamboo poles along the main streets and in the station; there are also fireworks, parades and concerts.

## Where to stay

Next to the station is the JR-run *Hotel Metropolitan Sendai* ホテルメトロポリタン仙台 (☎ 022-268 2525, 🖥 www.sendaimetropolitan.jp; from ¥12,200/D, ¥14,900/Tw; discounted for rail-pass holders), which has comfortable if not overly luxurious rooms.

Across the street from the nearby subway station is the upscale *Richmond Hotel Premier Sendai Eki-mae* リッチモンドホテルプレミア仙台駅前 (☎ 022-716 2855, 🖥 www.richmondhotel.jp/sendai-ekimae; ¥7000/S, ¥9000/D, ¥10,000/Tw). The lobby/reception is on the 5th floor and there's a restaurant (see Where to eat) in the basement. A 10-minute walk north of the station is *Richmond Hotel Sendai* リッチモンドホテル仙台 (☎ 022-722 0055, 🖥 www.richmondhotel.jp/sendai; ¥6000/S, ¥8200/D or Tw), another branch of the reliable chain, with reasonably spacious rooms, a coin laundry and restaurant open until 1am. You pay at a machine in the lobby, though human staff are also on hand.

*Hotel Monterey Sendai* ホテルモントレー仙台 (☎ 022-265 7110, 🖥 www.hotelmonterey.co.jp/sendai; ¥14,000/S, ¥24,000/Tw; breakfast ¥1700) is a good-value mid-range hotel with a European feel – it has a brick façade. A one-day pass for the hotel's 17th-floor **Sala Terrena** サラテレナ spa is ¥1230 for hotel guests. The Monterey is less than five minutes on foot from the Central Exit of Sendai station.

A newish place offering rooms of a high standard is *ANA Holiday Inn Sendai* ANAホリディ・イン 仙台 (☎ 022-256 5111, 🖥 www.anaholidayinn-sendai.jp; from ¥10,500/S, ¥11,600/D or Tw, ¥23,677/Tr; online discounts available); it's a 6-minute walk from the station's East Exit.

*Toyoko Inn Nishiguchi Hirose-dori* 東横イン仙台西口広瀬通 (☎ 022-721 1045, 🖥 www.toyoko-inn.com; from ¥6588/S, ¥7668/D, ¥8748/Tw, inc breakfast). Take the 2nd floor exit from the station and use the overground walkways to reach the other side of the main road, Ekimae-dori 駅前通り. Turn right and walk along Ekimae-dori and then left down Hirose-dori 広瀬通 and take the first right just before Basilica di Santo Stefano, a church built specifically for Western-style weddings. Walk along and the Toyoko Inn is on the left. If this is full look at the website for details of the other branches of this chain in Sendai.

*Comfort Hotel Sendai Higashiguchi* コンフォートホテル仙台東口 (🖥 www.choice-hotels.jp/cfsende; ☎ 022-792 8711; from ¥7000/S, ¥10,100/Tw) is five minutes on foot from the station's East Exit. The rooms and lobby area are fresh and the free breakfast offers more choice and quality than many other economical hotels.

HONSHU

*Bansuitei Ikoi-so* 晩翠亭いこい荘 (☎ 022-222 7885, 🖳 www.ikoisouryokan .co.jp; from ¥5700pp; breakfast ¥1000pp) has a smart wooden interior with both tatami and Western-style rooms. A big selling point is that the common bath turns into a Jacuzzi (which has, according to the owner, 'an ultrasonic massaging effect on your body recognised by the Health and Welfare Ministry'). It's near Kita Yoban-cho subway station, three stops from Sendai station. Take North Exit 2, turn right at the top of the steps that lead to street level, and walk for about eight minutes. The ryokan is on a quiet road off to the left, just before you reach Tohoku University Hospital.

See pp67-73 for general information about accommodation.

**Where to eat and drink**  Turn right as you take the central shinkansen ticket exit and double-back on yourself to reach **Gyutan-dori** (Beef Tongue St) and **Sushi-dori**, parades of beef-tongue and sushi restaurants. Grilled beef tongue, known as *gyutan-yaki* 牛タン焼, is a Sendai delicacy. Gourmets say the tongue loses fat and develops its taste when it is charcoal roasted. At street level there is a branch of

*Starbucks*, as well as bakeries and cafés that do good-value morning sets.

Another option in the station is the **S-Pal department store**, in the basement of which are restaurants (10am-11pm) and take-out food counters (10am-9pm). The floor is divided into three areas: S-Pal Kitchen (takeaway food items), S-Pal Sendai Miyage-kan (gifts and souvenirs) and the restaurant zone.

A curious fusion Sendai creation is the *mabo-yaki* マボ焼き, Japanese yakisoba (noodles) topped with spicy Chinese mabo-tofu (minced meat and tofu in chilli and bean sauce). Try **Shiron** 囍龍 (also known as Koufukisshou-shiron 口福吉祥 囍龍; daily 11am-2.30pm & 5.30-10.30pm; ¥1030 lunch, ¥1296 dinner), a glass-fronted restaurant which is on the 1st/ground floor (bus level) of the **PARCO** building. On the 9th floor here *Trattoria La Verde* トラット リア ラ・ベルデ (11am-11pm) offers typical pasta dishes as well as hit-and-miss fusion versions; expect to pay around ¥1300 for a main course.

For a variety of Japanese dishes at reasonable prices try **Hana** 波奈 (🖳 www .hana-group.co.jp; daily 11am-2.30pm & 5-11pm) in the basement of Richmond Hotel.

### Side trip by rail to Yamadera 山寺
Some 50km west of Sendai lies Yamadera, a hillside temple founded in 860 by the monk Jikaku Daishi and considered one of the holiest sights in northern Japan. The temple complex is 50 minutes by 'rapid' train (1/hr) along the JR Senzan Line to Yamadera.

Once you pass the urban sprawl of Sendai city, the scenery begins to open up as the train weaves between the hills and passes from village to village. Yamadera station is small and has some ¥600 lockers, although the adjacent restaurant *Enzou* will store luggage for free, though undoubtedly buying a drink/snack there would be appreciated.

From the station, follow the signposted route up towards Yamadera (also known as Risshaku-ji 立石寺; daily 8am-5pm; ¥300). Before the ascent, try the famous local 'power conjak' 力こんにゃく, chewy yam-cake-balls on a stick, from the stallholder. Give yourself an hour to climb the '1100' steps (there are frequent count markers); there's a handrail but some people buy wooden sticks to help with the ascent. The best views into the valley are from about two-thirds of the way up, at **Godai-do** 五大堂, a temple built like a stage, which doubles as a useful viewing platform out over the valley. Your goal at the top is **Okuno-in Temple** 奥の院, which contains a large golden Buddha. Being Japan, there is also a postbox near the top of the mountain.

## NIIGATA 新潟

Niigata is the largest city on the Japan Sea coast and was one of the first ports to welcome foreign trade when Japan reopened to the outside world in 1869 after nearly 230 years of self-imposed seclusion. It is known in Japan for the quality of its rice and seafood, and for its sake, which is produced in a number of breweries scattered across Niigata prefecture.

Visitors are put off spending time here because it is a major industrial city, and most press on without delay to nearby Sado-shima (Sado Island, see p362). But it's difficult to write the place off as just another identikit Japanese city; it has several places of interest, a coastal area, a river which offers another dimension to sightseeing as well as some quiet back streets.

Winters here are cold (the average temperature in January is 2.1°C) but summers tend to be hot and humid.

### What to see and do

A good place to start is across Showa Ohashi 昭和大橋 bridge, on the other side of the city to the station, at **Hakusan Park** 白山公園 (Hakusan-koen), reached by City Loop bus (see p360) from the station. Here stands **Hakusan Shrine** 白山神社 (Hakusan-jinja), a place of worship for more than 400 years, which is frequented by couples seeking the support of a God of Marriage enshrined within.

Also within Hakusan Park, but entered from a street just outside, is **Enkikan** 燕喜館 (daily except 1st and 3rd Mon, 9am-5pm; free), an old merchant's home that was moved here and transformed into a house for traditional Japanese arts such as tea ceremony and *ikebana* (flower arranging). It's a beautiful example of a traditional Japanese house and enjoys a view of the lotus pond. For ¥400 you'll be served a cup of Japanese tea in one of the tatami rooms.

Walking through the park and leaving the other side you'll come to the **Prefectural Government Memorial Hall** 新潟県政記念館 (Niigata Kensei Kinenkan; Tue-Sun 9am-4.30pm; free) which dates back to 1884. Used as the prefectural parliament for 50 years, it was apparently constructed in the same style as the Houses of Parliament in London, with Shinano-gawa in place of the River Thames. Old photos of assembly delegates show how the dress code has changed. In a group shot dated 1911 almost all the delegates are in traditional Japanese clothes. By 1931 the vast majority were in Western-style suits.

From here, it's an easy 10-minute walk to the central shopping area of **Furumachi** 古町, where you'll find plenty of places for lunch. For a (free) bird's eye view of the city, the sea and on a clear day Sado Island (see p362), head for the 19th floor of the **Next 21 Building** NEXT 21ビル (daily 11am-11.30pm; free), a landmark that's easy to spot because it's shaped like a pencil. Closer to the station is the new **Media Ship** メディアシップ (daily 8am-11pm; free) building, which has an observation gallery on its 20th floor that is relatively tourist-free. The lift/elevator is on the right of the entrance lobby.

The 31st-floor **observation gallery** (daily 8am-10pm; free) in Hotel Nikko Niigata (see p362) has the highest viewing point on the Japan Sea coast and is accessed via a dedicated express lift/elevator from the 1st/ground floor.

On the 5th floor of this building is **Niigata Bandaijima Art Museum** 新潟県立万代島美術館 (Niigata Bandaijima Bijutsukan; 🖳 banbi.pref.niigata.lg.jp; Tue-Sun 10am-6pm; ¥310), a modern gallery space with a small permanent collection. Take the City Loop bus (Toki Messe route); Hotel Nikko Niigata is the third stop from the station.

If the weather is cooperating, there can be no better way of seeing Niigata than on a relaxed cruise along the Shinano River. Ferries plough the water on a regular basis, stopping at various embarkation/disembarkation points along the way. Riding the **Shinano-gawa Water Shuttle** 信濃川ウォーターシャトル (🖳 www.watershuttle.co.jp) from Bandai City 万代シテイ (the closest stop to the station) to Furusato-mura ふるさと村 takes 45 minutes and costs ¥800 one-way. A one-day water shuttle pass costs ¥1800.

HONSHU

Particularly in the summer, a good mini-escape from the city is down by the coast in the area around **Niigata City Aquarium** 新潟市水族館マリンピア日本海 (Niigata Suizokukan Marinepia Nihonkai; 🖳 www.marinepia.or.jp; daily 9am-5pm, to 6pm occasionally in the summer; ¥1500, ¥1200 with the City Loop bus pass). The largest aquarium on the Japan Sea coast, it is home to 450 species of sea life, including a large number of endangered Humboldt penguins, and it stages dolphin shows. Both tourist City Loop bus services stop outside.

Don't miss **Gokoku shrine** 護國神社 (Gokoku-jinja), surrounded by pine trees, just a couple of minutes from the aquarium. It was built in 1945 to console the souls of the war dead. Instead of taking the bus back to the station from here, it's a very pleasant walk back into the city through quiet back streets filled with old wooden houses and privately owned craft shops.

See p362 for details about the side trip to Sado Island from Niigata.

## Practical information

**Station guide** Niigata is the terminus for the Joetsu shinkansen to/from Tokyo. The other main rail lines are the Shinetsu Line to Joetsu-Myoko, the Joetsu Line to Ueno (Tokyo) and the Uetsu Line that runs north to Akita.

The station is divided into the shinkansen side and regular JR lines side.

For the city centre, follow signs for the Bandai Exit. The shinkansen side has the most shops and restaurants, including the **CoCoLo** department store with several places to eat. Lockers are available on both sides. On the Bandai side of the station, just across from the TIC, is a station waiting room called – inexplicably – 'Banana', where you'll find seats, **lockers** (mainly of the small ¥300 variety, but also a few ¥500) and tablets with free **internet access** (daily 11am-7pm; 30 mins per person).

**Tourist information** The tourist information centre 新潟駅万代口観光案内センター (TIC; 🖳 www.nvcb.or.jp; daily 9am-6pm) is to the left as you take the main Bandai exit. The staff here have maps and leaflets for Niigata and can book same-day city accommodation. They also have information about ferries to Sado Island 佐渡島. Pick up a copy of the monthly *Niigata English Journal*, which contains restaurant reviews and listings for concerts, exhibitions and movies.

**Getting around** The central point for crossing over Shinano-gawa 信濃川 is Bandai Bridge 萬代橋. It's easy enough to walk around central Niigata but all city buses depart from the bus terminal outside the Bandai Exit of the station.

A better bet for getting to the main sights is to take one of the **Niigata City Loop buses** 新潟市観光循環バス (¥210, 1-day pass ¥500 inc small discounts at many tourist facilities), which operate on different circular routes around the city. Both services start and finish outside Niigata station; note that the stop-request buttons are on the ceiling.

An alternative means of transportation is the **water shuttle** (see p359) along the Shinano river.

**Festivals** Niigata Matsuri (7th-9th Aug) started as a festival to pray for the prosperity of the port and growth of the city; it still involves a procession and folk dancing over Bandai Bridge (on the 8th) and ends with a huge fireworks display over Shinano-gawa on the evening of the 9th.

In 2002 **Niigata Soh-Odori** (🖳 www .soh-odori.net), which was first celebrated over 300 years ago, was revived, and has been staged annually ever since in mid September. The highlight is a series of traditional and modern dances performed by large groups; the purpose of all the festivity is to wish for a good harvest.

**Where to stay** Closest to the station is *Toyoko Inn Niigata Ekimae* 東横イン新潟駅前 (☎ 025-241 1045, 🖳 www.toyoko-inn .com; from ¥5724/S, ¥7344/D, ¥9180/Tw), immediately on your right as you take the Bandai Exit. Reception is on the 4th floor.

On the left side of the Bandai Exit is *Niigata Tokyu REI Hotel* 新潟東急REIホ

Niigata

新潟

HONSHU

Key locations on map:

To Sado Island

Shinano-gawa Water Shuttle

Niigata Ferry terminal (for Sado Island)

Niigata Port Intnl Passenger Terminal

Akashi-dori

Hotel Nikko Niigata, Serena & Niigata Bandaijima Art Museum

Shinano-gawa Water Shuttle

Dormy Inn Niigata

Hotel Sunroute Niigata

Ryutu Bridge

Nishibori-dori

Toyoko Inn Niigata Ekimae

Central Post Office

Media Ship

B A N D A I

Niigata Station

Higashi-odori

Furumachi-dori

Masaya-koji

Bandai Bridge

Tengu

Shinano-gawa Water Shuttle

Niigata Tokyu REI Hotel

Next 21 Building

F U R U M A C H I

Yachiyo Bridge

Comfort Hotel Niigata Eki-mae

Tourist Information Center

Uonuma Kamazo Ponshukan

Higashinaka-dori

Shinano-gawa

Joetsu Shinkansen to Tokyo

Prefectural Government Memorial Hall

Niigata City Aquarium/ Marinepia Nihonkai

Gelateria Popolo

Gokoku Shrine

Hakusan Shrine/Park

Hakusan Park

Enkikan

Showa Ohashi Bridge

JR Echigo Line

Hakusan

0  250  500m

テル (☎ 025-243 0109, 🖥 www.tokyuho telsjapan.com; from ¥5000/S, ¥9600/D, ¥10,200/Tw; online discounts for advance booking; inc breakfast). Some of the rooms are for women only, with extra amenities including humidifier, face lotion, brush and hairband. Also near the station is *Hotel Sunroute Niigata* ホテルサンルート新潟 (☎ 025-249 8100, 🖥 www.sunroutehotel .jp; ¥8470/S, ¥6,500/D, ¥11,000/Tw), a good mid-range choice.

Five minutes on foot north of the station is *Dormy Inn Niigata* ドーミーイン 新潟 (☎ 025-247 7755, 🖥 www.hotespa .net/hotels/niigata; from ¥7190/S, ¥9190 /D); It's clean and efficiently run and like all branches of this chain boasts its own onsen and rotemburo and serves free Yonaki soba in the evening.

*Comfort Hotel Niigata Eki-mae* コン フォートホテル新潟駅前 (☎ 025-242 0611, 🖥 www.comfortinn.com; from ¥6200/S, ¥5700/D, ¥6200/Tw, inc break-fast) is a good mid-range option with rooms that are a cut above the usual business-hotel standard. The hotel is three minutes on foot from the Bandai Exit of JR Niigata station.

At the top end is *Hotel Nikko Niigata* ホテル日航新潟 (☎ 025-240 1888, 🖥 www.hotelnikkoniigata.jp; from ¥4800/S, ¥11,200/D, ¥11,900/Tw, exc breakfast), centrepiece of the redeveloped harbour area which includes the Toki Messe international convention centre. The tallest hotel on the Japan Sea coast enjoys a superb water-front location set back from the city centre. The rooms are spacious, have large win-dows and there's a choice of restaurants.

**Where to eat and drink** To sample two of Niigata's specialities – seafood and sake – head for *Uonuma Kamazo Ponshukan* 魚沼釜蔵 ぽんしゅ館 (🖥 www.sep-i .co.jp; 11am-11pm) next to the Hotel Mets outside the South Exit of the station. Their sake 'tasting set' 3種セット (¥1200 for three glasses) allows you to choose from different variants selected for that month and at lunchtime various set menus provide good value at around ¥1000. There is also a shop on the upper floor, where you can sample and purchase different sakes.

As a seaport, there's no shortage of excellent sushi places. At night, try lively *Tengu* 天狗 (Mon-Sat 6pm-3.30am), which literally translates as 'long-nosed goblin!'. Whichever sushi restaurant you end up in, do ensure you try the *toro* トロ – fatty tuna – and *nasu* なす (aubergine or 'eggplant' for Americans) – a Niigata speciality.

In the harbour area, it's worth taking lunch at *Serena* セリーナ (daily 11.30am-9pm), a modern all-day dining place on the 3rd floor of Hotel Nikko Niigata, where there are spectacular panoramic waterfront views through the bay windows. The buffet lunch is good value (¥2500) but the dinner is less so (¥4860).

Near the aquarium, drop by the Sea West 3 complex to sample what's probably the best hand-made ice-cream in Japan, at *Gelateria Popolo* ジェラテリアポポロ (🖥 www.web-popolo.com; daily 10am-7pm). Down here, and with trees covering the concrete blocks behind, it's hard to believe you're in a major industrial city.

### Side trip from Niigata

● **Sado Island** 佐渡島 The most popular trip is to Sado (🖥 www.visit sado .com), once a place of exile and now home to the world-famous **Kodo drum-mers** (🖥 www.kodo.or.jp). Ferries (🖥 www.sadokisen.co.jp; 5-7/day; 2½hrs; ¥2380 one way) and jet foils (5-9/day; 1hr; ¥6390 one-way, ¥11,560 return) depart from Niigata Port bound for Ryotsu 両津, the largest town on the island.

To reach Sado Ferry Terminal 佐渡汽船 新潟支店, take a bus from stop No 6 outside the station to its terminus at Sado Kisen 佐渡汽船. Before leav-ing Niigata station, pick up the English map of Sado Island; this contains infor-mation on bus routes on the island as well as sights, accommodation and restaurants.

## AOMORI 青森

The last major city before Hokkaido, Aomori is known for its red apples, considered to be the best in Japan, and for Nebuta Matsuri, one of the major summer festivals in Tohoku (not to be confused with Neputa Matsuri in Hirosaki, which is also known for its apples!). Even if you aren't here for the Nebuta you can see some of the floats.

Summer is mild but in winter snow becomes a fact of life for months on end. If visiting in the summer, look out for the phone boxes mounted well above street level with steps leading up to them. In winter, the steps – and sometimes much of the phone box – are buried in snow.

### What to see and do

There are a few attractions around the station but also make time to go to Sannai-Maruyama, site of a prehistoric settlement, and Aomori Museum of Art (see p366).

With the Nebura Matsuri so pivotal in Aomori's cultural image, head first to **Nebuta Warasse** ねぶたワ・ラッセ (⌨ www.nebuta.jp/warasse; May-Aug 9am-7pm, Sep-Apr to 6pm; ¥600), the modern crimson box to the left as you exit the station. The historical explanation of the Nebuta (p364) is limited, but the five very large Nebuta floats are impressive, displayed in a darkened hall and lit from within. The ancient legends depicted on the floats are explained in English.

Pass underneath the bay bridge to the **Memorial Ship** *Hakkoda-Maru* 八甲田丸 (⌨ aomori-hakkoudamaru.com; daily 9am-6pm, Nov-Mar to 4.30pm; ¥500), a former JR-operated ferry that ploughed the water between Aomori and Hakodate in Hokkaido for 80 years until it was retired in 1987 when the Seikan Tunnel was opened. You can climb aboard, look around and even put on a captain's jacket and cap and pose for photos. The ship has been preserved as it was, except that in the summer there's now a beer garden on the top deck.

Cross Aomori bay on the deckway (nicknamed the 'Love Bridge') to **ASPAM** アスパム (Aomori Sightseeing Products Mansion; ⌨ www.aomori-kanko.or.jp; daily 9am-10pm, goods corner to 7pm

(Apr-Oct) or 6pm (Nov-Mar)), the large triangular building (meant to resemble an 'A' for Aomori). There is an observation lounge (¥400) on the 13th floor and a panorama theatre (¥600) on the 2nd floor, where a 20-minute video of Aomori prefecture is introduced on a 360° screen. Dual tickets are ¥800, add in the *Hakkoda Maru* for ¥1100 and include both the *Hakkoda Maru* and Warasse for ¥1300; visits can be over multiple days. There are also free shamisen concerts (11.30am & 2pm; 30 mins) on the 2nd floor most days; these are worth attending.

For tired legs, visit **Machinaka-onsen** まちなかおんせん (⌨ www.aomoricenter hotel.jp; daily 6am-11pm; ¥420 plus ¥200 for towel); turn left at the second set of traffic lights and the onsen is on your left. Take your shoes off at the entrance and then buy a ticket from the machine. You need a ¥100 coin for the locker. There are several baths, including a Jacuzzi-style one and a *rotemburo*, as well as a sauna. The ergonomic lilo is a comfortable way to relax when you are thoroughly clean.

### Practical information

**Station guide** See p343 for details about transferring from Shin-Aomori to Aomori station. Aomori station is small with two sides, east and west. There are no lifts/elevators and only a one-way escalator so you need to carry your luggage when going down to the platforms. The main exit is on the east side. As you leave the ticket barrier, there is a **JR ticket office** (daily 5.20am-10.30pm) and **View Plaza Travel Service Center** (Mon-Fri 10am-5.30pm).

**Aoimori railway** 青い森鉄道 ticket office (daily 6am-10.50pm) is on the left by the station exit. See box p343 for details of using the pre-shinkansen line between Aomori and Hachinohe, now operated by Aoimori Railway (⌨ aoimorirailway.com).

There are some **lockers** (including a couple of ¥600 ones) between the station and the entrance to Lovina department store as well as a locker room (daily 5.30am-midnight) with lockers of all sizes on the left as you exit the station.

**Tourist information** The **tourist information desk** 青森市観光交流情報センター (daily 8.30am-7pm) in the bus terminal office on the left as you exit the station focuses on Aomori as the city, rather than the prefecture. Staff can advise on accommodation. There's another desk, 青森県観光連盟 (daily 9am-10pm), on the 1st/ground floor of **ASPAM**.

A useful website for information about Aomori city as well as other towns in the prefecture is 🖳 www.en-aomori.com.

**Getting around** The centre of Aomori is walkable but there is also a network of city buses. **Nebutan-go** ねぶたん号 (4-5/day; ¥500/1-day pass) runs in a loop from both Aomori and Shin-Aomori stations round the main tourist sights, including to Sannai-Maruyama Site and Aomori Museum of Art.

**Festivals Nebuta Matsuri** (🖳 www.nebuta.or.jp; 2nd-7th Aug) is one of the most popular and spectacular festivals in Japan. Every night, giant, colourful floats are paraded through the city – each depicting traditional Chinese and Japanese myths and legends – and on the evening of the final day a fireworks festival is held in the port area. The atmosphere of the city changes completely during the festival week. Thousands of visitors arrive and accommodation gets booked solid.

In recent years, a clash of old and new has played out; in 2015 a flotilla of *Star Wars* Nebuta were crafted but at the last minute removed from the main parade for not being traditional enough (and for potentially attracting *too* many visitors!).

**Where to stay** Convenient for the station is *Hotel Route Inn Aomori Ekimae* ホテルルートイン青森駅前 (☎ 0177-31 3611, 🖳 www.route-inn.co.jp; from ¥6300/S, ¥12,300/D, ¥13,300/Tw, inc buffet breakfast). It's not one of the newer hotels in the chain and the beds are firm, but some rooms have lovely views over the port, and the hotel also has a common bath so is good value overall.

Nearby is a branch of the ever-reliable Toyoko Inn chain: *Toyoko Inn Aomori-eki*

*Shomen-guchi* 東横イン青森駅正面口 (☎ 017-735 1045, 🖳 www.toyoko-inn.com; from ¥5724/S, ¥7884/D, ¥8964/Tw, inc breakfast). On a side street near the station is *Iroha Ryokan* いろは旅館 (☎ 0177-22 8689; from ¥4000/S, ¥6000/Tw), offering tatami rooms but no attached bathrooms or meals. It's a small place and gets booked up quickly.

*Aomori Center Hotel* 青森センターホテル (☎ 017-762 7500, 🖳 www.aomoricenterhotel.jp; from ¥6100/S, ¥10,500/D, ¥12,200/Tw, inc buffet breakfast), on top of Machinaka-onsen (see p363), has mostly single rooms, some of which are pretty compact, but rates include access to the onsen. *Hotel JAL City Aomori* ホテルJALシティ青森 (☎ 017-732 2580, 🖳 www.jalhotels.com/domestic/tohoku/ aomori; from ¥9300/S, ¥10,300/D, exc breakfast), is more upmarket, with an elegant lobby and large rooms; it is close to the ASPAM building. *Hyper Hotels Passage* ハイパーホテルズパサージュ (☎ 017-721 5656, 🖳 www.hyperhotel.co.jp; from ¥5980/S, ¥8980/Tw, ¥12,480/family, inc buffet breakfast) is fairly convenient for the station as well as city centre shops and restaurants. The single rooms are comfortable; the family rooms have a double bed and bunk beds. The breakfast is particularly extensive.

See pp67-73 for details about accommodation in general and also about facilities at chain hotels.

**Where to eat and drink** For a quick packed lunch, the 1st/ground floor of the **Lovina** ラビナ department store (daily 10am-8pm) has lots of options, including a branch of the tonkatsu-chain, *Saboten* さぼてん, which offers both sit-down meals and takeaway lunch boxes.

The basement of the **Auga** アウガ building (🖳 www.auga.co.jp), across the street from the station, has a fresh-fish market (5am-6.30pm). Sushi is naturally on offer at a couple of restaurants adjacent to the market area. Unsurprisingly there is an overwhelming smell of fish, so it's not a place to linger over a slow meal. There are also **fish and fruit/vegetable markets** along the road to the right of Auga.

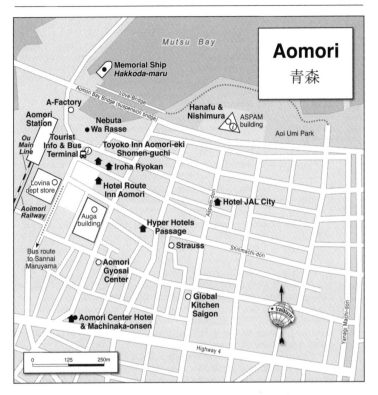

Aomori
青森

Mutsu Bay

Memorial Ship
Hakkoda-maru

Aomori Bay Bridge (suspension bridge)
Love Bridge

A-Factory

Aomori
Station

Hanafu &
Nishimura

ASPAM
building

Aoi Umi Park

Ou
Main
Line

Tourist
Info & Bus
Terminal

Nebuta
Wa Rasse

Toyoko Inn Aomori-eki
Shomen-guchi

Iroha Ryokan

Lovina
dept store

Hotel Route
Inn Aomori

Aspam-dori

Hotel JAL City

Aoimori
Railway

Auga
building

Hyper Hotels
Passage

Strauss

Shinmachi-dori

Bus route
to Sannai
Maruyama

Aomori
Gyosai
Center

Global
Kitchen
Saigon

★ trailblazer

Aomori Center Hotel
& Machinaka-onsen

Highway 4

Yanagi Machi-dori

0    125    250m

To create your own sushi/sashimi
bowl – *Nokke-don* のっけ丼 – go to
**Aomori Gyosai Center** 青森魚菜センタ
ー (🖥 www .aomori-ichiba.com/nokkedon;
daily 7am-4pm). First get a bowl of rice
(¥100/200 small/large) from one of the
stands on the left-hand side as you walk in
and then go round choosing your fish –
there is usually a huge variety to choose
from. You can also have miso and pickles;
tea is served free. Most of the fish sellers
have portions (¥100-250) already prepared.
  The **A-Factory** エーファクトリー
(daily 9am-8pm) is all about promoting
local produce, particularly apples. Food
options here include a sushi bar, cake shop
and soup stand; it would be a good place to
get food for a picnic.

*Global Kitchen Saigon* グローバルキ
ッチン居酒屋サイゴン (also known as
Saigon; 🖥 www.globalkitchensaigon.net;
Mon-Sat 5.30pm to midnight) is a small,
wooden-table restaurant which does food
from an array of international cuisines with
no discernible connection between them
but providing ample variety. It's further
south along the road from Hotel JAL City
and has an English sign.
  On the 14th floor of the **ASPAM**
building down by the port, *Hanafu* はなぁ
ふ (11am-6pm) serves reasonably priced
pasta and curry dishes as well as fish or
steak sets whilst offering impressive views
over Aomori and the bay. On the 10th floor,
*Nishimura* 西むら (Mon-Sat 11am-
9.30pm, Sun to 8.30pm), a casual Japanese

restaurant with low wooden tables, specialises in local fish dishes (a set meal costs around ¥2000).

For a decadent treat, try **Strauss** シュ トラウス (daily 10am-6.30pm); downstairs is a cake shop, but upstairs is a very smart café where waitresses in 1920s-style black-and-white uniforms serve slices of rich cake and various coffees. There's no better place to escape a freezing Aomori winter than here with a hot chocolate and apple strudel.

### Side trip by bus from Aomori

A 25-minute bus ride away on the edge of the Aomori are two attractions well worth making the effort to get to. **Aomori Museum of Art** 青森県立美術館 (💻 www.aomori-museum.jp; Jul-Nov 9am-6pm, Oct-Jun to 5pm, closed 2nd and 4th Mon of each month; ¥510) exhibits modern art with a focus on artists from Aomori prefecture. Like the archaeological site next door, the museum display spaces are excavated out of the ground. Expect gargantuan exhibition halls – the collection includes three impossibly large paintings by Marc Chagall – and endless corridors of local works. Apart from the Aleppo hall, there are few explanations in English.

The big draw of the museum is the colossal *Aomori-ken* ('ken' can mean both 'dog' and 'prefecture'), an 8.5m-high statue of a weeping dog peering into the museum that you can stand beneath and be photographed with (ask museum staff for a map for the convoluted access route; 'Aomori-ken' can be visited without paying the admission charge).

A well-signposted 10-minute walk from the art museum is the **Sannai-Maruyama Site** 三内山遺跡 (💻 sannaimaruyama.pref.aomori.jp; daily Jun-Sep 9am-6.30pm, Oct-May to 5.30pm; free), the site of a prehistoric settlement inhabited between 3900 and 2300BC. Visitors may enter the reconstructions of primitive buildings and the domes that preserve the excavated pits. All explanation signs are translated into English.

Do visit the adjacent **Jomon-jiyukan** 縄文時遊館, a modern facility containing both the (free) Sanmaru Museum and Jomon Theatre, which plays two informative documentary films on loop; pick up a pair of headphones for an English translation of the latter.

Ask at the TIC for an English bus timetable and board the Aomori City bus bound for Sannai Maruyama Iseki 三内丸山遺跡 from stop No 6. Alight at Kenritsu-bijutsukan-mae 県立美術館前 for the art museum (¥280), or Sannai-Maruyama Iseki-mae 三内丸山遺跡前 (the final stop) for Jomon-jiyukan (¥310). The Nebutan-go bus (see p364) also runs between Aomori station, Shin-Aomori station and the sites.

# HOKKAIDO

## Hokkaido – route guides

The northernmost of the major islands in the Japanese archipelago, Hokkaido represents one-fifth of the country's land mass, but is inhabited by only one-twentieth of the total population.

The island is the largest of Japan's 47 prefectures and is bordered by the Sea of Japan to the west, the Sea of Okhotsk to the north-east and the Pacific Ocean to the south. Hokkaido was colonised by the Japanese only in the middle of the 18th century; prior to that it was known as Ezo and was inhabited almost exclusively by the Ainu, an indigenous people who all but disappeared as more and more Japanese moved north from Honshu (see the box on p408).

Hokkaido is an island of stunning natural beauty, vast national parks with mountain ranges, volcanoes, forests, rivers, crashing waterfalls, hot springs, wildlife – and tourists. In the summer months, bikers, backpackers and cyclists descend on the island to feel what it is like to drive on the open road, unclogged by pollution, noise and urban development. Others come to escape the oppressive heat and humidity found elsewhere in Japan, to see cows, taste fresh Hokkaido milk, yoghurt and even Camembert-style cheese. In winter, when temperatures plummet and snow falls for months on end, skiers and snowboarders pour on to the slopes.

The good news for the rail traveller is that the shinkansen network now reaches Hokkaido; the bad news is that some lines on the island have closed. Spiralling costs, few passengers on remote lines and the difficulty of track maintenance in areas particularly exposed to the elements mean that some parts are no longer accessible by rail. But enough of the network remains to provide more than a glimpse of the spectacular natural environment. Don't expect frequent, lightning-fast services, particularly away from the major cities, but few other places in Japan offer such breathtaking scenery from the train window.

Shin-Aomori (see p343), on the tip of north-eastern Honshu, is the rail gateway to Hokkaido. The route in this chapter follows a loop around Hokkaido, starting from Shin-Aomori. Three weeks would be enough to enjoy the island without feeling rushed. For a briefer taste of what the island has to offer, the line between Abashiri and Kushiro (see pp382-7) has

*Through fragrant fields of early rice we went beside the wild Ariso Sea*
(MATSUO BASHO)

早稲の香や分け入る右は荒磯海

some of the most impressive scenery. Since Hokkaido is away from the major tourist areas, most visitors never make it this far but the views, if nothing else, more than repay the distance and effort. With the opening of the Hokkaido shinkansen it is even easier to make the journey through the Seikan Tunnel (see box below) so hopefully many more people will discover the charms of Hokkaido. (The extension of the shinkansen to Sapporo is expected to open in 2031.)

For further information about what to see and do on Hokkaido visit: 💻 en .visit-hokkaido.jp; 💻 www.hokkaidoexperience.com; or 💻 uu-hokkaido.com.

For details about using the rail route guide see p12.

## SHIN-AOMORI TO SHIN-HAKODATE-HOKUTO / HAKODATE
[Map 21, p370; Table 11, p508]

Distances from Shin-Aomori. Fastest journey time to Shin-Hakodate-Hokuto 61 minutes; to Hakodate 88 minutes.

### Shin-Aomori 新青森 (0km)                    [Aomori; see pp363-6]
The introduction of the Hayabusa shinkansen service in March 2016 means the journey time to Hakodate has been reduced by about an hour. (The fastest journey from Tokyo to Shin-Hakodate-Hokuto now takes just over four hours.)

Some Hayabusa services stop at **Okutsugaru-Imabetsu** 津軽いまべつ (38km), the only shinkansen stop on Honshu after Shin-Aomori. Soon after leaving Okutsugaru-Imabetsu the train enters the Seikan Tunnel and emerges from it about 15km before Kikonai.

### Kikonai 木古内 (75km)  Some Hayabusa services stop here, the first stop on Hokkaido – but the station does not have a code (see box p370). **Traveler's Center Road Station Misogi-no-Sato Kikonai** has a tourist information centre (daily 8am-6pm, later in peak season) and a restaurant, *Donan d'es* (daily 11am-2pm & 5.30-8.45pm) serving meals made with Hokkaido produce. The majority of the journey from here to Shin-Hakodate-Hokuto is in tunnels though there are some stretches on viaducts.

### Shin-Hakodate-Hokuto 新函館北斗 (H73; 148km)
This station started life in 1902 and was then called Hongo. In 1942 the name was changed to Oshima-Ono. In honour of the new shinkansen line it has been

---

❏ **Seikan Tunnel – a happy train partnership?**
The 53.8km-long Seikan Tunnel, under the Tsugaru Straits between Honshu and Hokkaido, is the longest underwater tunnel in the world. It is also the deepest at 140 metres below the sea bed. On top of that it was built as straight as possible and in a way that shinkansen tracks could be added; this long-term planning is now a reality, and the Seikan Tunnel is the only place in Japan with dual-guage tracks so both shinkansen and freight trains can share the tunnel. For this reason shinkansen trains, at least to start with, will go at no more than 140kph through the tunnel so that any freight train passing in the opposite direction isn't derailed by the shock of a speeding shinkansen.

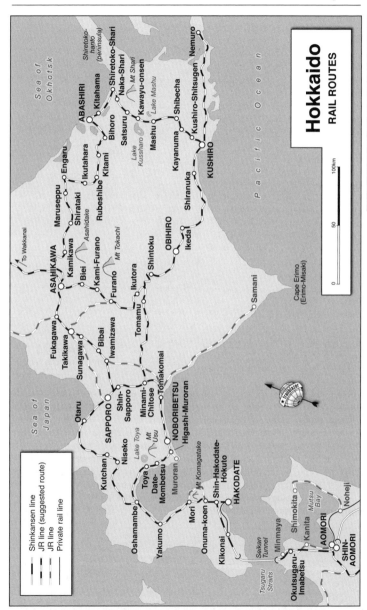

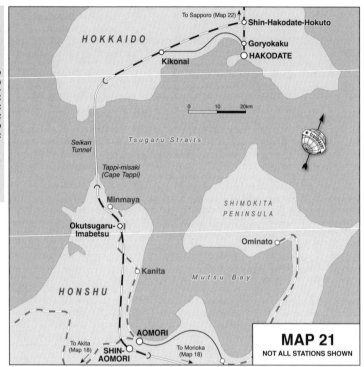

rebuilt with large windows and using locally sourced cedar trees and Hokkaido bricks; it has also been given yet another name. **Hokuto City Tourist Information Center** (🖳 hokutoinfo.com; daily 9am-7pm) is on the 2nd floor of the station building. The main exit is the South Gate. If in need of an ekiben for your onward journey visit *Bento Café 41° Garden* (daily 8am-8pm); the 41° refers to the latitude. Ekiben sold here feature local ingredients but there are also baked goods as well as drinks. There are **lockers** behind the escalator on the 1st/ground floor of the shinkansen side of the station.

If going **to Sapporo** change to a Hokuto/Super Hokuto LEX and pick up the route opposite. For **Hakodate** (see pp393-9) transfer to a local/rapid

❏ **Station codes**
To make life simpler for foreigners, JR Hokkaido has given every station a code based on an initial letter symbolising the name of the line and a number for the station so when you buy a ticket or make a seat reservation all you need to say is the code for the station. This guide lists these codes, for example Hakodate is 'H75'.

Hakodate-Liner 'relay' service; this is a very straightforward process. For both Sapporo and Hakodate connecting services depart about 10 minutes after shinkansen services arrive.

## HAKODATE / SHIN-HAKODATE-HOKUTO TO SAPPORO
[Map 22, p373; Table 14, p509]

Distances by JR from Hakodate. Fastest journey time: 3 hours 43 minutes.

**Hakodate** 函館 **(H75; 0km)** Pick up a Hokuto, or slightly faster Super Hokuto, LEX.

All trains stop at **Goryokaku** 五稜郭 (H74; 3km), see p399.

**Shin-Hakodate-Hokuto** 新函館北斗 **(H73; 18km)** All trains stop here. Transfer here (see p368) to a shinkansen if returning to Shin-Aomori.

**Onuma-koen** 大沼公園 **(H67; 28km)** Not all limited expresses stop here. To the right as you exit the small station is Onuma International Communication Plaza, a wooden building with a glass front, where there's a **tourist information counter** (daily 8.30am-6pm, Nov-Mar to 5.15pm). In the station there are a few ¥400 lockers.

One of the most beautiful, if foreboding, natural backdrops you're likely to come across in Japan is **Mt Komagatake**; it last erupted in a big way in 1640 when it killed more than 700 people. A minor eruption in 2000, which saw nearby areas covered in ash, proved that though Komagatake was dormant it is by no means extinct. There are hiking trails around the volcano, but you may prefer to admire the jagged peak from the safe distance of the lakes. Lake Onuma and two smaller lakes, Konuma and Junsainuma, were created when debris from an eruption of Komagatake settled as a natural dam. In winter the lakes freeze over and holes are cut in the ice for fishing.

Between April and November pedal **boats** (¥1400/30 mins), motor boats (¥1300/10 mins) and canoes (¥1400/hour) can be hired on the lakes. Alternatively, pleasure boats do 30-minute tours of Lake Onuma for ¥1100. A great way of seeing the lakes and taking in the spectacular surrounding scenery is to **rent a bike** (approx ¥500/hour, ¥1000/day). There are rental places in the station area, the most obvious being Friendly Bear, opposite the station.

The line passes between Lake Onuma (on the right) and the smaller Lake Konuma (on the left); it's a fleeting but superb last view of the two lakes. Soon enough though, the line becomes enclosed by trees.

Fittingly, the next stop for some limited expresses is called **Mori** 森 (H62; 50km); Mori means forest. Just before the station the train passes right by the sea. Mori, despite its name, is actually situated on the coast.

After leaving Mori the line begins to curve around Uchiura Bay. The track runs so close to the sea that you can see the different shades of blue in the water. Not all limited expresses stop at **Yakumo** 八雲 (H54; 81km). The line runs further from the sea along this stretch but look out to the left for views of the rolling green hills that are always featured on Japanese TV adverts for Hokkaido milk.

**Oshamambe** 長万部 **(H47; 112km)** All limited expresses stop here. Change here for the alternative route to Sapporo, via Niseko and Otaru on the Hakodate Line (see below). Hakodate Line trains depart from the same platform so transferring is easy, though you may have to wait a while.

For the continuation of the principal route to Sapporo, see p375.

### Alternative route to Sapporo via Otaru

**Oshamambe to Otaru**  The train from **Oshamambe** 長万部 (H47; 0km) to Otaru (6-7/day; 198 mins) is a one-car, one-man train. If you don't already have a ticket (or pass) pick up a numbered ticket (the number shows which station you got on at and therefore enables the driver to work out the fare) from the front of the train as you embark. Even though this is a local line announcements are in English.

One of the great features of this journey is that there are few tunnels, at least in the early section. Most of the time you can gaze out at the rural scenery as you gradually get closer to the tree-covered hills and the mountains.

At **Kuromatsunai** 黒松内 (S30; 20km) there is a small ski slope on the right – a sign of the greater things to come. Just before **Konbu** 昆布 (S26; 58km), an onsen resort, you get the first glimpse of **Mt Yotei** (1898m), which resembles Mt Fuji, to the left. It's a long-extinct volcano and the reason for the many hot springs in the area.

Even if you aren't listening to the train announcements, if you are looking out of the window you'll know when you've reached **Niseko** ニセコ (S25; 67.3km) because of the bright yellow bridge arching over its railway track. A year-round activity resort, Niseko has well-developed winter sport facilities and in summer offers white-water rafting, mountain-biking, rock-climbing, canyoning and trekking. Contact Niseko Adventure Centre (💻 nac-web.com), Niseko Hanazono Resort (💻 hanazononiseko.com/en), or Niseko Outdoor Adventure Sports Club (💻 noasc.com) for details.

Soon after leaving **Hirafu** 比羅夫 (S24; 74.3km; 💻 www.grand-hirafu .jp), another major ski resort, the urban spread of **Kutchan** 倶知安 (81km; S23; 💻 www.town.kutchan.hokkaido.jp/town) starts to appear. However, you also get compensatory views of Mt Yotei. By the time you reach **Shikaribetsu** 然別 (S20; 111.8km) the hills are behind you.

**Yoichi** 余市 (S18; 120.3km) is an increasingly popular tourist spot mainly due to its whisky distillery. There are lockers (¥300-500) at the station. The distillery is on the left-hand side as you walk down the main road heading from the station; en route you will find **Yoichi Tourist Association office** (Tue-Sun 9am-6pm), across from the plaza on the left-hand side. It has a good variety of pamphlets on local attractions. Continue straight on and you can't miss the imposing distillery building ahead. **Nikka Whisky Yoichi Distillery** 余市蒸溜 所 (💻 www.nikka.com/eng/distilleries/yoichi; daily 9am-5pm; free) was built in 1934 by Masataka Taketsuru and his Scottish wife, Rita. He chose this site because the environment seemed as similar as possible to Glasgow, in Scotland, where he had studied whisky-making. The distillery offers 20-minute tasting sessions of its malt whisky products as part of self-guided tours. Guided tours (Japanese only; 2/hr 9am-noon & 1-3.30pm) are also available.

HOKKAIDO

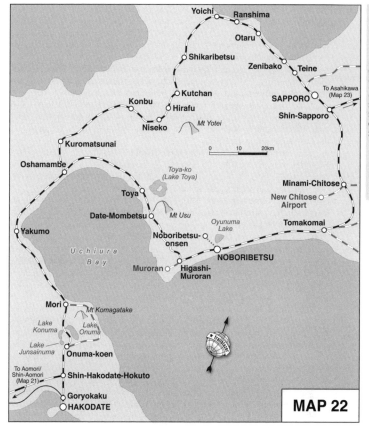

MAP 22

A little further along that road is **Yoichi Space Memorial Museum (Yoichi Dome)** 余市宇宙記念館（スペース童夢）(🖳 spacedome.jp; late Apr-Nov Tue-Sun 9am-6pm; ¥500). It is here because Mamoru Mohri, the first Japanese scientist who became a NASA astronaut, was born here. Attractions include a digital planetarium, models of the Hubble Space Telescope and the International Space Station as well as a life-size model of the Space Station's Kibo laboratory where two Japanese astronauts stayed. You can also learn about the life for astronauts in space and can buy space food at the shop. All signage is in Japanese though. As you walk around you are likely to spot the town's apple mascot everywhere.

After **Ranshima** 蘭島 (S17; 125.6km) the line runs near the coast.

**Otaru** 小樽 Otaru (S15; 140.2km) is a laid-back, compact port town surrounded by mountains and the sea. It is known for its many stone buildings (former warehouses and banks) as well as its canals and seafood. The canals perhaps explain the profusion of glass and 'Venetian art' stores by the waterfront. Along with the 'romantic slopes' leading the walker down to the shoreline, its literature and art museums all serve to project a cultivated image for its mainly domestic visitors.

To the right as you exit the ticket gates is a Twinkle Plaza Travel Center (daily 10am-6pm), Midori-no-madoguchi ticket counter (daily 6.30am-7pm) and **tourist information desk** (daily 9am-6pm). English tourist maps are available by the station exit if you arrive when the desk is closed. There is also a tourist information office (daily 9am-6pm) on Sakura Bridge in the canal area. There are **lockers** (¥400-700) to the left as you exit the ticket gates and the bus stands are to the right.

It is easy to walk around but **Otaru Stroller Bus** (1-3/hr; ¥210/journey, ¥750/day pass inc local buses) operates on several routes to the main sights. Alternatively, a rickshaw tour costs from ¥2000 (10 mins) for two people.

Rail fans will want to go **Otaru Transportation Museum** 小樽市総合博物館 (Otaru Kotsu Kinenkan; Wed-Mon 9.30am-5pm; ¥400, ¥500 for both sites), which is spread over two areas. The **Honkan** (Railway Museum) is built on the site of Hokkaido's first railway station and is filled with locomotives and carriages. There's even the chance to take a 400m ride on a steam locomotive from one end of the grounds to the other. To reach the museum take a bus from stop No 6 outside Otaru station to Kotsu Kinenkan-mae. The **Canal Building** branch (Ungakan; same hours; ¥300) explores the history of Otaru, the indigenous Ainu people, and the conservation movement in Otaru. It is about a 10-minute walk from the Honkan and is worth allocating some time for.

The **canal area** is lovely at any time of the day but particularly in the evening when the old-fashioned gas lamps are lit. Most of the warehouses have now been converted into shops, restaurants and museums, among them, on Sakaimachi-dori, are some glass workshops, a Museum of Venetian Art 北一ヴェネツィア美術館 (🖥 www.venezia-museum.or.jp; daily 8.45am-6pm; ¥700), and a Bank of Japan museum 金融資料館 (Tue-Sun 9.30am-5pm; free), where you can learn about banking and money and have the chance to feel the weight of a hundred million yen.

Conveniently, **Otaru Yuki Akari-no-Michi** 小樽雪あかりの路 (Snow Light Path Festival) is held at the same time as the Sapporo Snow Festival (see p404). Lanterns are lit in two particular parts of town and snow sculptures created (and also illuminated) but everywhere is atmospheric because of the snowy streets.

*Dormy Inn Premium Otaru* ドーミーインPREMIUM小樽 (☎ 0134-21 5489, 🖥 www.hotespa.net/hotels/otaru; from ¥6900/S, ¥9100/D, ¥11,600/Tw; ¥1500 breakfast) is on the left at the top of the road down to the canals and sea from the station. It has comfortable rooms as well as an onsen and sauna and serves a fantastic breakfast. *Authent Hotel* オーセントホテル (☎ 0134-27 8199; 🖥 www.authent.co.co.jp; ¥10,300/S, ¥13,600/D, ¥18,600/Tw, ¥27,900/Tr) is located on the first main boulevard running parallel to the east of the station's sea-facing road about halfway down on the corner.

Since Otaru is a fishing port it is not surprising that sushi/sashimi is popular here. For either, or both, head to **Sushi St** 寿司屋通り (Sushi-ya-dori); several of the larger shops have menus in English. For informal food options try the friendly **Otaru Beer** 小樽ビール, a German-style beer hall backing onto Otaru canal, or the more refined setting of **Otaru Bine** 小樽バイン (next to Otaru post office) for its Italian pasta and Hokkaido wine. There try a glass of Otaru Camberuari, an extraordinarily fruity local wine, that tastes like a peculiar blend of port and Koolaid. After that description, it shouldn't be, but is, a surprisingly quaffable tipple.

**Otaru to Sapporo**  Even if you aren't stopping in Otaru you will need to change train here. There are both local and semi-rapid services to Sapporo (at least 3/hr); some of the latter continue to Shin-Chitose Airport (2/hr).

Try to sit on the left for the best views of the sea and the coastline, until **Zenibako** 銭函 (S11; 155.8km). If here mid July-August, the new **Onze Harukayama Lily Garden** オーンズ春香山ゆり園 (🖥 www.onze-yuri.com; daily 9am-5pm; ¥800 plus ¥520 for optional cable car to summit) gives you another taste of floral Hokkaido with two terraces looking down the slope; the *Seagull restaurant* specialises in lily tempura. It takes 30 minutes to walk down from the summit. You can pick up the free shuttle bus to the garden from the station. After Zenibako the line turns inland and scenery becomes more industrial and urban. At **Teine** 手稲 (S07; 163.4km) there are views to the hills on the right if you look over the buildings but otherwise there is little of interest until you reach **Sapporo** (01; 174km), see pp399-406.

There is a long section of tunnels between Oshamambe and Toya, the next major stop.

**Toya** 洞爺 **(H41; 154km)**  All limited expresses stop here. The attraction hereabouts is **Toya-ko** 洞爺湖 (🖥 www.laketoya.com), a caldera lake formed by the collapse of a mountain following volcanic activity thousands of years ago. However, it lacks the charm of Onuma-koen (see p371) as huge lakeside hotels spoil the scenery and the atmosphere. That said, the lake itself is worth a look and onsen fans might enjoy an afternoon wallowing in a hot spring or two in some of the larger resort hotels.

There are lockers in the station. Turn right out of the station for buses to the lake (daily approx 1/hr; 17 mins; ¥320). **Toya-ko Visitor Center** 洞爺湖ビジターセンター (daily 9am-5pm) is near Toya-ko-onsen Bus Terminal and in the same place as the **Volcano Science Museum** 洞爺湖町立火山科学館 (9am-5pm; ¥600).

All limited expresses stop at **Date-Mombetsu** 伊達紋別 (H38; 167km), after which it's coast, then tunnels, then industrial blot, then **Higashi-Muroran** 東室蘭 (H32; 190km).

**Noboribetsu** 登別 **(H28; 207km)**  All limited expresses stop here. Noboribetsu comes from the Ainu word 'Nupurupetsu', meaning 'a cloudy river tinged with white'. A bus ride away from the station is **Noboribetsu-onsen** 登別温泉 (a hot-spring resort) that draws water from **Jigokudani** 地獄谷 (Hell Valley), the centre of which is a volcanic crater where steam rises from the earth. It was only in 1858, when a businessman who was mining sulphur realised there was money to be made from tourism, that the first public bath house was opened using hot water from the crater. Since then, tourism has taken off and the resort is now full of hotel blocks and tourist attractions. Despite this, Jigokudani is well worth seeing close up as are the geothermal springs of bubbling Oyunuma Lake. A visit here would not be complete, however, without a trip to one of the hot springs in the resort.

From Noboribetsu station, Donan buses run up to the terminal in Noboribetsu-onsen (daily approx 1/hr; 15 mins; ¥330). There is a small tourist office here and a couple more on the road to Jigokudani. All can provide a useful English map and guide to the area and advise on accommodation but cannot book it. The first you reach after the bus terminal is **Noboribetsu Tourist Association** 登別観光協会 (🖳 www.noboribetsu-spa.jp; daily 9am-6pm), a couple of minutes up the main road on the left-hand side.

In 1924 the area was designated '**Noboribetsu Primeval Forest**', a fitting description for the haunting landscape. Though you aren't allowed to walk around Hell Valley (not that you'd want to with the bubbling and smoke rising from the ground), there is a short promenade offering a close-up view. From early June to early August on Thursdays and Fridays, the '**Demon's fireworks displays**' allow you to 'enjoy experiencing the fable of Hell Valley as the demons carry spark-throwing columns of fire along the Demon footpath, hoping for happiness and taking away misfortunes'. Every night until 9.30pm, the Jigokudani pathway is illuminated as a 'Demon's fire trail' so it is worth exploring even if you have limited daylight hours in the resort. A far more satisfying walk takes you up into the hills above Hell Valley and down to the volcanic swamp that is the percolating **Oyunuma Lake** 大湯沼, where temperatures reach 130°C. Find the sign for 'Mountain-Ash Observatory' and walk up the path for 20 minutes to reach Oyunuma. Even in the rain the sight is impressive – it's magnificent in autumn and you can borrow winter boots from the **Noboribetsu Park Service Centre** 登別パークサービスセンター (daily 9am-4pm), near the entrance to Jigokudani, before your climb to witness the geothermal displays amidst the snowy backdrop.

Having seen the source there are plenty of opportunities to test out the water in one of the onsen hotels. The most popular baths, but also the most expensive (daily 9am-5pm; ¥2000pp for non residents), are at ***Daiichi Takimotokan*** 第一滝本館 (🖳 www.takimotokan.co.jp/english; from ¥18,090/S, ¥10,260pp if two sharing inc half board), the highlight of which are several *rotemburo*, which even have a drinks service – just pick up the phone in the booth by the main bath. Massage and beauty treatments are also available. This hotel is the last before Hell Valley.

***Takimoto Inn*** 滝本イン (☎ 0143-84 2205, 🖳 www.takimotoinn.co.jp; half board from ¥8250/S, ¥7170pp if sharing), which is right opposite, has none of the grandeur of its neighbour but provides good-value accommodation with free access to Daiichi's baths. To reach them cross the road (it is perfectly acceptable to do this in your yukata), go in the main entrance to the hotel and head left following the signs; it is a surprisingly long walk. There is also an onsen in the basement of the Inn, but no rotemburo. Some of the buses from Noboribetsu station stop right outside Takimoto Inn (and therefore opposite the Daiichi) so it is worth taking one of these to avoid the walk uphill from the bus terminal with heavy luggage.

A less elaborate but much better-value onsen is **Sagiriyu** さぎり湯 (daily 7am-9.30pm; ¥420), the only municipal hot spring in the resort. Conveniently it's next door to the tourist office by the bus terminal. Look for the purple hanging curtain and wooden entrance.

Noboribetsu also has more than its fair share of tacky theme-park entertainments, for which there is a combination Noboribetsu Theme Park ticket (¥3300pp/2 parks, ¥4500pp/3 parks). At the station, you can't miss the enormous and kitsch European-style castle; this is **Noboribetsu Marine Park Nixe** 登別マリンパークニクス (🖳 www.nixe.co.jp; daily 9am-5pm; ¥2450), a large aquarium with dolphin, sea lion and penguin shows plus an aqua tunnel.

**Noboribetsu Date Jidaimura** 登別伊達時代村 (☎ 0143-83 3311, 🖳 www .edo-trip.jp; Apr-Oct daily 9am-5pm, Nov-Mar to 4pm; ¥2900) is a reproduction Edo-period village. Of particular interest is the Ninja show involving a ninja sword duel, secret doors, a roped descent from the ceiling and a rather unconvincing earthquake scene. In the 'Scary Cat' house you have to be careful of the cat; it appears behind secret panels, its giant furry paw descends from the ceiling and it even hides inside a giant bell ready to pounce. Beware of the cat! The bus from the station to Noboribetsu-onsen stops here (8 mins; ¥330).

**Tomakomai** 苫小牧 **(H18; 248km)**   All limited expresses stop here. Tomakomai is a railway junction and port.

**Minami-Chitose** 南千歳 **(H14; 275km)**  All limited express services stop here. Change here for **Shin-Chitose (New Chitose) Airport** 新千歳 空港 (AP15; 🖳 www.new-chitose-airport.jp), three minutes away by local train. This is the nearest airport to Sapporo, handling both domestic and international flights. As you look out to the left, you should spot aircraft located very close to the railway tracks.

**Shin-Sapporo** 新札幌 **(H05; 308km)**  Some limited expresses make a brief stop here, but stay on the train until the Sapporo terminus.

**Sapporo** 札幌 **(01; 319km)**                                    [see pp399-406]

## SAPPORO TO ASAHIKAWA & ABASHIRI
### [Map 23, p379; Map 24, p381; Table 15, pp509-10]

Distances by JR from Sapporo. Fastest journey time to Asahikawa 80 minutes and from Asahikawa to Abashiri 3¾ hours.

Note that all the trains on this route from Sapporo stop in Asahikawa, but if continuing beyond that you will need to be on the Okhotsk LEX.

**Sapporo** 札幌 **(01; 0km)**  The views from the train are less than spectacular as far as **Iwamizawa** 岩見沢 (41km; A13), as it takes some time to leave Hokkaido's capital behind. From here on, the familiar wide green spaces start to open up once more. Some trains stop at **Bibai** 美唄 (A16; 46km) and **Sunagawa** 砂川 (A20; 64km).

The landscape is briefly interrupted by the small city of **Takikawa** 滝川 (A21; 84km), known throughout Hokkaido for its extremely heavy snowfall.

About 10 minutes after leaving Takikawa, the train crosses Ishikari-gawa; beyond **Fukagawa** 深川 (A24; 107km) is a series of long tunnels.

## Asahikawa 旭川 **(A28; 137km)** [see pp407-10]

Asahikawa is an important junction station for lines east to Abashiri, south to both Obihiro and Kushiro, and north to Wakkanai.

For Abashiri continue on, or if starting at Asahikawa join, the Okhotsk LEX that runs along the JR Sekihoku Line. It's worth making a seat reservation as there is only a limited number of carriages.

All the clichés of Japan being a nation of no open space and houses packed together like rabbit hutches collapse on this stretch of the journey. The train travels slowly enough to see some of the tiny stations along the way.

## Kamikawa 上川 **(A43; 185km)** Alight here for Sounkyo-onsen (see below).

### Side trip by bus to Sounkyo-onsen

In addition to the many ryokan at Sounkyo-onsen 層雲峡温泉 (🖳 www .sounkyo.net) there is one **public bath-house** Kurodake no Yu 黒岳の湯. Taking the **Daisetsuzan Sounkyo Ropeway** 大雪山層雲峡・黒岳ロープウ エイ from near the visitor centre (cable car; 9am-4pm, longer in peak periods; 3/hr; 7 mins; ¥1950 round trip) is an excellent way to take in the grandeur of Mt Kurodake (1984m), the jewel in Daisetsuzan National Park, an area also known as the Central Highlands of Hokkaido. From here (Station 5) you can then take a chair-lift (daily June to mid Oct & mid Nov to Apr; 15 mins; ¥600 round trip) to Station 7 leading to a final 200-metre hike (about 90 mins) to the peak. If you have hiking boots, time and the weather is fair, you could also hike the trails all the way from the bottom. Either way, the splendid views of Kurodake easily explain why the Ainu named the area Kamui Mintara, or 'Playground of the Gods'.

Buses (11/day; 35 mins; ¥870) to the main resort area are timed to meet most trains; enquire at the bus ticket office to the right as you exit the station.

After Kamikawa the predominant scenery is forest rather than open space. The track becomes hemmed in by trees on both sides and there are some semi-tunnels (with windows). There's one long tunnel about 15 minutes before arriving at Shirataki but then the countryside starts to open up again.

Some limited expresses do not stop at **Shirataki** 白滝 (A45; 223km), but even when passing through you'll see that the station is supposed to recall the railway of yesteryear, with a clock tower topped by a weathercock. Most limited expresses make a brief stop at **Maruseppu** 丸瀬布 (A48; 242km).

At **Engaru** 遠軽 (A50; 261km) the train waits a few minutes as everyone turns their seats around so as to continue facing the direction of travel. If you are feeling hungry there is a soba restaurant in the station.

Shortly after leaving **Ikutahara** 生田原 (A53; 278km) the train heads into the Jomon Tunnel.

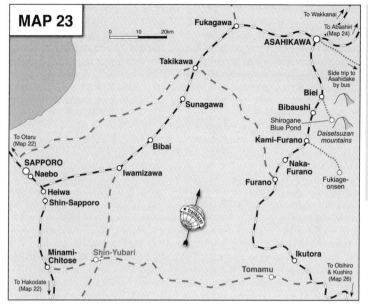

MAP 23

To Wakkanai
To Abashiri
(Map 24)

Fukagawa

**ASAHIKAWA**

0    10    20km

Takikawa

Side trip to
Asahidake
by bus

**Biei**

Sunagawa

Bibaushi

Shirogane
Blue Pond

*Daisetsuzan
mountains*

To Otaru
(Map 22)

Bibai

**Kami-Furano**

**SAPPORO**

Naka-
Furano

Naebo

Iwamizawa

**Furano**

Fukiage-
onsen

Heiwa

Shin-Sapporo

Minami-
Chitose

Shin-Yubari

**Ikutora**

To Obihiro
& Kushiro
(Map 26)

Tomamu

To Hakodate
(Map 22)

HOKKAIDO

**Rubeshibe** 留辺蘂 (A56, 299km) station is the closest to **Onneyu-onsen**
おんねゆ温泉 (🖥 www.onneyuonsen.jp), which is home to one of the world's
largest cuckoo clocks.

The wide plains seen during the early part of this journey return, with fields
on either side of the track. During the last few kilometres before **Kitami** 北見
(A60; 321.5km), the final major stop on the line to Abashiri, the surroundings
get a little more built up (for Hokkaido) and there's a long tunnel.

Services then call at **Bihoro** 美幌 (A65; 346km) and **Memambetsu** 女満別
(A67; 358km), which lies just at the edge of Lake Abashiri. From here, though
the track looks as if it will run right by the lake, trees block out any view and it
is only about four minutes before arriving in Abashiri that there is finally a
glimpse (on the left) of the northern tip of the lake. Just in case you miss it, the
conductor makes an announcement urging passengers to look out of the window
and savour the fleeting view.

**Abashiri** 網走 **(A69; 374.5km)** Abashiri (🖥 abashiri.jp/tabinavi) is the terminus of the JR Sekihoku Line from Asahikawa. In winter, people come here to
see blocks of drift ice on the Sea of Okhotsk. Ornate, hand-crafted snow and ice
sculptures are a highlight of the **Drift Ice Festival** in February.

Abashiri station is small but has some **lockers** (all sizes, but only a few
¥500 ones) and a coffee shop, as well as a **tourist information office** (daily
9am-5pm) on your right as you leave the station. Turning left as you exit the

station, you will soon find a **post office** branch (9am-5pm) and **ATM** (Mon-Fri 9am-5.30pm, Sat 9am-12.30pm). Continue just a little further for *Sukiya* すき 家 (daily 11am-11pm), an eel fast-food chain restaurant, replete with picture menus. If you have never eaten eel and are desperately hungry, make this your inexpensive initiation into the culinary world of Japanese *unagi*.

The main sights are around **Mt Tento** (207m), nationally designated a place of scenic beauty. A bus (daily May to mid Jan 9.30am-4pm; 6/day; ¥800 one-day pass) to these, with announcements in English, runs on a loop and departs from stop 2 outside Sukiya.

Taking the bus from Abashiri station, stop first at **Abashiri Prison Museum** 博物館網走監獄 (Hakubutsukan Abashiri Kangoku; ◻ www.kan goku.jp/world; Apr-Oct 8am-6pm; Nov-Mar 9am-5pm; ¥1050), halfway up Mt Tento. Abashiri Prison was first built in the 1890s, when Abashiri was a small, remote village, to help pioneer Japanese settlement in Hokkaido. This was primarily achieved through the use of prison labour in the hazardously gruelling work of building the Chuo-Doro road. This was seen as essential to counter the perceived growing imperial threat of the Russian Empire, now pressing the Far East via the Trans-Siberian Railway. The hard-labour system was modelled on France's 1810 Penal Code (as dramatised in the opening of the film *Les Miserables*). It was modernised in 1984 and the original cells and other buildings were relocated here. Today visitors are allowed to wander around the buildings, which include cell blocks, a court-house and bath-house, and get an idea of daily life for the prisoners and how tough it must have been, especially during the freezing winters. There are some stimulating touch-screen interactive displays in the large government building and a 'sensory theatre' performance projected in the Prison History Museum every 10 minutes (aim to arrive at 10 minutes past the hour for the English version).

The next stop on the bus route is **Okhotsk Ryu-Hyo (Drift Ice) Museum** オホーツク流氷館 (Apr-Oct 8am-6pm, Nov-Mar 9am-4.30pm, closed 29th Dec to 5th Jan; ¥540), which has a -12C 'Drift Ice Experience Room', where you are even encouraged to swing a cold wet flannel around to appreciate its chill as ice-block displays attempt to show what the Sea of Okhotsk is like in the dead of winter. Also look out for displays of the tiny endearing 'clione' fish (a bit like a translucent winged batman) found in local waters that has been embraced by the townsfolk as the 'Angel of the Drift Ice'. There is an HD cinema screen too depicting the four seasons of Abashiri plus impressive views of Lake Abashiri and the Sea of Okhotsk from the new Mt Tento Observatory on the 3rd, 4th and 5th floors.

Next, pick up the bus or walk 800m to the **Hokkaido Museum of Northern Peoples** 北方民族博物館 (Hoppou Minzoku Hakubutsukan; ◻ hop pohm.org; Tue-Sun Jul-Sep 9am-5pm, Oct-Jun 9.30am-4.30pm; ¥550, ¥800 inc temporary exhibitions; free headset and mini iPod provided). This museum seems to attract fewer people, which is a pity since it's perhaps the best, with exhibits relating not just to the Ainu, but also to minorities across the northern hemisphere. You can, for example, hear clips of over nine northern indigenous languages from around the world. The main hall displays everything from snow boots to a recreated Ainu winter home. Screens show footage of reindeer herding and hunting for fish by cutting holes through the ice. There are real environmental lessons to note here. For example, admire how Ainu snow-shoes are made from salmon skin, using the dorsal fins for traction on the soles, while lengthy seal intestines are utilised as containers for cooking oil.

A seasonal bus (Jan 20th–Mar 31st) to the Drifting Ice Boat Terminal departs from stop 1 outside Abashiri station. The *Icebreaker Aurora* 網走流氷観光砕氷船おーろら (🖳 ms-aurora .com/abashiri; 4-6/day; ¥3300) departs from the terminal on one-hour trips on the Sea of Okhotsk. 'Feeling the ice cracking beneath the ship's hull defies description,' reads the publicity. This trip is by far the best reason for paying a visit to Abashiri in the dead of winter.

There are two business hotels near the station. *Toyoko Inn Okhotsk Abashiri Ekimae* 東横 インオホーツク網走駅前 (☎ 0152-45 1043, 🖳 www.toyoko-inn.com; from ¥5724/S, ¥6804/D, ¥8964/Tw, inc breakfast with extra discounts in winter) is on the left as you leave the station. Just opposite the station is *Route Inn Abashiri Ekimae* ホテルルートイン網走駅前 (☎ 0152-32 1112, 🖳 www.route-inn.co.jp; ¥5800/S, ¥9550/D, ¥10,050/Tw, inc buffet breakfast); the rooms are reasonable but the beds can be hard.

If booked in advance a pick-up service from the station to *Abashiri Ryuhyo-no-oka Youth Hostel* 網走流氷の丘ユースホステル (☎/🖹 0152-43 8558, 🖳 www.jyh.or.jp; from ¥3250pp + ¥600 for non members, breakfast ¥630, evening meal ¥1050, or special meal ¥1500; 28 beds) can be arranged; alternatively a taxi costs under ¥800. The hostel is a small, clean, friendly place with mostly bunk-bed dorms and a good view over the Okhotsk Sea from outside. Cakes and tea are served at 8pm for anyone who wants to socialise. Be sure to pick up discount coupons from reception before you hit the Abashiri museums.

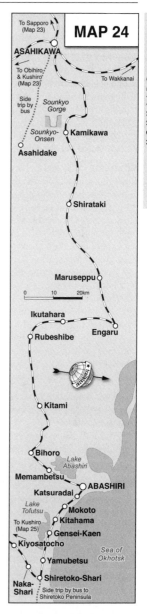

MAP 24

HOKKAIDO

## ABASHIRI TO KUSHIRO [Map 24, p381; Map 25; Table 16, p510]

Distances by JR from Abashiri. Fastest journey time: 3 hours 3 minutes.

**Abashiri 網走 (A69; 0km)** This route has some of the most stunning scenery but is not for anyone in a hurry. Only local trains run along the single-track Senmo Line that first heads east along the coast as far as Shiretoko-Shari, before turning south-west through Akan National Park towards Kushiro.

Once the train has emerged from the short tunnel just after **Katsuradai 桂台** (B79; 1.5km) there are great views out to the left of the Sea of Okhotsk.

**Mokoto 藻琴** (B77; 9km) station has a coffee shop with views out to sea, though the one at the next stop, Kitahama, is even better.

**Kitahama 北浜** (B76; 12km) Although only a few minutes out of Abashiri, Kitahama really is worth stopping at. There can be no better location to have a coffee than here, facing the Okhotsk sea, especially in winter when the water becomes a sheet of ice. The old railway seats and battered suitcase make this the ultimate *café* (Wed-Mon 11am to around 8pm) for passing travellers. The menu includes toast, pasta, and a daily set lunch. For an authentic taste of the sea, dive into a hot bowl of Okhotsk-style noodles, a delicious broth brimming with crab, prawns, salmon, scallop & cod roe (¥1200).

The station's waiting room is also worth seeing as it is covered with old railway tickets and business cards left by travellers.

Bird-watchers may want to stop here as it is only a 10-minute walk (turn left out of the station then take the first right fork) to the **Lake Tofutsu Waterfowl and Wetland Centre 濤沸湖水鳥・湿地センター** (🖳 tofutsu-ko .jp; Tue-Sun 9am-5pm; free) in Shirotori Park. The lake is a popular bird-watching spot in the winter months (particularly Oct-Nov & Mar-Apr) when whooper swan and grey heron are here. If the weather is uninviting, use the professional field scopes indoors.

After Kitahama, look out to the right for views of Lake Tofutsu. **Gensei-Kaen 原生花園** (B75; 17km) station is another popular spot for viewing the lake. If it's not too foggy you should be able to see Shiretoko Peninsula on the left in the distance, though the view is blocked in places by pine trees. After **Yamubetsu 止別** (B73; 26km) there's a long stretch without any stations.

**Shiretoko-Shari 知床斜里 (B72; 37km)** This is the nearest station to Shiretoko Peninsula and Shiretoko National Park.

**Side trip by bus to Utoro for Shiretoko Peninsula/National Park**
In 1964 most of **Shiretoko Peninsula 知床半島** was designated **Shiretoko National Park 知床国立公園** (🖳 www.shiretoko.asia). The area is considered an idyllic retreat from the man-made world, an unspoilt territory inhabited by wild eagles, brown bears and the world's largest owls; for this reason it was also declared a UNESCO World Heritage site in 2005.

Turn left as you exit the station for Shari bus terminal 斜里バスターミナル (under the archway that reads 'Welcome to Shiretoko'). Most buses run from here along the peninsula to the bus terminal at **Utoro** ウトロ (Apr-Oct 8/day, Nov-Mar 5/day; 60 mins; ¥1490, Shiretoko round-trip ticket ¥1800), from where it's about a 10-minute walk to the ferry terminal. The longest **ferry ride** (🖳 ms-aurora.com/shiretoko; June-Sep 1/day; 3¾hrs; ¥6500) goes all the way to Cape Shiretoko 知床岬 (inaccessible by road) and back. The Mt Io 硫 黄山 (late Apr to late Oct 4-6/day; 90 mins; ¥3100) option doesn't go as far.

Note that in winter many of the roads beyond Utoro into the national park are closed because of the amount of snow.

**Naka-Shari** 中斜里 **(B71; 42km)** Just after leaving the station a large and unsightly factory looms into view on the right-hand side. This eyesore aside, the journey from here is one of the best in Hokkaido. This is the only line on the

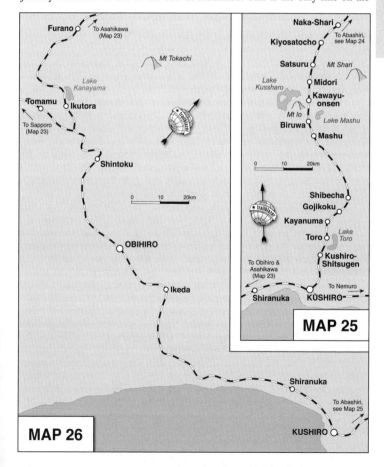

island that actually runs through a national park, between Lake Kussharo and the smaller but more mysterious Lake Mashu. Neither lake is visible from the train, though there are good access points to both along the way.

After **Kiyosatocho** 清里町 (B69; 49km) look on the left for the 1545m-high **Mt Shari** 斜里岳; it should be visible unless the summit is covered in cloud.

There's a long stretch between **Satsuru** 札弦 (B68; 57km) and **Midori** 緑 (B67; 65km) where trees very definitely outnumber people. Midori ('Green') station has a brown roof and blue trees painted on the side; it is the last stop before Akan National Park. The whole area, with the track surrounded by forest, is so lush and green that it is difficult to tell exactly where the national park officially begins. But about 10 minutes after leaving Midori the train passes through a tunnel. Emerging from this you are actually in Akan National Park.

**Kawayu-onsen** 川湯温泉 **(B66; 80km)**  Built in 1936, the old station master's office has been turned into an excellent *café*. It's tempting to while away an afternoon right here as there is also a **foot-bath** at the station, but with such magnificent scenery so close to hand it would be a shame to miss out. The **information desk** offer a free **left-luggage service** (8.30am-5pm) and you can pick up a cycle map there so you can explore the Teshikaga area; **cycles** can be rented for free but they must be returned by 5pm. Non-cyclists might consider purchasing a two-day **Eco Passport pass** (Jul-Oct; ¥1500) that will allow you to join the half-day **Lake Kussharo bus tour** (3-4/day) taking you on a long circular route, with brief photography stops, to Lake Mashu (approx 85 mins; you can leave the bus here) before going round Lake Kussharo and to the Bihoro Pass. The pass is also valid on local buses, the Lake Mashu sightseeing tour bus (see Mashu opposite) and securing discounts in local restaurants and attractions.

If the weather is good, do venture out by bike (although be advised the free station bikes are the standard basket-bearing 'mamachari' versions not renowned for their speed). From the station, head up to the main road and turn right onto Route 391. Go straight until the first set of lights and turn left onto Route 52. A few minutes down this road, on the left-hand side, is the stunning **Mt Io (Iwo)** 硫黄山, still very much an active volcano. If you don't see it first, you'll almost certainly smell it. Smoke pours out from different places around the mountain and the sulphur turns the rock a bright yellow. Most people take a brief closer look at the smoke then rush back, covering their mouths and noses. By the car park, the food offerings in the ubiquitous souvenir shop are plentiful so be bold and try an *onsen tamago* (eggs boiled in natural local hot springs) for ¥100, or a refreshing melon ice-cream (¥300).

Continue along the main road for another 2km until you reach the centre of Kawayu-onsen, known for its 'diamond dust'. This is crystallised water caused by steam from when the hot spring river freezes in the air when the temperature decreases below -20°C (usually seen mid Jan to late Feb). As you arrive in the centre, look for an orange Seicomart convenience store on your right. Then look on the left for a sign pointing to **Kawayu Eco Museum Center** 川湯エコミュ ージアムセンター (EMC; Thur-Tue Apr-Oct 8am-5pm, Nov-Mar 9am-4pm;

free); this shows films of the area's flora and fauna, has scale models of Akan National Park, and free tea and coffee. Ask for the *Let's Walk Around EMC* leaflet, with details of walks in the woods around the centre. You can then choose to take the more scenic forested path back to Mt Io (Iwo) car park on your return. There is also a free foot-bath near here.

Near the EMC is a small museum dedicated to local **sumo wrestler Taiho-san** 大鵬 (daily Oct-May 9am-5pm, Jun-Sep to 9pm; ¥420), who reached the rank of *yokozona*, sumo's highest, and claimed 32 tournament victories, twice winning six consecutive titles. Taiho-san was born in Sakhalin (now part of Russia) but moved to Hokkaido and attended school in Kawayu-onsen before leaving for Tokyo at 16 to begin his sumo apprenticeship. On display are all 32 tournament trophies won up to his retirement in 1971, along with photos and other memorabilia, including one of his oversized suits. Kawayu-onsen continues its link with sumo by hosting the annual Women's Sumo Championship.

Energetic cyclists might consider continuing for a further 3km to **Lake Kussharo** 屈斜路湖, where Kussie – the local equivalent of Scotland's Loch Ness Monster – is said to live. Signs are posted warning of bears in the woods. Around the lake are some outdoor hot springs (a few are free) as the lake is thermal, and summer activities on the lake include canoeing and kayaking although it feels mainly set up for young families. After the cycle tour head back to the station in time to pick up a train to **Mashu** station, as Mashu-ko Youth Hostel (see below) is a good place to stay.

**Biruwa (B65; 87km)** This is more of a portakabin than a station.

**Mashu 摩周 (B64; 96km)** A small station with a few ¥300 lockers by the exit and a helpful **tourist information office** (🖳 www.masyuko.or.jp; summer only daily 9am-5pm). There is a good **foot-bath** on your left as you emerge from the station. Here in the summer you can also buy your Eco Passport pass which allows you to pick up the Lake Kussharo bus tour (for both see opposite), or take a local bus (4/day) to Lake Mashu.

**Mashu-ko** 摩周湖 (Lake Mashu), 20km in circumference, is known as the lake 'of mystery and illusion'. No river flows in or out of it and it is completely surrounded by trees. The only way of seeing the lake is from elevated observation points, but the water is almost always shrouded in a blanket of fog. It's almost as if this mystical natural phenomenon becomes disgruntled by the unwanted attention, so cloaks itself in a mist to avoid the gaze of tourists.

*Mashu-ko Youth Hostel* 摩周湖ユースホステル (☎ 015-482 3098, 🖳 www.jyh.or.jp; dorm from ¥3300pp, ¥4200/S, ¥3900/3600/¥3300pp for 2/3/4 sharing, plus ¥500pp for non-YHA members; closed 1st-20th Dec), situated about halfway to the lake, is an ideal place to stay. Call ahead to arrange a pick-up from the station. Accommodation is Western style and there is a coin laundry and internet access (¥10 per minute). Hostel staff organise summer and winter activities including cross-country skiing and canoeing. Meals (dinner from ¥1300, breakfast ¥780) are served in *The Great Bear* restaurant (🖳 great bear.sakura.ne.jp) next to the hostel.

From Mashu-ko Youth Hostel, it's a 3-hour walk up the road that runs outside the hostel to the lake but it should be easy to hitch a lift with a fellow hosteller; alternatively take the bus (see p385).

Mashu station lies just outside Akan National Park but the views from the train remain tremendous, with long gaps between isolated stations. The next major sight is **Kushiro-Shitsugen National Park** 釧路湿原国立公園; it's a good idea to plan to spend a whole day on the journey between Mashu and the terminus at Kushiro.

The next stop is **Shibecha** 標茶 (B61; 121km), followed by **Gojikoku** 五十石 (B60; 130km), which is on the edge of Kushiro-Shitsugen National Park. The park is mostly marshland, inhabited by Japanese cranes. Though not as well known as Akan National Park it still has some beautiful scenery.

During the mating season (Jan-Mar), Japanese cranes perform elaborate mating dances on the snow-covered ground near **Kayanuma** 茅沼 (B59; 135km) station. Beyond Kayanuma there's a long stretch of track through marshland, so look out for swamp marshes on both sides.

**Toro** 塘路 **(B58; 142km)** Bikes can be rented (¥700/hr) from *Norroko & 8001* coffee bar in the station. Ask the owner for a map of the area, which includes Lake Toro, the major lake in the marshlands area.

Two minutes on foot from the station is *Kushiro Shitsugen Toro Youth Hostel* 釧路湿原とうろユースホステル (☎ 0154-87 2510, 🖳 www.jyh.or.jp; ¥3456pp, ¥4536 for non-members; breakfast ¥648, dinner ¥1080). It's a homely place with 14 beds and a good base for exploring the area and bird-watching.

**Kushiro-Shitsugen** 釧路湿原 **(B56; 152km)** All the stations along this stretch of the line are tiny wooden buildings. There are plenty of hiking opportunities around Kushiro-Shitsugen. Views from the train remain impressive until about 10 minutes before Kushiro, where modern life begins to encroach.

**Kushiro** 釧路 **(K53; 169km)** Kushiro is the terminus for the Senmo Line from Abashiri and also a stop on the Nemuro Line that runs east to Nemuro (see opposite) and west to Obihiro and beyond. Facing the Pacific Ocean, Kushiro is the most easterly city in Japan and is often enveloped in a sea fog. Most come here as a base to explore local marshlands.

Turn left after the ticket barrier to find lockers (all sizes) and a bakery/café. The staff at the **tourist information booth** (🖳 www.kushiro-kankou.or.jp); daily 9am-5.30pm) in the station may not speak English but can provide a map of the city. The horrendously kitsch chapel that sits incongruously outside the station is a fake, rented by couples for a white wedding.

**Kushiro City Museum** 釧路市立博物館 (Tue-Sun 9.30am-5pm; ¥470) is 15 minutes by bus from the station. Here you can get an overview of the city and the Kushiro-Shitsugen marshland you have just travelled through. There are also exhibitions on Ainu traditions and on the Japanese crane (the feathered variety). Several buses go to the museum from the bus terminal to the left as you exit the station. Get off at Kagaku-kan-dori.

**Kushiro City Art Museum** 北海道立釧路芸術館 (Tue-Sun 10am-5pm; free) showcases the work of local artists across formats and is a 20-minute walk from the station. Cross Nusamai Bridge 幣舞橋 and follow the signs. You will find the museum on the 3rd floor of the glass and concrete barrel-shaped tower.

*Route Inn Kushiro Ekimae* ホテルルートイン釧路駅前 (☎ 0154-32-1112, 🖳 www.route-inn.co.jp; from ¥6000/S, ¥10,150/Tw, ¥12,600/D, breakfast ¥1000) is opposite the station towards the left. *Kushiro Tokyu Inn* 釧路東急イン (☎ 0154-22 0109, 🖳 www.kushiro-i.tokyuhotels.co.jp/ja; from ¥6600/S, ¥12,000/Tw, ¥12,600/D, breakfast ¥1000) is just to the left across the street as you leave the station. *La Vista Hotel and Spa Resort* ラビスタ釧路川 (☎ 0154-31 5489; 🖳 www.hotespa.net/hotels/kushirogawa; from ¥7100/S, ¥9560/D, ¥10,620/Tw inc breakfast) is adjacent to Nusamai Bridge and opposite Fisherman's Wharf/Moo. Run by the Dormy Inn chain, it offers a popular rooftop spa, a hearty breakfast and complimentary coffee in the foyer.

*ANA Crowne Plaza Hotel Kushiro* ANAクラウンプラザホテル (☎ 0154-31 4111, 🖳 www.anacpkushiro.com; from ¥6500/S, ¥7000/Tw, ¥9000/D), directly across the street from MOO, offers the most upmarket accommodation in town. The best budget choice is the youth hostel at Toro (see opposite).

Kushiro is known for its soba shops, which serve **green soba**. The best are called Azumaya 東家 and usually have big white signs with 東 painted on their traditional facades. To call themselves an Azumaya soba shop, the chefs must have trained at the original restaurant, which is near Harutori Lake. The restaurant is relatively ancient for Hokkaido, having been established over a hundred years ago, and Emperor Hirohito once ate there; it also has a lovely bamboo garden. *Azumaya Nusamai* 東家ぬさまい (daily 11am-7pm), a small place across Nusamai Bridge, is not much to look at inside but the quality of the noodles (*zarusoba* ¥650) is spectacular; their tempura is also excellent.

Fifteen minutes down the main road that leads from the station is **Fisherman's Wharf MOO** フィッシャーマンズワーフMOO, a large waterside shopping and restaurant complex popularly known as **MOO**. In summer (end of May to end Oct) a big marquée is set up along the riverside here for *robatayaki*. Joe Woodruff (UK) says: 'It's a great experience – you buy a set of tickets at the till as you come in, then find a seat at one of the charcoal barbecues. There are about five stalls, all selling incredibly fresh seafood and meat, with a good selection of vegetables too. Once you've handed over your tickets you take the food over to your barbecue and cook it to your liking, although the wandering waiters will always give you a hand with anything if you need it'. Some locals prefer **Washo market** 和商市場 (a 2-min walk from the station) for this type of dining experience although it doesn't have the river views.

### Side trip to Nemuro, the easternmost tip of Japan
From Kushiro, JR Nemuro Line extends east to its terminus in Nemuro 根室 (🖳 www.nemuro-kankou.com). Nemuro and the surrounding area is known for its delicious seafood, variety of fauna, and for the view of the Habomai Islands, currently disputed territory with Russia. The section of line between **Monshizu** 門静 and **Itoizawa** 糸魚 is great for seeing the marshland.

Inspired by the many footpaths in the UK, Nemuro has set up its own network. The best access point for these is **Attoko station** 厚床駅 (7/day; 90-105 mins). For further details visit 🖳 www.nemuro-foottourism.com.

Trains to Nemuro (7/day) take just over two hours; it's then a further 40 minutes by bus (8/day; ¥1040 one-way) to Cape Nosappu (Nosappu-misaki) 納沙布岬.

## KUSHIRO TO SAPPORO (OR ASAHIKAWA)

Distances by JR from Kushiro. Fastest journey time: 3 hours 58 minutes.

### Kushiro to Shintoku                    [Map 26, p383; Table 17, p510]

**Kushiro 釧路 (K53; 0km)**  Pick up the Super Ozora LEX.

There are occasional glimpses of the Pacific Ocean during the first part of the journey. Some trains stop at **Shiranuka** 白糠 (27km).

**Ikeda 池田 (K36; 104km)**  The first major stop after Kushiro. Joe Woodruff (UK) says: 'Ikeda is famous (in Hokkaido anyway!) for its wine and dairy products and is a nice place to stop in the summer for a few hours. The landscape around the town is Hokkaido down to a tee – wide plains filled with fields and farms, and backed by dramatic mountains. The town is home to **Ikeda Wine Castle** 十勝ワイン工場 where you can sample some of the local tipple. It is not the best and there's not much to the "castle", but it might be worth a quick visit as it's very close to the station. The nicest thing to do in Ikeda, though, is to take a walk alongside the fields to **Happiness Dairy** ハッピネスデーリィ (daily Mon-Fri 9.30am-5pm, Sat & Sun to 5.30pm); it sells excellent ice-cream and cheese from Tokachi milk. There are a few strange ice-cream flavours which are surprisingly good – the pumpkin and potato flavours were delicious.'

Five or six minutes after leaving Ikeda, the train crosses Tokachi river. Look out for cows – a rare sight – on this part of the journey.

**Obihiro 帯広市 (K31; 128km)**  The Hidaka mountains lie to the south and west of Obihiro. Obihiro is best known for its unique version of horse-racing (see box opposite). At the end of the first week in February **Obihiro Ice Festival** features ice sculptures, fireworks and local street food.

There is a **tourist information office** (🖳 www.obikan.jp) on the 2nd floor of the Esta East building in the station and two hotels very close to the station. *Richmond Hotel Obihiro Ekimae* リッチモンドホテル帯広駅前 (☎ 0155-20 2255, 🖳 obihiro.richmondhotel.jp; from ¥5900/S, ¥6900/D, ¥7900/Tw) is to the left from the North Exit of the station. The upmarket *Hotel Nikko Northland Obihiro* ホテル日航ノースランド帯広 (☎ 0155-24 1234, 🖳 www.jrhotels.co .jp/obihiro; ¥14,000/S, ¥23,000/Tw, ¥25,000/D; small discount for rail-pass holders) is right outside the South Exit of the station.

Obihiro's food speciality is *butadon* 豚丼 (pork on rice, eaten in a bowl); the dish originated here and lots of restaurants serve it. It's definitely worth checking out the atmospheric *Kita no Yatai* 北の屋台 (approx 6pm to midnight), a small alleyway full of superb tiny restaurant-stalls serving traditional

❏ **Ban'ei racing – with 'draft' horses**
**Ban'ei Tokachi Obihiro Horse-Race Track** 帯広競馬場 (🖳 www.banei-keiba.or.jp;
Sat, Sun & Mon from 9.40am, first race 11am; ¥100), in Obihiro, is the only place in
the world where you can watch 'draft' horses (like carthorses) racing. The horses are
twice the size of thoroughbreds and they race (pulling a weighted sled) on a straight
200m track which has two small hills as obstacles.
    Races are held throughout the year, even in the snow and at night-time. Success
depends on the strength of the horse but also the skill of the 'jockey'. The stadium is
about a 15-minute walk from the station.

Japanese, Korean, Chinese and European food. Each place seats only a few people. The alleyway is about five minutes' walk from the North Exit of the station.

**Shintoku** 新得 **(K23; 172km)** The town of Shintoku is known for buckwheat soba (noodles) and you'll find buckwheat ice-cream, buckwheat tea as well as buckwheat soba lunch deals in some of the restaurants.

Shintoku is also at the junction of two lines: to continue to Sapporo stay on the Super Ozora LEX, which travels west along the Sekisho Line to **Tomamu** トマム (K22; 206km), **Shin-Yubari** 新夕張 (K20; 261km), **Minami-Chitose** (H14; 304.5km) and **Sapporo** (01; 348.5km). The section of line between Tomamu and Shin-Yubari is spectacular in the autumn months.

For Asahikawa, change to a local train and continue along the Nemuro Line to Furano, as described below, where you'll then need to change again.

## ▲ Shintoku to Asahikawa
            **[Map 26, p383; Map 23, p379; Tables 18 & 19, both p510]**
Stations along this line are spread out and there's a whole series of tunnels, one of the longest being about 25 minutes after leaving Shintoku.

After leaving **Ikutora** 幾寅駅 (T36; 210km), the train runs past **Lake Kanayama** 金山湖 on the right-hand side. The track then crosses the lake before entering a tunnel. After this, it's a pleasant ride through the hills and plains to Furano.

**Furano** 富良野 **(T30; 254km)** Furano is a junction station for the JR Nemuro Line to Shintoku and the JR Furano Line to Asahikawa.

Known for its powder snow in winter (late Nov to early May; 🖳 www.ski furano.com) and its fields of lavender (see p390) in summer, Furano is one of the most popular tourist resorts in Hokkaido. Traditionally appealing mostly to the domestic tourist, recent years have seen an explosion of interest from large groups of Chinese tourists.

There are lockers to the left of the station exit and a soba/udon counter (¥300-600). Staff at **Furano and Biei Tourism Centre** 富良野・美瑛広域観光センター (🖳 www.furano-kankou.com; daily 7am-6pm), at the station, can provide information about the area and accommodation. Outside the station towards the left, there is a bike rental spot (¥200/hr).

Three minutes on foot from the station, the rooms at **Sumire Inn** すみれ旅館 (☎ 0167-23 4767, 🖥 www4.plala.or.jp/furano-sumire; from ¥4300pp, ¥5500pp with breakfast, ¥6500pp inc half board; ¥300 for heater in winter) may look a bit old and tired but all the facilities are modern – the owner is friendly and keeps cats. For more upmarket accommodation try **Furano Natulux Hotel** 良野ナチュラクスホテル (🖥 www.natulux.com; from ¥9000/S but not available in winter, ¥20,520/D, ¥25,920/Tw; breakfast ¥1300; good-value packages available). The hotel, to the right as you leave the station, has a relaxation spa (free for guests 5-8.30am & 11am-midnight; non-residents 11am-11pm, ¥630).

*Yamadori* ヤマドリ (11am-3pm & 5-10pm), on the right as you walk to Sumire Inn, serves *yakiniku*. You cook your own meat (pork from ¥600) and vegetables (from ¥420) on a gas charcoal burner; they also do a Furano Cheese fondue (¥1680). **Furano Burger** ふらのバーガー (🖥 www.furanoburger.com; summer daily 11am-7pm, winter to 5pm though occasionally closed) is near Torinuma Park and is best reached by taxi from the station. It is well known and comes highly recommended for its burgers.

Lavender is big business in Furano; lavender ice-cream is available nearly everywhere and even the JR station has its name painted in purple above the entrance. The main attractions are lavender fields, dairy farms and cheese-making factories. The official **lavender-viewing season** is June to August; if visiting at this time ensure you have booked accommodation well in advance. During this period the Furano Biei Norokko train (3/day) stops at Lavender Field ラベンダー畑駅, a seasonally constructed station, and it is a short walk from there to **Farm Tomita** ファーム富田, one of the many lavender farms in the area. Be warned, the lavender-viewing trains (as well as local ones) can be extremely overcrowded in summer with large tour groups. If you can get around on foot instead, do so and you will likely see as much, if not a lot more. In peak season JR Hokkaido also operates various Twinkle Bus sightseeing routes (seat reservations essential) from Furano and Biei stations (daily Jun-Aug, less regularly in Sept/Oct; ¥1500); see the JR Hokkaido website for details.

▲ Transfer here to another local train along the Furano Line towards Asahikawa.

**Naka-Furano** 中富良野 **(F42; 262km)** The 15-bed **Furano Youth Hostel** ふらのユースホステル (☎/🖨 0167-44 4441, 🖥 jyh.or.jp; dorms ¥3450pp; rooms Oct to late June: ¥5610/S, ¥4530/4170pp for 2/3 sharing; rates inc breakfast and supper) is six minutes on foot behind the station here and highly recommended. Please note payment is in cash only. You can walk to the lavender fields from here if you don't mind stretching your legs.

After Naka-Furano, on your left are low hills and fields while in the distance to the right are the more impressive peaks of the Daisetsuzan mountains.

**Kami-Furano** 上富良野 **(F39; 269km)** The main reason to stop here, other than to visit the lavender and flower farms and for the Lavender and Fireworks Festival in July, is to go to one of the hot springs (see opposite) in Daisetsuzan National Park. For further information visit 🖥 www.kamifurano.jp.

## Side trip by bus to Fukiage-onsen

**Fukiage-onsen** 吹上温泉 is a completely natural (wild) hot spring where bathing is mixed and there are no admission fees. Follow the short path down from the bus stop to find the two pools nestled snugly on the hillside. Immerse yourself as you look up at the looming green foliage amidst the sounds of the racing river to enjoy what some visitors have claimed is Hokkaido's best onsen experience. If mixed bathing in the wild is not your thing, just down the road is *Fukiage-onsen Recreation Centre Hakuginso* 吹上温泉保養センター (🖳 www.navi-kita.net/shisetsu/hakugin; 10am-10pm; ¥600; no English spoken), with a variety of segregated baths (there is a swimsuit one for families) at different temperatures as well as a sauna and rotemburo affording views over the mountains. Buy a ticket from the vending machine in the entrance lobby and, afterwards, sample one of the 17 flavours of ice-cream from the vending machine as you exit to cool down.

If you fancy a night in the mountains you can stay here, either in a tatami mat room or in bunk-bed dorms (from ¥2600pp). Snacks are available but meals are not provided so bring food with you – there are cooking facilities (nominal charge). Camping pitches (¥500) are available in the summer.

To get to Fukiage-onsen take a Kami-Furano bus (3/day; 33 mins; ¥500); the bus terminates at **Tokachi-dake-onsen** 十勝岳温泉 (the stop is called Ryo-unkaku; 3/day; 46 mins; ¥500).

**Bibaushi** 美馬牛 **(F38; 278km)** There are opportunities here for a wide variety of outdoor sports. **Guide no Yamagoya** ガイドの山小屋 (🖳 www.yamagoya.jp; daily May-Nov from 8am-6pm but closed in rain), in the wooden building across the street from the station, is an outdoor pursuits centre which arranges canoeing and rafting trips, and guided mountain-bike rides out to Daisetsuzan National Park. From December to March the main activity is cross-country skiing. They also rent out electric-bikes (¥600/hr, ¥3000/day) and mountain-bikes (¥400/hr, ¥1500/day). Youth hostel guests (see below) get discounted rates. This place also has a café, showers, lockers and laundry.

The bright white house right outside the tiny station is *Bibaushi Liberty Youth Hostel* 美馬牛リバティユースホステル (☎ 0166-95 2141, 🖳 www.biei.org/liberty; closed early to mid Apr & mid Nov to mid Dec; dorm ¥4580pp, room from ¥5080pp), where accommodation is mostly in four-bed dorms. The couple who run the hostel are really welcoming and it's small enough to feel very homely. Evening meals are not available.

*Gosh* ゴーシュ (🖳 www.gosh-coffee.com; Wed-Mon 10am-5pm), about 800m from the station, is highly recommended for its home-made breads and cakes. It roasts its own coffee and is an atmospheric place, with lots of wood and brickwork, as well. It also serves European-style meals.

**Biei** 美瑛 **(F37; 285km)** The extremely helpful **tourist information centre** (🖳 www.biei-hokkaido.jp; daily May-Oct 8.30am-7pm, Nov-Apr to 5pm) is in the green-and-white building to the left outside the station. The lockers here (all sizes; ¥200-500) are available during office hours; bulky luggage can be left with the staff (¥420) between 10am and 6pm.

If descriptions of 'the greens of the rolling pastures, the delicate pinks of the potato flowers, the rusty yellows of the ripened seeds' appeal, Biei will be the perfect place to stop for an extended cycle ride (outside the snow season). The area is very hilly so be prepared for a bit of legwork, but your efforts will be rewarded with magnificent views. There are also plenty of small cafés and private art galleries to explore in and around the hills above the station.

**Matsuura** 松浦商店 (daily 9am-7pm, closed in wet weather), next to the tourist information centre, rents out mountain-bikes and ordinary bikes (¥600/200 for 1hr, ¥3000/1000 for 5hrs) and gives out cycling-tour maps. Another option is **Takikawa bike rental** 民宿 たきかわ (7am-6pm, ¥1500/all day, ¥3000/all day electric assist); here there are mountain-bikes as opposed to the typically heavy *mamachari* basket-bikes common elsewhere (although you may prefer storage to speed). The owner is also friendly. From the station, turn right along the main street (213) before turning right again into a side road once you have reached Idemitsu petrol station. Lighter mountain-bikes are definitely recommended for the terrain which is hilly in areas. Follow the numbered signposts on your map on what is billed the 'Panoramic Road'. Be sure to enjoy the floral displays at **Shikisa no Oka** 四季彩の丘, where you can see the extent of the lavender fields and also buy fruit and vegetables, eat melon ice-cream and hop on a buggy, wagon or golf cart to enjoy nature's work.

If cycling sounds like too much work, for a **free view** of the surrounding area go to the top of Biei Town Hall 四季の塔 (Shiki-no-Tou). The town hall is on the left at the second set of traffic lights heading straight from the station.

*Hotel L'Avenir* ホテルラ ヴニール (☎ 0166-92 5555, 🖥 www.biei-lavenir .com; ¥5500-9000pp inc half board), a concrete-looking building with Western-style en suite rooms, is a short walk from the station. *Biei Potato-no-Oka Youth Hostel* 美瑛ポテトの丘ユースホステル (☎ 0166-92 3255, 🖥 www.potatovil lage.com; closed late Nov to late Dec; dorm ¥6900pp; rooms ¥6900-17,800, plus ¥600 for non-YHA members; supper ¥1480, breakfast ¥780) is just over 4km from the station; if you call ahead, someone will pick you up.

*Family Restaurant Daimaru* ファミリレストランだいまる (daily 11am-3pm & 5-8pm, sometimes closed on summer evenings if food sells out) serves dishes using local produce as well as curry-rice and udon (mostly about ¥800). Walk down from the station and then turn first right at the traffic lights. Daimaru is towards the end on the right before the next set of traffic lights. In summer arrive early to beat the large tour groups that will descend on this popular spot.

### Side trip by bus to Shirogane Blue Pond

Take a No 39 Douhoku bus 道北バス (5/day; 26 mins; ¥500) to see the unusual Shirogane Blue Pond 白金青い池. This was created by chance as a result of attempts to control landslides in the area after Mt Tokachi erupted in 1989. The local authorities built a dyke to contain the volcanic mudflow and water got trapped here. The aluminium that seeped into the water makes it look blue in sunlight.

The bus continues to **Shirogane-onsen** 白金温泉, which is part of Daisetsuzan National Park.

From Biei, stay on the train for the rest of the journey along the Furano Line to Asahikawa. If you are on a local train there will be lots of stops!

## Asahikawa 旭川 (A28; 309km) [see pp407-10]

See p378 for routes from Asahikawa (in reverse) back to Sapporo and Hakodate.

HOKKAIDO

# Hokkaido – city guides

### HAKODATE 函館

The first major stop on a journey through Hokkaido, Hakodate is the third largest city on the island and was one of the first port cities in Japan to open to foreign trade in the 19th century. The first commercial treaty was signed with the USA in 1858, followed by similar agreements with Holland, Russia, Britain and France. Foreign consulates opened up near the port in order to oversee international trade, red-brick warehouses and churches were built, and many of the original buildings still stand as a reminder of the city's Western influence.

Its proximity to Honshu means Hakodate gets packed out in the summer when tourists come to eat fresh crab and gaze down at the 'milky way floating in the ocean', a lyrical description of the night view of the city from the top of Mt Hakodate.

### What to see and do

**Station area** Outside the station's West Exit is the busy **morning market** 函館朝市 (*asaichi*; 5am-noon, closed Sun in winter). Early in the morning the market-stall tanks are filled to bursting with fresh catches of crab and squid. Fruit (particularly musk melons) and vegetables are also big business. **Jiyu Market** 函館自由市場 (daily 5am to early afternoon), a 10-minute walk from the station, is smaller but is where chefs and restaurateurs go so expect the fish and other produce to be top quality.

**Memorial Ship** *Mashumaru* 摩周丸 (daily Apr-Oct 8.30am-6pm, Nov-Mar 9am-5pm; ¥500) is the old JR ferry that plied the water between Aomori and Hakodate in the days before the Seikan Tunnel (see box p368). It has a small museum; visitors can tour the bridge and radio-control room, and even put on the captain's jacket and gloves. The ship is geared more for those who might enjoy the nostalgic appeal of former seagoing vessels; there are better things to see and do in Hakodate.

**Motomachi** 元町 Motomachi is the city's old quarter, where the former consulate buildings were located. It is possible to see four of the 'sights' in the area for ¥840. However, two of these – the museums – have few labels in English and thus may be of less interest. Individual tickets cost ¥300, or ¥500 for two sights. All are open daily (Apr-Oct 9am-7pm, Nov to Mar to 5pm).

From Suehiro-cho tram stop cross the road and walk back a bit to reach the **Museum of Literature** 文 学 館 (Bungakukan), which has displays on the life and works of novelists, poets and journalists who are connected with Hakodate.

On the same side of the road but a little way past the tram stop, the **Museum of Northern Peoples** 函館市北方民族資料館 (Hoppo Minzoku-shiryokan) is housed in the former branch of the Bank of Japan. Displays include a collection of clothes and accessories worn by the Ainu as well as a number of ceremonial objects and everyday items such as a sled and fishing harpoons.

Five minutes' walk uphill from the museum is the **Former British Consulate** 旧イギリス領事館 (Kyu-Igirisu-Ryojikan; 🖳 www.hakodate-kankou.com/british/),

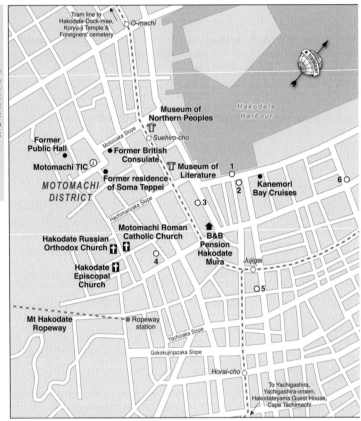

Tram line to
Hakodate-Dock-mae,
Koryu-ji Temple &
Foreigners' cemetery

O-machi

Hakodate
Harbour

Museum of
Northern Peoples

Motoizaka Slope

Suehiro-cho

Former
Public Hall

Former British
Consulate

Motomachi TIC

Museum of
Literature

1

Former residence
of Soma Teppei

MOTOMACHI
DISTRICT

2

Kanemori
Bay Cruises

6

Hachimanzaka Slope

3

Motomachi Roman
Catholic Church

Hakodate Russian
Orthodox Church

4

B&B
Pension
Hakodate
Mura

Jujigai

Hakodate
Episcopal
Church

5

Mt Hakodate
Ropeway

Ropeway
station

Yachizaka Slope

Gokokujinjazaka Slope

Horai-cho

To Yachigashira,
Yachigashira-onsen,
Hakodateyama Guest House,
Cape Tachimachi

which first opened in 1859. The building that stands today was constructed in 1913 and was used up to the closure of the consulate in 1934. Look out for the rusty 'Dieu et mon Droit' royal crest that used to hang on the consulate gate and for the account of how one consul's wife taught Japanese women the Western way of doing laundry. The video diorama on the 2nd floor is in Japanese but features a lovely scene of American sailors first meeting Japanese people and wanting to take a photo. The gift shop does a roaring trade in old-fashioned British products such as 'Ahmad tea' and 'Simpkins sweets', and the menu at

*Victoria Rose Tea Room* (9am-7pm, Nov-Mar to 5pm) includes a full tea with cakes and biscuits (¥1500).

A little further up the road is the **former residence of Soma Teppei** 旧相馬邸 (Kyu-Soma-tei; daily 9am-4pm; ¥500). This house was built (1908-11) by Soma Teppei, a very successful merchant, to a design that drew on both Japanese and Western traditions. There is much impressively detailed workmanship, including a handsome dining table and chairs; make sure you see the wooden lift/elevator that was installed so that food could be sent up to the 2nd floor from the kitchen. At the

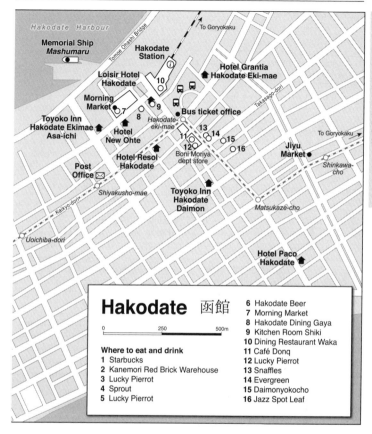

**Hakodate** 函館

0        250        500m

**Where to eat and drink**
1 Starbucks
2 Kanemori Red Brick Warehouse
3 Lucky Pierrot
4 Sprout
5 Lucky Pierrot

6 Hakodate Beer
7 Morning Market
8 Hakodate Dining Gaya
9 Kitchen Room Shiki
10 Dining Restaurant Waka
11 Café Donq
12 Lucky Pierrot
13 Snaffles
14 Evergreen
15 Daimonyokocho
16 Jazz Spot Leaf

time of writing there was little explanation in English, so if a member of staff offers to guide you round do accept the offer.

The **former Public Hall** 旧函館区公会堂 (Kyu-Kokaido) is a large Western-style building, completed in 1910, with a number of guest bedrooms (look out for the Emperor's toilet and bathroom) and a large hall on the 2nd floor that commands a great view of the harbour. Free concerts are held here occasionally between June and October.

Don't be surprised if you see Japanese women drifting around in ball gowns; for ¥1000 they can dress up and be photographed in front of an enlarged photograph

of the building that is downstairs in the billiard room.

Other sights to look out for in the area are **Motomachi Roman Catholic Church** カトリック元町教会 (Katoriku Motomachi Kyoukai), **Russian Orthodox Church** ハリストス正教会 (Harisutosusei Kyoukai; Mon-Fri 10am-5pm, Sat 10am-4pm, Sun 1-4pm; ¥200) and **Hakodate Episcopal Church** 函館聖ヨハネ教会 (Hakodate-yohane Kyoukai).

Mt Hakodate, 334m above sea level, offers a panoramic view of the city. **Mt Hakodate Ropeway** 函館山ロープウェイ (🖥 www.334.co.jp; ¥1200 return; times vary according to season; the ropeway doesn't operate in windy weather) runs up to the top from Motomachi. A cheaper way of reaching the summit is by bus from Hakodate station. In the summer months a bus service (see opposite) operates mostly in the evening, when, for 30 minutes a day, the view is considered one of the most spectacular in Japan and is a must-see. The cheapest way though is the walking path which is open from spring to autumn.

For great (and free) sea views (with Honshu in the distance) and crashing ocean waves, head out to **Cape Tachimachi** 立待 岬 (Tachimachi-misaki), the name of which is derived from words in Ainu meaning 'a rocky point where one waits for and catches fish'. Ride the tram to the terminus at Yachigashira 谷地頭 and then follow the signs. It is a 1km walk, partly uphill, and partly through a graveyard with memorials to various Hakodate poets. There are several trails over the hills if you want to continue walking. The well-maintained and signposted forest paths are a trail runner's paradise where your dirt-cushioned steps are often accompanied by the flutters of butterflies and unusual birds. Despite small print warnings of pit vipers, yellow hornets and poison ivy, you can run easily to the summit in well under an hour and enjoy the morning views before the ropeway opens. Along an upward path you will also find a monument dedicated to the memory of Ieyasu Tokugawa's retainers (follow the sign from the Cape) who fled here at the coming of the Meiji era. A poignant Chinese proverb is etched on the back of the stone that reads, 'The blood of those loyal to their lords turn blue after three years' indicating the inherent honour of fidelity.

If you want to relax after all the walking **Yachigashira-onsen** 谷地頭温泉 (daily apart from 2nd and 4th Tue of month; 6am-10pm; ¥420) is just off the slope down to Yachigashira tram stop. It has both indoor and outdoor baths,

If you take the tram to the Dock-mae どつく前 terminus on the other side of the peninsula and walk uphill from there, you can get more lovely views and also visit **Koryu-ji Temple** 高龍寺 and the

**Foreigners' cemetery** 外国人墓地 (Gaijin Bochi); both are a 10- to 15-minute walk from the tram stop and are worth the walk to even if they are closed. Another option is to take Bus Line 1 from Hakodate station and get off at Koryu-ji-mae 高龍寺前 from where the temple is a 3-minute walk.

At the back of the Kanemori Red Brick Warehouse shopping area at the water inlet, **Kanemori Bay Cruises** 金森ベイクルー ズ offer regular 15-minute loops (Apr-Nov daily 10am-5pm; ¥1500) around Hakodate Bay on the back of small open-topped vessels. You are given a bright yellow life-vest to wear.

See p399 for details of the side trip to Goryokaku from Hakodate.

## Practical information

**Station guide**  Hakodate station is bright, modern and serves as a welcoming gateway to the city. There is only one ticket barrier and it is on the same level as the platforms. Immediately to your left as you leave the ticket barrier are the **JR ticket office** and adjacent Twinkle Plaza travel agency. Both can handle rail-pass seat reservations. There is a post office **ATM** on the station concourse. The main exit is the Central Exit but for the morning market take the West Exit, to your right as you pass through the ticket barrier.

On the 1st/ground floor *King Bake* (daily 7am-7pm) is a decent bakery and *Café St* (daily 6.30am-8pm) serves spaghetti and pizza (¥600-950). Also in this area are some kiosks selling **ekiben** lunch boxes (specialising in crab).

For **lockers** (¥400 & ¥700; 6am-10pm) take the escalator up from the concourse; there is a change machine if you don't have the correct coins. Up here you'll also find *Dining Restaurant Waka* ダイニングレス トラン和華 (10am-9pm), whose menu includes soba (¥520) and tonkatsu curry-rice (¥950). Take a seat along the far window for excellent views of Mt Hakodate.

**Tourist information**  Hakodate Tourist Information desk (🖵 www.hakodate-kan kou.com; daily Apr-Oct 9am-7pm, Nov-Mar to 5pm) is in the far corner of the Twinkle

Plaza travel agency on the station concourse. Staff can provide a map, a 10% discount coupon for Mt Hakodate Ropeway and other key information, but **Motomachi TIC** (Apr-Oct 9am-7pm, Nov-Mar to 5pm) has a wider range of leaflets in English.

**Getting around** Hakodate's **tram/street car system** has been in operation since 1913 and it's still the best way of getting around the city. A one-day tram pass (¥600) is probably all you need but if you would like to travel on **buses** (except the bus to the airport) as well a one-day pass is ¥1000 (two days ¥1700). This also covers the seasonal bus service (late Apr to late Nov; 2-3/hr; 25 mins; ¥360 one-way) to the top of Mt Hakodate. Purchase the pass from either the tourist information desk or tram drivers. Individual fares (tram or bus) are ¥200-250.

Note that tram stops aren't always opposite each other so ensure you are waiting at the correct one for your destination.

**Festivals Hakodate Port Festival** (Aug 1st-5th) is the largest summer event in Hakodate and it includes parades, the Squid dance (Hakodate's speciality) and a fireworks display. **Goryokaku Festival** (21st-22nd May) commemorates the Battle of Hakodate (1868-9) and features a parade of people enacting scenes from that era. It is held at Goryokaku Fort (early July to early Aug, weekends; 75 mins).

**Where to stay** Convenient for rail users is *Loisir Hotel Hakodate* ロワジールホテル函館 (☎ 0138-22 0111; ☐ www.solarehotels.com/english/loisir; ¥9800/S, ¥15,730/D, ¥24,564/Tw, breakfast ¥1730), which offers upmarket accommodation and is near the West Exit of the station.

*Hotel Grantia Hakodate Ekimae* ホテル　グランティア函館駅前 (☎ 0138-21 4100; ☐ route-inn.co.jp; from ¥6100/S, ¥8000/D or family; breakfast from ¥800), part of the Route Inn chain, is to the left as you take the Central Exit. It has an onsen on the top floor.

Toyoko Inn (☐ www.toyoko-inn.com) has two branches here: *Toyoko Inn Hakodate Ekimae Asa-ichi* 東横イン函館

駅前朝市 (☎ 0138-23 1045; from ¥4800/S, ¥6800/D, ¥7800/Tw, inc breakfast) is three minutes on foot from the station, at the edge of the morning market, so you're perfectly placed for an early-morning walk around the stalls. *Toyoko Inn Hakodate Ekimae Daimon* 東横イン函館駅前大門 (☎ 0138-24 1045; from ¥5300/S, ¥6800/D, ¥7300/Tw, inc breakfast) is a 5-minute walk into town.

*Hotel Resol Hakodate* ホテルリソル函館 (☎ 0138-23 9269, ☐ www.resol-hotel.jp; ¥8600/S, ¥12,600/D, ¥14,600 inc breakfast) is close to the station and has reasonably spacious rooms and **Rakusis**, an aromatherapy salon where you can try a 60-minute Legs Drain for ¥10,300 to reactivate tired limbs. The lobby area offers free drinks in a pseudo living room setting.

*Hotel New Ohte* ホテルニューオーテ (☎ 0138-23-4561; ☐ www.homepage2.nifty.com/new-ohte; ¥4990/S, ¥6800/D, ¥8970/Tw). Those looking for a really cheap hotel option might try this ironically named establishment conveniently located adjacent to the morning market. Stuck in an early '80s timewarp, the elderly receptionist, as grey as the décor, wistfully remarked that they had been around a very long time but attracted no particular type of visitor. Ask for one of their family room options if there are several of you.

*B&B Pension Hakodate Mura* B＆Bペンション　はこだて村 (☎ 0138-22-8105; ☐ www.bb-hakodatemura.com; ¥5940/S, ¥9500/D; ¥10,800/Tw) is a pleasant pension near Hakodate Bay. Run by Sumiko (good English) and her husband, it has 13 basic rooms (35 guests is the maximum capacity so book ahead) and a nice central lounge area looking back on to the garden. A decent Western breakfast costs ¥850.

Open between April and October, *Hakodateyama Guest House* 函館山ゲストハウス (☎ 080-4503 9044, ☐ www.hakog-e.cloud-line.com; dorm ¥2980pp, from ¥3400pp in private room) is a delightful guest house which boasts some of the finest views across Hakodate and is a fantastic location for exploring the hillside around Mt Hakodate and Cape Tachimachi.

Inside it contains an interesting array of vintage furnishings including a wooden Yamaha piano, suspended yukata and old televisions. You can hire bikes for ¥500 a day and the locally sourced breakfast (¥850) is a real labour of love. To get there take Tram 2 six stops (10 mins) from the station to the terminus at Yachigashira 谷地頭 then follow the signs for the Guest House (or GH). **Yachigashira-onsen** (see p396) has a restaurant, though there are better culinary choices in town. If you go into town check when the last tram back to the Guest House leaves.

While *Hotel Paco Hakodate* ホテルパコ 函館 (☎ 0138-23 8585, 🖳 www .pacoweb.jp/hakodate; from ¥6680/S, ¥9700/Tw) is a fairly typical economical hotel and is about 10 minutes from the station, it is very convenient for Hakodate's Jiyu Market (see p393). Its greatest attraction, though, is the hot springs facilities in the building next to the hotel, which also has accommodation and restaurant facilities. The wide range of baths there are available free on presentation of your room key.

See also pp67-73 for general information about finding accommodation.

**Where to eat and drink** Both the morning market and Jiyu Market (see p393) are good places to hunt around for an impromptu meal; you can be sure that the fish is fresh.

*Hakodate Dining Gaya* 函館ダイニング 雅家 (daily 11am-2.30pm & 5pm to midnight) adjacent to the market is a recommended spot. Set over two floors, the contents of the seafood sets are freshly trawled and plucked from the visible tanks of swimming squid and crabs, although the waiter admitted that the freshest King Crab catches now demand higher premiums owing to recent Russian tax increases in their territorial waters. Blue-fin tuna sets (¥1000) and whole white-haired crab dishes (¥2500) are among the many seafood staples (sea urchins and whelks are also plentiful), but there are also plenty of reasonably priced meat offerings.

*Hakodate Beer* はこだてビール (daily 11am-10pm) is a lively place where you can try various meat and seafood dishes and wash them down with locally brewed beers. In the summer there's space to sit on a veranda outside. There are also restaurants and shops in the converted **Kanemori Red Brick Warehouse** 金森赤レンガ倉庫 buildings near Hakodate Beer. *Starbucks* スターバックス has also established itself opposite the Kanemori Red Brick Warehouse and is a popular spot.

*Sprout* スプラウト (Suparauto; daily noon-11pm) in **Motomachi** is a good place for an evening feed. This established European-themed restaurant, near the old Western churches, is big on atmosphere with its hanging gauze, relaxed jazz music and a genuinely impressive selection of wines to serve as a great antidote to a day spent on your feet. The owner will allow you to sample of one of the half-dozen open wines on the bar top before selecting your favourite (¥700-1000 glass) to accompany your meal or just to enjoy. The speciality garlic and prawn pizza (¥1450) is beautifully flavoursome and the Caesar Salad (¥850) fresh and plentiful. For around ¥1000 or less the usual spaghetti variations and other Italian-influenced offerings predominate despite the wider cosmopolitan pretensions of the menu.

*Daimonyokocho* 大門横丁 (daily 6pm to late) is two rows of small, informal shops serving everything from sushi to Asian cuisine. It's a very small area, less than five minutes on foot from the station, and a good place to look around for a bite to eat. There are more than 20 outlets, most with counter or table service.

One of the best cake shops in town is *Snaffles* スナッフルス, on the main street leading away from the station; choose a cake downstairs, go upstairs to sit and order coffee (from ¥300). There is another branch in the Kanemori Red Brick Warehouse area of Hakodate Bay where free samples are offered (although one is politely instructed not to walk and eat the samples).

*Evergreen* エバグリン (11am-3pm & 5-10.30pm) has an impressive array of seafood spaghetti dishes (¥500-700), steak & fries (¥700) as well as cheesecake, ice-cream and chocolate gateaux (¥400-500).

*Jazz Spot Leaf* ジャズ スポット リーフ (11.30am-5pm & 7pm to midnight), a little further down off the main strip is the typical Japanese illustration of its obsession with traditional jazz. The cosy but dark café is adorned with '60s memorabilia, images of American jazz greats, instruments and concert ticket stubs in a dark atmosphere with Miles Davis's seductive trumpet playing in your ears. Sit out or in to enjoy a great cocktail menu (¥600-800), standard spaghetti dishes (¥700) and decent coffee brewed at the bar in what appears to be a old-fashioned chemistry set before reading that Haruki Murakami novel.

*Café Donq* ドンク (daily 10am-7pm) in the basement of Bani Moriya department store offers a good selection of specialist breads, pastries (¥300-500), croissants and doughnuts as well as a small serviced seating area.

There are several branches of the *Lucky Pierrot* hamburger-and-curry fast-food chain around town. The one most worth visiting, if only for the bizarre year-round Christmas décor, lies close to the Jujigai tram stop. It's easy to spot as it's the only building covered in Christmas trees and Santa Claus faces although the looped Christmas tracks begin to jar after several minutes. The Lucky Pierrot (10am to midnight, Sat to 1am) closest to the station is on the far side of Boni department store. The menu at all includes coffee (¥200), hamburgers (¥350-800), curry rice (¥700) and some highly recommended flavoured milkshakes (¥350).

## Side trip by rail to Goryokaku

About 4km north-east of Hakodate station is Goryokaku 五稜郭, the first Western-style fort in Japan. Built between 1857 and 1864 as a strategic stronghold from which Hokkaido could be ruled, the fort is a pentagonal star shape (called 'the most beautiful star carved on earth'). Warriors from the fallen Tokugawa shogunate escaped from Honshu to Hakodate and occupied the fort in October 1868. Seven months later they gave themselves up to the Imperial Army, bringing both the Battle of Hakodate and Japan's feudal era to a dramatic end.

At the main entrance is the 60m-high **Goryokaku Tower** 五稜郭タワー (⌨ www.goryokaku-tower.co.jp; daily late Apr to late Oct 8am-7pm, late Oct to late Apr 9am-6pm; ¥840). It's a modern-day eyesore but does have an observation platform affording views over the remains of the fort and the city beyond. It is the site of a festival in May (see p397) but is also worth visiting in spring to see the blossom on the 1600 cherry trees planted here in the Taisho era.

To reach Goryokaku take the tram/streetcar to Goryokaku-koen-mae 五稜郭公園前 and then walk north along the main road for about 10 minutes. Look for signs to the fort; you'll soon see the concrete tower in front of you. Alternatively take a train from Hakodate to JR Goryokaku but the walk from the JR station is longer.

## SAPPORO 札幌

The biggest city in Hokkaido and venue for the 1972 Winter Olympics, Sapporo is frequently voted the city where most Japanese would like to live. It certainly feels relaxed and cosmopolitan, with green parks, 19th- and 20th-century red-brick buildings and a thriving entertainment district in Susukino.

It's also one of the easiest cities to get around, thanks to the north–south grid layout and subway trains.

If you need a further incentive to spend a couple of days here, time your visit to coincide with one of the many festivals, the most famous of which is the annual Snow

HOKKAIDO

Festival in February. Like the rest of Hokkaido, Sapporo receives a thick blanket of snow in the winter but summer is mild and provides the perfect opportunity for relaxing in the city's central Odori Park at one of the many beer gardens or concerts.

## What to see and do

**Akarenga** (Red Brick) is the nickname for the **Former Hokkaido Government Office Building** 北海道庁旧本庁舎 (daily 8.45am-5pm; free). Built in 1888, and modelled on Maryland State House and Massachusetts State House, it was gutted by fire and had to be completely rebuilt in 1911. The floral displays and pruned Japanese trees surrounding the building offer a lovely haven from the hustle and bustle. Inside (free entry) the historical exhibitions contain a couple of moving WWII exhibits such as a 'senninbari' cotton belt containing 1000 red stitches, each hand sewn by different members of the community as an amulet to avoid fatal bullets. Paradoxically, the photo of Emperor Hirohito, responsible for sending these men to fight in the first place, hangs upstairs in the Memorial Room as part of a sequence of framed images of various Hokkaido dignitaries. There is another small exhibition at the top of the grand staircase on the ongoing struggle for Hokkaido's return of the Four Northern Territories occupied by Stalin in the aftermath of WWII. You can add your name to the 87 million strong petition calling for their return.

One block south and slightly to the east is Sapporo's famous **Clock Tower** 時計台 (daily 8.45am-5pm except 4th Mon of month & 29 Dec-3 Jan; ¥200). If you don't see the clock immediately, you'll no doubt see the tourists lining up at the official photograph point in front of it. The building was originally used by the former Sapporo Agricultural College (now Hokkaido University) for graduation ceremonies and military drills. It has also been used as a post office and a library. The tower was constructed in 1878 but had to be redesigned when the clock that arrived from the USA was too big. Inside, the 1st/ground floor is used as an exhibition space. On the 2nd floor there is a model of the internal mechanism of the clock as well as a video about it; concerts are also staged here.

**Odori Park** 大通公園 (Odori-koen) stretches for 1.5km through the centre of the city between West 1 and West 12. In summer, people come here to relax, play games and hang out. From mid July the major breweries each erect their own beer garden along the length of the park anticipating month-long scenes of tipsy office workers celebrating the summer heat at the Bavarian-style tables. To save drinkers the effort of continually getting up, the beer companies often employ troupes of young, short-skirted saleswomen to patrol tables with large portable beer kegs strapped to their backs.

In the eastern corner of the park is the 147.2m-high **TV Tower** テレビ塔, built in 1957. It has an observatory (daily 9am-10pm; winter 9.30am-9pm; ¥720) but it's not really high enough for exceptional views. (The JR Tower at Sapporo station is much better; see p402). (Pick up a ¥100 discount coupon at the Tourist Information Centre at JR Sapporo or at the front desk of the Tokyo Dome Hotel Sapporo).

West of the Hokkaido Government Building are the **Botanical Gardens of Hokkaido University** 北海道大学植物園 (Apr-Sep Tue-Sun 9am-4pm, Oct-Nov to 3.30pm; ¥400), opened in 1886 and still the perfect place for a summer stroll. The ticket includes entry to a small Ainu museum in the grounds but there's a better museum devoted to preserving Ainu heritage and culture in a building called **Kaderu 2.7** かでる２・７ (N2 W7), across the street from the entrance to the gardens. On the 7th floor is a small **Ainu exhibition** (Mon-Sat 9am-5pm; free) with items of Ainu clothing and equipment used in daily life. Pop into the office next door to pick up a leaflet.

**Hokkaido Museum of Modern Art** 北海道立近代美術館 (🖳 www.aurora-net .or.jp/art/dokinbi; N1 W17; Tue-Sun 9.30am-5pm; ¥500) has works by Hokkaido artists as well as an exhibition of glass arts by French artists. The easiest way to get here is to take the JR Burari Sapporo Kanko Bus (see p404).

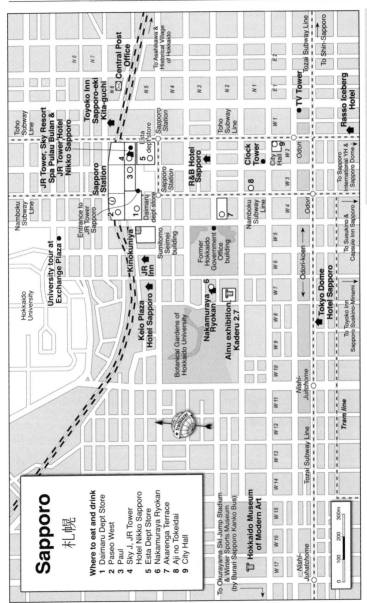

HOKKAIDO

**Sapporo**

札幌

**Where to eat and drink**
1  Daimaru Dept Store
2  Paseo West
3  Paul
4  Sky J, JR Tower
   Hotel Nikko Sapporo
5  Esta Dept Store
6  Nakamuraya Ryokan
7  Akarenga Terrace
8  Aji no Tokeidai
9  City Hall

Hokkaido Museum
of Modern Art

To Okurayama Ski Jump-Stadium
& Winter Sports Museum
(by Burari Sapporo Kanko Bus)

Nishi-
Juhatchome

| 0 | 100 | 200 | 300m |

Tozai Subway Line

Nishi-
Juhatchome

Tram line

To Toyoko Inn
Sapporo Suskino-Minami

To Susukino &
Capsule Inn Sapporo

Tokyo Dome
Hotel Sapporo

To Sapporo
International YH &
Sapporo Dome

Botanical Gardens of
Hokkaido University

Nakamuraya
Ryokan 6

Ainu exhibition,
Kaderu 2.7

Former
Hokkaido
Government
Office building

Odori-koen

Odori-koen

Namboku
Subway
Line

Keio Plaza
Hotel Sapporo

JR
Inn

Kinokuniya

Sumitomo,
Seimei
building

Hokkaido
University

University tour at
Exchange Plaza

Nnamboku
Subway
Line

JR Tower, Sky Resort
Spa Pulau Bulan &
JR Tower Hotel
Nikko Sapporo

Entrance to
JR Tower
Sapporo

Sapporo
Station

Daimaru
dept-store

Esta
dept-store

Sapporo
Station

R&B Hotel
Sapporo

Clock
Tower

City
Hall

Odori

Toho
Subway
Line

Toho
Subway
Line

Sapporo
Station

Sapporo
Station

Toyoko Inn
Sapporo-eki
Kita-guchi

Central Post
Office

To Asahikawa &
Historical Village
of Hokkaido

Tozai Subway Line

To Shin-Sapporo

TV Tower

Rasso Iceberg
Hotel

Sports fans might enjoy the **Okurayama Ski-Jump Stadium** 大倉山 ジャンプ競技場 (Okurayama Janppu Kyogijo; ¥500, or ¥900 inc ski-jump chair-lift; ¥100 discount with Burari bus ticket). The ski jump was used in the Sapporo Winter Olympics in 1972 and the chair-lift to the top is well worth doing if the weather is good for the stunning views of Sapporo from the observation gallery.

The **Winter Sports Museum** ウィンタースポーツミュージアム here has few signs in English but has enjoyable simulators for ski-jumping, cross-country skiing, luge, ice hockey and figure skating. The easiest way to get here is to take the JR Burari Sapporo Kanko Bus (see p404); alternatively take JR bus 14 (free for JR pass-holders) from Maruyama-koen subway station (Tozai Line) and get off at Okurayama-kyogijo-iriguchi bus stop (10-15 mins) followed by a 10-minute walk.

The 40,000-capacity **Sapporo Dome** 札幌ドーム (☎ 011-850 1020, 💻 www .sapporo-dome.co.jp; tours hourly 10am-4pm; 50 mins; ¥1000 or ¥1200 inc observatory) stadium is home to Consadole Sapporo football team and Hokkaido Nippon-Ham Fighters baseball team. The stadium is known for its grass pitch, which grows outside and is brought in on a hi-tech cushion of air when matches are played. Tours take in the stadium, bullpen, locker room and team director's room. An observatory (¥500) at the top of the dome, 53m above the stadium ground, is reached via an 'aerial escalator'. Take the Toho subway line to Fukuzumi station.

The free, guided tour of **Hokkaido University** 北海道大学 campus (formerly Sapporo Agricultural College; 💻 sapporo-flv.com; in English & Japanese; Wed & Fri-Sun 10-11.30am), led by volunteers, is an interesting diversion. The pleasant walk goes past the library, the showpiece Faculty of Agriculture building where Emperor Hirohito stayed in 1935, garden areas and the site where the first artificial snowflake was made. The tour also illustrates how the university tried to serve as a beacon for agricultural advancement in the unforgiving climate of Hokkaido by importing the agricultural expertise of Dr William Smith Clark from Massachusetts, a place with a similar climate. A local hero now, Clark's motto, '*Boys, be ambitious*' is etched beneath his statue and across numerous souvenir cakes in Sapporo. What is less well-known is that Clark, who stayed just under a year, taught all his classes in English, a language so poorly understood by his students that it led to a large number of them failing the course. Tours depart from the Exchange Plaza inside the main gates (Kita 8 Nishi 5) of the university; arrive 10 minutes early. The plaza is a 5-minute walk from the back of the station.

The top-floor observation platform inside the 38-storey landmark **JR Tower** JRタワー (💻 www.jr-tower.com/t38; daily 9.30am-11pm; ¥720), 160m above the South Exit of JR Sapporo station, offers unparalleled views of the city – and, for men, a possibly unique toilet experience (see box below). Take the lift/elevator from the **Stellar Place** complex at Sapporo station to the 6th floor of the tower and then transfer to a special lift to the 38th floor.

If you want to soak weary limbs after a day spent traipsing around the city, **Sky Resort Spa Pulau Bulan** スカイリゾートスパ「プラウブラン」 (daily 11am-11pm; ¥2800, hotel guests ¥1600, inc towels) boasts modern and minimalist single-sex

---

❏ **Toilet in the sky – men only!**
Why not take a comfort break at the top of the city's highest building? The men's toilets at the JR Tower's 38th-floor observation room are walled with glass. According to the designer, Junko Kobayashi, 'one is supposed to do it as if one is taking a leak into a river from the top of a bridge' – well, you can certainly imagine you are taking a leak onto the city below. Sadly the women's loos have no view at all! However, it is possible for women to get an idea of what the experience is like from the disabled toilet.

hot-spring facilities on the 22nd floor of **JR Tower Hotel Nikko Sapporo** JRタワーホテル日航札幌 (see p404). It has a variety of pools, Jacuzzis, and a Finnish sauna, but best of all is the Karuna air massage bath. Massage and spa-treatment packages are also available (a 40-minute massage plus use of the spa is ¥6500); expect to be in the same room as other customers. Take the lift from the 1st/ground-floor hotel lobby.

In the evening, the place to head for an eyeful of Japan by night is the **Susukino** すすきの entertainment district. Billed as the 'largest amusement area north of Tokyo', the area boasts between 4000 and 5000 bars and restaurants, all of which rely on the evening trade when the district is flooded by businessmen. Although it's the red-light area of Sapporo, in February it's also a site for the Snow Festival (see p404). Take the subway to Susukino.

See pp406-7 for details of side trips from Sapporo.

### Practical information

**Station guide** The station has two main exits: north and south; take the South Exit for all the main sights as well as for the JR Tower, buses and taxis. The station itself is divided into two halves, Paseo East and Paseo West, with JR ticket offices and Twinkle Plaza travel agencies on both sides. You can also access the platforms from both sides.

The best bet when leaving a train and wanting to head for the centre of Sapporo (or for the tourist information office) is to leave the platform area and enter the station concourse via the west side. **Lockers** (including enormous ¥600 ones) are located all over the station, but particularly in the passageway which connects the east and west sides.

JR Hokkaido operates an **Information Desk** (daily 8.30am-8pm) in Dosanko Plaza on the west concourse. Rail passes can be exchanged here, rail-pass holders can make seat reservations and you can buy a JR Hokkaido Pass (see pp35-6), as well as the one-day Sapporo-Otaru Welcome Pass (see p407). Of course you can also use any other JR ticket, or Twinkle Plaza, office to

> ### ❏ Sapporo orientation
> Thanks to Sapporo's grid system, it's easy to find your way almost anywhere in the city. Nearly all addresses include a grid reference, so a building at 'N1 W3', for example, is  one block north and three blocks west of the grid apex on the eastern corner of Odori-koen in the city centre.

book tickets/make seat reservations. There are many English leaflets to collect here to help you plan your time in the city.

The station is home to a flagship **Daimaru** 大丸 department store, **Sapporo Stellar Place** 札幌ステラプレイス (❏ www.stellarplace.net; daily 10am-9pm; restaurants 11am-11pm) shopping mall, restaurant and cinema complex, and the magnificent tower which houses **JR Tower Hotel Nikko Sapporo** (see Where to stay).

**Tourist information** The **Hokkaido-Sapporo Tourist Information Center** (❏ www.welcome.city.sapporo.jp; daily 8.30am-8pm) is next to the JR Information Desk (see Station guide) on the west concourse of the station adjacent to the Paseo West dining entrance. There are plenty of useful English leaflets to pick up here for the whole of the city and Hokkaido.

**Getting around** Sapporo has a modern **subway** system with three lines – Namboku, Tozai and Toho – that interconnect at Odori station, one stop south of Sapporo station. There is a minimum subway fare of ¥200; 1-day subway passes (¥830) are sold at subway vending machines.

On Saturdays, Sundays and national holidays, you can pick up an unlimited subway pass, called the Donichika, for ¥520. The passes are available in the stations from designated vending machines, not the usual ticket machines.

The 'Common-Use One-Day Card' (¥1000) is valid on the subway, tram (see below) and most buses.

The 8.5km **tram/streetcar** line intersects with the subway at Susukino but does not actually go to Sapporo station; it serves the south-west part of the city and is likely to be of most interest to tram fans.

JR's **Burari Sapporo Kanko Bus** ぶらりサッポロ観光バス (Apr-Nov 12/day; ¥200/journey; ¥500/day pass inc discounted entry to some attractions) operates on a fixed route and stops at the main sights including the Winter Sports Museum. Buses depart from stand 6 in the bus terminal to the left as you leave the station on the south side.

**Shin-Chitose Airport** 新千歳空港 is about 30km south of the city centre. Both the Airport Express train (2-4/hr; approx 36 mins) and the Super Kamui LEX (1/hr) connect the airport with Sapporo; the Super Kamui continues on to Asahikawa.

**Festivals** The biggest event of the year is the **Snow Festival** (Yuki Matsuri; 6th-12th Feb), when hordes of tourists flock in to see the huge ice sculptures on display in Odori-koen and the main street in Susukino.

**Yosakoi Soran Festival** (see box below) in June brings together thousands of dancers from all over Japan, who compete in front of a crowd of nearly two million to win over the judges with their own interpretations of a dance rhythm that originated in Kochi (see p472).

In summer the **Pacific Music Festival** (Jul-Aug), which was founded by Leonard Bernstein, draws young musicians from all over the world to stage a series of mainly classical concerts around the city. Some performances are free. Lawson Station convenience stores sell tickets (see box p84), or ask at the tourist information centre.

**Where to stay** The plushest place in town is the 350-room *JR Tower Hotel Nikko Sapporo* JRタワーホテル日航札幌 (also known as Sapporo Sky Resort; N5 W2; ☎ 011-251 2222, 🖥 www.jrhotels .co.jp/tower; from ¥18,000/S, ¥26,000/D, ¥34,000/Tw, inc breakfast; rail-pass holders receive a moderate discount). It's part of the JR station and the tower also houses a hot spring spa and an observatory (for both see p402). The rooms are on the 22nd-36th floors; all are well equipped and come with large windows. If a wide view is important ask for a corner room (120° view) and if you want to see the trains ask for a room facing the tracks; the views from these are particularly amazing. The helpful concierge speaks good English.

*Keio Plaza Hotel Sapporo* 京王プラザホテル札幌 (N5 W7 ; ☎ 011-271 0111; 🖥 www.keioplaza-sapporo.co.jp; from ¥8500 /S, ¥13,000/D or Tw) is a short walk from the station and feels the type of hotel that was constructed before the economy crashed and business budgets grew tighter, although it still represents very good value. Far more personal than a business hotel, the large lobby area contains an admittedly old-fashioned bar and restaurant but its show-case basement swimming pool using natural underground water (10am-9pm; ¥1000-1500, extra charge includes gym and sauna, free gym use before 9am) is certainly a unique selling point.

Those on a tighter budget should try *JR Inn Sapporo* JRイン札幌 (N5 W6; ☎ 011-233 3008, 🖥 www.jr-inn.jp; from ¥9400/S or D, ¥11,400/Tw, inc breakfast). The Inn is about a 4-minute walk from the station's West Exit and offers stylish rooms with full-length windows. It has a pillow 'library': if you are not happy with the pillow on your bed you can choose from the selection on the 1st/ground floor.

---

❏ **Yosakoi Soran Festival**
This festival is an astonishing spectacle – the vibrant colours of the dancers' costumes twinned with the rhythmic steps and the chanting is a mesmerising sight. Teams come from all over the country, and even from China and Taiwan, to attend and dance their extravagantly patterned socks off for days on end. **Joe Woodruff** (UK)

*Nakamuraya Ryokan* 中村屋旅館 (N3 W7; ☎ 011-241 2111, 💻 www.naka mura-ya.com; from ¥6825pp room only; breakfast ¥1575, dinner ¥3150) is a typical Japanese inn with en suite tatami rooms. It's in the city centre, on the road between the Botanical Gardens and Hokkaido government buildings.

*Toyoko Inn* (💻 www.toyoko-inn.com) has several branches in the city. Most convenient for the station is *Toyoko Inn Sapporo-eki Kita-guchi* 東横イン札幌駅北口 (N6 W1; ☎ 011-728 1045; from ¥6480/S, ¥7480/D, ¥8480/Tw, inc breakfast). If you prefer to be closer to the nightlife, *Toyoko Inn Sapporo Susukino Minami* 東横イン札幌すすきの南 (S6 E2; ☎ 011-551 1045; ¥6600/Tw, ¥11,000/Tr) would be a better bet. There are no single rooms but the rooms are larger than average and have kitchenettes.

Another good budget pick is *R&B Hotel Sapporo* R＆Bホテル札幌北 (N3 W2; ☎ 011-210 1515, 💻 sapporo.randb.jp; from ¥5880/S, ¥7380/Tw, inc breakfast). The rooms have wide beds and check-in is automated (with a key card). *Rasso Iceberg Hotel* ラッソアイスバーグホテル (S2 W1; ☎ 011-290 3000, 💻 www.rasso.co.jp /iceberg; from ¥6090/S, ¥9240/D or Tw, inc breakfast) is clean and well located. Rasso stands for 'Resort and Spending Special Offtime'!

The best budget choice by far is *Sapporo International Youth Hostel* 札幌国際ユースホステル (☎ 011-825 3120, 💻 www.youthhostel.or.jp/kokusai; dorm room ¥3200pp, ¥3800pp in private room; breakfast ¥630). The family-size tatami rooms as well as the Western-style dorms are very comfortable and kept spotless. All rooms are equipped with individual lockers; in the basement there's a hot spring bath and coin laundry. From the station, take the Toho subway line to Gakuen-mae station and follow the signs for Exit No 2.

For an authentic Japanese capsule experience try *Capsule Inn Sapporo* カプセル・イン札幌 (☎ 011-251 5571, 💻 cap suleinn-s.com; ¥2800, or ¥1200 for a 6hr rest; baths ¥600) in Susukino and watch 'Salarimen' recover from their night on the town. One block north of Susukino subway Station (Exit 1). Turn right at the branch of Kentucky Fried Chicken.

Adjacent to the night activities in Odori Park is the *Tokyo Dome Hotel Sapporo* 東京ドームホテル 札幌 (☎ 011-261 0111, 💻 www.tokyodome-hokkaido-sapporo.com; ¥14,000/S or D, ¥25,000/Tw, ¥36,000/Tr) with good restaurant options.

See pp67-73 for general details about finding accommodation.

**Where to eat and drink** At **Esta** 札幌エスタ, the department store on the left as you take the South Exit of the station, there's a dedicated ramen 'village' on the 10th floor, where you can try the local Sapporo ramen at *Aji no Tokeidai* 味の時計台 (11.30am-11pm; ramen from ¥750); the delicious noodle broth is made from *miso* (fermented soybean paste) and is rich with garlic and butter. There's another branch of *Aji no Tokeidai* opposite Sapporo Grand Hotel (N1 W4), where you can sit at the counter and watch the chefs. The reasonable prices and large portions mean both places gets crowded at lunchtime. An English menu is available. Also on the 10th floor of **Esta** is *Soup Curry Lavi* スープカレー lavi (5-10pm; from ¥1200), which does the Hokkaido speciality – soup curry.

*Paul's* ポールズカフェ, by the JR Tower Nikko Hotel Exit, serves excellent baguettes and teas for lunch and is part of the new European artisan imports that are making their way into stations in Japan.

The 8th floor of **Daimaru** department store, built into the JR station building, is filled with restaurants doing sushi, tonkatsu and Italian food, and there's also the all-you-can-eat buffet at *The Buffet* ザ・ブッフェ (daily 11am-5pm, ¥1490; 5.30-10pm, ¥2150).

There is a great variety of eateries on both the basement and 1st/ground floors of the **Paseo West** side of the station. *Kitamaru* 北○ boasts Japanese cuisine in season (mostly seafood and vegetables) in a chic modernist setting. Specialising in whelks, grilled oysters and potatoes, and sea urchins this venue is pleasantly surprising. Sushi sets also available and white horsehair crab ¥1980. English menus are available although they do include a mackerel dish asking you to 'Savour the flavour of fatty'. Next door to this is *O Neill's* (11am-11pm) Irish Pub screening football and serving a variety of Japanese beers to the mainly male clientele. You can also purchase fish & chips here for ¥500. *Sombrero Mexicano*, on the basement floor, serves vegetable and bacon burritos (¥950) and chicken fajitas for ¥1380.

*Sky J* (5.30pm to midnight) on the 35th floor of JR Tower Hotel Nikko Sapporo (see Where to stay) is a romantic and atmospheric place for a drink or meal. If you get there before 8pm, the ¥750 cover charge is waived. There is often a mellow musical accompaniment on the piano.

A really decent dining area to try is in the newly opened **Akarenga Terrace** 赤れんが テラス (daily 8am-10pm) adjacent to the Former Hokkaido Government Office Building (see Where to go). It boasts a modernist setting and a mixture of indoor and outdoor dining options including a food court on the 3rd floor. Also try *Tsuruga Buffet Dining* (2nd floor) where you can eat as much Japanese food as you like for ¥2400 (90 mins) at lunch, or ¥4200 (120 mins) for dinner. Here, you can also try *Brooklyn Parlor Sapporo* for a good selection of gourmet hamburgers, steaks and hotdogs from about ¥1500. On the 2nd floor terrace you can enjoy looking at outside scenes in a relaxed and partly leafy setting. There are also Italian options, a soup stand and a Chinese restaurant.

For a budget lunch with a view, head for **City Hall** 市役所, where *Aozora* あおぞら (N1 W2; Mon-Fri 9am-5pm) on the 19th floor has simple meals such as chicken with rice or noodles for ¥700-800. There's a similar menu at *Lilac* ライラック (Mon-Fri 10am-6pm) on the 18th floor.

*Nakamuraya Ryokan* 中村屋旅館 (see Where to stay; 11.30am-2pm & 5-9pm) offers traditional Japanese meals as well as *bento* that you can take out or eat in; expect to pay from ¥1000.

### Side trips from Sapporo

● **Hokkaido Museum (Mori no Charenga)** 北海道博物館森のちゃれんが (🖳 www.hm.pref.hokkaido.lg.jp; Tue-Sun May-Sep 9.30am-5pm, Oct-Apr to 4.30pm; ¥600, ¥1200 for joint entry to Historical Village of Hokkaido; ¥280 audio guide) Newly reopened in 2015 after a revamp, the prefectural museum, sitting within **Nopporo Forest Park** 野幌森林公園, charts the long historic arc of Hokkaido's 1.2 million years as 'the crossroads of North-East Asia'. It tells the story of the island's unique cultural, natural and environmental history through large displays and bold dioramas of Ainu culture. Main text boards are in English with smaller individual labels in Japanese only but you can pick up plenty of information, such as why Sapporo gets nearly twice as much snowfall as St Petersburg. Take a train to Shin-Sapporo and then pick up the 'Shin 22' bus (9-12/day; 15 mins; free for JR pass-holders) from platform 10 towards the Historical Village and get off at the museum stop.

● **Historical Village of Hokkaido** 北海道開拓の村 (May-Sep daily 9.30am-5pm, ¥830; Oct-Apr Tue-Sun to 4.30pm ¥680; 🖳 www.kaitaku.or.jp) is also in Nopporo Forest Park. A large number of buildings from the Meiji and Taisho periods (mid 19th to early 20th century) have been restored and moved here. It's a very atmospheric place to wander around and there are explanations in English. The main entrance to the village is through the old Sapporo railway station, in use from 1908 to 1952.

Although the village is the main attraction of Nopporo Forest Park there are also 30km of forest trails to explore. Sapporo Tourist Information Center has a map detailing footpaths and distances along various routes.

Three buses a day run to the village from Sapporo station (60 mins; No 3 JR bus, free for rail-pass holders), but as for the museum it is quicker to take a train to Shin-Sapporo and then pick up a bus (see opposite).

● **Otaru (S15)**  The attractive port city of Otaru (see pp373-5) is easily reached in 30 minutes by rapid train west along the Hakodate Line.

If you don't have a rail pass, consider buying JR Hokkaido's **Sapporo-Otaru Welcome Pass** (¥1700 valid for 1/day), which is available only to tourists from abroad and allows unlimited travel on JR services between Sapporo and Otaru, as well as on all subway lines in Sapporo itself. The pass comes with an illustrated sightseeing map of Otaru. A one-way journey from Sapporo to Otaru costs ¥640, ¥950 on a Rapid Airport service and with a seat reservation, so the Sapporo-Otaru Welcome Pass is only definitely good value if you travel on the Rapid Airport service, stop off en route a couple of times and/or use the metro in Sapporo.

● **Asahiyama Zoo**  JR Hokkaido (🖳 www2.jrhokkaido.co.jp/global/english/ travel) offers an **Asahiyama Zoo Ticket** which includes the journey from Sapporo (8/day; ¥6130 unreserved seat on a limited express) to Asahikawa, bus to the zoo and zoo entry (see p411). The ticket is valid for four days.

The Asahiyama Zoo train (weekends & holiday periods 1/day; extra ¥520 for a reserved seat); has three cars (Ground of Hokkaido, Tropical Jungle, Savanna of grassland) and runs between Sapporo and Asahikawa.

## ASAHIKAWA 旭川市

Despite the backdrop of the Daisetsu mountain range, Asahikawa is not an attractive place by Hokkaido's standards. The second biggest city in Hokkaido after Sapporo serves mainly as a transport hub and a gateway to both Daisetsuzan National Park and to Asahiyama Zoo. However, it is a pleasant place to walk around.

### What to see and do

One of the main reasons for visiting Asahikawa is for side trips to Asahidake in Daisetsuzan National Park and to Asahiyama Zoo (for both see p411). Also out of town is **Kawamura Kaneto Ainu Memorial Hall** アイヌ記念館 (Jul & Aug daily 8am-6pm, Sep-Jun 9am-5pm; ¥500), a very small museum with a few exhibits on Ainu traditions. The museum was founded by Kenichi Kawamura, an 8th-generation Ainu who has campaigned for many years for greater recognition of Hokkaido's indigenous population (see box p408). It's a 10-minute bus ride (bus No 24; 2/hr; ¥200) from bus stop No 14 outside Seibu department store near the station. En route you

may catch a glimpse of one of several Christian churches. Get off at Ainu Kinenkan-mae アイヌ記念館前, walk back to the main junction to turn left and you will find the entrance on the left-hand side. There is a good opportunity to purchase Ainu souvenirs here.

If you have time in Asahikawa itself it is worth walking along the main street to **Tokiwa Park** 常盤公園 (7-jo-dori, 2-5 chome) - on your way look out for the sculptures, particularly the saxophonist and cat. (If you are keen on sculptures ask at the tourist information centre for details of the various sculptures around town.) The park, Asahikawa's oldest, is a pleasant place to stroll in, especially during the spring cherry blossom season, and contains a small lake on which it is possible to rent a boat in the summer. While there have a look around the wood-craft themed **Hokkaido Asahikawa Museum of Art** 北海道立旭川美術館 (Tue-Sun 9.30am-5pm; ¥170, additional charge for temporary exhibitions). You can also buy some beautiful holographic Japanese art postcards at the coffee shop, and staff will even provide an egg timer if you are a stickler for having your tea brewed to the precise second.

**AEON Mall** イオンモール (daily 9am-9pm inc food court; 4th floor cinema and restaurants 10am-10pm) complex opened in April 2015 and gives a much-needed lift to the cityscape. The mall entrance can be found at the North Exit of the station. Boasting an impressive area of specialist food stores, one of the largest wine shops in Hokkaido, a supermarket, food court, cinema and fashion goods, this is a modern mall that draws international shoppers, judging by the frequent announcements in Chinese. Look out for coupon books and other special promotions for overseas shoppers when you present your passport and receipts at the counter on the 1st/ground floor.

Head up the escalators to the 4th floor and turn left into the 'Soyu Game Field' amusement area and allow your eyes and ears to be overwhelmed by some of the latest and most sophisticated Japanese game technology around. Exit and continue

---

### ❑ The Ainu: fight for survival

When Kenichi Kawamura visited the National Museum of Natural History in Washington, USA, in April 1999, for an exhibition of Ainu artefacts, he was joined by the late Japanese prime minister, Keizo Obuchi. Kawamura overheard the prime minister enquire of another visitor to the museum, 'Are there still Ainu in Hokkaido?'

One of the world's least-known aboriginal cultures, the Ainu have long been almost invisible to the outside world. In a speech to the United Nations in 1992, a representative of the Ainu people told how the Japanese government had 'denied even our existence in its proud claim that Japan, alone in the world, is a "mono-ethnic nation"'. The Ainu originally populated parts of northern Honshu as well as Hokkaido, living in small communities of up to 10 families, fishing from the rivers and hunting bear – a sacred animal in Ainu tradition – in the forests.

There was never any question of land rights until the *wajin* (Japanese) moved further north, calling the Ainu 'dogs' (the Japanese word for dog is *inu*) and forcing them off their land. The only work that some could find was manual labour with logging companies – thus the Ainu found themselves in the extraordinary position of having to earn a living by destroying the very land on which they had lived.

In 1899, the Hokkaido Former Aborigine Protection Law was passed, giving the island's governor power to 'manage the communal assets of the Ainu people for their benefit', on the pretext that the Ainu were unable to manage these assets themselves. Almost a century was to pass until the law was repealed in 1997, replaced with a new act to promote Ainu culture and return assets that had been 'managed' by the prefectural government. Endless legal wrangles over the exact amount and how it should be paid suggest a quick resolution is unlikely.

There has been some attempt to revive Ainu traditions and in particular the Ainu language, now spoken by fewer than a dozen elderly people. Weekly Ainu language radio courses have started and storytellers are being trained to continue the Ainu oral tradition. In 1994, Shigeru Kayano became the first Ainu to win a seat in the Upper House of the Japanese Parliament, and in a landmark 1998 ruling a Hokkaido judge recognised the indigenous status of the Ainu people for the first time.

Kayano died in 2006, just short of his 80th birthday and not long before a picture book he wrote about the Ainu, *The Ainu and the Fox*, was published for the first time in English. Kayano wrote the story, based on an Ainu legend, in 1974 for elementary schoolchildren. During his lifetime he also compiled an Ainu-language dictionary and recorded folk tales. Nobody yet knows if all this was too little too late to save the Ainu from cultural extinction.

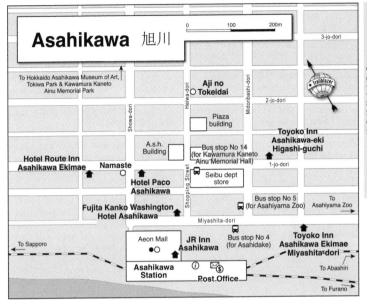

**Asahikawa** 旭川

0    100    200m

To Hokkaido Asahikawa Museum of Art,
Tokiwa Park & Kawamura Kaneto
Ainu Memorial Park

3-jo-dori

2-jo-dori

Aji no
○ Tokeidai

Piaza
building

*trailblazer*

HOKKAIDO

Toyoko Inn
Asahikawa-eki
Higashi-guchi

A.s.h.
Building

Bus stop No 14
(for Kawamura Kaneto
Ainu Memorial Hall)

Hotel Route Inn
Asahikawa Ekimae    Namaste

Seibu dept
store

1-jo-dori

Hotel Paco
Asahikawa

Bus stop No 5
(for Asahiyama Zoo)

To
Asahiyama Zoo

Fujita Kanko Washington
Hotel Asahikawa

Miyashita-dori

Bus stop No 4
(for Asahidake)

Toyoko Inn
Asahikawa Ekimae
Miyashita-dori

Aeon Mall
● ○

JR Inn
Asahikawa

To Sapporo

Asahikawa
Station

To Abashiri

ⓘ ✉ $
Post Office

To Furano

Helwa-dori · Showa-dori · Midoribashi-dori · Shopping Street

straight to reach the restaurants offering
both traditional and cosmopolitan 'fayre'.

**Practical information**
**Station guide** Asahikawa station is a real
pleasure to be in as there is wood everywhere – the area is known for its wood
industry – and because of the feeling of
space here. The central area has a **post
office** (Post Station; Mon-Fri 9am-6pm, Sat
& Sun to 5pm) with an **ATM** (same hours)
and a **hotel information desk** (daily 2-
6pm). The North Exit has West and East
gates and there are **lockers** (all sizes) by
both. Take the West Gate for JR INN
Asahikawa and the main part of town.
There is also free wi-fi in the station.

For sustenance there is a café, an
*ekiben* stand (take away or eat in udon from
¥300), and at the West Gate end of the station is the AEON Mall complex (see p410).

**Tourist information** The **tourist information centre** (daily Jun-Sep 8.30am-7pm,
Oct-May 9am-7pm) is on the 1st/ground

floor of the station by the East Gate concourse. There are lots of leaflets and staff
can help with bus timetables and other
queries. For information about Asahikawa
visit 🖳 www.asahikawa-tourism.com.

**Getting around**    Walking around
Asahikawa is easy as all the roads in the
central area are on a grid. The first road
going west to east in front of the station is
Miyashita-dori but from then on the main
roads are numbered 1-jo-dori (No 1 Street)
to 10-jo-dori by the river. Each block north
to south is a 'chome'; 7-chome is to the left
of the main pedestrianised shopping street
from the station and on the right is 8-chome.
**Buses** depart from stops spread around the
roads in front of the station. Bus stand No 6
for the zoo is on Midoribashi-dori, which
runs to the right of Seibu department store.

**Festivals    Asahikawa Winter Festival**
(Asahikawa Fuyu Matsuri; around 8th-12th
Feb) is not as vast or commercial as
Sapporo Snow Festival (see p404), but it's

just as impressive so is worth making time for. The World Ice Sculpture Competition brings together international teams who compete to build giant sculptures. Some are built along the pedestrianised shopping street (Heiwa-dori) and others are by the river (Asahibashi); a 10- to 15-minute walk from the end of Heiwa-dori. Every year one of these is used as a stage for a variety of performances. A fireworks display takes place on the opening night.

**Where to stay** The newly opened 11-storey *JR Inn Asahikawa* JR イン旭川 (☎ 0166-24-8888, 🖳 www.jr-inn.jp/asahikawa; from ¥13000/S, ¥15,000/D, ¥17,00Tw, ¥24000/Tr), conveniently connected by a lift/elevator to the adjoining AEON Mall and railway station (North Exit), is a very comfortable place to stay that emphasises Hokkaido's frontier identity through stylish wooden interiors, calm-inducing spot lighting, and magnificent views above the city streets. The rooms feel as much Nordic as Japanese and you can choose from 21 varieties of pillow, relax in the well-furnished guest lounge and library with supply of complimentary coffee and enjoy the fine prospect from the upstairs hotel onsen as you unwind after a hard day. Breakfast vouchers for Saint Marc Café on the 1st/ground floor of AEON Mall are provided.

There are two branches of **Toyoko Inn** (🖳 www.toyoko-inn.com) within three minutes' walk of the station. *Toyoko Inn Asahikawa Ekimae Ichi-jo-dori* 東横イン旭川駅前一条通 (☎ 0166-27 1045; from ¥6804/S, ¥8300/D, ¥8800/Tw, inc breakfast) is at 1-jo-dori, 9-chome and *Toyoko Inn Asahikawa-eki Higashi-guchi* 東横イン旭川駅東口 (☎ 0166-25 2045; from ¥6804/S, ¥8300/D, ¥8800/Tw, inc breakfast) is at Miyashita-dori, 10-chome.

Conveniently located across the road from the AEON Mall, the *Fujita Kanko Washington Hotel Asahikawa* 藤田観光ワシントンホテル旭川 (☎ from ¥4000/S, ¥6500/D, ¥7000/Tw. *Hotel Paco Asahikawa* ホテルパコ旭川 (☎ 0166-23 8585, 🖳 hotelpaco.com; from

¥7700/S, ¥11,500/D or Tw) is busier with smaller rooms but does boast a pleasant onsen spa.

A block further west along 1-jo-dori is *Hotel Route Inn Asahikawa Ekimae* ホテルルートイン旭川駅前 (☎ 0166-21 5011, 🖳 route-inn.co.jp/english; from ¥5600/S, ¥8500/D, ¥9550/Tw); it's a 5-minute walk from the station.

See pp67-73 for general details about finding accommodation.

**Where to eat and drink** The **AEON Mall 4th floor restaurant plaza** offers an abundance of good-quality choices although be sure to arrive by 9pm as some establishments stop serving early. *Grand Farm Buffet* グランファームビュッフェ (10am-5pm ¥1500, 5-10pm ¥1850) offers a wide variety of food including tempura, chicken, vegetables and squid; ask for an English menu. *Soup Curry Lavi* スープカレーLavi (10am-10pm) offers 'Sapporo soul food' such as soup curry (from ¥1030). *Mia Bocca* ミアボッカ (10am-10pm, lunch to 5pm) offers Italian-style dishes (pizza from ¥980). Elsewhere in the plaza, the unmissably huge crab indicates where you can enjoy ¥1400 crab sets, or ¥900 crab sushi for a genuine taste of Hokkaido's seafood. The piazza area, just outside the West Gate of Asahikawa station, often fills with an all-you-can-eat-and-drink beer garden in the summer, sometimes accompanied by bands.

*Namaste* ナマステ (Mon-Sat 11am-10pm, lunch to 3pm; 1-jo-dori, 6-chome), across the road from Hotel Parco, offers Nepalese food that comes highly recommended for its chicken and vegetable curry (¥980). Choose the amount of spiciness and a choice of rice or naan bread as part of your set. Also try their lassi (¥300).

Asahikawa is proud of its local version of the Sapporo ramen dish, where the pork is stewed in *shochu*. Try it at the branch of *Aji no Tokeidai* 味の時計台 (🖳 www.ajino-tokeidai.co.jp; 11am-10pm; 2-jo-dori, 8-chome); there is a handy picture menu.

## Side trip by train to Asahiyama Zoo

Asahiyama Zoo 旭川市旭山動物園 (🖳 www5.city.asahikawa.hokkaido
.jp/asahiyamazoo; late Apr to mid Oct daily 9.30am-5.15pm (last entry 4pm)
early Nov to early Apr Fri-Tue 10.30am-3.30pm (last entry 3pm), closed for a
few weeks in Apr and Dec 30-Jan 1st; ¥820, passport valid for a year ¥1020)
is Japan's northernmost zoo and is a good opportunity to see chimpanzee and
orangutans plus some of the animals native to Hokkaido, including the brown
bear and red fox.

The zoo's design and layout is also good as it enables visitors to see the
various animals in unusual ways: an underwater tunnel gives access to the penguin tank and in the aquarium seals swim up through a tunnel into a large tank.

To reach the zoo, take an Asahikawa Denkikidou 旭川電気軌道 bus (No
41 or 47; 2/hr; 40 mins; ¥440) from stop No 6 outside Asahikawa station. (See
also p407).

## Side trip by bus to Asahidake

Alpine flowers bloom in spring on the slopes of Asahidake 旭岳 (Mt Asahi) in
**Daisetsuzan National Park** 大雪山国立公園, the highest mountain in
Hokkaido. In winter, powder snow attracts skiers keen to take advantage of
Japan's longest skiing season, from December to early May.

Access to the mountain is by bus from outside Asahikawa station to the
resort of Asahidake-onsen 旭岳温泉 (stop No 4; 3/day; 80 mins; ¥1320).
Buses terminate at **Asahidake Ropeway** 旭岳ロープウェイ (🖳 wakasa
resort.com; 3-4/hr; 9am-5pm, to 4pm in winter, longer in summer; closed 7th-
17th May & 30th Nov-10th Dec; Jun-mid Oct ¥2900 round trip, mid Oct-May
¥1800), which takes you up to 1600m.

Before going up the mountain, pop in to **Asahidake Visitor Center** 旭岳
ビジターセンター (Jun-Oct daily 9am-5pm, Nov-May Tue-Sun to 4pm), on
the main street just before the ropeway entrance. Here you can pick up a map
and get a weather forecast. From the ropeway's top station a gentle 1km walk
leads to Asahidake's main lookout point, with smoke pouring out from rock
turned yellow by the sulphur.

From the lookout point it's a further 2.6km to the **summit** (allow two
hours up and one to get back) which, at 2290m, is sometimes covered in cloud.
It's advisable to wear strong trainers or hiking boots as the path is rocky.

The 16-bed *Daisetsuzan Shirakaba-so Youth Hostel* 大雪山白樺荘青年
旅舎大雪山白樺荘ユースホステル (☎ 0166-97 2246, 🖳 shirakabasou-asahi
dake.com; dorm from ¥6890pp, private room ¥7940pp; breakfast ¥760, dinner
¥1260, onigiri rice ball ¥420) is less than five minutes on foot down the main
road from the ropeway station. Camp-jo-mae bus stop, the stop before the
ropeway terminus, is right outside the hostel.

A place that has been highly recommended is *Hotel Bearmonte* ホテル
ベアモンテ (☎ 0166-97 2321, 🖳 www.bearmonte.jp; from ¥7000pp). It has a
variety of indoor baths and *rotemburo*; rates depend in part on which way your
room faces as some views are better than others.

The hotel is about three minutes' walk from the base of the ropeway. If
you have booked at least four days in advance the hotel will offer a free shuttle bus from in front of Esta department store in Asahikawa.

# KYUSHU

## Kyushu – route guides

Despite its modern-day reputation as something of a backwater, Kyushu's history has been more linked with the West than any of the other main islands. The port of Nagasaki, in particular, was the only place in the country where trading with the outside world was permitted during Japan's nearly 300 years of self-imposed isolation under the Tokugawa shogunate.

Today, the majority of visitors to Kyushu pause briefly in **Fukuoka**, the island's capital, before making a beeline for **Nagasaki**, the second city in Japan to be hit with an atomic bomb in 1945. But if you're prepared to devote more time to seeing the island, it really is worth travelling further south. Perhaps because of its relatively mild climate, Kyushu feels more relaxed and the people more laid-back than on Honshu. This may also have something to do with the popularity of *shochu*, a strong spirit found in every bar that becomes even stronger and more popular the further south you go.

A trip down the west coast brings you to the shochu capital, **Kagoshima**, sometimes described as the 'Naples of the East' because of its bay and neighbouring **Sakurajima**, one of the world's most active volcanoes; unlike Naples the city is virtually crime-free. And right in the centre of the island, a perfect side trip by rail from either the east or west coasts, lies formidable **Mt Aso**, where visitors can peer over the top of an active volcanic crater as long as there isn't too much volcanic activity.

Nagasaki can be seen in a couple of days but allow at least a week more if you're travelling down either coast and planning to fit in a visit to Mt Aso as well. For general information about Kyushu visit 🖳 www.visitkyushu.org.

Kyushu can be reached easily by rail from Honshu via the Tokaido/Sanyo shinkansen lines (see box opposite). Beyond the shinkansen, JR Kyushu runs an efficient network that will take you just about anywhere and uses limited expresses on most of its lines.

For details of JR Kyushu's rail pass see box p30 and p36, for suggested itineraries p46 and for information about using the rail route guide see p12.

山の温泉や裸の上の天の川

*Hot spring in the mountains: high above the naked bathers the River of Heaven*
(SHIKI MASAOKA)

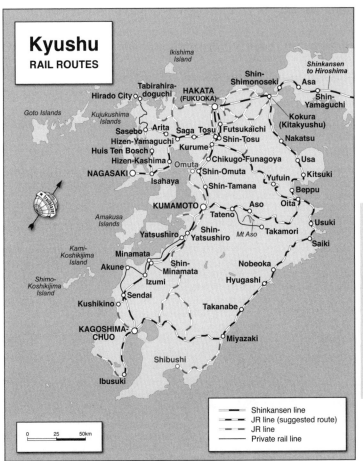

**Kyushu**
**RAIL ROUTES**

*Ikishima Island*

*Shinkansen to Hiroshima*

Shin-Shimonoseki

Asa

Tabirahira-doguchi

**HAKATA (FUKUOKA)**

Hirado City

Shin-Yamaguchi

*Goto Islands*

*Kujukushima Islands*

Kokura (Kitakyushu)

Sasebo  Arita  Saga  Tosu  Futsukaichi

Hizen-Yamaguchi  Shin-Tosu  Nakatsu

Huis Ten Bosch  Kurume

Hizen-Kashima  Chikugo-Funagoya  Usa

Omuta

**NAGASAKI**  Shin-Omuta  Yufuin  Kitsuki

Isahaya  Shin-Tamana  Beppu

**KUMAMOTO**  Aso  Oita

Tateno

*Amakusa Islands*  Shin-Yatsushiro  *Mt Aso*  Takamori

Yatsushiro  Usuki

*Kami-Koshikijima Island*  Minamata  Saiki

Akune  Shin-Minamata  Nobeoka

*Shimo-Koshikijima Island*  Izumi  Hyugashi

Kushikino  Sendai

Takanabe

**KAGOSHIMA-CHUO**

Miyazaki

Shibushi

Ibusuki

======= Shinkansen line
=-=-=-= JR line (suggested route)
= = = JR line
——— Private rail line

0   25   50km

K Y U S H U

---

## ❏ Shinkansen services to, and within, Kyushu

The only shinkansen services which run all the way from Tokyo to Hakata are the Nozomi for which the Japan Rail Pass is not valid. Mizuho, Sakura and Kodama services to Hakata start in Shin-Osaka; the Mizuho and Sakura continue to Kagoshima-chuo. There are Green Cars on the Sakura shinkansen but not on either the Mizuho or Tsubame; the Tsubame operates between Hakata and Kumamoto and occasionally to Kagoshima-chuo.

The Japan Rail Pass is valid on all services in Kyushu except Mizuho, but the JR Kyushu Pass is valid on Mizuho services. For more details see box p30 and p36.

## SHIN-YAMAGUCHI TO HAKATA (FUKUOKA) BY SHINKANSEN
[Map 27; Table 3, p505]

Distances from Tokyo by shinkansen. Fastest journey time from Shin-Yamaguchi: 45 minutes.

**Shin-Yamaguchi** 新山口 **(1027km)** All Kodama, some Nozomi and a few Sakura/Hikari stop here. Shin-Yamaguchi is the point of connection with the route guide around Western Honshu.

All Kodama stop at **Asa** 厚狭 (1062km). Kodama and a few Sakura/Hikari stop at **Shin-Shimonoseki** 新下関 (1089km) before heading into the tunnel for the journey through the narrow Kammon Straits to Kyushu.

**Kokura** 小倉 **(1108km)** All services stop at Kokura's sleek, modern station. Kokura made the American military's shortlist as the next A-Bomb target following the attack on Hiroshima, but cloud cover over the city on the morning of 9th August 1945 meant the plane carrying the bomb was forced to change direction and headed instead towards Nagasaki. Kokura is part of a wider area called Kitakyushu.

From Kokura, the shinkansen line continues on to Hakata (Fukuoka) and the Nippo Line runs along the east coast. LEX and local trains to Hakata run on the Kagoshima Line. JR West runs the shinkansen tracks at Kokura, so if you're changing from the shinkansen follow the signs for 'JR Kyushu Lines'.

The main station concourse, with a central plaza and large TV screen, is on the 2nd floor. There is a **tourist information centre** (daily 9am-7pm) here by the South Exit and also one on the 1st/ground floor (KitaKyushu City Tourism Information Corner; daily 9am-6pm) by the North Exit. Staff at both can provide you with an English map, general information and a food-focused walking map (in Japanese only). There are also two **JR ticket offices**: one is to the left as you leave the shinkansen ticket barrier; the other, larger one is on the main concourse. **Lockers** can be found behind the entrance to the monorail on the main station concourse. More can be found downstairs on the 1st/ground floor.

● **What to see and do** **Kokura Castle** 小倉城 (⌨ www.kokura-castle.jp; daily 9am-5pm, Apr-Oct to 6pm; ¥350), a 1990 reconstruction of the original 1602 building, is a 15-minute (and well-signed) walk from the South Exit of Kokura station. Inside are exhibitions about the history of the castle and what life was like living there in the Edo period. The nearby **Kokura Castle Japanese Garden** 小笠原会館 (daily 9am-5pm, Apr-Oct to 6pm; ¥300) is very small and may be a disappointment unless you are here in the autumn when the maple trees would be at their best. However, the entrance ticket includes access to a traditional wooden samurai-style house, with Shoin-style architecture, built out over the garden's pond; for ¥500 extra you can be served a bowl of green tea and a Japanese sweetmeat by shuffling, kimono-clad women. Also included in the ticket is the **exhibition zone** which contains artefacts based on culture and traditions in Japan, as well as Japanese manners; it is definitely the place to go to learn how you should be behaving in Japan.

A very different attraction is the **TOTO Museum** TOTO ミュージアム (🖳 www.toto.co.jp/museum); museum Tue-Sun 10am-5pm, showroom Thur-Tue 10am-5pm). Toto started making flush toilets and sanitaryware in 1917 and in 2015 opened a museum here to showcase the company's products over the years. It is a nicely designed building: in the showroom on the 1st/ground floor you can see – and also touch – what's hot and new on the market in terms of kitchens, bathrooms and washrooms as well as products for seniors. The museum is on the 2nd floor: the exhibits in the 10 rooms focus on how the various products are manufactured and the history of plumbing with enough information in English to get the most important points. There are, of course, proper toilets you can use should the need arise. The easiest way to get there is by bus (No 21, 22 or 43 from Platform No 3, or bus No 25 from Platform No 4; approx 15 mins; ¥190) from the Bus Center on the Castle Exit side of Kokura station.

The straddle-beam **Kitakyushu monorail** 北九州モノレール, which departs from JR Kokura on a 20-minute (8.8km) journey to Kikugaoka 企救丘 (4-6/hr; ¥290) in the suburbs, is an enjoyable experience. The entrance and ticket machines are on the main concourse of Kokura station. The journey gives an elevated perspective to the city and lovely views of the surrounding hills. Also look out for the racecourse (horse-racing) on the right after Keibajomae 競馬場前 station. Rail buffs in particular might also like to do the side trip to Kyushu Railway History Museum at Moji (see p416).

The main festival, **Wasshoi Hyakuman Matsuri** わっしょい百万夏祭り is held around the town on 2nd & 3rd August every year. Dances, parades, floats and the usual fireworks at the end.

● **Where to stay and eat** There are plenty of business hotels around the station but the most convenient place to stay is *Station Hotel Kokura* ステーションホテル小倉 (☎ 093-541 7111, 🖳 www.station-hotel.com; from ¥9300/S, ¥16,500/D, ¥17,500/Tw inc breakfast) as it is built into the JR station building. You can access the hotel from the main concourse of the station (Kokura Castle side) though the reception desks are on the 1st/ground floor.

Cheaper and nearly as convenient is *Nishitetsu Inn Kokura* 西鉄イン小倉 (☎ 093-511 5454, 🖳 www.n-inn.jp/hotels/kokura; from ¥6400/S, ¥9300/D, ¥12,400/Tw inc buffet breakfast), three minutes from the South Exit. The rooms are en suite but there is also a large common bath.

Kokura's speciality is *yaki-udon* (similar to yakisoba, see p499, but using fried udon); it is served at several places in the city which are shown on the map you can pick up at the TIC. One such place is ***Ishin*** いしん (daily 11.30am-10pm), 10 minutes on foot from the South Exit. It is on the left-hand side very near the end of Uomachi Shopping Mall (before it becomes Tanga Market); the entrance is behind a red *noren* (curtain) and the restaurant is downstairs. The atmosphere is a bit like a coffee shop and they serve okonomiyaki as well as yaki-udon; expect to pay around ¥1000.

If you fancy experiencing real local flavours, try making your own *daigaku-don* (student rice bowl) at ***Daigaku-don*** 大學丼食堂 (10am-5pm) in **Tanga Market** 旦過市場 (Tanga Ichiba; daily, but most stalls closed on Sunday). Buy your rice first in a donburi bowl (¥100-300), then go to one of the many market stalls outside to purchase toppings from the vocal traders before returning to eat. Unsurprisingly, it was local university students who started this practice. Tanga Market is at the end of Uomachi Shopping Mall.

### Side trip by rail from Kokura

For **Kyushu Railway History Museum** 九州鉄道記念館 (Kyushu Tetsudo Kinenkan; ⌨ www.k-rhm.jp; daily 9am-5pm except 2nd Wed of month & 2nd Wed & Thur in July; ¥300, ¥240 with a Sugoca card, see box p66), operated by JR Kyushu. While much smaller than the museums at Omiya (see pp321-2), Kyoto (see p256), or Nagoya (see p202), it is nicely laid out and has mini-trains, modelled on real types. To get there take a JR Kagoshima Line (3-5/hr; 13 mins) train to **Mojiko** 門司港, a few minutes' walk from the museum. The port town here, **Moji** 門司, has a number of historic buildings including the station which dates from 1914, though it is under renovation until March 2018.

Families flock to northern Kyushu to visit **Space World** スペースワールド (⌨ www.spaceworld.co.jp; hours vary daily so check website; ¥4320/day pass) theme park; it even has its own station (JR Space World) five stops (10 mins) from Kokura along the JR Kagoshima Line. In addition to space-themed attractions there are rollercoasters and water rides.

From Kokura it's one more stop by shinkansen to Hakata. If heading down the east coast (on the route starting on p426), change trains at Kokura rather than at Hakata, otherwise you'll have to backtrack.

### Hakata (Fukuoka) 博多 (福岡) (1175km)　　　　　　　[see pp434-40]

It's mostly tunnels on the short journey between Kokura and Hakata; in the brief snatches of daylight it's surprising to see how lush and green the countryside is.

Hakata is the terminus for the Tokaido/Sanyo shinkansen and the starting point for JR Kyushu's shinkansen service south to Kumamoto and Kagoshima. It is also the name of the JR station for the city of Fukuoka.

## HAKATA (FUKUOKA) TO NAGASAKI　　　　　[Map 28; Table 20, p511]

Distances by JR from Hakata. Fastest journey time: 1¾ hours.

**Hakata** 博多 (0km)　A blueprint for an extension of the shinkansen line to Nagasaki was drawn up in 1973 and some construction has happened but it is

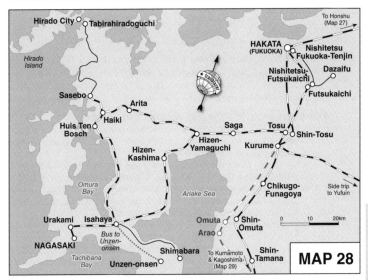

likely to be years before the extension is operational. For now, the fastest way is on the Kamome LEX from Hakata along the JR Kagoshima and Nagasaki main lines. If going to Tosu, Saga, Hizen-Yamaguchi or Arita you can also take the Midori LEX (1/hr).

**Futsukaichi 二日市 (14km)** Some trains stop at this hot spring resort. Of far more interest is neighbouring **Dazaifu**, home to Tenmangu Shrine and the impressive Kyushu National Museum; for full details see pp440-1.

**Tosu 鳥栖 (29km)** There are few facilities at Tosu station, apart from a small branch of the *Trandor* bakery and a convenience store.

From Tosu, the Nagasaki Line heads west towards Nagasaki; this is the route followed here. For details of the shinkansen services from Shin-Tosu (3 mins on JR Nagasaki Line) south to Kumamoto and Kagoshima, see p421.

**Saga 佐賀 (54km)** Everyone passes through Saga on their way to Nagasaki, but in November many get off the train here as it is the venue for the **Saga International Balloon Fiesta** 佐賀インターナショナルバルーンフェスタ (🖥 www.sibf.jp/e).

The **tourist information centre** (Mon-Fri 8.30am-6pm, Sat & Sun to 5pm) is by the South Exit. Staff here have an accommodation list and can help book somewhere to stay if necessary but if you are coming for the balloon fiesta you should book well in advance. There are lockers on the concourse.

Two convenient places to stay are *Toyoko Inn Saga Ekimae* 東横イン佐賀駅前 (☎ 0952-23 1045, 🖥 www.toyoko-inn.com; ¥5076/S, ¥7776/D, ¥8856/Tw),

which is immediately to your right as you take the station's South Exit, and
**Comfort Hotel Saga** コンフォートホテル佐賀 (☎ 0952-36 6311, 🖳 www
.choice-hotels.jp/cfsaga); from ¥7200/S, ¥10,300/D), by the North Exit.

## Hizen-Yamaguchi 肥前山口 (68km)

This is the junction for the branch line
to Sasebo; this line can also be used as an alternative route to Nagasaki (see
below). The Kamome LEX continues from Hizen-Yamaguchi on the main line
via Hizen-Kashima to Nagasaki; for the continuation of this route see p420.

### Alternative route to Nagasaki via Arita and Sasebo

If you have the time this route includes a scenic coastal journey and a chance
to see the wonderful pottery in Arita, visit historic Hirado via Sasebo, and/or
go to the theme park at Huis Ten Bosch.

For Arita and Sasebo/Hirado make sure you are on a Midori LEX. For
Huis Ten Bosch take a Huis Ten Bosch LEX, though this also stops at Arita.

● **Arita**  The Arita area is known for hand-made pottery, **Arita-yaki** 有田焼
(also known as Imari-yaki 伊万里き as it was exported from Imari port),
which was first produced in and around Arita 有田 (🖳 www.arita.jp/en).
Porcelain manufacture in Japan started because a Korean potter, who came
here in 1616, discovered kaolin (an essential clay for porcelain) at Izumiyama
Quarry. The milky-white ceramic pieces made here became highly prized by
the Dutch East India company and other European traders. Before leaving the
station pick up a map at the **information office** (daily 9am-5pm).

**Kyushu Ceramic Museum** 九州陶磁文化館 (Kyushu Toji Bunkakan; 🖳
saga-museum.jp/ceramic; Tue-Sun 9am-5pm; free) offers a well-designed history of Japanese porcelain development as well as exhibiting some fine contemporary pieces; the museum's large ceramic musical clock box and unique
porcelain toilet cubicles are worth the visit alone. Also fun to see here are the
porcelain dolls showing children posing in a huge variety of ways. On the walk
along the road from the station you will cross a bridge festooned with elaborate ornamental pottery. Take the pedestrian overpass and go up the steps on
the left to the entrance. At nearby **Gallery Arita** ギャラリー有田 (daily 9am-
7pm) you can choose what cup you would like for your tea or coffee from the
2000 on display. You can also eat reasonably priced lunch sets (¥1350) served
on colourful Arita-yaki and buy authentic porcelain souvenirs from the impressive shop. To get to the gallery from the museum go back to the station side of
the overpass and down on the right-hand side; Gallery Arita is a little way
along on the left – look for the enormous vase outside. There may also be a
rather unmissable Mini car.

**Arita Ceramics Fair** 有田陶磁の里プラザ (29th Apr to 5th May) is held
along the main street with stalls set up on either side. It offers the chance to
pick up a variety of bargains as long as you are prepared to jostle with the
crowds.

From Arita take an eastbound Midori LEX if wanting to backtrack to
Hizen-Yamaguchi for the route to Nagasaki, or for Shin-Tosu, see p421.
Alternatively pick up a westbound Midori LEX for Sasebo/Hirado, or a west-
bound Huis Ten Bosch LEX for the theme park (see opposite).

All LEX services stop at **Haiki** 早岐 (108km); this is the last chance to
change train if not on the correct service for your chosen destination.

● **Sasebo/Hirado** Sasebo 佐世保 is a very pleasant port town and a great place for a breath of fresh sea air and a stroll along the promenade before continuing on to either Hirado, or Nagasaki. Its deep harbour means it was an important base for the Japanese Imperial Navy and therefore one of the possible targets in WWII for the atomic bomb.

British travellers in particular, but anyone interested in history, may also like to go north from Sasebo to **Hirado** 平戸 (🖥 www.city.hirado.nagasaki.jp) as that is where William Adams (see p168 & p431), the first British person to reach Japan, worked, lived and passed away. At Sasebo change to Matsuura Railway for **TabiraHiradoguchi** たびら平戸口 (approx 1/hr; 87 mins; ¥1220; JR rail passes not valid). From TabiraHiradoguchi it is a 15-minute taxi ride to Hirado city centre across Hirado Bridge. Alternatively walk for 10 minutes to Hiradoguchi Sanbashi Bus Terminal and take the bus to Hirado.

**William Adams** took the Japanese name of Miura Anjin and he was instrumental in developing foreign trade here. You can find his grave in Sakigata Park which, significantly, has a nice view of the port. Hirado Dutch Trading Post was founded in 1609 with the efforts of William Adams. A reconstructed warehouse now tells the history of international trade in Hirado. The castle and the stunning old Matsura Historical Museum are other good places to visit. The former house of William Adams now houses the shop of a 500-year-old sweet-manufacturing business where you can literally taste the international history of this little port town.

From Sasebo take the JR Seaside Liner (13/day; approx 94 mins; ¥1650) to Nagasaki; the line joins the Nagasaki Line at Isahaya; see p420. See also box p428 for details of the Aru Ressha train that runs on this route seasonally.

● **Huis Ten Bosch** Huis Ten Bosch ハウステンボス (🖥 www.huisten bosch.co.jp; hours vary according to the season; 1-day passport ¥6200, 12-17 years ¥5200, 4-11 years ¥3800; 2- and 3- day passports also available, some attractions not included), the Dutch theme park overlooking Omura Bay northeast of Nagasaki, is one of Kyushu's most popular attractions for vacationing Japanese.

The idea for this bizarre recreation of tulip fields and windmills came from Yoshikuni Kamichika, who visited Holland in 1979 and decided to build a city in Japan that would combine Dutch city planning with Japanese technology. The aim was to make the site a living, working, eco-friendly city 'to last 1000 years'. What you find is much more of a Disney resort, with hotels, rides and attractions, canals, shops that sell clogs, and a cast of real Dutch who dress up in traditional costume and become walking photo opportunities. Whilst the theme is basically Dutch, attractions include a Japanese Ghost Story Hall and restaurants serving food from around the world.

If you would like to stay the night there is a rather unusual option: ***Henna Hotel*** 変なホテル (🖥 www.h-n-h.jp/en; ¥39,960/Tw) literally means Strange Hotel and it is a world first in that robots welcome you and provide many services such as taking your luggage to your room. If this doesn't appeal, or is full, there are three normal hotel options (accommodation including breakfast and a 2-day pass starts from ¥16,500pp; see the website for details).

From Huis Ten Bosch take the JR Seaside Liner (13/day; 76 mins) to Nagasaki; the line joins the Nagasaki Line at Isahaya, see p420.

After **Hizen-Kashima** 肥前鹿島 (83km) the line follows the coast, affording great views of the Ariake Sea on the left side. The train briefly comes to a halt every now and then to allow the train returning to Hakata to pass. The view is occasionally blotted out by the odd tunnel and gradually the train moves more inland before arriving at Isahaya.

## Isahaya 諫早 (129km)

Isahaya is a gateway to **Shimabara Peninsula**, which juts out east of Nagasaki into the Ariake Sea. Attractions here include the scenery; the hot-spring resort of Unzen-onsen; and Shimabara, a castle town.

Buses to **Unzen-onsen** are operated by Shimatetsu 島鉄 (🖥 www.shima tetsu.co.jp; 1/hr; 80-90 mins; ¥1300 one way) and leave from the bus terminal directly opposite Isahaya station.

For **Shimabara** turn right out of the JR station; the entrance to the private Shimabara Railway is between Mister Donut and the Joyroad travel agency. Purchase tickets from the ticket machine in the JR station (Isahaya to Shimabara 1-2/hr; approx 65 mins; ¥1330; JR rail passes are not valid).

### Side trips from Isahaya

● **Unzen-onsen** Unzen-onsen 雲仙温泉 (🖥 www.unzen.org/e_ver) is a compact and relatively unspoilt onsen town situated in one of Japan's oldest national parks: Unzen-Amakusa National Park 雲仙天草国立公園. About 350 years ago, during the time of religious persecution in Japan, 30 Christians were sent to Unzen for refusing to renounce their faith and were thrown into the boiling hot springs here. Mt Unzen 雲仙岳 is an active volcano that last erupted in 1995. Over the years It has caused many deaths, but it is considered safe now.

*Unzen Kanko Hotel* 雲仙観光ホテル (☎ 0957-73 3263, 🖥 www.unzen kankohotel.com/english; from ¥23,000pp inc half board) offers both luxury and history, the latter because it opened in 1935, a year after the national park was designated, and it was the first hotel in Japan to be specifically built for foreign tourists. Thus it is Western in style but it does have its own onsen.

● **Shimabara** Shimabara Railway runs from Isahaya around the peninsula, stopping at Shimabara 島原 (🖥 www.city.shimabara.lg.jp) on the eastern side. Being a port town it was a place where many Christian missionaries came and also died due to persecution. It is also an attractive castle town: the white-walled five-storied **Shimabara Castle** 島原城 (🖥 shimabarajou.chicappa.jp; daily 9am-5pm; ¥540) is a far larger structure than most castles, though like many it is not the original having been rebuilt in 1964. The museum in the castle keep has a number of Christian artefacts from the time of the Shimabara rebellion – when peasants, many of whom were Catholics, protested about the increase in taxes – as well as the history of Shimabara itself. The castle is a 5-minute walk down the road in front of the station.

For the last 10 minutes of the journey to Nagasaki the train goes at full speed and there's one long tunnel about five minutes before arrival.

## Urakami 浦上天 (152km)

When it first opened in 1897, Urakami was Nagasaki station. But the growth of the downtown port area and land reclamation meant traffic shifted further away so a decision was made to construct a new Nagasaki station; in 1905 the station's name was changed to Urakami.

The atomic bomb exploded at 11.02am on 9th August 1945 over this district; Urakami is the nearest JR stop to the A-Bomb Museum and Peace Park (see p442).

**Nagasaki 長崎 (154km)**  [see pp441-8]

## HAKATA (FUKUOKA) TO KAGOSHIMA-CHUO BY SHINKANSEN
[Map 28, p417; Map 29; Table 21, p511]

Distances by JR shinkansen from Hakata. Fastest journey time: 79 minutes.

Tsubame services stop at all stations on this route, though some only go to Kumamoto; Sakura stop at most stations; and Mizuho only stop at Kumamoto.

There is not much to see on this journey – mostly you are in a tunnel, or there is a barrier obscuring the view – but occasionally there are glimpses of farmland (mostly rice fields) and wooded hills.

**Hakata 博多 (0km)** [Fukuoka, see pp434-40]

**Shin-Tosu 新鳥栖 (29km)**  All Tsubame and most Sakura stop here. This is where you should transfer to the JR Nagasaki Line, especially if coming from Kumamoto or Kagoshima as it saves backtracking all the way to Hakata, for Nagasaki. When the planned extension of the shinkansen line to Nagasaki is open this will be the junction station.

If you do stop here, on the station concourse there is a **Family Mart** and a waiting room; there is also an ekiben and soba stand by the local trains entrance.

**Kurume 久留米 (36km)**  All Tsubame and most Sakura stop here. Kurume is a pleasant place to walk around if you have time before continuing to Yufuin or Oita (see p422). Your first port of call should be the **tourist information centre** (🖥 www.kurume-hotomeki.jp; daily 9am-7pm), at the back of the souvenir shop opposite the exit to the shinkansen tracks; the staff speak English and are very friendly.

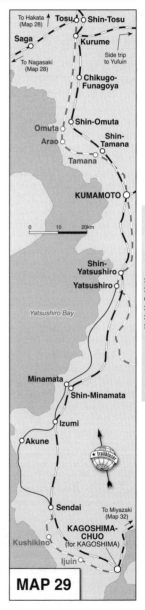

MAP 29

KYUSHU

With a map in hand head for the Suitengu (West) Gate 水天宮（西）口 of the station and turn left, then right at the first set of traffic lights and turn right again at the end of Suitengu-dori 水天宮通り and walk along parallel to Chikugo river 筑後川. **Suitengu Shrine** 水天宮 (💻 www.suitengu.net) dates from 1650 and its location by the river means it is a guardian shrine for marine traffic as well as housing the god of safe childbirth.

From here head back along the river towards **Bairin-ji** 梅林寺. You will be able to see it from the riverbank; climb up the rather overgrown steps. The temple is where ascetic (Zen Buddhist) monks come to train and for this reason you can't go into the buildings – indeed the doors are firmly closed – but the grounds are a pleasant place for a stroll. Retrace your steps to the riverbank and walk along it, under the shinkansen and local line railway tracks and past the Bridgestone and Asahi factories, then look for another set of overgrown steps. Climb up and join the road heading left; soon you will walk past the remains of **Kurume Castle** 久留米城 and **Sasayama shrine** 篠山神社. Turn right here (if you don't go into the castle grounds first) and then right at the traffic lights and from there follow the main road back to the east side of the station. Before you go into the station look out for the **huge tyre** – its diameter is four metres – symbolising the importance of the Bridgestone company to the town. The founder of the company was called Shojiro Ishibashi; Ishibashi literally means 'stone bridge' but he transposed the name for the company he created.

The most convenient place to stay is **Kurume Station Hotel** 久留米ステーション (☎ 0942-36 1122, 💻 ksth.com; ¥5150-5550/S, ¥8200-8700/Tw, ¥10200-10800/D; breakfast ¥500); it is on the left if facing the station, behind the bus terminal. A feature of this hotel is the range of massage and other relaxing treatments (from ¥4000/40 mins) on offer.

There are **lockers** (¥300-600) in the waiting room and there are several restaurants (okonomiyaki 11am-10pm; yakitori 11am-2pm & 5-11pm; udon ramen 11am-11pm; and sashimi 11am-2pm & 5pm to midnight) on the 2nd floor by the Machinaka (East) Exit of the station but the tuna bowl 鉄火丼; ¥700) at *Kiyomatsu* 清松 (daily 11.30am-11pm) is highly recommended. Kiyomatsu is in the orangey-yellow building, beyond the car park, visible from the top of the escalator to the East Exit.

### Alternative route to Yufuin

Kurume station is the point of interchange for the Kyudai Line that cuts across Kyushu (west to east), stopping at the hot spring resort of **Yufuin** (see pp428-30) before terminating in **Oita** (see p427-8). The Yufu and Yufuin no Mori LEX (both approx 3/day) run to Yufuin (about 96 mins) and on to Oita (about 2¼hrs).

Only Tsubame stop at **Chikugo-Funagoya** 筑後船小屋 (51.5km), **Shin-Omuta** 新大牟田 (69km) and **Shin-Tamana** 新玉名 (90km). Make the most of the views as soon as the train passes through more tunnels with fleeting glimpses of tree-clad hills before you reach the built-up area signalling you are getting near Kumamoto.

## Kumamoto 熊本 (118km)
[see pp448-54]
All shinkansen stop here. Change here for the scenic journey across Kyushu to Oita, via the dramatic Mt Aso caldera (see below).

### ❏ Stop press
The Kumamoto earthquakes (see p448) severely damaged the line to Aso/Oita and the Minamiaso Line (see p424); local services now operate on parts of the line inland from Kumamoto and Oita, but it will be a while before the line reopens fully. Check 🖳 www.jrkyushu.co.jp for updates.

### Side trip by rail to Mt Aso
[Map 31, p429]
A trip to the Aso Tableland with its spectacular mountain scenery and the chance to peer over the edge of a volcanic crater makes an excursion to the centre of Kyushu a highlight in Japan. You can also take the scenic line round the south side of Mt Aso, see p424.

Access to the tableland is via Aso station on the JR Hohi Line. Take the Kyushu Odan Tokkyu LEX (4/day; about 67 mins; 50km) to Aso station 阿蘇駅; all other services are local and require several changes of train. In the latter part of the journey the train passes through the Aso valley and its rice fields. In the distance, the craters come into view a while before the train arrives in Aso.

**Aso station** is the gateway to Aso National Park. The JR ticket office (daily 6.30am-6.40pm) is on the right as you exit the ticket barrier and **Aso Information centre** (daily 9am-5pm) is on the left. The English-speaking staff here provide a very good map of the area around the station as well as general information about Aso-san including bus timetables to get there. They can also help book accommodation and arrange pick-up services from the station to your hotel, particularly if there isn't a convenient bus service. You can store luggage here (daily 9am-5pm; ¥300 per bag) if it won't fit into a locker – there are **lockers** (¥300-700) in the corridor to the right by the station exit – and even rent a bike (¥900/day).

**Mt Aso** 阿蘇山 (Aso-san) actually refers to the whole caldera area and all five of its peaks (Nakadake, Takadake, Nekodake, Kijimadake and Eboshidake). All of these are contained within the enormous outer crater that is the Aso tableland. The most accessible and impressive is **Nakadake** 中岳火口, the only active volcano, reached by a combination of bus and ropeway. If conditions allow you can peer over the edge of the crater and see the bubbling green liquid below. The last big eruption at Nakadake was in 1979. However, the ropeway to the crater is often closed because of volcanic activity and sometimes when it is too foggy.

To reach the crater take a bus (see p424) to **Aso-san Nishi** 阿蘇山西 and then transfer to **Aso-san ropeway** 阿蘇山ロープウェー (daily Mar-Oct 8.30am-6pm, Nov to 5pm, Dec-Mar 9am-5pm; every 8 mins; ¥750/1250 one-way/return trip) to **Kakonishi** 火口西, which is just beneath the crater. The walk up to the crater from there is a rather gentle 108 metres; instead consider taking the terracotta footpath that hugs the roadside (20 mins) as it provides a relatively quick and physically undemanding opportunity to survey the wondrous landscape. It's an extraordinary experience to stand at the edge of the crater. Some slopes in this area provided exterior shots for Ernst Blofeld's missile silo in the 1967 James Bond film, *You Only Live Twice*. More recently, concrete bunkers have been built in the event of a sudden eruption; experts

KYUSHU

suggest that at the first sign of danger it's best to run backwards, looking at the crater, so as to dodge pieces of volcanic debris.

If the ropeway is closed the bus may only go as far as **Kusasenri** 草千里, a large grassy plateau which you can explore either on foot or on horseback (9am-4pm; ¥1500/5 mins, ¥4000/20 mins, ¥5000/25 mins). At **Aso Volcano Museum** 阿蘇火山博物館 (Aso-kazan Hakubutsukan; 🖳 www.asomuse.jp; daily 9am-5pm; ¥860) you can see footage of major eruptions and there are real-time cameras for a close-up of the crater without having to peer over the edge yourself, though in reality you may not see much. There are also exhibits about the area's history, geology and flora/fauna.

Nine **buses** a day run from the bus stop outside Aso station up to Kusasenri (¥570) and Asosan-nishi (¥650; ¥170 from Kusasenri). The journey takes 30-40 minutes and the last bus from Aso station leaves no later than 3pm.

The homely and very pleasant *Aso Backpackers Hostel* ASOバックパッカーズホステル (☎ 0967-34-0408, 🖳 www.aso-backpackers.com; ¥2800pp/dorm; ¥5500/S, from ¥6000 for two sharing a room) is near the station. Facilities are kept spotless, wi-fi is free and there are mountain views from most rooms. They don't serve meals but there is a kitchen. You also get a ¥100 discount for the nearby, cosy **Yumeno-yu** 夢の湯 (daily except every 1st & 3rd Mon 10am-9pm; ¥400; towels ¥200) onsen.

Useful websites for further information are: 🖳 www.kyusanko.co.jp/aso and 🖳 www.asocity-kanko.jp.

[See Stop Press box p423] For views of Aso-san from the southern side you can take the scenic 17.7km **Minaimaso Railway** 南阿蘇鉄道 from JR **Tateno** 立野 station, a stop on all LEX services, to Takamori 高森 (approx 14/day; 32 mins; ¥470). There is no ticket office at either Tateno or Takamori so you need to pay the driver on the train. Torokko (open-air trains) run twice a day in the summer months. Another reason for travelling on this line is that you pass through (and can stop at) the station with the longest name in Japan: Minami-Aso-Mizuno-Umareru-Sato-Hakusui-Kogen 南阿蘇水の生まれる里白水高原, though it is usually referred to as Hakusui-Kogen. Be aware that the trains can get very crowded with tour groups.

To continue from Tateno/Aso to Oita, or Beppu (for details on both see pp426-8), get back on a Kyushu Odan Tokkyu LEX.

## Shin-Yatsushiro 新八代 **(151km)** All Tsubame and most Sakura stop here.

### Alternative route on the Hisatsu Orange Railway

The sections of pre-shinkansen railway line which run between Hakata and Yatsushiro (via Kumamoto) and from Sendai to Kagoshima-chuo are still operated by JR Kyushu. However, the section between Yatsushiro and Sendai is run by a private company, Hisatsu Orange Railway 肥薩おれんじ鉄道 (🖳 www.hs-orange.com; 8/day; fastest journey 2hrs 25 min; ¥2620). JR passes are not valid on this route so it is best to take the shinkansen, especially if speed is a factor. However, if scenery is your priority do consider this route even if you only do a section such as from Izumi (see opposite) to Sendai (¥1450; 14/day; fastest journey 63 mins compared to about 10 mins on a shinkansen). Proof that the scenery is good is that the luxury Seven Stars train (see box p97) travels on this line between Yatsushiro and Kagoshima-Chuo to see the sun set.

Note that many of the stations are unmanned so you need to collect a ticket from the machine in the train and pay the driver as you get off the train.

At Sendai you can pick up the shinkansen to Kagoshima-chuo.

Unfortunately nearly all the journey from Shin-Yatsushiro to Kagoshima-chuo is through tunnels.

**Shin-Minamata 新水俣 (194km)** All Sakura and Tsubame call here. The station is connected to the Hisatsu Orange Railway (see opposite).

If you look carefully you get brief glimpses of the sea to your right and also – but only between November and March – you might see some Siberian cranes (see below).

**Izumi 出水 (210km)** All Sakura and Tsubame call here. It is a small station also with a connection to the Hisatsu Orange Railway (see opposite).

Izumi is a paradise for bird-watchers particularly during the winter months when it is home to around 10,000 Siberian cranes. If you're here then staff at the **information office** (🖳 www.izumi-navi.jp; daily 8.30am-7pm), opposite the ticket barrier, can advise on access to the **Crane Observation Centre** ツル 観察センター (daily Nov to end Mar 9am-5pm; ¥210) set in a 245-hectare wildlife protection area. In addition to the rooftop terrace observatory there is an exhibition about cranes including some documentary videos. If the seasonal sightseeing excursion bus (Dec-Feb only; 6/day; ¥1000) continues to operate it will leave from the West Exit; alternatively a taxi costs about ¥4500. Cycles can be rented from the station (¥300/4hrs, ¥100 per additional hour), though they must be returned by 5pm.

In the summer months you can see the cranes come to life on the big screen at the Dome Theater in **Crane Park Museum** ツル博物館 クレインパークいずみ (Nov-Mar daily 9am-5pm, Apr-Oct Tue-Sun to 5pm; ¥320). The park is a short walk from the station.

Whilst here make time to go to **Izumi-fumoto Bukeyashiki-ato** 出水麓武家屋敷, an area of preserved Edo-period samurai residences which are free to enter (daily 9am-5pm). They are a 25-minute walk from the station or less by bicycle (maps available from the information office) but they are also a stop on the seasonal sightseeing bus (see above).

***Hotel Wing International Izumi*** ホテルウィングインターナショナル出水 (☎ 0996-63 8111, 🖳 www.hotelwing.co.jp/izumi; ¥5500/S, ¥7000/D, ¥7700/Tw inc buffet breakfast) provides Western-style accommodation and is only a minute's walk from JR Izumi station.

After Izumi, some services stop at **Sendai** 川内 (243km) before hurtling into tunnel after tunnel on the way to the Kagoshima-chuo terminal. Sendai is where the Hisatsu Orange Railway ends and the JR Kagoshima Line restarts.

**Kagoshima-chuo 鹿児島中央 (289km)**                    [see pp455-60]
Kagoshima-chuo station is the main rail terminal for the city of Kagoshima. **Kagoshima station** 鹿児島駅 is one stop further along but you'll probably only pass through it if heading towards Miyazaki (see p426) on the JR Nippo Line.

**Alternative route back to Hakata**
Instead of returning to Hakata the same way, it's possible to cut across Kyushu via the JR Nippo Line (120 mins by Kirishima LEX; 10/day) to Miyazaki (see p433), then follow the route described below in reverse. The first part of the journey is particularly scenic and if the weather is good make sure you sit on the right-hand side of the train for views of Sakurajima as you go around the bay. From around Hayato the train goes inland but it is still a very pleasant journey.

The Nichirin Seagaia LEX goes from Miyazaki to Hakata (see Table 22, p511). If on a Nichirin you will need to change at Oita or Beppu.

## KOKURA TO MIYAZAKI      [Map 30; Map 32, p431; Table 22, p511]

Distances by JR from Kokura. Fastest journey time: 4 hours 34 minutes.

**Note**: Although it's possible to start a journey down the east coast from Hakata, if coming from Honshu you'll save a lot of time by changing on to a limited express at Kokura.

**Kokura 小倉 (0km)**  The Nichirin Seagaia only goes once a day to Miyazaki so the chances are you will need to take a Sonic to Beppu, or Oita, and change there. If on the 883 version you may be amused by the headrests that make you look like Mickey Mouse. Sit on the left-hand side for views of the coast.

The Nichirin Seagaia doesn't stop at Usa or Kitsuki but Sonic services stop at all or some of the following: **Yukuhashi** 行橋 (25km), **Unoshima** 宇島 (45.2km), **Nakatsu** 中津 (52km), **Yanagigaura** 柳ヶ浦 (69km), **Usa** 宇佐 (76km), where American visitors may wish to photograph the torii-framed station signs, though here Usa is in hiragana うさ ('Usa' is pronounced Oo-sa), and **Kitsuki** 杵築 (99km).

**Beppu 別府 (121km)**  Beppu produces more hot-spring water than any other onsen town in Japan so don't come here with the classic image of the rustic hot spring in mind. It's a sprawling city and amongst the mass of concrete buildings lie many hot springs that have to be seen to be believed.

Apart from the onsen most people come here for the eight '**burning hells**' 地獄 (*jigoku*; daily 8am-5pm; ¥400 for one; pass for all eight ¥2100); these are onsen that you look at rather than bathe in because the water is far too hot. Each jigoku has a different feature. The six in the Kannawa 鉄輪 area of town are: Umi 海, best known for its 200m-deep pond of boiling hot cobalt blue water; Oniishi Bozu 鬼石坊主, with bubbles of hot grey mud thought to resemble the shaven head of a monk; Yama 山, ponds of steaming water and a mini zoo; Kamado かまど, 'cooking pot' hell with a bright red demon as a mascot; Oniyama 鬼山地獄, also home to 100 crocodiles; Shiraike 白池, with ponds of hot milky white water. The other two are on the other side of the Noda Tunnel: Chinoike 血の池, known for its ponds of steaming blood red water; and Tatsumaki 竜巻, where a geyser erupts every 20 minutes or so.

**Beppu Tourist Information Office** (🖳 www.city.beppu.oita.jp; daily 9am-5pm) is by the East Exit of the station. The staff there will give you a map of the jigoku area and a bus timetable and guide you to where to get the bus. A one-day pass costs ¥900 which gives a saving of ¥10 if you go to both 'hell' areas. If you just go to Kannawa, the main area, it would be cheaper just to pay the bus fare (¥330) to and from the station as long as you don't mind a bit of walking. There is a myriad of bus services some with much longer routes than others. The best to take to Kannawa are Nos 5, 7 and 9 (around 17 mins); for Chinoike and Tatsumaki Jigoku take bus No 26 (around 30 mins; 2/hr) from the station and the No 21 from there back to the station.

If you are not going to have a hot sand-bath in Ibusuki (see pp461-2) you may also like to have a one while in Beppu: the oldest (the current building dates from 1938), most famous and possibly the most characterful place for both a **sand-bath** 砂湯 (*suna-yu*) and an onsen is **Takegawara-onsen** 竹瓦温泉 (bath 6.30am-10.30pm ¥100, additional charges for soap etc ¥50-100; branded towel ¥320; sand-bath 8am-10.30pm ¥1030). Takegawara-onsen is a 10-minute walk from the station. Alternatively, **Beppu Beach Sand-bath** 別府海浜砂湯 (daily except fourth Wed of month; Mar-Nov 8.30am-5pm, Dec-Feb 9am-4pm; ¥1030; towel ¥320; locker ¥100) is near Rokushoen 六勝園 bus stop (bus No 26).

There is no shortage of places to stay the night; the tourist information office will be able to give you information.

As the train pulls away, the left side affords stunning views back across the bay towards the city. Look carefully and you may spot white steam puffing out of the many spas dotting the steep hillside beyond.

**Oita** 大分 **(133km)** The main reason for stopping here is for a side trip to Yufuin (see pp428-30) and/or to Aso (see p423-4). However, if you have the time you may like to discover the art museum, or go to the onsen on the top of JR Oita City station; the reconstructed station opened in 2015.

❏ **Aru Ressha – luxury sweet train**
Aru Ressha 或る列車 (🖳 www.jrkyushu-aruressha.jp; 1/day, mostly weekends; from ¥20,000pp one-way based on two people travelling together) is a luxury train that operates between Oita and Hita (Aug-Oct) and between Sasebo and Nagasaki (Nov-Mar). Passengers are served sweets, cakes and baked goods using seasonal food from the region. The 'train of dreams', as the train had long been known among railway fans, was revived by designer Eiji Mitooka, based on a model crafted by the late Nobutaro Hara, who was a model railway creator.
    Tickets can be booked through a JR Kyushu Travel Center, but at times it is chartered by tour operators. Eiji Mitooka also designed the Seven Stars (see box p97).

**Oita City Tourist Information Center** (TIC; 🖳 www.oishiimati-oita.jp; daily 8.30am-7pm) is to the left as you come through the ticket gate. Staff can provide maps and give information about accommodation. Next to the TIC is a **JR Kyushu Travel Center** (Mon-Fri 10.30am-7pm, Sat & Sun to 6pm). There are plenty of places at which to eat in the station, both on the main concourse and in Bungo Niwasaki Ichiba 豊後にわさき市場 (7am-11pm), where there is also a supermarket (9.30am-10pm). There are more options on the 4th floor of AmuCityDining (11am-10pm). There are **lockers** (mostly ¥300 size but a few large ¥600 ones) at the Ueno-no-mori (South Gate) end of the concourse.

**Oita Prefectural Art Museum** 大分県立美術館 (OpAm; 🖳 www.opam .jp; daily 10am-7pm, Fri & Sat to 8pm; ¥300, additional charge for special exhibitions), also opened in 2015. The director's aim is that it is seen as a playground and a place where everyone will enjoy seeing art – even people who wouldn't normally go to an art gallery. Exhibits include bamboo craft, ukiyo-e, ceramics and contemporary Japanese art. It is a 15-minute walk from the North Exit of the station.

A highlight at *JR Kyushu Hotel Blossom Oita* JR九州ホテルブラッサム 大分 (☎ 097-5788 8719; 🖳 www.jrk-hotels.co.jp/Oita; from ¥14,100/S, ¥19,500/D or Tw), which opened in 2015, is the roof-top open-air onsen (**City Spa Tenku** daily 11am-midnight; hotel guests also 6-9.30am; ¥1500, free for guests) with wonderful views – if the weather is good! It is to the right of the Funai-chuo (Central) Gate Exit, though it can be accessed from the station. Reception is on the 8th floor; the rooms are on the 9th-21st floors.

**Side trip by rail to Yufuin**                        **[see Map 31]**
**Yufuin-onsen** 由布院 offers a tranquil, rural antidote to Beppu's commercial hedonism, though it must be said that in recent years it has become rather touristy. Nestling at the base of Mt Yufu, **Yufuin town** 湯布院 not only boasts a variety of onsen but an assortment of craft shops, a picturesque pond (Kinrinko), art galleries and museums to enrich both soul and body. In fact the culture starts right in the station with a changing exhibition of artwork in the waiting room. The **tourist information office** (🖳 yufuin.or.jp; daily Mar-Oct 8.30am-6pm, Nov-Feb 9am-6pm) is on the left of the ticket gate and next to the waiting room. The staff may give you a 'walking map' though it really only shows the hotels and ryokan so make sure you ask for the main map of Yufuin

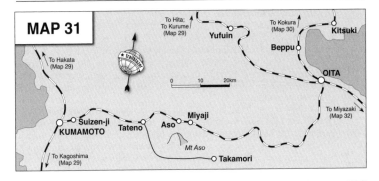

as well. At the time of research the maps included some museums that had closed and didn't include some that had opened, but the staff can mark those on for you if a new map hasn't been produced by the time you are here. The staff can also give you details of the onsen (many with rotemburo) that you can visit for the day, as well as information about the many ways to see the town from the station: on a horse-drawn carriage tour (50 mins; ¥1600pp); in a replica English classic car (1/hr; 50 mins; ¥1350pp) called Scarborough; in a rickshaw pulled by a man (from ¥4500pp/30 mins); or on a bike/electric bike (from ¥400 for 2hrs, ¥1000/day) – though since the town is pretty compact walking is straightforward and free.

Most of the places of interest are along the way to Kinrinko. At the slightly kitsch **Yufuin Trick Art Museum** 湯布院トリックアート迷宮館 (Meikyukan; 🖥 www.trick3dart-yufuin.com; Mar-Sep 9.30am-5.30pm, Oct-Feb to 5pm; ¥850) nothing is as it seems and everything offers fun, bizarre, photo opportunities. Go with another person as some of the exhibits only work if someone can actively be part of them. The museum is set back from the road on the right-hand side so keep an eye out as you walk along.

**Yufuin Showa Kan** 昭和館昭和レトロテーマパーク (🖥 www.yufuin-syowakan.jp; daily 9am-5pm; ¥500) is a museum full of nostalgic memories for Japanese who lived in the Showa era, particularly the mid 1950s to mid 1960s; the museum has exhibits from all aspects of life as well as a recreated classroom, post office, living room in a house, sweet shops and much more. Even if you don't go into the museum you will know where you are as there are several exhibits outside such as a period Coca-Cola vending machine.

Further up the road you will eventually reach the turning to the right for the popular **Kinrinko** 金鱗湖, a lake with some koi and, at times, birds skimming the surface. A great place to admire the lake views or simply relax with a book is the bankside terrace of **Café La Ruche** カフェ外観 (11.30am-3pm & 6.30-9pm), which serves good European-style sandwich lunch sets (¥1270) or soups (from ¥540) as well as Yufuin 'red egg roll' cake (¥594).

There are plenty of other options of places for snacks or a meal as you walk towards Kinrinko but one of the more unusual is **Snoopy Chaya** スヌーピー 茶屋, a Peanuts-themed *matcha* (green tea) café (daily 10am-5pm) where a matcha ice-cream costs ¥380, a cake from ¥390 and a Snoopy Matcha parfait is ¥950. Main meals are also available as are Snoopy products.

If you were to make one expensive splurge on a ryokan during your trip to Japan, try *Hotel Kamenoi Besso* 旅館亀の井別荘 (☎ 0977-84 3166; 🖳 www.kamenoi-bessou.jp; from ¥43,000/S, ¥35,750pp for two sharing inc half board) near the edge of Kinrinko. It's an idyllic and luxurious retreat. You can either stay in a Japanese-style cottage room (sleeping 2-4 people), or a Western-style room in the main building. Each room boasts a private natural onsen but there are also two rotemburo. If booked in advance they will meet guests at the station.

A cheaper option and an easy walk from the station is *Sansuikan* 山水館 (☎ 0977-84 2201, 🖳 www.sansuikan.co.jp; from ¥17,000pp inc half board). It is notable for having its own brewery; the (delicious) beer is only sold in Yufuin so do try it while you are here. The two baths are rotated morning and evening (between men and women) because only one has a proper rotemburo. Some rooms are Western style and some Japanese. The evening meal is served in private cubicles; the food is good but not outstanding.

The main reason to stay at *Makiba no Ie* 牧場の家 (☎ 0977-84 2138, 🖳 ryosoumakibanoie.wix.com/yufuin; from ¥14,190pp inc half board) is the fact that the accommodation is in separate huts and there are two wonderful open-air baths. The main building is old and characterful and the food delicious. The huts sleep up to five people and the one nearest the road is the cheapest. It is about a 10-minute walk from the station: walk along Ekimae-dori, at the first major junction turn right along the road with a torii gate; a few minutes after crossing the river you will see Makiba on the right-hand side. Look for the kanji engraved in a large stone on the left-hand side of the entrance.

Both the Yufu LEX and Yufuin-no-mori LEX run to Yufuin about three times a day (approx 48 mins), though the latter is much more comfortable and enjoyable; reservations are essential but the journey is free with a JR pass. Local JR Kyudai Line trains are more frequent but take around an hour.

### Side trip by rail to Mt Aso                [see Map 31, p429]

[See Stop Press box p423]  Oita is also where you can change to the JR Hohi Line (also known as the Aso Kogen Line) that cuts across Kyushu to Kumamoto via the stunning volcanic peaks of **Mt Aso tableland** (see pp423-4). Kyushu Odan Tokkyu LEX (4/day; all JR passes accepted) runs to **Aso** station (98km; about 108 mins) before terminating in Kumamoto (another 50km; additional 71 mins). All other services are local and require several changes of train.

Very soon after leaving Oita the train starts a gradual climb into the mountains and forest scenery takes over. As the train chugs down the single-track line there are long stretches where it passes small clusters of houses separated by fields and mountains. Heading towards Aso station, the craters that make up the Aso range should be visible in the distance.

## Usuki 臼杵 (169km)  Usuki's main attraction is the exquisite array of Heian/Kamakura-era **Stone Buddha carvings** 臼杵石仏 (Usuki Sekibutsu; daily 6am-6pm; ¥540) carved serenely into a remote hillside.

From the station take a bus bound for Miemachi 三重町 (4/day; approx 20 mins; ¥310) and alight at the Usuki Sekibutsu stop; the first statues are a 5-minute walk away. Additional bus services (6/day) go from the Jyohoku 敘北

bus stop which is a 700-metre walk (approx 10 mins) from Usuki station. Pick up a map from the information centre (🖳 www.usuki-kanko.com; daily 9am-3pm; if closed ask at the JR ticket counter) in the station. Alternatively borrow a free bike from the station-master's collection and cycle to the Buddhas or use it, or your own two feet, to explore the narrow historic lanes, temples and castle remnants of this charming coastal town. William Adams (see p419) first arrived here in April 1600; it was the start of his love affair with Japan. At that time the town was called Bongo, not Usuki.

The next stop is **Tsukumi** 津久見 (179km). As you approach **Saiki** 佐伯 (198km) there are good views out to sea on the left side.

The views become more spectacular as the train leaves the coast and begins to thread its way inland through the hills. However, the verdant landscape enjoyed so far on the journey abruptly disappears as the train pulls in to Nobeoka station.

**Nobeoka** 延岡 **(256km)** Many people stop here for the side trip to Takachiho (see p432), but a 15-minute walk from Nobeoka station takes you to **Imayama** 今山 where you can see the tallest statue (17m-high) of Kobo Daishi (see p156) in Japan; the statue is called **Imayama Daishi** 今山大師, meaning 'great master of Imayama'. **Nobeoka Taishi Festival** 延岡大師祭 is held here over three days in April to celebrate the anniversary of Kobo Daishi's death. To get to Imayama walk along the road straight opposite the station (passing the Route Inn hotel on your left) and then turn left at the first major road. Soon on your right you will see some steps leading up to Imayama.

Nobeoka (🖳 www.city.nobeoka.miyazaki .jp) was put on the literary map by Japanese author Natsume Soseki, who mentions the place in his most famous novel, *Botchan*, and its cultural history is also evident in its **Noh Theatre** which is in the ruins of the castle. Performances are held here in October.

There is an ***udon restaurant*** (9am-8pm) and a Mini Convi (6.20am-8pm) convenience store in the station. ***Hotel Route Inn Nobeoka Ekimae*** ホテルルートイン延岡駅前 (☎ 0982-12 1300, 🖳 www.route-inn.co.jp; ¥6600/S, ¥9550/D, ¥10,550/Tw) is opposite the station. The rate includes a buffet-style breakfast and access to an onsen bath.

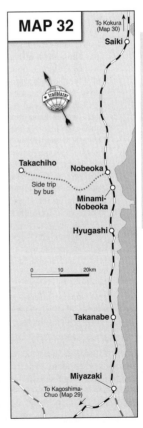

MAP 32

To Kokura (Map 30)

Saiki

trailblazer

KYUSHU

Takachiho — Nobeoka

Side trip by bus

Minami-Nobeoka

Hyugashi

0  10  20km

Takanabe

Miyazaki

To Kagoshima-Chuo (Map 29)

## Side trip by bus to Takachiho

Formerly services on the Takachiho Railway Line took travellers on one of the most scenic mountain railways in Japan to Takachiho 高千穂, a mountain town known for its spectacular gorge. But in 2005 Typhoon Nabi washed away two of the line's major bridges, and with it, any chance of the locally funded line resuming business. Now the most practical route is to take the Miyako bus (🖥 www .miyakoh.co.jp/bus/express/takachiho.html; approx 1/hr; 80-90 mins; ¥1740) from Platform 1 of **Nobeoka Bus Center** 延岡バスセンター (the blue building on the right of Nobeoka station); the views en route are equally splendid.

**Takachiho Gorge** 高千穂峡 (Takachiho-kyo) was formed by the gradual erosion of lava that once flowed from Mt Aso (see pp423-4). You can rent a boat and row around the gorge (daily summer 7.30am-6pm, rest of year 8.30am-4.30pm; 30 mins, ¥2000; up to three people per boat); there's also a 600m walking trail. The gorge is lit up at night between mid July and early September.

Taxis wait by the bus station in Takachiho for the chance to take you to the gorge; you can order a return taxi from the ticket booth there. However, the fare (from ¥720) is expensive for the journey so if the weather is OK rent an electric bike (¥300/hour) from Shinwa Rent-a-cycle by the former railway station. The **tourist office** (🖥 takachiho-kanko.info; daily 8.30am-5.30pm), look for the 'i' sign, is opposite the bus station. Their quad-bike ('buggy') option (¥1300/hr) offers a more adventurous yet environmentally incongruous alternative. Luggage can be left here all day for ¥300.

Takachiho is also known for *yokagura* 夜神楽 ancient dances which re-enact scenes from Japanese mythology. Traditionally, performances of yok-agura take place in local people's homes and tend to last from early evening through to the following morning. Plenty of sake keeps everyone awake into the small hours. Tourists are welcome at these performances, which are organised at the weekend between November and February. Alternatively, a one-hour version is performed at the cedar-lined **Takachiho Shrine** 高千穂神社 (Takachiho Jinja; nightly 8pm; tickets ¥700 at the shrine). From the bus stop, turn right up the slope then left at the main road. The shrine is a 10- to 15-minute walk from the bus stop on the right-hand side.

The only 'rail' service now is the **open-air torokko**, which goes by the name SuperCart スーパーカート (10am-4pm; 1-2/hr; 30 mins; ¥1200). The torokko goes across the 105m-high **Takachiho Tekkyo** 高千穂鉄橋 (iron bridge) and is popular because of the views.

There are several places to stay in town. Closest to the bus centre is ***Imakuni Ryokan*** 今国旅館 (☎ 0982-72 2175, 🖥 imakuniryokan.co.jp; from ¥8000pp); it offers some en suite accommodation in Japanese-style rooms. Details of other places are available on the tourist office's website or at the tourist office itself.

The short journey between Nobeoka and **Minami-Nobeoka** 南延岡 (260km) takes you alongside a mass of pipes that connect up the Asahi Kasei factories. **Hyugashi** 日向市 (277km) is the station for Hyuga, a port town with a number of beaches popular with local surfers. The line between Hyugashi and **Takanabe** 高鍋 (314km) is one of the most rewarding parts of the journey. There are fantastic views of the coastline on the left as the train runs for one stretch just a few metres from the shore.

**Miyazaki** 宮崎 **(340km)** The resort city of Miyazaki is known for its long hours of sunshine and mild climate, and pulls in domestic tourists keen to enjoy relaxing weekend escapes from the daily grind.

Miyazaki's modern station is small and easy to find your way around. The staff at the **tourist information counter** (🖳 www.city.miyazaki.miyazaki.jp; daily 9am-6pm) in the station can provide you with a walking map and brochures about the town and surrounding area. There are **lockers** (¥300-700) opposite and also outside the East Gate side of the station. There are several options for a snack.

**Miyazaki Science Center** 宮崎科学技術館 (Cosmoland; 🖳 cosmoland .miyabunkyo.com; Tue-Sun 9am-4.30pm; ¥540, ¥750 inc planetarium) focuses on space and has one of the world's largest planetariums. Even if you aren't interested in visiting it is worth the short walk to see the 40m-high (actual size) model of an H-1 rocket outside the museum. From the East Exit of the station turn first right on to Hokenjomae-dori and then it is hard to miss.

Don't leave Miyazaki without trying the local speciality: *chicken nanban* チキン南蛮, pieces of fried chicken served with a sweet-and-sour sauce. Ask for the *chicken nanban teishoku* (set meal) at the famous *Ogura Honten* おぐら本店 (11am-5pm), off Tachibana-dori Higashi.

*JR Kyushu Hotel Miyazaki* ＪＲ九州ホテル宮崎 (☎ 0985-29 8000, 🖳 www.jrk-hotels.jp/Miyazaki; from ¥10,800/S, ¥16,200/D, ¥17,300/Tw), whose nickname is 'Kiten', is connected to the station. The reception desk (front) is on the 8th floor and the rooms are on floors 9-14.

The most luxurious place to stay is *Sheraton Grande Ocean Resort* シェラトン・グランデ・オーシャンリゾート (☎ 0985-21 1133, 🖳 www.seaga ia.co.jp; from ¥17,350/S or D, ¥24,950/Tw, rooms up to ¥168,450) at **Phoenix Seagaia Resort**. Every room has an ocean view and facilities include numerous restaurants and bars, a fitness centre, spa and pool, and a free shuttle bus service to local beaches such as Jinko beach (good for swimming). Even if you don't stay here, it's worth stopping for an early evening drink at the 42nd-floor **Top Bar 'Stella'** トップバー「ステラ」 (5pm to midnight; table charge ¥1000); the bar has nearly 200 brands of shochu and affords unparalleled views of the ocean, coastline and Miyazaki city in the distance – a quite extraordinary experience at dusk.

Part of the same resort but offering slightly cheaper accommodation is *Sun Hotel Phoenix* サンホテルフェニックス (☎ 0985-39 3131, 🖳 www.seagaia .co.jp; from ¥15,800/Tw; Japanese-style accommodation also available); it is set amidst the pine forests along the Hitotsuba coast.

All the Nichirin LEX services to Miyazaki continue to **Miyazaki Airport** 宮崎空港 (Miyazaki Kuko), a 9-minute journey.

From Miyazaki, instead of retracing your steps, take a Kirishima LEX (10/day; 2hrs) along the JR Nippo Line to Kagoshima (see pp455-60) and then follow the route (in reverse) from p425. The journey on the Nippo Line is very scenic in parts, particularly around Kirishima and also when you get near to Kagoshima and can see Sakurajima in the distance across the bay.

# Kyushu – city guides

## FUKUOKA/HAKATA 福岡/博多

Fukuoka, literally 'Happy Hills', was one of the first areas of Japan to come into contact with foreign culture, due to its proximity to the Asian mainland. Both the city's JR station and the port are called Hakata not Fukuoka, a confusion of names that dates back to the time when the city was divided into the merchants' district (Hakata) and the old castle town (Fukuoka).

The city has a relentless energy, but feels more laid back and manageable than Tokyo or Osaka. At the weekend, people flock here from all over Kyushu and further afield to take advantage of Fukuoka's abundant shopping, eating and entertainment facilities. There are a good few cultural sights as well, making a stopover in Fukuoka an excellent introduction to the rest of the island.

### What to see and do

Any visit to Kyushu should start with a trip to Kyushu National Museum (see pp440-1) for an introduction to the history of Asia and Fukuoka's role in it; whilst there visit Dazaifu where the God of learning and literature is enshrined.

If your time here is limited, and if you're not in town for Hakata Gion Yamakasa Festival (see p438), it's worth paying a visit to **Hakata Machiya Folk Museum** 博多町屋ふるさと館 (🖳 www .hakatamachiya.com; daily 10am-6pm; ¥200), a regional cultural-heritage centre where you can learn about life in Hakata, particularly in the Meiji and Taisho eras, and watch a 15-minute film (2/hr) of the raucous highlights of the festival. There is a crafts workshop area and you can also learn about the Hakata dialect. The museum is a 10- to 15- minute walk from JR Hakata station. **Kushida-jinja** 櫛田神社 (daily 4am-10pm; free), where the Hakata Gion Yamakasa Festival is based, is a short walk

from the museum. The shrine was first built in 757 but, as is so common in Japan, it was destroyed by fire; what you see today dates from 1587 when Hideyoshi Toyotomi rebuilt it. Also worth visiting is **Tocho-ji** 東長寺 (daily 9am-5pm); this temple was established by Kobo Daishi (also known as Kukai; see p156) in 806. On the 2nd floor you can see the largest seated Buddha in Japan but it dates from the 1990s. Ben Storey & Alex Chambers commented: 'If you are here at the right time you might be able to see the prayer burning ceremony. Smoke, drums and loud chanting make it a captivating assault of all the senses!'.

For more background history go to **Fukuoka City Museum** 福岡市美術館 (🖳 museum.city.fukuoka.jp; Tue-Sun 9.30am-5.30pm; ¥200); the museum traces the history of Fukuoka, right back to the Yayoi period when the introduction of rice farming led to fights between villages and the beginning of the age of warfare. The star exhibit is the gold seal of a Chinese Emperor, discovered in 1784 on nearby Shikanoshima island. There aren't many labels in English but headphones can be rented (free; bring your passport) for an English commentary. To reach the museum, take bus No 306 from stand No 5 or 6 in Hakata Bus Terminal to Hakubutsukan kita-guchi (4-6/hr; ¥230; about 30 mins). This bus goes via Fukuoka Dome, Hawks Town and terminates outside Fukuoka Tower.

The 234m-high **Fukuoka Tower** 福岡タワー (🖳 www.fukuokatower.co.jp; daily Apr-Sep 9.30am-10pm, Oct-Mar to 9pm; ¥800, 20% discount for foreigners) is the tallest seaside tower in Japan and its 123m-high observation deck is open to the public. The 3rd floor boasts a designated 'Lovers' Sanctuary' with a heart-shaped flower arch. At night the tower is illuminated; the colours and designs change according to the season.

**Ohori Park** 大濠公園 (Ohori-koen) is dominated by a turtle-inhabited boating lake and a Noh theatre. It is home to **Fukuoka City Art Museum** 福岡市美術館 (Fukuoka-shi Bijutsukan; 🖥 www.fukuoka-art-museum.jp); Tue-Sun 9.30am-5.30pm, Jul & Aug to 7.30pm; permanent exhibition ¥200), which has some superb exhibits. However, the museum is closing for restoration from September 2016 to March 2019. Several buses go to the park and museum area but the most convenient is bus No 13 from Hakata Bus Terminal; get off at Fukuoka-shi Bijutsukan Higashiguchi from where it is a 3-minute walk.

**Fukuoka Asian Art Museum** 福岡アジア美術館 (FAAM; 🖥 faam.city.fukuoka .lg.jp); Thur-Tue 10am-8pm; permanent exhibition ¥200) is a modern gallery on the 7th floor of the **Hakata Riverain** 博多リバーレイン complex. Artists in residence from across Asia display their own works and there is also a small permanent collection of contemporary Asian art. Take the subway to Nakasu-Kawabata 中洲川端 (on the Hakozaki and Kuko lines).

The **harbour** area is the place to escape from the built-up city centre and get a sense of the historical and modern-day importance of the port to the regional economy. Take bus No 99 (15 mins; ¥230) from bus stop E across the street from the Hakata Exit of Hakata station. The bus drops you close to **Bayside Place Hakata** ベイサイドプレイス博多 (🖥 www.baysideplace .jp), the perfect place to start a tour of the port area's trendy shops and waterfront cafés.

For an alternative perspective on the city, the **short train/ferry excursion** is recommended. Take a local train on the JR Kagoshima Line from Hakata station to Kashii 香椎 (LEX 1/hr, 6 mins; local train 6/hr, 11 mins). Change on to a local train on the JR Kashii Line and travel to the terminus at Saitozaki 西戸崎 (2-3/hr; 24 mins). This is a pleasant ride out along a narrow peninsula but the best part is the boat journey (1-2/hr; ¥430 one-way) from the ferry terminal at Saitozaki back to **Hakata Port Ferry Terminal** 博多ポートフェリーターミナル. On this short ride there are great views of the skyline and bay area – you are unlikely to miss Fukuoka Tower.

**Practical information**
**Station guide  Hakata station** was rebranded JR Hakata City (🖥 www.jrhakatacity.com) when the shinkansen line opened and it is a lovely station to arrive at – or depart from – though getting around it can be a little confusing. Hakata Exit is the main exit for the city and the Chikushi Exit is for JR Kyushu Hotel Blossom Fukuoka. There are also separate entrances for the shinkansen (2nd floor) and the ordinary lines (1st/ground floor concourse level).

The entrance to the subway for downtown Fukuoka (the Tenjin district) and the airport is via an escalator in the middle of the concourse. There are several **JR ticket desk**s (Midori-no-madoguchi) on the main concourse – all of them can organise (railpass) seat reservations. A branch of **JR Kyushu Travel Agency** (Mon-Fri 10am-8pm, Sat & Sun to 6pm) is on the station concourse near the Chikushi Exit. There are **lockers** all over the station – it is not therefore surprising that one reader sent us this warning: 'If you use the lockers be sure to really remember where they are…'

A central part of the station complex on the Hakata side is **AMU Plaza Hakata** アミュプラザ博多, with a Hankyu department store (1st-8th floors) and a branch of Tokyu Hands (1st-5th floors). There are restaurants (see Where to eat) on the 9th and 10th floors as well as T-Joy Hakata, a multiplex cinema. The **roof garden** つばめの杜ひろば (Tsubame no Mori Hiroba), with over 10,000 painted tiles, is an excellent place to get a view of Hakata and the surrounding area. There is a railway shrine (Tetsudo-jinja), a miniature Tsubame train and track, as well as a garden area with some vegetables growing, let alone a selection of restaurants. If that does not provide enough options the **Food Market**, in the basement, is full of cheap places to eat – from Western-style family restaurants to fast food and okonomiyaki – as well as convenience stores. *(Cont'd on p438)*

*(Cont'd on p438)*

KYUSHU

To
Saitozaki

● International
Ferry Terminal

Hakata Port
Ferry Terminal ●

● Bayside
Place Hakata

Fukuoka
Kokusai
Center

Naka-gawa

★ trailblazer

Fukuoka Asian
Art Museum
(Hakata Riverain)

Fish
market

NAGAHAMA

To Yatai stalls

Nakasu
Kowabata

Central
Post Office

Showa-dori

Ichiran
(Nakasu)

Meiji-dori

Yatai
stalls

Tenjin

Nanotsu-dori

Tenjin
Core

TENJIN

Nishitetsu-Fukuoka
(Tenjin) Station

IMS building

Terrassa,
Sushi Isogai

Akasaka

Meiji-dori

Tenjin Bus
Center

To Fukuoka City Art Museum
(Ohori Park), Fukuoka Tower
& Fukuoka City Museum

DAIMYO

Daimaru
Department
Store

# Fukuoka / Hakata

福岡 / 博多

Nishitetsu
Tenjin-Omuta
line

To Futsukaichi
& Dazaifu

## ❏ Fukuoka – a shopping paradise for some

Fukuoka is Kyushu's shopping capital and **Tenjin** 天神, accessible by subway from Hakata Station, marks its centre. If there was ever an entire department store dedicated to teenage girls, **Tenjin Core** 天神コア (🖳 www.tenjincore.com; daily 10am-8pm) fits the bill although its alternative style in some sections is more typical of Tokyo's Harajuku district.

Wander just a little way west from here to reach trendy **Daimyo** 大名, a chic enclave of local stores and designer-label shops where you'd be lucky to find anyone aged over 30. Its narrow streets are filled with an eclectic mix of shops selling everything from snowboards to fashion haircuts.

Set away from all this is **Canal City** (see p440), a city within a city of shops, restaurants, food courts, thrill rides and multiplex cinema. Another option is **Bayside Place Hakata** (see p435). However, you don't even have to leave Hakata station to find a shopping paradise: **Hankyu** and **Tokyu Hands** department stores (see Station guide) sell virtually everything.

Non Japanese also benefit from the tax-free status and the fact that tax is now refunded immediately.

*(Cont'd from p435)* **Nishitetsu Fukuoka (Tenjin)** is the terminal station for the private Nishitetsu Line; it is in Tenjin, the main shopping district. The rail tracks are on the 2nd floor, Nishitetsu's bus terminal is on the 3rd floor, and Tenjin subway station in the basement – along with a massive shopping arcade.

**Tourist information** The **tourist information centre** (🖳 yokanavi.com/eg; daily 8am-9pm) is on the Hakata City station concourse (street level). You can pick up a map to the city from the leaflet section by the side of the information centre as well as other guides in English to attractions in the city and a restaurant guide. However, note that this only includes a few of the many restaurants and eating places in the city.

**Fukuoka Tenjin Tourist Information Centre** (daily 10am-6.40pm), on the 1st/ground floor at Nishitetsu Fukuoka (Tenjin) station, can provide information about accommodation and also a leaflet about Daizafu and Kyushu National Museum.

**Getting around** If you are planning to go to Kyushu National Museum and/or Dazaifu it is worth getting a **Fukuoka Tourist City Pass**: the particularly useful feature of the Fukuoka City and Dazaifu option (¥1340) is that it permits unlimited travel for a day on Nishitetsu trains and buses as well as the Fukuoka City subway, JR trains and Showa buses. The Fukuoka City option (¥820) is valid only for travel in the city centre and does not include use of Nishitetsu trains. Ask for a leaflet at the tourist information centres; only people with a non-Japanese passport are eligible for these passes.

If you only expect to travel around in the central area the cheapest way is using **Nishitetsu's Loop bus** (¥100 per journey); this runs frequently between Hakata Station and Tenjin station via Canal City.

Nishitetsu (🖳 www.nishitetsu.jp) also offers a **Green Pass** (¥700 one-day pass), or a **Green Pass Dazaifu** (¥1500) for unlimited travel on its extensive services in the defined zones but you are restricted to

using its services and it is less good value. An English guide to the loop-bus system is available from the tourist-information desk at Hakata station.

Local buses depart from inside **Hakata Bus Terminal** 博多交通ターミナル (🖳 www.f-kc.jp; also known as Fukuoka Bus Center/Fukuoka Kotsu Center); it is on the right-hand side as you leave Hakata Station's Hakata Exit. City buses depart from street level and highway buses from the 3rd floor of the bus terminal.

There are three **subway** lines (all operate daily 5.30am-12.30am); the most useful is probably the Kuko Line which connects the airport with Hakata, Tenjin and Ohorikoen. Fares range from ¥200 to ¥350 depending on the zones in which you travel. A one-day pass (¥600) gives unlimited travel and discounts on some attractions.

**Fukuoka Airport** 福岡空港 (Fukuoka Kuko; 🖳 www.fuk-ab.co.jp) has three domestic terminals and an international terminal. It's only two stops on the Kuko subway line (¥260) to Hakata station. Free shuttle buses link the domestic and international terminals.

**Festivals and events** The biggest annual event is **Hakata Gion Yamakasa** (1st-15th July), the climax of which is a float race through the city; seven teams carry their respective floats a distance of 5km.

The biggest sporting event is the **Kyushu Grand Sumo Basho**, the last tournament of the annual sumo calendar (see p61). It takes place in November at Fukuoka Kokusai Center.

**Where to stay** Fukuoka has some world-class hotels at prices that would be impossible to find in Tokyo, as well as some cheap but clean business hotels.

*Hakata Green Hotel Annex* 博多グリーンホテル アネックス (☎ 092-451 4112, 🖳 www.hakata-green.co.jp/annex; from ¥7200/S, ¥11,200/D or Tw, inc breakfast) is outside the Chikushi Exit of Hakata station. It's a low-key but smart place with a coin laundry and a Family Mart convenience store next door. There are two more branches nearby if this one is full.

Also near Hakata station, and of a similar standard, are branches of other popular chains: **Hotel Route Inn Hakata Ekimae** ホテルルートイン博多駅南 (☎ 092-477 8885, 🖥 www.route-inn.co.jp; from ¥7800/S, ¥10,350/D, ¥14,500/Tw); **Toyoko Inn Hakata-guchi Ekimae** 東横イン 博多口駅前 (☎ 092-451 1045, 🖥 www.toyoko-inn.com; from ¥5616/S, ¥7560/D, ¥9180/Tw inc breakfast) and **Comfort Hotel Hakata** コンフォートホテル博多 (☎ 092-431 1211, 🖥 www.comfortinn.com; from ¥8900/S, ¥12,400/Tw, inc continental breakfast).

*Hotel Active! Hakata* ホテルアクティブ！博多 (☎ 092-452 0001, 🖥 www.hotel-active.com/hakata; from ¥6800/S, ¥9800/D, ¥12,500/Tw, inc buffet breakfast) has compact modern rooms with a designer feel – great if you like variations on black – plus two single-sex spas. There are also coffee dispensers, drink vending machines and a coin laundry. To get there from Hakata station walk down the road with the brick-coloured building on the left. Turn second left (a 7-Eleven store is on the corner) and then first right. The hotel is a little way down on the left.

JR Kyushu rail-pass holders get discounted rates at *JR Kyushu Hotel Blossom Fukuoka* JR九州ホテルブラッサム福岡 (☎ 092-413 8787, 🖥 www.jrk-hotels.co.jp; from ¥13,000/S, ¥19,500/D, ¥21,600/Tw). It is more luxurious than a standard business hotel, with larger-than-average rooms and a general feeling of spaciousness. It's only a 3-minute walk from the Chikushi Exit of the station.

Top of the range is *Grand Hyatt Fukuoka* グランドハイヤット福岡 (☎ 092-282 1234, 🖥 fukuoka.grand.hyatt.com; from ¥15,200/S, ¥21,200/D), in Canal City; it's *the* place to stay in Fukuoka. Large bathrooms feature a bath you can definitely sink into – with a small TV screen you can watch while soaking in the tub – and a separate shower. Hotel facilities include a gymnasium, swimming pool and saunas. Ask about special offers or promotional packages. Also in Canal City is a more economical alternative, *Canal City Fukuoka Washington Hotel* キャナルシ

ティ福岡ワシントンホテル (🖥 fukuoka.washington-hotels.jp; from ¥8200/S, ¥12,000/D, ¥14,000/Tw inc breakfast), with wi-fi, automated check-out machines and a coin laundry. However, many of the rooms are small.

See p73 for details of **Japan Experience**'s rental apartments/houses in Fukuoka.

For general details about accommodation options see pp67-73.

**Where to eat and drink** Hakata is particularly associated with **yatai** 屋台 (street stalls) and also with ramen made with a pork bone broth called tonkotsu 豚骨. Yatai can generally be found in the Tenjin area in front of the department stores, by the river in Nakasu, and in Nagahama near the fish market. The stalls are usually set up around 6pm but may not really get going till 7pm or later. However, don't expect to see any, or many, if the weather is bad. Most serve ramen, gyoza and tempura and it is not considered polite to share dishes.

The popular **Ichiran chain** 一蘭 (🖥 www.ichiran.co.jp) has combined both yatai and restaurant on the 1st/ground floor of its headquarter building in Nakasu 中洲 (daily 10am-midnight), on Meiji-dori, right by Nakagawa (Naka river). The yatai is inside, so it is more 'yatai-style' than real yatai, but it is a good alternative if there aren't any real yatai. The menu includes their trademark dish, tonkotsu ramen 豚骨ラーメン (¥490). Whatever ramen you order you'll be given a sheet to fill out (ask for the English version), specifying exactly how firm you want your noodles to be, whether the broth should be weak or strong tasting, how rich it should be, how much garlic you want, how spicy the sauce should be and whether you want additional pork or vegetables – and also if you want Ichiran's original spicy red sauce! If you finish your noodles and want more you can ask for a refill 替え玉 (*kaedama*). A side dish that many people have with, or before, their ramen is gyoza 餃子 (¥790 for 8). This branch is near Nakasu-Kawabata station on the subway, or Higashi Nakasu bus stop on the No 12 bus route from Hakata station.

KYUSHU

Restaurants on the 9th and 10th floors of **AMU Plaza** アミュプラザ in the station serve all kinds of cuisine: Japanese, Korean, Chinese, Indian, Mexican and Italian. The branch of *Ippudo* 一風堂 (🖳 www.ippudo.com; 11am-10pm), on the 10th floor, has tasty ramen for ¥700-900. For Italian food try *37 Pasta* 37パスタ (9th floor; daily 11am-11pm); beer fans should go to *A&K Beer & Food Station* A&K ビア&フード ステーション (10th floor; daily 10am-11pm), for its wide range of beers. The lifts/elevators up to the restaurants are in the central area to the left of JR Hakata City building.

**Deitos** デイトス by the Chikushi Exit has a Gourmet Street (B1F ie first floor of the basement; daily 11am-11pm) with a range of Japanese and Western dishes, a Japanese-style pub street (1F; 11am-11pm) and a noodle street (2F; 11am-9pm). *Tonkatsu Hamakatsu* とんかつ浜勝; B1F), in Gourmet Street, is a great place to try tonkatsu; it has menus and explanations in English and, like most tonkatsu places, they will refill your miso soup and give you extra rice and cabbage free of charge.

**Canal City** キャナルシティ (🖳 www.canalcity.co.jp) has a good selection of restaurants on its basement level, including the popular *Dipper Dan* ディッパーダン crêperie-cum-gelateria (daily 10am-11pm), whose blueberry cheesecake crêpes and Hokkaido chocolate ice-cream are much sought after. On the 5th floor there is a *Ramen Stadium* ラーメンスタジアム (11am-11pm) with several ramen restaurants from around the country; a bowl of ramen costs from ¥700.

At **Daimaru** department store 大丸デパート in Tenjin there's take-out food on the 2nd floor of the basement (B2F); there is also a selection of restaurants on the 5th and 6th floors in the East Building.

In the **IMS Building** イムズビル (Inter Media Station) in Tenjin try the smart but relaxed Spanish restaurant *Terrassa* テラッサ (11am-11.30pm, lunch 11.30am-2.30pm) on the 12th floor, which does excellent sherry-braised chicken and fine desserts. On the 13th floor *Sushi Isogai* すし磯貝 (11am-3pm & 5pm-midnight) offers a range of twin-roll plates (¥200-580) and many sushi specialities plus great views across the city.

### Side trip by rail to Dazaifu

Once the political heart of Kyushu and the town where the god of learning and literature is enshrined, Dazaifu 大宰府 is an easy day trip from Fukuoka but can equally well be visited en route to Nagasaki, Kumamoto or Kagoshima.

Dazaifu's key draw is its **Tenmangu Shrine** 天満宮, which dates from 1591 and was built in memory of Michizane Sugawara who was known as the 'god of learning' and who died on the site in 903AD. A popular sight is the photogenic red Taiko bridge arcing over Shinji pond. The shrine is a 5-minute walk from the station; pick up a map from the tourist information centre (daily 9am-5pm) by the station – alternatively follow the crowds down the paved street to the right from the station!

Afterwards, follow the escalators and pulsing light tunnel to reach the striking **Kyushu National Museum** 九州国立博物館 (Kyushu Kokuritsu Hakubutsukan; 🖳 www.kyuhaku.com; Tue-Sun 9.30am-5pm; ¥420, under 18s free; pick up a free audio guide on the 4th floor), built in the shape of a blue wave. The museum aims to provide a 'new perspective on Japanese culture, in the context of Asian history'. The permanent exhibition is on the 4th floor; the exhibits are varied and well displayed with plenty of labels in English. The room showing how the images of Buddhas vary throughout the world and at different times historically is fascinating. Special exhibitions (additional cost) are on the 3rd floor. On the 1st/ground floor there is an area where children can learn about Asian culture and also a souvenir shop.

After you leave the museum, turn left and walk down the slope and steps (rather than back through the tunnel and escalator) to **Komyozen-ji** 光明善寺 (daily 8am-4.30pm; ¥200), where you can enjoy the tranquility of the temple's Zen gardens. The overhanging trees that shade the upright stones, the mossy perimeters and raked gravel all make for spectacular viewing, especially in the autumn.

There are several options for getting to Daizafu. If you have a JR rail pass and don't want to buy a Fukuoka Tourist City Pass take a JR train (LEX, rapid or local) from Hakata to **Futsukaichi** 二日市 (track 7; frequent service; 10-28 mins). From here it's four/ten minutes by bus/on foot to the private Nishitetsu Futsukaichi station for the short journey to Dazaifu (2-5/hr; ¥150; 5 mins; JR rail passes not accepted). Without a JR pass this route would cost ¥430 if you take a local or rapid train. However, assuming you have the version of the Fukuoka City Tourist Pass (see p438) that includes Dazaifu, the easiest way to get to Dazaifu is to take the subway from JR Hakata to Tenjin (Kuko Line) and then a Nishitetsu Tenjin–Omuta Line train from Nishitetsu Fukuoka (Tenjin) station to Nishitetsu Futsukaichi where you transfer to Platform 1 for the train to Daizafu. Without a city pass this route would cost ¥600.

Dazaifu station has a **tourist information counter** on the right after the barriers, as well as large luggage lockers.

## NAGASAKI 長崎

*'I cannot think of a more beautiful place. There is a land-locked harbour; at the entrance are islands … the ship winds up the harbour which is more like a very broad river, with hills on either side levelling down towards the extreme end where the town of Nagasaki stands.'*
So wrote Elizabeth Alt, wife of William Alt, a 19th-century English merchant who lived and traded in Nagasaki. Nagasaki's history as a centre of international trade and its long period of contact with the West are still the reasons why tourists pour into the city, but it was the dropping of the second atomic bomb here on 9th August 1945 that ensured

Nagasaki would become known throughout the world. More people were killed in this one blast than in all the bombing raids on Britain throughout WWII. Like Hiroshima, Nagasaki is now home to a Peace Park and Atomic Bomb Museum, both of which record huge numbers of visitors every year.

### What to see and do

For sightseeing purposes it's useful to consider Nagasaki as a city of two halves. North of the station, in the Urakami district, is the Atomic Bomb Museum and Peace Park. Around the station and to the south of it is everything else – from the fascinating

KYUSHU

---

❏ **Japan's first railway?**
Though most history books conclude that the first official railway line in Japan was built between Shimbashi and Yokohama (see pp88-9), the estate of the 19th-century Scottish expat Thomas Glover (see box p445) begs to differ. In a corner of Glover's House a sign reveals that in 1865 the Scotsman purchased the 'Iron Duke', claimed to be Japan's first steam locomotive, and laid a 400m-long track in Nagasaki. He used Japanese coal to power the engine and opened the line to an astonished public. It was not until 1872, seven years after the opening of this mini railway, that the Shimbashi–Yokohama Line opened for business.

Museum of History and Culture and the Museum of the 26 Martyrs to Dejima, the island enclave which was the only point of contact with the outside world during Japan's period of national seclusion (1641-1859) and on the hills overlooking the harbour, is Glover Garden, with some 19th-century Western-style homes. One day would be just enough to visit both parts but it's preferable to allow a couple of days.

See p419 for details of the side trip to **Huis Ten Bosch**: from Nagasaki take a JR Seaside Liner (1/hr; 85 mins; ¥1470, JR rail passes valid) to JR Huis Ten Bosch station. Additional local services (116 mins) also operate on the JR Omura Line.

**Urakami district** The atomic bomb dropped on Nagasaki at 11.02am on 9th August 1945 was meant for the city of Kokura (see p414). Poor visibility meant the plane carrying the bomb circled three times over Kokura before changing course for Nagasaki, where cloud also hampered visibility. A chance break in the clouds just after 11am sealed the city's destiny. It's estimated that over 73,000 (of a 240,000 population) were killed either instantly or in the period up to the end of 1945 and nearly 75,000 injured. The bomb was intended for Nagasaki Shipyard but exploded instead over Urakami 浦上天, a centre of Christian missionary work in Nagasaki since the latter half of the 16th century. As the bomb was dropped, a service was underway at Urakami Cathedral; all that's left today is a melted rosary (now on display in the A-Bomb Museum) and one piece of the cathedral wall, in the nearby Hypocenter Park. Today, Urakami is home to the Peace Park and Atomic Bomb Museum.

**Nagasaki Atomic Bomb Museum** 長崎原爆資料館 (Nagasaki Genbaku Shiryokan; 🖳 nagasakipeace.jp; daily 8.30am-5pm, to 6pm in summer; ¥200; audio guide ¥145) is a high priority, though the constant stream of school groups can be wearing. As you pass into the first hall, the scene immediately transforms to the precise moment that the bomb was dropped – a clock ticks and black-and-white images of the devastation appear on screens. Among

the most memorable exhibits are: the glass bottles melted together from the heat of the blast; the burnt-out remains of a school-girl's lunchbox; and the photo of a mother and her baby who were at Urakami Railroad Station at the time of the impact. Nearby is the moving **Nagasaki National Peace Memorial Hall for the Atomic Bomb Victims** 国立長崎原爆死没者追悼平和祈念館 (daily May-Aug 8.30am-6.30pm, Sep-Mar to 5.30pm; free). In addition to the striking memorial you can read testimonies, in English, from survivors. Directly down the hill from the museum, and next to the main street, is the **Atomic Bomb Hypocenter** 原爆落下中心地, marking the exact spot over which the A-bomb exploded.

The nearby **Peace Park** 平和公園 is filled with statues and memorials given to the city as a gesture of peace from all over the world; many are from former Eastern bloc countries. The centrepiece is a giant **Peace Statue** 平和祈念像 – a man with his right hand pointing to the threat of the atomic bomb, his extended left hand symbolising peace and his eyes closed, as in prayer, to remember the souls of the dead. The statue was erected 10 years after the bombing and is now the backdrop for the annual peace ceremony held on 9th August. Throughout the year, visiting school parties hold their own peace ceremonies in front of the statue.

The nearest tram stop for the Atomic Bomb Museum is Hamaguchi-machi (on tram No 1 or 3). From there cross Urakami-dori and walk uphill along St Paul St. For the Peace Park and Hypocenter the nearest tram stop is Matsuyama-machi. However, it is easy to walk between these sights.

**Nagasaki station area** Nagasaki's importance as a historical centre for Christianity in Japan is most apparent at Oura Catholic Church (see p445) below Glover Garden and at the **Memorial to the Martyrdom of the 26 Saints of Japan** 日本十六聖人殉教地 in Nishizaka-machi, honouring the four Spanish missionaries, one Mexican, one Indian and 20 Japanese Christians who were crucified here in 1597.

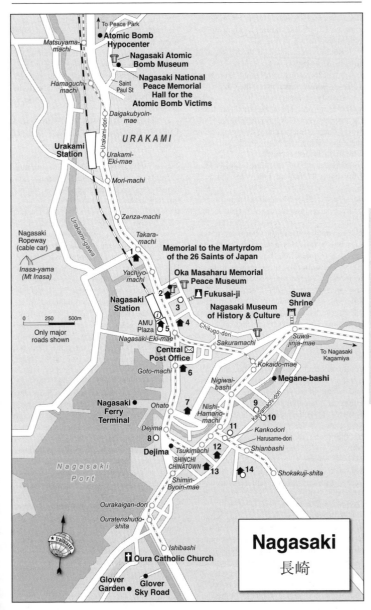

To Peace Park

● Atomic Bomb Hypocenter

Matsuyama-machi

☗ Nagasaki Atomic Bomb Museum

Nagasaki National Peace Memorial Hall for the Atomic Bomb Victims

Hamaguchi-machi

Saint Paul St

Daigakubyoin-mae

URAKAMI

Urakami Station

Urakami-Eki-mae

Mori-machi

Zenza-machi

Nagasaki Ropeway (cable car)

Inasa-yama (Mt Inasa)

Takara-machi

1

Memorial to the Martyrdom of the 26 Saints of Japan

Yachiyo-machi

Oka Masaharu Memorial Peace Museum

2 ☗   🏯 Fukusai-ji

Nagasaki Station

3

Nagasaki Museum of History & Culture

Suwa Shrine

0   250   500m
Only major roads shown

AMU Plaza

5

4

Chikugo-dori

☗

Suwa-jinja-mae

Nagasaki-Eki-mae

Sakuramachi

To Nagasaki Kagamiya

Central Post Office ✉

6

Kokaido-mae

Goto-machi

Nigiwai-bashi

● Megane-bashi

● Nagasaki Ferry Terminal

Ohato

7

Nishi-Hamano-machi

9

Kanyamachi-dori

Dejima

8 ○

10

11

Kankodori

Dejima

Tsukimachi

12

Harusame-dori

SHINCHI CHINATOWN

Shianbashi

13

14

Shokakuji-shita

Shimin-Byoin-mae

Ourakaigan-dori

Ouratenshudo-shita

★ trailblazer

Ishibashi

✝ Oura Catholic Church

Glover Garden ●   ● Glover Sky Road

KYUSHU

Nagasaki Port

**Nagasaki**
長崎

It's a very simple memorial, a few minutes' walk east from the station, heading up the road to Nishizaka 西坂公園.

Behind the memorial is the **Museum of the 26 Martyrs** 日本二 十六聖人記念館 (🖥 www.26martyrs.com; daily 9am-5pm; ¥500), which explains the path of Christianity in Japan from Francis Xavier to the Meiji era. The museum is small but its displays contain unique religious artworks such as the painting of *Our Lady of the Snows* depicting Mary, mother of Jesus Christ, on Japanese paper.

Very much off the tourist trail is **Oka Masaharu Memorial Peace Museum** 岡まさはる記念長崎平和資料館 (Tue-Sun 9am-5pm; ¥250), which focuses on Japan's actions before and during WWII in Korea, China & South-east Asia. It's not an easy place to visit, some of the photos are shocking, but it provides a very different perspective to that offered at the 'official' A-Bomb Museum. The museum was founded in memory of the late Protestant minister and peace activist Oka Masaharu (1918-94), who devoted much of his life to relief efforts for Korean atomic bomb survivors in Japan. The signs are in Japanese and Korean but you will be given a leaflet with some English and there's a detailed ¥300 booklet in English outlining the history and controversies; the photos that line the walls tell their own story. It receives few visitors and is not included in any of the tourist guides or brochures produced by the city. It is also a little hard to find, though if you look carefully for the kanji there are signs on the roads by the Martyrs Memorial/ Museum: follow these and you'll find it just past the memorial on the right side of the road as it bends left at the top. The museum is in an ordinary-looking white building but with the kanji on the front above the entrance and below a wide window.

**Fukusai-ji** 福済寺 is a striking temple because it consists of a 60ft/18m-high Kannon (goddess of mercy) statue standing on top of a turtle. The temple was founded by Kakukai, a Chinese Buddhist monk, in 1628. The original was destroyed by the A-bomb in 1945 but the temple was rebuilt and it is the largest Chinese temple in Nagasaki. Inside the Kannon statue is a Foucault pendulum which is suspended over the remains of thousands of the Chinese people who died as a result of the atomic bomb. The bell outside tolls at 11.02 as a reminder of the terrible event in 1945. Fukusai-ji is near the station though the walk to it, like many things in Nagasaki, is all uphill.

**Nagasaki Museum of History and Culture** 長崎歴史文化博物館 (Nagasaki Rekishi Bunka Hakubutsukan, 🖥 www .nmhc.jp; daily 8.30am-7pm, closed 3rd Tue of the month; ¥600) is fascinating. Exhibits focus on Nagasaki's history, particularly topics concerning its links, largely through trade, with its neighbouring countries and also Asia, but also the influence the Chinese living in Nagasaki had on the city. The collection is very well laid out and has English labelling in some places though you will be given a comprehensive leaflet. However, if you are offered a guided tour by a museum volunteer do accept. The closest tram stop to the museum is Sakura-machi; follow the signs from there.

**Suwa shrine** 諏訪神社 (Suwa-jinja; daily all day) is a 5-minute walk uphill from Suwa Jinja-mae tram stop. You will see the steps when you get off the tram; there are 193 from the first o-torii gate. Suwa shrine dates from 1624 and is particularly known for its Kunchi Festival (see p446). However, it is also of interest because of the many, amusing, lion-dog statues here; their job is to protect the god of the shrine. The drum in the drum tower is sounded twice a day as a purification ritual.

**Megane-bashi** 眼鏡橋, otherwise known as 'spectacles' bridge', is one of many characterful bridges along Nakashima-gawa.

## South of Nagasaki station Glover Garden グラバー園 (🖥 www.glover-gar den.jp; daily 8am-6pm, till 9.30pm in holiday periods; ¥610), an area of late 19th-century Western-style houses, with accompanying gardens, built on a hill overlooking Nagasaki harbour, is usually swamped with visitors so it is worth getting there early. The harbour views from the hillside repay

the ticket cost, even if some of the houses are not overly exciting for Western visitors.

Thomas Glover's house is the oldest-surviving wooden Western house in Japan and it was constructed by Hidenoshin Koyama, who also built Oura Catholic Church. All the houses here are furnished and there are plenty of labels in English. Before leaving you pass through **Nagasaki Traditional Performing Arts museum** which has exhibits from the various festivals held in the city; dynamic footage of October's Kunchi Festival, held at Suwa shrine (see opposite) is also shown.

To reach Glover Garden, take tram No 1 (bound for Shokakuji-shita) from Nagasaki station and change at Tsukimachi to tram No 5. There are two entrances to Glover Garden: if you get off the tram at Ouratenshudoshita you will go to Glover Garden Gate No 1; however, if you stay on the tram to Ishibashi, the next stop and also the terminus, you can then reach Glover Garden Gate No 2 entrance by taking the **Glover Sky Road** グラバース カイ ロード, a 'slope lift' (elevator; free) which travels diagonally up five floors – an unusual experience.

If you use Glover Garden No 1 entrance look out for **Oura Catholic Church** 大浦天主堂 (Oura Tenshudo; daily 8am-6pm; ¥300), built by French missionaries in 1864 and one of the oldest wooden churches in Japan; it is dedicated to the 26 Martyrs (see p442).

From 1641 to 1859 the then island of **Dejima** 出島, just off Nagasaki, was Japan's sole point of contact with the outside world as the base for trade with the Dutch East India Company. A reconstruction of the Dutch enclave (daily 8am-6pm; ¥510) opened in 2000 to mark the 400th anniversary of relations between Japan and the Netherlands and continues to expand. It currently includes replicas of over 25 buildings, 10 of which have been restored to their early 19th-century appearance using notes and records from the time as well as items discovered during excavation of the area. However, this being the 21st century, earthquake proofing has also been installed. The restored buildings, including the Chief Factor's Residence, are now open and include an excellent museum recounting the story of the Dutch traders who were forced to live in isolation on the island. The plan is eventually to recreate Dejima's traditional fan-shape, surrounded by water on all sides. Take tram No 1 three stops south from Nagasaki station to Dejima; the stop is right outside the reconstructed complex. Cross over and walk towards the sea for Dejima Wharf (see Where to eat).

The Chinese have also been here since the 17th century and at times have formed the biggest foreign community in Nagasaki.

---

❏ **Thomas Glover – the 'Scottish Samurai'**

Best known of all the 19th-century residents of Nagasaki was the man whom the garden is named after, Thomas Glover. Born in Scotland in 1838, Glover moved to Nagasaki in 1859, married a Japanese woman and involved himself in a number of key Japanese businesses, including helping to set up the Japan Brewery Company in July 1885, predecessor to today's Kirin Brewery. Look out for the *kirin*, a mythical creature that sports a bushy moustache remarkably similar to Thomas Glover's, on cans and bottles of Kirin beer.

Thomas Glover is also credited with bringing the railway to Japan (see box p441), but his role selling armaments to the samurai, which helped them overthrow the Tokugawa shogunate, is what let him to acquire the nickname 'Scottish Samurai'. His Japanese wife is also believed to be the inspiration for Puccini's opera, *Madam Butterfly*.

An account of Thomas Glover's incredible life can be found in Alexander McKay's *Scottish Samurai* (Edinburgh, Canongate Press, 1997).

Despite this, and even though there are many Chinese temples around the city, **Shinchi Chinatown** 新地中華街 covers a surprisingly small area.

A good end – or beginning – to a tour of Nagasaki would be to take **Nagasaki Ropeway** 長崎ロープウェイ (🖵 www.nagasaki-ropeway.jp; daily Mar-Nov 9am-10pm, Dec-Feb to 9pm; 5 mins; 3-4/hr; ¥720 one-way, ¥1230 return) up Mt Inasa 稲佐山 (Inasa-yama) to enjoy a panoramic view of the city. The best time to go is at night when the city is lit up. Look back over the dark hills for a strange and slightly eerie contrast to the bright lights that dazzle below. Take Nagasaki Bus No 3 or 4 from Nagasaki station and get off at Ropeway-mae, or take tram No 1 or 3 two stops north from the station to Takara-machi. From here, follow the main road underneath the railway line and over Urakami-gawa. Cross the river, turn right and follow the road round until you see a shrine entrance on your left. Walk through the entrance gate and turn left to find the entrance to the ropeway.

## Practical information
**Station guide** Nagasaki station incorporates a tourist information centre (see below), hotel (see Where to stay), AMU Plaza department store (see Where to eat) and a plaza under a giant canopy. There is only one exit (Central Exit) and it's on the same level as the platforms. For **lockers** turn left after the ticket barrier, skirt around the JR Kyushu travel agency and follow the station building round.

**Tourist information** Nagasaki City Tourist Information Center (TIC; 🖵 www.at-nagasaki.jp; daily 8am-8pm) is in the waiting room to your right as you exit the ticket barrier. Pick up a map to the city which includes details about the tram network, a tram pass if you plan to use the tram network, and the *Discover Nagasaki Visitor Guide*. Another useful source of information is 🖵 visit-nagasaki.com.

**Getting around** Nagasaki is known for its *chin chin densha* チンチン電車, old-fashioned **trams/streetcars**, that have been

trundling around the city since 1915, and which are by far the best means of getting around. They are operated by **Nagasaki Electric Tramway** 長崎電気軌 (Nagasaki Denki Kido; ☎ www.naga-den.com), known as **Nagaden**, and there are four lines which are colour coded. Services operate every 5-10 minutes (6.30am-11pm). One-day tram passes (¥500) are available from the TIC and some hotels but not on board the trams themselves. Individual rides cost a flat ¥120 (ensure you have the correct change – if you don't, use the machine at the front of the tram to get change). If you don't have a pass and want to change tram-line at Tsuki-machi ask for a transfer ticket ('*norikae onegaishimasu*').

**Festivals** The main event in Nagasaki is the annual **peace memorial ceremony** on 9th August. However, there are several other festivals here, in particular **Kunchi Festival** which has been held on 7th-9th October since 1634 and is based around Suwa Shrine (see p444), and **Nagasaki Lantern Festival** which is held over 14 days during Chinese New Year so the dates vary each year.

**Where to stay** Several of the chain hotels in Nagasaki have more than one branch so if the one listed here is full look at the relevant website for details of other branches.

*JR Kyushu Hotel Nagasaki* JR九州ホテル長崎 (☎ 095-832 8000, 🖵 www.jrk-hotels.co.jp/en/Nagasaki; from ¥10,800/S, ¥19,500/Tw, inc breakfast) is the most convenient place to stay as it is built into the station complex. Reception is on the 2nd floor and there is a direct link on the 5th floor to the restaurants in AMU Plaza. The rooms are well equipped and the de luxe rooms are spacious. At the time of research the let down here was the breakfast which is eaten in the Royal Host Restaurant, opposite the entrance to the hotel.

*Best Western Premier Hotel Nagasaki* ベストウェスタンプレミアホテル長崎 (☎ 095-821 1111, 🖵 www.bestwestern.co.jp/nagasaki; ¥15,000/S, ¥26,000/Tw) is a top-end hotel with a choice of restaurants, great panoramic views from the bar, and its own hot-spring facilities. The rooms are spacious, particularly those on the executive floor. There is also a ladies-only floor.

There are three cheaper business hotels near the station. The closest are *APA Hotel Nagasaki-ekimae* アパホテル長崎駅前 (☎ 095-820-1111, 🖳 www.apahotel.com; from ¥7000/S, ¥10,000/D, ¥13,000/Tw inc breakfast) and *Hotel Cuore Nagasaki Ekimae* ホテルクオーレ長崎駅前 (☎ 095-818 9000, 🖳 www.hotel-cuore.com; from ¥6400/S, ¥7800/D, ¥9800/Tw), situated across the street from the station, which offers the usual line in clean, no-frills rooms. Solo women travellers can also choose a ladies-only floor.

A bit further away, by the Goto-machi tram/streetcar stop, is the ever-reliable chain hotel, *Toyoko Inn Nagasaki Ekimae* 東横イン長崎駅前 (☎ 095-825 1045, 🖳 www.toyoko-inn.com; from ¥6048/S, ¥9288/Tw or D, inc breakfast).

*Hotel Dormy Inn Nagasaki* ドーミーイン長崎 (☎ 095-820-5489, 🖳 www.hotespa.net/hotels/nagasaki; from ¥6790/S, ¥8290/D, inc breakfast) is a 2-minute walk from the Tsukimachi tram stop and conveniently located for Chinatown and Glover Garden. The hotel boasts stylishly furnished modern rooms, an excellent onsen and free yonaki soba in the evening.

The nearby *Hotel JAL City Nagasaki* ホテルJAL シティ長崎 (☎ 095-825-2580, 🖳 www.nagasaki.jalcity.co.jp; from ¥8500 /S, ¥13,000/Tw) is a more upmarket business option with a good range of facilities and excellent location.

*Comfort Hotel Nagasaki* コンフォートホテル長崎 (☎ 095-827 1111, 🖳 www.choice-hotels.jp/nagasaki; ¥5500/S, ¥8000/D, ¥10,500/Tw, inc simple breakfast) is good value and well located for Chinatown and Dejima.

The modern *Richmond Hotel Nagasaki Shianbashi* リッチモンドホテル長崎思案橋 (☎ 095-832-2525, 🖳 nagasaki.richmondhotel.jp; ¥8300/S, ¥11,900/D, ¥16,800/Tw) is a short trot along a side street from the Shianbashi tram stop and offers stylish, high-quality rooms. Downstairs is a decent adjoining Italian restaurant (see Where to eat).

*Nagasaki Kagamiya* 長崎かがみや (☎ 095-895-8250, 🖳 www.n-kagamiya .com; ¥2300pp in mixed 4-bed dorm, ¥4000/S, ¥5600/D; annex Japanese-style rooms 4-7 sharing ¥2800pp; rates inc a simple breakfast) is a delightful family-run hostel that offers an authentic Japanese experience at budget prices. It is located a 5-minute walk from Hotarujaya tram stop (Tram line No 3 from Nagasaki station; 12 mins).

This small inn and its kimono-clad young owners know the importance of a warm welcome and even offer the chance to rent a kimono for the day (from ¥5000; 11am-7pm). They speak English and the inn does not operate a curfew. A basic map is available at the TIC but the website has clearer photos for navigation.

For details about accommodation in general see pp67-73.

**Where to eat and drink** Nagasaki is known for *champon* ちゃんぽん and *saraudon* 皿うどん; both are noodle dishes served with lots of meat, seafood and vegetables but the former has a soup and the latter a sauce. A good place to try these in the station area is *Matsunaga* まつなが (daily 5pm to midnight) where both dishes cost ¥880; also on the menu is whale くじら (*kujira*) served in a variety of styles (from ¥680). To reach Matsunaga cross the road from the station (use the overground pedestrian walkway); it is at the far end (on the right-hand side) of the street with lanterns. The menu has an English translation.

In the station itself the obvious place to head is the 5th-floor Gourmet World in **AMU Plaza** アミュプラザ department store. Here you'll find a good range of restaurants (generally open daily 11am-10pm): amongst the various ones serving Japanese food here is *Sushi Katsu* すし活, a kaiten sushi-ya. Other options are a soba restaurant うまや; *Milan* ミラン Indian curry house; and a branch of the Italian chain *Capricciosa* カプリチーザ. A *Trandor* bakery is on the station concourse.

Another good area for places to eat is **Harusame-dori** 春雨通り, particularly between Kanko-dori and Shianbashi tram stops. For the best wood-fired oven-cooked pizza, go to **Pizzeria Margherita** ピッザレ ーアマーグレータ (daily 11am-10pm, lunch 11am-4pm; pizzas from ¥980); it is on the left side if walking from Kanko-dori tram stop to Shianbashi and is on the 2nd floor but is well signed. Nearby is a branch of **CoCo Curry House** (11am to midnight) with various curry rice options from ¥700. Also **Shougun Sushi Bar** with sushi from ¥100 and **Men-do Maruyoshi** (11am-3am) serving ramen (from ¥600).

Popular with Nagasaki residents and visitors alike, **Hamakatsu** 浜勝 (daily 11am-10.30pm) is the place to eat tonkatsu. Seating is at tables or along the counter; alternatively, a take-out box of tonkatsu sandwiches costs ¥850. The *orandakatsu* set (¥990) of breaded pork and Gouda cheese symbolises the city's international influences. It's a 5-minute walk along **Kajiyamachi-dori** 鍛冶市通り, the road to the left at the back end of Shianbashi tram station if coming from Kanko-dori. Look for a white building, beige wooden sign and lantern hanging outside. Just opposite is **Tarafuku-Asa** 多ら福亜紗 (daily 5-11pm) whose dark wooden interiors and sunken tables offer an atmospheric setting to sample the daily menu. Try the hoke grilled fish (¥480) or eel (¥740) washed down with a satisfying warm Kiku-Masamune sake (¥370). This is a good-value restaurant even if not geared for English speakers.

On the other side of Harusame-dori and adjoining Richmond Hotel is **Yako Hai** 夜光杯 (daily 5-11pm), where a broad range of Italian dishes (around ¥1000) is served to customers at stylish banquettes.

A lovely place for a meal, or to watch the sunset over a drink after a hard day of sightseeing, is at one of the harbourside bars, cafés and restaurants at **Dejima Wharf** 出島ワーフ. A delicious *salmon donburi* サーモン丼 (rice bowl) from **Dejima Asaichi** 出島朝市 costs ¥1130 and a *jige donburi* 地げ丼, containing a range of local seafood, costs ¥1720. Alternatively have a *tempura teishoku* 天婦羅定食 (¥1350).

The other food for which Nagasaki is known is **castella** カステラ, a delicious sponge cake introduced to Japan by the Portuguese in the 16th century. You are bound to find some in cake shops and supermarkets.

---

## KUMAMOTO 熊本

Halfway down the west side of Kyushu, Kumamoto once flourished as a castle town; today the (reconstructed) castle still rates as the city's biggest tourist draw.

In April 2016 the area around Kumamoto and east towards Mt Aso suffered a series of powerful earthquakes; the first ever to hit Kyushu on such a scale and also the first magnitude 7 quake since the Great East Japan earthquake in 2011. Fortunately the number of fatalities was minimal but the damage caused to buildings including the castle was considerable.

### What to see and do

There are several places of interest in Kumamoto but rail fans will also want to fit in time for some of the side trips on the D&S (sightseeing) trains which operate from here (see pp454-5).

To get an overview of the history of Kumamoto and the castle, start with a visit to **Sakuranobaba Josaien** 桜の馬場城彩苑 (⌨ www.sakuranobaba-johsaien.jp; daily Mar-Nov 8.30am-6.30pm, Dec-Feb to 5.30pm; ¥300, ¥600 with castle entry), a 'historical culture experience facility'. Most signs are in Japanese but look out on the floor for circles where you can stand for an explanation in English, German, Korean and Chinese. Children in particular may also like the chance to sit in a sedan, ride a model horse and try on kimonos.

**Wakuwaku Za Story Palace**, on the 2nd floor, is a theatre where episodes from Kumamoto's history are acted out in Japanese, but an English translation is available. Also in the complex are shops and restaurants selling local food and drinks (see p454).

To get to Sakuranobaba Josaien either take the tram to Hanabata-cho or Kumamoto-jo Shiyakusho-mae, or the Castle Loop bus to stop No 8 or 16.

A shuttle bus (6-8/hr; 3 mins) goes from Sakuranobaba Josaien up to Hohoatego-mon, the main gate to the castle; alternatively it is a short, uphill walk. (Note: due to the extensive earthquake damage the castle was closed when this book went to the printer; check with the TIC before visiting.) Kumamoto Castle 熊本城 (daily Mar-Nov 8.30am-6pm, Nov-Mar to 5pm; ¥500, or ¥640 inc entry to the Former Residence of Hosokawa-Gyobu) was completed between 1601 and 1607, but most of its fortifications were destroyed during the Seinan Civil War of 1877. The main castle tower was reconstructed in the 1960s to look as similar as possible to the original fortification. The castle is still an impressive sight, especially when lit up at night (until 11pm), but the number of buildings now is nothing compared to what there were originally. Unusually the castle is entered through a 'Passage of Darkness' (Kuragari-Tsuro) with stone walls on either side and straddled by Honmaru Goten Palace, the residential part of the castle. Once inside you can visit the donjon (main castle tower) where there are displays on the history of the castle and the region and take in the view from the top. The reconstructed living areas in Honmaru Goten Palace are the real highlight of any visit to the castle; the rooms are on a large scale and the screens (partitions) have been painstakingly recreated based on ancient documents; the mass of gold-leaf used makes them almost dazzling to look at.

If you go to the castle from the station take the Castle Loop bus; it stops at Ninomaru Parking Area (stop No 9) close to the main entrance.

A short walk from the castle buildings (or stop No 11 on the Castle Loop bus), but still within the vast grounds, is the Former Residence of Hosokawa Gyobu (Kyu-Hosokawa-Gyobutei, 旧細川刑部邸; daily Mar-Nov 8.30am-6pm, Nov-Mar to 5pm; ¥300, or ¥640 with castle entry); a samurai residence painstakingly reconstructed during the mid 1990s. It's an elegant building and is worth the entrance fee to walk (or squeak) your way along the wooden corridors and around the maze of tatami rooms and imagine what it must have been like to live like a samurai, though there are few artefacts to see.

Kumamoto's other hotspot, Suizen-ji Jojuen 水前寺公園 (daily Mar-Nov 7.30am-6pm, Dec-Feb 8.30am-5pm; ¥400) was originally a teahouse garden for the Hosokawa family; it was created in the 17th century. The site was chosen because beautifully clear spring water flows into the pond here and this was of course good for making tea. Sadly for some reason the water dried up after the 2016 earthquake, but hopefully it will be flowing again by the time you visit. Apart from the pond the main point of interest is a grass mound in the shape of Mt Fuji. If you go in the afternoon you are more likely to be able to enjoy it all in peace as the flag-waving tour guides with their groups will probably have gone.

Also in the grounds are Izumi Shrine 出水神社, built in 1878 and a popular venue for New Year celebrations, and a Noh theatre; firelit performances are staged here during the summer festival, 11th-13th August. Take the tram to Suizenji-koen-mae; walk back to the first road to the right and then turn right when you see the torii gate and a street lined with shops. The closest entrance to the park is at the end of this road. Alternatively, rail-pass holders can save a few yen on the tram fare by taking a local train on the JR Hohi Line from Kumamoto to Shin-Suizenji (10 mins), from where it's a short walk (follow the tram line) to the garden.

The trendiest art space in town is Kumamoto Contemporary Art Museum 熊本市現代美術館 (🖳 www.camk.or.jp; Wed-Mon 10am-8pm; free except for special exhibitions). The museum provides exhibition space for local artists but they also have works from foreign artists. The entrance is on the 3rd floor – take the escalator up from street level – and the museum is in the same building as Hotel Nikko Kumamoto (Toricho-suji tram stop).

(Cont'd on p452)

KYUSHU

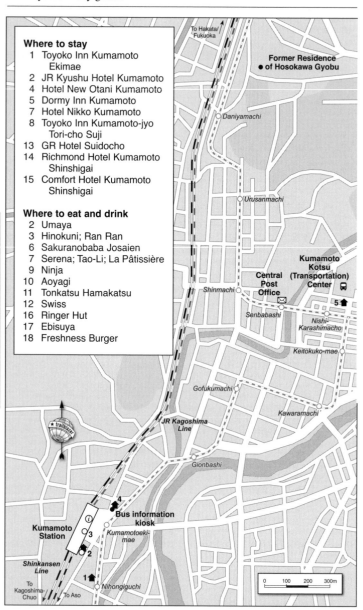

**Where to stay**
1  Toyoko Inn Kumamoto Ekimae
2  JR Kyushu Hotel Kumamoto
4  Hotel New Otani Kumamoto
5  Dormy Inn Kumamoto
7  Hotel Nikko Kumamoto
8  Toyoko Inn Kumamoto-jyo Tori-cho Suji
13  GR Hotel Suidocho
14  Richmond Hotel Kumamoto Shinshigai
15  Comfort Hotel Kumamoto Shinshigai

**Where to eat and drink**
2  Umaya
3  Hinokuni; Ran Ran
6  Sakuranobaba Josaien
7  Serena; Tao-Li; La Pâtissière
9  Ninja
10  Aoyagi
11  Tonkatsu Hamakatsu
12  Swiss
16  Ringer Hut
17  Ebisuya
18  Freshness Burger

To Hakata/Fukuoka

Former Residence of Hosokawa Gyobu

Daniyamachi

Urusanmachi

Kumamoto Kotsu (Transportation) Center

Central Post Office

Shinmachi

Senbabashi

Nishi-Karashimacho

Keitokuko-mae

Gofukumachi

Kawaramachi

JR Kagoshima Line

trailblazer

Gionbashi

4
Bus information kiosk

Kumamoto Station

3
Kumamotoeki-mae

2

Shinkansen Line

To Kagoshima-Chuo

To Aso

1
Nihongiguchi

0  100  200  300m

KYUSHU

# Kumamoto

熊本

Kumamoto Castle

Sakuranobaba Josaien

6

Shiyakusho-mae

Tsuboigawa

Torichosuji

Kamitori

Kamitori

Kumamoto Contemporary Art Museum

7

8

Daiei dept store

9

Suido-cho

10

11

12

Former residence of Lafcadio Hearn

Kumamotojo-mae

Shimotori Arcade

13

Ginza-dori

Denpokyoku-mae

17  16  15

Sun Road  Shinshigai

14

Karashima-cho

18

Shira-kawa

Kotsukyoku-mae

Highway 3

To Suizen-ji Jojuen garden & Izumi Shrine

KYUSHU

## ❏ Basashi – an acquired taste

*That evening I learned that raw horsemeat was a speciality of the area… I went to a little restaurant near Kumamoto station with my mind made up to try some. It was disappointingly stringy, and having come straight out of the refrigerator, was hard with bits of ice. I sat for a long time sipping beer, waiting for the horsemeat to thaw, while the only customer in the restaurant had a conversation with the owner.*
**Alan Booth**, *The Roads to Sata*, Kodansha International, 1985

Kumamoto's big culinary draw doesn't sound the most appetising of regional specialities; the main problem with *basashi* 馬刺し (raw horsemeat), however, is not so much the taste but that most places offering it are prohibitively expensive. You could easily spend around ¥10,000pp dining at a restaurant specialising in the stuff.

If you decide to try some it's best to go to a butcher who will probably prepare it so it is ready to eat. That way you'll get to try Kumamoto's speciality at a fraction of the prices charged in basashi restaurants.

*(Cont'd from p449)* Behind Tsuruya department store in the city centre (stop No 11, Toricho-suji, on the Castle Loop bus) is the **former residence of Lafcadio Hearn** 小泉八雲熊本旧居 (Koizumi Yakumo Kumamoto Kyukyo; Tue-Sun 9.30am-4.30pm; ¥200). Hearn is better known as a one-time resident of Matsue (see p312), from where he moved to Kumamoto in 1891. He lived in a house owned by a local samurai family, now in the middle of the downtown shopping area. The house is very small but it's still worth going inside; panels in English tell the story of how Hearn, who was born on the Greek island of Lefkas (Levkas), arrived in Yokohama in 1890 at the age of 40 on an assignment for *Harper's* magazine. He spent the rest of his life in Japan, living in Matsue and then spending three years in Kumamoto teaching English. Later he moved to Kobe and in 1896 became a Japanese citizen. Yakumo Koizumi, as Hearn was called after his naturalisation, died suddenly of a heart attack on 26th September 1904.

### Practical information
**Station guide** The shinkansen station (West Gate) is connected to the original station by an underpass. If transferring to the local line take the exit on the left when you reach street level. If heading for Kumamoto go straight ahead.

The sights and hotels are on the Shirakawa (East) Gate side so you will almost definitely need to use the underpass. As well as places to eat (see Where to eat), convenience stores and all the usual station facilities, there is a small bank of **lockers** opposite the tourist information counter on the East Gate side, and more are available at the end of the concourse, close to the convenience store. Also at the station are some **ATMs** which accept foreign-issued debit/credit cards.

**Tourist information** There is a tourist information centre (TIC; 🖳 www.kumamoto-icb.or.jp and 🖳 www.manyou-kumamoto.jp; daily 8am-7pm) on each side of the station. At both staff can give you a list of accommodation and a restaurant guide in

English; they also provide city maps and sell the bus/tram passes.

**Getting around** The **tram/streetcar** 熊本市電 (Kumamoto Shi-den) is the easiest way to get around. There are two lines – Kumamoto Station line (A-Line) and Kamikumamoto line (B-Line) and the stops get you close to most of the attractions. A one-day pass costs ¥400 (¥150 per journey) and can be bought at either of the TICs at the station or on board any tram. However, if you don't plan to go to Suizen-ji, or to travel around in the evening, you may prefer to use the **Kumamoto Castle Loop bus (Shiromegurin)**, which does a loop around town (8.30am-5pm; 2-3/hr; ¥150 flat fare, or ¥400 one-day pass) from Kumamoto station, stopping en route at the castle and other attractions in the city centre. There is a screen at the front of the bus with English information on the castle and other sights.

**Kumamoto Kotsu Center** 熊本交通センター is the main bus station; it is in the centre of town and all buses pass through here. The Kotsu Center is stop No 7 (Platform A Location 6) and 17 (Platform B Location 20) on the Castle Loop bus.

The **bus information kiosk** バス案内所 (daily 7.50am-4pm) to the left outside JR Kumamoto station has bus timetables but in Japanese only.

**Festivals** The biggest annual event is the **Hi-no-Kuni** (Country of Fire) festival, which takes place 11th-13th August and features a fireworks display and late-night folk dancing.

**Aki no Kumamoto Oshiro Matsuri** (Kumamoto Oshiro Autumn Festival), held during the first fortnight of October, includes all sorts of events centred around the castle, including *yabusame* (horseback archery), martial arts, food fiestas, and a Noh performance.

**Where to stay** *JR Kyushu Hotel Kumamoto* JR九州ホテル 熊本 (☎ 096-354 8000, 🖳 www.jrk-hotels.co.jp/en/Kumamoto; from ¥8460/S, ¥16,200/Tw, inc breakfast; rail-pass holders get a small discount), immediately on your right as you exit via the Shirakawa (East) Gate side of the station, is undoubtedly the most convenient place to stay. If you like watching trains come and go, ask for a room facing the tracks; the sound-proofing is excellent and the windows allow a superb view of the tracks and indeed station life. The baths are also larger than in many hotels.

On the left side outside the station is *Hotel New Otani Kumamoto* ホテルニューオータニ熊本 (☎ 096-326 1111, 🖳 www.newotani.co.jp; from ¥12,705/S, ¥17,325/D or Tw); it has all the facilities you'd expect of this top-class hotel chain including several restaurants.

Other alternatives include a branch of the Toyoko Inn chain (🖳 www.toyoko-inn.com). *Toyoko Inn Kumamoto Ekimae* 東横イン熊本駅前 (☎ 096-351 1045; from ¥5184/S, ¥6264/D, ¥8424/Tw) is just behind the JR hotel but is best reached by walking on the left side of the taxi rank. Follow the rank round to the right, past the police station and cross the road to the hotel; it's not easy to miss as it's the tallest building in the area. It is worth paying for a panoramic view though sadly none really faces the castle.

*Dormy Inn Kumamoto* ドーミーイン熊本 (☎ 096-311-5489, 🖳 www.hotespa.net/hotels/kumamoto; from ¥7000/S, ¥11,000/D or Tw) is a short walk from Karashima-cho tram stop and is right opposite the Kotsu Center (see opposite). Like all Dormy Inns it has an onsen bath – the one here is on the roof – and serves an excellent breakfast and Yonaki soba (9.30-11pm; free to guests). Recommended.

Two slightly cheaper options are: *GR Hotel Suidocho* ジーアールホテル水道町 (☎ 096-211 2222, 🖳 www.gr-suidocho.com; from ¥6700/S, ¥9500/D inc buffet breakfast), part of the Green Rich Hotel chain, and *Toyoko Inn Kumamoto-jyo Tori-cho Suji* 東横イン熊本城通町筋 (☎ 096-325 1045; from ¥5480/S, ¥7980/Tw), which is in front of Suido-cho tram stop.

Other good business-hotel options include: *Richmond Hotel Kumamoto Shinshigai* リッチモンドホテル熊本新市街 (☎ 096-312 3511, 🖳 www.richmondho

tel.jp/kumamoto; from ¥9400/S, ¥14,900/D or Tw, inc breakfast), in the covered Sun Road Shinshigai Arcade, and *Comfort Hotel Kumamoto Shinshigai* コンフォートホテル熊本新市街 (☎ 096-211 8411, 🖳 www.comfortinn.com; ¥5700/S, ¥10,800/D or Tw, inc breakfast), which offers all-day coffee in the lobby. The hotel is down a fairly narrow lane off the arcade – it is on the left-hand side if walking from Karashima-cho tram stop.

A luxurious option, and considered the best in town, is *Hotel Nikko Kumamoto* ホテル日航熊本 (☎ 096-211 1111, 🖳 www.nikko-kumamoto.co.jp; from ¥13,600/S, ¥20,800/Tw; discount packages often available). It has larger-than-average rooms (some on the 10th floor with a view of Kumamoto Castle); the twin rooms have a separate toilet and bathroom. There's a choice of restaurants and you're ideally placed to visit the Contemporary Art Museum, since it's located on the 3rd and 4th floors of the building.

For further details about facilities in chain hotels and finding accommodation in general, see pp67-73.

**Where to eat and drink** There are dining options on both the shinkansen and the local train sides of the railway station. On the local train side go to the 2nd floor for eat-in restaurants. Amongst these *Hinokuni* 本の素材 (11am-9pm) which serves *basashi* (see box p451); if you would like to try a bit but aren't sure you will like it, have the *kara-age teishoku* (¥1350) as that way there will be other things to eat if you don't like the basashi. Also here is a branch of *Ran Ran* らん蘭 (daily 11am-9pm), where you can eat delicious ramen for about ¥750.

Aside from the usual fast-food joints around the station, a good place to eat in the immediate station vicinity is *Umaya* うまや (daily 7am-10/11pm); it is on your right as you leave the station and is attached to JR Kyushu Hotel Kumamoto. It's a modern take on an *izakaya*, with the option of sitting at the counter and having your food grilled in front of you. Great-value set lunch menus cost from ¥750.

KYUSHU

In the **covered shopping arcades** (Sun Road Shinshigai and Shimotori) in the city centre there's a good selection of cafés, restaurants and fast-food places.

On the left near the Karashima-cho entrance to **Sun Road Shinshigai** (⌨ www.shinshigai.com) is *Ebisuya* えびすや, a simple place which has a happy hour between 7pm and 8pm where beer (Suntory) is ¥300 instead of ¥560. It also serves some delicious yakitori. Also on this side is a branch of *Ringer Hut* リンガーハット 熊本新市街店 (⌨ www.ringerhut .co.jp; daily 11am-4am) which specialises in ramen (from ¥700).

At *Freshness Burger* ハンバーガーカフェフレッシュネス (⌨ www.fresh nessburger.co.jp; daily 9am-10pm), on the other side of the arcade, the burgers (from ¥360) are cooked to order and the freshly squeezed lemonade is very refreshing.

Options in **Shimotori Arcade** (⌨ shi motoori.com) include *Swiss* スイス (10am-midnight, Sat & Sun to 1am), a bakery/café serving simple meals and cake-and-coffee sets; and *Ninja* 忍者 (daily 6pm to late) where all the staff are dressed as ninjas and entertain guests with ninja magic tricks. The food is typical izakaya fare and there's a good selection of drinks. It's next to a McDonald's and is signed in English.

For more of a local flavour try *Aoyagi* 青柳 (⌨ aoyagi.ne.jp; 11.30am-2pm & 5-10pm). The menu, available in English, includes a variety of *basashi* (horse-meat) dishes as well as another local speciality – lotus root filled with mustard 辛子蓮根 (*karashi renkon*) but also sushi, sashimi and tempura. Expect to pay at least ¥2000 for the food but you are unlikely to be disappointed. It is on the right-hand side of Shiromicho St if walking from Shimotori Arcade. Opposite it is a branch of *Tonkatsu Hamakatsu* とんかつ浜勝 (daily 11am-midnight) which, as its name suggests, serves tonkatsu; kare tonkatsu costs ¥990.

If you've a big appetite, it's worth considering the all-you-can-eat buffet lunch at *Serena* セリーナ (11.30am-2.30pm; Mon-Fri ¥2300, Sat & Sun ¥2500), a brasserie-style restaurant on the 2nd floor of Hotel Nikko Kumamoto. On the same floor is an excellent Chinese restaurant, *Tao-Li* 桃李 (11.30am-3.30pm & 5.30-10pm), where the cheapest lunchtime set menu is ¥1400. *La Pâtissière* ラ・パティシエール (daily 10.30am-7.30pm, Sat & Sun to 7pm) bakery on the 1st/ground floor is good for a sweet treat to eat in or take away.

**Sakuranobaba Josaien** 桜の馬場城彩苑 (see p448) also has a variety of options: a meal at *Ginnan Buffet* (daily 11am-2.30pm & 5-10pm; ¥1500/2000 lunch/evening) is the best way to try a range of local dishes but *Asotei Yamamichaya* specialises in *basashi* (see box p451) and *Yumeakari* serves noodles and light meals.

## Side trips by rail from Kumamoto

Kumamoto is the starting point for some enjoyable sightseeing trains, called D&S (Design & Story) by JR Kyushu.

● **SL Hitoyoshi** This SL (Mar-Nov Fri-Sun and national holidays in this period; 1/day; 2½hrs each way; ¥2640 one-way) was restored in 2009 in order to celebrate the 100th anniversary of the JR Hisatsu Line. This line originally connected Kumamoto and Kagoshima; it was built inland, through the Kirishima mountains and along the Kuma river, so that it couldn't be attacked by any foreign navies. There is no longer a direct service between Kumamoto and Kagoshima on the Hisatsu Line but it is still possible to follow the original – very scenic – route. The SL Hitoyoshi goes to Hitoyoshi via Yatsushiro and Shin-Yatsushiro. The three cars have maple and rosewood furnishings and include an observation lounge, a reading area and a buffet counter for snacks – you can even buy a locomotive-shaped cookie (¥360) – and drinks. The train stays at Hitoyoshi for a lunch break but there are also options at stations en route to try local food specialities.

● **Aso Boy! Kuro** [See Stop press box p423] The Aso Boy! Kuro (most Sat & Sun plus daily in holiday periods; 2/day; 80 mins; ¥2380 one-way plus ¥200 for a panorama seat) is a Limited Express service that runs from Kumamoto to Miyaji 宮地 (see Map 31, p429) and consists of four carriages. Cars No 1 and No 4 have the panorama seating – the driver sits in an elevated position so passengers can reserve the seats at the front and see the driver's usual view – and Car No 3 (Kurochan) is the car for families as it has a play area, a small library and a Kuro Café. Be aware that there are a couple of switchbacks on the journey so you have to wait while the driver goes back and forth.

JR rail passes are valid on both services but reserved seats are essential. Since these services are popular it is worth booking early but you still may be able to get a seat if booking the day before.

● **A-train** So called partly because of the famous jazz tune *Take the A-train* but also because it has a bar on it (for adults), this train operates between Kumamoto and Misumi 三角 (mostly at the weekends (about 3/day; 40-45 mins). The bar is in Car 1; there are also some ordinary seats here. Car 2 has some booths, sofa seats and wooden seats facing the window for children.

## KAGOSHIMA 鹿児島

Kagoshima is on the eastern side of the Satsuma Peninsula, facing Kinko Bay, and is the southern terminus of the Kyushu shinkansen. The island of Sakurajima, with its brooding volcano, lies just 4km away. The volcano's proximity means umbrellas are sometimes needed to keep off the dust and ash blown across to the mainland. Don't be surprised to find a thin coating of ash on the streets on some days.

If Sakurajima dominates the skyline, historically it is the Shimazu family who have dominated the political map of Kagoshima. Successive generations of the family ruled the Satsuma domain (province) from 1185 through to the Meiji Restoration in 1871.

As the southern gateway to Japan, Kagoshima was also the place where missionary Francis Xavier landed on 15th August 1549. As his ship approached the city, Xavier is said to have been filled with excitement on seeing what he thought was the cross of Jesus Christ, but which turned out to be the sign of the ruling Shimazu family. Little of Xavier's legacy is left today since the church he built was bombed during the Pacific War (1941-5).

### What to see and do

Apart from visiting Sakurajima (see p461), or going to Ibusuki for a sand-bath (see pp461-2), both of which are highly recommended, Kagoshima's big draw is **Sengan-en** 仙巌園, also known as **Iso-teien** 磯庭園 (🖳 www.senganen.jp/en/senganen; daily 8.30am-5.30pm; ¥1000 inc garden and Shoko Shuseikan Museum). The 50,000-square-metre landscape garden was constructed in 1658 as a residence for Mitsuhisa Shimazu, 19th lord of the ruling Shimazu family. Even though it was designed as a 'borrowed scenery' garden with Sakurajima as a backdrop there aren't many places where you can get a good view of the garden with Sakurajima, though it is easy to see Sakurajima itself. The main highlight of the garden is the bamboo grove though cat fans may prefer to visit the shrine dedicated to cats, especially as there aren't many such shrines in Japan. Unless it is a lovely sunny day, or you are really keen to have some exercise, it is not worth walking all the way up the Nature Trail to the observation point. The City View tourist bus from Kagoshima-chuo station stops outside the main entrance; it's stop No 9 on the Shiroyama/Iso route, or stop No 6 on the Waterfront route.

After visiting the garden take a quick look at the adjacent **Tsurugane shrine** 鶴嶺神社, dedicated to the members of the Shimazu family who reigned over Kagoshima for many years. One of the deities enshrined here is Princess Kameju. Born in 1571, she was the third daughter of the 16th Shimazu Lord; Kameju became known as the guardian of female beauty. Legend has it that a woman who prays at the shrine will become even more beautiful.

Tickets for Sengan-en are also valid for **Shoko Shuseikan Museum** 尚古集成館 (🖳 www.shuseikan.jp; daily 8.30am-5.30pm), across from the entrance to the garden on the site of the former factory used by the Shimazu family to manufacture iron and glassware; it is the oldest Western-style factory in Japan. Inside, the history of the Shimazu family is told in great detail (with plenty of labels in English).

In central Kagoshima the main attraction in the **Museum of the Meiji Restoration** 維新ふるさと館 (🖳 www.ishinfurusatokan.info; daily 9am-5pm; ¥300) is a waxwork show, during which a model of Takamori Saigo (see box p458) rises from the floor/grave and the story of his life is retold in dramatic fashion. The soundtrack is in Japanese only but the headphones you are given with the 'voice guide map' (audio guide) can be plugged into a socket below your seat. There is much else of interest here including learning about the Goju education system and also that Nariakira Shimazu, a member of the Shimazu clan, designed the Hi no Maru, the Japanese national flag. Take the City View bus from Kagoshima-chuo station; the museum is the first stop on both the Shiroyama/Iso and the Waterfront routes.

The best place for views of Kagoshima and Sakurajima is the observation point (daily; free) on **Mt Shiroyama** 城山, in Shiroyama-koen 城山公園. From the bus stop walk up to the observation area. The colour of the volcano on Sakurajima is supposed to change seven times a day so if it burns bright red and orange for too long it's at least reassuring to know you're on high ground (107m above sea level): Shiroyama itself consists almost entirely of volcanic deposit. It is also known as the place where Takamori Saigo died (see p458). Take the City View bus from Kagoshima-chuo station to stop No 7 on the Shiroyama/Iso route.

**Kagoshima City Aquarium** 鹿児島市水族館 (🖳 www.ioworld.jp; daily 9.30am-6pm; ¥1500), next to Sakurajima Ferry Terminal, is in the building with a roof that looks like a rough copy of the Sydney Opera House. Most of the attractions are geared to children, but the range of fish in the main tank and the dolphins (fed three times a day) are why most people visit. Take the City View bus from Kagoshima-chuo station to stop No 13 (Kagoshimasuizokukan-mae) on either the Waterfront or the Shiroyama/Iso routes. Close by is **Dolphin Port** ドルフィンポート (🖳 www.dolphinport.jp), where you'll find waterfront restaurants and shops on two levels, a large foot-bath (*ashi no yu*) and views out to Sakurajima. This is a good place to chill out, have a meal (see Where to eat) and enjoy the views. Take the City View bus from Kagoshima-chuo station to stop No 15 on the Shiroyama/Iso route, or stop No 14 on the Waterfront route.

For a good view of Kagoshima from the station area head for the 6th floor of **AMU Plaza** department store, where you'll find the entrance to **Amuran** アミュラン (daily 10am-10.45pm; ¥500pp, ¥1200 for whole gondola ie up to four people; tickets from the machine by the entrance), a bright red ferris wheel 観覧車. A rotation takes about 15 minutes; should you wish to see in every direction wait for one of the two gondolas that are completely transparent. Also on the 6th floor is a 10-screen multiplex cinema and games arcade.

---

❏ **A rather taxing journey**
In the 17th/18th centuries feudal lords had to go to Edo (Tokyo) every two years to pay their taxes. The Shimazu family had the furthest to go since they had to travel from Kagoshima; the journey took them 40-60 days which is an amazing contrast to the 6 hours 20 minutes it would now take on a Nozomi/Mizuho shinkansen service.

## Practical information

**Station guide** The southern terminus for the shinkansen from Fukuoka/Hakata is **Kagoshima-chuo**. It is also a stop on the JR Kagoshima main line and the JR Ibusuki-Makurazaki Line. **Lockers** (all sizes) are easy to find on the main concourse. There is also the usual selection of food outlets (see Where to eat) and tourist information (see below). There are two exits: the Nishi-da (West) Exit and the Sakurajimaguchi (East) Exit; the latter is the main one. **Kagoshima station** is the southern terminus of both the JR Kagoshima and the JR Nippo main lines but since most services go to Kagoshima-chuo you are unlikely to need to go there.

**Tourist information** The **tourist information counter** (TIC; 🖳 www.kagoshima-kankou.com; daily 8am-8pm) is on the main station concourse. Staff can provide maps of Kagoshima and Sakurajima, as well as a *Gourmet Guide* showing restaurants and cafés. They can also assist with accommodation reservations, arrange tickets for Sakurajima sightseeing tours (see p461) and sell one-day travel passes (see below).

**Getting around** Kagoshima's **tram/streetcar** network is the best way of getting around. The flat fare is ¥170 but a **one-day pass** (¥600) allows you to board all city tram and bus services as well as the retro **City View tourist bus** (flat fare ¥190), which does two different circuits: the Shiroyama and Iso route (9am-5.20pm; 2/hr), and the Waterfront route (8.40am-4.40pm; 7/day). Both routes start and end at bus stops No 8 & 9 outside the station. Pick up a route map from the tourist information counter. Alternatively get a **Welcome Cute pass** (1-/2-day; ¥1000/1500); this includes the above as well as travel on both the Sakurajima ferry and Island View Tour bus (see p461).

**Kagoshima Airport** (🖳 www.koj-ab .co.jp; mostly domestic flights) is served by buses (2-6/hr; 40 mins; ¥1250) from stop No 4 outside Kagoshima-chuo station.

**Festivals** Two major festivals are the **Natsu Matsuri** (Summer Festival) at the end of July and **Ohara Matsuri** in early November. Fireworks are a feature of the Natsu Matsuri and the main event at the Ohara Matsuri is a dancing parade which starts from the centre of the city and heads towards the Sakurajima pier.

**Where to stay** *JR Kyushu Hotel Kagoshima* JR九州ホテル鹿児島 (☎ 099-213 8000, 🖳 www.jrk-hotels.co.jp/Kagoshima; from ¥10,800/S, ¥19,500/Tw or D, buffet breakfast ¥1000) is the closest hotel you can get to the train platforms. It can be reached along the slope to the right of Seattle Coffee/Gourmet Yokocho off the main concourse. Alternatively, turn left after going through the ticket barrier and follow the sign as you head towards the Nishida (West) Exit. The rooms are compact but clean and comfortable.

There are several branches of the Toyoko Inn chain (🖳 www.toyoko-inn .com). For *Toyoko Inn Chuo-eki Nishiguchi* 東横イン鹿児島中央駅西口 (☎ 099-814 1045; from ¥5184/ S, ¥6264/D, ¥7884/Tw) follow signs for the Nishida (West) Exit, the hotel is on the right just beyond JR Kyushu Hotel Kagoshima. If this is full, consider the *Chuo-Eki Higashiguchi* 東横イン中央駅東口 branch (same rates), a 4-minute walk to the right from the East Exit. Two branches in central Kagoshima are: *Toyoko Inn Kagoshima Tenmonkan No 2* 東横イン鹿児島天文館2 (☎ 099-224 1045; from ¥4860/S, ¥6480/D, ¥8316/Tw, inc breakfast), which is between the Takamibaba and Tenmonkan-dori tram stops, and *Toyoko Inn Kagoshima Tenmonkan No 1* 東横イン鹿児島天文館1 (☎ 099-219 1045; from ¥4644/S, ¥6264/D, inc breakfast), a minute's walk south from Takamibaba stop.

*Hotel Urbic Kagoshima* ホテルアービック鹿児島 (☎ 099-214 3588, 🖳 www .urbic.jp; from ¥7500/S, ¥10,500/Tw, inc breakfast) is a decent business-hotel choice located in front of you as you take Kagoshima-chuo station's Nishida Exit.

*Chisun Inn Kagoshima* チサンイン鹿児島 (☎ 099-227-5611 🖳 www.solarehotels.com; from ¥7800/S, inc buffet breakfast) is well located. *(Cont'd on p460)*

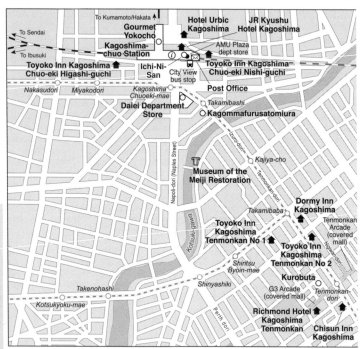

## ❏ Takamori Saigo

It's impossible to walk very far around Kagoshima without seeing statues and monuments dedicated to the many people who have played a part in the city's, and in Japan's, history; of these the name Takamori Saigo is probably what you will see most. Points of reference such as the 'Birthplace of Saigo', 'House where Saigo was resuscitated', 'Cave where Takamori Saigo hid' and 'Place where Takamori Saigo died' can all be seen. Laid out around town is the chronicle of one man's life, his journey from humble birth to a glorious if tragic death.

Takamori Saigo (1827-77) was born into a lower-class samurai family in the province of Satsuma (now Kagoshima), the eldest of seven children. In 1868 he became one of the leading figures in the battle to defeat the shogunate and restore power to the Meiji Emperor. It wasn't long before Saigo's loyalties were stretched between support for the new power base and his unerring allegiance to the large numbers of samurai in Satsuma who were being deprived of their status by Imperial edict.

His change of heart reached a dramatic climax in 1877 when Saigo gathered a 15,000 strong army and announced his intention to march on Tokyo. He never even managed to leave Kagoshima as he died on Mt Shiroyama at 7am on 24th September 1877 after a defiant last stand against the government he had helped to found.

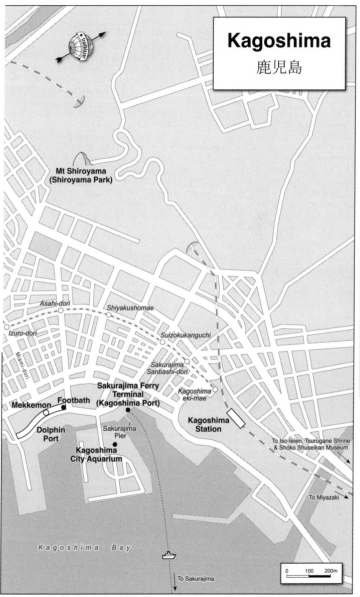

# Kagoshima

鹿児島

Mt Shiroyama
(Shiroyama Park)

Asahi-dori

Shiyakushomae

Izuro-dori

Suizokukanguchi

Miami-dori

Sakurajima
Sanbashi-dori

Sakurajima Ferry
Terminal
(Kagoshima Port)

Kagoshima
eki-mae

Mekkemon    Footbath

Sakurajima
Pier

Kagoshima
Station

Dolphin
Port

To Iso-teien, Tsurugane Shrine
& Shoko Shuseikan Museum

Kagoshima
City Aquarium

To Miyazaki

Kagoshima   Bay

0    100    200m

To Sakurajima

KYUSHU

*(Cont'd from p457)* It is a minute's walk from Tenmonkan-dori tram stop. Like most hotels the rooms aren't particularly big but they are clean and the location is great.

*Dormy Inn Kagoshima* ドーミーイン鹿児島 (☎ 099-216 5489, 🖳 www.hotespa .net/hotels; from ¥7000/S, ¥10,000/D or Tw), part of the ever-reliable chain which offers brilliant value: an onsen/rotemburo on the roof, excellent buffet breakfast; free yonaki soba in the evening; and free laundry (though not drying).

*Richmond Hotel Kagoshima Tenmonkan* リッチモンドホテル鹿児島天文館 (☎ 099-239 0055, 🖳 tenmon kan.richmondhotel.jp; from ¥7700/S, ¥11,000/D, inc breakfast) is an upmarket business hotel in the Tenmonkan shopping district. The hotel's staff wear sleek black uniforms; the single rooms have large double beds, and there is room service (6-11pm) from the hotel restaurant.

For further details about finding accommodation in general see pp67-73.

**Where to eat and drink** The main specialities of Kagoshima are **kurobuta** 黒豚 (black pork) – the pigs are a (now rare) breed from Berkshire, England, and they are fed on a sweet-potato diet – and **satsuma-age** 薩摩揚げ (deep-fried fishcake), also known as *tsuke-age*, which is good as a snack. The very useful *Gourmet Guide* map (see p457) will show you where you can eat kurobuta and the many other kinds of restaurants in Kagoshima.

Possibly the most convenient if you are in the station is *Ooyama* 大山 in **Gourmet Yokocho** グルメ横町 (restaurants open daily at least 10am-11pm), next to the entrance to JR Kyushu Hotel Kagoshima on the station concourse. The menu includes tonkatsu and shabu-shabu made with both black and white pork; a very tasty sirloin kurobuta tonkatsu set is ¥1250. The staff don't speak much English but are helpful and may try to show you how to eat the various dishes the 'Japanese way'. Also in Gourmet Yokocho you'll find a revolving sushi bar (*Mawaru*), a pasta & pizza place (*Trattoria Budonoki*), a coffee and cake shop (*Seattle*) and a ramen place (*Zabon*).

There are lots of restaurants on the 5th floor (most open daily 11am-11pm) of **AMU Plaza** アミュプラザ, department store next to the station complex. Take the Sakurajima (East) Exit; you can't miss the building since it's the only one with a large red ferris wheel protruding from the roof. One of the most popular places here is *Ichi-Ni-San* いちにいさん, which serves a range of Japanese dishes from shabu-shabu to tonkatsu (from ¥750).

**Kagommafurusatoyataimura** かごっまふるさと屋台村 (Kagomma Hometown Gourmet Village; 🖳 www.kago shima-gourmet.jp) is an atmospheric place with 25 stalls, each selling a range of local specialities and seating no more than about eight people. Some stalls open at lunch (approx 11.30am-2pm) but all are open in the evening by 6pm and stay open till midnight or later. If you are feeling brave you can try *tori-sashi* (chicken sashimi) at *Oyasai Okoku* (stall No 5). There is a leaflet in English listing all the stalls and what they serve.

Within the covered malls – **Tenmonkan G3 (Sen-nichi) arcade** 天文館G3アーケード and **Tenmonkan Hon-dori arcade** 天文館本通りアーケード – that lead off from Tenmonkan-dori tram stop are a variety of restaurants with everything from fast-food (Western and Japanese) to places such as *Kurobuta* 黒福多 (Tue-Sun 11.30am-2.30pm & 5.30-10pm), on the first road to the right of G3 arcade. The menu includes delicious kurobuta tonkatsu かごしま黒豚 (from ¥1500) including some in a black *panko* (breadcrumb) covering (from ¥1600).

*Mekkemon* めっけもん, on the 1st/ground floor at Dolphin Port (see p456), is a popular sushi restaurant with a lively atmosphere and excellent food for the price (¥100-500 per dish). You may have to wait a short time for a seat but the staff are very welcoming and this places comes highly recommended.

For **self-catering** try **Daei** department store ダイエーデパート opposite the station, or the basement of AMU Plaza, which also has a food court.

## Side trips from Kagoshima
**By ferry to Sakurajima** Smoke, dust and ashes billowing out from Sakurajima 桜島 are a common-enough sight in Kagoshima but the last major eruption was in 1946. The worst eruption of the 20th century was in 1914, when three million tonnes of lava buried eight villages and turned the island into a peninsula, completely filling a 400m-wide and 70m-deep sea. The worst eruption in recent memory – but tiny in comparison to 1914 – was in 2013, when ash from Sakurajima rose over 5000 metres (approx 16,400ft) in the sky; at the time of research the most recent dramatic eruption was on 5th February 2016, but fortunately there were no injuries then, or in 2013.

The **ferries** (daily 1-6/hr; 15 mins; 24 hours a day; ¥160, bicycle ¥270) to Sakurajima take cars, bicycles and foot passengers and depart from the Ferry Terminal フェリーターミナル near Kagoshima Aquarium – follow the signs to whichever boat will go next. You pay on arrival at Sakurajima and must have the correct change; if you need it there is a change machine by the ticket collector.

The **Sakurajima Island View Tour Bus** (daily 9am-4.35pm; 8/day; 60 mins round trip; ¥120-440 per journey, or ¥500/one-day pass) departs from Sakurajima port and stops at the main sights on the western side of the island, including the Visitor Centre and several lookout points. At the latter the bus stops for 5-15 minutes so it is possible to have a quick look and then get back on the same bus rather than waiting for another. Tickets are available on the bus or at TICs in the area.

**Yunohira Observatory** 湯之平展望所 (at 373m) is the best place for views of the mountain and the surrounding area. If you don't fancy sitting on a bus you can walk up here following the road; expect it to take about an hour.

Before leaving the Ferry Terminal on the Sakurajima side, go to **Sakurajima Information Center** (daily 8.30am-5pm) for a map and cycle rental (¥300/hour). However, the better source of information is **Sakurajima Visitor Center** 桜島ビジターセンター (🖳 www.sakurajima.gr.jp/svc; daily 9am-5pm). Turn right out of the Ferry Terminal and follow the road round the coast for about 10 minutes. The Visitor Center has a model of Sakurajima, an explanation of the ecosystem, displays of volcanic rock and footage of previous eruptions. There are labels in English and the film (11 mins) is subtitled in English.

In the park outside there is a 100m-long *ashi-yu* (**foot-bath**; daily 9am to sunset; free) – walk out of the door opposite the one you came in by and head towards the sea but slightly to the left. Towels are not provided but it shouldn't take long for your feet to dry after a soak. It is certainly a relaxing experience and will set you up for the walk back. Alternatively (for ¥500) you can dig your own foot-bath on the beach; ask for details at the Visitor Center.

Whilst on Sakurajima look out for *komikan* 小みかん, these are small but sweet tangerine oranges; the climate and volcanic ash mean these grow well here. They are both fresh and dried and also used to flavour ice-cream, sweets and cakes. Look out for them in souvenir shops on the island.

**By rail to Ibusuki** A day trip to Ibusuki 指宿 (🖳 www.city.ibusuki.lg.jp) combining a journey on the **Ibusuki-no-Tamatebako** train (also known as Ibutama; LEX 3/day; 51 mins; ¥2130 inc seat; free with a Japan Rail or JR Kyushu rail pass but seat reservation essential; local trains generally 1-2/hr,

66-75 mins) with the chance to have a **sand-bath** (like a sauna but covered in sand), in Japan's only naturally hot sand, is highly recommended.

Both the train's name, which means Ibusuki Treasure Box, and its paint-work – the side that faces the sea is painted white and the land side black – are inspired by a folk tale. In this tale, a character called **Taro Urashima** opens a treasure box, whereupon white mist curls out of the box and his own hair turns from black to white; as you enter the train white mist duly comes out above the doors.

The train has two cars: in both there is a variety of seats – some are swivel seats facing the window, some are like mini sofas and arm chairs; the rest are traditional. There is also an area where children can play as well as books to read. Souvenir photographs (both on the platform and on the train) are free.

Once the train has left the Kagoshima suburbs the scenery improves; if the weather is good, Sakurajima is visible most of the time. The **tourist information centre** (daily 9am-6pm) in the station has a map of the area and information about accommodation if you decide to stay in this onsen town, though it can seem a bit of a ghost town out of the tourist season.

A sand-bath at **Sunamushi Kaikan 'Saraku'** 砂むし会館砂楽 (🖳 saraku.sakura.ne.jp; daily 8.30am-8.30pm; ¥920, towel rental ¥200) is a truly wonderful experience, and has the added benefit that it is meant to improve circulation and relieve conditions such as arthritis, asthma, rheumatism, 'alimentary disorder' and 'sensitivity to cold'. However, if you're pregnant or have high blood pressure you shouldn't have one. From the station either take a **bus** (1-2/hr; ¥140) from the stop on the left along the road straight ahead from the station, or walk (15-20 mins).

The entrance to Saraku is on the 2nd floor (take the escalator). At the ticket office you will be given a yukata; you can rent a towel if you don't have one. Having changed into your yukata, follow the signs to the sand-bath on the beach. You will be allocated a space and staff will cover you with the hot black sand. You are recommended to stay for only 10 minutes, after which you get up (not an entirely easy process) and shake yourself down before heading back in for a shower followed by a bath in the onsen. If it is a sunny day and the tide is out you may be able to have a sand-bath outside – on the beach – but usually they are inside. The top floor of the building has massage chairs, a restaurant and an observatory.

If you are already missing the onsen effect by the time you get back to Ibusuki station, join the locals at the foot-bath in front of the station.

Finally, a great place for a meal is ***Kurobuta Kyodo Cuisine Aoba*** 黒豚と郷土料理 青葉 (11am-2.30pm & 5-10pm); in fact it has been recommended by two different readers. There is a menu in English: highlights are 'plenty of hearty dishes, some fantastic vegetable sides such as chargrilled broad beans that are a must and the local black pork was tasty'. If you don't have the chargrilled broad beans try the broad-bean ice-cream. Go left along the main road outside the station and Aoba is very soon on the left.

If the Ibutama is fully booked, or the return journey time isn't convenient, local trains (1-2/hr; about 75 mins; ¥1000) provide an additional option for getting between Kagoshima-chuo and Ibusuki.

# SHIKOKU

## Shikoku – route guides

Shikoku ('Four Provinces') takes its name from the provinces into which the island was once divided. The old provinces of Sanuki, Tosa, Iyo and Awa are known today as the prefectures of Kagawa, Kochi, Ehime and Tokushima, though you'll still come across the original names.

Predominantly rural, Shikoku has everything that the current image of Japan does not: wide open spaces, forests, country villages and a dramatic natural landscape. However, the island is not just a provincial backwater. There's plenty to see and it's worth devoting at least a week to completing the loop route described below, which passes through all four prefectures. Though a number of road bridges link Shikoku with Honshu, the only entry/exit point by rail is across the Inland Sea via the Seto-Ohashi Bridge (see p464).

This route starts in Okayama, taking the Marine Liner train across the bridge to **Takamatsu** where you can savour a trip to Ritsurin-koen, one of the largest gardens in Japan, or have a day trip to **Naoshima**, an island known for its open-air art and art museums. From Takamatsu either continue east to **Tokushima**, home to the famous Awa-odori summer dance festival and then return to the main route at Awa-Ikeda, or head west to **Kotohira**, home to an interesting shrine, Kompira-san, and then south to Kochi. **Kochi** is known for its manga museum as well as for its Yosakoi summer dance festival. The route continues in a clockwise direction to **Uwajima**, with its bullfights and fertility shrine, then on to **Matsuyama**, the largest city on the island and the access point for a visit to **Dogo-onsen**, Japan's oldest spa town. The last part of the journey covers the route from Matsuyama back towards Okayama on Honshu.

See p36 for details of the passes available in Shikoku and see p47 for itinerary ideas. It's worth noting that though plenty can be accomplished on a rail tour of Shikoku, the more isolated parts of the island can be reached only by bus (often infrequent), or by hiring a car.

On most weekends between April and September (except in June, because of the rainy season) open-air carriages トロッコ (*torokko*) are attached to some of

冬星の旅青鷺は番なり

*Winter stars –*
*just two grey herons*
*as I journey by*
(MINAKO KANEKO)

---

❏ **Shikoku 88 temple pilgrimage**

Pilgrims who embark on the circuit of Shikoku's 88 temples 四国八十八箇所 (Shikoku Hachijuhakkasho) are following in the steps of Kobo Daishi, the Buddhist saint who was born in Zentsuji (see p468) and first walked around the island. However, he now lies in eternal meditation at Koya-san on Honshu, home to the Shingon sect of Buddhism founded by him in the 9th century. Most *henro* (pilgrims) visit Koya-san (see pp156-8) either before or after completing the Shikoku pilgrimage. It's not necessary to follow precisely in Kobo Daishi's steps by walking between the temples. There are no rules to prevent modern-day pilgrims using public or private transport. Indeed, many of the pilgrims you see in the temples today, dressed in traditional white and carrying sticks to help them along the way, have a minibus waiting in the car park ready to whisk them off to their next destination.

The pilgrimage does not have to be completed in one visit, so many make return trips to Shikoku over a number of years. Some, however, such as the Buddhist monks who walk the circuit for spiritual cleansing, do it the hard way.

A few of the temples are mentioned in this guide but for more information see ⌨ www.88shikokuhenro.jp (Japanese only) or ⌨ www.shikokuhenrotrail.com.

---

the most scenic rail lines in Shikoku. Shiman Torokko, one of the most popular torokko services, runs every year between Tokawa and Ekawasaki (see p474). Apart from this the routes change annually to take in a variety of lines, so check in advance through JR Shikoku's website. Torokko carriages carry an additional charge (about ¥310), which is not covered by the rail pass; seat reservations should be made in advance (from any JR ticket office) anyhow.

See also p12 for details about using this guide. A useful resource for planning a trip is ⌨ www.tourismshikoku.org.

Note that apart from on the main routes, limited express services on Shikoku may only have a few reserved seats because they are only in part of a carriage not a whole carriage, so book early if you want to be sure of having a seat; also because the train may only have two cars anyhow.

## OKAYAMA TO TAKAMATSU [Map 33, p467; Table 23, p512]

Distances by JR from Okayama. Fastest journey time: 53 minutes.

### Okayama 岡山 (0km) [see pp297-301]
Take the Marine Liner rapid train along the Seto-Ohashi Line, which runs direct to Takamatsu across the Seto-Ohashi bridge. On its way the train calls at **Senoo** 妹尾 (8km), **Hayashima** 早島 (12km) and **Chaya-machi** 茶屋町 (15km).

### Kojima 児島 (28km) The last stop on Honshu before the train crosses **Seto-Ohashi** 瀬戸大橋. The bridge, or rather series of bridges, spans 9.4km; it was opened in 1988 having taken nearly a decade to build and with a construction bill of ¥1,120 billion. The view from the train as it crosses the bridge is certainly impressive, though it is eclipsed by the scale and design of the bridge itself.

The first stop after crossing the bridge is **Sakaide** 坂出 (Y08; 51km).

### Takamatsu 高松 (Y0, T28; 72km) [see pp480-5]

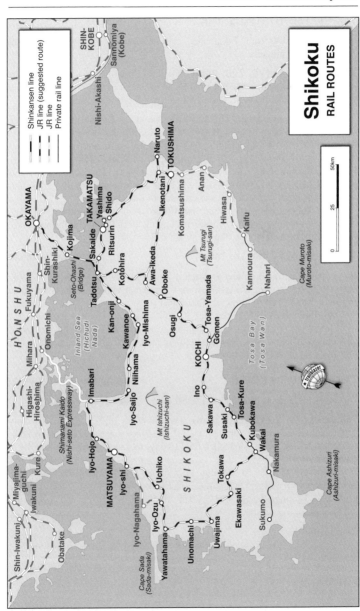

**Shikoku**
RAIL ROUTES

Shinkansen line
JR line (suggested route)
JR line
Private rail line

0    25    50km

SHIKOKU

## TAKAMATSU TO TOKUSHIMA                    [Map 33; Table 24, p512]

Distances by JR from Takamatsu. Fastest journey time Takamatsu to
Tokushima: 65 minutes.

**Takamatsu** 高松 **(Y0, T28; 0km)**  For those looking for a more leisurely
route around Shikoku, Tokushima makes an excellent cultural diversion before
you rejoin the Takamatsu to Kochi route at Awa-Ikeda (see p469).

From Takamatsu take a Uzushio LEX bound for Tokushima. All of these
stop at **Ritsurin** 栗林 (T25; 4.3km), but only local trains stop at Ritsurin-koen
Kitaguchi 栗林公園北口, the closest station to Ritsurin-koen (see p480). Most
then call at **Yashima** 屋島 (T23; 9.5km) and all at **Shido** 志度 (T19; 16.3km).
From **Sambommatsu** 三本松 (T12; 38km) the scenery gets better. Some trains
stop at **Hiketa** 引田 (T10; 45.1km). After that the train weaves through isolated forested slopes with the inevitable stretch of tunnels.

After **Itano** 板野 (T07; 58km) most trains stop at **Ikenotani** 池谷 (T04,
N04; 64.2km) where you may consider changing for the Naruto Whirlpools (see
pp489-90). The next stop is **Shozui** 勝瑞 (T03; 66.9km).

### Tokushima 徳島 (M0, T0; 75km)                          (see pp486-9)

If continuing to travel around Shikoku it is sensible to go to **Awa-Ikeda** 阿波
池田 (D22, B25; 74km; see p469), from where you can pick up the route guide
to Kochi, rather than returning to Takamatsu.

The Tsurugisan LEX (6/day) takes about 74 minutes from Tokushima and
local trains (8/day) take around two hours to wend their way alongside Yama-
gawa to Awa-Ikeda. After Awa-Ikeda the scenery gets better – on balance it is
best to sit on the right-hand side.

## TAKAMATSU TO KOCHI                        [Map 33; Table 25, p512]

Distances by JR from Takamatsu. Fastest journey time: 130 minutes.

**Takamatsu** 高松 **(Y0, T28; 0km)**  The Shimanto LEX (5/day) is the only
service direct to Kochi along the Dosan Line. Since there are only a few services consider taking an Ishizuchi LEX (16/day) to Tadotsu and changing there
on to a Nanpu LEX to Kochi.

Most services stop at **Sakaide** 坂出 (Y08; 22km), **Utazu** 宇多津 (Y09;
26km; see p480) and/or **Marugame** 丸亀 (Y10; 29km; see pp479-80). The line
divides at **Tadotsu** 多度津 (Y12, D12; 33km; see p479): the Ishizuchi LEX

---

❏ **Station codes**
To make life simpler for foreigners, both JR Shikoku and the private rail companies
here have given every station a code number so that when you buy a ticket or make
a seat reservation all you need to say is the code number for the station. This guide
also uses these codes, for example Naruto is 'N10'. Stations that are the junction of
lines often have two codes eg Takamatsu is 'Y0, T28'.

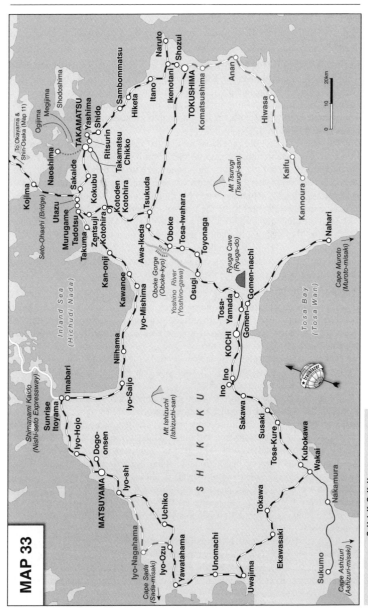

**MAP 33**

heads west along the Yosan Line towards Matsuyama (see pp490-4); the Shimanto and Nanpu LEX continue south along the Dosan Line to Kochi and beyond.

**Zentsuji 善通寺 (D14; 39km)** Zentsu-ji 善通寺 (🖥 www.zentsuji.com; daily 7am-5pm) is the birthplace of Kobo Daishi (also known as Kukai), the first Buddhist monk who made a pilgrimage on foot around Shikoku (see box p464). He built the temple here in 807, though the present buildings date from 1699. The temple is now the 75th on the 88-temple circuit and one of the busiest because of its link with Daishi.

The extensive temple precincts are divided into two areas. In **Garan**, the first area you reach from the station, there is a 45m-high 5-storeyed pagoda, completed in 1884 for the 1050th anniversary of Kobo Daishi's death. The Kondo (main hall) is also here but possibly of more interest are the rakan (statues of Buddha's disciples), with their incredible range of expressions, on the left of the Kondo. Mie-do Hall, said to be the very spot where Kobo Daishi was born in 774, is in the other area; turn left in front of the Kondo and walk over the bridge to **Tanjoin**. There is a lot to explore and there are plenty of labels in English.

Zentsu-ji is a 20-minute walk along the main road which runs away from the station; when you reach an open plaza turn right. There is no TIC at the station but there is a branch of the 7-Eleven convenience store.

**Kotohira 琴平 (D15; 44km)** Kotohira is an ideal place to break your journey for a few hours and visit the shrine of Kotohira-gu 金刀比羅宮, better known as **Kompira-san** こんぴらさん, the affectionate name for the guardian deity of seafarers. Rail fans may also like to stop here to see the station as it dates from the Taisho era (1912-26) and is Western in style. On a more practical note there are **lockers** (¥600), though it's cheaper (¥400) to leave large luggage with the staff, and a Kiosk; there is no TIC but you can pick up a pictorial map in Japanese by the ticket counter.

To get to Kompira-san turn left out of the station and walk along till you see a torii gate and covered shopping street on your right. Turn right down this road and it will lead to the start of the 1368 steps you will need to climb to reach the highest point – Kompira-san has was built on the slope of Mt Zozu ('Elephant's Head'), hence the need to climb. The steps are gradual with flat parts in between and there are also lots of distractions en route in the form of souvenir shops, snack stands and cafés/restaurants as well as places where you can buy walking sticks, so it really isn't too challenging. However, if the thought of all these steps already tires you a sedan ride up the first 365 steps costs ¥6800. The reward for making it up the first 785 steps to the main shrine is a view over the valley below.

It's a further 583 steps to **Okusha Shrine** 厳魂神社 the Inner Sanctuary, from where the view can extend as far as the Seto-Ohashi bridge. In addition to the view and the lovely shrine buildings, look out for *Malt's Mermaid*, an experimental solar-powered boat which was used in 1996 to cross the Pacific. It is truly bizarre to have a real boat so high above sea level and so far from the sea.

Before or after making the ascent, drop in at **Kompira Oshibai** 金毘羅大
芝居, also known as **Kanamaru-za** 金丸座 (🖥 www.konpirakabuki.jp; Wed-
Mon 9am-5pm; ¥500), the oldest wooden kabuki theatre in Japan. Built originally in 1835, it later became a cinema before falling into disrepair. It was
restored in 1976 and as long as you are not here when there are performances
you can go behind the scenes, tour the dressing rooms and under the stage itself.
Since there is no electricity all the stage effects are done by manpower including lifting the actors up on to the stage, or making the stage revolve.

If you decide to go to the theatre on your way to Kompira-san turn left after
climbing the first 22 steps and then follow the road ahead up a small hill. Just
before a big bend in the road there are some steps on the right – these lead up
to the ticket office for the theatre and the theatre itself. Alternatively continue
round the bend and you will see the theatre on your right.

Originally there were three entrances; the one on the left-hand side was for
the middle classes, the tiny one in the middle was for the commoners, and the
one on the right for the upper classes. Now there is just one entrance and you've
guessed it – it is the one originally used by the commoners. If someone offers
to guide you round, do accept as you will learn some fascinating facts about
how performances are staged, as well as about kabuki in general.

Kabuki is staged here only once a year, during April, as that is when the climate is the best due to the lack of air-conditioning or heating. There are shows
then twice a day for 16 to 19 days; each lasts about three hours. Tickets cost
¥7000-13,000 and are best booked through a travel agency.

Pick up a Shimanto or Nanpu LEX. Reservations are recommended as some
trains run with fewer carriages, making it a scramble for the non-reserved seats.

Local trains stop at **Tsukuda** 津久田 (B24, D21; 72km) which is the first
junction with the Tokushima Line.

**Awa-Ikeda** 阿波池田 **(D22, B25; 77km)** This is a stop for most LEXs so is
the main interchange station for the Tokushima Line (see p466).

From Awa-Ikeda, the Dosan Line continues south towards the area's big
sight, Oboke Gorge. Unfortunately, many of the passengers who use the limited express train to commute to Kochi shut the curtains and sleep through some
of the best views. If you don't want to miss out, reserve a window seat (both
sides of the train have superb views).

**Oboke** 大歩危 **(D27; 99km)** **Oboke Gorge** 大歩危 (Oboke-kyo) – or
'canyon' as some Japanese signposts call it – is one of Shikoku's hidden highlights. Since not all limited expresses stop here it is best to plan ahead, especially if you want to have a seat reservation for your onward or return journey
as the station is not manned, so you can't make reservations there. Allow two
hours to walk to Oboke, have a boat trip and a quick visit to the museum.

There are **lockers** at the station (¥300-500) and an **information desk** (Tue-
Fri 8.30am-3.30pm, Sat, Sun and holidays to 5.30pm), where you can pick up a
map even if it is not always manned when officially open. A somewhat unusual
feature is the 'LoveLove' (RabuRabu) らぶらぶベンチ bench on the platform;

one of a few JR Shikoku has installed at stations around the island. If you want to get closer to someone this is the place to come. Also on the platform is a sample *kazurabashi* (a bridge made from mountain vines); there used to be lots of them in the area but now there are only three.

The starting point for sightseeing boat tours along Yoshino River is about 1km from the station. Walk up to Oboke Bridge above the station, cross it, turn right and walk along parallel to the gorge; lorries thunder past on the road so it is not a pleasant walk though it is easy. If you prefer, a taxi costs about ¥2000.

If walking you will pass '**Lapis Oboke**' ラピス大歩危 (🖥 www.miyoshi navi.jp; Mar-Nov daily 9am-5pm), a modern building overlooking the gorge. Inside is a café, information centre, souvenir shop and Museum of Rocks and Minerals (¥500) well as a Yokai Museum (¥500) with life-size models of ghosts/monsters from local folklore. If these museums appeal stop here, but if your goal is the boat trip continue walking until you see a big car park with another large building on the gorge side by it. In here is the ticket office for the gentle 30-minute **Oboke Ravine Pleasure Boat trip** 大歩危遊覧船 (Oboke Yuransen; 🖥 www.mannaka.co.jp; daily 9am-5pm or earlier if not busy; ¥1080) as well as a restaurant and souvenir shop. No rowing is required – all you have to do is sit back and admire the views and the amazing geology; however, the commentary is in Japanese only. Note that it can be chilly out of the summer season and you have to take your shoes off and sit on the bottom of the boat.

For more information about the many things to see and do in this area, the Iya Valley, including white-water rafting and trekking, see 🖥 oboke-iya.jp. Both are on offer at Tosa-Iwahara (see below) so, if interested, get off the limited express here and take a local train (8/day; 7 mins) to the first stop.

♦ **Tosa-Iwahara** 土佐山田 (**D28**)  Less than 100m from the station is Australian-run **Happy Raft** ハッピーラフト (🖥 www.happyraft.com), which offers white-water rafting (mid-Mar to Oct from ¥9000/day, ¥5500pp/half-day) and canyoning (Jul-Oct from ¥9000pp/half-day) adventures on the Yoshino River. For full details, as well as information about accommodation if you want to stay nearby, see their website.

To continue your journey south take a local train to Osugi (see below) or Tosa-Yamada and pick up a LEX for the final stretch of the journey to Kochi.

Not all limited expresses stop at **Osugi** 大杉 (D32; 120km) but they do at **Tosa-Yamada** 土佐山田 (D37; 144km).

**Gomen** 後免 (**D40; 149km**)  Gomen is also a stop on the Gomen–Naharai Line of the Tosa Kuroshio Railway, a third-sector railway company. Tosa's Gomen station links with Gomen-nachi 後免町 (1-2/hr; 2 mins; ¥210), the eastern terminus of the tram/streetcar line from Kochi, so tram fans may like to get off here and transfer to Gomen-nachi for the tram ride to Kochi (2-11/hr; approx 40 mins; ¥460); see opposite about the various My-Yu passes on this line.

**Kochi** 高知 (**D45, K00; 160km**)  Kochi is known for its mild climate, long days of sunshine, and relaxed, friendly atmosphere. Ryoma Sakamoto (see p111), Ryuichi Yokoyama, one of Japan's most famous cartoonists, and Takashi Yanase, who created Anpanman, the superhero whose head is full of bean-filled bread, were all born in Kochi so there are statues and reminders of them everywhere. You are likely to have arrived here on an Anpanman train anyhow.

● **Station guide and information** Arriving at the impressive but airy structure of Kochi station, you will find some **lockers** (including large ¥600 ones) to the right after going through the ticket gates, and more through the Anpanman Terrace; Anpanman fans should also listen out for the station melody here (see box p102). Turn left out of the ticket gate for the bus terminal and JR buses to Matsuyama (see pp490-4). Kochi's well-informed **tourist information counter** (TIC; 🖥 www.attaka.or.jp; daily 9am-5pm, accommodation information 8.30am-7.30pm), and with English-speaking staff, is housed in Tosa Terrace, the wooden edifice to the right side of the station's Central Exit. For information about things to see and do in Kochi prefecture visit 🖥 visitkochijapan.com.

● **Getting around** Kochi's old but efficient **tram/streetcar system**, called the **Tosaden** とさでん (🖥 www.tosaden.co.jp; approx 6am-9.30pm; 2-11/hr), comprises two lines which intersect at Harimayabashi in the city centre. At 25.3km it is the second largest tram system in Japan and in all there are 76 stations. City-centre rides cost ¥200 per journey; a one-day **My-Yu pass** (valid for trams and My-Yu buses in the city centre area) costs ¥600, but is only ¥300 for anyone with a foreign passport. The pass is available from the TIC, or the IC shop at Harimayabashi. This pass is excellent value, but if you want to make the most of the whole tram/streetcar system get a ¥1000 pass, or for two days it is ¥1600; either way passes are half-price for foreign-passport holders. If you don't have a pass and are changing tram lines at Harimayabashi, ask for a *norikae-kippu* の りかえきっぷ; this allows you to transfer without paying again. The trams have been brought from all over the world; each has a different design and interior layout and even though many are old fashioned on the outside, inside they have LED displays with stops in English and some have video ads. The **Tosaden tram terminus** is on the main road that runs parallel to the front of Kochi station (turn right out of the ticket gate). The **bus stand** is on the right outside Kochi station; JR Shikoku buses to Matsuyama (see p473) depart from here.

● **What to see and do** Completed in 1611, **Kochi Castle** 高知城 (Kochi-jo; 🖥 kochipark.jp; daily 9am-5pm; ¥420) at the end of Otesuji-dori, is the city's big sight and one of a dozen original Japanese castles remaining, though its specific claim to fame is that it is the only castle still with all its Edo-period architecture in the main citadel. Among its many defensive elements (ironically never used) are holes for dropping stones on assailants, and spikes, on the northeast corner, referred to as 'ninja repellents'. There's a fine view from the top floor of the donjon, but as in most castles the stairs are very steep. Take a tram from the station to Harimayabashi (4 mins) and then change to the Shinai Line to Kochijomae (4 mins).

    **Yokoyama Ryuichi Memorial Manga Museum** 横山隆一記念まんが館 モバイルサイト (🖥 www.bunkaplaza.or.jp/mangakan; Tue-Sun 9am-6pm;

¥410) celebrates the work of the late Yokoyama, who died in 2001. His best-known comic-strip character, Fuku-chan, made his debut in a national newspaper in 1936 and was only retired in 1971. Comics' fans will be in heaven in the attached **manga library** (free entry). The museum is in Culport かるぽーと (Kochi City Culture Plaza; 3rd-5th floors), a 3-minute walk from Saenbacho tram stop.

**Yosakoi Festival** (🖳 www.yosakoi.com) is a high-energy dance event involving over 14,000 people divided into teams. Each team can choreograph their own dance so the festival has a contemporary feel. The festival (9th-12th Aug) is held on streets in central Kochi, approximately 15 minutes' walk south from the station. A similar event is held in Sapporo (see p404). If you can't be here for the festival make time to visit **Kochi Yosakoi Museum** 高知よさこい 情報交流館 (Kochi Yosakoi Joho Koryukan, also known as Kochi Yosakoi Information Interchange Hall; 🖳 www.honke-yosakoi.jp; Thur-Tue 10am-6.30pm; free), at the end of Harimayabashi Shoutengai arcade, on the left side before reaching Harimayabashi crossroads. Even though the labels are mostly in Japanese there is a lot to see and the video (Japanese commentary only) with clips from various years shows the variety of costumes, dances and music. Another room has a Blu-Ray DVD of the current year's event. Amazingly despite the terrible rain in the 2015 festival the participants' enthusiasm didn't wane. If you are inspired you can also put on a costume and have a go at dancing.

● **Where to stay and eat** If you want to stay near the station try *Comfort Hotel Kochi Ekimae* コンフォートホテル高知駅前 (☎ 088-883 1441, 🖳 www.choice-hotels.jp/cfkochi; from ¥5400/S, ¥7400/D, ¥9800/Tw, inc buffet breakfast). The rooms are very spacious and come with ergonomically designed pillows. There are also laundry facilities here.

A short way up the main road that heads away from the station towards the Harimayabashi crossroads is *Kochi Pacific Hotel* 高知パシフィックホテル (☎ 088-884 0777, 🖳 www.kochi-pacific.co.jp; from ¥5100/S, ¥7000/D or Tw), a business hotel with a range of accommodation as well as a restaurant and café.

*Richmond Hotel Kochi* リッチモンドホテル 高知 (☎ 088-820 1122, 🖳 kochi.richmondhotel.jp; from ¥6900/S, ¥13,100/D or Tw, inc breakfast) is a trendy outfit near lots of bars, with fashionably tailored staff, modern décor and pleasingly spacious rooms. It is in Obiyamachi 帯屋町, a covered arcade next door to a branch of *Doutor Coffee*.

Kochi proudly claims to have the highest consumption of *bonito* (skipjack tuna) in Japan. It is available at many restaurants here and can be eaten in many ways but *katsuo no tataki* 鰹のタタキ, where the bonito is seared briefly and then sliced and served with spring onion or ginger, is popular.

*Tosa Ichiba* 土佐市場 (Tue-Sun 11am-9.50pm), in Obiyamachi, has a feast of plastic window-display models and does well-priced set meals (from ¥1000, platters for several sharing up to ¥12,000) including katsuo no tataki. Tosa Ichiba is on the left when you reach the first crossroads if walking from Harimaya-dori – look for the picture of the whale on the sign outside and the fish tank inside. There are several other places here offering similar options.

Some of the set meals at restaurants here include *kujira* (whale); if you prefer not to eat this check if kujira (鯨、くじら) is included in your chosen meal.

At **Hirome Market** ひろめ市場 (🖥 www.hirome.co.jp; generally daily 8am-11pm but each stall's hours may vary), an indoor food mall on Otesuji-dori, a 5-minute walk from Ohashi-dori tram stop, you can sit at picnic tables and enjoy snacking on a cornucopia of food and drink from any of the approximately 60 stalls.

## KOCHI TO KUBOKAWA AND UWAJIMA

Distances by JR from Kochi. Fastest journey time: 3 hours 10 mins.

### Kochi to Kubokawa                    [Map 33, p467; Table 26, p512]
If you're in a hurry to get to Matsuyama consider taking a JR Shikoku bus (5/day; approx 3hrs; ¥3600/one-way, JR rail-pass holders free) from outside Kochi station, so you can skip the next (slow!) part of the journey by train.

**Kochi** 高知 **(K00, D45; 0km)**  From Kochi, pick up the Nanpu LEX, which continues along the Dosan Line to Kubokawa.

**Ino** 伊野 (K07; 11km) has been a paper-making town for over a thousand years, using water from Niyodo River. It is the terminus for one of Kochi's tram/streetcar lines, so enthusiasts might consider getting here by tram (2-3/hr; approx 50 mins; ¥460), especially if you have a valid My-Yu pass (see p471).

After **Sakawa** 佐川 (K13; 28km) there are rice fields everywhere you look. Kochi's mild weather and heavy rainfall means that it's the first place in Japan to harvest the year's crop.

Approaching **Susaki** 須崎 (K19; 42km) it's something of a shock to come across factories, concrete buildings and industry. The next stop is at **Tosa-Kure** 土佐久礼 (K22; 53km).

**Kubokawa** 窪川 **(K26, TK26; 72km)**  The JR Dosan Line terminates here. From here, the private Tosa Kuroshio Railway's Nakamura Line runs further south to **Nakamura** 中村 (TK40). The JR LEX (Nanpu, Shimanto and Ashizuri) services continue along this line, though rail-pass holders have to pay between Kubokawa and Nakamura. After Nakamura the private Tosa Kuroshio Line is called the Sukumo Line.

▲ To follow the next part of this rail route, change trains at Kubokawa and connect with the rural JR Yodo Line, which runs along Shimanto-gawa (Shimanto River) before terminating in Uwajima.

If you don't have a rail pass take a ticket when boarding the train and pay the fare when you get off. No limited expresses run along this line.

### Kubokawa to Uwajima                    [Map 33, p467; Table 27, p512]
The Yodo Line is one of the most scenic and rural in Shikoku; most of the stops are barely stations – just places where the train pulls up, often on the edge of a field. In theory, since the line between Kubokawa and **Wakai** 若井 (5km; the first stop after Kubokawa) runs on the private Tosa Kuroshio Line, rail-pass

SHIKOKU

holders should pay a ¥200 supplement. However, since nobody checks your ticket until you arrive in Uwajima, this additional fare may be forgotten.

It takes around two hours for the train to pull in to Uwajima. En route it occasionally fills up with schoolchildren but then just as quickly empties again. For part of the way the line follows the course of Shimanto-gawa, claimed to be the 'last great virgin river in Japan'. No man-made dams have been built near it; unimpeded by mechanical barriers, the water is probably the clearest you'll see anywhere. Even though the chugging of the train can be sleep-inducing, the scenery is worth staying awake for, as you'll see farmers working in the fields and storks in water-logged rice paddies. More often than not, the railway line has been cut between fields, so you can stare right down at the cauliflowers, cabbages and individual rice plants. After **Ekawasaki** 江川崎 the line leaves Shimanto-gawa and winds its way towards the Pacific Ocean, crossing into Ehime prefecture on its way to Uwajima.

If you are in luck you will be able to travel on either the Tetsudo Hobby, Kaiyodo Hobby, or Shiman Torokko, train, though none of these operates daily year-round so check in advance. The **Tetsudo Hobby train** 鉄道ホビートレイン, Japan's slowest shinkansen, started service in 2014. This is a normal diesel car train that has been converted to look like a 0-series shinkansen, the first generation bullet train, on the outside. Inside it is like a museum showcasing a variety of model trains (exhibits change periodically) but the seats are genuine 0-series shinkansen seats. Despite this, don't expect to go more than 85kph. This is possibly the closest that Shikoku – the only major island with no official shinkansen or plans for one – will get to having a shinkansen. The **Kaiyodo Hobby train** 海洋堂ホビートレイン is a very colourful train with dinosaurs painted on the outside and various forms of sealife inside as well as showcases with changing exhibitions. These hobby trains operate between Kubokawa and Uwajima.

Between 22nd July and 31st August the **Shiman Torokko** しまんトロッコ (see p464) operates between **Tokawa** 外川 (G32; 103km) and **Ekawasaki** 江川崎 (G34; 115km).

**Uwajima 宇和島 (G47, U28; 150km)** Uwajima station has platforms on the same level as the exit. The station itself is very spartan. Only small **lockers** are available but the staff at the ticket barrier may allow you to store large luggage. The **tourist information booth** (🖳 uwajima-tourism.org; daily 9am-6pm) is inside the station and has maps and leaflets.

**Taga Shrine** 多賀神社 (Taga-jinja; daily all day; free) is a fertility shrine with **Dekoboko Shindo** 凸凹神堂 (daily 8am-5pm; ¥800), a Sex Museum. The museum, a 3-storeyed building in one corner of the shrine, is wall-to-wall penises, in various shapes and sizes, though the emphasis is on the huge. The phallic models, pictures and works of art leave nothing to the imagination. Labels are in Japanese but it's not as if much explanation is needed.

Uwajima's other big attraction is **bull fighting** 牛相撲 (togyu; 🖳 www.tougyu.com); togyu is also known as ushi-sumo, literally cow/bull sumo. These contests are strictly bull against bull – no human risks getting hurt – and take place a few times a year at the Municipal Bull Fighting Ring 市営闘牛場 (2nd Jan, first Sun in Apr, 24th Jul, 14th Aug, second Sun in Nov; ¥3000). At other times, a film of the fighting is shown (Mon-Fri 8.30am-5pm; ¥500).

**Uwajima Castle** 宇和島城 is about a 15-minute walk from the station (turn right out of the station, then left on Highway 56 at the main junction), but then it is about another 15 minutes to reach the top. It is called a *hirayamashiro* 平山城 (a castle on a hill surrounded by a plain) as it was built on a 80m-high hill in Shiroyama Park 城山公園. The 3-storey structure dates from the Edo period and the main keep 天守閣 (*tenshukaku*; Tue-Sun 9am-4pm; ¥200) is one of twelve in Japan that is still an original. There is no exhibition to speak of inside the castle, though if you are happy to climb the steep steps to the top there is a good view. The grounds are extensive so there is plenty to explore.

Nearby also is **Tensha-en** 天赦園 (daily Apr-June 8.30am-5pm, July-Mar to 4.30pm; closed Mon mid Dec to Feb; ¥300), a typical Japanese garden with a pond in the middle; the best time to be here is in spring/early summer for the wisteria and iris.

If you need somewhere to stay, the JR-operated *Hotel Clement Uwajima* ホテルクレメント宇和島 (☎ 0895-23 6111, 🖥 www.jrhotelgroup.com; from ¥7128/S, ¥11,880/D, ¥12,474/Tw; tatami rooms ¥17,820; 10% off all rates with a JR rail pass) is immediately above the station. Standard rooms have modern furnishings; there are also some tatami rooms.

*Kadoya* かどや (🖥 www.kadoya-taimeshi.com; Fri-Wed 11am-2.30pm & 5-9pm, Thur 5-9pm), a well-known sashimi restaurant, is on Nishiki-machi, the main strip as you leave the station. As the road doglegs, go straight on and the restaurant is on the right-hand side after you cross the first side street. Dishes include sashimi sets (from ¥2000), pork tonkatsu, tempura sets (both ¥1500), and steak sets (¥2200).

## UWAJIMA TO MATSUYAMA　　　　　　[Map 33, p467; Table 28, p513]

Distances by JR from Uwajima. Fastest journey time: 1¼ hours.

**Uwajima** 宇和島 **(U28, G47; 0km)**　From Uwajima, pick up the Uwakai LEX, which runs along the Yosan Line to Matsuyama. The first stop is **Unomachi** 卯之町 (20km).

**Yawatahama** 八幡浜 **(U18; 35km)**　Yawatahama is now the final stop for one of the routes of the **Iyonada Monogatari** 伊予灘ものがたり (🖥 iyonada monogatari.com; fare inc reserved seat ¥2260 each way, Japan Rail Pass valid, JR Shikoku pass extra charge ¥980; additional charge for meals), Shikoku's first sightseeing train. Tickets can be bought from JR ticket offices, or travel agencies. The train has two cars and it operates on the coastal route (see p476) to Matsuyama; services generally operate at the weekends and in holiday periods.

**Iyo-Ozu** 伊予大洲 **(U14, S18; 48km)**　This castle town, called **Ozu** 大洲, is just one of three remaining spots in Japan where traditional **cormorant fishing** can be seen on Hiji-kawa river (June to mid Sep).

SHIKOKU

The rail line divides at Iyo-Ozu, with a choice of either the **inland route**, which this guide follows (served by limited express or local train), or the **coastal route** (served by local trains and now the Iyonada Monogatari). If you're on a limited express and want to follow the coastal route, this is the last place you can change before the lines diverge.

Taking the coastal route (local trains 9/day; approx 70 mins), the line follows Hiji-gawa river to Iyo-Nagahama and the sea, then heads slowly up the coast before converging with the inland line just before Iyo-shi station. If the weather is good and you have the time, this is a pleasant option.

**Uchiko 内子 (U10; 59km)** Between the Edo and Meiji periods, Uchiko prospered as a manufacturing centre for Japanese paper and wax. Today it is known for the streets of **preserved old houses** 町並み, one of which is called Yokaichi. Here some of the buildings are open to the public as museums or coffee shops.

There are lifts/elevators from platforms 1 and 2 down to street level. The station has small **lockers** only but you may be able to leave your bags at the adjoining café for a small charge. At **Tabirian** (daily 9am-4pm), to the right of the station exit, you can pick up a walking map if you haven't already downloaded one from 🖳 www.iyokannet.jp.

Outside the station is a **steam locomotive** (C12 231) that ran on the Uchiko Line between 1969 and 1970, transporting cargo between Uchiko and Iyo-Ozu. Built in 1939, its overall accumulated mileage would be enough to circumnavigate the globe 33 times.

To reach the main sights (all open daily 9am-4.30pm) from the station, walk ahead to the second set of lights, then turn left along Honmachi-dori. Turn first left off Honmachi-dori for Uchiko's kabuki theatre, **Uchiko-za** 内子座 (¥400). Built in 1916 and restored in 1985, it is similar in design to the theatre at Kotohira (see p469), with a revolving stage and seats for up to 650. The theatre is now used on about 60 days a year for kabuki, puppet shows, films and concerts. You will be given a leaflet in English explaining everything.

To find the **Museum of Commercial and Domestic Life** 内子町歴史民俗資料館 (Rekishi Minzoku Shiryokan, also known as Uchiko History Museum; ¥200), a folksy recreation of a 1920s family-run pharmaceutical business; look for the mannequins staffing the pharmaceutical counter on the right as you head up Honmachi-dori. Inside, you can wander freely among the wax figures seated on the upstairs tatami mats, but it's more atmospheric than instructive.

Continue walking along Honmachi-dori to reach the more informative **Japanese Wax Museum** 木蝋資料館　上芳我邸 (Mokuro Shiryokan Kamihagatei; ¥500 inc entry to Kami-Haga, see below), in the heart of the Yokaichi 八日市 area. The production cycle and international role of Uchiko's wax industry is proudly outlined (in English) through an interesting variety of dioramas, artefacts and local products. Adjoining the wax museum, the **Kami-Haga Residence** 上芳我家 beautifully illustrates the prosperity the industry brought to one of the major producer families in the early 1900s.

**Iyo-shi** 伊予市 **(85km)**  This is the point at which the coastal and inland rail lines re-converge for the final part of the journey to Matsuyama.

**Matsuyama** 松山 **(U0, Y55; 97km)**                    **[see pp490-4]**
Matsuyama, the largest city on the island and a castle town, is perhaps best known for the Dogo-onsen hot-spring baths (see pp494-5).

## MATSUYAMA TO OKAYAMA                    [Map 33, p467; Table 28, p513]

Distances by JR from Matsuyama. Fastest journey time: 2 hours 35 mins.

**Matsuyama** 松山 **(U0, Y55; 0km)**  The final part of the journey around Shikoku; the Shiokaze LEX runs direct from here back to Okayama. If returning to Honshu, make sure you're sitting in car Nos 4-8 as car Nos 1-3 split off at Tadotsu and head to Takamatsu (if you have a seat reservation, you'll already be in the correct part of the train).

Between Matsuyama and **Iyo-Hojo** 伊予北条 (18km), the line roughly parallels the main 196 trunk road but there are occasional views of the Inland Sea out to the left. About 20 minutes after Iyo-Hojo you should see, also out to the left, the Nishi-Seto Expressway (see below) linking Shikoku with Honshu.

**Imabari** 今治 **(Y40; 50km)**  Imabari is the starting point for the **Nishi-Seto Expressway**, also known as the **Shimanami Kaido**. Completed in 1999, the bridge uses six small islands as staging posts and runs across the Inland Sea to Onomichi. The bridge was originally just for vehicles, but is now a popular cycling route (see p279). If this appeals you can rent a bicycle at a couple of places near Imabari station: JR Imabara station **Rent-a-cycle terminal** レンタサイクルターミナル (daily 8.30am-5pm; from ¥500/day) is 100 metres to the left from the station's West Exit. The **Giant Store** ジャイアントストア (🖥 giant-store.jp/imabari; Wed-Mon 9am-7pm; see p279 for details and prices), in the station building, has an extensive range of good-quality bicycles to choose from so they are the most expensive option. You can also rent a bicycle at **Sunrise Itoyama** サンライズ糸山 (🖥 www.sunrise-itoyama.jp; Apr-Sep 8am-8pm, Oct-Mar to 5pm; bicycle ¥1000/day, electric assist bicycles ¥1500/day, tandem bicycles ¥1200/day; ¥1000 deposit required, refunded if bicycle returned here), the official starting point for the route on this side of the bridge. However, since the bus service from the station to Sunrise Itoyama is infrequent it is easier to rent a bicycle near Imabari station.

**Imabari District Sightseeing Information Centre** (daily 9am-7pm), marked on some maps as Question & Answer office, is by the West Exit (1st/ground floor) of the station. There is a 7-Eleven/Kiosk and a branch of *Willie Winkie bakery* in the station. Imabari is the main towel-producing city in Japan; several are on display at the station so it is hard to miss its claim to fame.

**Imabari Castle** 今治城 (daily 9am-5pm; ¥500) was built in 1602 and is one of three castles in Japan with sea water in its moat; another of these seaside castles on Shikoku is Takamatsu Castle (see p481). Imabari Castle is about a 15-minute walk from the station.

***Imabari Urban Hotel*** 今治 アーバン ホテル (🖳 www.imabari-urban-hotel.com; from ¥6300/S, ¥11,000/D, ¥12,000/Tw; Japanese style from ¥5500/S, ¥10,500/14,500 two/three sharing) offers both Western- and Japanese-style accommodation and is conveniently located near the station. There are also several other hotels around the station.

### Iyo-Saijo 伊予西条 (Y31; 80km)

The **Railway History Park** 鉄道歴史パーク at the station features the Shikoku Railway Culture Center (🖳 s-trp.jp; Thur-Tue 9am-6pm; ¥300). Shinji Sogo, who comes from Saijo, is known as the 'father of the bullet train' as it was he who first promoted the idea of a super-express train and persuaded the relevant authorities that one should be built. He is honoured in a memorial museum here and there is an 0-series shinkansen. The museum contains railway memorabilia and opportunities for visitors to 'drive' some trains and ride on a rail-gauge bicycle; for full details see the website.

If you happen to be passing this way around 14th-17th October, drop in on the town's autumn **festival**. The highlight is a parade of portable shrines through the city on the morning of the 15th. Conveniently, Niihama (see below) holds a festival at around the same time.

### Niihama 新居浜 (Y29; 91km)

The floats that get paraded around town during **Niihama's Taiko Festival** (16th-18th Oct) weigh around two tonnes each and require 150 people to carry them. The physical effort involved is possibly equalled by the amount of sake and beer drunk.

The limited express next calls at **Iyo-Mishima** 伊予三島 (Y23; 116.8km) and **Kawanoe** 川之江 (Y22; 122km), which is the last stop before the train crosses the border from Ehime back to Kagawa prefecture.

### Kan-onji 観音寺 (Y19; 138km)

This is the best stop for **Kotohiki Park** 琴弾公園, known for its massive and mysterious coin shape called **Zenigata** (see box below), carved about two metres deep in the sand. Kotohiki Park is about

---

#### ❏ The Zenigata – a coin shape carved in the sand

There are several stories about how the **Zenigata suna-e** 銭形砂絵 came to be in Kotohiki Park (see Kan-onji above). Some claim the coin carving is at least 350 years old, while others say it only dates back 130 years. Another theory is that the coin was and remains to this day a UFO base (a Japanese version of crop circles?), while others attribute it to the miracle-working of Kobo Daishi (see box p464). However, the common consensus is that it was completed in just one night by locals in 1633 as an unusual gift to the feudal lord of the area, Takatoshi Ikoma, who was to arrive the next day on a tour of inspection. Everybody knew that his lordship had to be pleased and a huge coin in the sand seemed the perfect answer. With a circumference of 345m, the biggest mystery is why the design does not disappear in the rain or wind.

A great time to be here is for the sunset, but also every evening the sculpture is lit up till 10pm. Twice a year the coin is reshaped by a group of volunteers who have orders shouted to them by one person commanding a bird's eye view. A 2-day **Zenigata Festival** is held around 20th July (Maritime Day), with a fireworks display and dance contest in Kotohiki Park.

a 20-minute walk north-west of the station: go straight ahead out of the station, over a bridge and turn left at the first traffic lights, then first right at the next traffic lights and then left and right again at subsequent traffic lights. Then cross the bridge over Saita-gawa and turn left again. Soon on the right a road leads uphill towards the observatory platform 銭形展望台; even though getting up there is quite a walk the views repay the effort. Retrace your steps and when you reach the bottom turn right for the World Coins Museum and to see the Zenigata at ground level. The **World Coins Museum** 世界のコイン館 (Sekai-no Coin Kan; daily 9am-5pm; ¥200) has coins and currency notes from all over the world and is a fascinating place to visit. It seems that Queen Elizabeth II features on more notes than any other individual.

There is no tourist information centre in Kan-onji station but there is a Kiosk and also a branch of *Willie Winkie* bakery to the right of the station.

Between **Takuma** 詫間 (Y14; 152km) and Tadotsu there are great views of the many tiny islands in the Inland Sea.

### Tadotsu 多度津 (Y12, D12; 162km)
Tadotsu is a junction for the Yosan Line between Matsuyama and Takamatsu, and the Dosan Line to Kochi. This is where the railway network on Shikoku began in 1889, when the first steam locomotive ran 15.5km from Marugame to Kotohira via Tadotsu.

As soon as the Shiokaze LEX stops, a lightning-fast decoupling takes place, allowing the front half (car Nos 4-8) to continue on to Okayama, while the remainder wait a couple of minutes before starting off for Takamatsu.

### Marugame 丸亀 (Y10; 166km)
Marugame is a former castle town that is also known for its *uchiwa* 団扇 (non-bending fans), which have been produced here since the Edo era. The town now churns out 80,000,000 uchiwa every year – 90% of the domestic market.

The **tourist information office** (🖥 www.city.marugame.kagawa.jp; Mon-Fri 9.30am-6pm, Sat & Sun 10am-5pm) is by the station exit. The staff can give you a map of the town (in English). On the 2nd floor is an Anpanman Torokko play area as well as some cafés and restaurants. There are **lockers** to the left of the exit and branches of Kiosk and Ace One in the station.

Right outside the station in a striking modern building is **Marugame Genichiro Inokuma Museum of Contemporary Art** 丸亀市猪熊弦一郎現代美術館 (MIMOCA; 🖥 www.mimoca.org; daily 10am-6pm, closed on occasional days; ¥300). The permanent exhibitions on the 2nd floor display the works of Genichiro Inokuma (1902-93), who attended school in Marugame before eventually moving to New York for 20 years and then Hawaii. His works are unusual in that most are on paper rather than canvas. The museum also has special exhibitions of contemporary art.

**Marugame Castle** 丸亀城 (daily 9am-4.30pm; grounds and Marugame City Museum free; castle keep ¥200) was built in 1597 on a hill overlooking the city. Thus, like Uwajima Castle (see p475), it is called a *hirayamashiro* (a castle on a hill surrounded by a plain). It is one of the twelve original wooden castles still existing in Japan. Its design may not be unusual but the mason who built the ramparts certainly was: legend records that he always worked naked. The museum in the castle has exhibits about all aspects of Marugame's history. You can see how Marugame's Uchiwa fans are made at **Uchiwa Studio Take** うちわ工房「たけ」 (Thur-Tue 10am-4pm; free), inside the castle's grounds. However, get there by at least 3pm as after that they start packing up, though you can buy fans till closing time.

The castle is about a 10-minute walk from the South Exit of the station.

**Utazu** 宇多津 **(Y09; 169km)**  The final stop in Shikoku before the train turns to cross the Seto-Ohashi Bridge and heads for Okayama. If you're not returning to Honshu and haven't yet changed trains, this is the last chance to do so.

**Kojima** 児島 **(187km)**  First stop back on Honshu, and the point where the JR Shikoku staff are replaced by their counterparts from JR West.

**Okayama** 岡山 **(214km)**                                      [see pp297-301]

# Shikoku – city guides

## TAKAMATSU 高松

Capital of Kagawa Prefecture for over a century and a former castle town, Takamatsu has transformed itself into a major business and tourism centre for the 21st century with the regeneration of the port area behind JR Takamatsu station. The hugely ambitious decade-long land reclamation project, dubbed 'Sunport Takamatsu', changed the face of the city beyond recognition.

### What to see and do

The garden at Ritsurin-koen is Takamatsu's biggest draw, but even if you aren't an art fan a day trip to Naoshima (see pp485-6) is highly recommended.

**Ritsurin-koen** 栗林公園 (🖳 ritsurin garden.jp; daily Apr, May & Sep 5.30am-6.30pm, June-Aug to 7pm, Oct 6am-5.30pm, Nov 6.30am-5pm, Dec & Jan 7am-5pm, Feb 7am-5.30pm, Mar 6.30am-6pm; ¥410), a strolling-type landscape garden, enjoys a dramatic setting at the foot of Mt Shiun. The garden dates from 1625 but was added to over the next hundred years by various *daimyo*. It was opened to the public in 1875 and now covers an extensive area and contains six ponds and 13 mounds; the

latter are great for overviews of the garden. Nominally the garden is divided into two areas: the Hokutei (Northern) and Nantei (Southern), but there is no real division between the two. *Kikugetsu-tei* 掬月亭 (Moon-Scooping Pavilion; 9am-4.30pm), in Nantei, is a restored tea house which was first built in 1640; it's thought that moon-viewing parties were once held here but you can now pop in for a cup of *matcha* (¥700) or *sencha* (¥500) tea.

Also within the grounds are two interesting museums. **Shoko Shoreikan** 商工奨励館 (Commerce and Industry Promotion Hall; daily 8.30am-5pm; free) has various exhibitions, including one about the history of Sanuki udon (see p484). **Sanuki Folkcraft Museum** 讃岐民芸館 (Sanuki Mengeikan; Wed-Sun 8.30am-5pm; free) contains many interesting items including a model portable shrine as well as various ceramics and masks.

For a chance to feel like a *daimyo* have a **boat ride** (2/hr; from 9am to 4pm, later in summer; ¥610) on the South Pond. Tickets must be bought at the main ticket office.

To ensure you have as much peace as possible in the garden, go early.

The North Gate entrance of Ritsurin is only 240m (a 3-minute walk) from JR Ritsurin-koen Kita-guchi station so that is the best option for JR pass-holders; take a local train from Takamatsu on the Kotoku Line (towards Tokushima). Kotoden's Ritsurin-koen station (2-4/hr; ¥190) is a 10-minute walk from the main entrance but buses (from stand No 4 or 5 outside Takamatsu station; 5-7/hr; ¥240) stop at Ritsurin-koen-mae, only a minute's walk from the main entrance.

**Takamatsu Symbol Tower** 高松シンボルタワー, on your left as you leave the station, dominates everything else in the station vicinity. The tower is an office building (Tower Building), but is connected to a lower building (Hall Wing) in which Maritime Plaza has shops and restaurants (see Where to eat). Take the lift/elevator in the Tower Building up to the 8th-floor viewing platform (🖳 www.symboltower .com; daily 10am-8pm; free). On a cloudless day you'll get unparalleled views of the city and out over the Inland Sea. There is a viewing lobby on the 30th floor inside Alice (see Where to eat); it is free to go there between 10am & 11am and 3-5pm.

Back at street level consider taking a leisurely stroll out to **Red Lighthouse** 赤灯台 (Aka-todai, also known as Seto Marker); it is so called because it is made of red glass bricks. It's a popular place to hang out in the summer, but is not very obvious until you get quite close.

**Tamamo-koen** 玉藻公園 (Western Gate Apr-Sep 5.30am-6.30pm, Oct-Mar 7am-5pm; Eastern Gate Apr-Sep 7am-6pm, Oct-Mar 8.30am-5pm; ¥200), by the harbour and next to Takamatsu-Chikko station (Kotoden Kotohira Line), is a large park where **Takamatsu Castle** once stood. The castle was built in 1590 and some of the original turrets remain but what makes it noteworthy is its unusual proximity to the sea. Waves crashed against the northern ramparts until 1900, when land was reclaimed to construct a new harbour but the moat has sea water in it. The park is a very pleasant place to stroll around.

Located on the far side of Tamamo-koen, **Kagawa Prefectural Museum** 香川県立ミュージアム (daily 9am-5pm; ¥410) charts the history of Kagawa but is also an art museum and at times has exhibitions of Western artists. An English audio-guide is provided for the more interesting 3rd floor History Gallery, where you can enjoy dioramas of a Yayoi period pit dwelling and an early 20th-century school classroom.

**Takamatsu City Art Museum** 高松市美術館 (Tue-Sun 9.30am-5pm, Tue-Sat to 7pm during special exhibitions; ¥200; additional charge for special exhibitions), housed in a modern building and reopened in spring 2016 after a year of renovation, has a worthwhile permanent collection of mostly contemporary Japanese art. The galleries are small but exhibits are changed every few months. The museum occasionally stages concerts.

**Practical information**

**Station guide** Takamatsu station has a nickname – **Sanuki Udon** – which you will see on station signs here; this is to promote the local food speciality (see p484). You don't even need to go through the ticket gate to have some udon; there is a stand on the left side of the platform concourse though it is only open at peak times. Immediately to your left after going through the ticket barrier are some **lockers** (including large ¥600 ones). To your right is the JR ticket office. Take the East Exit for the main sights and the South Exit for the bus terminal.

**Tourist information** There is an **information booth** (Takamatsu City Tourist Information Plaza JR Takamatsu Station Satellite; daily 9am-6pm) in the corridor leading to the South Exit of the station but the main **information centre** (🖳 www .takamatsu.or.jp; daily 9am-6pm) is in a building on the left-hand side of the square in front of the main station exit. The helpful staff can advise on trips to the islands and on accommodation in Takamatsu, but booking is at a separate desk. Another website worth looking at is 🖳 www.city.takamatsu .kagawa.jp.

**Getting around** Though you may want to take a train to Ritsurin-koen, the best

SHIKOKU

way of seeing the city centre is on foot, or on two wheels. The **bicycle rental system** here is one of the best anywhere as you can keep a bicycle for up to 24 hours. The initial charge is ¥100 but if you keep the bicycle for over six hours (and up to 24) you need to pay an additional ¥100. To reach the rental place at the station take the lift/elevator on the right after you leave the station and go down to B1. Turn left and you will find the registration area (daily 7am-10pm). You will need photographic proof of your identity (ie a passport or identification card). After that you will get a card – and won't need your ID again – and will also be given details of the bicycle rental ports around town.

**Train** services are provided by both JR and the private Kotoden Railway (see box below); both operate in and around Takamatsu.

The best way to reach the **ferry terminals** from Takamatsu station is to go up the escalator next to JR Hotel Clement Takamatsu; a sign above says 'Pedestrian access to Takamatsu Port'. Going this way means you don't have to cross any roads.

**Festivals** The biggest annual event is **Sanuki Takamatsu Festival** (12th-14th Aug), when thousands of costumed locals dance through the main streets (anyone is welcome to join in) and there are large-scale fireworks on the 13th. The **Setouchi International Art Festival** (🖳 setouchi-artfest.jp) is held every three years in Takamatsu and on Naoshima and other islands in the Inland Sea; events in 2016 continue until November.

**Where to stay** Right outside the station, *JR Hotel Clement Takamatsu* JR ホテルクレメント高松 (☎ 087-811 1111, 🖳 www.jrclement.co.jp; from ¥14,256/S, ¥24,948/D, ¥26,136/Tw) is dwarfed by the neighbouring Symbol Tower but is still a skyscraper by Takamatsu standards. It's easily the most de luxe place to stay in town. Not surprisingly there are several restaurants here (see Where to eat).

Away from the station area there are two branches of the popular Toyoko Inn chain (🖳 www.toyoko-inn.com). The newer *Toyoko Inn Takamatsu Hyogomachi* 東横イン 高松兵庫町 (☎ 087-821 1045; from ¥6264/S, ¥7344/D, ¥9072/Tw, inc Japanese breakfast), is five minutes on foot from the station. The original *Toyoko Inn Takamatsu Nakajincho* 東横イン 高松中新町 (☎ 087-831 1045; from ¥5075/S, ¥6156/de luxe single, ¥7236/D or Tw) has especially good de luxe single rooms, which are very spacious and include a separate seating area.

*Hotel Fukuya* ホテル福屋 (☎ 087-851 2365, 🖳 www.hotel-fukuya.com; from ¥6912/S, ¥11,880/Tw, Japanese-style tatami rooms from ¥13,068/17,820 two/three sharing) is a 10- to 15-minute walk from the station. The open-plan lobby sets the tone and rooms are also veering on the spacious, particularly the Japanese-style ones – the bathrooms remain tiny though.

For a taste of luxury, try *Rihga Hotel Zest Takamatsu* リガホテルゼスト高松 (☎ 087-822 3555, 🖳 www.rihga.com/kagawa; from ¥7000/S, ¥13,200/D, ¥15,200/Tw, ¥25,100/de luxe Tw, ¥25,200/sleeps four). The rooms in the main

---

❏ **Kotoden – trainspotters' paradise**

Kotoden ことでん (🖳 www.kotoden.co.jp; approx 6am-11pm; fares from ¥190; 2-3/hr) operates three railway lines in and around Takamatsu: services on the Kotohira and Nagao lines start from Takamatsu-Chikko; its Shido Line starts from, and all services stop at, Kawara-machi 瓦町, its main station which is beneath Flag フラッグ department store in the city centre. Particularly among trainspotters – called *tetsudo mania* (railway enthusiasts) in Japanese – Kotoden is known as a good place to photograph some of Japan's oldest trains still in service. The company has bought old rolling stock from cities such as Tokyo and Osaka and put them back into service on its lines. The oldest train dates back to 1925.

To Red Lighthouse & Mikayla

Takamatsu Symbol Tower ○1 / ○2

Sunport Takamatsu

Ferries to Naoshima & Shodoshima — Takamatsu Port

High-speed boats to Naoshima & Shodoshima; ferries to Megijima and Ogijima

⛴3

Mizuki-dori

Takamatsu Station

TIC ⓘ

△4 ⓘ

JR Kotoku, Yosan & Dosan lines

Takamatsu-chikko

□5 Tamamo-koen

Remains of Takamatsu Castle

🏛 Kagawa Prefectural Museum

Seto ohashi-dori

Kenchomae-dori

Chuo-dori

Kotoden Kotohira line

Katahara-machi

🏠6 Post Office ✉

🏠7 Hyogomachi ○ Katahara-machi 🏠10

○9

🏠8 ○11

Bijutsukan-dori

Marugamemachi

Raion-dori (Lion Street)

Ferry-dori

🏛 Takamatsu City Museum of Art

Il Gosen

🏠12

Chuo Park

Covered arcade

🏠13

Minamishinmachi

Chuo-dori

Kotoden Shido line

Kawara-machi

Flag dept store

Kikuchan-dori

Tokiwagai

Covered arcade

Kanko-dori

Kotoden Nagao line

🏠14

Hachiman-dori

Kotoden Kotohira line

JR Kotoku line

Ritsurinkoen Kitaguchi

North ● entrance

Mt Shiun

Ritsurin

Shoko Shoreikan 🏛 🏛 Sanuki Folkcraft Museum

Ritsurin-koen

Main ● entrance

To Kikugetsu-tei

Ritsurinkoen

★ trailblazer

SHIKOKU

0  100  200  300m

# Takamatsu

高松

**Where to stay**

3 JR Hotel Clement Takamatsu
6 Toyoko Inn Takamatsu Hyogomachi
7 Hotel Fukuya
8 Rihga Hotel Zest Takamatsu
10 Takamatsu Hotel Sakika
12 Daiwa Roynet Hotel Takamatsu
13 Dormy Inn Takamatsu
14 Toyoko Inn Takamatsu Nakajincho

**Where to eat and drink**

1 Alice, Szechwan (Tower Building)
2 Freshness Burger, Udon Takumi Goshiki (Maritime Building)
3 Vent, Bar Astro
4 UCC Café Plaza
5 Beer Pub Station' Irish Pub the Craic
9 Hanamaru
11 Ten Yasu

building are adequate, but those in the newer annex are de luxe and there's a combination Western/tatami room that can sleep four; the hotel also has three restaurants.

As a member of the YHA/HI, *Takamatsu Hotel Sakika* 高松ホテルサキ カ (☎ 087-822-2111, 🖳 www.netwave.or .jp/~nmimatsu; member/non-member from ¥3990/4590pp; breakfast ¥778, evening meal ¥1167) is a good budget option (and not a bunk bed in sight). It mixes Japanese- and Western-style accommodation and is spacious and has more character than a business hotel. Wi-fi and washer/dryer facilities are available. Note that reception (front) is not always well attended, check-in closes at 11pm and they don't store luggage. Book in advance as there are only 21 rooms. Meals are served in the New Grand Mimatsu building, two minutes away on foot. Follow the left-side path to the hotel entrance.

*Dormy Inn Takamatsu* ドーミーイン 高松 (☎ 087-832 5489, 🖳 www.hotespa .net/hotels/takamatsu; from ¥8995/S, ¥13,990/D, inc breakfast) is part of the reasonably priced but excellent-quality business hotel chain. As in all branches there is an onsen (both indoor and outdoor); there's free wi-fi and free yonaki soba in the evenings. Almost opposite, but in **Marugame-machi** 丸亀町 shopping street, is *Daiwa Roynet Hotel Takamatsu* ダイワ ロイネットホテル高松 (☎ 087-811 7895, 🖳 www.daiwaroynet.jp/takamatsu; from ¥8300/S, ¥12,760/D or Tw, ladies room from ¥9830; rates inc buffet breakfast). The rooms are on floor Nos 8-12; Ladies rooms have foot massagers and facial steamers.

For details about accommodation on Naoshima see p486 and in general see pp67-73.

## Where to eat and drink

Takamatsu is known for **Sanuki udon** 讃岐うどん, named after the Sanuki region in Kagawa Prefecture. The main feature of the udon noodles, served al dente, is the 'smooth texture and strong body'; the broth is made from bonito and kelp. Not surprisingly there are several places where you can eat this in Takamatsu. Good places to look for somewhere to eat are the long, covered shopping streets – Hyogomachi, Marugamemachi and Minamishinmachi. The branch of *Hanamaru Udon* はなまる うどん (🖳 www.hanamaruudon.com; daily 11am-9pm) in **Hyogomachi** 兵庫町店 serves delicious Sanuki udon (small ¥300-450, medium ¥400-550, large ¥500-650) with a variety of toppings; a medium-sized curry udon costs ¥550. There are other branches of Hanamaru in Takamatsu.

There are several restaurants on the 2nd floor of JR Takamatsu station serving both Japanese and Western food; for the latter *UCC Café Plaza* ユシーシーカフェプ ラザ (daily 7.30am-9pm) serves meals from ¥710. JR Hotel Clement Takamatsu has a good-value all-you-can-eat buffet meal in its informal brasserie café/restaurant *Vent* ヴァン (11.30am-2.30pm ¥1800; 6-9pm ¥2900), on the 1st/ground floor, but it also has Chinese, Japanese and Italian restaurants which offer more upscale dining. For a drink with a view try the 21st-floor *Bar Astro* バーアストロ (5pm to midnight), where you can sip cocktails (around ¥1450) while admiring the sunset over the harbour area.

On the 30th floor of **Tower Building** タワービル (in the Symbol Tower complex) is *Alice* アリス (☎ 087-823 6088; 11.30am-3pm & 5-10pm), a French restaurant whose full name is 'Alice in Takamatsu by Queen Alice'. You pay for the stunning views as much as the excellent nouvelle cuisine (set dinner menus from ¥6300, à la carte main dishes from ¥2200). They also offer wedding receptions and other events so the restaurant may be closed. One floor below is *Szechwan* スーツァン (11am-3pm & 5-10pm; dishes from ¥1500; lunch/evening set menu ¥3200/4300), a good Chinese place.

In **Maritime Plaza** マリタイムプラ ザ (🖳 www.maripla.jp), on the 2nd floor of Hall Wing, you'll find a branch of the fast-food joint *Freshness Burger* フレッシュ ネスバーガー (10am-9pm; burgers around ¥790); all the burgers are made to order and include vegetarian options. There are several restaurants on the 3rd floor: for Sanuki udon try *Udon Takumi Goshiki* うどん匠 郷屋敷 (daily 11am-10pm) – delicious *yaki-udon* costs here ¥1200; other options on this floor include ramen, fried chicken, sushi and Chinese. Most places are open daily 11am-9pm.

*Mikayla* ミケイラ (☎ 087-811 5357, 🖥 www.mikayla.jp; daily 11am to midnight, lunch 11am-2pm, café 2-4pm, evening meal 5-10pm), also part of the **Sunport Takamatsu** complex, is out on the pier and has a terrace café which affords great views over the Inland Sea. The lunch menu includes pasta or curry rice (from ¥980); if in the mood to splash out have 'surf and turf' (¥5200). The set menu in the evening costs ¥5400 but pasta/pizza dishes cost from ¥1000 and the food is excellent. The terrace is also a great place to relax with a cocktail at sunset and watch people strolling along the promenade. Booking is advisable in the evening. Mikayla is about a 5-minute walk from JR Takamatsu station.

*Ten Yasu* てんやす (11am-9pm) is a delightfully traditional tempura house with dishes from ¥1200 and set meals for ¥6000. Look out for the large Japanese trees and bushes at the entrance.

If passing through Takamatsu-Chikko station late in the day stop at '*Beer Pub Station' Irish Pub the Craic* アイリッシュ パブ ザ クラック ことでん (Wed-Sat 5-9pm, Sun 3-8pm) for a drink or snack; it is a small stand where you can get Guinness (¥600) and other beers as well as hot coffee (¥300); takeaway is also available. To soak up your beer, try some 'bone-in chicken' こ だわりの骨付鳥 (¥950; chicken thighs grilled with the bone in), a speciality of the region.

## Side trips from Takamatsu

**By boat to Naoshima** Naoshima 直島 (🖥 www.naoshima.net), an island in the Inland Sea, is home to a truly impressive art and cultural complex called **Benesse Art Site Naoshima** ベネッセアートセイト直島, the centrepiece of which is the superb **Benesse House** ベネッセハウス (🖥 www.benesse-art site.jp; daily 8am-9pm; ¥1030); this is both a contemporary art museum – designed by leading architect Tadao Ando and focusing on 'the coexistence of nature, art and architecture' – and a hotel (see below). The complex also includes **Lee Ufan Museum** 李禹煥美術館 (Tue-Sun Mar-Sep 10am-6pm, Oct-Feb 10am-5pm; ¥1030), which has works by Korean artist Lee Ufan, and **Chichu Art Museum** 地中美術館 (same hours as Lee Ufan Museum; ¥2060), which has works by Claude Monet, James Turrell and Walter de Maria and is mostly underground. You can, though, see a lot of wonderful art works without paying anything. As you approach Miyanoura Port you can't miss the *Red Pumpkin* by Yayoi Kusama but there is lots more to see, including Kusama's *Yellow Pumpkin*, spread around the area by Benesse House. Art fans should consider staying the night in *Benesse House*; there is a range of accommodation in super-swanky purpose-built rooms (from ¥27,000/D or T) overlooking the Inland Sea; see the website for details.

The **Art House Project** 家プロジェクト (🖥 www.benesse-artsite.jp/ en/arthouse; Tue-Sun 10am-4.30pm; ¥410 for one house, ¥1030 for six houses), in the Honmura 本村 district of the island, consists of a number of houses converted to be, or show, works of art. The ticket lists the many options so you can choose where to go.

The island is also a place of pilgrimage for fans of James Bond. James Bond is no stranger to Japan: most of *You Only Live Twice*, starring Sean Connery opposite the characters Tiger Tanaka and Kissy Suzuki, was set and filmed in the country; see p274. But it may come as a surprise to learn that there is a small museum – **007: The Man With the Red Tattoo Museum** ダ ブルオーセブン博物館 (🖥 www.007museum.jp; daily 9am-5pm; free but

SHIKOKU

donations appreciated) – here particularly devoted to promoting Naoshima as a location if a film is ever made of the 007 novel *The Man With the Red Tattoo* by American author Raymond Benson (Hodder & Stoughton, 2002); the novel was set in Japan, much of it on Naoshima itself, hence its relevance as a location. The museum also displays information on Benson and other authors who have contributed to the Bond legacy, as well as memorabilia connected to the 007 franchise.

Before you leave the island, don't forget to enjoy an artistic soak in the gloriously eccentric bath-house, I□湯(**Yu**) (Tue-Fri 2-9pm, Sat, Sun & holidays 10am-9pm; ¥510), a very short stroll up the narrow lane, opposite the port, that bisects the village. Created by artist Shinro Otake, the architecture reverses notions of interior and exterior and may explain why your hot bath takes place in the shadow of a giant elephant called Sadako. Note that neither a towel nor soap is provided.

**Shikoku Kisen** 四国汽船株式会社 operates ferries to Miyanoura Port (🖳 www.shikokukisen.com; 5/day; 40-60 mins depending on the tides; ¥520 each way) and also high-speed boats (30 mins; 1-3/day; ¥1220 each way). There is a **tourist information centre** (daily 8.30am-6pm) in the Miyanoura Port terminal building where you can pick up a map to the island and its many attractions; staff here will also help with the many accommodation options if you decide to stay the night. You can rent a bicycle from a number of places but it is probably easiest to get the Town Bus to Tsutsuji-so つつじ荘 (1-2/hr; ¥100). From Tsutsuji-so a free shuttle bus (13-15/day) takes you to Benesse House. Get off the Town Bus at Nokyo-mae 農協前 for the Art House Project.

**By boat to Megijima** Takamatsu is also an access point for other islands in the Inland Sea. Megijima 女木島, also known as Onigashima 鬼ヶ島, has a huge cave – **Daidokutsu** 大洞窟 (Oni's Cave; daily 8am-5pm; ¥500) – said to have been used as a pirate den and also to have been visited by Momotaro (see box p297). Follow signs to the ticket office キップノリバ from where you can either take a bus (5/day; ¥300 each way), or rent a bicycle (¥300-600; electric assisted ¥700, both for 4hrs). Close to Megi port is a small village full of atmospheric narrow streets some of which lead down to a sandy beach. Megijima is only a 20-minute ferry ride (6/day) from Takamatsu. Services also go to Megijima's neighbouring island, **Ogijima** 男木島.

**By train to Kotohira** Kotohira (see pp468-9) is easily reached by either JR train (LEX 42 mins, local 50 mins) or, if you don't have a JR Pass, on the Kotoden Kotohira Line (2/hr; 62 mins; ¥620) from Takamatsu Chikko station.

## TOKUSHIMA 徳島

You might not immediately think of Rio when you see Tokushima, but the city believes its annual dance festival is as big as Brazil's carnival. Quiet for most of the year, Tokushima comes alive in August when it hosts the Awa-Odori.

### What to see and do

If you miss the Awa-Odori festival, you can experience its highlights year-round at **Awa-Odori Kaikan** 阿波おどり会館, home to both the Awa-Odori Museum, a hall where there are regular performances of the festival dance, and the base station for Bizan Ropeway (cable car) up to Mt Bizan. It is generally worth getting a combination ticket: return trip on the ropeway plus the museum/museum and afternoon dance ¥1120/1620); or museum and afternoon dance ¥800.

The **museum** (🖥 www.awaodori-kai kan.jp; daily 9am-5pm, closed every 2nd and 4th Wed; ¥300), on the 3rd floor, presents the history, costumes and instruments of the Awa-Odori dance though all the labels are in Japanese. The person at the ticket desk can give you some notes in English but they are very general. Awanokaze, the resident troupe, perform the dance for real in the 2nd-floor dance hall (Mon-Fri 2pm, 3pm & 4pm, weekends and holidays also at 11am; 40 mins; ¥600 afternoon); in the evenings other dance troupes perform (daily 8pm; 50 mins; ¥800).

Go to the 5th floor for **Bizan Ropeway** 眉山ロープウエイ (daily 9am-5.30pm, to 9pm in summer; 2-4/hr; 6 mins; ¥610 one-way) up **Mt Bizan**. At the top there are impressive views of the city whether you are here during the day or at night. Bizan Park is also pleasant to walk around.

The Kaikan is a 10-minute walk down Shinmachibashi-dori, the main thoroughfare leading away from the station;

From **Hyotanjima Cruise Boat Pier** ひょうたん島周遊船乗降口, along **Shinmachi Riverside Park** 新町川水際公園 promenade, you can take a very good-value **boat trip** (dep daily every 40 mins 11am-3.40pm, in Jul & Aug also 5-7.40pm; free but ¥200 for insurance) along the Shinmachi and Suketoh rivers round Tokushima's island centre. Even though it is not particularly scenic you do go under lots of very low bridges which is fun as you always think you will hit your head. There are two kinds of boat; if in luck yours will be the stylish one with leather seats.

**Tokushima Castle Museum** 徳島城博物館 (Tue-Sun 9.30am-5pm; ¥300), within **Tokushima Central Park** 徳島中央公園, charts the 267-year history of the Tokushima clan's hilltop castle until it was demolished during the Meiji Restoration. Entrance is worth it just to see the full-length *Senzan-Maru* cruising vessel from feudal Japan's civil-war period, the only *daimyo* vessel left in Japan. Entrance includes admission to **Omotego-ten Garden** 表御殿庭園 (¥50 on its own), a dry landscape garden featuring an impressive pond and rock garden that you can clamber

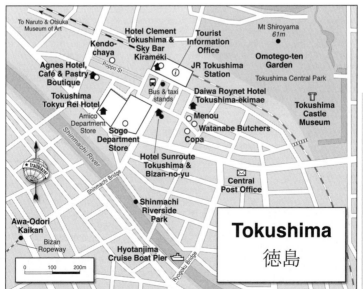

SHIKOKU

over. From the station, turn left and hug the railway line until you see a little pedestrian bridge crossing the tracks; climb up and over this and then turn left for the museum and garden.

The spectacular Naruto Whirlpools (see opposite) are easily reached from Takamatsu and make an excellent side trip.

## Practical information

**Station guide** The station only has one exit. There are some **lockers** on the concourse but walk down to the basement level for large ones. **Clement Plaza** クレメント プラザ (🖳 www.clementplaza.com; daily 10am-8pm) shopping complex is on the left side of the concourse from the ticket gates; there are several restaurants (daily 11am-9.30pm) on the 5th floor and a branch of *Starbucks* on the 1st/ground floor.

**Tourist information** The tourist information office (🖳 www.city.tokushima.toku shima.jp; daily 10am-6pm) is on the 6th floor; take one of the lifts/elevators on the right-hand side by the station exit.

**Getting around** Tokushima is easy to navigate on foot.

**Festivals** The city's fame lies squarely with its 400-year-old **Awa-Odori dance festival**, staged during the O-bon celebrations (Aug 12th-15th; be sure to book accommodation in advance if arriving in this period). The festival encapsulates the city's cultural identity and has a relaxed vibe. Anime fans come here in the autumn for **Machi-Asobi** (🖳 www.dedao-tokushi ma.com); many of the events are held on Mt Bizan (see p487).

**Where to stay** For accommodation with style, *Hotel Clement Tokushima* ホテルク レメント徳島 (☎ 088-656-3131, 🖳 www .hotelclement.co.jp; ¥15,444/S, ¥19,008/D, ¥26,136/Tw; buffet breakfast ¥1880) is a convenient choice as it is located just to the right of the station exit. As with many hotels rates for online reservations can be much less and packages may include breakfast. The rooms (7th-17th floors) are a good

size but the ones facing the tracks can be noisy if you like having the window open. To the left of the station is *Daiwa Roynet Hotel Tokushima-ekimae* ダイワロイネッ トホテル徳島駅前 (☎ 088-611 8455, 🖳 www.daiwaroynet.jp; from ¥8380/S, ¥10,460/D, ¥15,460/Tw, inc buffet breakfast); it has a variety of rooms, including some 'Ladies' rooms', and provides all the facilities you would expect.

*Hotel Sunroute Tokushima* ホテルサ ンルート徳島 (☎ 088 653 8111, 🖳 sunrou te-tokushima.com; ¥10,000/S, ¥15,960/D or Tw, inc buffet breakfast) offers stylish and comfortable accommodation; the rooms are on the 4th-10th floor. A particular feature is the tranquil 11th-floor **Bizan no yu** びざんの湯 hot spring bath, which is free for guests (non-residents 7am-noon ¥520, noon-8pm ¥720). The hotel entrance is to the right of the branch of Tully's Coffee on the 1st/ground floor. Take a lift to the reception desk on the 3rd floor.

Another decent option is *Agnes Hotel* アグネスホテル (☎ 088-626-2222, 🖳 www.agneshotel.jp; from ¥6018/S, ¥12,037/Tw, inc good buffet breakfast); it is quite a small hotel but it is stylish and minimalist in design. See also Where to eat.

*Tokushima Tokyu REI Hotel* 徳島東 急REIホテル (☎ 088-626-0109, 🖳 www .tokushima.rei.tokyuhotels.co.jp; from ¥5900/S, ¥9400/D or Tw; buffet breakfast ¥1342) is part of the reliable business hotel chain. The rooms are on the 9th-11th floors (above Amico department store).

See also pp67-73.

**Where to eat and drink** The broth for Tokushima's ramen is made from a sweet/salty pork belly stock with soy sauce; traditionally the ramen is served with a raw egg on top. A good place to try some is *Menou* 麺王 (daily 11am to midnight); purchase a ticket from the machine outside (ramen from ¥500). Such is its reputation for delicious ramen that locals feel it is always worth the wait if there is a queue. If you get tired of waiting there are several other options on this road including *Watanabe Butcher's* わたなべ精肉店 (5.30pm-1am), which describes itself as a

'Station Front Wine Bistro'. The menu includes *yakiniku* and *teppanyaki* (around ¥3500); cheaper options are burgers (¥980) and a colourful salad (¥680). There is a wide selection of wines.

**Sogo department store** そごう徳島店 in the far right corner of the station square has a medley of restaurants on the 9th floor including Italian and Chinese (daily 11am-9pm). The blandly named but popular *Family Restaurant* ファミリーレストラン offers the best value with a vast range of rice, udon and spaghetti sets from ¥900 to ¥1600. Don't be put off by the long queues outside as the cavernous restaurant has brisk service. Also on this floor is a tonkatsu restaurant, *Tonkatsu Marukatsu-tei* とんかつまるかつ亭 (expect to pay around ¥1500), and a pasta place called *Dear* ディアー, where pasta/pizza cost around ¥800. The 10th floor (roof) offers a free view of Tokushima and a play area for kids. If self-catering go to the **supermarket** in the basement.

Agnes Hotel (see Where to stay) has a *pastry boutique* ペストリーブティック (daily 11am-9pm; cakes and pastries around ¥500) as well as a *café* カフェ (daily 7am-9.30pm); the latter offers pasta dishes and the Agnes Curry (both from

¥1100) as well as a variety of main dishes (from ¥2100).

For a quiet drink, try the friendly *Copa* コパ bar (daily 6.30pm-1am), which has interesting photo pastiches of arty/Euro-culture on the walls and serves a decent choice of beer (¥600) and spirits as well as unusual cocktails such as beer and tomato juice (¥600). The atmosphere is intimate and conducive to conversation. Go past Menou (see opposite) and keep walking until you see the English sign on the right side of the road. Another option for a drink is *Sky Bar Kirameki* スカイバー 煌 (daily 6pm to midnight), on the 18th floor of Hotel Clement Tokushima (see Where to stay). It offers great views across the city, but do sit at the bar if you want to avoid the ¥750 table fee on top of your cocktail (around ¥1000). The hotel also has several upmarket restaurant options.

There are a few options along **Poppo-machi** ポーポー町, the covered shopping street to the right of the station: at *Kendo-chaya* けんど茶屋 (daily 9am-8pm, to 10pm during the Awa-Odori) Tokushima ramen costs ¥650 and a Tokushima donburi (rice bowl) is ¥700. It's on the right-hand side as you walk from the station; look for the straw dolls outside.

## Side trips from Tokushima

● **Naruto Whirlpools** 鳴門の渦潮 (Naruto no Uzushio)  Guaranteed to get your fellow mariners gasping with delight, the phenomenon of the colliding Pacific Ocean and Seto Inland Sea currents, whipping the waters of the narrow Naruto straits into a series of frothy vortexes, is a great experience. Boat tours are best enjoyed during the faster spring tidal periods, when they can measure 20 metres across and 2 metres deep. Failing that, ensure you are there during the 90-minute morning or evening low/high tide to see them at their most active. Visit Tokushima tourist information office for daily tide times.

**Naruto Kanko Kisen** 鳴門観光汽船 operates 30-minute tours on both *Wonder Naruto* (🖳 www.uzusio.com; daily 9am-4.20pm; every 40 mins; ¥1580) and *Aqua Eddy* (daily 9.15am-4.15pm; 2/hr; 25 mins; ¥2260; book online at least four days ahead); this is a smaller (and more cramped) vessel but its lower level allows for an underwater view of the spinning eddies. Both leave from Kameuro-kanko-ko pier 亀浦観光港 in Naruto-koen. **Uzushio Kisen** うずしお汽船 (🖳 www.uzushio-kisen.com; daily 8am-4.30pm; 2/hr; 20 mins; ¥1550) also operate boat trips from the same pier.

Above the whirlpools, **Onaruto bridge** 大鳴門橋 offers a 450-metre long glass-floor-viewing walkway, **Uzu-no-michi** 渦の道 (Mar-Sep 9am-6pm, Oct-Feb to 5pm, closed every 2nd Mon Jun, Sep, Dec & Mar; ¥510); even though the experience is less dramatic than being on the boat, the advantage is that you can stay as long as you like.

From JR Tokushima take the local train to Naruto (14-17/day; about 35 mins), then hop on a bus to Naruto-koen 鳴門公園 (No 21 or 27; 13-18/day; 20 mins; ¥270) from outside the station.

● **Otsuka Museum of Art** 大塚国際美術館 This museum (💻 www.o-muse um.or.jp; Tue-Sun 9.30am-5pm; ¥3240) is a must for art lovers. It is the largest permanent exhibition space in Japan and contains over a thousand impressive reproductions of Western masterpieces (such as Leonardo da Vinci's *Mona Lisa*, Van Gogh's *Sunflowers* and Picasso's *Guernica)*, all recreated on specially manufactured ceramic boards, as well as its very own full-scale Sistine and Scrovegni chapels. Comfortable footwear is strongly recommended as a total circuit can involve a 4km walk. Regular gallery talks are held, some even provided by 'Art', a diminutive robot who speaks four languages and points his own professorial laser beam!

Get off the Naruto-koen bus at Otsuka Kokusan Bijutsukan-mae 大塚国際美術館前. The museum entrance is up and around the adjacent road turning on the left. If going on to the whirlpool tours, take the next bus (or simply walk 15 minutes up the road). If planning to visit this museum and have a boat tour do check the whirlpool tide times when deciding what to do first.

## MATSUYAMA 松山

Matsuyama, the largest city on the island, became prominent as a castle town in the 17th century. In recent years it has benefited greatly from the road link (from nearby Imabari) across the Nishi-Seto Expressway to Honshu.

### What to see and do

Two priorities are Matsuyama Castle and nearby Dogo-onsen (see pp494-5). Both could be done in one day, but an overnight stay would be more relaxing.

**Matsuyama Castle** 松山城 (💻 www .matsuyamajo.jp; daily 9am-5pm; ¥510, joint admission/return ropeway ticket ¥1020) is at the top of Katsuyama Hill 勝山 (132m-high) in the city centre. Construction was completed in 1627 but, like other castles in Japan, it has suffered various misfortunes since: struck by lightning on New Year's Day 1784, the donjon and other buildings burnt to the ground. They were reconstructed in 1854 – but the donjon was made a 3-storey rather than 5-storey building – only to suffer bomb damage during WWII. Today, the castle is reached by taking either the **ropeway** ロープウェイ (cable car), or a cutesy **chair-lift** リフト. Both operate daily (8.30am-5pm,

ropeway to 6pm in August; ¥510 return) but the chair-lift operates continuously so you don't need to wait long; also it is much more fun as long as the weather is good. It's difficult to imagine what the castle lords who occupied this fortification would have made of the sight of people gliding up the hill in moving chairs but it's safe to assume that as intruders they'd have been easy targets.

Even if you avoid the cost of the ropeway/chair-lift by walking up the hill there's still a fair way to go before you reach the donjon, let alone climbing up inside it, which is probably the main purpose of your journey. However, the views of the city and surrounding area, with mountains on one side and the Inland Sea coastline on the other, make the effort worthwhile. Aside from that there are lots of labels in English and several things to see. The castle is a popular place so don't expect to be on your own. The nearest tram/streetcar stop for the journey up to the castle is Okaido; from there it is a short walk along Ropeway Street to the base of the ropeway/chair-lift.

A couple of minutes north of Minami-Horibata tram stop is **Ehime Prefectural Art Museum** 愛媛県美術館 (💻 www .ehime-art.jp; Tue-Sun 9.40am-6pm; ¥300) which houses a permanent collection of Japanese and Western art alongside special exhibitions (separate charge). In amongst the traditional scrolls depicting cormorant fishermen are some intriguing sculptures such as Jean Arc's *Gur*. At the opposite end of the upper floor gallery, significant space is devoted to local art work. **Bansui-so** 萬翠荘 (Tue-Sun 9am-6pm), a French-style building, was built in 1922 by a former feudal lord; today it functions as an annex to the Prefectural Art Museum. Entry to the 1st/ground floor is free but the 2nd floor houses temporary exhibitions for which the charge varies. The nearest tram stop is Okaido.

Popular with couples in search of a romantic view of Matsuyama is **Kururin ferris wheel** 大観覧車 (also known as Kanran-sha; Apr-Dec 11am-10pm, Oct-Mar 11am-7.30pm, last ride 15 mins before ride closes; ¥500/ride, or ¥1000 per 4-seat gondola; free for foreign tourists), an unmissable landmark (eyesore?) perched on the 9th floor of Iyotetsu Takashimaya department store, above Matsuyama-shi station. This is worth a go for the views of the city; the best time is at dusk, when you'll witness the sun setting over the city.

The **Botchan train** 坊っちゃん列車 (6/day; ¥500 per journey, additional ¥300 if you have a 1-day pass), described as being 'a small matchbox-like train' in Soseki's novel, *Botchan*, is a great way to get to, or return from, Dogo-onsen (see pp494-5). You can buy a ticket from Iyotetsu Ticket Center (daily 6am-11pm) at Mastuyama-shi station, or from the Botchan shop at Dogo-onsen, or on the train. In general the journey is jerky and noisy but fun. Make sure you arrive in time to see the previous train arrive at the Matsuyama-shi terminus, or hang around when it reaches Dogo-onsen, so that you can see the staff disconnect the carriages and manually turn the loco around. Botchan also operates from Komachi station (2/day) to Dogo-onsen. The trains today are diesel replicas of the original Botchan train which was the first small-size steam locomotive in Japan; it was imported from Germany in 1888 and was used for 67 years. If you don't have

time to have a journey on one you can see the original train on the far right corner of Botchan Square if looking from Matsuyama-shi station.

### Practical information

**Station guide** The **ticket office** (daily 5am-11pm) at JR Matsuyama station is combined with the travel agency. There's an *udon and soba* (daily 11am-6pm; ¥300-500) stand by the ticket barrier. **Lockers** (all sizes) are behind the udon/soba stand and also to the right of the station exit.

Do not confuse JR Matsuyama station with **Matsuyama-shi** 松山空 station; the latter is the main station in Matsuyama for services operated by Iyotetsu. There are lockers there and a convenience store; the station is connected to Iyotetsu Takashimaya department store.

**Tourist information** Matsuyama **Tourist Information Center** (TIC; ☐ en .matsuyama-sightseeing.com; daily 8.30am-8.30pm) is in the kiosk to the left as you face the station exit. A quirk of this place is that from 8.30am to 5pm it functions only as a tourist information office and cannot help with accommodation reservations. However, from 5pm to 8.30pm hotel reservation staff take over. If you time your arrival for around 4.30pm you may get the best of both worlds. **Dogo Tourist Office** (daily 8am-5pm) is across the street from the tram terminus at Dogo-onsen (see pp494-5). In both places you can pick up leaflets about Matsuyama as well as Dogo-onsen and also buy the local travel passes. You should be also able to pick up a copy of *What's Going On?* (☐ home.e-catv.ne .jp/wgo), a monthly guide to events in Matsuyama. The latter is also available in some hotels.

**Getting around** The easiest way of travelling around Matsuyama is on one of the Iyotetsu **tram/streetcar** lines (daily 6am-10pm; 3-12/hr; ¥160 flat fare, ¥500/800 1-/2-day pass). There are five routes (Nos 1, 2, 3, 5 and 6); there is no No 4 because 'shi' (4) means death in Japanese. Enter at the back and pay as you leave at the front. Passes can be bought from the TIC at JR Matsuyama station, or at Iyotetsu Ticket Center at Matsuyama-shi station. An additional ticket is required to ride on the Botchan train (see p491). Note that for some places the tram announcements in English are the translation of the Japanese name, not the name you actually see on the signs or on some maps.

**Festivals** The highlight of **Matsuyama Festival** (11th-13th Aug) is a night-time parade of samba dancers. The event is kicked off by a fireworks display on 10th August.

**Where to stay**  *Terminal Hotel Matsuyama* ターミナルホテル松山 (☎ 089-947 5388, 🖥 www.th-matsuyama.jp; from ¥4950/S, ¥8220/D or Tw; Western or Japanese breakfast ¥650), a JR hotel (see box p71), has functional rooms and is near the JR station and right by the tram stop.

Also near the JR station is **Sky Hotel** スカイホテル (☎ 089-947 7776, 🖥 www.shikoku-sky.com; from ¥6800/S, ¥11,000/D, ¥12,000/T; buffet breakfast ¥1000), with comfortably sized, though slightly tired, rooms.

*Hotel JAL City Matsuyama* ホテルJALシティ松山 (☎ 089-913 2580, 🖥 my jmyj.co.jp; from ¥7800/S, ¥8148/D or Tw; buffet breakfast ¥1500) is within walking distance of the JR station and is a cut above the standard business hotel. Reception staff are friendly and pro-active.

As Shikoku's biggest city, Matsuyama is not short of top-class hotels. *ANA Hotel Matsuyama* 全日航ホテル松山 (☎ 089-933 5511, 🖥 www.anahotelmatsuyama .com; from ¥7695/S, ¥13,680/D or Tw) has a great location, opposite the castle and in the centre of town. The spacious rooms have wide-screen TVs, mini bars and room service. Across the street is *Matsuyama Tokyu REI Hotel* 松山東急REIホテル (☎ 089-941 0109, 🖥 www.matsuyama.rei.tok yuhotels.co.jp; from ¥8200/S, ¥12,400/D, ¥14,400/Tw, inc buffet breakfast), with a bright interior and smartly decorated rooms.

A good budget option, a short way from the Okaido shopping arcade, is *Hotel*

*Top Inn* ホテルトップイン (☎ 089-933 3333, 🖥 www.top-inn.com; from ¥4100/S, ¥5830/D). A basic business hotel with simple rooms (and room service); Japanese-style rooms (sleeping up to three people) are also available. A bonus is that it is near the sights and tram stops.

*Toyoko Inn Matsuyama Ichibancho* 東横イン 松山一番町 (☎ 089-941 1045, 🖥 www.toyoko-inn.com; ¥5724/S, ¥7884/D, ¥8640/Tw, inc breakfast), a branch of the reliable chain hotel, is in the city centre; the Katsuyama-cho tram stop is outside the hotel.

For details about accommodation at Dogo-onsen see p495; for general accommodation information see pp67-73.

**Where to eat and drink**  *O-oiritei* 大入亭 (daily 6-11pm, Sun & holidays noon-2pm) is a small cramped izakaya that specialises in sashimi – ask for the *o-sashimi mori awase* お刺身盛合せ, a splendid plate of up to 15 types of sashimi – but also has a wide variety of grilled and fried foods. The menu is in Japanese and prices vary according to the daily catch, but expect to pay an absolute minimum of ¥1680pp for the main sashimi course. Be aware that this place is very hidden; soon after entering the covered Okaido 大街道 arcade, turn left down a narrow alley after McDonald's and with the Flying Scotsman (see below) on the right-hand side. Follow the alley as it doglegs right then left. Look for the white kanji sign low on the right side. At the alley entrance lies the mock railway carriage of the *Flying Scotsman* フライングスコッツマン (daily 8.30am-11pm), a fine choice for a lunchtime sandwich. Hamburger sets (¥660) and toasted sandwich sets (¥860) complement the cold choices. Find a peaceful booth to munch away in and let the period interiors turn your thoughts back to the golden age of steam.

The menu at *Himawari* ひまわり (daily 11am-3am, lunch to 5pm) includes *takoyaki* (from ¥400) and *mitsuyamataki* (like okonomiyaki; from ¥820); lunch sets cost ¥720-950. You can eat in or take-away and since it is open till the early hours it is a great place for a late-night snack.

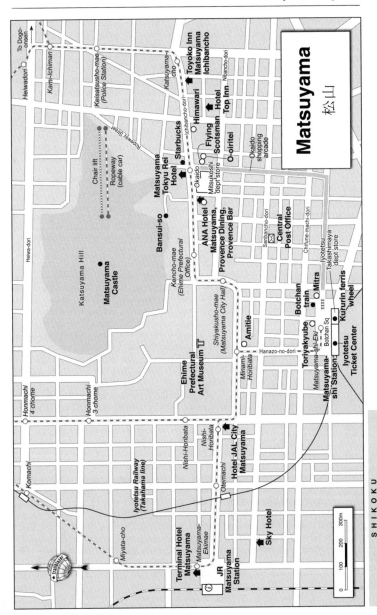

# Matsuyama

松山

**To Dogo-onsen**

Heiwadori

Kam-Ichiman

'Keisatsusho-mae (Police Station)'

Katsuyama-cho

Toyoko Inn Matsuyama Ichibancho

Ichibancho-dori

Nibancho-dori

Himawari

Top Inn Matsuyama Hotel

Flying Scotsman

O-oiritei

Okaido shopping arcade

Chair lift

Ropeway (cable car)

Ropeway Street

Starbucks

Matsuyama Tokyu Rei Hotel

Okaido

Mitsukoshi dept store

Bansui-so

Katsuyama Hill

Heiwa-dori

Matsuyama Castle

Kencho-mae (Ehime Prefectural Office)

ANA Hotel Matsuyama, Provence Dining, Provence Bar

Sanbancho-dori

Central Post Office

Chifune-machi-dori

Takashimaya dept store

Iyotetsu

Shiyakusho-mae (Matsuyama City Hall)

Botchan train

Mitra

Kururin ferris wheel

Amitie

Honmachi 4 chome

Honmachi 3 chome

Ehime Prefectural Art Museum

Minami-Horibata

Toriyakyube

Matsuyama-shi-Eki

Botchan Sq

Hanazo-no-dori

Iyotetsu Ticket Center

Matsuyama-shi Station

Komachi

Iyotetsu Railway (Takahama line)

Nishi-Horibata

Nishi-Horibata

Hotel JAL City Matsuyama

Otemachi

Sky Hotel

Terminal Hotel Matsuyama

Miyata-cho

Matsuyama-Ekimae

JR Matsuyama Station

**SHIKOKU**

0    100    200    300m

Trailblazer

***Toriyakyube*** とりや久兵衛 (daily 11.30am-2.30pm & 5pm to midnight) serves a variety of yakitori (¥120-250) as well as various grilled vegetables including aubergines, potatoes and onions. Donburi (¥650) is also available. It is by bus stop No 8 in Botchan Square. On the eastern edge of the square lies ***Mitra*** 三トラ (Tue-Sat 11.30am-2pm & 6pm-2am; Sun 11.30am-2pm & 6pm to midnight), a 1st/ground-floor dining bar that tries to bring an edge of European sophistication to a young demographic. Its menu offers Italian fare such as creamy pasta (¥880) and pizza (¥800) as well as fried rice (¥900). Drinks are a standard ¥500 (¥380 if ordering food) and there is an excellent range of wines. The terrace is pleasant in the summer and offers a nice oasis in the city. There are several other options around the square.

Opposite Ehime Prefectural Art Museum (see p490) on the main road is ***Amitie*** アミテイエ (lunch 11.30am-2pm, tea 2-4.30pm, evening meals 5.30-10pm), an odd cross between an antique shop and French bistro. Diners enjoy a good choice from a changing daily menu, such as grilled fish and continental desserts. Mains start at ¥1200; cakes/pastries around ¥800.

Many hotels have restaurants: ANA Hotel Matsuyama (see Where to stay) has a good choice including ***Provence Dining*** プロヴァンスダイニング (11.30am-2pm & 5.30-10pm), an Italian restaurant with a lunch/dinner menu for ¥1950/2800. Also on the 14th floor is ***Provence Bar*** プロヴァンスバー (6.30pm to midnight) which provides a panorama of the neon cityscape and is a good place to sit and reflect on the day's discoveries over a cocktail (¥1150).

## Side trip to Dogo-onsen 道後温泉

Twenty minutes by tram from Matsuyama is the ancient spa town of Dogo. Today, Dogo is geared up to the tourist trade but a trip to the bath-house is an excellent way to unwind after a day's sightseeing and offers a unique experience if you get the Tama-no-yu ticket (see below). The hot spring dates back 3000 years and according to legend was discovered when a white heron put its injured leg into hot water flowing out of a crevice in some rocks. **Dogo-onsen bath-house** 道後温泉本館 (Dogo-onsen honkan; 🖳 www.dogo.or.jp) was built in 1894 and is said to be the inspiration for the bath-house of the Gods in Miyazaki's animated classic *Spirited Away*. The hot spring is now deemed one of the three most famous in Japan.

For the best atmosphere and to see the bath-house illuminated visit in the evening; last entry is about 30 minutes before closing time. Tickets for the no-frills 1st/ground-floor bath, called **Kami-no-yu** 神の湯 (Water of the Gods; daily 6am-11pm), cost ¥410, but there is no soap or shampoo, nor are you given a towel though one can be hired for ¥60. The 2nd floor has the more exclusive **Tama-no-yu** 霊の湯 (Water of the Spirits; daily 6am-10pm) bath. For ¥840 you are: given a towel and yukata; served Japanese tea and a rice cracker after your bath; have an area to relax in; and you can also go down to Kami-no-yu which is worth doing as it is a far more characterful bath. The highlight though is the guided tour (in Japanese only but you will be given notes in English) of the Yushinden (see opposite). All of this applies for the ¥1250 option but for that instead of the rice cracker you have a *Botchan Dango* – a dumpling-shaped sweetmeat, that Natsume Soseki, author of *Botchan*, used to eat when he worked in Matsuyama; or for ¥1550 the same but with a private room (with balcony) for relaxing in.

You can safely deposit items alongside your clothes in the free wooden lockers at the bath entrances. Wear the key on your wrist as you enter the baths. It is rather a warren of rooms inside but the staff will show you where to go.

Since the actual baths here are not that exciting, and in peak hours can be incredibly crowded, you may prefer just to come for the fascinating guided tour (¥260) of the **Yushinden** 又新殿, a special area in the bath-house constructed for any visiting Emperor, or male members of the Imperial family. Both the Taisho and Showa emperors have visited as well as some crown princes, but empresses/princesses aren't allowed to bathe here. The area is absolutely stunning with *fusuma* (sliding screens) covered in gold foil. There is a separate entrance, bath and toilet for the Emperor; the latter has never been used as Imperial visits have always been short. The Emperor is the only person who is allowed to bathe wearing some clothes – a silver silk bath robe is provided.

Take a tram (No 5 from Matsuyama station, or No 3 from Matsuyama-shi) bound for Dogo-onsen. The old-fashioned terminal here is a 1986 reconstruction of the original (1911) European-style building. From the tram station, walk through the covered L-shaped **Dogo Haikara-dori** 道後ハイカラ通り shopping arcade to reach Dogo bath-house; turn right when you reach the locally popular but less well known (and less crowded) **Tsubaki-no-yu** 温泉椿の湯 bath-house (Mon-Fri 9am to midnight, Sat & Sun from 7am; ¥650-750) on your left. Keep walking for Dogo bath-house; it's opposite the exit to the arcade.

Back near the tram/streetcar stop, be sure to stop and observe the exquisite workings of the **Botchan Karakuri clock** 坊ちゃんからくり時計 each hour (daily 8am-10pm). The roof rises to reveal traditionally clad figures from a bath-house scene in Soseki's novel as they gently spin to a playful musical score. You can also dip your feet into the adjoining **foot-bath**.

If you decide to stay in the area there are several options: *Yamatoya Honten* 大和屋本店 (☎ 089-935 8880, 🖳 www.yamatoyahonten.com; from ¥20,000pp inc half board; room-only rates on request) is definitely the place to stay if you can afford it. It's all kimonos and shamisen music in this upmarket ryokan, which even stages daily performances at its own Noh theatre. The ryokan also has its own attractive outdoor hot spring. Most rooms are tatami style though there are some Western singles and two twins. Advance booking is highly recommended. *Old England Dogo Yamanote Hotel* オールドイングランド道後山の手ホテル (☎ 089-998 2111, 🖳 www.dogo-yamanote.com; from ¥10,000/S, ¥14,000/D or Tw, inc breakfast; rates can be as high as ¥42,000/D or Tw, inc half board) exudes luxury and impresses from the moment you approach it. This is a place which tries, and to some extent succeeds, to recreate the atmosphere and décor of an Edwardian English country house so don't come here for an authentic Japanese experience. If you can't be bothered to walk around the corner to Dogo-onsen bath-house, you can soak in the hotel's own spa. It's great for an unusual one-night escape. *Hotel Patio Dogo* ホテルパティオ・ドウゴ (☎ 089-941 4128, 🖳 www.patio-dogo.co.jp; from ¥7665/S, ¥11,550/D, ¥14,700/Tw, see website for discounts; breakfast ¥750) also has Western-style accommodation and is right across from the far side of the bath-house if coming from the tram.

A great place to eat after a bath is *Dogo Uotake* 道後 魚武 (🖳 www.dogo-uotake.com; 11am-11pm); the menu includes several *teishoku* (set meals) some of which have *taimeshi* 鯛めし (sea-bream rice) a speciality of the area; a sashimi/tempura teishoku costs ¥1800. Also worth trying here is the delicious **Dogo beer** 道後ビール, brewed by Dogo Brewery in Matsuyama and designed to be drunk after a bath. Dogo Uotake is on the left side, near the top of the arcade, if returning to the tram.

# APPENDIX A: GLOSSARY

## GENERAL

**Asa-ichi** 朝市 morning market

**Ashi-yu** 足湯 foot-bath

**-basho** 場所 place where a sumo tournament is held

**-bashi** 橋 bridge

**Bento** 弁当 lunch box (*see also* Ekiben)

**Bunraku** 文楽 puppetry

**Cosplay** コスプレ costume play ie dressing as a character from anime or manga

**Daimyo** 大名 feudal lord

**Depachika** デパチカ food hall in department store

**-dera** 院 temple (Buddhist)

**-dori/odori** -道リ street

**Ekiben** 駅弁 station lunch box (see box p102; *see also* Bento)

**Front** フロント reception desk in a hotel

**Gaijin** 外人 foreigner

**-gawa** 川 river

**Geisha** 芸者 person trained to entertain at a party (usually a woman)

**Geta** 下駄 wooden clogs

**-gu** 宮 shrine (Shinto)

**Hanabi** 花火 fireworks

**Haiku** 俳句 poem of 17 syllables

**Hanami** 花見 cherry-blossom viewing

**Hanten** 半纏 or はんてん a jacket worn over a yukata (*see* Yukata)

**Henro** 遍路 pilgrims

**Hibakusha** 被爆者 A-bomb survivors

**Hiragana** ひらがな (see p500) syllabary for writing Japanese words

**Ikebana** 生け花 flower arranging

**-in** 院 temple (Buddhist)

**Izakaya** 居酒屋 Japanese-style pub/bar

**-ji** 寺 temple (Buddhist)

**Jidohan-baiki** 自動販売機 vending machine

**-jinja** 神社 shrine (Shinto)

**Jinrikisha** 人力車 pulled (cycle) rickshaws, common in tourist areas

**-jo** 城 castle

**Kaiseki-ryori** 懐石料理 a traditional multi-course meal each course of which will be small but aesthetically pleasing

**Kaisoku** 快速 rapid train

**Kaiten-zushiya** 回転寿司 a conveyor-belt sushi restaurant

**Kami** 神 spirit/deity in Shinto religion

**Kanji** 漢字 Chinese characters used to write the Japanese language

**Katakana** カタカナ syllabary for writing non-Japanese words (see p501)

**Kissaten** 喫茶店 a coffee shop where morning sets (see p74) as well as tea, coffee, cakes, sandwiches & light meals are served.

**-ko** 湖 lake

**Koban** 交番 police box

**-koen** 公園 park

**Koi** 鯉 a carp (fish)

**Konbini** コンビニ convenience store (see box p84)

**Koto** 琴 Japanese harp

**Koyo** 紅葉 autumn leaves

**Kyuko** 急行 express train

**Maiko** 舞子 trainee geisha; often called a *geiko* 芸子 in Kyoto

**Manga** 漫画 / マンガ comic

**Manga kissa** 喫茶店 A café with manga/video games; *see also* Kissaten

**Matsuri** 祭 festival

**Meishi** 名刺 business card

**Mikoshi** 神輿 portable shrine particularly used in Shinto festivals

**Minshuku** 民宿 place to stay, similar to a B&B (see p69)

**Morning set / service** モーニングセット / サビス a coffee shop's breakfast; usually coffee, boiled/fried egg and toast

**Noren** 暖簾 split curtain in front of Japanese-style restaurant or shop that shows it is open for business

**Onsen** 温泉 hot-spring resort (*see also* Rotemburo)

**Oshibori** おしぼり or お絞り hot (or cold) wet towel used to refresh yourself before/after a meal

**Robatayaki** 炉端焼き / ろばたやき a kind of *izakaya* but the food is displayed in a counter and customers point to what they want cooked (on a grill)

**Rotemburo** 露天風呂 open-air hot-spring bath (*see also* Onsen)

**Ryokan** 旅館 Japanese-style hotel (see pp71-2)

**Sento** 銭湯 public bath

**Shamisen** 三味線 wood instrument covered in cat skin with three strings made of silk

**Shide** 紙垂, 四手 A paper streamer that is used in Shinto rituals and is often placed in front of a shimenawa (see below).

**Shimenawa** 注連縄 A rice-straw rope which marks the line between a sacred place where gods are enshrined and the outside world. They are also meant to ward off evil spirits.

Shimenawa are found at Shinto shrines

**Shinkansen** 新幹線 super express, or bullet, train

**Shohizei** 消費税 consumption tax (see box 79)

**Shoji** 障子 sliding paper screen

**Shojin ryori** 精進料理 vegetarian food served and eaten by monks in temples

**Shokudo** 食堂 canteen, dining hall

**Taiko** 太鼓 drum

**-taisha** 大社 shrine

**Tatami** 畳 traditional Japanese mat made from rice straw and used as flooring

**-teien** 庭園 garden

**Teishoku** 定食 set meal

**Tenshukaku** 天守閣 donjon; the tower or keep of a castle

**Tetsudo mania / otaku** 鉄道 マニア / オタク railway enthusiast; some like to take photos of trains others prefer to ride on them

**Tokkyu** 特急 limited express train

**Tokonoma** 床の間 alcove in a room containing a Japanese fan, vase or scroll

**Torii** 鳥居 gate at entrance to Shinto shrine

**Torokko** トロッコ open-air carriage on a train

**Ukai** 鵜飼 cormorant fishing; traditional fishing method

**Waraji** 草鞋 giant straw 'sandals' at temples which are meant to act as a charm to ward off evil spirits

**Yabusame** 流鏑馬 horseback archery

**Yakuza** やくざ Japanese mafia

**-yama** 山 mountain

**Yokozuna** 横綱 the highest rank in sumo

**Yukata** 浴衣 cotton garment worn as nightwear; also a summer kimono

**Zazen** 座禅 Zen (Buddhist) meditation

## FOOD AND DRINK

### Food

**Basashi** 馬刺し Raw horsemeat (see box p451).

**Butadon** 豚丼 See Donburi.

**Curry rice (kare raisu)** カレーライス A Japanese take on Indian curry. The sauce is more like gravy than curry but it's a cheap, filling meal.

**Dango** 団子 Dumpling-shaped sweetmeat or confection.

**Donburi** 丼 A bowl of rice topped with chicken and egg (**oyako-don** 親子丼), strips of beef (**gyudon** 牛丼), or pork (**butadon** 豚丼) cooked in a slightly sweet sauce. These restaurants are easy to spot as the counter is usually full of businessmen and meal tickets are bought from vending machines at the entrance; a very cheap meal.

**Ebi-fry** エビフライ Deep-fried prawns.

**Edamame** 枝豆 Soy beans, often served as a snack in izakaya (see opposite).

**Fugu** 鰒 Fugu, also known as blow fish, or puffer fish, 河豚 is notorious as it can be fatal if eaten when not correctly prepared. Only chefs who have qualified after several years of training can serve fugu but still, very occasionally, there are reports of death-by-fugu. Fugu is generally served as sashimi, as a fish jelly or deep fried.

**Gunkan-zushi** 軍艦巻 Rice surrounded by dried seaweed and shaped into a container which is filled with such as salmon roe (**ikura** イクラ), sea urchin (**uni** うに、ウニ) and **natto** (see Natto).

**Gyutan-yaki** 牛タン焼き Grilled beef/ox tongue, a Sendai speciality (see p358).

**Gyudon** 牛丼 See Donburi.

**Gyoza** 餃子 Dumplings filled with meat and vegetables.

**Inari-sushi** 稲荷寿司 The cheapest kind of sushi; rice is covered with **abu-rage** (deep-fried tofu; 油揚げ).

**Kaiten sushi-ya** 回転寿司 Conveyor-belt sushi restaurant. A tank containing live fish often signifies the restaurant is run by a fishmonger so the fish should be the best.

**Kaki-fry** カキフライ Deep-fried oysters

**Kakigori** かき氷 Crushed ice served with different fruit flavours.

**Kani** 蟹 Crab, which is usually served in dedicated crab restaurants, recognisable from the giant crab with moving pincers above the entrance.

**Kare raisu** カレーライス See Curry rice.

**Katsudon** カツ丼 A bowl of rice with tonkatsu (see p499) on top, covered with a slightly sweet sauce (*see also* Donburi).

***Katsuobushi*** かつおぶし A kind of fish (bonito) which is smoked and dried and then used to make dashi, a stock for soup.

***Kitsune-udon*** きつねうどん Udon (see opposite) served with deep-fried thinly sliced tofu.

***Kushikatsu*** 串カツ Deep-fried bits of meat on a skewer (like a kebab).

***Meron pan*** メロンパン Melon-flavoured buns.

***Misoshiru*** みそしる, みそ汁 Miso soup; served with practically every Japanese dish, miso (soybean paste) is a staple ingredient in Japanese cuisine. In Nagano there's even a shop where you can try miso-flavoured ice-cream (see p210).

***Mochi*** 餅 A rice cake; a special type of mochi is eaten to celebrate New Year.

***Nabe*** 鍋 A kind of Japanese hot pot; chicken, beef, pork or seafood mixed with vegetables and cooked in a large pot at your table.

***Natto*** 納豆 Fermented soy beans. Foreigners are often asked if they like *natto*. Answering 'yes' will shock most Japanese since foreigners are supposed not to like it.

***Nigiri-sushi*** 握り寿司 Slices of fresh fish, shellfish, or a sweet Japanese-style omelette (***tamago-yaki***, 卵焼き) on small, oval-shaped rice balls.

***Nori/nori-maki*** 海苔巻き Dried seaweed/seaweed-covered sushi.

***Okonomiyaki*** お好み焼き Japanese savoury pancake with vegetables and meat, cooked on a grill; in some places you cook it yourself.

***Onigiri*** おにぎり Triangles of rice wrapped in a sheet of nori (seaweed) with fillings such as salmon, tuna or pickled plum (see Umeboshi). A popular convenience-store snack.

***Oshi-zushi*** 押し寿司 Rice in a box covered with a mixture of fish, pickles, seaweed and other delights; common as a bento/ekiben (see box p102).

***Oyako-don*** 親子丼 See Donburi.

***Ramen*** ラーメン Stringy yellow noodles served in a miso- or soy-based soup/broth with meat/vegetables; a popular cheap meal or late-night snack. Many restaurants let you specify if you want hard, or soft, noodles, additional toppings such as pork or

vegetables; they also offer ***kaedama*** 替え玉, unlimited refills of noodles.

***Sashimi*** 刺身 Slices of raw fish such as tuna (***maguro*** マグロ), eel (see Unagi), mackerel (***saba*** さば、鯖), prawn (***ebi*** えび、海老) and salmon roe (***ikura*** イクラ); not to be confused with sushi (see below).

***Shabu-shabu*** しゃぶしゃぶ Thinly sliced beef cooked at your table with vegetables and served with a special sauce.

***Shoyu*** しょうゆ 醤油 Soy/soya sauce; fermented soy/soya beans with water and salt; an essential condiment for most meals.

***Soba*** そば Thin buckwheat noodles eaten hot in a soup/broth, or cold when the noodles are dipped into a separate sauce made from soy, mirin (rice wine for cooking) and sake.

***Somen*** そうめん Noodles served cold and eaten only in the summer.

***Soup curry*** スープカレー As the name implies this is a curry-flavoured soup; it is a popular dish in Hokkaido and the advantage is that you can say how spicy you want your soup to be. It is served with a variety of meat and vegetables.

***Sukiyaki*** すき焼き Sliced beef with vegetables grilled in a special iron pan at your table.

***Sushi*** すし, 寿司 The general name for slices of fresh fish (*see* Sashimi) on a bed of rice. The most common kind is ***nigiri-sushi*** but other common ones are ***temaki-sushi***, ***nori-maki*** and ***inari-sushi*** (see relevant entry). Add soy sauce (and wasabi) to taste and eat with a few slices of pickled ginger.

***Takoyaki*** たこ焼き Pieces of octopus in batter; popular at summer festivals.

***Temaki-sushi*** 手巻寿司 A cone shape of dried seaweed filled with rice, fish and vegetables such as avocado, that is big enough to hold in your hand. This style is not traditionally Japanese

***Tempura*** 天ぷら Prawns/fish/vegetables deep fried in batter; served with a dipping sauce.

***Tendon*** 天丼 Tempura served on a bowl of rice.

***Teppanyaki*** 鉄板焼き Meat and fish cooked on an iron griddle.

***Tofu*** 豆腐 Soybean curd, delicious when dipped in soy sauce.

*Tomorokoshi* (焼き)ともろこし (Grilled) corn on the cob.

*Tonkatsu* トンカツ A pork cutlet, which is dipped in breadcrumbs and deep fried. Comes as either *hirekatsu* (ヒレカツ; pork fillet) or *rosukatsu* (ロースカツ; pork tenderloin). Always served with miso soup, rice and a mass of shredded cabbage; it is acceptable to ask for more cabbage or rice.

*Tonkotsu* 豚骨 Do not confuse tonkatsu (above) with tonkotsu which is a pork broth used in ramen, particularly in Kyushu.

*Udon* うどん Wheat-flour noodles, much thicker than soba, served hot in a broth.

*Umeboshi* うめぼし、梅干し Sour, pickled plums

*Unagi* 鰻 Eel, basted in soy and sake sauce, cooked over a charcoal fire and served on a bed of rice. Traditionally eaten in the summer as stamina food for beating the heat.

*Viking* バイキング The Japanese word for a buffet meal.

*Wanko soba* わんこそば Bowls of good-quality soba, served with side dishes and traditionally eaten in a competition where diners race to scoff the most noodles; a speciality of the Morioka area.

*Wasabi* わさび Hot mustard, similar to horseradish, served with sushi and sashimi.

*Yaki-imo* ヤキイモ、焼き芋 Baked sweet potato.

*Yakiniku* 焼き肉 Grilled meat, usually beef

*Yakisoba* 焼きそば Pork mince and vegetables with fried (but soft) soba; popular at summer festivals. The soba can also be served crunchy ie deep fried (*kata-yakisoba* 固焼きそば). Also served with udon (*yaki-udon* 焼きうどん).

*Yakitori* 焼き鳥 Chunks of chicken (wing, leg, heart, liver) and/or vegetables (usually leeks and pepper) on a skewer, either dipped in a sweet and savoury sauce made from sake, *mirin* (rice wine for cooking), stock and soy sauce, or a salty seasoning, and cooked over a charcoal fire. Yakitori is found at dedicated restaurants, *izakaya*, or at street stalls during festivals.

### Drink

● **Beer** *Asahi Superdry* アサヒスーパードライ and *Kirin* キリン (see box p445)

are rivals for the title of 'nation's favourite beer'. Other popular brands are **Sapporo** サッポロ and **Suntory** サントリー. In recent years the number of micro-breweries has expanded; try Yufuin beer, see p430, and Dogo Beer, p495. See p77 for details about beer gardens ビアガーデン.

● **Soft drinks** In addition to standard fruit juices/fruit juice drinks there is a huge range of soft drinks in Japan with seasonal versions appearing at the relevant time of year. Some of the most popular drinks are: *Calpis* カルピス, a milk-based soft drink popular with children (its name was changed to 'Calpico' when launched overseas); *CC Lemon* CCレモン, a fizzy lemon-flavoured drink; *Pocari Sweat* ポカリスエット, an energy drink; and *Yakult* ヤクルト, a 'lactic acid bacteria beverage' or, if you think it sounds more appealing, a fermented milk drink.

● **Sake** 酒 Often refers generally to alcoholic drinks, while 'Nihonshu' 日本酒 is more specifically what is known in the West as sake (pronounced sa-kay). Made from particular kinds of white rice (not the rice which is eaten) which has been fermented. Sake is served hot or cold and, as with wine, comes in a range of qualities. Amazake 甘酒 is a sweet form of sake and is usually less alcoholic. A more recent development is sparkling sake.

● **Shochu** 焼酎 A strong spirit, particularly popular in Kyushu, made from grain/potato. *Chu-hai* チューハイ is shochu served with carbonated water and lemon or lime.

● **Tea** Cups of *o-cha* お茶 (green tea) or *houji-cha* ほうじ茶 (brown tea) are served free in some Japanese restaurants. **Ko-cha** 紅茶 is Western-style tea; Earl Grey and English Breakfast are common in many hotels, while fruit- and peppermint-flavour tea infusions are also widely available. *Mugi-cha* 麦茶 (barley tea) is served cold in the summer and is popular as a cooling drink but it can also be served hot.

● **Whisky** ウイスキー No bar would be without bottles of Suntory whisky, the leading domestic brand. But really high-class establishments only serve imported Scotch (particularly Johnny Walker).

# APPENDIX B: USEFUL WORDS AND PHRASES

## General words and phrases

| | | | |
|---|---|---|---|
| Good morning | *ohaiyoo gozaimasu* | Good evening | *kombanwa* |
| Good night | *oyasumi nasai* | Hello | *konnichiwa* |
| Please* | *dozo, onegaishimasu* or *kudasai* | Goodbye | *sayonara* |
| Thank you | *domo arigato* | Yes (see p82) | *hai* |
| (very much) | (*gozaimashita*) | No | *iie* |
| No thanks | *kekko desu* | I don't understand | *wakarimasen* |
| Excuse me / I'm sorry | *shitsureishimasu / sumimasen* or *gomen nasai* | | |

| | |
|---|---|
| What's your name? | *O-namae wa nan desu-ka* |
| My name is ............. | *Watashi wa ............. desu* |
| Where do you live? | *Doko ni sunde imasu ka* |
| I'm from Britain / America / Canada / Australia / New Zealand | *Igirisujin / Amerikajin / Kanadajin / Australiajin / New Zealandjin desu* |
| Do you speak English? | *Anata wa eigo ga hanasemasu ka* |
| Please write it down for me | *Sore o kaite kudasai* |
| Could you repeat that please? | *Mo ichido itte kudasai* |
| How much does it cost? | *Ikura desu ka* |
| Where is an ATM? | *ATM (genkin jodo azukebaraiki) wa doko desu-ka* |

*\*Note: onegaishimasu* and *kudasai* are used with a noun or when requesting/receiving something; *dozo* can be used without a noun and when giving something away.

## Day/time

| | | | | | | |
|---|---|---|---|---|---|---|
| Monday | *getsuyobi* | 月曜日 | yesterday | *kino* | 昨日 |
| Tuesday | *kayobi* | 火曜日 | morning | *asa* | 朝 |
| Wednesday | *suiyobi* | 水曜日 | afternoon | *gogo* | 午後 |
| Thursday | *mokuyobi* | 木曜日 | evening | *yoru* | 夜 |
| Friday | *kinyobi* | 金曜日 | day | *hi / nichi* | 日 |
| Saturday | *doyobi* | 土曜日 | month | *gatsu / tsuki* | 月 |
| Sunday | *nichiyobi* | 日曜日 | year | *nen/toshi* | 年 |
| today | *kyo* | 今日 | hour | *ji* | 時 |
| tomorrow | *ashita* | 明日 | minute | *fun / pun* | 分 |

### Hiragana chart

| a | ka (ga) | sa (za) | ta (da) | na | ha (ba/pa) | ma | ya | ra | wa |
|---|---|---|---|---|---|---|---|---|---|
| あ | か（が） | さ（ざ） | た（だ） | な | は（ば／ぱ） | ま | や | ら | わ |
| i | ki (gi) | shi (ji) | chi (ji) | ni | hi (bi/pi) | mi | | ri | |
| い | き（ぎ） | し（じ） | ち（ぢ） | に | ひ（び／ぴ） | み | | り | |
| u | ku (gu) | su (zu) | tsu (zu) | nu | hu (bu/pu) | mu | yu | ru | (w)o |
| う | く（ぐ） | す（ず） | つ（づ） | ぬ | ふ（ぶ／ぷ） | む | ゆ | る | を |
| e | ke (ge) | se (ze) | te (de) | ne | he (be/pe) | me | | re | |
| え | け（げ） | せ（ぜ） | て（で） | ね | へ（べ／ぺ） | め | | れ | |
| o | ko (go) | so (zo) | to (do) | no | ho (bp/po) | mo | yo | ro | n |
| お | こ（ご） | そ（ぞ） | と（ど） | の | ほ（ぼ／ぽ） | も | よ | ろ | ん |

## Numerals and counting systems

| | | | | | | | | | |
|---|---|---|---|---|---|---|---|---|---|
| 1 | ichi | 一 | 11 | ju-ichi | 十一 | 21 | ni-ju-ichi | 二十一 |
| 2 | ni | 二 | 12 | ju-ni | 十二 | 22 | ni-ju-ni | 二十二 |
| 3 | san | 三 | 13 | ju-san | 十三 | 100 | hyaku | 百 |
| 4 | shi / yon | 四 | 14 | ju-shi / ju-yon | 十四 | 101 | hyaku-ichi | 百一 |
| 5 | go | 五 | 15 | ju-go | 十五 | 200 | ni-hyaku | 二百 |
| 6 | roku | 六 | 16 | ju-rokku | 十六 | 1000 | sen | 千 |
| 7 | shichi / nana | 七 | 17 | ju-shichi / nana | 十七 | 1001 | sen-ichi | 千一 |
| 8 | hachi | 八 | 18 | ju-hachi | 十八 | 2000 | ni-sen | 二千 |
| 9 | kyu / ku | 九 | 19 | ju-kyu | 十九 | 10,000 | ichi-man | 一万 |
| 10 | ju | 十 | 20 | ni-ju | 二十 | 20,000 | ni-man | 二万 |

There are many different counting systems in Japanese. The most useful to know are (based on counting from one to five):

● **People**: hitori / futari / san-nin / yon-nin / go-nin
● **Nights (stay in a hotel/minshuku etc)**: ippaku / nihaku / sanpaku / yonpaku / gohaku
● **Flat thin objects such as tickets**: ichimae / nimae / sanmae / yonmae / gomae
● **Cylindrical-shaped objects such as bottles of beer/wine or glasses (of drink)**: ippon / nihon / sanbon / yonhon / gohon
● **Floors of a building**: ikkai / nikai / sankai / yonkai / gokai

## Directions

| | | | | | | | | |
|---|---|---|---|---|---|---|---|---|
| North | *kita* | 北 | West | *nishi* | 西 | (Go) left / right | *hidari / migi (itte)* | |
| South | *minami* | 南 | East | *higashi* | 東 | (Go) straight on | *massugu (itte)* | |

| Where is ...? | *... wa doko desu ka* | ... はどこですか |
|---|---|---|
| the train station | *Eki ...* | 駅 ... |
| the ticket office | *Midori-no-madoguchi ...* | みどりの窓口 ... |
| the bus stop | *Basu noriba ...* | バスのりば ... |
| a tourist information office | *Kanko annaijo ...* | 観光案内所 ... |
| the tram stop | *Romendensha noriba ...* | 路面電車のりば ... |
| a toilet (*see also* box p78) | *O-tearai* (polite) / *toire* (informal) | お手洗い／トイレ... |
| (male / female) | | （男／女） |
| a taxi stand | *Takushi noriba ...* | タクシーのりば ... |

### Katakana chart

| a | ka (ga) | sa (za) | ta (da) | na | ha (ba/pa) | ma | ya | ra | wa |
|---|---|---|---|---|---|---|---|---|---|
| ア | カ（ガ） | サ（ザ） | タ（ダ） | ナ | ハ（バ／パ） | マ | ヤ | ラ | ワ |
| i | ki (gi) | shi (ji) | chi (ji) | ni | hi (bi/pi) | mi | | ri | |
| イ | キ（ギ） | シ（ジ） | チ（ヂ） | ニ | ヒ（ビ／ピ） | ミ | | リ | |
| u | ku (gu) | su (zu) | tsu (zu) | nu | hu (bu/pu) | mu | yu | ru | (w)o |
| ウ | ク（グ） | ス（ズ） | ツ（ヅ） | ヌ | フ（ブ／プ） | ム | ユ | ル | ヲ |
| e | ke (ge) | se (ze) | te (de) | ne | he (be/pe) | me | | re | |
| エ | ケ（ゲ） | セ（ゼ） | テ（デ） | ネ | ヘ（ベ／ペ） | メ | | レ | |
| o | ko (go) | so (zo) | to (do) | no | ho (bo/po) | mo | yo | ro | n |
| オ | コ）ゴ） | ソ（ゾ） | ト（ド） | ノ | ホ（ボ／ポ） | モ | ヨ | ロ | ン |

## Railway vocabulary

| English | Japanese (romaji) | Japanese |
|---|---|---|
| adult / child | otona / kodomo | 大人 / 子供 |
| aisle (seat) | tsuro (gawa no seki) | 通路（側の席） |
| arrival | tochaku | 到着 |
| berth | shindai | 寝台 |
| conductor | shashosan | 車掌さん |
| departure | shupatsu | 出発 |
| entrance / exit | iriguchi / deguchi | 入り口 / 出口 |
| express train | kyuko | 急行 |
| fare adjustment office | ryokin seisanjo | 料金精算所 |
| Green car | guriin-sha | グリーンカー |
| handicapped person | karada no fujyu na hito | 身体の不自由 |
| limited express train | tokkyu | 特急 |
| local train | futsu | 普通 |
| luggage | nimotsu | にもつ |
| no-smoking car | kin-en-sha | 禁煙車 |
| ordinary class car | futsu-sha | 普通車 |
| platform | platthomu | プラットホーム |
| railway line | sen | 線 |
| railway lunchbox | ekiben | 駅弁 |
| rapid train | kaisoku | 快速 |
| refund | haraimodoshi | 払い戻し |
| reservation | yoyaku | 予約 |
| reserved seat | shitei-seki | 指定席 |
| sleeper train | shindaisha | 寝台車 |
| smoking car | kitsuen-sha | 喫煙車 |
| station | eki | 駅 |
| ticket / transfer ticket | kippu / norikae-kippu | きっぷ / 乗り換えきっぷ |
| ticket gate | kaisatsu-guchi | 改札口 |
| timetable | jikoku hyo | 時刻表 |
| Travel Service Center | ryoko senta | 旅行センター |
| trolley | wagon service | ワゴンサービス |
| underground / subway / metro | chikatetsu | 地下鉄 |
| unreserved seat | jiyu-seki | 自由席 |
| window seat | madogawa no seki | 窓側の席 |

## Railway/travel phrases

| | |
|---|---|
| How can I get to [Kyoto] from here? | [Kyoto] e ikitai desu. Doyatte ikimasu ka. |
| I'd like to reserve a seat on the next train to [Kyoto] | Tsugi no densha de [Kyoto] ni ikimasu. Zaseki o yoyaku shitai desu. |
| What time does the train to [Kyoto] leave? | [Kyoto] e ikimasu. Tsugi no densha wa nan-ji desu ka. |
| Which platform does the train to [Kyoto] leave from? | [Kyoto] e ikimasu. Platform wa nan-ban desu ka. |
| Excuse me, does this train go to [Kyoto]? | Sumimasen, kono densha wa [Kyoto] ni ikimasu ka |
| Can you tell me where my seat is? | Watashi no seki wa doko desu ka |
| Where is the Lost and Found office? | Otoshimono (or wasuremono) o shimashita. Doko e ikeba ii desu ka |
| Can I have a one-day pass? | One-day pasu o kudasai. |

(If the person you are speaking to doesn't understand *One-day pasu* try *Ichinichi joushaken*)

## Accommodation (*see also* Numerals and counting systems, p501)

| | |
|---|---|
| I'd like to book a single / double / twin room (Western-style hotel) | Shinguru / daburu / tsuin no heya o yoyaku shitai desu. |

(Since in Japanese-style accommodation the number of people who can share a room depends on how many futon can be laid out it is best to say how many people want to share.)

| | |
|---|---|
| I'd like a Japanese- / Western-style room | Washitsu / Yoshitsu onegaishimasu |
| I'd like a room but no meals | Sudomari onegaishimasu |
| What is the rate? | Ikura desu ka |

**Accommodation** (*cont'd*)

| | |
|---|---|
| Does the rate include breakfast / supper? | *Choshoku / yushoku tsuki desu ka* |
| Where is the reception desk? | *Front wa doko desu ka* |
| Where is the (Japanese-style) bath? | *O-furo wa doko desu ka* |
| Can I check-in? / I'd like to check out | *Check-in dekimasu ka / Check-out shimasu* |
| Do you accept Amex / Visa card? | *Amekkusu / Viza kaado de ii desu ka* |
| Can I leave my luggage here? | *Nimotsu o azuketemo ii desu ka* |
| Can I borrow a LAN cable? | *Lan cable o kashite kudasai.* |
| What time is breakfast / supper? | *Asa-gohan / Ban-gohan wa nan-ji desu ka* |

**Restaurant**  **Resutoran**

| | |
|---|---|
| I'd like to make a reservation | *Yoyaku onegai shimasu.* |
| Do you have a menu in English? | *Eigo no menyuu wa arimasu ka* |
| Can I have the English menu please | *Eigo no menyuu o kudasai.* |
| What is this? | *Kore wa nan desu ka* |
| I'd like this, please | *Kore o kudasai* |
| What time does the restaurant open? | *Resutoran wa nan ji kara desu ka* |
| What time does the restaurant close? | *Resutoran wa nan ji made desu ka* |
| Can I have some more water / tea? | *Omizu / ocha o kudasai.* |
| Can I have some more cabbage / rice please? (for a tonkatsu meal, see p499) | *Kyabetsu / gohan, okawari kudasai* |
| Can I have more noodles (see p498). | *Kaedama onegai shimasu.* |
| I don't eat meat / I don't eat fish | *Niku wa tabemasen / Sakana wa tabemasen* |
| I am a vegetarian. I only eat vegetables / I only eat vegetables and fish | *Bejitarian desu. Yasai dake tabemasu / Yasai to sakana dake tabemasu* |

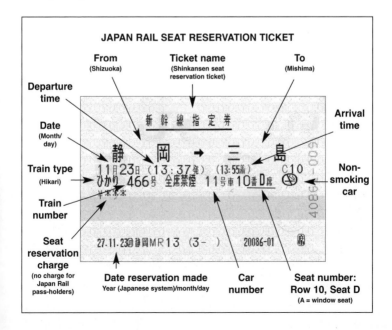

**JAPAN RAIL SEAT RESERVATION TICKET**

**From** (Shizuoka)

**Ticket name** (Shinkansen seat reservation ticket)

**To** (Mishima)

**Departure time**

**Date** (Month/day)

**Train type** (Hikari)

**Train number**

**Seat reservation charge** (no charge for Japan Rail pass-holders)

**Arrival time**

**Non-smoking car**

新 幹 線 指 定 券

静　岡　→　三　島

11月23日 (13:37発) (13:55着) C10
ひかり 466号 全席禁煙 11号車 10番D席

27.11.23㊞静岡MR13 (3- )　20086-01

**Date reservation made**
Year (Japanese system)/month/day

**Car number**

**Seat number: Row 10, Seat D** (A = window seat)

# APPENDIX C: JR SERVICE SUMMARIES

The details contained in this appendix give an idea of the JR services available for the main routes covered. For the actual times you will need to look at online versions (see box p94), the timetable summary in English, or the Japanese Timetable (see box below).

## USING THE SERVICE SUMMARIES IN THIS GUIDE

Frequencies and approximate journey times for services on the main routes described in this book are provided below. Note that the actual journey length always depends how many stops there are; **the times quoted are given as a guideline only**.

The main text focuses on shinkansen and limited express (LEX) services; details for local/rapid trains are included only when there are few limited express (LEX) services, even though these also operate on most routes.

Most services listed operate daily year-round, but sometimes there are additional seasonal services and also services at weekends can differ – these variations are not noted.

Even though a service may seem to operate frequently often this is because there are lots of services in the morning and evening; during the day the service may be limited and for that reason it is not described as an hourly service.

For the majority of routes only the main stations are listed.

### Table 1: Narita Airport to/from Tokyo/Ofuna/Ikebukuro via Narita Express (N'EX)

| From Terminal 1 成田空港ターミナル1 | | From Terminal 1 成田空港ターミナル1 | |
|---|---|---|---|
| Terminal 2[1] ターミナル2 | 1-2/hr; 1 min | Terminal 2[1] | 1-2/hr; 1 min |
| Tokyo[2] 東京 | 1-2/hr; 1hr 9 mins | Tokyo[2] 東京 | 1-2/hr; 1hr 9 mins |
| Shinagawa 品川 | 1-2/hr; 1hr 19 mins | Shibuya 渋谷 | 1-2/hr; 1½hrs |
| Musashi-Kosugi 武蔵小杉 | 1-2/hr; 1hr 22 mins | Shinjuku 新宿 | 1-2/hr; 1hr 35 mins |
| Yokohama 横浜 | 1-2/hr; 1hr 43 mins | Ikebukuro 池袋 | 1-2/hr; 1hr 40 mins |

**Notes**:
[1] If you land at Terminal 3, you need to transfer to Terminal 2 for rail services.
[2] Trains divide/join up at Tokyo (since you have to have a seat reservation you are likely to be in the correct part of the train).

From Yokohama services continue to **Totsuka** 戸塚 (18/day; 1hr 55 mins) and **Ofuna** 大船 (18/day; 2hrs).

From Narita services operate between 7.44am and 9.44pm. To Narita there are services between 5.30am and 7pm from Ofuna and 6.45am and 7.30pm from Ikebukuro.

---

### ❏ How to use the Japanese Railway Timetable

You will find at least one copy of the Japanese timetable (see pp98-9) in ticket offices, or travel service centres. The route maps on the colour pages at the front of the timetable use kanji so you need to know the kanji for where you are and where you want to go – this guide now provides kanji for all station names so even if they are not shown in the service summaries here, you can find them in the text.

Find the route map which covers the area you are travelling in and then the places you want to travel between. Finally, look for the number which appears immediately above or below it. This refers to the corresponding page in the timetable. For major services two numbers are given – one for each direction.

Working your way around the Japanese timetable can take time but is rewarding and also it is by far the most reliable way of checking train times.

## Table 2: Kansai Airport to/from Shin-Osaka/Kyoto via Haruka LEX

Kansai Airport 関西空港 (Journey times quoted are to/from Kansai Airport)

| | |
|---|---|
| Tennoji 天王寺 | 1-2/hr; 35 mins |
| Shin-Osaka 新大阪 | 1-2/hr; 52 mins |
| Kyoto 京都 | 1-2/hr; 1¼hrs |

● Services operate between 6.30am and 10pm from Kansai Airport and 5.45am and 8.15pm to the airport. In the early morning services from Kansai also call at Hineno; in the evening services to Kansai call at Hineno.

**Local/rapid services**
● JR Kansai Airport Rapid Service (1-3/hr) calls at Rinku Town, Hineno, Tennoji and Osaka but not Shin-Osaka.
● From both Osaka and Shin-Osaka there are frequent local/rapid trains to Kyoto.

## Table 3: Tokyo to/from Hakata (Fukuoka) by Tokaido/Sanyo shinkansen

| | Nozomi[1] | Hikari[2] | Kodama[3] |
|---|---|---|---|
| Tokyo 東京 (Journey times quoted are to/from Tokyo) | | | |
| Shinagawa 品川 | 2-6/hr; 7 mins | 2/hr; 7 mins | 1/hr; 7 mins |
| Shin-Yokohama 新横浜 | 2-6/hr; 18 mins | 2/hr; 18-20 mins | 1/hr; 20 mins |
| Odawara 小田原 | | 7/day; 35 mins | 1/hr; 40 mins |
| Atami 熱海 | | 3/day; 40 mins | 1/hr; 50 mins |
| Mishima 三島 | | 5/day; 45 mins | 1/hr; 1hr 2 mins |
| Shin-Fuji 新富士 | | | 1/hr; 1hr 11 mins |
| Shizuoka 静岡 | | 1/hr; 60 mins | 1/hr; 1hr 28 mins |
| Kakegawa 掛川 | | | 1/hr; 1hr 47 mins |
| Hamamatsu 浜松 | | 1/hr; 1½hrs | 1/hr; 2hrs 3 mins |
| Toyohashi 豊橋 | | 9/day; 1hr 23 mins | 1/hr; 2hrs 20 mins |
| Nagoya 名古屋 | 2-6/hr; 1hr 40 mins | 2/hr; 1hr 44 mins | 1/hr; 2hrs 49 mins |
| Gifu-Hashima 岐阜羽島 | | 1/hr; 2hrs 2 mins | 1/hr; 3hrs |
| Maibara 米原 | | 1-2/hr; 2hrs 10 mins | 1/hr; 3hrs 20 mins |
| Kyoto 京都 | 2-6/hr; 2hrs 9 mins | 2/hr; 2hrs 40 mins | 1/hr; 3hrs 48 mins |
| Shin-Osaka 新大阪 | 2-6/hr; 2hrs 24 mins | 2/hr; 2hrs 58 mins | 1/hr; 4hrs 4 mins |

| | | Journey times to/from Shin-Osaka | |
|---|---|---|---|
| | | Hikari[2] | Kodama[3] |
| Shin-Kobe 新神戸 | 2-4/hr; 2hrs 52 mins | 1-2/hr; 13 mins | 8/day; 13 mins |
| Nishi-Akashi 西明石 | | 1/hr; 23 mins | 8/day; 23 mins |
| Himeji 姫路 | 2/day; 3hrs 9 mins | 1-2/hr; 29 mins | 8/day; 35 mins |
| Aioi 相生 | | 1/hr; 48 mins | 8/day; 48 mins |
| Okayama 岡山 | 2-4/hr; 3½hrs | 1-2/hr; 55 mins | 8/day; 1hr 10 mins |
| Shin-Kurashiki 新倉敷 | | | 8/day; 1hr 25 mins |
| Fukuyama 福山 | 11/day; 3¾hrs | 1-2/hr; 1¼hrs | 8/day; 1hr 40 mins |
| Shin-Onomichi 新尾道 | | 8/day; 1¾hrs | |
| Mihara 三原 | | 8/day; 2hrs 10 mins | |
| Higashi-Hiroshima 東広島 | | 8/day; 2hrs 17 mins | |
| Hiroshima 広島 | 2-4/hr; 4hrs | 1-2/hr; 1hr 26 mins | 8/day; 2½hrs |
| Shin-Iwakuni 新岩国 | | 8/day; 2¾hrs | |
| Tokuyama 徳山 | 7/day; 4hrs 23 mins | 8/day; 3hrs 10 mins | |
| Shin-Yamaguchi 新山口 | 11/day; 4½hrs | 10/day; 2hrs | 8/day; 3½hrs |
| Asa 厚狭 | | 8/day; 3hrs 52 mins | |
| Shin-Shimonoseki 新下関 | | 5/day; 2hrs 10 mins | 8/day; 4hrs 5 mins |
| Kokura 小倉 | 2-4/hr; 4¾hrs | 1-2/hr; 2hrs 20 mins | 8/day; 4¼hrs |
| Hakata (Fukuoka) 博多 | 2-4/hr; 5hrs | 1-2/hr; 2hrs 38 mins | 8/day; 4hrs 35 mins |

[1] **Nozomi services** operate from Tokyo to Shin-Osaka/Hakata but the Japan Rail Pass is not valid and it is not possible to pay a supplement to use them. If travelling without a rail pass,

note that all Nozomi services have three non-reserved carriages (and therefore no compulsory seat-reservation charge). The first service from Tokyo leaves at approx 06.00, the last to Shin-Osaka/Hakata leaves at approx 21.20/18.50. **Mizuho** services from Shin-Osaka to Kagoshima-chuo are shown in Table 21 on p511.

[2] **Hikari** services operate from Tokyo to Shin-Osaka/Okayama. Services start from Tokyo at approx 06.30, the last to Shin-Osaka/Okayama leaves at approx 20.00/16.00. **Sakura** services from Shin-Osaka to Hakata/Kagoshima-chuo are also shown in Table 21, p511.

[3] **Kodama** services operate from Tokyo to Nagoya/Shin-Osaka and from Shin-Osaka to Hakata. Services from Tokyo start at approx 07.00; the last to Shin-Osaka leaves at approx 19.30.

### Table 4: Tokyo to Kanazawa by shinkansen

|  | **Kagayaki** | **Hakutaka** | **Asama** |
|---|---|---|---|
| Tokyo 東京 (Journey times quoted are to/from Tokyo) |  |  |  |
| Ueno 上野 | 10/day; 5 mins | 14/day; 5 mins | 18/day; 5 mins |
| Omiya 大宮 | 10/day; 25 mins | 14/day; 25 mins | 18/day; 25 mins |
| Kumagaya 熊谷 |  |  | 16/day; 38 mins |
| Takasaki 高崎 |  | 12/day; 50 mins | 16/day; 54 mins |
| Karuizawa 軽井沢 |  | 10/day; 1hr 6 mins | 16/day; 1hr 18 mins |
| Ueda 上田 |  | 8/day; 1hr 25 mins | 16/day; 1hr 36 mins |
| Nagano 長野 | 16/day; 1hr 25 mins | 13/day; 1hr 38 mins | 18/day; 1hr 49 mins |
| Iiyama 飯山 |  | 11/day; 1hr 50 mins |  |
| Joetsu-Myoko 上越妙高 |  | 14/day; 2hrs |  |
| Itoigawa 糸魚川 |  | 14/day; 2¼hrs |  |
| Kurobe-Unazukionsen 黒部宇奈月温泉 |  | 14/day; 2½hrs |  |
| Toyama 富山 | 12/day; 2hrs 20 mins | 14/day; 2¾hrs | **Tsurugi** **Times from Toyama** |
| Shin-Takaoka 新高岡 |  | 14/day; 2hrs 52 mins | 18/day; 8 mins |
| Kanazawa 金沢 | 12/day; 2hrs 32 mins | 14/day; 3hrs 10 mins | 18/day; 23 mins |

● See Table 11 (p508) for additional services between Tokyo and Omiya.

Additional services between Tokyo and Takasaki are provided by Toki, Tanigawa/Max-Tanigawa services to Niigata.

### Table 5: Nagano to/from Nagoya via Matsumoto on Wide View Shinano LEX

Journey times quoted are to/from Nagano 長野

| | |
|---|---|
| Shinonoi 篠ノ井 | approx 1/hr; 8 mins |
| Matsumoto 松本 | approx 1/hr; 50 mins |
| Shiojiri 塩尻 | approx 1/hr; 1hr |
| Nagiso 南木曽 | 4/day; 1hr 55 mins |
| Nakatsugawa 中津川 | approx 1/hr; 2hrs 5 mins |
| Tajimi 多治見 | approx 1/hr; 2hrs 34 mins |
| Nagoya 名古屋 | approx 1/hr; 3hrs |

**Local/rapid services**
● Local trains operate about 9-10/day between Nagano and Nakatsugawa
● From Nakatsugawa to Nagoya there are 1-2/hr

### Table 6: Toyama to Nagoya via Takayama on Wide View Hida LEX

Toyama 富山 (Journey times quoted are to/from Toyama)

| | |
|---|---|
| Inotani 猪谷 | 4/day; 38 mins |
| Hida-Furukawa 飛騨古川 | 4/day; 1¼hrs |
| Takayama 高山 | 4/day; 1½hrs |

**Local/rapid services**
Local trains from Toyama to Takayama (Takayama Line) 8-11/day; likely to have to change train at Inotani

● The Wide View Hida LEX services from Toyama operate through to Nagoya (4hrs).

### Table 6: Toyama to Nagoya *(cont'd)*

Takayama 高山 (Journey times quoted are to/from
 Takayama)

| | |
|---|---|
| Gero 下呂 | 10/day; 45 mins |
| Mino-Ota 美濃太田 | 10/day; 1¾hrs |
| Unuma 鵜沼 | 3/day;  1hr 56 mins |
| Gifu 岐阜 | 10/day; 2hrs 9 mins |
| Nagoya 名古屋 | 10/day; 2½hrs |

**Local/rapid services**
● Local trains (Takayama
Line) from Takayama to Mino-
Ota 8/day
● Local trains (Takayama Line)
from Mino-Ota to Gifu 2/hr
● Local/rapid trains (Tokaido
Line) Gifu to Nagoya 8/hr

### Table 7: Kanazawa to/from Kyoto and Osaka on Thunderbird LEX

Kanazawa 金沢 (Journey times quoted are to/from Kanazawa)

| | | |
|---|---|---|
| Fukui 福井 | 1-2/hr; 45 mins | Shirasagi 1/hr; 45 mins |
| Tsuruga 敦賀 | 1-2/hr; 1hr 22 mins | Shirasagi 1/hr; 1hr 22 mins |
| Kyoto 京都 | 1-2/hr; 2¼hrs | |
| Shin-Osaka 新大阪 | 1-2/hr; 2½hrs | |
| Osaka 大阪 | 1-2/hr; 2¾hrs | |

● Shirasagi LEX runs from Kanazawa to Nagoya (8/day); services stop at all stations to
Tsuruga; from there the train goes via Nagahama (3/day); Maibara and Gifu to Nagoya.

### Table 8: Nagoya to Shingu/Kii Katsuura on Wide View Nanki LEX

Nagoya 名古屋 (Journey times quoted are
 to/from Nagoya)

| | |
|---|---|
| Suzuka 鈴鹿 | 4/day; 44 mins |
| Tsu 津 | 4/day; 58 mins |
| Matsusaka 松阪 | 4/day; 1¼hrs |
| Taki 多気 | 4/day; 1hr 27 mins |
| Kumano-shi 熊野市 | 4/day; 3¼hrs |
| Shingu 新宮 | 4/day; 3hrs 36 mins |
| Kii-Katsuura 紀伊勝浦 | 3/day; 3hrs 55 mins |

**Local/rapid services**
● Rapid Mie Nagoya to Taki
1/hr
● Taki to Shingu (Kisei Line)
8/day
● Shingu to Kii-Katsuura – see
Table 9

### Table 9: Shingu to Shin-Osaka (and Kyoto) on Kuroshio LEX

Shingu 新宮 (Journey times quoted are
 to/from Shingu)

| | |
|---|---|
| Kii-Katsuura 紀伊勝浦 | 7/day; 15 mins |
| Taiji 太地 | 7/day; 22 mins |
| Kushimoto 串本 | 7/day; 50 mins |
| Susami 周参見 | 7/day; 1hr 25 mins |
| Shirahama 白浜 | 7/day; 1hr 47 mins |
| Kii-Tanabe 紀伊田辺 | 7/day; 2hrs 8 mins |
| Gobo 御坊 | 7/day; 2hrs 37 mins |
| Yuasa 湯浅 | 1/day; 2hrs 47 mins |
| Wakayama 和歌山 | 7/day; 3hrs 10 mins |
| Hineno 日根野 | 9/day; 3hrs 20 mins |
| Tennoji 天王寺 | 17/day 3hrs 58 mins |
| Shin-Osaka 新大阪 | 17/day; 4hrs 12 mins |
| Kyoto 京都 | 2/day; 4hrs 47 mins |

**Local/rapid services**
● Shingu to Kii-Katsuura
(Kinokuni Line) 10/day
● Kii-Katsuura to Kii-Tanabe
(Kinokuni Line), 6/day
● Kii-Tanabe to Gobo
(Kinokuni Line), 1/hr
● Gobo to Wakayama
(Kinokuni Line), 1-2/hr
● Wakayama to Hineno;
Hineno to Tennoji/Shin-Osaka/
Kyoto various services but
approx 2-6/hr

● For additional services between Hineno/Tennoji
and Shin-Osaka, see Table 2, p505.

**Notes**: Journey times quoted are all approximate. Not all stops are listed.

## Table 10: Shin-Yamaguchi to Matsue (and Tottori) on Super Oki LEX

Shin-Yamaguchi 新山口 (Journey times quoted
   are to/from Shin-Yamaguchi)

| | | |
|---|---|---|
| Yuda-onsen 湯田温泉 | 3/day; 10 mins | |
| Yamaguchi 山口 | 3/day; 14 mins | |
| Tsuwano 津和野 | 3/day; 1hr 2 mins | |
| Nichihara 日原 | 3/day; 1hr 12 mins | |
| Masuda 益田 | 3/day; 1hr 35 mins | **SM** |
| Gotsu 江津 | 3/day; 2hrs 25 mins | SM 4/day |
| Yunotsu 温泉津 | 2/day; 2hrs 38 mins | |
| Odashi 大田市 | 3/day; 2hrs 55 mins | SM 4/day |
| Izumoshi 出雲市 | 3/day; 3hrs 20 mins | SM 4/day |
| Shinji 宍道 | 3/day; 3hrs 32 mins | SM 1/day |
| Tamatsukuri-onsen 玉造温泉 | 2/day; 3hrs 40 mins | SM 2/day |
| Matsue 松江 | 3/day; 3hrs 50 mins | SM 4/day |
| Tottori 鳥取 | 1/day; 3hrs 23 mins | SM 4/day |

**Local/rapid services**
**Yamaguchi Line**
● Shin-Yamaguchi to Yamaguchi, 1-2/hr
● Yamaguchi to Tsuwano, 7/day
● Tsuwano to Masuda 7/day

**San-in Line (local and rapid)**
● Masuda to Izumoshi 14/day
● Izumoshi to Matsue 25/day
● Matsue to Yonago 28/day
● Yonago to Tottori 20/day

● The Super Matsukaze (**SM**) LEX operates between Masuda and Tottori; the journey times
are similar to those on the Super Oki.

## Table 11: Tokyo to Shin-Hakodate-Hokuto by shinkansen (Hayabusa)

Tokyo 東京 (Journey times quoted are to/from Tokyo)

| | | | |
|---|---|---|---|
| Ueno 上野 | 1-2/hr; | 5 mins | Yamabiko 1-3/hr; Nasuno 16/day (5 mins) |
| Omiya 大宮 | 1-2/hr; | 24 mins | Yamabiko 1-3/hr; Nasuno 16/day (24 mins) |
| Oyama 小山 | | | Yamabiko 11/day; Nasuno 16/day (42 mins) |
| Utsunomiya 宇都宮 | | | Yamabiko 1-3/hr; Nasuno 16/day (50 mins) |
| Nasu-Shiobara 那須塩原 | | | Yamabiko 11/day; Nasuno 16/day (70 mins) |
| Koriyama 郡山 | | | Yamabiko 1-3/hr; Nasuno 5/day (1½hrs) |
| Fukushima 福島 | | | Yamabiko 1-4/hr; 1hr 40 mins |
| Sendai 仙台 | 1-2/hr; | 1hr 32 mins | Yamabiko 1-3/hr; 1hr 55 mins |
| Furukawa 古川 | 3/day; | 1hr 50 mins | Yamabiko 10/day; 2hrs 13 mins |
| Ichinoseki 一ノ関 | 4/day; | 2hrs | Yamabiko 10/day; 2hrs 32 mins |
| Shin-Hanamaki 新花巻 | 3/day; | 2hrs 35 mins | Yamabiko 10/day; 3hrs 3 mins |
| Morioka 盛岡 | 1-2/hr; | 2¼hrs | Yamabiko 10/day; 3hrs 16 mins |
| Ninohe 二戸 | 10/day; | 2hrs 41 mins | |
| Hachinohe 八戸 | 1/hr; | 2hrs 50 mins | |
| Shin-Aomori 新青森 | 1-2/hr; | 3hrs 10 mins | |
| Okutsugaru-Imabetsu 青森 | 5/day; | 3hrs 40 mins | |
| Kikonai 木古内 | 8/day; | 4hrs 10 mins | |
| Shin-Hakodate-Hokuto 函館 | 10/day; | 4hrs 18 mins | |

● See Table 4 for additional services between Tokyo
and Omiya.
● The Hayate (3/day) operates between Tokyo and
Morioka and the first stop is always Sendai; there
are additional services in peak seasons.
● The times in brackets eg (5 mins) apply to both
the Yamabiko and Nasuno.

❏ **Shinkansen marathon**
The journey from Shin-
Hakodate-Hokuto to
Kagoshima-chuo can be done
in just over 12 hours: take a
Hayabusa to Tokyo then
change to a Hikari (see Table
3) and at Shin-Osaka change
to a Sakura (see Table 21).

   Without a Japan Rail Pass
this would cost ¥48,220, but
to save time you could take a
Nozomi from Tokyo.

## Table 12: Aomori to Akita on Tsugaru LEX/ Resort Shirakami

Aomori 青森 (Journey times quoted are
to/from Aomori)

| | |
|---|---|
| Shin-Aomori 新青森 | 5/day; 7 mins |
| Hirosaki 弘前 | 5/day; 33 mins |
| Owani-onsen 大鰐温泉 | 5/day; 46 mins |
| Odate 大館 | 5/day; 1hr 13 mins |
| Higashi-Noshiro 東能代 | 5/day; 1hr 55 mins |
| Akita 秋田 | 5/day; 2¾hrs |

**Local/rapid services**
● Aomori to Hirosaki (Ou Line) 22/day
● Hirosaki to Akita (Ou Line) 11/day; may have to change train at Odate.

## Table 13: Akita to Niigata on Inaho LEX

Akita 秋田 (Journey times quoted are
to/from Akita)

| | |
|---|---|
| Kisakata 象潟 | 3/day; 54 mins |
| Sakata 酒田 | 7/day; 1hr 26 mins |
| Amarume 余目 | 7/day; 1hr 37 mins |
| Tsuruoka 鶴岡 | 7/day; 1hr 48 mins |
| Atsumi-onsen あつみ温泉 | 7/day; 2hrs 7 mins |
| Murakami 村上 | 7/day; 2hrs 48 mins |
| Sakamachi 坂町 | 7/day; 2hrs 57 mins |
| Niigata 新潟 | 7/day; 3hrs 34 mins |

**Local/rapid services**
● Akita to Sakata local (Uetsu Line) 9/day
● Sakata to Murakami (Uetsu Line) 7/day
● Murakami to Niigata (Uetsu/ Hakushin Line) 14/day

## Table 14: Hakodate/Shin-Hakodate-Hokuto to Sapporo on Hokuto/Super Hokuto LEX

Hakodate 函館 (Journey times quoted are
to/from Hakodate)

| | |
|---|---|
| Goryokaku 五稜郭 | 7/day; 5 mins |
| Shin-Hakodate-Hokuto 函館 | 7/day; 19 mins |
| Onuma-koen 大沼公園 | 7/day; 29 mins |
| Mori 森 | 7/day; 47 mins |
| Oshamambe 長万部 | 7/day; 1hr 27 mins |
| Toya 洞爺 | 7/day; 1hr 51 mins |
| Higashi-Muroran 東室蘭 | 7/day; 2hrs 18 mins |
| Noboribetsu 登別 | 7/day; 2½hrs |
| Tomakomai 苫小牧 | 7/day; 2hrs 54 mins |
| Minami-Chitose 南千歳 | 7/day; 3hrs 11 mins |
| Shin-Sapporo 新札幌 | 7/day; 3hrs 39 mins |
| Sapporo 札幌 | 7/day; 3hrs 48 mins |

**Local/rapid services**
● Hakodate to Mori (Hakodate Line) 10/day
● Mori to Oshamambe (Hakodate Line) 6/day
● Oshamambe to Higashi-Muroran (Muroran Line) 4/day
● Higashi-Muroran to Tomakomai (Muroran Line) 13/day
● Tomakomai to Sapporo (Chitose Line) 20/day
● Minami-Chitose to Sapporo 3-4/hr local/Rapid Airport Line (Airport Line service starts in Otaru).

● The Suzuran LEX starts in Muroran and operates 6/day to Sapporo

## Table 15: Sapporo to/from Asahikawa & Abashiri on Okhotsk LEX

Sapporo 札幌 (Journey times quoted are to/from
Sapporo)

| | |
|---|---|
| Iwamizawa 岩見沢 | 4/day; 28 mins |
| Takikawa 滝川 | 4/day; 59 mins |
| Fukagawa 深川 | 4/day; 1hr 14 mins |
| Asahikawa 旭川 | 4/day; 1hr 38 mins |
| Kamikawa 上川 | 4/day; 2hrs 22 mins |
| Engaru 遠軽 | 4/day; 2hrs 43 mins |

**Local/rapid services**
● Asahikawa to Kamikawa (Sekihoku Line) 7/day
● Kamikawa to Engaru (Sekihoku Line) 2/day

*(Cont'd on p510)*

*(Cont'd on p510)*

## Table 15: Sapporo to/from Asahikawa & Abashiri *(cont'd from p509)*

| | |
|---|---|
| Rubeshibe 留辺蘂 | 4/day; 4hrs 23 mins |
| Kitami 北見 | 4/day; 4hrs 38 mins |
| Abashiri 網走 | 4/day; 5½hrs |

**Local/rapid services**
*(cont'd from p509)*
● Engaru to Kitami (Sekihoku Line) 5/day
● Kitami to Abashiri (Sekihoku Line) 10/day

● The Super Kamui LEX (1-2/hr) operates from Sapporo to Asahikawa. One service an hour starts at /continues to New Chitose Airport

## Table 16: Abashiri to/from Kushiro
### (Note: there are no regular limited express services on this route)
Abashiri 網走 (Journey times quoted are to/from Abashiri)

| | |
|---|---|
| Kitahama 北浜 | 5/day; 16 mins |
| Shiretoko-Shari 知床斜里 | 7/day; 47 mins |
| Kawayu-onsen 川湯温泉 | 5/day*; 1hr 32 mins |
| Mashu 摩周 | 5/day*; 1hr 39 mins |
| Toro 塘路 | 5/day*; 2hrs 32 mins |
| Kushiro 釧路 | 5/day*; 3hrs 3 mins |

**Notes:** Journey times quoted are all approximate. Not all stops are listed.

* = additional service (1/day) for Kushiro starts at Shiretoko-Shari

● The services shown are the only direct services between Abashiri and Kushiro.
● The SL Fuyu no Shitsugen (see box p92) and Kushiro Shitsugen Norokko LEX (2/day weekends and holiday periods; from Toro) also operate on this route.

## Table 17: Kushiro to Shintoku (and Sapporo) on Super Ozora LEX
Kushiro 釧路 (Journey times quoted are to/from Kushiro)

| | |
|---|---|
| Ikeda 池田 | 6/day; 1¼hrs |
| Obihiro 帯広市 | 6/day; 1hr 4 mins |
| Shintoku 新得 | 6/day; 2hrs 3 mins |
| Minami-Chitose 南千歳 | 6/day; 3hrs 28 mins |
| Shin-Sapporo 新札幌 | 6/day; 3hrs 49 mins |
| Sapporo 札幌 | 6/day; 3hrs 58 mins |

**Local/rapid services**
● Kushiro to Obihiro (Nemuro Line) 6/day
● Obihiro to Shintoku (Nemuro Line) 13/day
● No local trains on route from Shintoku to Sapporo via Minami-Chitose.

● The Super Tokachi LEX (5/day) operates from Obihiro to Sapporo

## Table 18: Shintoku to Furano [Services are direct and local or rapid]
Shintoku 新得 (Journey times quoted are to/from Shintoku)

| | |
|---|---|
| Furano 富良野 | JR Nemuro Line 6/day; 1hr 37 mins |

● Services continue to/start from Takikawa; see Table 15, above.

## Table 19: Furano to Asahikawa
### (Note: no limited express services)
Furano 富良野 (Journey times quoted are to/from Furano)

| | |
|---|---|
| Naka-Furano 中富良野 | 12/day; 10 mins |
| Kami-Furano 上富良野 | 12/day; 20 mins |
| Bibaushi 美馬牛 | 12/day; 33 mins |
| Biei 美瑛 | 12/day; 40 mins |
| Asahikawa 旭川 | 12/day; 73 mins |

**Seasonal service**
The **Furano Biei Norokko** operates between Biei and Furano in the lavender/flower season (June to mid July weekends, mid July to Oct daily; 3/day, 1/day to/from Asahikawa).
At this time, **Lavender Farm** ラベンダー畑 station is open between Naka-Furano & Kami-Furano.

### Table 20: Hakata (Fukuoka) to/from Nagasaki on Kamome LEX

Hakata 博多 (Journey times quoted are
   to/from Hakata)

| | |
|---|---|
| Futsukaichi 二日市 | (Midori/HTB only) |
| Tosu 鳥栖 | 1-2/hr; 22 mins; |
| Saga 佐賀 | 1-2/hr; 42 mins |
| Hizen-Yamaguchi 肥前山口 | 1-2/hr; 50 mins |
| Hizen-Kashima 肥前鹿島 | 1-2/hr; 58 mins |
| Isahaya 諫早 | 1-2/hr; 1hr 42 mins |
| Urakami 浦上 | 1-2/hr; 1hr 57 mins |
| Nagasaki 長崎 | 1-2/hr; 2hrs |

**LEX notes**
The **Midori LEX** (1/hr) oper-
ates between Hakata and
Sasebo; the **Huis Ten Bosch**
(HTB) LEX (5-9/day) operates
between Hakata and Huis Ten
Bosch. All services stop at sta-
tions between Hakata and
Hizen-Yamaguchi.

### Table 21: (Shin-Osaka and) Hakata to Kagoshima-chuo by Sakura, or Tsubame (T), shinkansen

Shin-Osaka 新大阪 (Journey times quoted are to/from Shin-Osaka)[2]

| | | | From Hakata |
|---|---|---|---|
| Shin-Kobe 新神戸 | 17/day; 13 mins | | |
| Okayama 岡山 | 17/day; 45 mins | | |
| Hiroshima 広島 | 17/day; 1hr 31 mins | | |
| Kokura 小倉 | 17/day; 2hrs 20 mins | | |
| Hakata (Fukuoka) 博多 (福岡) | 17/day; 2hrs 41 mins | | |
| Shin-Tosu 新鳥栖 | 17/day; 2hrs 53 mins | 1-2/hr; 13 mins | (T) 1-2/hr; 13 mins |
| Kurume 久留米 | 17/day; 3hrs | 1-2/hr; 17 mins | (T) 1-2/hr; 17 mins |
| Shin-Omuta 新大牟田 | | | (T) 1-2/hr; 35 mins |
| Shin-Tamana 新玉名 | | | (T) 1-2/hr; 43 mins |
| Kumamoto 熊本 | 17/day; 3hrs 21 mins | 1-2/hr; 38 mins | (T) 1-2/hr; 50 mins |
| Shin-Yatsushiro 新八代 | 7/day; 3hrs 36 mins | 1/hr; 50 mins | (T) 3/day; 67 mins |
| Shin-Minamata 新水俣 | 7/day; 3hrs 48 mins | 1/hr; 1hr 3 mins | (T) 3/day; 81 mins |
| Izumi 出水 | 7/day; 3hrs 54 mins | 1/hr; 1hr 11 mins | (T) 3/day; 88 mins |
| Sendai 川内 | 17/day; 4hrs | 1/hr; 1hr 19 mins | (T) 3/day; 100 mins |
| Kagoshima-chuo 鹿児島中央 | 17/day; 4hs 10 mins | 1/hr; 1hr 26 mins | (T) 3/day; 112 mins |

● Mizuho services (7/day; valid with a JR Kyushu Pass but not a Japan Rail Pass) call at
Shin-Kobe 13 mins; Okayama 51 mins; Hiroshima 80 mins; Kokura 2hrs 28 mins; Hakata
1¾hrs; Kumamoto 3hrs; and Kagoshima-chuo 3¾hrs.

● See also Table 3 for additional services between Shin-Osaka and Hakata

### Table 22: Hakata (Fukuoka) & Kokura to Miyazaki on Sonic/Nichirin & Nichirin Seagaia (NS)

Hakata 博多 (Journey times quoted are to/from Hakata)

| | | |
|---|---|---|
| Kokura 小倉 | NS 1/day; 1hr | Sonic 1-2/hr; 52 mins |
| Nakatsu 中津 | | Sonic 1-2/hr; 1hr 27 mins |
| Usa 宇佐 | | Sonic 1/hr; 1hr 42 mins |
| Beppu 別府 | NS 1/day; 2hrs 20 mins | Sonic 1-2/hr; 2hrs 12 mins |
| Oita 大分 | NS 1/day; 2hrs 32 mins | Sonic 1-2/hr; 2hrs 21 mins |

| | | |
|---|---|---|
| Oita 大分 | | (Journey times quoted are to/from Oita) |
| Usuki 宇宿 | NS 1/day; 3hrs 4 mins | Nichirin 1/hr; 33 mins |
| Saiki 佐伯 | NS 1/day; 3hrs 31 mins | Nichirin 1/hr; 1hr |
| Nobeoka 延岡 | NS 1/day; 4hrs 41 mins | Nichirin 1/hr; 2hrs |
| Miyazaki 宮崎 | NS 1/day; 5hrs 36 mins | Nichirin 1/hr; 3hrs |

● All NS/Nichirin services continue to Miyazaki Airport (a 9-minute journey).

## Table 23: Okayama to/from Takamatsu by Marine Liner

Okayama 岡山 (Journey times quoted are to/from Okayama)

| | | | |
|---|---|---|---|
| Kojima 児島 | ML 2-3/hr; 23 mins | Shiokaze 1/hr; 19 mins | Nanpu 1/hr; 21 mins |
| Sakaide 坂出 | ML 2-3/hr; 40 mins | | |
| Takamatsu 高松 | ML 2-3/hr; 55 mins | Uzushio LEX 2/day; 60 mins | |

● The Marine Liner (ML) is a rapid train rather than a LEX but it is the easiest way to get from Okayama to Takamatsu. The service operates between 5.30am and midnight.

## Table 24: Takamatsu to/from Tokushima by Uzushio LEX

Takamatsu 高松  (Journey times quoted are to/from Takamatsu)

| | | |
|---|---|---|
| Ritsurin 栗林 | 1/hr; | 4 mins |
| Ikenotani 池谷 | 12/day; | 57 mins |
| Tokushima 徳島 | 1/hr; | 1hr 10 mins |

> **Uzushio LEX notes**
> Two services a day start/end in Okayama (119 mins) via Kojima, Takamatsu, Ritsurin and Ikenotani (1/day).

## Table 25: Takamatsu to Kochi/Kubokawa on Shimanto/Nanpu (N) LEX

Takamatsu 高松 (Journey times quoted are to/from Takamatsu)

| | | |
|---|---|---|
| Sakaide 坂出 | 5/day; 14 mins | |
| Utazu 宇多津 | 3/day; 24 mins | (N) 9/day |
| Marugame 丸亀 | 5/day; 31 mins | (N) 9/day |
| Tadotsu 多度津 | 5/day; 34 mins | (N) 9/day |
| Zentsuji 善通寺 | 5/day; 40 mins | (N) 9/day |
| Kotohira 琴平 | 5/day; 45 mins | (N) 9/day |
| Awa-Ikeda 阿波池田 | 5/day; 68 mins | (N) 9/day |
| Oboke 大歩危 | 5/day; 87 mins | (N) 9/day |
| Osugi 大杉 | 3/day; 106 mins | (N) 5/day |
| Tosa-Yamada 土佐山田 | 5/day; 126 mins | (N) 9/day |
| Gomen 郷免 | 5/day; 131 mins | (N) 9/day |
| Kochi 高知 | 5/day; 139 mins | (N) 9/day |

> **Local services**
> ● The **Yosan Line** (local and rapid services) operates between Takamatsu and Iyo-Saijo (3/hr), so on this route between Takamatsu and Tadotsu.
> ● The **Dosan Line** (1-2/hr) operates between Tadotsu and Kubokawa.

● Some Shimanto services from Takamatsu join the Nanpu (Okayama to Kubokawa) at Utazu. Also one Shimanto a day goes to Kubokawa (3hrs 22 mins)

2 The Ishizuchi LEX (Takamatsu to Uwajima) stops at all stations between Takamatsu and Tadotsu (16/day).

## Table 26: Kochi to Kubokawa on Ashizuri (A) / Nanpu (N) LEX

Kochi 故知 (Journey times quoted are to/from Kochi)

| | |
|---|---|
| Ino 井野 | (A) 5/day (N) 2/day; both 10 mins |
| Kubokawa 窪川 | (A) 5/day (N) 2/day; both 65 mins |

> **Local services**
> On the Dosan Line between Kochi and Ino there are 1-2/hr; and to Kubokawa 6/day.

## Table 27: Kubokawa to Uwajima on local train

Kubokawa 窪川 (Journey times quoted are to/from Kochi)

| | | |
|---|---|---|
| Tokawa 十川 | 7/day; 42 mins | 1 No LEX services operate on this line, |
| Ekawasaki 江川崎 | 7/day; 1¼hrs | (the Yodo Line) |
| Uwajima 宇和島 | 7/day; 2hrs 35 mins | |

---

**Notes**: Journey times quoted are all approximate. Not all stops are listed.

## Table 28: Uwajima to Matsuyama on Uwakai LEX

Uwajima 宇和島 (Journey times quoted are to/from Uwajima)

| | |
|---|---|
| Yawatahama 八幡浜 | 16/day; 35 mins |
| Iyo-Ozu 伊予大洲 | 16/day; 47 mins |
| Uchiko 内子 | 16/day; 57 mins |
| Iyoshi 伊予市 | 16/day; 73 mins |
| Matsuyama 松山 | 16/day; 82 mins |

**Local services**
Uwajima to Matsuyama (Yosan/Uchiko Line) 7/day; Uwajima to Yawatahama (10/day); Yawatahama to Iyoshi 15/day; Iyoshi to Matsuyama 1-3/hr.

## Table 28: Matsuyama to Okayama on Shiokaze LEX

Matsuyama 松山 (Journey times quoted are to/from Matsuyama)

| | |
|---|---|
| Imabari 今治 | 14/day; 36 mins |
| Iyo-Saijo 伊予西条 | 14/day; 58 mins |
| Niihama 新居浜 | 14/day; 66 mins |
| Kan-onji 観音寺 | 14/day; 1hr 43 mins |
| Tadotsu 多度津 | 14/day; 2hrs |
| Marugame 丸亀 | 14/day; 2hrs 4 mins |
| Utazu 宇多津 | 14/day; 2hrs 17 mins |
| Okayama 岡山 | 14/day; 2hrs 48 mins |

**Local services**
● Matsuyama to Iyo-Saijo (Yosan Line) approx 1/hr; Iyo-Saijoto Kan-onji approx 1/hr.
● Kan-onji to Okayama (Seto-Hashi Line) 2/day, but 4/day from Utazu.

● The Shiokaze LEX divides at Utazu; part of it becomes the Ishizuchi LEX (17/day) and goes to Takamatsu. The Ishizuchi LEX from Takamatsu joins up with the Shiokaze LEX at Utazu.

## Map key

| | | |
|---|---|---|
| | 🏛 Museum/Gallery | ▬▬ Shinkansen line |
| | ✚ Church/cathedral | ▬ ▬ JR line (suggested route) |
| | 卍 Buddhist Temple | ▬ ▬ JR line |
| 🛏 Where to stay | ⛩ Shinto Shrine | ▬▬ Private (non-JR) |
| ○ Where to eat | 🚌 Bus station/stop | ▬□▬ Railway station |
| ✉ Post office | ⛴ Ferry/boat trip | ▬○▬ Tram/metro/subway line |
| ⑤ Bank/money exchange | ✗ Airport | ⋯⋯ Bus route |
| ① Tourist information | ⚱ Monument/memorial | ▭ Park |
| 📖 Bookstore | ● Other | |

# INDEX

## OTHER GUIDES FROM TRAILBLAZER – see opposite for full list

### Trans-Siberian Handbook
*Bryn Thomas & Anna Cohen Kaminski,* 9th edn, £15.99
ISBN 978-1-905864-56-0, 528pp, 90 maps, 40 colour photos
Ninth edition of the most popular guide to the world's longest rail journey. ● Kilometre-by-kilometre route guides and maps covering the entire routes of the Trans-Siberian, Trans-Manchurian and Trans-Mongolian railways ● City guides and maps – Moscow, St Petersburg, Ulaanbaatar, Beijing and 25 towns in Siberia. *'Definitive guide'* Condé Nast Traveler

### Trans-Canada Rail Guide
*Melissa Graham,* 5th edn, £12.99
ISBN 978-1-905864-33-1, 256pp, 34 maps, 30 colour photos
Covers the entire route from coast to coast – for all budgets.
● Mile-by-mile route guides
● City guides and maps – ten major stops including Quebec City, Montreal, Toronto, Winnipeg, Jasper & Vancouver.
*'Invaluable'* Daily Telegraph

❏ **Manhole cover sightseeing**
Most visitors to Japan have a list of temples, shrines, castles, gardens or onsen they want to visit. However, there is much more to look out for including the colourful and entertaining manhole covers you can see on the streets in almost every town and city. Manhole covers are a fact of life and generally provide a very functional service, but in Japan local governments have used them as a way to promote the attractions in their area. As you walk along keep an eye on the

ground and you never know what you will see. One place with a wonderful range of manhole covers is Yuda-onsen (see p282). This manhole cover is for *osui* おすい (dirty water) from Kawaguchi-ko-cho (Kawaguchi-ko town).

# TRAILBLAZER TITLE LIST

Adventure Cycle-Touring Handbook
Adventure Motorcycling Handbook
Australia by Rail
Azerbaijan
Coast to Coast (British Walking Guide)
Cornwall Coast Path (British Walking Guide)
Corsica Trekking – GR20
Cotswold Way (British Walking Guide)
The Cyclist's Anthology
Dales Way (British Walking Guide)
Dolomites Trekking – AV1 & AV2
Dorset & Sth Devon Coast Path (British Walking Gde)
Exmoor & Nth Devon Coast Path (British Walking Gde)
Hadrian's Wall Path (British Walking Guide)
Himalaya by Bike – a route and planning guide
Inca Trail, Cusco & Machu Picchu
Japan by Rail
Kilimanjaro – the trekking guide (includes Mt Meru)
Moroccan Atlas – The Trekking Guide
Morocco Overland (4WD/motorcycle/mountainbike)
Nepal Trekking & The Great Himalaya Trail
New Zealand – The Great Walks
Offa's Dyke Path (British Walking Guide)
Overlanders' Handbook – worldwide driving guide
Peddars Way & Norfolk Coast Path (British Walking Gde)
Pembrokeshire Coast Path (British Walking Guide)
Pennine Way (British Walking Guide)
Peru's Cordilleras Blanca & Huayhuash – Hiking/Biking
The Railway Anthology
The Ridgeway (British Walking Guide)
Sahara Overland – a route and planning guide
Scottish Highlands – The Hillwalking Guide
Siberian BAM Guide – rail, rivers & road
The Silk Roads – a route and planning guide
Sinai – the trekking guide
South Downs Way (British Walking Guide)
Thames Path (British Walking Guide)
Tour du Mont Blanc
Trans-Canada Rail Guide
Trans-Siberian Handbook
Trekking in the Everest Region
The Walker's Anthology
The Walker's Haute Route – Mont Blanc to Matterhorn
West Highland Way (British Walking Guide)

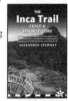

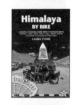

For more information about Trailblazer and our
expanding range of guides, for guidebook updates or
for credit card mail order sales visit our website:

## www.trailblazer-guides.com

**(Opposite, p525)  Map – Around Tokyo**

**(Overleaf, pp526-7) The diversity and style of Japan's trains never fails to impress**
*Photos from left*

**Row 1**
• The **E7 shinkansen**, operated by JR East, runs between Tokyo and Kanazawa; JR West operates the W7, a similar train, on this route (© AU).
• **Coupled Hayabusa and Komachi shinkansen** run together between Tokyo and Morioka; at Morioka the Komachi goes to Akita and the Hayabusa continues to Shin-Aomori/Shin-Hakodate-Hokuto (© AU).
• The **Narita Express (N'EX)** operates between Narita Airport and various stations in the Tokyo area (© AU).
• **Dr Yellow** is the nickname for the trains that test the condition of the track and overhead cables on Tokaido/Sanyo shinkansen lines (© AU).
• The **N700** is the fastest shinkansen between Tokyo and Hakata, the N700A which looks exactly the same also operates on this route (© CJRC).

**Row 2**
• At the start and end of routes it is common to see **cleaners** waiting for a train to arrive so they can clean it and get the seats facing the right direction – often in about seven minutes – before it leaves on its next journey (© AU).
• The best way to get around Matsuyama is on one of its **trams** but taking the **Botchan**, a diesel replica of a mini steam locomotive that operated here in the early 20th century, is a great way to reach Dogo-onsen (© AU).
• The **Super Hokuto** runs between Hakodate and Sapporo (© AU).
• The **A-train** is named after the jazz tune *Take the A-train* and also because it is for adults as it has a bar; it operates from Kumamoto to Misumi (© KU).
• The **Yufuin no Mori** (Hakata to Beppu via Yufuin) looks great externally but also has a stylish wooden interior (© AU).

**Row 3**
• A **700-series shinkansen** passing through Atami station (© KU).
• The **Shonan monorail** is a suspended monorail and it operates between Ofuna and Shonan-Enoshima (© AU).
• **Yamanote Line** trains operate in a circular route around Tokyo (© JRL).
• Odakyu's '**Romance Car**' is a limited express train that is used on three routes from Shinjuku including to Hakone-Yumoto (© AU).
• The **East-i shinkansen** is JR East's equivalent to the Dr Yellow (© AU).

**Row 4**
• The **Hanayome Noren** is one of JR West's sightseeing services and it is probably the most lavishly decorated of all the sightseeing trains as it has gold-leaf (© KU).
• The driver of the **SL Hitoyoshi**, one of JR Kyushu's sightseeing trains (called D&S), prepares for a journey from Kumamoto to Hitoyoshi (© AU).
• **Nitama**, the second cat in the world to be a station master, is on duty at Kishi station (© RZ).
• The **SL Banetsu Monogatari** (Aizu-Wakamatsu to Niigata) is one of JR East's steam locomotive services and also one of their many 'Joyful Trains' (© JH).

Photo credits: (© AU) Anna Udagawa; (© CJRC) courtesy Central Japan Railway Company); (© KU) Kazuo Udagawa; (© JRL) Jill & Roderick Leslie; (© RZ) Ramsey Zarifeh; (© JH) James Hodgson

**(p528) Map – Japan: Major JR Lines**

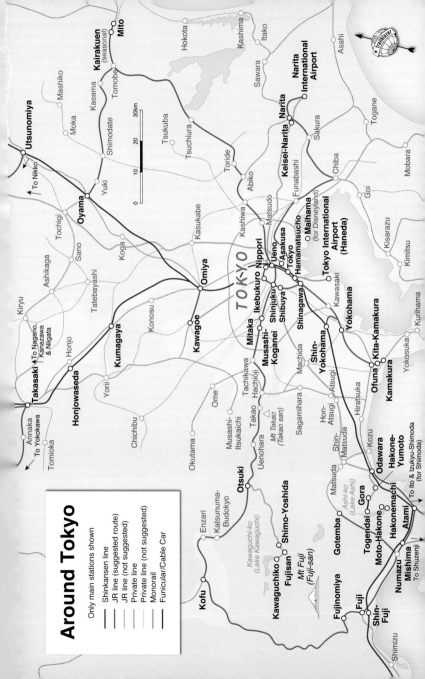

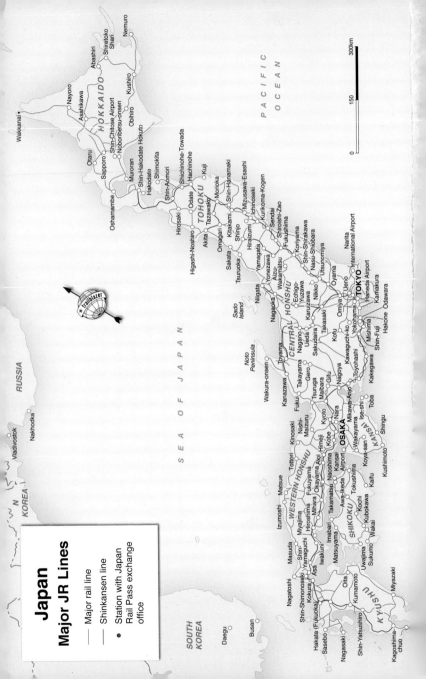

# Japan
## Major JR Lines

— Major rail line
— Shinkansen line
● Station with Japan Rail Pass exchange office

0   150   300km